GEORGE ALLEN

Pantstowne shoppers shook hands with Charley Harraway (*left*), running back with the Washington Redskins, when he appeared at the shop at 5550 Norbeck Road, Rockville, Maryland. Harraway is shown with Pantstowne owner Ed Richman and his son, Mike. Photo by Raymond Crowell. Courtesy of the author.

GEORGE ALLEN

A FOOTBALL LIFE

MIKE RICHMAN FOREWORD BY DICK VERMEIL

University of Nebraska Press
Lincoln

Manufactured in the United States of America

The University of Nebraska Press is part of a land-grant institution with campuses and programs on the past, present, and future homelands of the Pawnee, Ponca, Otoe-Missouria, Omaha, Dakota, Lakota, Kaw, Cheyenne, and Arapaho Peoples, as well as those of the relocated Ho-Chunk, Sac and Fox, and Iowa Peoples.

♾

Library of Congress Cataloging-in-Publication Data
Names: Richman, Michael, 1961– author. |
Vermeil, Dick, writer of foreword.
Title: George Allen: a football life / Mike
Richman; foreword by Dick Vermeil.
Description: Lincoln: University of Nebraska Press,
[2023] | Includes bibliographical references and index.
Identifiers: LCCN 2023005950
ISBN 9780803249684 (hardback)
ISBN 9781496238160 (epub)
ISBN 9781496238177 (pdf)
Subjects: LCSH: Allen, George, 1918–1990. | Football
coaches—United States—Biography. | Washington
Redskins (Football team)—History. | Los Angeles
Rams (Football team: 1946–1994)—History. |
BISAC: SPORTS & RECREATION / Football |
BIOGRAPHY & AUTOBIOGRAPHY / Sports
Classification: LCC GV939.A53 R54 2023 |
DDC 796.332092 [B]—dc23/eng/20230518
LC record available at https://lccn.loc.gov/2023005950

Set in Lyon Text.

To my parents, Ilene and Ed Richman, who gave me the motivation and drive needed to excel in life. My mother instilled in me a love for history and storytelling, and my father introduced me to the world of sports. Those interests have inspired me to pursue my literary work of today.

Contents

Illustrations

Foreword

Dick Vermeil

I'm truly honored to be invited to write the foreword for this biography of George Allen. He was a very special person, as well as a very special NFL coach. His career winning percentage of .712 places him in an elite group of only three men to win more than 70 percent of their regular-season games: Vince Lombardi, John Madden, and George Allen.

George was a coach who was always thinking ahead of the curve. The fact that he contacted me, interviewed me, then hired me as the first-ever special teams coach in 1969, while he was coaching the Los Angeles Rams, proves my statement to be true.

Even though I worked only one year for George in 1969 (I moved on to become the offensive coordinator at UCLA for Tommy Prothro in 1970), he really impacted my coaching career. Fortunately for me, George and I remained good friends after I went to UCLA. During the time period that he was out of coaching, George would spend a week with me and my staff in my Eagles training camps. Needless to say, we all picked his brain. His communication skill with his players was outstanding. He had a way of telling them what they needed to hear in a manner that united the thinking process of the entire team. Consequently, they trusted his judgment and process. His detailed preparation in every phase of the game was exceptional. In fact, I believe this was one of the areas of head coaching in which George was way ahead of most of the league. For example, I remember coming down the elevator in the hotel on the way to a Saturday practice in Chicago prior to playing the Bears. George asked me if I knew where the sun would be at kickoff time so I could alert the kick-off returners of what to expect. I thought he was kidding, but he wasn't! Therefore, while on the field that Saturday, I checked out the sun position so I could tell my returners what to expect and how to shade their eyes as the ball came to them.

In another example of George's detailed approach to preparation, he had me travel to every Baltimore Colts preseason game in 1969, when it didn't conflict with our own game, to study tight end John Mackey's split from his offensive tackle. We opened with the Colts in Baltimore. George wanted to find out if he could predict a run or pass based on Mackey's split. With this thought, I studied every snap Mackey played in the preseason, as well as most of the snaps that he took in games the year before. I ended up with the knowledge that Mackey's split made no difference. There was nothing we could use to gain a defensive edge versus the Colts. When I gave George my final report, telling him there was nothing we could use, he said, "Great—the conclusion is there is no conclusion." I was a little confused by his statement, but he was satisfied!

George never hesitated to do something that hadn't been done before in the NFL. For instance, I believe he was the first coach to go to a fifth defensive back, taking out a linebacker in obvious passing downs and using what everyone has gone on to call a "nickel back." From there, the dime defense evolved with six defensive backs. We were playing the 49ers in a preseason game, and George decided during the week to take out two linebackers on long-yardage passing downs against quarterback John Brodie to see how it would work. Well, it did work, and the multiple defensive back coverage schemes started to grow as the season went on. Today the concept is in everyone's coverage package. This is one of the reasons George's defensive teams were so good at taking away what offenses were doing, although the schemes required really experienced safeties to execute his plans. In 1969 we had two veteran safeties who no longer could really run like they used to, Eddie Meador and Richie Petitbon. But George needed very smart, experienced safeties to get the coverages called under pressure. George always said that what the safeties lacked in speed, they would make up in knowing where the ball was going prior to the snap. This probably would not be possible in today's game, in that the offensive schemes are so much more sophisticated, and everyone's game plan includes so much more offense each week, though I wouldn't doubt that George would find a way.

Because of George, I always had great respect for the so-called older player who was supposedly "over the hill." I remember early in my Eagles coaching days signing two-time Pro Bowl offensive lineman Woody Peoples, who the 49ers thought was finished, because I knew what George would do—sign him—let 'em play. I did, and Woody played very well for us for four years. We also took the George Allen approach in trading for defensive end Claude Humphrey. He had retired after four games in 1978 because he became frustrated while losing in Atlanta. In 1979 Claude posted fourteen sacks and played equally well for us for two more years, including our Super Bowl year in 1980. Not only did he play well, but he became a symbol of what a true NFL pro really was. Later we applied the same George Allen philosophy when I coached in Kansas City and president and general manager Carl Peterson signed offensive tackle Willie Roaf, who was coming off two major knee surgeries in New Orleans. He ended up playing in four Pro Bowls in a row for the Chiefs. Not bad for an old man! Thank you, George Allen.

George's family concept within his teams was also very influential throughout my coaching career. Once you earned the right to play for George, he sort of added you, for that period of time, to his George Allen family. He talked about team family all the time, believing if everyone deeply cared for each other, they wouldn't want to let the other guy down. When you win 70 percent of your games, something had to be the difference maker. For George, it was his football family, and he ingrained it in his players to really hate losing. There are two statements I remember him making to the team following a loss, and he was sincere about both: "Losing is worse than dying. You have to get up the next morning and face it all over again!" and "Playing like we did today, we should all donate our game checks to charity."

I could go on and on writing about George, but I won't. Mike Richman has taken on that challenge himself, and I believe you will really enjoy the read. George had his own way of leading, and I don't think anyone will ever duplicate his leadership skills. Only George could be George Allen. I will always be indebted to George for what I learned from him about being a head coach in the NFL. Thank you, Coach Allen!

Preface

No authoritative biography has been written on George Allen. That fact dominated my thinking when I considered writing this book. How could that be? Shouldn't his legacy be honored? Who was this legend? Allen certainly isn't the only coach enshrined in the Pro Football Hall of Fame. He didn't even win an NFL Championship as a head coach, and he posted only a 2-7 postseason record. Some of his contemporaries, namely Vince Lombardi, Don Shula, Tom Landry, John Madden, and Chuck Noll, hold much loftier spots in NFL lore. Yet, his life deserves to be explored because he was a fascinating figure who left a lasting imprint on the National Football League.

In no uncertain terms, I told myself that I was the person to take on this project. A native Washingtonian, I lived through the Redskins' Sonny Jurgensen–led offensive explosion of the 1960s. But those Redskins, despite being so entertaining, were no better than mediocre. It wasn't until Allen arrived in the nation's capital in 1971, declared "the future is now," and immediately coached the Redskins to their first playoff appearance in a quarter century that I became hooked.

I lived vicariously through that team, which Allen took to the playoffs five times in the '70s, including an appearance in Super Bowl VII. In addition to Allen, names such as Billy Kilmer, Sonny Jurgensen, Charley Taylor, Chris Hanburger, Brig Owens, Larry Brown, Ron McDole, Ken Houston, Pat Fischer, and Diron Talbert—most of whom were members of Allen's "Over the Hill Gang"—became seared into my train of thought. To me, these men were larger-than-life figures. It was a treat to hang out with Redskins fullback Charley Harraway when he made a promotional appearance at my father's men's clothing store after the '71 season (a photo of that visit faces the title page of this book). My life became so linked to that Redskins team that I'd have major emotional swings based on their fortunes on a given Sunday. On back-to-back Sundays in December 1972 at RFK Stadium, the Redskins turned in the most memorable victories of the Allen era in DC: 16–3 over the Packers in the NFC divisional playoffs and 26–3 over the Cowboys in the NFC Championship Game. The latter win was his crowning moment in his twelve seasons as an NFL head coach. I was at both games.

In decades of researching and writing about the Redskins and NFL history, as well as interviewing many players who were once part of Allen's teams in college and the pros, plus other people who crossed paths with him, I've come to understand why he was a special man who left a special coaching legacy. I hope that, after reading this book, you will, too.

Prologue

DRIVEN TO SUCCEED

"My life is football—football morning, noon, and night. I've put it ahead of my family, which is wrong. But if you want to be totally successful, that's the way you have to do it. I'd do the same thing no matter what job I had."[1]

That, in a nutshell, was George Allen: tenacious, relentless, and inextricably linked to the game of football. Many coaches may think football comes before family, but they don't advertise it. Allen did.

No story better epitomizes Allen's priorities in life than the fib he told at Veterans Stadium in Philadelphia on September 30, 1973. Redskins ball boy Bruce Allen—the coach's son—wore a credential that kept him confined to an area between the 35-yard lines on the sidelines. That day, Bruce roamed outside of the zone and yelled distracting signals toward Eagles quarterback Roman Gabriel. A referee stopped play and escorted him back to his father.

Referee: "Is this a member of your staff?"

Allen: "I've no idea. He must be one of those people [the Eagles] gave us as ball boys."

Referee: "If this happens again, it's a fifteen-yard bench misconduct penalty."

Allen: "Thank you."[2]

"We looked over at Bruce and said, 'Your dad denied you as a son,'" Redskins safety Brig Owens, who started in that game, said only half in jest.[3]

From the sidelines, where Allen would often adjust the bill of his cap, lick his fingers, clap his hands, and even flap his arms at times, he projected a sort of innocuous image. He never cursed, usually saying "gosh almighty," "gosh darn," or "cripes sakes" to express frustration. Beneath that veneer, though, was a man eager to vanquish his opponents. He operated from the premise that "I will know you better than you know yourself."

Fueled by his cult-like devotion to football, Allen established himself as one of the first NFL coaches to be known as a workaholic. A self-made man who learned the value of hard work while growing up in the depths of the Great Depression, he toiled fourteen to sixteen hours a day, combed through the most arcane details, and studied game films meticulously to find an edge on his opponents.

In a 1973 article he penned for *Sports Illustrated*, Allen explained that winning, which he often described as "the science of being totally prepared," is predicated on an elementary concept: "If I've succeeded, it's because I outwork most people. Work is simply a synonym for effort, and as I tell my players, 'A hundred percent is not enough.' The average American pictures himself as an extremely hard worker. Sociologists and psychologists have shown, however, that most persons are really operating on less than half power. In terms of effort, they may never get over 50 percent, although they think of themselves as 90 percent producers. Therefore, to get 100 percent you must aim for 110 percent. The world belongs to those who aim for 110 percent."[4]

In truth, Allen's blueprint for success—in his words—consisted of a series of other important elements besides hard work:

> First, there's that hunger to succeed. It isn't because of the paycheck or a new automobile or a bigger house. It's just that you want to succeed so badly that everything else becomes secondary.
>
> Your attitude controls your destiny. Whether it's the last-minute loss in a football game or the loss of a key contract, you can't let anything pull you down. You've got to believe that you're going to win, and you've got to believe that you're going to succeed—and you will. Usually, people who don't make it have the wrong attitude. They're blaming somebody else or something else, whatever that might be.
>
> If you don't have self-discipline, you're not going to make it. You're not going to be in shape or mentally sharp if you're out late carousing. The only way to have an organized work schedule is through self-discipline.
>
> Live in the present. That's almost like the slogan I had with the Washington Redskins: The future is now.[5]

Allen's philosophy on winning translated into many victories on the football field. In twelve seasons of NFL coaching, he posted a 116-47-5 regular-season record (.712 winning percentage) and a 118-54-5 mark, including playoffs (.680). Both percentages are No. 3 all-time records for coaches with at least one hundred career victories. His teams made the playoffs in seven of twelve seasons, a mark that might have been 100 percent in today's era of seven playoff teams, including three wild card spots, per conference. Plus, he's the only coach in NFL history not to suffer a losing season in more than ten years of coaching. In twenty-one years in pro football, including his first seven as the defensive coordinator and head talent scout for the Chicago Bears, he was part of only two losing teams: the '60 and '64 Bears. He also coached winning teams in his two seasons in the United States Football League and in seven of his ten seasons in the college ranks.

Losing just wasn't in George Allen's DNA.

"Every time you win, you're reborn," he often said. "When you lose, you die a little."

His players and members of his family saw how deflated he was after a rare loss. "If it was a Redskins home game, and we won, we'd go to [popular DC restaurant] Duke Zeibert's after the game," said Allen's oldest son, George Felix Allen. "It would be a great celebration. If we lost, the heck if we're going out. It was like a funeral. You'd get in the car and drive home, and everyone would be quiet and glum. It truly was like a wake."[6]

In addition to his winning percentage, Allen is remembered as an innovator in two of football's three phases—defense and special teams—where he changed the way the game is played and how it's understood. On defense, he perfected bold schemes, such as the nickel and dime packages, that are part of the fabric of today's game. The nickel called for five defensive backs and the dime six.

With Allen as their defensive coordinator, the '63 Bears won the NFL Championship with one of the stingiest defenses in NFL history. Following the 14–10 win over the Giants, Allen's players carried him off the field because of his defensive wizardry, a remarkable honor for an assistant coach. When he was head coach with the Rams and Redskins, his defenses were often among the best in the NFL, first with the "Fearsome Foursome" in LA, then the "Over the Hill Gang" in Washington.

There's the old saying that offense scores points, defense wins ball games. Allen took that to heart. "No one ever won a championship without a great defense," he said on the eve of the Redskins' 14–7 loss to Miami in Super Bowl VII in January 1973, his only Super Bowl appearance. "That applies to the [New York] Yankees, even when they had their great hitting teams. It applies to basketball, with the Celtics. It applies to [hockey, with] the Toronto Maple Leafs. It goes right down the line."[7]

Allen also outfoxed the rest of the league when it came to special teams. At a time when the concept of special teams and the potential of those units to swing the outcome of a game was not taken seriously, Allen was far beyond his coaching brethren. His special teams impacted games with blocked kicks, clutch kick returns, and forced turnovers. He depended on those units for at least two wins per season and elevated that once-anonymous sector of football to new levels of respect.

"At the time, special teams were just becoming recognized," said one of Allen's most impactful special teamers, Bill Malinchak, who blocked four punts in the '70s. "They were always kind of a filler between possessions. It was like, 'Send a bunch of guys in, let's get this over with.' George Allen said, 'Here's an opportunity.'

"We would dominate special teams in every phase. People recognized that we were really making a difference in games, if not just outright winning them."[8]

In terms of his roster composition, Allen preferred seasoned veterans over inexperienced players and rookies, believing battle-tested players would in theory be less likely to make mental mistakes on the field. As a head coach, especially in the nation's capital, "Trader George" dealt a slew of draft picks to build his veteran-dominated rosters. He simply felt that veterans would better meet the immediacy he felt was needed to win. Besides that, no unfettered free agency system or salary cap existed at the time, meaning fewer roster spots were open to rookies because most players stayed with the same team year after year.[9] "I want to look in my locker room and see bald old men, guys who have been through it—winners," Allen once said.[10] And it was his view that "you're never over the hill, because there's always another hill to climb."[11]

Perhaps the greatest paradox about Allen is that he also showed a razor-sharp eye for rookie talent. As Chicago's head talent scout from '59 to '65, he drafted three players who are enshrined today in the Hall of Fame: tight end Mike Ditka, middle linebacker Dick Butkus, and running back Gale Sayers. In what many consider the greatest draft in NFL history, he picked Butkus and Sayers with back-to-back selections in the first round in '65, placing him in the conversation of the best general managers ever.

Yet, for all of his attributes, achievements, and accolades, Allen could not escape controversy. Having angered management with his player personnel and spending moves, among other decisions, he was fired four times by one team—the Rams—and was released by the Redskins, although one can argue the latter was not a firing. Plus, in one of the most bizarre incidents in NFL history, Bears owner George Halas accused him of breach of contract and took him to court. Halas won the case but released Allen from his contract so he could take the head coaching position with the Rams in '66.

Amid all of this turbulence, Allen insisted on doing things his way and vowed that he would have fun while coaching. Asked in a '75 interview with the *Washington Star* how long he figured on coaching, he responded, "I haven't thought of that. I enjoy it. It isn't work for me. I'd rather come to Redskin Park than go out and play golf. As long as I have my health and can do a good job and make a contribution, I'd like to coach because I can't picture myself being retired. I've spent so much time in football that I'm not really qualified for anything else. It's been my whole life."[12]

George Allen literally coached until the day he died. For a man with a life-long devotion to the game of football, nothing could have been more fitting.

1

Humble Beginnings

When one looks back on the football coaching exploits of George Allen, certain characteristics about him inevitably take shape: his exceptional work ethic, his ultracompetitiveness, and his unyielding quest for perfection. Those traits defined him to the core.

It's not too difficult to pinpoint why he became so driven or the origin of his Type A personality. Growing up poor during the Great Depression likely played a significant role. The way he described it, his hunger to succeed existed from the very beginning.

"I was born motivated," Allen wrote in his 1990 book, *Strategies for Winning*. "Not everyone is. But I believe motivation can be passed on and acquired, like a vaccine."[1]

George Herbert Allen was born on April 29, 1917, in a home at 62 Fulton Street in Detroit. His birth certificate identifies his father, Earl Allen, as a "machinist auto worker" and his mother, Loretta Hannigan Allen, as a "housewife." By his teenage years, George would be called on to help support the family, which welcomed a second child, Virginia, in 1921. But the Allens seemed financially comfortable for the time being.[2]

Earl and Loretta had moved to Detroit from the town of Rensselaer, New York, on the east side of the Hudson River opposite the state capital, Albany. In the 1800s many Dutch immigrants settled in Albany, Rensselaer, and other nearby areas. Rensselaer is today the only New York State site devoted to Dutch culture and is home to Crailo, the museum of the colonial Dutch in the Hudson River valley. Earl and Loretta were both of Irish descent, with Earl also possessing Dutch lineage.

By the turn of the century, millions of Americans were migrating to the country's rapidly growing cities in search of economic opportunity. Detroit, which had evolved into a mecca of industrial production led by auto companies, held a wealth of potential jobs. The city's population skyrocketed in the first half of the twentieth century, with waves of European and Canadian immigrants, as well as residents of southern U.S. states, seeking work in the booming car industry.

The Allens took notice, although when they relocated to Detroit is unclear. Their home in 1917 at 62 Fulton Street was in a blue-collar industrial area in the southwestern part of the city.[3] Many working-class people settled there around the end of World War I.

That same year, the Allens headed east to the Detroit suburb of Grosse Pointe Shores, which by the early twentieth century had become a popular destination for the rich and powerful. Their residence was on Lake Shore Road, which featured some imposing mansions on multiacre estates, with architecture so grand that one house resembled an "early English Renaissance Castle" and cost $2 million to build, the equivalent of about $40 million today.[4] Members of the Ford family—the auto-manufacturing dynasty—owned some of the mansions. Grosse Pointe Shores as a whole was trending upscale, with a fair number of residents listing themselves as professionals, merchants, or industry owners of some sort. One called himself a "capitalist."[5]

Other people such as Earl Allen were there to service the wealthy. He and his family resided at 1025 rear Lake Shore Road. The "rear" in the address likely meant they lived in a cottage on the property or in an apartment above the garage.[6]

Earl Allen was a chauffeur for a successful businessman named Edgar H. Houghton, who lived with his family in the main residence at 1025 Lake Shore Road.[7] Houghton, a Canadian immigrant who became an American citizen, managed the Lawrence Publishing Company before becoming secretary-treasurer of the *Michigan Farmer*, an agricultural publication. Having a car and being able to afford a chauffeur made him quite upper class for that time.

Houghton thought highly of Earl Allen as an employee and penned a letter of recommendation for him on January 20, 1920: "The bearer, Earl R. Allen, has been in my employ for three years. I have found him to be perfectly honest in every way and a consistent worker. I cheerfully recommend him, and I am certain that he will ably fill any position he may accept. He is taking a vacation for three months, while I am away in Florida, and I will gladly take him back on my return if he will accept the position."[8]

In addition to being a chauffeur, Earl spent time as a car mechanic at a local Ford plant. Loretta was a domestic worker. The family's 1025 rear Lake Shore Road residence was across the street from the estate where the family of Edsel Ford, the only son of automobile mogul Henry Ford and the president of the Ford Motor Company at the time, began residing in 1928.

According to the 1930 U.S. Census, the Allens relocated about six miles north, to 23511 Allor Boulevard in St. Clair Shores, Michigan, a bedroom community with many workers in the Detroit auto industry. It was also a transport site for "rum running," the illegal business of shipping alcohol during the Prohibition era. The 1930 Census says Earl Allen was still a chauffeur for a "private family." He also played the saxophone and performed in clubs. The Allens owned a radio, which at the time meant they were probably in the middle-class portion of the socioeconomic spectrum.[9]

But the Great Depression, which began in 1929, shook the nation, causing steep declines in industrial output and employment. Many companies laid off workers, and Detroit was hit hard. Some fifteen million Americans were out of work by the nadir of the Great Depression, in 1933.

Earl Allen struggled, although not entirely because of the tight economy. In an incident that prevented him from working, he suffered a debilitating head injury on the Ford assembly line. At the same time, he was a heavy drinker, a pattern that his son observed. George Allen never drank alcoholic beverages in excess in his life, limiting his consumption to a blackberry brandy or a beer that he shared with his wife. "My father's determination not to drink and to make sure his children did not drink much could be because his father drank too much," said the oldest of George Allen's four children, George Felix Allen.[10]

With Earl Allen out of work and the country in the throes of the Great Depression, George Allen stepped up in his teens to keep the family afloat. He worked odd jobs, whether it was planting potatoes in a field for ten cents a day or picking berries. Like many other young people during the Great Depression, he found a way to produce income for the family.

Amid these turbulent times, the roots of his determination to succeed were born. He also developed the intestinal fortitude needed to overcome adversity. "That's how he grew up, having to work hard, be responsible, and work as many hours and do the best you can," George Felix Allen said. "He had to be resourceful through it all. He tried to find whatever work he could no matter what and do it well."[11]

Greg Allen, the second of his four children, said, "Work was the way you survived and acquired food, basics. He overcame being down in life. He and his family were poor."[12]

George Allen's mother, Loretta, also was behind his quest to excel. She grew up on the poor side but possessed a lot of "fire and drive," said

Jennifer Allen, the youngest of George Allen's four children. "She was very intense, like a motivator, and pushed him to be the best he could be." George's sister, Virginia, was "super-successful" and graduated as valedictorian of her high school class, Jennifer said.

Jennifer couldn't remember a time when her father complained about the difficulties he faced in his childhood: "He would only say that we kids didn't really realize what we had. He knew how to work. He tried to instill that. All of us are really strong workers. We have his work ethic. He had this great quote: 'Do what you love because what you love is where you'll be successful. Don't worry about trying to figure out how to make money.'"[13]

George Allen did just that. Harboring a love of sports, especially the thrill of competition, he began dreaming of a career in athletics, a wild thought considering that the nation had experienced such a drastic economic decline. Something more lucrative and stable, like law or medicine, seemed much more practical.

"I was always interested in every sport and played football, basketball, baseball, and track," he said in the 1972 book *The Future Is Now*. "I played some hockey because we lived right near Lake St. Clair, and we used to go out and play and skate for six, seven, eight, nine hours a day. I liked the outdoors. I liked to fish and hike and camp and all those sports.

"I felt that if you make a living by being in sports, what a great way it would be. And everything that I did real early was to try and learn more, to learn more about all sports. We were just an average family, so I never had much of an opportunity to have the greatest clinics and teaching like we have nowadays. We didn't have any organized programs. I don't recall having any organized sports except for when we got to high school."[14]

Allen showcased his athletic versatility at Lake Shore High School in St. Clair Shores. While attending the school from 1933 to 1937, he earned nine varsity letters—three in football, three in basketball, and three in track. He ran the 440-yard sprint and did the long jump in track, setting a school record in the latter with a distance of 22 feet, 2 inches. He was all-conference in football, playing end on offense and defense in a single-platoon system. He was also all-conference in basketball, captaining the Shorians for two seasons, 1935 and 1936.[15] "My best sports were really basketball and track," Allen said in *The Future Is Now*. "I wasn't very big. I only weighed about 148, 150 pounds."[16]

Allen's basketball and football teams made winning a habit. The Shorians prevailed in nineteen straight games at one point on the court. In football, Allen contributed to a juggernaut that outscored its opponents by 351 points in capturing seventeen of eighteen games in the mid-1930s. The school won the 1936 bi-county league championship.

Allen especially admired his football coach, Carlton Worden, describing him as an excellent teacher, well organized, and self-disciplined. "My outstanding coach, Carlton Worden, played a group of sophomores and kept them together while building the team," Allen wrote in an article he penned for the *Sports Fans' Journal* in the 1980s. "This group of athletes stayed together for three years with tremendous success. Most everyone played at least two sports and some three. So we all stayed in shape the year 'round."[17]

At right end on offense, Allen focused on blocking first and receiving second in Lake Shore's single-wing setup. He caught three touchdown passes. On defense, "I never thought of coming out or being substituted," he wrote. "Our team really won with an outstanding running game and a powerful defense."

In a sign of his appreciation for special teams, an element of the NFL that he would revolutionize, he noted, "We also had good special teams and, in those days, special teams were not something you worked on regularly. But ours were good, and we won games by blocking kicks and returning punts for big plays."

As Allen entered his senior year at Lake Shore High, his parents and sister returned to Rensselaer, New York, because they needed the support of Earl's parents, with whom they lived. But his parents determined that it was important for George to stay in Michigan. It's unclear if they made that decision so he could finish his high school education and athletic endeavors at Lake Shore, so he could retain his odd jobs and send money home, or both.

He lived with a family that the Allens knew through their Catholic parish. The father of the family was an executive at Chrysler and helped get Allen a job as a messenger at the company. While there, he improvised in a bid to stay in shape. "My father soon discovered that it was more efficient to run the stairs than take the elevator for his errands," Jennifer Allen said. "He also learned that he had little desire to pursue a job in the auto industry."[18]

Allen's decision to challenge himself physically and his understanding of the importance of health and fitness were a harbinger of things to come. With the help of the family he lived with, he set up just behind the high school a community gym, carved out of the storage space of a storefront. He envisioned a place where kids could lift weights, jump rope, use medicine balls, and stay in shape. He charged a nominal fee to use the gym.

Allen himself stayed committed to a rigid daily exercise routine even into his waning years, whether by running, biking, swimming, or doing calisthenics and other exercises. "My father firmly believed that in order to stay strong mentally, you needed to stay strong physically if you hoped to compete and succeed in any field," Jennifer said.[19]

Upon graduating from high school in 1937 at the age of twenty, Allen hoped a career in sports would be his ticket to success. "I was thinking, 'Gee, this would be great, if you could get the right job this would be a great way to make a living," he said in *The Future Is Now*. "I used to go to all the games, University of Detroit, Detroit Lions, University of Michigan. It was in the back of my mind, but I think that it's in the back of every guy's mind. I can remember at that time that this was something I wanted. Whether I could get it or not, I didn't know."[20]

Allen found out during his college years, when he earned a half dozen varsity letters in a cross section of sports, including football, basketball, track, and wrestling. But higher education would be a drawn-out process. He began at age twenty-three and didn't finish until he was nearly thirty-one because he had to work odd jobs to meet financial demands. He sent some of the money to his sister in Rensselaer so she could help support their parents.

In the fall of 1940, Allen began taking classes at Michigan Normal College (now Eastern Michigan University) in Ypsilanti, a few miles west of Detroit. The school's 1943 *Aurora* yearbook indicates that he concentrated on physical education and ran track, played basketball, and served on the board of the Men's Union. He also belonged to Phi Delta Pi, a social organization.[21] He left Michigan Normal in the spring of 1943.

Meanwhile, with World War II raging, Allen joined the U.S. Navy and enlisted in the V-7 Naval Reserve Midshipmen's School program on November 16, 1942. The eight-month program, which included an indoctrination school and a boot camp for officer candidates that consisted of Marine Corps drill instructors, was meant to prepare him for the U.S. Navy V-12 College Training Program.

The V-12 program aimed to generate a large number of officers for the U.S. Navy and Marines to help meet the demands of the war. The federal government paid tuition to colleges and universities so young men, many of whom were from low-income backgrounds and could not afford college, could study with the goal of becoming ensigns in the U.S. Naval Reserve or second lieutenants in the Marines.

The program's main goal was to "give prospective Navy officers the benefits of a college education in those areas most needed by the Navy." The participants were to complete a degree in their major and supplement their academic work with navy classes. Between July 1, 1943, and June 30, 1946, more than 125,000 V-12 candidates enrolled in 131 colleges and universities.[22]

Allen's first stop in the V-12 program was at Alma College, a tiny liberal arts school in Alma, Michigan. The school has no records of his major or any of his other experiences. A 1957 résumé of his indicates that he played on the football team but does not list his position.[23]

However, the following write-up in a 1994 Alma football encyclopedia sheds light on his years at the college: "Allen's association with Alma is somewhat mysterious. College news bureau releases on many occasions have mentioned that he was an end on the 1943 Scot squad. Careful research by [longtime Alma director of publications] Gordon Beld and this author of college records and the *Alma Record* fail to provide any mention of Allen as a football squad member. However, Rex Roseman, left halfback on the 1943 team and a member of the Scot Hall of Fame, says Allen was a member of the team. The author met George Allen at the Capital City Airport on April 25, 1968, to transfer Allen to the third annual Alma College all-sport reunion that evening, where he was to be guest speaker. Allen confirmed that he had been a football player but remembered very little about his playing days at the college. He did remember that Alma seemed 'very small' at the time."[24]

Separately, Allen is mentioned several times in "Cat Chatter," a gossip column in a campus publication. The 6-foot, 160-pound young man with blue eyes and jet black hair was a hit with the ladies.

"To all new students—George Allen was a mighty sharp specimen before his hair grew out to that waving stage (meaning waving in the breeze, straight out)," according to one write-up. "We are afraid it will seriously cramp his style. One helpful suggestion has been made—that he tie it down firmly with a kerchief every night upon retiring, and it will soon get the habit."

Another nugget read, "For the benefit of George Allen fans, he doesn't date up here because, quote, 'I have to study so much, and, well, Saginaw is such a nice town!'"

Then there was this write-up: "Well, kids, 'the fleet's in' . . . that means new material for columns like this one . . . that is, as soon as we get all the new names and faces catalogued . . . so far, from casual observation, we appoint . . . Hank Brennan as successor to George Allen, female heart throb number one."[25]

Allen took his good looks to Marquette University in Milwaukee, studying there from 1944 to 1945. He played end on the school's football team in '44. But in a sharp detour from his aspirations for a career in athletics, he enrolled in the dentistry school and belonged to Psi Omega, an international dental fraternity.[26] His notice of separation from thc navy on December 23, 1945, lists dentistry as his preference for additional training.[27] It's unclear why he considered dentistry as a career path.

"I recall him telling me about his interest in dentistry," Jennifer said. "But I can't imagine him being a dentist. I couldn't see him spending time staring into a person's mouth cleaning their teeth."[28]

As part of the V-12 program, Allen also made his way to Princeton University, the prestigious Ivy League school in New Jersey, and to the U.S. Naval Hospital Corps School in Farragut, Idaho. At the naval hospital, he earned a graduation certificate on August 31, 1945, for having "satisfactorily completed the prescribed course of instruction for the HOSPITAL CORPS." He also received a certificate of award as part of the hospital's softball team.[29]

Allen met many famous people in life. Such was the case at Princeton, where he had an exchange with the brilliant scientist Albert Einstein. Einstein lived in the town of Princeton from 1933 until his death in 1955. Despite never serving on the university's faculty, he led a seminar on the mathematics of relativity and helped students with math problems.

Einstein is often mistakenly connected with the U.S. project to build the atomic bomb that ended World War II. In reality, he didn't participate in the project, although he was key to facilitating its development through his theory of relativity, which explained the energy released in the bomb.

One day toward the end of the war, Allen's competitive instincts consumed him: he was determined to challenge Einstein to a game of checkers. In a wide-ranging 1989 conversation with Steve Guback, who reported on Allen's Redskins for the *Washington Star* in the '70s and served as the information officer for the President's Council on Physical Fitness and Sports when Allen chaired that body in the '80s, Allen explained how he met Einstein in hopes of beating him in checkers:

"I was a pretty good checkers player and won some tournaments and even played a guy named Steve Rubin who was champion of the world. He beat me decisively. But there weren't many people that could beat me. And I could play a few games, maybe eight moves by the numbers. So I heard that Albert Einstein was a good checkers player. I thought, 'Boy, oh boy, would I love to play Albert Einstein in a checker game.'"[30]

On a Sunday morning after church, Allen boarded a bus with another navy midshipman, Bill Nuse, en route to Einstein's house at 112 Mercer Street in Princeton. But the bus took them only so far, and they had to trudge through the snow to reach his house. Allen knocked repeatedly on the door before an elderly woman opened it. She didn't speak English and motioned for the two young men, who were in their navy uniforms, to wait.

"We waited for what seemed like twenty minutes but was probably only about ten," Allen remembered. "She let us in and pointed to go in the living room by the fireplace. We just stood there and looked around and didn't even sit down. She came in and told us in broken English the best we could understand that Einstein would be down very soon.

"Then I heard the biggest noise. You talk about an earthquake. I thought, 'Oh my. He's fallen down the stairs. I hope he didn't get hurt.' It was a rattle and rumble. And all at once I see this guy come bursting into the living room. He was in sweat clothes, baggy stuff, a sweat shirt, could even have been pajamas, but I don't think it was, big whiskers, hair flying all over the place, and eyes lit up.

"I told him, 'Mr. Einstein, thank you for allowing us to come into your home. The reason I'm here is I heard you're a good checkers player. This is one of my favorite games, and I'd be honored to play you in a game of checkers.' He laughed and said, 'No, I'm not a good checkers player. People say a lot of things about me that aren't true.' So when he said he wasn't a good checkers player, then I wanted to play him even more. I said, 'Well, I'd like to play you just one game for the fun of it.' He said, 'I don't even have a board. Did you bring a board?'"

Allen didn't bring a board, either, a lack of preparation that would be antithetical to how he carried himself in life. So the checkers game was not to be. But before the two midshipmen left, Einstein had a parting message.

"As we were going to the door," Allen said, "Einstein said the war is going to end very soon: 'BOOM, BOOM.' A big noise, he spread his arms. We didn't know what he meant, but of course he was telling us that it was the atomic bomb. That was about 1944, '45, so Einstein had to be pretty old then. But he still was nimble and alert. It's one of the big thrills of my life."

Jennifer Allen said her father's moxie in wanting to challenge a genius to an intellectual game was one of his defining features. "It was so gutsy and so my dad: 'Why not, why can't I try that, why can't I show up?' It's a sense of hope. My dad always had hope."[31]

The end of the war didn't mean an end to Allen's educational pursuits. Two months after separating from the navy in December 1945, he enrolled at the University of Michigan in Ann Arbor, where his commitment to college finally paid off with both a bachelor's and a master's degree.

True to form, Allen was also a jock at Michigan. He played intramural basketball for the fraternity Phi Sigma. He was good, too. The school newspaper, the *Michigan Daily*, noted that in a 72–16 romp of Acacia, the "trio of Van Lenpe, George Allen, and Ben Pipp accounted for a total of 56 markers."[32] Allen also earned a "reserve" letter on the Wolverines' 1946 varsity wrestling team and served as vice president of the Men's Physical Education Club. Plus, he joined Sigma Delta Psi, a national honorary athletic and scholastic fraternity with demanding entry requirements.

"To get in," Allen said in *The Future Is Now*, "you had to have a B average, and you had to swim 100 yards in one minute, twenty-five seconds, do a 10-second handstand, climb a 25-foot rope in, I think, twelve seconds, do the 120-yard high hurdles in sixteen seconds, throw a baseball 250 feet, punt a football forty-five yards, run a mile in five minutes, run the hundred in eleven [seconds] flat, put a 16-pound shot thirty feet, do a 17-foot long jump, and high jump five feet."[33]

Having exhausted all of his college football playing eligibility, Allen considered his next best option: coaching. He had already acquired some experience. In what appears to be his first football coaching stint, he served as line coach for the sophomore team at nearby Ann Arbor High School in the fall of '46. His 1957 résumé notes that the team won a championship, but the school has no record of that.[34]

In the months leading up to the 1947 season, Allen asked legendary Wolverines coach H. O. "Fritz" Crisler if he could join his staff. Not a bad idea. Allen would learn from not only a proven winner but also one of the premier coaches in college football history. At the time, the Wolverines stood as one of the top teams in the country and featured All-Americans up and down the roster.

In ten seasons under Crisler (1938–47), Michigan posted a phenomenal 71-16-3 record for a winning percentage of .805, today the second-best mark in school history, and won two Western Conference championships. (It was also called the Big 9 Conference at the time.) His 1947 team went 10-0, including a 49–0 demolition of Southern California in the Rose Bowl. The Wolverines finished that season ranked first in the country, and Crisler was named national coach of the year.

Crisler rejected Allen's coaching request. But Allen refused to take no for an answer and arranged another appointment to see Crisler, who was also the school's athletic director. This time, Allen improvised when making his request. "I was washing dishes and doing bus boy work at the student union," Allen told Steve Guback. "So I said, 'Coach Crisler, I'm making $85 a month on the GI Bill, and I've got my room and board [covered] for washing dishes and bus boy work. I'll pay you $60 a month to coach at the University of Michigan and help you on the team in any capacity.' I figured I could do that and get by. He looked at me and laughed and laughed and said, 'No, I can't do that.'

"Two weeks later, I got a call from someone saying Fritz Crisler wants to see me. Boy oh boy, what a thrill that was. I went in his office, and he said, 'George Allen, I have a job for you. You don't have to pay me, but we're going to pay you.' So I said, 'Coach, what is it?' He said, 'Michigan is going to field a 150-pound football team, and I'd like you to be the line coach.' I said without hesitation, 'It's a deal!' That's how I got my start there.

"How many guys would do something like that?" Allen asked rhetorically in reference to his bold offer.[35]

His timing was impeccable. Michigan was slated to be part of an experimental 150-pound league that included Ohio State, Illinois, and Wisconsin. In a four-game season, the Wolverines would play each of the three other schools, with two games against longtime rival Ohio State.

The head coach of Michigan's lightweights was Cliff Keen, an assistant to Crisler. Keen was better known as the school's wrestling coach. On the mats, his Wolverines compiled a 276-88-11 record in dual meets from 1925 to 1970. They were two-time NCAA runners-up and won thirteen Big 10 championships.

For the career in sports that Allen had dreamed of since his youth, this was the break he needed. The opportunity would open important doors for him in the competitive world of football coaching.

2
The Roots of His Genius

George Allen was born and grew up in Michigan. He attended high school and spent most of his college years there, including some at the University of Michigan. Now he was in the genesis of his storied life as a football coach at where else but the University of Michigan.

What could have been more apropos?

It was the spring of 1947. Not only was Allen getting his start as an assistant for Michigan's 150-pound lightweight team, but he was doing it at a school with an entrenched football tradition amid a sea of color and pageantry, all of which was punctuated by Michigan's famous fight song, "The Victors."

While pursuing a bachelor's degree in physical education at the school, Allen had a whistle in his mouth and a clipboard in his hands. He was handling line duties for the lightweight football team, which in a few months would kick off its first season. Its head coach was Cliff Keen, the school's wrestling coach and an assistant to varsity head football coach Fritz Crisler. Some 115 students, including a slew of talented players, tried out for the team, which the press often referred to as the "midget footballers" or the "little Wolverines."

"What amazed Keen and me was that so many excellent athletes came out for the team—all-state, all-conference players, outstanding track men, and athletes in other sports who were too small to play varsity ball," Allen, who was Keen's only assistant, wrote in an article he penned for the *Sports Fans' Journal* in 1987. "One of the main reasons we had such a good turnout was because World War II had just ended, and every school was loaded with service veterans. It was an excellent experiment to give more players a chance to compete from the student body of 16,000. One-hundred-fifty-pound football had been played in the Ivy League and service academies, and Crisler, who had coached at Princeton, saw how successful it had been."[1]

While serving as the lightweights' line coach, Allen was also a graduate assistant to Crisler, who allowed him to observe varsity practices and even gave him a varsity playbook.[2] At the 1947 spring practices, Allen tracked the varsity coaches in how they handled specific circumstances. A review of his copious notes from some of the practices provided a snapshot of the meticulousness and sharp attention to detail with which he'd approach his head coaching roles in the coming years. It made perfect sense that the phrase "winning is the science of being totally prepared—there is no detail too small" long stood as one of his coaching mantras.

Crisler led the varsity practices, which included such assistants as Keen, Benny Oosterbaan, Jack Blott, and Forrest "Butch" Jordan. At the first spring practice on April 14, 1947, Allen wrote, "first item I noted was that all coaches were on the field early before the players. This seems to impress players and develops an attitude of promptness.

"At this time, I have an idea that should be extremely useful to anyone coaching. I'm going to take each position and interview players at that position with experience on all details that are essential [for] doing a good job on the field. This applies to [the] Michigan system single wing.

"Crisler stressed inflection of voice for quarterbacks and a leadership—commanding attitude.

"Benny Oosterbaan had all backs and ends going out for passes. [He] also had one man spinning who was the fullback. Crisler walked from group to group observing procedures."

Regarding an April 15 practice, Allen wrote, "I talked with Oosterbaan concerning space of backs before and after shift. Here's the way I understand it before shift: Backs assume upright stance, that is, semi-erect position—feet in line—normal spread—weight on balls of feet—both knees bent—buttocks lower than his shoulders—straight back—his head up, eyes focused on ball, both hands resting on knees, with arms straight—but relaxed."[3]

All the while, Allen witnessed a Michigan squad that crafted one of its most glorious college campaigns ever: a 10-0 regular season followed by a 49–0 shellacking of Southern California in the Rose Bowl. A No. 1 post-bowl ranking from the Associated Press cemented the 1947 Wolverines as one of the greatest teams in college football history.

Michigan's lightweights earned bragging rights, too. They finished 3-1, destroying Ohio State, 39–0, in the season finale to tie Wisconsin for the conference championship. One of the team's best players was Frank Whitehouse, who played quarterback, halfback, end, and punter.

The *Michigan Daily*, the student newspaper, covered the team consistently, with Allen receiving his share of props. After the Wolverines' season-opening win over Illinois, the newspaper reported that the victory was of "great satisfaction" to Cliff Keen and George Allen. "The performance of the line was especially outstanding," Keen stated. "Several goal-line stands nullified long Illini drives that would have resulted in touchdowns. Although Illinois made more first downs than we did, our line came through in the punches and held."[4]

Two decades later, Keen told of Allen's drive for perfection in an article in the *Ann Arbor News*: "Allen was a stickler for details. I honestly felt he tried to give our players too much detail for the relatively short time we had practice. But he thought football day and night."[5]

That would be a familiar description of George Allen in the years to come.

While coaching the lightweights, Allen also devoted time to his academic work. Realizing that his ability to communicate was a fundamental tool in coaching and teaching, he minored in English and took courses at Michigan in public speaking, organization, and administration.

"Clark Shaughnessy, who invented the T-formation, was a brilliant coach but ineffective as a communicator," Allen wrote in his 1990 book, *Strategies for Winning*. "Communication is more important than knowledge. George Halas, the father of pro football, did not have Shaughnessy's great knowledge. But he had enough, and he was an excellent communicator and motivator with his own methods."[6]

In June 1947 Allen earned a bachelor's degree in education with a teacher's certificate in physical education. From there, he set out to finish a graduate-level program in education. Rather than taking the easy road—six hours of audit—he chose to write a thesis, producing a masterpiece in the process. He showcased his passion for football, his incredible foresight, and his instincts for the game that proved so valuable in the coming years. In his thesis, "A Study of Outstanding Football Coaches' Attitudes and Practices in Scouting," he focused on an element of not only football but sports in general that has long been considered critical to a team's success.

Allen typed the three-hundred-page thesis by himself. He mainly focused on scouting an opponent and showing an ability to think out of the box, coupled with a meticulous approach—traits that were synonymous with his coaching style down the road. He understood the importance of fleshing out some of the most esoteric details, such as how many scouts should attend a game and where they should sit in the stadium to gain the best angle for evaluating an opponent. The thesis included thirty-eight conclusions and eight recommendations, as well as neatly laid out tables, charts, and diagrams.

In the thesis, Allen claimed to be the first person to undertake an analysis of football scouting of such magnitude: "Upon a preliminary review of the problem, it was found that no study comparable to this one in scouting had been made," he wrote. "It, therefore, became evident that investigation of the problem would contribute to a very little-known field. In addition, the writer's coaching experience in football provided the interest for studying the effects of scouting. Finally, it was desirable to include thoughts and attitudes of leading football coaches with experience so that younger colleagues might gain the benefit of their experience.

"Scouting, like any other profession, requires proper training if coaches are to get the full value from this essential phase of football. No member of the coaching staff should be selected with more painstaking care than the scout. The development of football in the past few years throughout the United States places even more emphasis on the importance of the scout, his obligations to the head coach, and to each and every player on the squad. Men of exceptional character, intelligence, sportsmanship, and a comprehensive knowledge of football will materially aid both scouting and football. It is hoped that such a high type of leadership will be available for the future direction of football as a school sport."[7]

To support his research, Allen wrote letters to fifty-two college coaches and four pro coaches, many of whom he had read about and who had inspired him to pursue a career in coaching. He solicited opinions on how the coaches approached the art of scouting, asking four sets of questions:

> "To what extent do you use scouting reports? By this I mean, how much emphasis do you place on your scouting material?"
>
> "What do you consider more important in your scouting report—the defensive or offensive maneuvers?"
>
> "How many scouts would you like to have to cover a game adequately? From what angle of the stadium would you have them view the game? Would you keep them together or separate them?"
>
> "To what extent has scouting been responsible for the success you have achieved? Can you recall a game where scouting has played a major factor in your winning?"

Allen also requested that the coaches send examples of scouting report forms that they used, all of which he included in the thesis.

Forty-six coaches responded, including established college icons in Crisler, Army's Colonel Earl "Red" Blaik, Notre Dame's Frank Leahy, Duke's Wallace Wade, and Rice's Jess Neely, and future coaching luminaries, such as Georgia Tech's Bobby Dodd. All four of the pro coaches wrote back, and two of them, Chicago's George Halas and Green Bay's Earl "Curly" Lambeau, were founding fathers of the National Football League.

Allen, in one of his main conclusions, wrote that "coaches, as a rule, scout extensively and place great emphasis on it. Thirty-three, or 72%, of the coaches selected for this study regarded the scouting of opponents as extremely important, and believed it was well worth the time, effort, and expense involved. Since competition is so keen in modern football, coaches attach high value to scouting information for game preparation."

In another telling statistic, Allen noted that 41 percent of the coaches who responded said the aspect of scouting that should be emphasized the most pertains to both offense and defense. Forty percent said offense, 11 percent defense, 4 percent personnel, and 2 percent offense, defense, and personnel. Two percent had no comment.

Most of the respondents sounded cordial and appreciative of Allen for pursuing an analysis of scouting. A few asked to see the finished product.

Said Georgia's Wally Butts, "I think that every ball game is more or less won by the scouting report turned in by a competent man. We at Georgia think that scouting is just as much a part of football as the actual work on the field."

Virginia's Arthur Guepe noted, "Depending on the situation, we use anywhere from one to three scouts per game and try to see each opponent at least twice. If our opponent is an important rival, naturally, we shall put more time on him."

John DaGrosa of Holy Cross gave one of the most thorough responses. It included a diagram of an opponent's alignment that explained how many times that team called a certain play to a given spot (run or pass), how many yards were gained, and who passed, received, and carried the ball.

DaGrosa also detailed how comprehensive scouting of the Boston College Eagles made the difference in a season-ending 13–6 Holy Cross win in 1946. He told how his Crusaders used a 7-2-2 defense against the Eagles after scouting them in seven games, saying no other team had used the 7-2-2 against Boston College all season. He noted that "on a pet play the

Eagles had used several times for long gains," a Holy Cross defensive guard was in the right spot to make a game-saving tackle in the final minutes that preserved the 13–6 victory.

In the pros, Cleveland's Paul Brown thanked Allen for his "nice letter." He answered all four questions and said he could recall "many examples" when scouting data were the key factor in winning a game. Brown also referred back to his high school coaching days: "When I was coaching at Massillon High School [in Massillon, Ohio], we used to play on Friday nights while our opponent, Canton-McKinley, played on Saturday afternoons. This enabled our entire staff to scout them week after week, and we usually had their offense down to a fine point by the time we were to play them. It aided us greatly in defensing them and in the success we had in playing them."

The gruff George Halas chimed in with some pertinent observations:

> Dear Sir:
>
> Naturally, you can realize how busy I have been and, as a matter of fact, still am. I am also apologizing for my failing in not writing you sooner.
>
> First, we make very good use of scouting reports by our own scouts. We recognize scouting of rival teams as highly essential for the success of our organization. Second, it is difficult to state which is more important, the scouting report or the offense or defense maneuver. This all depends on the particular team we scout and their style of play. Fourth, do you use more than one scout per game? Yes, sometimes we use three men for scouting a particular game. Fourth, while I hesitate to say that a particular scouting report was a major factor in winning a particular game, on a number of occasions they have been especially important for us.

This was likely the first interaction Allen had with Halas, the Bears' owner and head coach and the face of the organization. But it wouldn't be the last. Starting in about a decade, the two would be together over the course of seven full NFL seasons (1959–65), with Allen coming to see Halas as his chief mentor.

Allen, a prolific writer who would complete about a dozen books on football, used much of the information from his master's thesis for a 1953 book called *How to Scout Football*. He earned a master's degree in education at Michigan in February 1948 and pursued coursework toward a doctorate in education at Michigan in the summer of 1948. But he came up short in earning the doctorate at both Michigan and the University of Southern California, where he took classes later in life.

For George Allen, the time had arrived to put into action the idea that had surfaced in his childhood: a career as a football coach. With name recognition from his previous coaching gigs, he was interviewed by several high schools in Michigan, two of which offered a job as head football coach. But he declined those offers. He felt that high school coaching would stifle his chances of advancing to college football or the pros.[8] His goal was to coach football at the University of Michigan, which offered him a job as assistant track coach. But the school's track coach, Don Canham, wouldn't allow him to carry double duties, so he turned the track offer down.

Allen then became creative. To pinpoint schools he thought might be interested in hiring him, he poured through a national directory, the *Blue Book of College Athletics*, which listed nearly a thousand schools and their addresses. With his customary thoroughness, he prepared more than eight hundred form letters to schools for a position as an assistant, including ones he had never heard of. Michigan allowed him to use its stationery because he had been line coach for the 150-pound lightweight team.[9] Canham, who attended graduate school at Michigan at the same time as Allen, wrote in his 1996 book *From the Inside: A Half Century of Michigan Athletics*, that his wife helped Allen type some of the letters. Allen became friends with Canham, who served as Michigan's athletic director from 1968 to 1988.[10]

Allen received two answers from colleges interested in interviewing him: Trinity College in Hartford, Connecticut, where the head coach was Dan Jessee, and Morningside College in Sioux City, Iowa, which was coached by Les Davis. "I had heard of Dan Jessee and Trinity, but I had never heard of Morningside," Allen once said. "When I called Trinity, the job was already filled. So that left only Morningside."[11]

Allen's journey to Sioux City was tumultuous. "When I flew in there, I came by the way of Omaha [Nebraska], and I hadn't eaten breakfast," he said. "I didn't have a lot of money, and I hadn't done a lot of flying. I ended up getting really sick on the plane. It was a really bumpy ride from Omaha to Sioux City, really rough weather."

Allen surprised the six people who met him at the airport: "I said, 'I'm sorry, but I don't think I'm in very good shape to have an interview. So they took me to a hotel. The doctor gave me a pill, and I went to sleep. I don't know how long I slept. When I woke up, it was the next morning, and I thought, 'Oh boy, oh boy, what a way to start a job.' Then I had to stay there an extra day."

The interview still took place. On April 20, 1948, Allen met with Morningside president Earl Roadman and a board consisting of faculty and athletic department personnel.[12] "I was interviewed altogether by about twenty-five different people," he remembered. "In the last meeting after they asked me a lot of questions, I pulled an envelope out of my pocket. I always liked to write on envelopes, and I had ten questions. Then they asked me to leave the room."[13]

Soon after, Allen was offered his first college coaching job. But it wasn't as an assistant. Raised as a Catholic, he was asked to become the head football coach at a private, liberal arts school that was founded in 1894 by the Methodist Episcopal Church and had an enrollment of about 1,500 students. "I was caught off guard when the president offered me the head coaching job," Allen wrote in *Strategies for Winning*. "I pointed out that they had a head coach, Les Davis, and I had not come there to apply for his job. I was told that Davis was going to retire, and that the head coaching job was mine on the condition that I was willing to coach track as well. So I had come full circle on the subject of track."[14]

Davis left Morningside to become the sports director at radio station WNAX in Yankton, South Dakota. He had guided the Maroons for two seasons, finishing 3-5-1 in 1946 and 4-4 in 1947. He was also relinquishing his duties as Morningside's athletic director and head baseball coach, as well as his faculty position in physical education. Al Buckingham, Morningside's basketball coach, would take over as athletic director.[15]

Before saying yes to Morningside, Allen spoke with two men he knew from Michigan: his mentor Fritz Crisler and Don Canham. Crisler told him to take the job before the school changed its mind. He thus accepted the position and an annual salary of $3,900. He asked school officials if they'd also hire an assistant coach for $500, saying that "for one man to turn this around is a big order."[16] After the school obliged, he named Bill Pritula, a star tackle on Michigan's 1947 national championship team, as the Maroons' line coach.

In May 1948 Morningside welcomed Allen with a flattering write-up in the school alumni publication, *The Morningsider*: "An announcement by athletic director Les Davis after meeting with President Earl A. Roadman and the athletic committee of the board of trustees has revealed the signing of George Allen, assistant coach at the University of Michigan, as head grid mentor of the Maroons.

"He has been extensively trained in the single-wing, unbalanced line formation that took Michigan to the Rose Bowl.

"The new Maroon mentor comes here highly recommended by Fritz Crisler, former head coach at Michigan, and by Benny Oosterbaan, current head mentor there. Crisler says, 'I believe Allen has superior qualities as a football coach. He is conscientious, loyal, and industrious.'

"Coach Allen will report for duty at Morningside in mid-August, but he was on the campus May 17 when he was honored at a dinner in the Women's Residence Hall at 7:00 p.m. Sixty of the outstanding athletes of the surrounding territory were present to get acquainted with the Morningside College coaching staff. Colored pictures of the New Year's Day Rose Bowl game between Michigan and the University of Southern California were shown by Mr. Allen at the dinner."[17]

In one of his first trips from Ann Arbor to the Morningside campus, Allen had to call an audible because he could not afford a car. So he asked a car rental agency if he could drive one of its new vehicles to Sioux City. The agency only had an old milk truck that needed to be transported seven hundred miles west, to Omaha, Nebraska, which is about a hundred miles south of Sioux City. Allen agreed to drive the milk truck. Once in Omaha, he persuaded the company to let him drive on to Sioux City, from where, as the story goes, a milkman drove the truck back.[18] Similar to how he persuaded Crisler to consider him as an assistant coach, this was a vintage George Allen improvisation: maintain bold ideas and an unwillingness to take no for an answer in order to achieve what you want.

On the coaching front, Allen's moment had arrived. At age thirty-one, he was grabbing the head coaching reins for the first time. His debut intersected with a period when American football was rising in popularity, after emerging from a stretch when both pro and college football were still impacted by the urgent demands of World War II, in which many pro and college football players served. NFL roster shortages led to franchise mergers, and rumors circulated that the league was in jeopardy of folding. During the war, many colleges abandoned football, including Morningside, leaving the NFL with a much leaner talent pool from which to recruit. The Maroons suspended their program for two seasons before reviving it in 1945.

Three years later, George Allen became the twelfth coach in the history of Morningside football.

3

From America's Heartland to Southern California

Upon arriving in Sioux City in 1948, George Allen was focused on transforming Morningside football into an entertaining product and a consistent winner. The Maroons were coming off three straight nonwinning seasons and a 0-4 campaign in the North Central Conference (NCC), which they had won only once since its inception in 1922. For the most part, they were a conference doormat, a warm-up for more formidable opponents.

In contrast, two schools, North Dakota and Iowa State Teachers College (later known as the University of Northern Iowa), had ruled the NCC with thirteen championships between them. The Iowa school had captured five straight prior to Allen's arrival at Morningside, tying Augustana College in 1942 and South Dakota in 1947. (The conference did not compete from 1942 to 1945 during World War II.) North Dakota State and South Dakota State rounded out the NCC field.

Allen hoped to pull off a few surprises in 1948. In a manner that became more known in his NFL coaching days, Allen dove into the assignment with tunnel vision. He lived and breathed Morningside football, showing a fanaticism and a level of intensity rarely if ever before seen at the Sioux City school. He never stopped grinding in his quest to amass knowledge about the art of coaching. "I would collect statistics from all major colleges," he once said. "Then I would determine the ten best offensive and ten best defensive teams. I'd write to the coaches and ask for game films to study. I would drive my car, at my own expense, to as many coaching clinics as I could. Everything I did was an attempt to know more about coaching."[1]

Dick Weikert, a Morningside fullback who played for Allen in 1950, had a front-row seat to Allen's attention to detail: "He was very concentrated on making that operation as near perfect as you can get. He knew that if he did things right with his offense, it was going to work, and it usually did pretty well. If everybody carried out their jobs just like with any team, things were going to work right. He worked awfully hard at that. Football was his life pretty much at the time. Personality-wise, he was very good to get along with, answering questions and things like that."[2]

Allen inherited a 1948 Morningside team that sported some talented players. They included junior halfback Connie Callahan, who would go down as one of the greatest offensive players in Morningside history, as well as sophomore fullback Bob Hooks and senior end Leon "Shorty" Shortenhaus. All three earned first-team all-conference honors.

In one of his first strategic moves, Allen switched the Maroons from the T formation to the more daring Michigan-style single-wing formation, which was known for its razzle-dazzle, deception, and trickery. The Michigan-style setup included a spinning fullback, who would take the snap and spin and then hand off, or fake, the ball to the right halfback, left halfback, or the quarterback coming at him and keep the ball.

Allen quickly embarked on finding skilled players not only to run the single-wing formation but also to improve other facets of the team. He made trips east to look for potential recruits in Chicago and his hometown of Detroit, eventually signing a host of players from those cities. "I always used to go to state and city high school (track) meets in Detroit," he said in *The Future Is Now*. "We got a lot of our players that way. I got a fullback, a tackle, and a defensive back just by going to the finals of the city meet in Detroit one year."[3] He scouted players even before leaving for Morningside, bringing with him a reported nine high school graduates from Michigan and Ohio.[4]

He also wrote letters to prospective recruits, touting the program and what he had to offer as a coach, and to current players to maintain lines of communication. In separate letters dated May 21, 1948, he congratulated Callahan and Hooks for making the all-conference team in 1947 and shared thoughts on how they would fit into the single-wing offense.

"I believe the single-wing, as we will use this fall, will give you an opportunity for many long runs and offer many passing opportunities," he told Callahan, who co-captained the '48 team with Shortenhaus. "I'm planning to use you at tail. Your deception and faking at this spot with the [fullback] is essential, as you undoubtedly noticed by watching [star Michigan halfback and quarterback Bob] Chappius."

In his letter to Hooks, Allen wrote, "As you know, Michigan's single wing is built around the spinning of the [fullback]. From all reports, I've heard you spin well. I hope you practice it this summer. Your ball handling must be clever and spinning complete. As you probably noticed, watching [Michigan fullback Jack] Weisenburger, we use the complete spin—ball coming to [the fullback] on left leg. . . . Your first step is with the right foot on a 45-degree angle. You have two fakes on many plays—to tail and wing."[5]

Allen also implemented coaching methods that helped the Morningside program mature. He involved himself in studying films of opponents, hoping to find the slightest crack he could exploit. As an incentive, he launched a Morningside alumni award to honor the team's most improved player after every season.

By the time practice opened, Allen had recruited another assistant. George Johnson, another starting tackle on Michigan's 1947 team, coached Morningside's ends during eleven days of two-a-day practices, before returning to Ann Arbor to pursue his master's degree in industrial engineering.

When Allen was on the Morningside campus, the initially car-less rookie coach resorted to riding his bike everywhere, including to practice. He vowed he wouldn't buy a car until he posted his first winning season. Sure enough, after his 7-3-1 season in 1949, he bought a 1949 red Ford convertible, a car he still drove in '57 when he became a Los Angeles Rams assistant.[6] According to a write-up in a school publication, the *Collegian Reporter*, "The young man you see riding a bicycle around the campus isn't a transfer student as many seem to think but is our new football coach, Mr. George Allen."[7]

With Morningside not exactly exhibiting signs of a school committed to becoming a football powerhouse, Allen personally had to seed the football field so there'd be grass. He also created a set of weights for his players by filling Maxwell House coffee cans with cement. He attached the cans to the opposite ends of a metal bar so it resembled a barbell.[8]

The Morningside Maroons kicked off the '48 season by hosting Midland at their home field, Public Schools Stadium. They made it look easy, winning 33–0. Hooks, Dave Waleryszak, and Bob Fulton caught touchdown passes, and Loren Moll ran 70 yards for another score.

Allen couldn't have asked for a better start. "Coach George Allen's grid charges partly mastered the intricate Michigan single-wing offense in a brief eleven-day practice period," the *Collegian Reporter* revealed. "It was their deceptive ball handling and superior physical condition that gave them the lopsided victory over the ragged Midland team."[9]

The Maroons subsequently lost consecutive games to North Dakota, Iowa State Teachers College, and Omaha University. They looked particularly inept in a 33–0 loss to Iowa State Teachers. "It was definitely not the Maroons' night as the Panthers capitalized on fumbles, blocked punts, and interceptions to run up the high score," *The Morningsider* reported.[10]

Injuries weren't helping. Callahan hurt his ankle against Iowa State Teachers, sidelining Morningside's triple-threat halfback for the rest of that game and the Omaha game. His running mate, Hooks, twisted his ankle in the second quarter of a 13–6 loss to Omaha.

Moll picked up the slack against North Dakota State in Fargo, running for 14- and 26-yard touchdowns in a 22–7 victory that marked the Maroons' first conference win since 1946. Then came two more setbacks: 21–14 to Augustana and 14–7 to South Dakota in the Maroons' homecoming game.

Allen's troops responded by tallying another conference win, 18–13, this one on the road over South Dakota State. In the season-ending game, a 38–7 loss to Bowling Green left Allen with a 3-6 mark overall and a 2-4 record in the North Central Conference in his first year at Morningside. Still, he gained a reputation as a demanding, no-nonsense coach. "You either did it his way or you didn't play," recalled Shortenhaus in a 1989 article in the *Burbank Leader*. Shortenhaus, a senior during Allen's first year, went out in style by posting first-team all-conference honors. "Having George Allen as a coach was really a memorable experience in my life," he said.[11]

Although 1948 marked the end for Shortenhaus's playing career, he never relinquished his ties to Morningside or Allen. The two remained good friends for decades and reunited on the coaching front in the late 1980s, when Shortenhaus convinced Allen to spend time with the Maroons as the honorary coach for the first George Allen Classic, played in Sioux City in 1989.

Allen summarized his first season at Morningside in a letter he penned for *The Morningsider* in November 1948: "Considering the fact that our boys had to learn the intricate Michigan single-wing system, which has taken the champion Michigan team years to master, our record is understandable. During the past season, Morningside won two conference games, which was two more than in 1947; defeated two teams which Morningside had not beaten in 11 years; and except for an early game fumble, might have trounced the highly rated Coyotes from [the University of] South Dakota. When the percentages were figured, the Maroons had the best offensive and defensive record of teams tied for fourth place in the North Central Conference."[12]

He also issued a call for bigger and more talented players: "The quality of football depends upon the quality of the players. We were outweighed and outmanned in every contest last fall. We must have bigger and better men if we hope to improve our record in 1949. This is where you can aid your college, as well as the student you recommend.

"If you know an outstanding athlete in your area—contact him. Get his name and send it to the athletic department, or have the boy himself write us. We will follow up [with] each prospect and inform you of our progress."

Although the 1949 season was Allen's primary concentration, he couldn't help but be distracted by the presence of someone at a spring function on the Morningside campus: a young woman visiting from the North African country of Tunisia. Her name was Henrietta Lumbroso. She would become a pillar in his life and the "unbreakable rock" of the Allen family.

Lumbroso was the daughter of Felix Lumbroso and Eugenie Garcin. The Lumbrosos were part of a Sephardic Jewish family that most likely fled Spain and went to the Italian Peninsula during the Spanish Inquisition in the late fifteenth or early sixteenth century—when Jews and Muslims were ordered to convert to Catholicism or leave Spain. In the nineteenth century, as Italy was developing strong political, economic, and social ties to Tunisia, tens of thousands of Italians migrated across the Mediterranean to the North African country. In 1881 French forces seized control of Tunisia, launching a bid by European powers to colonize the African continent. Tunisia remained a French protectorate for the next seventy-five years.

The Lumbrosos thrived in a country with a large Italian community. Felix Lumbroso, a successful businessman based in the capital, Tunis, imported wine and spirits and exported olive oil. Both of Henrietta's parents were Jewish, and "Etty" herself was raised Jewish. Educated and worldly, she was fluent in English, French, Italian, Arabic, Spanish, and Latin.[13]

But during World War II, Tunisia was caught in the North African campaign. Units from two of the Axis powers—Germany and Italy—battled Allied troops, mostly from Britain and the United States, across the Sahara Desert, with fighting in Morocco, Algeria, Tunisia, Libya, and Egypt.

In Europe, Germany's military defeat of France led to the establishment of the "Vichy regime," in which the pro-fascist government of unoccupied France and its territories collaborated with Nazi Germany. The government imposed antisemitic legislation on the nearly half million Jews of Tunisia, Morocco, and Algeria (the latter being two other French colonies in North Africa). French police organized raids to capture Jews in North Africa, where enslavement camps surfaced in Morocco, Algeria, Tunisia, and Libya, an Italian colony. During their six months in Tunisia, the Germans interned an estimated five thousand Jewish men in these labor camps, and Jewish businesses were confiscated.

Tunisia was the only Arab country occupied by the Germans, and some Tunisian Jews were deported and killed in Europe. SS troops from the Nazi Party's elite corps rounded up Jews in Tunis, where at some point Felix Lumbroso was imprisoned. The Allen family has no record of whether the man also known as "Popop" was sent to a labor camp or how long he was detained before his release.

"The way my mother explained it, Popop was rousted out of bed in the dark of the night by the Nazis and put in prison," George Felix Allen recalled. "She said it was either because he was part of a French Resistance movement or because he was a prominent businessman. The Nazis had plans to exterminate the Jews in North Africa—the same hideous killing of the Jews that they pulled off in Germany, Poland, and elsewhere. They weren't able to effectuate it because they were run out of there by British and American forces."[14]

Efforts to liberate Tunisia began in early 1943, as the Allies gradually cut off Germany's supply bases and squeezed Axis forces into a pocket along the country's Mediterranean coast. On May 7, 1943, British troops captured Tunis, and the Americans seized Bizerte, the last port held by the Axis. The Germans surrendered a few days later, marking the end of the North African campaign.

Henrietta never forgot the significance of the date May 7, 1943. In a letter to her four children five years before her death in 2013, she described the terrifying circumstances that she and her family faced while the Nazis occupied Tunisia: "Today is a very important date. That is the day the Germans and [General Erwin] Rommel's army surrendered, and the Allies liberated us from them. I remember seeing the previously arrogant German officers who used to come and eat at the restaurant [in the building] where we lived. The owner was a customer friend of Popop, and he let us stay in some spare rooms he had there. He also lived there. The officers used to come in, click their heels together, and say 'Heil Hitler.' We had to keep smiling, so we wouldn't look suspicious. We left our Tunis home and sheltered ourselves at the restaurant [in the city of Carthage] thinking we might be safer from the bombing, not knowing the German headquarters were nearby. . . . So on this day, we saw the same officers come down the hill with their buttons off their jackets and arms up. After them came the first English and American tanks, chanting, 'Remember the day, the seventh of May.'

"Oh my!!!!! What a joyous day! Funny I remember the day but not the year. Still have a mental block about some dates. Excuse the sequence of my story, as I am still very emotional thinking about it! However, I am glad I remember all of it very clearly. It makes me appreciate my life now even more! I hope none of you experience anything similar. Even though the Allies bombed us, we were grateful for all who liberated us from the Nazi occupation. That was the beginning of the end of the war with Germany!"[15]

During the war, Henrietta Lumbroso volunteered at a hospital to help wounded Allied soldiers. There, she met a British officer who influenced the Lumbroso family to visit the United States. "My mom and her parents befriended the officer," Greg Allen explained. "They had him over for dinner at the house. He became part of their family and would come over and socialize. Then one day he said, 'Let me know if you ever want to go to America,' because he had friends in Sioux City, Iowa. That was the connection to come over and visit the U.S."[16]

The Lumbrosos made their way to Sioux City, where Etty met George Allen on the Morningside campus. They dated briefly, and after she returned to Tunisia, they corresponded for more than a year and fell in love in the process.

Allen, who once sent a telegram to Etty saying, "I'd like to have you as my teammate," proposed to her after Morningside's 1950 season. Around Christmas, he flew in a propeller plane more than five thousand miles, to New York, Paris, and Tunisia, to pop the question, probably encountering a lot of turbulence along the way.[17] Or did he travel to the North African country for another reason?

According to an article in the *Collegian Reporter*, "Rumor has it that he was hunting for some foreign football players that wouldn't be eligible for the draft." The publication further noted that "Coach Allen must have thought Iowa looked pretty bleak because immediately upon returning he warmed up his red convertible and made tracks toward Dallas, Texas, to attend the national coaches' convention. When he had a moment to spare, he filed his application for the now vacant coaching job at Kansas State College."[18]

Before they took their vows, George and Etty made a pact. They agreed to never tell his parents that he was marrying someone who wasn't an Irish Catholic. She would eventually be baptized as an Episcopalian, and they raised their kids in the Presbyterian Church.[19] "My dad wasn't allowed to marry anyone who wasn't an Irish Catholic and who was Jewish," Greg Allen said. "His family thought she was Protestant, and they were upset that he wasn't marrying an Irish Catholic. They both kept it a secret."[20]

The two married in Sioux City on May 26, 1951, with the *Sioux City Journal* capturing the details and elegance of the wedding ceremony: "Miss Etty Lumbroso, Sioux apartment hotel, daughter of Mr. and Mrs. Felix Lumbroso of Tunis, North Africa, and George Herbert Allen, son of Mr. and Mrs. Earl R. Allen of Rensselaer, N.Y., were married at 4 o'clock Saturday afternoon at the home of Mr. and Mrs. C.E. LaGrave, 3834 Country Club Boulevard. [Morningside president] Dr. Earl A. Roadman read the service.

"The bride wore an ice blue shantung ensemble with matching accessories. Her flowers were pink roses and lilies-of-the-valley. . . . Harry Gamage, head football coach at the University of South Dakota, was Mr. Allen's best man. . . . Mr. and Mrs. Allen will travel to Niagara Falls, New York city, and Florida on their wedding trip."[21]

George and Etty remained a couple for nearly four decades, until his death at age seventy-three on December 31, 1990. Along the way, Etty developed a strong admiration for many of her husband's characteristics, including his work ethic, his honesty, his respect for women, his refusal to curse, and even his "square" personality.[22] She also liked his "love notes."

"My father was always occupied with thinking of football," George Felix Allen said. "I remember my mother saying he'd diagram plays on his napkin, but she didn't realize that at first. He had these *X*s and *O*s and arrows going around, guards pulling and blocking. At first, she thought these were love notes of some sort. She knew nothing about American football whatsoever. She obviously learned about it."[23]

In 1959, less than a decade into their marriage, Etty learned something else about her husband. "He told me that he was 41, four years older than he said when we met," she said, as recorded in the 2005 book *Papa Bear: The Life and Legacy of George Halas*. "I could tell he was so embarrassed. It took him time to get through college. He served in the Navy and went to Marquette, Alma College, and finally Michigan."[24]

George Allen also made himself appear younger in his professional life. A résumé of his from the 1950s, for example, indicated that he was born on April 29, 1922, exactly five years after his real birthdate in 1917. With his good looks, he could pass for being considerably younger. The year of his birth was reported differently over the years, with the book *The Future*

Is Now noting that he was born in 1922, while other media sources said he was born in 1918. The years 1918 to 1990 are engraved on his tombstone in the cemetery where he's buried in Rancho Palos Verdes, California.

Meanwhile, Allen's Morningside Maroons took a major leap toward respectability in 1949 with their most remarkable season since the school's only North Central Conference championship, in 1923. They finished 7-3-1 and tied North Dakota for third place in the conference at 3-2-1. South Dakota State and Iowa State Teachers tied for first at 5-1. The conference voted to play a complete round-robin schedule starting that year.

The glorious season came after Allen staged the most intense spring practice campaign in Morningside's history: six weeks of daily workouts, five days a week, two and a half hours a day, with an intrasquad scrimmage every Saturday. The spring practices, he said, were an "absolute necessity for the school's existence in the North Central Conference." In his view, they were imperative for fundamentally preparing his squad to compete against the much larger rosters of the conference's state schools. "If you work hard in the spring, the rest will take care of itself," he often said.[25]

The coach issued a call for players, hoping to get seventy to report to spring workouts. "Any boy who has ever played football or who has the slightest notion that he would like to play football should report," he wrote in *The Morningsider*. "It's impossible to become proficient in football by just practicing in the fall—because of the time element. You need five or six weeks of intensive drills in the spring to net results. [The 1949] squad will be determined on the results of our spring football campaign. Also, those making the early season training table will be selected on the basis of spring drills."[26]

In addition to working on fundamentals, Allen liked to test his players' intestinal fortitude. Jim Fowler, a Morningside end who played for Allen in 1950, recalled the coach's use of a practice drill called the "slaughter box." "You'd line up people on both sides about 10 yards apart," Fowler explained. "The back would take the ball and run, and the lineman had to meet him head-on. We had a lot of injuries, so the coaches finally stopped it."[27]

By the season opener, the offense was "geared and polished for the rugged 11-game schedule this fall," according to an assessment in *The Morningsider*. "Much improvement was shown over last fall by many players during spring workouts, and many men were switched to different positions [that] the coaching staff thought they could more capably fit."[28]

Allen continued patterning his offense around the dizzying, multiple-ball-handling, single-wing system that he had brought with him from Ann Arbor. Talented backfield players, such as senior Connie Callahan, junior Bruce Pickford, and sophomores Oscar Jones (one of at least three Black players on the 1949 team) and Bob Hansen, helped execute the single-wing. Callahan, the Maroons' 5-foot-11, 170-pound triple threat (running, passing, punting), was nothing but outstanding, turning in one of the best seasons in the country. A vastly improved Maroons defense also produced its share of dominant performances.

Fowler remembered how the coach went to great lengths to perfect the single-wing: "He would get out a tape measure after the players shifted in the single-wing. If they were off three or four inches, they had to run laps. Everything was very precise. If the single-wing wasn't working the way he thought it should be, he'd spend a lot of time talking to Fritz Crisler about all of the variations and all of the things they could do to make it work better."[29]

Dick Weikert said the coach worked hard on the spinning aspect of the single-wing: "He made sure your spacing was right because it was much like the T. It was strictly a phantom operation. In other words, you faked everything and tried to hide it from the opposition. We also played the single-wing in high school. But it wasn't quite as precise as George's style of the Michigan single-wing. Ninety percent of it spun off of the fullback, who would either give it to the left half, the right half, or keep it for himself. Allen's strong point was working very closely on things like being in the correct formations and doing the right fakes at the right time."[30]

The offense often looked well oiled. Case in point: Morningside rushed for 227 yards without throwing a pass in a 20–0 season-opening victory over Buena Vista, its second straight year of kicking off the season with a nonconference win. Callahan ran for two touchdowns, and Oscar Jones, a fullback described by *The Morningsider* as "fleet-footed," ran 44 yards for a score.

Then came Morningside's biggest triumph in Allen's three seasons at the Sioux City school: a 12–0 victory over North Dakota in Grand Forks. In the Maroons' first win ever on the road against North Dakota, Morningside scored on long touchdown drives in the second and fourth quarters, with Jones and Callahan finding the end zone. But credit for the upset went mostly to a "charging [defensive] line which kept the 'Fighting Sioux' effectively bottled," according to *The Morningsider*.[31]

The Maroons also crafted two long touchdown drives against South Dakota State, of 87 and 94 yards, but were tripped up, 27–20. They roared back with three straight wins—26–7 over Augustana, 39–20 over North Dakota State, and 34–7 over Concordia—to sport a 5-1 record overall, 3-1 in the conference. Their first North Central Conference championship since 1923 was in sight.

In addition to a smooth-running offense led by the running and passing of Callahan, who scored two touchdowns against Augustana, Allen's hard-charging defense had also become a staple of the team. The powerful unit allowed an average of only 9 points in the first six games, with two shutouts, as it bottled up opposing elevens. The unit prevented North Dakota State from moving the ball in the first three quarters and carried out a goal line stand in the 27-point smashing of Concordia. Today, this dominant pattern doesn't appear surprising. The Allen coaching doctrine as it evolved would call first and foremost for reliance on defense and special teams, especially when he reached the pro ranks.

But the Maroons, beset by injuries to key players, could only muster a 2-2-1 mark over their last five games, ending the year with a 28–14 loss to Quincy College.

Callahan capped his college career in style, amassing breathtaking statistics that season: 2,006 yards rushing and passing, the most in the country in 1949 and the second-highest in college football history at the time, not far behind Georgia's Frankie Sinkwich, who totaled 2,187 in 1942. Callahan's 1,284 yards on the ground were third highest in the nation, and his 43.7-yard punting average was also one of the best in the country. He completed 55 of 103 passes for 722 yards, scored 96 points, and played all but 10 of a possible 660 minutes.[32]

The Associated Press named Callahan to the Little College All-American Team, making him only the third Morningside player to earn such a distinction. He was also selected most valuable player in the North Atlantic Conference and first-team all-conference, as was senior guard and team captain Bob Gregorvich. He was inducted into Morningside's sports hall of fame in 1969 based on his feats in both football and baseball.

In a 1952 submission for the "Best Player" series in the *Saturday Evening Post*, Allen touted Callahan as the best player he ever coached—but not only because of the lofty statistics he produced on the field. "This great athletic ability was not his only asset," Allen wrote. "His attitude on and off the field was also remarkable. The lithe 170-pounder could take the punishment of a vicious tackle without recrimination. When smashed to the turf, he would be the first player to jump up and form the huddle. This [indefatigable] ball carrier never lost his poise on offense or defense.

"In the years that he played for Morningside College in Sioux City, Iowa, he *NEVER* once missed a practice nor asked for any time out during a contest."[33]

By the end of the '49 season, Allen had become a popular name in the head coaching market. The *Collegian Reporter* noted that "several schools" tried to lure him but that he rejected each offer, his intention being to stay in Sioux City for the 1950 season. The report said North Dakota State and the Case Institute of Technology in Cleveland had both sent out feelers.[34] This marked the start of a parade of colleges that expressed interest in hiring him over the years.

"I was interviewed for eighteen college jobs, including Idaho, Brigham Young, Kansas State, and Harvard," Allen once said. "I was in the final four for Harvard, Houston, Iowa, Case Tech in Cleveland. I was offered coaching jobs at North Dakota State and North Dakota University. Red Sanders hired me as an assistant at UCLA and died [in 1958]. George Munger offered me a job at Penn. Wally Butts offered me the end coaching job at Georgia. Earl Blaik offered me a job at West Point and then said, 'No, you won't be here long enough.'" The University of Kentucky, the University of Colorado, and the University of Arizona also expressed interest in Allen down the road.[35]

In 1950 Allen's big test was compensating for the loss of Callahan, a once-in-a-lifetime player. He had a host of varsity lettermen to work with, as well as a solid share of the players from the Maroons' 1949 undefeated freshman team.

Morningside opened with a new opponent on the schedule, Mankato State Teachers College in Minnesota, which Allen called the best season-opening team the Maroons had faced in his three years at the school. He was right. Unlike the two previous season-opening shutouts by a combined 53 points, the Maroons eked out a 14–13 victory that was decided in the final seconds when Mankato State missed an extra point.

South Dakota State, the eventual conference champions, then crushed Morningside, 31–7, with a devastating ground game that totaled 372 yards and fueled drives of 75 and 90 yards. It wasn't pretty for Allen's gridiron bunch. Things looked dicey the following week in the home opener at

Public Schools Stadium. North Dakota was on the cusp of victory with a 13–6 lead and possession of the ball in the last two minutes. But the Maroons recovered a fumble and took over on North Dakota's 45-yard line. Senior halfback Loren Moll, the "new Connie Callahan," ran 34 yards on the next play, shortly before scoring on a short touchdown run. His extra point accounted for a 13–13 tie.

The result left the Maroons at 1-1-1, not exactly the successful path they were on in '49. But the resilient team won five of its last six, starting with two conference wins on the road: 13–7 over North Dakota State and 60–6 over Augustana. Moll victimized Augustana with four touchdown passes and a 60-yard run for another score. Teammate Bruce Pickford scored three times, and Oscar Jones found the end zone twice. The 54-point margin of victory was the largest in Allen's three years at Morningside.

The Maroons made it three in a row with what Allen called his second-greatest all-time thrill at Morningside behind the 12–0 win over North Dakota in 1949. This time, they blanked South Dakota for their first win over the Coyotes in sixteen years in the annual rivalry. Afterward Allen presented a game ball to Morningside president Earl Roadman, who had never seen his Maroons beat the Coyotes since coming to Morningside in 1936. The score and the date of the game, as well as autographs of all of the Morningside players, were inscribed on the ball.[36]

The next week, the Maroons lost any chance for a second-place conference finish when they suffered a 13–7 loss to Iowa State Teachers, which took second at 4-2. Morningside closed out the season by upending two nonconference opponents. After a scoreless first half against Omaha, the Maroons scored three touchdowns to notch a 20–6 win, before rolling over a lighter Iowa Wesleyan squad with 399 yards rushing and twenty-one first downs in a 33–12 rout.

So went Allen's third season at Morningside: 6-2-1 with a fourth-place conference finish at 3-2-1. Morningside's defense placed first in the conference in points allowed (11.7), a feat the Maroons would never achieve again. The conference folded in 2008.

With the touch he would display as a turnaround artist at several coaching stops, Allen had revitalized a fledgling Morningside football program. In his first three seasons, the Maroons posted an impressive 16-11-2 overall record (.593 winning percentage), 8-8-2 in the North Central Conference.

A few weeks after the 1950 season, Allen's right-hand assistant coach, Bill Pritula, resigned. Then came much bigger news. Allen announced his own resignation in August 1951 and said he had accepted the head coaching position at Whittier College, a small school in Southern California.[37]

Why did Allen feel compelled to leave? The *Sioux City Journal* reported that he voiced frustration with Morningside's decision to curtail spring football and the sharp decline in the school's enrollment, which meant fewer students to try out for the football team.[38] About eight hundred students were enrolled at the school at the start of the 1950–51 academic year, nearly 50 percent fewer than the previous year. The precipitous drop was partly because more than 60 percent of the students were enrolled through the GI Bill, and they had made their way through the college in the five years after the end of World War II and graduated by June 1950.[39]

With Morningside being the smallest school in the conference in terms of enrollment and with seven state schools on the schedule in 1951, Allen envisioned a continuous uphill battle. Plus, school officials were expected to limit the number of his assistant coaches in '51. He was guaranteed two regular assistants at Whittier.

Morningside president Earl Roadman accepted Allen's resignation with regret. "He has done an excellent job and has achieved an enviable place in the community," Roadman said at the time. "He leaves with our best wishes and hopes for as much success at Whittier as he had here." Allen praised Roadman for his support and wished his replacement good luck: "To my successor, whoever he may be, and to the present and future Maroons, I extend my sincere good wishes."[40]

His successors achieved what he didn't. Clayton Droullard's 1954 team tied South Dakota State for the conference championship at 5-1, and Dewey Halford coached the 4-1-1 Maroons to an undisputed conference title in '56, their third and final championship in the history of the North Central Conference. Other than that, neither coach rewrote Morningside's record books. Droullard won 50 percent of his games in four seasons, and Halford won 44 percent in nineteen seasons.

The time had come for Allen to go west to much sunnier pastures at Whittier, southeast of Los Angeles. For a position that called for a man who is "clean morally, one who can take his place in the college family and the community, and one that is proficient in the field of physical education," Whittier officials selected him from a pool of more than forty applicants.[41]

Allen would work for every penny of his $4,800 annual salary. In addition to football, he accepted the role of baseball coach and a demanding teaching schedule that included courses in anatomy, kinesiology, physical education, wrestling, volleyball, tennis, golf, and the theory of football. On top of those challenges, he took classes at the University of Southern California toward a doctorate in education, a program he had started at Michigan.

Like Morningside, Whittier was a tiny private liberal arts college with an enrollment of about 900 full-time students when Allen arrived, down from a post–World War II high of nearly 1,400.[42] The Quakers founded it as the Whittier Academy in 1887, the same year they founded the town of Whittier. The school was named after John Greenleaf Whittier, a prominent Quaker, poet, and leader in the abolitionist movement.

Whittier faced tough Ivy League–caliber competition—about the same level of talent as the North Central Conference. But Allen felt the school was in an area that offered a lot more in terms of recruiting and exposure. Whittier belonged to the National Association of Intercollegiate Athletics (NAIA) and played in the Southern California Intercollegiate Athletic Conference (SCIAC), which in football also included Pomona-Claremont College, Cal Tech, Occidental College, and the University of Redlands.

Unlike Morningside, the purple-and-gold-clad Whittier Poets—an appropriate nickname for a school named after a poet—had been a highly successful program. They were coming off seasons of 6-4 in 1948, 8-1 in 1949, and 10-1 in 1950, winning the conference championship in '49 and placing in a three-way tie for first in '50. They capped the 1950 season with a 27–14 win over a Mexican all-star team in the first annual Aztec Bowl in Mexico City.

A Whittier coaching legend had guided the Poets to their lofty status. Wallace "Chief" Newman, who was part Native American (from the Luiseño people), posted a 103-67-13 record in nineteen seasons (.606 winning percentage). He won seven conference championships outright and tied once for the championship in 1950.

Newman, an All-American college football player at Southern California in the 1920s, suffered only four losing seasons, but two of them were right after World War II. He came under pressure from Whittier alumni and fans who charged that his offenses were boring, but he responded with the three aforementioned winning seasons that preceded Allen's arrival.

Newman's decision to retire opened the door for Allen to take over the football and baseball teams. In football, Allen's assistants included Danny Tebbs and Bill Soeberg, both standouts from Newman's teams in the 1930s, as well as two star linemen from Newman's latter years as Poets coach: Evan McKinney and Bill Payne.

As in the case at Morningside, Allen planned to use the Michigan single-wing on offense. Newman had also employed a variation of the single-wing and the short punt formation, an offensive weapon in that era that presented the triple threat of running, passing, and punting.

About sixty players showed up on the first day of practice on September 10, 1951. They came in contact with a demanding, conservative-minded football coach who stressed the fundamentals of the game, namely blocking and tackling. Allen, who lived nearby so he could walk or ride his bike to the school, was also big on conditioning. He wasted no time drawing up a rigorous practice schedule, with a special emphasis on calisthenics in the early sessions to help get his players in shape for the season opener.

Bill Harris, a freshman when Allen arrived in 1951, would go on to play four seasons at Whittier as an end. He recalled how the new coach used almost every waking minute in preseason practice to prepare his troops. "His idea of football was to keep us busy," said Harris, who also ran track at Whittier for four seasons. "He brought us in two weeks early and kept us busy from 8:00 a.m. to 9:00 p.m. He was a taskmaster. You'd have your first meeting at 7:00 a.m., be on the field at 8:00, go to lunch at 11:00, then you'd practice in the afternoon until 5:00, then go get some dinner and practice until about 10 o'clock. It was three a day for the first two weeks because we didn't have any classes the first two weeks."[43]

In an era when many football coaches refused to let their players drink water during practice as a way of testing their manhood, Allen was no different. It made his grueling practices in the hot Southern California temperatures even more unbearable, Harris remembered: "He was wrong, of course, but it was hard not having any water out there. I'd see guys wring the sweat out of their towels and drink that. We'd do anything for water out there. That was a disaster. He was just a tough guy and a tough coach."

The *Quaker Campus*, the school newspaper, reported a few days into Allen's first round of practices that he had painted a nonflattering portrait of his players' devotion to conditioning in comparison to those in the Midwest during his coaching days at Morningside. "The fellows in the Midwest are hungrier than you boys out here," Allen told his troops during a chalk talk.

The newspaper also noted that Allen wasn't directing his comments only at the Whittier players "but was generalizing on the oft-debated question of Midwest gridiron supremacy, as observed in the Rose Bowl escapades of Pacific Coast elevens the past five years." Midwest schools had not only knocked off their Pacific Coast foes in the five most recent Rose Bowls. They also won seven of the next eight. Allen believed the dominance was all due to "conditioning."[44]

For the season opener at Whittier's Hadley Field, Allen wanted an opponent he thought the Poets could beat so they could gain confidence. He thus scheduled a military team, Submarine Force U.S. Pacific Fleet (SUBPAC). "I said, 'Oh, boy, these guys are on a submarine, no way they can play football,'" he told the *Los Angeles Times* decades later. "How could they work on their kicking game?"

Final score: 50–0 SUBPAC.

Allen was beside himself: "After the game, I went up to their coach and said, 'How did you guys get so good out at sea?' He said, 'These guys have never been on a submarine. All they do is eat steaks and practice.'"[45]

Whittier lost key players to injury in the humbling defeat, which kicked off a four-game losing streak in an eventual 2-7 season. The number of losses tied Whittier's all-time mark for the most in one football campaign.

What fueled the decline? Allen had inherited a team with less talent than Newman's successful postwar squads. Many of their impact players were battle-tested veterans who had returned after serving in World War II. One of them was Herman Reed, whom the *Quaker Campus* described as a "battering ram" and the "big negro fullback from Monrovia" in Southern California. Reed, who earned second-team all-conference honors in 1949, was among a series of quality players who had departed by the time Allen arrived.[46] In addition, Allen had to hustle on the recruiting trail to spot talent, while Newman had had the luxury of waiting for players to come to him. "Chief had a lot of players who had played football for him and became coaches throughout Southern California and in Orange County, so they sent good football players his way," said Al Stoll, a two-way lineman on Newman's '48 team.[47]

The 1951 squad wasn't void of talent. Halfback Ray Dezember, an accurate passer and shifty runner, quarterbacks Jack Pickering and Norm Haack, fullback Bob Dunham, and lineman and team captain Don "Rock" Rothrock highlighted the Poets' list of standout players.

As the season wound down, the man known as both the "Poet Pilot" and Professor Allen penned a thought-provoking article for the *Los Angeles Times* headlined "Are the Fans Ruining Football?" Essentially, he charged that a win-at-all-costs attitude perpetrated mostly by crazed alumni was leading to a revolving door on the coaching front. He pointed out that nearly three dozen prominent coaches lost their jobs after the 1950 season, whereby "in almost every case pressure from the fans was the underlying cause.

"I realize full well that we coaches are to blame for some of this hysteria," Allen wrote. "But we are its victims as well. And if we have created a Frankenstein monster which is destroying not only the coaches but the game, we are powerless to stop it. Only the fans can do that—and they are too overwrought.

"Carried away by his emotions, the rabid fan will accept nothing less than victory. Too often his demands are backed up by college authorities and voiced by sports writers. The harried coach must please not only all these people, but outsiders as well—among them gamblers who are busy betting on the notorious point system. If the coach of a 21-point favorite clears his bench and wins by only 14 points, he'll hear about it."[48] By then, Allen was a pro at showcasing his prolific writing skills. Starting in his days at Morningside, he had been a contributor to coaching and physical education publications. By the midway mark of his six-year stint at Whittier, he was writing a monthly column for *Coach & Athlete Magazine* and had freelanced for *Scholastic Coach*, *Mentor*, *People Today*, and the *Saturday Evening Post*, among a series of other magazines. He had also authored two books: *How to Scout Football*, an updated version of his master's thesis at Michigan on the importance of scouting, and the *Encyclopedia of Football Drills*.[49]

How did Allen perfect his ability to put his thoughts coherently on paper? For one, he was a voracious reader who absorbed the words of countless football coaching peers and other notable sports figures. He yearned to open his mind to the teachings and experiences of others. His vast library of books by college football coaching legends included the *Principles of Football* by John Heisman (1921), *Rockne's Football Problems* by Knute Rockne (1926), *Touchdown!* by Amos Alonzo Stagg (1927), *Modern Football: Fundamentals and Strategy* by Herbert Orin "Fritz" Crisler (1949), and *How to Play Football* by Bud Wilkinson (1955), as well as a sea of magazine and newspaper articles. "He was really into kind of the science of football," Bill Harris said of Allen.[50]

Plus, Allen participated in coaching clinics to learn more about his craft and to network with others in the profession. While at Morningside, for example, he was the featured speaker at the Iowa Coaching Clinic in 1949. But the school never had enough money in its budget to pay his way in full to attend clinics. He thus asked local companies to each kick in fifty dollars for his expenses, with the college also contributing a few dollars. "I always sat in the front row at the lectures and met a lot of coaches that way," Allen wrote in *Strategies for Winning*. "One year, 1951, at the old Commodore Hotel in New York, they gave me the job of registration chairman. I thought it was an honor until no one else would accept it. I worked so hard and took it so seriously that I was sick for a week with the flu and a sore throat after I returned to Morningside."[51]

With his customary out-of-the-box thinking, Allen circumvented the fundraising problem that he had experienced at Morningside by inviting coaches to attend his own daylong clinic at Whittier. A few weeks before the start of the '53 season, he kicked off the first annual Whittier College football clinic. More than two hundred coaches came from colleges, junior colleges, high schools, and military installations. The guest speakers in the coming years included head coaches Jess Hill (USC), Red Sanders (UCLA), Bob Bronzan (San Jose State) and Jordan Olivar (Yale), Los Angeles Rams assistants William Battle and Maurice "Clipper" Smith, and Washington Redskins assistant Wayne Millner, a star end in his playing days who entered the Hall of Fame in '68. Allen was so creative that he linked the clinic to the East-West Shrine college football all-star game, which was played in the San Francisco area at the time, and persuaded one of the teams to train on the Whittier campus.[52]

By keeping his name front and center in the world of football coaching, Allen became well known and respected. Just after the '51 season, he received the honor of becoming the only small-college coach who was asked to join the coaches' football rules committee of the American Football Coaches Association (AFCA) for 1952. He began by attending the organization's annual winter meeting in January 1952.[53] He was later appointed to the Motion Pictures Committee and the Ways and Means Committee to Restore Football at Institutions of the AFCA, as well as to an NCAA rules committee, which was a panel that included such coaching giants as Tennessee's General Bob Neyland, Army's Earl Blaik, and Georgia Tech's Bobby Dodd.

At an NCAA conference in 1951, Allen crossed paths with a man who would become a good friend and an influential figure in his life for years to come. This person would also go down as one of the most brilliant yet polarizing American politicians ever: Richard Milhous Nixon.

Nixon, a diehard football and sports fan, was a guest speaker at the 1951

NCAA conference.[54] He was anxious to meet the head football coach at Whittier, his alma mater and the school where he'd played football in a reserve role in the early 1930s. After getting to know one another, the two engaged in a deep discussion on *X*s and *O*s. At the time, Nixon was a U.S. senator from California who would soon be chosen as Dwight Eisenhower's vice presidential running mate on the Republican ticket in the 1952 presidential election, when Eisenhower won handily over Democratic opponent Adlai Stevenson.

From a young age, Nixon loved football. He wasn't big enough or strong enough to make a meaningful impact at Whittier, but he was a tenacious player who gave 100 percent effort. Standing 5 feet 11 and weighing no more than 150 pounds, he played on the offensive line. But he was slow and uncoordinated and just didn't have the athletic, jock-like look of a football player. The only time he saw action was in the waning minutes of a game "that was already safely won or hopelessly lost," he admitted in his 1978 autobiography, *RN: The Memoirs of Richard Nixon*.[55] In practice, he was often relegated to serving as a tackling dummy, sort of like Rudy Ruettiger, the pint-sized yet feisty walk-on at Notre Dame in the 1970s who overcame insurmountable odds to finally see action in a real game.

Through it all, Nixon's passion for football never waned. "My happiest memories of those college days involve sports," he wrote in his autobiography. "As a 150-pound seventeen-year-old freshman, I hardly cut a formidable figure on the field, but I loved the game—the spirit, the teamwork, the friendship."[56]

While a freshman at Whittier, Nixon sought ways to overcome his inferiority on the football field and gain respect from his peers. Along with Dean Triggs, a transfer student at Whittier, he co-founded a men's fraternal organization at the college called the Orthogonian Society. The jock-like group catered mainly to athletes, especially football players with less visibility, such as linemen, of which Nixon was one, as well as working-class students. Players at other positions that received much more exposure, such as quarterbacks and halfbacks, were welcome, too. The Orthogonians' charter focused on developing a "campus spirit" by building camaraderie among the members, who went together to ball games or to the beach. Orthogonian, partly a derivative of a Latin word, means "straight shooter."

Nixon, a history major at Whittier, was the Orthogonians' first president. He also served as president of Whittier's student body before graduating near the top of his class in 1934 and beginning law school at Duke University.

Al Stoll, a longtime Orthogonian who graduated from Whittier in 1949, surmised that Nixon possibly started the Orthogonian Society to compensate for the fact that he was a nonfactor on the field. "It may have been a little lonely, and the fact that he was an Orthogonian, that may have helped him being part of the team," Stoll said in a 2018 interview. "A lot of his friends were Orthogonians, and they may have made him feel a lot more at home than if he were just a player on the bench."[57]

A lot of the guys who played under Allen were also Orthogonians, including Pat Putnam, Rod Burroughs, Norm Haack, Ray Dezember, and the Harris brothers, Bill and Ben. There were a number of Black members, too, such as the Reed brothers, Herman and Charlie, both of whom played under Coach Newman. Nixon wanted Black students to be part of the organization.

"The Orthogonians were very close," Stoll said. "We were criticized sometimes by the women because we were so close and kind of clannish. At some events, we would always stick together."

Nixon's history with the Orthogonian Society is worth delving into. It speaks to both the leadership skills he would show later in life as a representative in Congress, a senator, and the thirty-seventh U.S. president, as well as to the fierce determination he put forth to rise above bleak circumstances. Although Nixon warmed the bench while playing for Newman, with whom he developed a strong friendship, he credited the coach more than anyone else with instilling in him a refusal to give up. Newman hated to lose, a sentiment Nixon also harbored.

George Allen also took losing extremely hard. He and Nixon, who had similar values, beliefs, and personalities, mirrored each other in other ways, too. Both men came from modest backgrounds and grew up amid financial hardship: Allen during the Great Depression and Nixon in the 1920s, after the failure of his family's ranch in Yorba Linda, California. They understood the need to work hard so their families could stay afloat, and they acquired a sense of industriousness and earnestness that never waned. And despite rising to the highest echelons of power in their respective professions, they embraced a blue-collar mentality and felt a closer connection to the common person than to the rich and elite.

It's been told over the years that the two football-loving buddies first met when Allen became coach of the Redskins in 1971 and Nixon was in his third year in the White House. That's obviously not true. But their mostly apolitical friendship took on a whole new dimension when they intersected in the nation's capital and became inextricably linked by one play in an NFL game with major implications in 1971.

For now, Allen had family matters to concentrate on. While preparing for the 1952 season, he and Etty welcomed their first child, on March 8, 1952: George Felix Allen. He was named after his father and Etty's father, Felix Lumbroso. Two more children joined the family before the decade was out, Greg in 1954 and Bruce in 1956. The couple's fourth child, Jennifer, was born in 1961.

Toward the end of his first season as Whittier's baseball coach, in which the Poets posted a 13-13 mark and a 6-4 record for second place in the conference, Allen turned his attention mostly to football. Spring practice opened on May 1, with workouts continuing daily for about three weeks. "Prospects are improving every day," Allen said at the time. "We're going to be a lot better than last year. With all our freshmen of last year having a season's experience, we cannot help but improve."[58]

As an incentive for non-letter winners from the prior year, Allen decided that the most improved player in that group would receive a trophy following the intersquad game on May 24. He said it would be an annual award. On the assistant coaching front, the second-year coach strengthened his staff by hiring Jerry Burns—a quarterback who had played sparingly on Michigan's 150-pound, freshman, and varsity teams and who later served as head coach at Iowa and with the Minnesota Vikings—and Beach Leighton, a former split T quarterback at the University of Virginia.

The fifty players who appeared for the opening of preseason practices in mid-September followed the same rigorous schedule as the previous season. Allen would ask no less. Whittier's 1952 football prospectus included a very measured assessment of the squad: "The Poets are still awfully young, green, and overmatched. They'll be improved over last year—if tailback George Sackman can make it physically, the offense will perk along considerably better—and should up the 1951 win mark by one or perhaps two. But surely no more." It didn't help that Whittier's best lineman, Chuck Stone, had left to serve in the navy.[59]

In contrast, the *Quaker Campus* radiated with optimism: "The team is shaping up rapidly and barring injuries or late draft calls, should be one of the top Poet elevens in many a season. Nearly twenty lettermen return from last year's aggregation—joined with some eight or ten transfers—should make Whittier a [conference] powerhouse."[60]

Which one was more accurate?

The Poets finished 9-1, one of the best records in school history, and won the conference championship with a 4-0 mark. It was Allen's greatest season in his six years at the Southern California school. They opened with a 7–6 upset of Santa Barbara, with Jack Fox's spectacular 14-yard touchdown catch in the third quarter and Bob Dunham's conversion accounting for Whittier's points. Allen dedicated the win to someone near and dear to his heart: "To my wife Etty; for appreciation in victory; support in defeat; Whittier 7, Santa Barbara 6." The Poets dropped the next game, 38–26, to San Francisco State, but then reeled off seven straight wins. The streak included a 14–6 victory over the Occidental Tigers. The winner in the annual cross-town rivalry earns a pair of bronze mounted football cleats—otherwise known as the "Shoes Trophy."[61]

Two weeks later, Whittier dismantled a highly favored Cal Polytechnic squad, 42–20, to spoil the Mustangs' homecoming. The win sparked bedlam in the Poets' locker room and prompted Allen to say, "Never in my five years of varsity coaching has a team turned in as great a game as this. Never has one exhibited more fight, more never-give-up spirit, or more poise under terrific fire." A 46–7 walloping of Redlands marked the Poets' seventh straight win and secured their 4-0 conference record. They ended the season with a 21–14 loss to Fresno State.[62]

The 8-2 record was short-lived in a good way. A few weeks after the season finale, San Francisco State forfeited its win over Whittier because one of its players, Al Endriss, was later found ineligible to compete. The *Los Angeles Times* reported that Endriss had signed a pro baseball contract in 1950. San Francisco State thus declared him not eligible to play college football.[63]

So 9-1 it would be. It was quite a display by Allen's bunch. They amassed more than 3,000 yards in rushing and passing and outscored opponents, 274–131. Senior halfback, tailback, and team captain Ray Dezember was virtually a one-man show, earning first-team all-conference honors on offense and defense. The 5-foot-7, 156-pounder posted team highs in passing yards (468) and touchdown passes (9) and was second in rushing yards (411), receiving (13 catches, 167 yards), and interceptions (7). He also led the team in punting, punt returns, and kickoff returns. He and Occidental's

Gordon Wells were the only players named first-team all-conference on offense and defense.

Poets quarterback Hal Jones, end Jack Fox, and guard Jack Killian joined Dezember on offense, with halfback Bob Dunham and guard Jack Cummings also earning first-team recognition on defense. Fox—perhaps the greatest receiver of Allen's Whittier era—led the Poets through the air (21 catches, 346 yards). Dunham intercepted a team-high 10 passes and paced Whittier in scoring with 62 points, about half on touchdown conversion kicks. Halfback Bryan Smith, who led the team with 450 rushing yards, and halfback Rod Burroughs, who was second in total yards behind Dezember, also crafted big years.

But Dezember was the unbreakable workhorse. Soon after Allen's stint ended at Whittier, he named Dezember his best back on both offense and defense in his six years at the school. He also labeled Dezember his most inspirational player.[64]

As much as the offense excelled in '52, Allen's teams were really predicated on strong defenses that made offenses fight for every yard. His '52 defense allowed only 10.3 points a game, with tackle Don Rothrock leading the way. His defenses in his six years at Whittier yielded 14.2 points a game, with ten shutouts. "George's defenses were pretty well known back in his college days," said Max Fields, a back who played at Whittier in '56 and '57. "He was an outstanding defensive coach. A lot of stunting with him. You didn't know where the linebackers were coming from."[65]

The success of Allen's defense back then isn't surprising, given that he emphasized defense to the max during his NFL coaching years, even pioneering critical strategy aspects. His Whittier special teams, another phase of the game that he modernized in the pros, also made their share of impact plays. His 1955 team, for one, tallied an abundance of blocked kicks. After that season, he was invited to speak at an NAIA football conference on the keys to blocking and returning punts. Also, similar to his days at Morningside, he relied a lot on the quick kick, which was popular at the time, in hopes of catching defenses off guard and pinning opponents deep in their own territory.

"He was the first guy I know of that had special teams," Bill Harris said. "He had an assistant coach who worked with us on special teams two or three times a week. You were on special teams if you were kicking, punting, or receiving the ball. When they were kicking, you'd send in the special teams to rush the kicker."[66]

Norm Haack played at Whittier during the same period as Harris: 1951 to 1954. A quarterback and running back, he also saw time on special teams. "We worked on blocking punts, and I was one of the blockers," Haack recalled. "You could work on that forever. You didn't get many opportunities to block a punt. But I did block one, which was very exciting."[67]

Haack and Harris were two of many Whittier players who respected Allen as a coach. Haack described him as a "very kind gentleman" who never cursed: "I don't think anybody ever heard him swear. But he was forceful, direct, and he knew what he wanted. If you understood that, you got along well with him."[68]

Harris found Allen to be very inspirational and praised him for simply teaching fundamentals: "A lot of coaches don't teach fundamentals. I didn't really know how to block when I was in high school. You figured that all you needed to do was hit the guy in front of you. He showed you. You just dip your shoulder and come up under the guy and lift him and drive him back 10 yards. That's why we had a good championship team. He taught fundamentals to everybody.

"We wanted to go out there and win it for him. The captain of the 1952 team was a guy named Ray Dezember. Ray inspired people, but the coach inspired, too. We had two leaders, one was the coach, and one was Ray Dezember."[69]

But not everyone was fond of the relatively quiet but intense coach. "You either did it his way, or you didn't do it," Haack said in retrospect. "I went to a reunion some time ago and talked to some players who didn't like him because he was very demanding. But I never saw him berate anybody. He wasn't that type of coach."[70]

Based on accounts from players in the Allen era, Stoll said "it's kind of a split" in how people felt about him: "Some guys really loved George Allen. Others that played for him were good athletes just like the guys that loved Allen. But they made fun of George because he was very staid in what he said and, of course, he was a defensive-minded coach. Some players, the wideouts and ends, didn't like that because they were more offensive minded. They liked the more wide-open game."[71]

A wide-open game just wasn't going to happen on Allen's watch, although the winning would continue. He guided the Poets to a 6-3-1 mark in 1953, when a slew of his players suffered knee injuries. Despite the success, was he getting the bug to leave Whittier? In the early months of

'54, the *Los Angeles Times* reported that he flew to Idaho to be interviewed for the head coaching job at the University of Idaho.[72]

Allen stayed at Whittier, but his Poets fell to 3-6-1 in 1954. They rebounded with an 8-2 season in 1955 that included a second-place finish in the conference at 3-1. This, after the *Quaker Campus* gave a pessimistic preseason outlook on a team with only six lettermen returning.

"Coach Allen, who will add some unbalanced split T to the Michigan single wing this year, looks forward to a plenty tough season," the school newspaper reported. "Playing the same ambitious schedule against schools like San Diego and Chico State, in addition to SCIAC schools, Allen will face dimmer prospects this year than last season because of a lack of experienced depth."[73]

Allen sidestepped the negativity. In 1955 preseason notebooks, he spelled out how his players could determine their fate on the field: "A real champion will prove his right to be called a champion not by talk but by action." He called for "aggressiveness, concentration, determination, obedience, reliability, and harmonious concentration."[74] His inspired Poets responded by capturing their first six games, including a 7–0 win over Occidental, to regain the Shoes Trophy after coming up short in 1953 and 1954, and a 14–7 win over a tough Cal Tech team.

"It's the best conditioned squad I ever had," Allen said in accounting for the 6-0 start, "and Carl Palmer, our captain, has been a good inspirational leader. You know how important a good start is. Well, we played Santa Barbara in our first game, and I had no idea what would happen.

"Santa Barbara had beaten us last year and had two lettermen back for every position this time. Somehow, we won, and on their field, too. That started the boys off. Then they beat Chico State, a strong team which was unbeaten at the time and which had drubbed us, 34–14, last year. I'd say every game we've played has been a surprise."[75]

In the win over Occidental, Whittier's defense put a stranglehold on the Tigers' offense, limiting star quarterback Jack Kemp to 8 yards on 3 of 6 passing, before he was injured in the third quarter.[76] Perhaps Allen impacted his subpar performance. The Whittier coach liked to rattle Kemp from the sideline when the rivals collided, calling him names like "spaghetti arm."[77] In reality, Kemp's right arm was dangerous. As a senior at Occidental in 1956, he threw for more than 1,100 yards, was named all-conference, and made the honorable mention Little College All-American Team.[78]

Picked in the seventeenth round of the 1957 NFL draft by the Detroit

Lions, Kemp fooled many NFL experts who had passed over him. In a standout ten-year career, mostly in the upstart American Football League, he threw for more than 21,000 yards, twice earning first-team All-Pro honors, and played in seven Pro Bowls. At the height of his career, he quarterbacked the Buffalo Bills to AFL championships in '64 and '65. One of his Buffalo teammates was defensive end Ron McDole, a cornerstone on Allen's "Over the Hill Gang" of the Redskins in the '70s.

With the 6-0 Poets enjoying a special season in '55, a Pomona-Claremont team on a four-game winning streak nipped Whittier in a battle for conference supremacy, 14–13. In a tug of war, "the defenses were immovable, holding and fighting, rocking and socking, with neither team taking great advantage of the other," as the *Quaker Campus* put it. The Poets led, 13–7, in the waning minutes. But the Sagehens drove inside Whittier's 5-yard line. The Poets prevented Pomona from piercing the end zone for the next seven plays, with a few penalties extending the drive. But the Sagehens ran for a touchdown and kicked the extra point to tally the win.

There's no such thing as a moral victory. But the Whittier faithful declared that they were "satisfied" at the end of the game. "I was proud to be part of Whittier at the game Saturday," George Allen told the *Quaker Campus*. "I was proud of the team and proud of the student body. I have never in my whole career seen a group of students so much behind a team. The spirit was terrific. They paid a great tribute to the team when they yelled 'satisfied' after it was all over."[79]

But the loss prevented the Poets from winning the conference championship. They dropped their next game to LA State, before beating Redlands and San Diego State to close out an 8-2 season, 3-1 in the conference. Pomona finished 4-0 to take the SCIAC title.

The season was one for the books for George Allen and his Whittier Poets. What keyed their turnaround from 3-6-1 in 1954 to 8-2 in 1955? For one, the '55 defense was stifling, posting three shutouts and holding opponents to 7 points or fewer in all eight wins. Plus, the Poets possessed a wealth of savvy, experienced players—just the prescription Allen used to gain success in his pro coaching years.

John McNichols, who began playing at Whittier as a junior in 1954 after two years at East Los Angeles Junior College, remembered that, when he arrived, Whittier "got a bunch of good football players all at one time." He was one of nine junior college players that Allen recruited, and all of them contributed in some capacity to the success of the '55 team, he noted. In addition, he said, four starters on the '55 team had served in the military, giving them time to mature physically. One of them was tackle Chuck Stone, who spent his freshman and sophomore years at Whittier, went into the service, and returned to Whittier as a junior at age twenty-two. He was one of seven Poets to earn all-conference distinction in 1955.

"Thank God Chuck went into the service and came out as a junior two years older and more mature as a player and a man," said McNichols, who played fullback and linebacker. "Chuck played tackle right in front of me on offense. For almost every yard I gained, I could thank Chuck. When you're eighteen, nineteen, twenty, you see that a couple of [additional] years make a difference.

"George always liked the older guys. He always liked the mature player. When I came in out of junior college, he started a guy ahead of me that had been with him. That's the way Coach Allen worked. He always started the vets, and he did that in the pros. When he was with Washington, he liked the older, experienced guys. They knew they were going to get to play. He got a lot out of guys maybe more than some other coaches might have because of that."[80]

The '55 team also benefited from the solid play of two-way tackle Bob Blechen, a pillar on the line. Allen considered Blechen one of the two best defensive tackles he coached at Whittier, along with Don "Rock" Rothrock. He also thought Blechen was the smartest player he ever coached, an apparent reference to his academic feats.[81] Blechen makes for a remarkable story. He was drafted by the Detroit Lions in 1956 but didn't make the cut, then failed to make it in the Canadian Football League. From there, the ageless wonder played defensive tackle on California semipro teams into his sixties. He was ultimately inducted into the American Football Association Hall of Fame, which honors semipro and Minor Football League players.

McNichols explained that Allen also recruited two young assistant coaches who were instrumental in the success of the 1955 team: Al Abajian and Frank Clayton. Both men had recently played at USC and assisted at Whittier only in '55.

"Our defensive schemes came with Al Abajian," McNichols said. "He introduced defenses to George that worked for us because there was a lot of stunting and slanting. Coach let him do it. I remember our calls. George thought things should be colorful. Our stunts were blueballs and snatch.

They would be called in the huddle. To young college boys, I guess that was pretty funny. George thought you should make things a little colorful."[82]

Shortly after the 1955 season, rumors again surfaced that other schools were interested in Allen. The *Los Angeles Times* reported that Brigham Young University was considering him as head coach and Notre Dame as an assistant. A few days later, the newspaper noted that Allen would remain at Whittier.[83] "I like my work here at Whittier College and am happy to remain here," Allen said.[84]

But that sentiment changed after a 4-3-3 season in 1956. In January 1957 Allen tendered his resignation to Whittier president Paul Smith and Roy Newsom, head of the school's athletic board, before leaving for St. Louis to attend the American Football Coaches Association convention. The resignation was effective June 1.[85] The *Quaker Campus* reported that he was considering several coaching offers but was undecided on his future plans.

"My decision to leave Whittier College is based solely on a desire to spend my full time in coaching football," Allen said in a statement. "It has been a real pleasure to work here. I have found many happy friendships with members of the faculty, student body, alumni, and especially the fine men on our football teams. Although I have enjoyed my teaching assignments as a professor of physical education, I would prefer giving up teaching for my first love, which is coaching."[86]

In a 1974 interview with the *Washington Post*, Allen said his personal clock was telling him that his time as a football coach at Whittier had expired: "I gave myself ten years [of college coaching]. I felt that if I didn't have a good job in ten years, then maybe I should consider something else."[87]

President Smith admitted he was sorry to lose Allen, who had coached the Poets to a 32-22-5 (.577 win percentage) mark over six seasons, 14-8-2 in the SCIAC. "But for a man who loves coaching as much as he does, I can appreciate his desire to want to spend his full time in coaching," Smith said. "I believe there are few men who have as complete a knowledge and sense of organization of the game of football as George Allen."[88]

But was it Allen's decision to depart? A local sports columnist, Howard Seelye of the *Palos Verdes News*, speculated in 1966, after Allen was named head coach of the Rams, that he may have been pressured to leave Whittier. "He was disliked by the players, and alumni grumbled about the good old days with Chief Newman," Seelye wrote. "Even though Whittier College never fires a coach, the inside report is that Allen was asked to submit his resignation, or at least hints were given in that direction."[89]

Those days with Coach Newman featured much more offensive firepower, which is what some of the players on Allen's team wanted, according to a source with close ties to that era of Whittier football. "It was mainly the older players," said the source, who requested anonymity. "They stated to the school administration, 'If he's back, we're not back.' There were enough that complained that the school didn't hire him back."[90]

The disgruntled players considered Allen's offense old-fashioned and unimaginative, with one player describing it as "3 yards and a cloud of dust." The Michigan single-wing formation was becoming outdated, and one game, a 14–14 tie with Pomona in '56, included about twenty punts. "[Some players] weren't having as much success as they thought they should be having," the source said. "I don't have firsthand knowledge of [Allen being pressured to leave]. But I know it happened because it got around on the squad."

John McNichols, an Orthogonian who entered graduate school at Whittier in 1956 and stayed in contact with a lot of his former teammates, knew nothing about a player rebellion against Allen. He added, though, "We weren't necessarily surprised when George resigned. If he hadn't resigned, he would have been fired."[91]

Allen had fallen out of favor with Whittier's booster club, which "liked him a lot for a long time," McNichols said. "Then, I think the honeymoon might have ended. He may have gotten carried away with his importance and perhaps went too far with some things. Rules and regulations may not have been George's long suit."

McNichols was referring to Allen's use of shady practices. He described one situation in which the football team, while traveling by bus to a game in Arizona, stopped at a store on Whittier Boulevard. "George went into the store and got a radio and a bunch of batteries," McNichols said. "I have a vivid memory of this. He's walking back to the bus with these things in his hands, with the store manager hollering at him saying, 'Wait a minute! You haven't paid us for that stuff!' George told him to charge it to Whittier College and got to listen to music on the way to Arizona. I saw it happen."

Allen also stretched the limits on financial benefits for some players, McNichols remembered. He said when Allen recruited him out of junior college in 1954, the coach promised him a special package covering tuition and books and added, "Now, don't tell anybody what you're getting because I have only a few of these kinds of deals." McNichols later learned that Mickey Bevilacqua, a tailback who transferred from Pasadena City College to Whittier and was all-conference in '55, as well as seven other junior college transfers, received the same deal from Allen.

Plus, McNichols recalled, Allen sidestepped the player substitution rule, although he was not alone in doing so. At the time, if a player was on the field at the start of a quarter, he could play until he came out but couldn't go back in until the next quarter. The coaches monitored his return to the game. "George would ask, 'You haven't been in this quarter, have you?'" McNichols said. "You both knew you'd been in because he started you. I don't think we ever got penalized. But that rule was eventually changed to where you had to report to an official. Some coaches would assume with a small *a* that you hadn't been in yet. There was disregard for that rule in general, and I don't think it was an accident. It was done by design until you got caught."

After his playing career at Whittier, McNichols had a brief tryout with the Baltimore Colts, before coaching football for more than two decades in high school and small colleges, including Whittier in the late 1970s. Despite his accounts that paint Allen as unethical in some respects, he also voiced admiration for the coach.

"I liked him as a man," McNichols said. "He always treated me well as a player and a coach. The other guys that I know—and I know lots of them—would pretty much say the same thing. You knew who you were dealing with. Basically, he was just a good guy who may tell you what you want to hear, whether it's true or not. A lot of us went into coaching and teaching, and we learned some things from George about how to do things and how not to do things. At the end of my senior year, he called me into his office and said, 'The Colts want to talk to you.' He sat me down and handed me his phone. He didn't have to do that, but he did. I'd be hard-pressed to say anything bad about the coach. It'd be hard to be angry at him. He's the person to me that I've described to you."

Decades later, a school librarian with access to the records of then-Whittier president Paul Smith found nothing during a search that documented the circumstances behind Allen's resignation. It does seem a bit odd that a man with such an admirable coaching record in six seasons at Whittier—a .577 winning percentage with one conference title—would be pressured to resign. It's not like Whittier was a football powerhouse bidding for a national championship year after year. At the same time, why would Allen quit without a coaching job lined up? Perhaps he had something in the works with the Los Angeles Rams, for whom he served as an assistant in the '57 season.

Bill Harris, who played for Allen at Whittier from 1951 to 1955, sensed the coach's desire to advance to the pro ranks. He said Allen visited the Rams' summer training camp in Redlands, about an hour east of Los Angeles, and came to know Sid Gillman, the Rams' head coach from 1955 to 1959. "He showed an inclination for that," Harris remembered. "Anytime the NFL would come to LA for meetings, he'd try to be a part of it. He wanted to meet people. I could see he wanted to find greener pastures."[92]

While coaching at Whittier, Allen ran a boys camp during the summer months in the Sierra Nevada of central California. While working there, he was allowed to break away to visit the Rams' summer training camp in Redlands.[93]

"I know that he went to the Rams' camp and would sit in on staff meetings," said Max Fields, who played at Whittier in 1956 and 1957.[94] McNichols recalled his presence there as well. "I'd go out there and watch the Rams practice all the time," McNichols said. "Coach Allen was often there."[95]

The players who apparently rebelled against Allen got their wish. His successor, Don Coryell, was an offensive mastermind and showed signs of the genius he would display in the NFL in decades to come. He immediately replaced the Michigan single-wing offense with the I formation in Whittier's backfield, with the tailback behind the fullback and the quarterback under center. The then-revolutionary setup turned the Poets into a prolific rushing team in '57. He later used a spread formation that called for more passing.

Whittier's Coryell-designed electric offenses made defenses dizzy. In his three seasons with the Poets, he posted a 21-5-1 record and three conference championships. His 1959 Poets led all NAIA schools in total offense, averaging 461.4 yards per game.

Under Coryell, Max Fields went from a spinning fullback under Allen in 1956 to an unstoppable halfback in 1957. Fields said he averaged 9.2 yards a carry in 1957, when he earned first-team all-conference honors, and fellow halfback Len Peden went for 9.1 yards a pop. He noted that in 1960, Coryell's lone year as an assistant at Southern Cal, the Trojans began using an I-formation setup that would help catapult USC running backs like O. J. Simpson, the Heisman Trophy winner in 1968, to fame.

"He brought the I formation to us," said Fields, an assistant to Coryell at

Whittier in '58 and '59. "The guys I played with weren't large but extremely quick. Our line was very, very quick. It was a much faster game."[96] Fields ran through some "huge, huge" holes, said Pat Putnam, a blocking back who played three seasons for Allen and one for Coryell at Whittier.[97]

The San Francisco 49ers drafted Fields in 1958, but he never played in the NFL because of an injury. Although his two Whittier coaches were polar opposites in philosophy, he's grateful to have played for both. Allen and Coryell are today members of Whittier's Purple & Gold Hall of Fame.

"I can't say enough good things about both of those guys," Fields said. "Both of them were strictly football. The thing I thought was quite interesting is that after I played for George, I would hear from him. I was lucky to get some feedback from him. Both guys cared for their players."[98]

McNichols also saw a stark similarity in both coaches. In addition to playing under Allen for two seasons at Whittier, he was invited by Coryell to practice with the Poets' freshman team. "Allen and Coryell stressed fundamental football," McNichols observed. "We didn't always have the biggest players, but we had players that were probably better prepared to play the game than some other people might have been. We didn't lose very many ball games. Coach Allen and Coach Coryell were winners."[99]

Allen and Coryell crossed paths years later. The two were NFC East rivals in the '70s, when Allen coached the Redskins and Coryell coached the St. Louis Cardinals (now Arizona Cardinals). In fourteen seasons as an NFL coach, Coryell posted a 111-83-1 mark (.572) and was dubbed "Air Coryell" for his high-flying, passing-dominated offenses.

Coryell's successor at Whittier, John Godfrey, went 120-67-6 over twenty seasons with nine conference titles. That means Allen's predecessor, Coach Newman, as well as Coryell and Godfrey, were all much more successful than him at the Southern California school. For coaches with at least three seasons at Whittier, Coryell and Godfrey are first and second in school history, with winning percentages of .796 and .634, respectively. Newman is third at .598.

Still, Allen's 48-33-7 record (.593) over nine seasons in the college ranks is nothing to gloss over. But all of that was now behind him. His sights were on the NFL in what would mark the beginning of a storied chapter in his extraordinary coaching career.

4

At the Car Wash

After nearly a decade of head coaching in the college ranks, George Allen wondered, what next? He figured he'd accomplished everything possible while holding the reins of the Morningside and Whittier football programs. Now, with the early months of 1957 upon him, the uncertainty of when and where he'd land his next coaching gig dominated his thinking.

Although he had resigned as Whittier's football coach in January 1957, he stayed on to coach the baseball team for a seventh season. He had strong aspirations of coaching in the NFL but didn't limit himself to the pros. He also heard from North Dakota State, a conference rival when he coached at Morningside. He expected to get an offer to coach the Bison, although it's not clear whether it was as head coach or an assistant.

When the telephone rang, though, it wasn't North Dakota State's athletic director but the man he'd acquainted himself with at the Los Angeles Rams' summer camp in Redlands, California: Sid Gillman. The Rams' head coach had something to tell him. "He just offered me a job on his staff, and I decided to take it," Allen told the *Washington Post* in 1974.[1]

In a press release, Rams general manager Pete Rozelle announced Allen's hiring on April 19, 1957—the same Pete Rozelle who later became NFL commissioner and one of the most powerful figures in pro football history. Gillman, who was then entering his third season as Rams coach, said the thirty-nine-year-old Allen would be "a strong addition to our coaching staff."

"George has been a college coach for nine years," Gillman said in the press release, "and is recognized throughout the coaching fraternity as having one of the really fine football minds among the young coaches [in] the country today. He will work with the offensive backs and ends where we feel his experience and knowledge will be of real benefit to our squad."[2]

Gillman first saw potential in Allen at the Rams' summer camp in 1955. The precocious Allen was "noticed at the time as the only non-professional coach who had such a strong desire to learn that he was allowed to move in with the Rams' coaches, living with them for weeks on end, even watching game films in a garage," William Gildea and Kenneth Turan wrote in *The Future Is Now*. "Every day, he followed Gillman from movie projector to squad meeting to late-night strategy session until the Ram coach gave in to sleep, sometimes at 3 a.m."

"At first, I thought the kid was a little kooky," Gillman quipped to Gildea and Turan. "But then I discovered that what he did was part of an overall plan that made a lot of sense. He is a talented and very smart fellow."[3]

The two developed a mutual respect and even spent time together away from the football field, such as in June 1956, when the Allen family hosted Gillman and his wife, Esther, for dinner. Allen was approaching his final season at Whittier at the time:

"It is needless to say that we sincerely enjoyed your very kind hospitality the other evening," Gillman told Allen in a thank-you letter. "May I say that I think you have one of the finest families it has ever been our pleasure to meet.

"Please convey our thanks and appreciation to Etty and [her sister] Lillian—we think they are splendid people.

"Best wishes for a great season this coming year."[4]

Getting hired by the Rams was an enormous break for a man who once had an ambiguous future as a football coach. On the surface, though, it seemed like an awkward fit. A defensive-minded small-college coach with conservative philosophies on offense—or "3 yards and a cloud of dust," as one of his Whittier players put it—would assist in coaching one of the most explosive NFL offenses of that era.[5]

The offense was predicated mostly on an aerial attack that amassed yards and points. From 1949 to 1951, the Rams had twenty-nine straight games of at least 300 total yards. They appeared in the NFL championship game all three seasons, losing to the Eagles and Browns in 1949 and 1950, respectively, and defeating the Browns in '51. The Rams led the NFL in scoring from 1950 to 1952 and finished third in scoring from 1954 to 1956. They returned to the NFL championship game in 1955, Gillman's first season coaching the Rams, and again lost to the Browns, the true juggernaut of that era.

So when news broke that Allen had signed with the Rams, John McNichols and his good friend Chuck Stone were stunned. Both men had played at Whittier under Allen and were key to the Poets team that finished 8-2 in 1955.

"We were shocked that he would jump from Whittier into the NFL,"

McNichols said in hindsight. "I could have heard Chuck Stone without the phone. With his big, bellowing voice, he was saying, 'Can you believe it?!' He was literally screaming in his surprise that Coach Allen had been hired by the Rams. Whittier wasn't necessarily the launching pad for getting into NFL coaching. Whittier in those days was NAIA, which today would be NCAA Division 3. That's down the ladder a few rungs."[6]

But Allen overcame his lack of exposure at Whittier by using a clever strategy to promote himself to NFL coaches. "George made a good point of meeting people," McNichols said. "My senior year, he took a group of us he thought may have a chance to play on the next level to spend a little bit of time with the 49ers and Colts when they were in our area to play the Rams. George used us perhaps as bait. But it did us some good. And it obviously did him some good because he got hired by the Rams."

To Lyle Gillman, her father's decision to tap Allen as the offensive ends coach sounded logical when considering Sid Gillman's philosophy in a coaching career of more than forty years. "He based a great offense partly on a defensive mind-set," she explained. "He would want George Allen to coach the ends and backs. He always had great defensive coaches to make his offensive players aware of what defenses could be presented and to make his offenses more effective."[7]

When Allen joined the Rams, two of the superstars from the team's offensive highlight reel, quarterback Bob Waterfield and receiver Tom Fears, had already departed. But two other future Hall of Famers, quarterback Norm Van Brocklin and receiver Elroy "Crazy Legs" Hirsch, were still there. Such players as backs Jon Arnett, Tommy Wilson, Joe Marconi, and Tank Younger, as well as ends Leon Clarke and Bob Boyd, were also under Allen's purview.

Allen's stay was brief. The Rams won their last two games in a 6-6 campaign in which they finished fourth in the Western Conference. Shortly after the season ended, he cut ties with the Rams. The *Los Angeles Times* reported that Allen had resigned but gave no reason why. The newspaper indicated that his replacement was Bill Swiacki, who had assisted with the Giants and Lions after a five-year NFL career as a receiver.[8] Separately, the *Los Angeles Times* noted that defensive line coach Lowell Storm, the only other Rams assistant to leave after the '57 season, resigned to accept a new position that he refused to disclose.[9] Were these departures related in some way, and why did Allen walk away without another coaching gig lined up? More than sixty years later, answers to both questions are very difficult to pin down. Interestingly, Gillman worked as a Redskins scout in '76, Allen's sixth year of coaching in the nation's capital.[10]

Despite the brevity of his pro coaching introduction, Allen had the opportunity to learn from one of the greatest innovators and most influential figures in NFL history: Sid Gillman.

After compiling a 79-18 record in ten seasons in the college ranks, Gillman coached the Rams for five seasons, with a 28-31-1 overall mark. He was fired after going 2-10 in 1959, but his pro coaching career took off after that. In 1960 he became head coach of the Los Angeles Chargers in the upstart American Football League (AFL). Under his direction, the pass-happy Chargers played in five of the first six championship games in the freewheeling, bombs-away AFL, which was a preview of the pass-first NFL of today, and won one championship, in 1963. Gillman, meanwhile, established himself as a leading mind on passing theories and tactics and as the "father of the modern passing game." He believed in passing first to set up the run.

In all, Gillman compiled a 123-104-7 record (.541 win percentage) in eighteen seasons as an NFL head coach for the Rams, Chargers, and Houston Oilers. Many of the top coaching proponents of the pass adopted elements from his playbook or his disciples. His coaching tree includes such luminaries as Don Coryell, Al Davis, Chuck Noll, Joe Gibbs, Bill Walsh, John Madden, and Tom Flores.

Should George Allen also be remembered as part of the Gillman coaching tree? It's hard to pinpoint whether he absorbed any of Gillman's offensive imagination because of his religious-like devotion to defense in the NFL, although in 1960 he published a book, *How to Train the Quarterback*. On the other hand, Gillman's industriousness had to have rubbed off on Allen, whether it was during the time Allen coached at Whittier and visited the Rams' summer training camp or during his brief coaching stint under Gillman or both.

Gillman was a workaholic, with coaching being his main hobby. The joke was that the only thing he seemingly knew how to do was work. He was addicted to the movie projector, becoming one of the first coaches to study game footage. He had realized the importance of doing so all the way back in the mid-1930s, when he borrowed football segments from newsreels at a movie theater in his hometown of Minneapolis and played them on his own projector. "If they ever make movies illegal, I'll quit football," he once said.[11]

Allen undoubtedly had a similar if not stronger work ethic. His near 24/7 in-season commitment to football was a by-product of his studiousness, meticulousness, copious note taking, and reliance on the projector as it rolled in the late-night hours.

But after he departed from the Rams in '57, his coaching career ground to a halt. Suddenly, he was disconnected from his top passion. He tried to regain his footing by circulating his name through the coaching ranks. For example, he contacted the career placement office at his alma mater, the University of Michigan, where school officials forwarded his résumé to Texas A&M and other colleges. Nothing broke for him.[12]

With the breadwinner of the Allen family out of a coaching job, Allen and Etty, along with their young sons George, Greg, and Bruce, experienced lean economic times. He sought creative ways to keep the family financially afloat. In 1958 he bought a percentage of a car wash on Ventura Boulevard in Encino, California, where the family had relocated after his departure from Whittier. Called the Rams Car Wash, it was touted as "The Most Modern Car Wash in the World." Company promos noted that the facility offered a "beauty shine, waxing, upholstery, and steam cleaning," in addition to a weekly drawing for two 50-yard-line tickets to a Rams football game.[13]

Allen made the business as festive as possible, remembered his oldest son, George, who was five at the time: "He had these plastic pennants, yellow, red, blue, all these colors. I remember there were so many cars with chrome bumpers. Think back to the 1950s and how much chrome was on cars."[14]

But the business struggled, putting a clamp on the Allen family's finances. The younger George Allen told of his mother's "parsimonious" approach when it came to buying food and other household items: "She wouldn't buy bags of oranges. She'd buy one orange or two oranges. That's all that could be afforded. My parents were very resourceful. Those days, heck if I could be eating sheep brains and tongue and liver and so forth. That's the type of food we would eat back then. My mother was a good cook."

The elder George Allen looked for other sources of income. He agreed to be the exclusive sales manager for Power Plus golf clubs in the Southern California counties of Ventura, Los Angeles, Orange, Riverside, and San Bernardino. The deal called for him to earn 5 percent on his golf club sales in those counties and a minimum of $700 each month as a draw against commission.[15] "I know he had golf clubs like an itinerant merchant," George Felix Allen said. "It must have been an arrangement with Rawlings because we had some Rawlings golf clubs. He wasn't selling them at a golf store or at a country club."[16]

Allen also began selling footballs on commission for a sporting goods manufacturer, the Voit Rubber Corporation, which made a nineteen-ounce weighted training football to strengthen a quarterback's arm and a twenty-three-ounce ball to strengthen a center's wrist. A regulation football weighed about fifteen ounces at the time. A company promo read, "Develop new highs in performance and efficiency with the new overweight training balls—POWER-ARM for passers and POWER-WRIST for centers—perfected by Voit with technical assistance by George Allen, author of [the] *Encyclopedia of Football Drills*."[17] "As kids in Encino, those were the footballs we played with," George Felix Allen recalled. "They were painful to catch when the nose of the ball hit your hands, even when we'd throw them only short distances."[18]

All along, George Allen never forgot his first professional love—coaching—and he maneuvered to get back in the game. He took a bus, for example, to an NFL meeting in Phoenix in hopes of meeting Bears owner and coach George Halas and other influential league figures and then landing a job.

He also visited NFL teams to introduce Voit's weighted football. At the Bears' 1958 training camp at St. Joseph's College in Rensselaer, Indiana, he bumped into Chuck Mather, a first-year running backs coach. Before, Mather had served as head coach at the University of Kansas for four seasons and at Massillon High School in Ohio, where he won fifty-seven of sixty games and six state titles.

It's not clear if Allen and Mather knew each other prior to Allen's arrival at the training camp, although the two developed a strong friendship. "Our family went over to their home several times in the off-season," George Felix Allen said. "He had a daughter who was pretty and older than me."[19]

While in Rensselaer, Allen asked Mather to arrange a meeting with Halas so the sporting goods sales rep could pitch his weighted football. "Halas didn't want any part of them," Mather said in *Papa Bear: The Life and Legacy of George Halas*. "When he got home [in Encino], Allen wrote me a letter telling me how lucky I was to coach pro football. I felt sorry for George on that basis."[20]

Shortly after the season kicked off, Mather spoke to Halas again about bringing Allen in to debrief the Bears' coaching staff about the Sid Gillman–coached Rams, the team Allen had just left. Chicago's schedule included two games against the Rams, and Mather thought Allen could provide insight into the strategy and signals of their offense. Halas liked the idea and hired Allen as a consultant. The Bears crushed the Rams at Wrigley Field, 31–10, but lost two weeks later in Los Angeles, 41–35.

"I'm sure he was there just like [assistant coach] Clark Shaughnessy was to break down film, break down different plays," said famed NFL historian Joe Horrigan, who knew Halas personally. "That's why Halas hired him: 'Tell me what Sid Gillman does to win.' He was so impressed with Allen's football knowledge and skills."[21]

Halas didn't want anyone to know that he had debriefed Allen, although word on another bit of news slipped out. "To the surprise of Los Angeles writers, George Allen, former Ram assistant coach and before that head coach of Whittier, appeared in the Chicago Bear camp today," the *Los Angeles Times* reported on October 20, 1958, the day after the first game against the Rams. "It was learned that George Halas will announce that Allen has been hired as player personnel director and assistant coach."[22]

But no hiring was announced, and Halas ordered Mather to "get him the hell out of here." So Allen again returned to California without a coaching job. But Mather continued trying to persuade Halas to hire him. With the recent death of Bears personnel director Frank Korch, Mather believed the Bears could use a man with Allen's smarts. "George knows a lot of personnel guys," Mather told Halas. "He'd be a good personnel guy."[23]

Halas acquiesced. After an 8-4 season with a second-place finish in the Western Division, the Bears announced on December 22, 1958, the hiring of Allen as an assistant coach and director of player personnel.[24] A little more than two months later, on March 1, 1959, he signed a three-year contract at $9,000 per year.[25]

George Allen was back in the coaching business.

5

Doing It George's Way

After selling his interest in the LA car wash, Allen renewed his midwestern roots in Chicago, coming face-to-face with the man who a decade earlier had contributed to his master's thesis at Michigan on the importance of scouting in football. He would learn much more from "Papa Bear" and the "Grand Old Man of the NFL" and came to see George Halas as his top coaching mentor.

Halas was a larger-than-life figure in the NFL and in sports. He was aligned with the Bears from 1920 until his death at age eighty-eight in 1983, with roles including owner, coach, player, promoter, ticket manager, and head of the grounds crew—sometimes all at the same time. (He stepped away from coaching three times: 1930–32, 1942–45, and 1956–57.) He collected six NFL Championships in a forty-year coaching career that ended in 1967. His 318 regular-season wins and 324 total victories were long-standing NFL records until Don Shula snapped both marks in 1993. Only six of Halas's forty teams finished below .500. In 1963 he was named a charter member of the Pro Football Hall of Fame, which sits on George Halas Drive in Canton, Ohio, on the site where the league was founded.

It's widely believed that Halas invented pro football, although that's a bit of a stretch. He was present at a 1920 meeting in a Hupmobile auto showroom in Canton, where prospective team owners discussed launching a new pro football league. He represented the Decatur (Illinois) Staleys, one of fourteen teams in the new American Professional Football Association. At the behest of Halas, the league changed its name to the National Football League in 1922, the same year the Staleys became the Chicago Bears.

Halas was a major influence on the growth of the game. He was the first to hold daily practices, study game film, employ scouts, have his games broadcast on radio, and use a public address system to keep fans in the stadium apprised of numbers like down and distance. To make the run-oriented sport more exciting, he collaborated in the mid-'30s with Redskins owner George Preston Marshall, another NFL pioneer, to promote a rule that permitted forward passing anywhere behind the line of scrimmage. Before, the quarterback had to be at least 5 yards behind the line before throwing the ball.

Halas was a great athlete, too. He had played football, basketball, and baseball at the University of Illinois before enlisting in the navy in 1918, less than a year before the end of World War I. He reported to the Great Lakes Naval Training Center in Illinois for officers training and became part of one of the best service football teams in the country as a player and coach. In the 1919 Rose Bowl, that team beat Mare Island, 17–0, with Halas catching a 32-yard touchdown pass and returning an interception 77 yards. He was named the game's most valuable player.

Later in 1919, Halas went to spring training with the New York Yankees. A right fielder, he appeared in a dozen Yankees games that season but batted just .091 with two singles in twenty-two at bats. The following year, with a newly acquired player named Babe Ruth playing right field for the Yankees, he opted not to report for spring training.[1]

He instead played for the Canton Bulldogs, a semipro football team. With a college degree in civil engineering, he also took up employment with the Chicago, Burlington and Quincy Railroad and the A. E. Staley Manufacturing Company in Decatur, Illinois. He played and coached football for the Staleys-turned-Bears through the 1920s. In 1921 the owner of the financially struggling Staley company, Augustus E. Staley, handed over ownership of the football team to Halas. The same year, Halas moved the team to Chicago and won his first NFL Championship.

Halas retired as a player and coach at the end of the 1920s and tapped Ralph Jones, his freshman football coach at Illinois, to be the Bears' head coach. Jones coached for three seasons, with his last one ending in an NFL Championship in 1932. But Halas seized the coaching duties from him, and, with the franchise teetering on the brink of collapse during the Great Depression, he bought out his fifty-fifty ownership partner, Edward "Dutch" Sternaman, to assume full ownership.

It was a precarious time for the Bears and the NFL, which had decreased to eight teams in 1932, following a high of twenty-two in 1926. To keep the Bears afloat, Halas signed promissory notes to such players as Red Grange ($1,000), Bronko Nagurski ($500), and Joe Savoldi ($500), as well as Ralph Jones ($1,500). The Bears owed about $12,000 to their creditors at one point.[2]

But the league recovered from its financial hardships. Halas righted his ship, too, with the Bears rising to the rank of perennial power. From 1932 to 1946, they appeared in nine championship games, winning five times with Halas as coach. Heartley "Hunk" Anderson and Luke Johnsos coached the Bears team that won the crown in 1943, when Halas served as a navy lieutenant commander in the Pacific during World War II.

Those Bears, known as the "Monsters of the Midway," maintained a classic rivalry with the Washington Redskins, the team Allen would coach decades later. The rivals clashed four times in the NFL championship game—1937, 1940, 1942, and 1943—with each winning twice. While the players on the two sides flat-out disliked each other, Halas and George Preston Marshall carried on a love-hate relationship. Both men had combustible personalities and nearly exchanged blows when a melee developed on the Redskins' sidelines during the '37 championship game, a 28–21 Redskins win.

Like Marshall, Halas ran the Bears with an iron fist. Maintaining tight control was his modus operandi. What he said was the bottom line, and he refused to tolerate disobedience and insubordination. He despised losing, and few people dared challenge his ire when he did. He was respected and feared. "He'd fine himself if he was late for a meeting or practice," George Trafton, a Bears Hall of Fame center who played in the NFL's early years, once said. "You had better be there, and you had better be on time."[3]

At the same time, Halas had an uncanny way of earning unwavering loyalty from his players and others around him. George Allen, too, gave Halas loyalty—up until a contentious stage in their relationship. From Halas, he learned about the need to control and the importance of paying attention to the smallest details, and he acquired a win-at-all-costs mentality and the owner's notorious paranoia—all for better or worse. He was synonymous with those characteristics in his twelve years as an NFL head coach with the Rams and Redskins. One time, Allen watched Halas choose sides on the field to shield his receivers' eyes from the sun.[4] Prior to Super Bowl VII, when his Redskins squared off against the Miami Dolphins, Allen tapped an assistant to chart the sun so it wouldn't be in his players' eyes during the game.

Allen also enjoyed a front-row view of the long hours Halas worked as part of his commitment to winning. In the early years of the NFL, Halas was the only coach who treated the game as a fifteen-hour-a-day, year-round job.[5] He believed in the creed, "Always go to bed a winner."

"On one Saturday, I spent the whole day in the office," Halas once said.

"Then I went to the game, when we played the Cardinals and lost. I was pooped. I was ready for bed when I remembered that phrase. So I jumped on my exercise bike and rode my 2½ miles. I was a winner."[6]

According to *Papa Bear: The Life and Legacy of George Halas*, Allen's wife, Etty, said, "George told me that when everyone else left the office, he and Mr. Halas still would be there. He said Halas would always turn off the lights when he left a room. 'I'm the one paying the bill,' he'd say."[7] George Felix Allen remembered that the "smart principle" of saving electricity and money when there was no need to light a room was incorporated into the Allen home as a "wise, efficient way of living."[8]

In his assistant, George Allen, Halas saw someone who possessed a similar dedication to the profession. He was particularly impressed with the young man's smarts and attention to detail. Even before signing on with the Bears, Allen had already proven to be a conscientious man who performed his coaching duties with painstaking attention to detail, a characteristic that would help solidify his reputation for having an unbreakable obsession with football. How much more of that industriousness did he acquire by being in the company of Halas? "I can only surmise that it spurred him on to more of that," George Felix Allen said.[9]

Said NFL historian Joe Horrigan, author of *NFL Century: The One-Hundred-Year Rise of America's Greatest Sports League*, "They probably wouldn't agree with me, but I think their personalities were very similar. George Halas worked just as hard as George Allen ever did. He lived and breathed the game. He had to work hard. He was the owner, the promoter, the general manager, the coach. He had no time off. Allen assumed all of those responsibilities short of ownership."[10]

All the while, the student developed tremendous respect for the resident patriarch of the NFL. "I think everyone idolized Halas," George Felix Allen said. "He was one of the founders of the NFL. In retrospect, everyone revers and appreciates him. He still has a lot of records that folks have not yet passed. So anybody in football is going to respect Papa Bear Halas as an owner, as a coach, and as a founder of the league, and for his creativity, his vision, and the fact he was a very hard worker. Obviously, he expected everyone else to work hard. My father had that same sort of attitude. He was fortunate that George Halas gave him so many responsibilities."[11]

Halas was also well known as a frugal man who preferred paying his players as little as possible. He was a tough negotiator. Born in 1895 and raised by thrifty, hardworking parents who had immigrated to the United

States in the 1860s from Bohemia (today part of the Czech Republic) and settled in Chicago, he had seen NFL franchises run by owners with deeper pockets than his go out of business. Knowing how overspending could cripple a franchise, he remained committed to a fiscal austerity plan that he saw as responsible to himself and to his franchise.

One time, a player about to be cut from the Bears begged Halas for some cash so he could buy milk for his kid. The parsimonious owner is said to have replied, "What's his address? I'll send a quart."[12]

In Halas's last NFL championship game, in 1963, the Bears defeated the New York Giants, 14–10. Bears defensive end Ed O'Bradovich intercepted a screen pass in the third quarter to set up the winning touchdown, one of five Chicago interceptions on the day. After the season, he hoped to capitalize on his clutch play when meeting with Halas in search of a bigger contract. Instead, he fell victim to Halas's obstinacy and curmudgeonly personality.

"If you went to him looking for a raise of whatever amount, his answer was always no," O'Bradovich said of Halas in a 2019 interview. "Not no with an explanation. It was two letters, N-O, no. And 'by the way, don't let the door hit you in the backside when you're leaving.'"[13]

One night the following season during training camp when the coaches were exiting the "purple room," where they congregated after practices and games, O'Bradovich told Halas he wanted to speak with him. "We met in his office," O'Bradovich said, "and I made my play: 'Coach, this, that, etc.' He said no. I said, 'What do you mean, no?' He said, 'I said no. You're not getting a nickel.' I said, 'Coach, if I don't make that interception, we don't win the championship. You don't wear that ring that's on your hand.' He said, 'Bullshit.' I said, 'What do you mean bullshit? I did it. Nobody else did it.' He said, 'No, I'm not giving you a dime. That's it.' As I'm walking out of his room, he said, 'By the way, kid, normally if somebody leaves camp, it's [a fine of] $100 a day. But for you, I'll make it $200. Have a good night.'"

In his head coaching roles, Allen didn't show the same miserliness when it came to authorizing player salaries and bonuses. In fact, he spent and overspent to the point that it irritated the NFL owners he worked under: the Rams' Dan Reeves and the Redskins' Edward Bennett Williams. Allen was also more rational and analytical than the impulsive and crusty Bears owner, and his motivational skills were much better. In fact, Allen is widely regarded today as one of the greatest motivational coaches in NFL history.

In the early months of his new job, Allen lived in Chicago while the rest of his family—Etty and sons George, Greg, and Bruce—remained in Encino, California. (The Allens' fourth child, Jennifer, was born in 1961.) In late spring 1959, the family left Encino and migrated the more than two thousand miles east to Chicago.

"My father drove the entire family of five in a 1951 faded blue Ford Victoria from California to Chicago, with side trips to Las Vegas and the Grand Canyon," recalled George Felix Allen, who had just finished first grade. "We took old Route 66 from Flagstaff, Arizona, to Chicago. Bruce was a little over two years old and slept in the back window ledge. All of that was completely unsafe by today's nanny standards.

"We lived awfully cramped in a dingy, hot hotel in Chicago in the late spring and summer months, generally a miserable existence. By the time second grade started for me, we had moved into a house in Deerfield," a suburb of Chicago.[14]

Allen rode the train to and from work without missing a minute of preparation time. "I'd bring my books and study the players then," he told the *Chicago Sun-Times* in 1988. "I had a special seat on the train in the section up above. Then I worked Saturdays and sometimes half days Sundays in the offseason. We were well-prepared."[15]

Allen was the newest member of a Bears coaching staff with decades of NFL coaching and playing experience. Five of the assistants had been NFL head coaches: Luke Johnsos, Clark Shaughnessy, Phil Handler, Joe Stydahar, and Paddy Driscoll. The other assistants were Chuck Mather and Sid Luckman, the quarterback of the Bears' championship teams in 1940, 1941, 1943, and 1946. Luckman, who is in the Hall of Fame, threw for 14,686 yards and 137 touchdowns in his twelve-year career—team records that stood for more than sixty years. He and Allen became close friends.

As a Bears assistant for seven full seasons, Allen would take on three roles: head talent scout, defensive coordinator, and general manager without title. Halas first assigned the newcomer to focus solely on personnel matters. With a proven understanding of the importance of scouting and the willingness to invest the excruciatingly long hours needed to find quality talent, the articulate, enthusiastic, and charismatic Allen seemed like a perfect fit to oversee the team's player drafts. The position required him to persevere to find the players he wanted by spending weeks at a time outside of Chicago.

"The whole family spent a lot of time on the road," George Felix Allen remembered. "We spent a lot of time in New Orleans because of the Sugar Bowl or in Florida for the Orange Bowl or the Tangerine Bowl. He would talk to certain players the Bears were considering drafting. We knew where the best fireworks were near Chattanooga, Tennessee. We'd all be loaded up in our Ford Country Squire. While driving, we'd listen to country music. Once in a while, there'd be a good motivating preacher on, and we'd listen to that. Or if we were driving in the summer, we'd listen to baseball games."[16]

In player personnel, Allen carved a name for himself and proved to be a master recruiter. In addition to the Bears' use of a scouting service called BLESTO, which gathered data on college players, Allen's keen eye for talent was critical to rounding the team into championship shape.[17] Most of the players on its '63 championship roster were acquired during Allen's stint as chief talent evaluator through the draft, trades, or free agency. He relied mainly on the draft, which he later mostly shunned during his head coaching stints in LA and Washington, where he much preferred proven veterans over untested rookies. Of the thirty-seven active players on the Bears late in the '63 season, twenty-five came via the draft, ten by trade, and two by free agency. Nine of the twenty-five draftees were in their first or second season at the time. None of the other sixteen had been in the league more than four years.[18] The infusion of talented youth helped give the Bears a leg up on their NFL competition.

Allen accomplished this at a time when the NFL was undergoing a paradigm shift. Buoyed by the thrilling 1958 championship game—Baltimore's 23–17 overtime win over the New York Giants entered the living rooms of millions of viewers and produced a marriage between television and football—the league experienced unprecedented growth and visibility. Men like Allen were under more pressure than ever to hit a bull's-eye with their personnel decisions.

During the '60s, the NFL's so-called golden era, the league grew exponentially and surpassed baseball as the nation's No. 1 spectator sport. Regular-season attendance vaulted from 3.1 million in 1959 to nearly 9 million in 1969. Concurrently, television revenue ballooned due to a series of lucrative deals between the NFL and the TV networks. The league had increased to sixteen teams by the mid-1960s and twenty-six by 1970.

The era was also unconventional when it came to securing college talent. Allen and other NFL general managers faced serious resistance from a new league in hot pursuit of premier players: the American Football League (AFL). Created by a group of wealthy businessmen dubbed "The Foolish Club," the AFL became one of the greatest success stories in sports history. The league kicked off in 1960 with eight teams, mostly in major media markets. Men with incredibly deep pockets owned some of those teams.

The NFL and AFL began holding simultaneous drafts in 1960, the start of a Cold War–era cold war that featured counterespionage, spying, and deceit to secure the best college talent. The rival leagues enlisted babysitters to prevent the top players from signing with another team, an effort that became known in the NFL as "Operation Handholding." The AFL went all out to corner potential big-name first-round draft picks with contracts generally more lucrative than what NFL teams offered. To avoid antitrust lawsuits and contract violations, the new league mostly avoided targeting current NFL players.

"The babysitters would stay with the players," NFL historian Joe Horrigan said. "Teams would hide them in hotels. Guys were jumping out of windows to escape. There's all sorts of stories about cars and booze and women. As one guy said, 'And some of it was true.'"[19]

In a snapshot of the AFL's aggressiveness, running back Billy Cannon and safety Johnny Robinson, both from Louisiana State, and Mississippi All-American fullback Charlie Flowers signed deals with the new league on the field after Ole Miss beat LSU in the Sugar Bowl on January 1, 1960.[20] Cannon, Robinson, and Flowers were also among a number of players who had first signed contracts with NFL teams before changing their mind for the AFL.[21] The New York Giants, in fact, lost in court in an effort to retain Flowers. During the trial, Giants co-owner Wellington Mara accused the AFL of "bribery, fraud, and double-dealing."[22]

In addition to Robinson, a series of other future Hall of Famers opted for the AFL, including Alabama quarterback Joe Namath (1965). His decision to play in the new league had the greatest ramifications of all of the players who signed with AFL teams. Drafted by the NFL's St. Louis Cardinals and AFL's New York Jets in 1965, Namath accepted an unprecedented $427,000 package from Jets owner Sonny Werblin. His signing came shortly after the AFL's $36 million, five-year television deal with NBC, allowing the upstart league to prosper. Overall, the '65 draft cost pro football teams an estimated $25 million for college players, with about $7 million going to the top twenty.[23]

These circumstances led the leagues, both of which wanted to avoid an extended and costly bidding war, to call a truce. The AFL-NFL merger, announced in June 1966, called for a common draft, a championship game, and one entity under the banner of the National Football League. The new-look NFL kicked off in 1970 with two thirteen-team conferences, the National Football Conference (NFC) and the American Football Conference (AFC).

The key figure in forcing the merger, which put pro football on a path to become a multibillion-dollar industry, was Al Davis. As a Chargers assistant coach in the AFL's first three seasons, Davis worked alongside the team's top scout, Don Klosterman, in evaluating college prospects and luring them to the AFL.

In 1963 Davis was named coach and general manager of the AFL's Oakland Raiders. He led the '63 Raiders to a 10-4 mark and won unanimous AFL Coach of the Year honors. After compiling a 23-16-3 record over three seasons in Oakland, he was named AFL commissioner in April 1966 and escalated the war with the NFL. "We will fight for players," the brash and gritty Davis, who grew up in Brooklyn, New York, said at the time. "We will do a-n-y-t-h-i-n-g we think necessary."[24]

George Allen, who first crossed paths with Davis at a coaching clinic in 1963 and maintained a cordial relationship with him in the coming decades, was in the thick of the NFL-AFL drama, although his first draft, 1959, was an AFL-free event. It featured a second-round pick who crafted an outstanding career: Tulane's Richie Petitbon. An all-conference quarterback as a senior, Petitbon transitioned to safety upon entering the NFL and played fourteen seasons, including two with the Allen-coached Rams and two with the Allen-coached Redskins. A four-time Pro Bowl selection who intercepted forty-eight passes, he was a first-team All-Pro safety on Chicago's '63 championship team.

In 1960 Allen used his first-round pick on fast and agile Syracuse guard Roger Davis, whom United Press International had named college lineman of the year after Syracuse's 11-0 national championship season in '59. Allen was on the spot in reeling him in, according to the *Chicago Tribune*: "Davis, 6 foot 3 inches and 230 pounds, was signed by assistant Coach George Allen in the presence of Davis' parents in Dallas, where he starred in Syracuse's 23–14 victory over Texas in the Cotton Bowl game on Friday." The AFL and the Canadian Football League were also eyeing Davis, but he chose the Bears because he wanted to "play with the best or not play at all."[25] He became a key piece on Chicago's remodeled offensive line and started all but one game for the Bears in 1963.

Then, with a first-round pick in 1961, Allen nabbed his first NFL superstar: Pittsburgh's 6-foot-2, 230-pound end and linebacker Mike Ditka. Halas liked tough-as-nails players. Few players have epitomized the toughness of the Bears as much as Mike Ditka. A native of the steel mill town of Aliquippa, Pennsylvania, he possessed an exceptional work ethic and competitiveness from growing up with a very strict father who demanded nothing but the best. His father, Mike Sr., a steel mill worker of Ukrainian ancestry, didn't "spare a rod" if one of his kids failed to comply, as Ditka put it.[26]

Halas envisioned Ditka playing tight end on offense. "Ditka will play the closed end," the Bears' coach told reporters in January 1961. "We are counting on his blocking to give our running game a big lift."[27] But Ditka became more than a blocker and excelled on the receiving end early in his rookie season. Linebackers tried to hold him as he came off the line of scrimmage to slow him down, a tactic they could get away with in those days. He lined up next to the offensive tackle at the time.

The coaches then repositioned him in a three-point stance on the line of scrimmage a few yards from the tackle. He could now release inside or outside, with defenders uncertain of his plans. With his ability to accelerate, he became so dangerous that in 1961 he caught fifty-six passes for 1,076 yards and a career-high twelve touchdowns, earning NFL Rookie of the Year honors. His 19.2-yard average per catch was also a career-high stat. It was just a glimpse of the brilliance that he would show in his twelve-year Hall of Fame career.

Ditka credited Allen with convincing Halas to position him away from the tackle. The move made Ditka the NFL's first modern-era tight end. "He talked Mr. Halas into it," Ditka said of Allen in a 2019 interview. "[Allen] said, 'He's going to be a tight end, we're going to throw the football to him, and he'll also be a great blocker for us.' It couldn't have worked out better for me. I don't know what he saw—I caught eleven passes my senior year in college. I couldn't catch. But we didn't throw the ball, we ran the ball. And I was a good blocker.

"At first [in the NFL], the linebacker was jamming me inside into the defensive end. It was hard to get out of there. So [Allen] said, 'Here's what we're going to do. We're going to flex you open about 5 yards, give you a two-way release.' He did all that. I was the first tight end that really flexed open. My quarterback, Billy Wade, loved to throw the ball to me."[28]

Hall of Fame middle linebacker Sam Huff, one of Ditka's contemporaries, explained that linebackers often double-teamed Ditka because he was so difficult to stop as he released off the line. "He was a hell of a player," said Huff, who played his first eight years with the Giants and last five with the Redskins. "He was as fast as our linebackers. He basically could have played linebacker if he wanted to, and a lot of times he wanted to get on the defensive side of the ball. He was a really tough player. He came off the ball, and he punched you. He hit you with his helmet."[29]

The Houston Oilers also drafted Ditka in the first round of the AFL's 1960 draft, so Allen kept the Heisman Trophy finalist in his sights to make sure he signed with the Bears. "George was a great guy, a very smart guy," Ditka said. "He kind of babysat me. He almost moved in with me for a while to make sure that I signed with the Bears. He basically came to Pittsburgh and talked to me and said, 'We want to fly you to Chicago to meet with Mr. Halas.' I flew to Chicago, and we sat down at his desk. It was very simple. [Halas] said, 'We'd really like to have you. You're not going to play defense.' I thought I was going to be a linebacker. 'You're going to play tight end.' That sounded pretty intriguing."[30]

Baylor's Ronnie Bull also wanted to showcase his talents in the NFL rather than the new league. Toward the end of the '61 season, both the Bears and the AFL's Dallas Texans drafted him with first-round picks. The *Chicago Tribune* reported that Texans owner Lamar Hunt appeared to have the inside track on signing the 6-foot-2, 200-pound Bull, who had played halfback, fullback, and safety at Baylor.[31] But that belief was only because the rookie was from Texas, Bull said years later.[32]

Allen's babysitting prior to Bull's decision to ink a deal with the Bears was the epitome of cunning and determination. After Bull was named MVP of the Gotham Bowl in New York City on December 9, 1961, following a 24–9 Baylor win over Utah State, Allen arranged for a cab to take him and his wife to New York's LaGuardia Airport. From there, they'd fly to Chicago and be the Bears' guests at their upcoming game against Cleveland, after which Bull would sign a contract. At least that's what Allen envisioned. But a snowstorm in the Midwest caused cancellation of multiple flights, and the Bulls considered returning to their hotel room.

"Each time they'd wash out a flight," Allen said in *Sports Illustrated* on October 14, 1963, "Ronnie would say, 'Well, I guess we'll go back to the hotel now. I'm kinda tired out.' I could just see him getting back to the hotel in time to take a long-distance phone call from Lamar Hunt. So I'd say, 'Let's just try one more flight, and we'll go in and have some ice cream while we wait.' We must have had six quarts of ice cream."[33]

Allen and the Bulls eventually found a late-night flight to Chicago. But after the Browns game, Bull didn't sign like Allen had hoped, and he instead returned home to Waco, Texas. Allen later flew to Love Field in Dallas, where he met up with Bull and tried to convince him to sign, even though Bull had already agreed to terms with the Texans.[34] In the end, Bull dictated the terms of a contract with the Bears and got what he wanted: a three-year, no-cut deal that paid $20,000, $21,000, and $22,000. "George and I hit it off pretty good," Bull said in a 2019 interview. "I felt very comfortable around him. He wasn't pushy. He just tried to sell the Bears."[35]

In a *Sports Illustrated* article, an unnamed Bears official was quoted as saying that "everybody thought Halas was nuts to draft Bull."[36] Bull was unaware who made that remark, but he believed it was predicated on the thought that the Bears probably needed help on defense more than offense. He wanted to play on offense in the pros, which was another reason he wasn't inclined to sign with the Texans, who would have positioned him at safety, he said.

"In the first place, we were sure he wouldn't leave Texas, so we'd be wasting a draft choice," the unnamed Bears official said. "But George was a little bit on the spot. Nothing much had happened around here," referring to the fact that the Bears hadn't won an NFL Championship since 1946, "and [Allen] felt Bull would be a big help to the team, either on offense or defense. Nobody has ever released any figures, but my guess would be that George didn't exactly impoverish the boy when he signed him."[37]

Bull evolved into another key piece to the championship puzzle. Positioned at fullback, he rushed for 363 yards on 113 carries and caught 31 passes for another 331 yards to earn NFL Rookie of the Year honors in 1962.

But Halas, Allen, and the Bears' coaching staff knew full well they needed to acquire more than just highly touted rookies. They also found players in the lower rounds of the twenty-round draft that impacted the success of the '63 team, among them flanker John "Bo" Farrington in the sixteenth round in 1960, defensive back Bennie McRae in the second round and defensive end Ed O'Bradovich in the seventh round in 1962, and offensive tackle Steve Barnett in the second round in 1963.

Larry Glueck, a highly touted defensive back from Villanova picked in the third round in '63, also chose the NFL over the AFL because he wanted to play in the more established league. The San Diego Chargers drafted him in the AFL's fifth round, but he signed with the Bears. "We wanted him badly," Allen said at the time. "He's got good size—6-feet-2-inches and 197 pounds—just right for a defensive halfback."[38]

Allen and the Bears lost out to the AFL on a few draft picks. In 1961 they selected Grambling's 6-foot-9, 340-pound defensive tackle Ernie Ladd in the fourth round, while the Chargers took him in the fifteenth round. In a victory for the Chargers' savvy recruiting team of Al Davis and Don Klosterman, the man known as "The Big Cat" chose San Diego and produced a star-studded career, with three first-team All-Pro seasons and four Pro Bowl appearances. He later gained fame as a pro wrestler.

In 1963 the Bears and the AFL's Buffalo Bills drafted Michigan State All-American center Dave Behrman, who signed with the Bills. That year, the Bears and the AFL's Denver Broncos selected University of Washington halfback Charley Mitchell, who chose the Broncos. In 1965 the Bears and Chargers each drafted Tennessee defensive end Steve DeLong in the first round. He played seven seasons in San Diego, making the Pro Bowl once, before ending his career in 1972 with the Bears.

"The competition and losing players you drafted to the AFL bothered my dad," Bruce Allen said in retrospect. "He was happy when there was talk that there could be a merger between the two leagues. That meant at least you weren't going to lose a player you drafted."[39]

The loss of Ladd, however, led to the acquisition of another player who made an enormous impact on the '63 team. The *Chicago Tribune* reported that while inquiring about Ladd, Allen asked Grambling coach Eddie Robinson if he had any good defensive backs. Robinson told of one player, Roosevelt "Rosey" Taylor, prompting Allen to ask if he was fast. "Well, he stays up there with anybody we got," Robinson replied. When Allen discovered that Taylor was keeping up with Olympic track prospects, he quickly signed him to a free agent contract.[40]

Decades later, Taylor gave a somewhat different take on how he ended up signing with the Bears. He said the Bears weren't recruiting him, but when he learned they were after Ladd, he called Allen and offered his services. Taylor, who played safety, cornerback, and running back at Grambling, led the country's small college defensive backs in interceptions with twelve in 1960. "I told him that I can play offense or defense,"

Taylor remembered. "He asked, 'Can you make my team?' I said, 'I can make your team.'"[41]

After signing as a free agent in '61, Taylor remained with the Bears for eight and a half seasons, establishing himself as one of the finest defensive backs in the game. He played twelve seasons overall, including a banner year in '63, when he earned first-team All-Pro and Pro Bowl honors.

"I don't think Allen expected me to become a ball player," Taylor said. "He just went along with me, day to day, week to week, and I turned out to be a player that he wanted. At that time, [cornerback] J. C. Caroline was the big name in the defensive backfield. He wanted me to strive to be like J.C. I heard years later that he told his players that a guy from a little, all-Black college down in southern Louisiana made my team."

Allen's pursuit of Ladd and Taylor established a pipeline to Eddie Robinson at Grambling that would pay big benefits some twenty years later when Allen coached in the United States Football League. Such recruitment also carried importance because Grambling and other historically Black colleges and universities (HBCUs) were a relatively untapped source of NFL talent at the time. "He loved the fact that he was one of the first NFL [general managers] to go down to Grambling," Bruce Allen said.[42]

From the time the NFL began integrating its rosters after World War II, teams tended to pursue Black players from predominantly white schools. But Allen and the other NFL scouts began recognizing the potential talent pool at HBCUs, although not to the same extent as AFL general managers like Al Davis. In the 1960s the new league aggressively recruited HBCU players, about a dozen of whom were eventually enshrined in the Hall of Fame. The AFL couldn't afford to overlook those schools, hoping to find gems the NFL did not scout. AFL rosters averaged 17 percent more Black players than NFL teams from 1960 to 1962. From then on, the NFL took notice.

"They didn't have a choice," said Charles Ross, author of the 1999 book *Outside the Lines: African Americans and the Integration of the National Football League*. "The NFL knew the AFL wasn't going away, so it had to start recognizing that the AFL was going to be around and why it was going to be around. They were playing a brand of football [that focused on] throwing the ball, they had a television contract, they were doing revenue sharing, and they were scouting and bringing players from these historically Black schools that possessed a tremendous amount of talent."[43]

It's hard to tell if Allen and the Bears were any more aggressive than other NFL teams in pursuing Black players. In addition to signing Taylor as a free agent, the Bears recruited nearly ten Black gridders while Allen led the personnel department from 1959 to 1965. That list included at least two from historically Black colleges—Bo Farrington (Prairie View A&M) and Charlie Bivins (Morris Brown College)—and some from larger schools, including Bennie McRae (Michigan) and Billy Martin (Minnesota). Other Black players, including offensive tackle Herman Lee and running back Willie Galimore—both from the same HBCU (Florida A&M)—and J. C. Caroline from Illinois were on the roster when Allen arrived.

Allen's keen eye for talent was also on display on the trade market, where he gave a snapshot of the successful wheeling and dealing he'd show on a much larger scale in later years. He used his favorite philosophy of trading draft choices for experienced players: a pick to the Redskins, just before the 1959 season, for linebacker Larry Morris, who was a pillar on the '63 Bears defense; a pick to the Steelers, before the 1960 season, for guard Ted Karras, who became regarded as one of the best pass blockers in the NFL; a pick in the '62 off-season to the Steelers for Bobby Joe Green, who maintained his standing as one of the league's best punters, finishing second in the NFL in '63 with a 46.5 average; and a pick to the Rams, just before the '62 season, for bruising fullback Joe Marconi, who led the Bears in rushing in 1962 and 1963.

Two acquisitions in the 1961 off-season are also notable. First, the Bears gave the Rams defensive back Erich Barnes and a high draft choice or a player to be named in exchange for seven-year veteran quarterback Billy Wade, in a trade that also involved the Giants.[44] Wade responded by throwing sixty-eight touchdowns and for nearly 10,000 yards over the next four seasons, starting every game in '63. Cornerback Dave Whitsell took a more circuitous route to Chicago. After being traded from the Vikings to the Giants, he was dealt to the Redskins. But he refused to report to Washington and was sent to the Bears. He intercepted twenty-six passes over the next six seasons in Chicago, including six in '63. Whitsell also "blossomed into a deadly tackler as a Bear, winning the right cornerback position in a defensive secondary that was destined to become the finest in football," the *Chicago Tribune*'s Cooper Rollow wrote in June 1964.[45]

So how much credit does George Allen deserve for spotting the myriad talent that arrived in Chicago on his watch? That's impossible to pinpoint, given the tremendous depth of knowledge and coaching experience on the team's staff and the probability that everyone provided input to some extent. In his 1979 autobiography, Halas didn't credit Allen for the personnel decisions that molded the Bears into a championship-caliber squad. Then again, Halas held a life-long grudge against Allen after his controversial exit from the Bears following the '65 season. Instead, the owner-coach patted himself on the back by writing, for example, "I sought strong linemen and linebackers," before mentioning some of the players that "we picked up."[46] You can bet, though, that Allen was a powerful voice in the personnel decisions, especially when considering the comments of some of the players he drafted in Chicago.

"Probably, George's greatest skill was recognizing talent and knowing how to get the talent to produce," Richie Petitbon said in retrospect. "He just had a way with people in which he got the most out of them. That's all you can ask from a coach."[47]

Allen's attention to detail when dissecting the strengths and weaknesses of players also impressed Ronnie Bull: "George lived in the film room, so he had a good idea of the players who were needed. He recognized talent and that there was talent to be developed. That was a sense he had of football. He watched an unbelievable amount of film. He knew all the strong points and all the weak points, and he knew the players that he was recruiting pretty well." Only one person, however, made the final decision on who was offered a contract. "That was Halas," Bull said without hesitation.[48]

The players Allen helped acquire teamed with a solid core that included three future Hall of Famers—defensive end Doug Atkins, defensive tackle Stan Jones, and middle linebacker Bill George. Atkins and Mike Ditka made the prestigious NFL Films "NFL 100 Greatest" team that was announced in 2019 to coincide with the league's one-hundredth season. The savvy Bill George was known as one of the first "quarterbacks" on defense. Toss in players like linebacker Joe Fortunato; defensive linemen Fred Williams, Earl Leggett, and Bob Kilcullen; cornerback Bennie McRae; fullback Rick Casares; offensive lineman Bob Wetoska; and quarterback Rudy Bukich; plus Willie Galimore, J. C. Caroline, and Herman Lee, and you had one well-rounded team.

Allen ended up coaching many of the defensive players that he had scouted or inherited. While he retained his personnel duties, Halas also tapped him to assist the team's defensive coordinator, Clark Shaughnessy, before the '62 season.

At the time, Chicago's defense was seeking consistency and an identity. In an 8-4 Bears season in 1959, Allen's first full year with the team, the defense held opponents to under 200 points for the first time since 1948. That figure rose to 299 in a 5-6-1 season in 1960 and to 302 in 1961, when the Bears finished 8-6 in the first year of the fourteen-game season.

Who better for Allen to learn from than Shaughnessy? He had a brilliant and imaginative mind on football theories and tactics and was a man with more than four decades of experience as a football coach and consultant. On the college level, he had served as head coach at Tulane, Loyola of the South, Chicago, Stanford, Pittsburgh, and Maryland. His 10-0 Stanford Indians posted a No. 2 national ranking in 1940 at the height of his college coaching career. In the NFL, he was periodically an advisor to the Bears from 1937 to 1962, an advisory coach to the Redskins in the mid-'40s, and the Rams' head coach in 1948 and 1949. His Rams went 14-7-3 overall, with a 14–0 loss to the Eagles in the 1949 NFL championship game. He returned to the Bears as a technical advisor in 1951, with the team noting by '58 that he specialized in defense.

Shaughnessy's creativity led him to experiment with blitz packages that called for linebackers and linemen to rush from multiple angles, as well as a move to vary the number of players on the defensive line. He emphasized man-to-man coverage in the secondary but had the foresight to merge that approach with popular zone or umbrella techniques to create combo-style pass coverages.

Like a mad scientist testing an assortment of substances in the lab, Shaughnessy was constantly thinking of ways to outwit opponents. He spent a lot of time diagramming new plays on his own and was "always doodling," said Joel Bussert, a former NFL vice president who did extensive research on Shaughnessy.[49]

To Hall of Fame lineman Stan Jones, who played in Chicago from 1954 to 1964, Shaughnessy was a genius. "It was like having Albert Einstein work with first-year algebra students," Jones said in *Papa Bear: The Life and Legacy of George Halas*. "He went to the board with his back to everyone. He never used an eraser, just the back of his arm. He'd be up there breaking chalk and writing all those things."[50]

For all of his imagination on defense, Shaughnessy is regarded as one of the greatest innovators in football history because of his work on the offensive side of the ball. He revolutionized the game by reviving and modernizing the T formation, which called for a player to take the snap right behind the center, with two runners in the backfield. The T became an explosive tool that influenced college and pro teams to shift from the single-wing. Prior to the 1940 NFL championship game, Halas hired Shaughnessy as a consultant to implement the T, which the Bears used to obliterate the Redskins that day, 73–0.

While working alongside Shaughnessy in Chicago, Allen learned a lot from the man twenty-five years his senior. "We'd go to the movies together, eat together, ride in planes together—and all the time we'd be talking football," Allen once said. "I learned some things to do and some things not to do."[51]

As astute as he was about football, Shaughnessy had his faults. The professorial man would sometimes overthink himself by disguising his strategies in terms and colors that were almost impossible for his players to decipher, remember, and execute, such as "hossy-gee-shuffleback mini-blast" and "blue dot dash cherry go." Bears defensive end Doug Atkins, for one, had five different places to go after lining up in a scheme called "slam, slide, slue, smooch."

Plus, while Shaughnessy was a staunch proponent of man-to-man pass defense, Halas favored zone coverage with the linebackers dropping back to help in the defensive backfield. Shaughnessy, who could be very controlling, also kept Halas in the dark on some of his strategies and refused to tell the Bears' owner who was and wasn't playing well. His stubbornness and insistence on doing things his way created friction with Halas. The two strong-minded men maintained a solid but sometimes confrontational relationship.[52]

"Shaughnessy loved to blitz," Bussert said. "I mean he loved to blitz! I can remember writers somewhat sarcastically saying the Bears would blitz on first and second down and sack the quarterback for a 10-yard loss. They'd blitz on third down, and they're in man to man, and the quarterback completes a 35-yard pass. That's an exaggeration, but he was blitz-happy. He had all kinds of blitzes. That was part of the problem. They gave up too many big plays, and Halas didn't like that."[53]

It all came to a head in 1962, when Allen's coaching responsibilities increased on defense as Shaughnessy fell out of favor with Halas. The old man was especially disenchanted with Shaughnessy following the Bears' 8-6 season in 1961, when Chicago finished with a ninth-ranked NFL defense that yielded 302 points and 4,449 yards.

Allen believed in a basic 4-3 setup with a strong pass rush, not a crazy alignment that could potentially handcuff players. He was confident that the Bears possessed an outstanding front four that could pressure the quarterback consistently and make life easier for the rest of the defense. He also favored a zone defense in which linebackers would drop back to help the four defensive backs, all of whom were assigned a designated area, instead of the single- or double-teaming of runners and receivers. He revolutionized the game by implementing the "nickel" defense, with five defensive backs, and the "dime" defense, with six defensive backs.

With Allen assisting, the defense came into its own in a 9-5 season in 1962. Led by the front four of ends Doug Atkins and Ed O'Bradovich and tackles Earl Leggett, Fred Williams, and Stan Jones, who provided quality minutes after starring on the offensive line in his nearly decade-long career; the linebacking trio of Bill George in the middle and Joe Fortunato and Larry Morris on the outside; and the secondary of cornerbacks Dave Whitsell and J. C. Caroline and safeties Richie Petitbon and Rosey Taylor, the defense formed a tight chemistry that carried over to the '63 season. The powerful 6-foot-8, 275-pound Atkins, whom Allen turned loose as a pass rusher, together with Fortunato and Petitbon, made the Pro Bowl, as did tight end Mike Ditka.

In 1962 Chicago's fifth-ranked defense allowed the league's lowest completion percentage (46.8) and 14 touchdown passes, compared with 27 in 1961. The defense also intercepted 23 throws, with Petitbon posting a team-high 6, including a 101-yard return for a touchdown. Whitsell was right behind him with 5. O'Bradovich led the NFL with 5 fumble recoveries, while Leggett tallied 4.

On paper, Allen was still assisting Shaughnessy. But the two had drifted apart—literally. In *Papa Bear: The Life and Legacy of George Halas*, author Jeff Davis quotes *Chicago Tribune* sportswriter Cooper Rollow as saying that one day while covering a Bears practice, he saw Allen and Shaughnessy at opposite ends of the field, noting that "they separated themselves because they couldn't stand each other."

"I talked to George for a while about the new zone he was putting in with a nickel, dime, and stuff like that," Rollow said in the book. "That since has become the way to play over the years. Then, I went down to Shaughnessy and asked, 'What do you think of all this?' 'Well, you won't win by setting up a silly little bunch of zones all over the field. I'll tell you that,' Clark said."[54]

Halas thought some of Shaughnessy's ideas were ridiculous. Midway through the '62 season, Shaughnessy called for a new defensive strategy in which the right tackle would move next to the left tackle as the signal was called. Halas replied, "Clark, you cannot do that. The offense will see the hole, call a play on a quick count before you can adjust, and come roaring through."[55] Separately, in the 2004 book *'63: The Story of the 1963 World Champion Chicago Bears*, Rosey Taylor said Halas objected to Shaughnessy's idea of unleashing him on a safety blitz, a relatively new concept in the NFL at the time.[56]

All the while, Shaughnessy disliked being told what to do and ran out of patience. With the 7-4 Bears on a three-game winning streak, he left the team inconspicuously on November 29, 1962, and resigned a few days later without explaining why. Allen took over as the Bears' top defensive coach without title for the last three games.[57]

"Clark severed his association with the Bears by his own doing," Halas told reporters. "But let's don't any of us forget all the many contributions he has made over the years."[58]

Perhaps Halas gave his "long-time crony," as the *Chicago Tribune* characterized Shaughnessy, a nudge toward the exit door.[59] According to NFL historian Joe Horrigan, "Clark was a student of the game. He was George Halas's 'I'm going to read all the books and develop all the methods. You approve them and tweak them, whatever you want to do.' That's what George Allen was, and all of a sudden he's a younger version of Clark Shaughnessy. And I'm sure George Halas says, 'I don't need two Clarks.' They had already battled enough, Shaughnessy and Halas. He says, 'I've got my new Shaughnessy,' and put him in there."[60]

Several months later, Shaughnessy apologized for his sudden departure.[61] But by then he was way off the team's radar. With his exit came a fresh mind on defense.

"Clark was an old-time coach and did things kind of the old way," Mike Ditka explained. "George infused the defense with a lot of new things. He understood that you played the game a certain way, with four down linemen, including two tackles and two ends, three linebackers, two safeties, and two corners. The game of football has evolved a lot since then, and George had a lot to do with that. He created a lot of change in the game."[62]

The difference between Shaughnessy and Allen was like "day and night," according to Ed O'Bradovich: "I think Clark Shaughnessy, and with all respect, my God, he was there forever and had done so many great things with that defense. But it was time. I'm thinking that he knew it because when he left, there was no big deal about him leaving, and all of a sudden, he's not there, and George Allen was. Allen was in charge and boom, bang, it was like, 'Okay, you have ten seconds to think of the adjustment, now we've got to go.' It was unbelievable. Clark was gone. Everything left with him. And that next week, we got a defensive book with a breakdown of who we were going to play. Holy Christ. I'll never forget it."[63]

That "book" was more like a monstrosity that broke down every detail of the upcoming opponent's offense and dwarfed the size of Shaughnessy's reports, O'Bradovich recalled. That's actually not surprising, given that Allen was always fanatical about game preparation.

"The day George Allen took over, we got a dictionary," O'Bradovich remembered. "He handed it out in the meeting, and everybody said, 'What the hell is this?' Every game. He had everything the other team did—in good weather, bad weather, typhoons, it made no difference. George had everything down to a science, and he would put the time in. Boy, let me tell you something. That guy worked all night, day after day after day, and he got a lot of great rewards, being with the Rams, the Redskins, and the President's Council on Physical Fitness and Sports under President Reagan."

In addition to making his players hit the books, Allen streamlined the Bears' approach on defense, discarding Shaughnessy's baffling schemes and sticking to the fundamentals. "He basically reversed a lot of things that Shaughnessy had done," O'Bradovich said. "[Shaughnessy] would have Doug Atkins so far wide out in a three-point stance. If the offense snapped the ball and the quarterback dropped back, the offensive tackle didn't even have to block him. Same with me when I played on the other side. What was his theory with all of that? I have no idea. But Allen totally changed everything when he came in."

In the final stretch of the '62 season, the Bears faced two of the league's elite teams—the Giants and Lions—and the lowly Rams. Playing before home crowds each week at Wrigley Field, Allen's defense collected six interceptions and ten sacks for a loss of 102 yards, validating his belief in a strong pass rush. In a 26–24 loss to the Giants, the defense harassed star quarterback Y. A. Tittle, who was "rushed harder and more persistently than by any other opponent this year," George Strickler of the *Chicago Tribune* wrote.[64] It was a harbinger of things to come for the rest of the NFL. The Bears followed with wins of 30–14 over the Rams and 3–0 over the Lions. The latter game resembled a defensive slugfest, with the Bears' defense tallying five sacks and stifling two desperate fourth-quarter rallies to secure the win.

The 2-1 finish left the 9-5 Bears in third place in the Western Conference behind the 13-1 Packers and the 11-3 Lions. The Giants captured the Eastern Conference, meaning the NFL championship game would pit the Packers and Giants against each other for the second straight year. The Packers made it two in a row with a 16–7 win.

More than any team, the Bears were fixated on the Packers, the crème de la crème of the NFL. By the end of the '62 season, Green Bay had appeared in three straight NFL championship games, starting with a 17–13 loss to the Eagles in 1960. The reason: Coach Vince Lombardi. After five seasons as the Giants' offensive coordinator, a period when New York appeared in two NFL title games, winning once, he took over a moribund Packers franchise that went 1-10-1 in 1958 and hadn't posted a winning season in a dozen years. He immediately transformed the Packers into winners starting with a 7-5 season in '59, when he was named NFL Coach of the Year. His leadership skills, abrasive coaching style, ability to get the most out of his players, and belief in doing easy things with consistent excellence—such as his often-devastating power sweep—elevated the Packers to an elite level. He won five NFL Championships in his ten-year coaching career, including two Super Bowls, and is spoken of as the greatest NFL coach ever.

Lombardi and Halas, two of the ten coaches later selected for the NFL Films "NFL 100 Greatest," became fierce rivals, with Lombardi gaining the upper hand. Halas went only 5-13 against Lombardi by the time both coaches stepped down after the '67 season, although his five wins were the most of anyone who faced the Packers legend. Lombardi tormented Halas as early as 1956, when he called the Giants' plays on offense. That year, he ran Frank Gifford, Mel Triplett, and Alex Webster on the power sweep in the NFL championship game to help crush the Bears, 47–7. Halas was widely believed to be calling the shots, although he was on coaching hiatus that season. By the end of the '62 season, the Packers had beaten the Bears five straight times by an average of 27 points, with routs of 49–0 and 38–7 in 1962.

Meanwhile, Halas came to despise everything about the Packers. Bruce Allen, who assisted in ball-boy duties at Bears training camps in the mid-'60s and became known as "Little Bear Bruce," said Halas and the Bears organization strongly believed the Packers spied on his team's practices, which were then out in the open in Grant Park in central Chicago.

Halas's antipathy for the Packers was not lost on Bruce in other ways, too. Once, he sat in the back seat of a car when Halas, riding with George Allen in the front, voiced his anger: "He looked through the rearview mirror at me and said, 'You're spying on our conversation,'" Bruce recalled. "I said, 'No, I'm just listening.' He looked at my dad and said, 'I'm going to teach him his first cuss word.' So he looked at me and said, 'I'm going to tell you the worst word in the whole world. You only use this against the worst people in the entire world. Never use this and never say it in front of your mom or any girls. The word is Packer. It's the worst thing to be called a Packer. That's your cuss word.' Oh, shit. I was calling everybody Packers. I learned my first cuss word from Coach Halas."[65]

In the words of Bill Curry, a Packers center in 1965 and 1966, the only NFL coach Lombardi ever talked about was Halas, but some of it was in admiration: "It was almost obsessive. We'd be getting ready to play the Bears, and Lombardi would say, 'Look at that old son of a gun. I ought to hate him, but I just love him. I just love that old rascal because he founded this league. But we still want to destroy him. We want to kill him.'"[66]

In '63 Halas knew the road to the NFL Championship went through the Packers. So did George Allen. They would make the most of the opportunity to show everyone which of the two teams deserved bragging rights.

6

"Allen Never Should Have Left"

Advancing in the coaching ranks is often an incremental process. So it went for George Allen, whose defensive prowess impressed George Halas so much that Halas elevated him in coaching authority soon after the 1962 season.

On February 12, 1963, Halas officially named Allen Chicago's head defensive coach, noting the Bears' significant improvement against the pass under the umbrella of Allen's zone defenses in '62. Halas also said Allen would continue in his role as the team's top scout.[1] A few days later, Halas named Joe Stydahar, a five-time All-NFL lineman who had played on the Bears' championship teams in 1940, 1941, and 1946, to assist Allen on defense with a focus on the line. Halas hoped Stydahar would improve a defense that yielded 4.7 yards per carry in '62, one of the worst marks in the league. "We want to bring our running defense up to our pass defense, in which we led the league," Halas said. "We are confident Stydahar can help us. Nobody ever ran very far against Joe."[2]

Although a sense of optimism permeated the organization heading into the '63 season, critics were saying Halas's best years were behind him, that he was too old at age sixty-eight, and that he should retire. But he stayed put. Coming off a year highlighted by five wins in the last six games, Halas, his coaching staff, and the players sensed that these Bears were built for a championship run, with a well-balanced defense that looked outstanding on paper and an offense that showed just as much talent. "We finished really strong in 1962," running back Ronnie Bull said. "We felt if we could carry that over, we had a very good chance of winning it."[3]

One day Halas asked Allen to be frank in explaining how good the defense really was. "Coach, on paper we have the best group coming to training camp that I have ever seen since I have been with you," Allen replied. "The competition for starting positions will be strong. We will separate the wheat from the chaff, but this will give us good depth at all positions. If we can stay healthy, we will be very good. I've spoken to the players, and they all have promised to report in good shape. They recognize how important that is. [Middle linebacker] Bill George told me last night he's ready to kick some ass. Bill told me he feels our team will be much better with a simple 4-3 defense, rather than the multiple sets Shaughnessy used the past couple of years. He felt it has been too confusing to many of the players."[4]

In training camp at St. Joseph's College in Rensselaer, Indiana, Halas embarked on modernizing the Bears' defense and focused on improving the team's run-stopping ability. Allen and Stydahar tweaked the defensive line. Doug Atkins and Earl Leggett remained positioned at end and tackle, respectively. But Stan Jones, a standout guard on offense for most of his nine previous seasons, replaced Fred Williams at left tackle at Allen's request. Bob Kilcullen played at the other end in place of the injured Ed O'Bradovich, who had a stomach ailment, and Maury Youmans, who was recuperating from a knee injury.[5] Halas also adopted a new motivational approach. Believing his players had become too "soft" and pampered, he implemented a "get-tough policy" designed to make the Bears a top contender and began cracking the whip. He wanted to return to his "1940 type of discipline," a championship year for a rugged Bears team known as the "Monsters of the Midway."[6]

Allen witnessed the ornery side of Halas, as the foul-mouthed owner-coach whipped his Bears into shape during two-a-day practices. "I'd watch the Bears' practices at training camp," George Felix Allen said. "Halas had a bad hip, so he'd move around a lot in a golf cart. At the beginning of practice as all of the players were warming up, he had them running around in a circle. He's just cussing away at them, saying all sorts of things, calling them everything you could think of. So he sees me and another kid just standing there watching and says, 'Hey, you boys, take this football and go play on the other field.' He realized young kids should not be hearing what he's saying to these grown men."[7]

The year 1963 evolved into a special one for Halas on several fronts. Just before the season, he was inducted into the inaugural class of the Pro Football Hall of Fame in Canton, Ohio, where he had helped give birth to the NFL more than four decades earlier. The initial class of seventeen NFL greats included fellow league pioneers Joe Carr, Earl "Curly" Lambeau, George Preston Marshall, and Bert Bell, plus Bears legends Bronko Nagurski and Red Grange, both of whom Halas had coached.

The Packers had won six NFL Championships with Lambeau as head coach. They now sought a third straight title under Lombardi, a feat not accomplished since the league began playing championship games in 1933. With the steady play of quarterback Bart Starr, running backs Jim Taylor and Paul Hornung behind linemen Jim Ringo, Jerry Kramer, Forrest Gregg, and Fuzzy Thurston, and a defense featuring end Willie Davis, middle linebacker Ray Nitschke, and safety Willie Wood, the '62 Packers scored a league-high 415 points and allowed a league-low 148. "The Packers and the Bears have always been big rivals," Richie Petitbon said years later. "Green Bay had just won two straight championships, so that just made it even more of a rivalry."[8]

Speaking at training camp, Halas called the Packers a "great ball club" but added that "even great clubs get beat."[9] Sure enough, the college all-stars embarrassed the Packers, 20–17, at Chicago's Soldier Field to open the '63 preseason. But Lombardi's troops won their last five exhibition games, the only team to do so, scoring the second-most points (136) and allowing the fewest (58). They were the consensus media pick to win the Western Conference, with the Giants taking the Eastern Conference—this, despite the NFL's move to level indefinite suspensions on Hornung, a triple-threat halfback and the NFL's most valuable player in 1961, and on Lions defensive tackle Alex Karras, the bulwark of Detroit's famed defensive line and, like Hornung, one of the best at his position. An extensive NFL investigation determined that both players had bet on NFL games. (The suspensions were lifted after the '63 season.)

"True, Hornung is suspended as a result of the betting probe," the Associated Press reported, "but the Packers still have the powerful running of Jim Taylor and company, Bart Starr's steady hand at quarterback, a bruising defense, and the great offensive line led by center Jim Ringo.

"In short, they're loaded. So loaded that coach Vince Lombardi recently predicted they would win again. There are fourteen games blocking their path to the playoff game on the home field of the Western Division champions. But it's like picking against the [New York] Yankees to say they won't make it."[10]

The Bears, in contrast, endured a topsy-turvy 3-2 preseason, with wins over the Giants, Redskins, and Colts and losses to the Cardinals and Packers. The Packers overpowered Chicago, 26–7, marking their eighth straight victory over the Bears, including three exhibition games. On a bright note, the Bears' run defense looked much stingier than the unit that had yielded 4.7 yards a carry the previous season.

George Allen, for his part, refused to leave anything unturned in his bid to prepare for the mighty Packers and the rest of the grueling schedule. He came to know Green Bay's offense better than any coach in the league outside of Lombardi and his staff. With one for every team, Allen the perfectionist maintained thick notebooks that broke down all of their plays on offense. He then transferred that information onto index cards that he used to create defensive game plans. He also reviewed hours and hours of game films on the Packers and other teams in hopes of finding anything he could exploit.[11] George Felix Allen recalled spending a lot of time watching his father analyze films with microscopic precision during his coaching days with the Bears.

"When watching football films, I'd like to watch the whole play," the coach's eldest son recalled. "With those reel tapes, he'd click the buttons so the tape goes back and forth and reverse and forward. He'd watch everyone power off the line of scrimmage. Every play would take almost thirty minutes. It would seem interminable just to go through one play. Plus, the projector would make that screeching sound when you reverse it and go back again and reverse it and go back again. It was the meticulousness of the study. I couldn't take it. But he made me appreciate his attention to the minutiae and detail of who's getting off the line or crossing the line, as well as figuring out the first motion and which way they move and all of that. He tried to detect tendencies and footwork and the synchrony of players, particularly offensive linemen and backs. My father would always have his defenses prepared. When opponents are in an offensive set in a specific down-and-distance scenario, [he'd know] the plays they're likely to run.

"Looking back on it, I understand why he was studying plays in endless detail. It was part of his success: preparation and hard work to make sure he was able to educate his players on whatever they needed to be more successful."[12]

Allen dissected the Packers' offense to a T for the season opener in Green Bay. Chicago's defense gave up only 150 yards and forced five turnovers, including four interceptions, in a 10–3 win that shattered the Packers' "invincibility," as the *Chicago Tribune* put it.[13] The Packers never advanced past Chicago's 33-yard line. Bears linebacker and defensive co-captain Joe Fortunato took congratulations afterward for calling a perfect game that handcuffed the Packers, while Chicago's offense was praised for its conservative game plan that featured short swing passes aimed at grinding out yardage.

Halas, who received the game ball, called the win the greatest team effort in Bears history. "This effort today culminates months of planning," he said in a raucous postgame locker room. "The coaches have worked hundreds of hours toward this one game. But the victory belongs to the players. They were ready physically, and they were ready mentally."

Linebacker Bill George said, "I knew damned well we'd do it. We wanted this game. We had to have it."[14]

Although the Bears were neck and neck with Green Bay the rest of the season, they were never out of first place in the Western Conference. They opened the season with a 5-0 streak that included victories over the Lions and Colts and ended with a 52–14 destruction of the lowly Rams. At the same time, the Bears' simplified defense took shape; it was a swarming, opportunistic unit that established itself as one of the greatest defenses in NFL history. Offenses encountered tough going against a defense that through five games limited opponents to 380 yards rushing (76 per game), compared with 837 (167.4 per game) at the same point in 1962; 48 points (9.6 per game); and 64 first downs (12.8 per game) and that had intercepted 19 passes (3.8 per game).

Allen attributed the rise of the '63 defense to avoiding anything cute, sticking to the basics, and repetition. "We cut down and simplified a lot of things in the last couple of games [in 1962]," he said in *The Future Is Now*. "We simply try to eliminate mistakes, concentrate on not giving up the easy score, the long run, or the long pass.

"Then we work on the A-B-Cs. Every day in camp we stressed fundamentals, all of them, the techniques and everything basic. That's the laborious part of the game, but it's what pays dividends. You don't beat yourself."[15]

As part of the simplification, Allen and other assistants implemented "Buz" and "Rub," terms for two of the Bears' main defensive maneuvers. Both were meant to improve coordination between different facets of the defense. "Buz" meant the linebackers dropped back to help the defensive backs with passes and runs, and "Rub" meant an improvement in teamwork between the linebackers and front four, or the "rush men," as the coaches called them.[16]

Without hesitation, Ed O'Bradovich credited Allen as the brains behind the dominance, noting that some of Allen's schemes that were bewildering defenses had never been seen in the NFL. "There's no question about it," he said in retrospect. "We were doing things where nobody else in the league knew what the hell we were doing. Offenses couldn't figure us out. We had such a complicated blitz package and a plan to take out opposing receivers. It was unbelievable. And we all knew we had a hell of a team. I guarantee if we didn't have George Allen, we never would have won the world championship in 1963. Everybody on the whole forty-man roster, including special team guys, respected George Allen and loved him. We just went out there with the belief we're going to shut everybody down. The way we played, we thought, 'They're not going to get a touchdown, they're not going to score.'"[17]

O'Bradovich explained, for instance, that when a running back tried swinging out of the backfield from the strong or weak side for a short reception in the flat, the Bears' defense would take him down before he could make the catch. "When you played the Chicago Bears, you couldn't do that," he said. "When a running back tried to get through, if he had the ball or if he didn't, then the term was 'you ground them.' You don't let him get through and take that little 7-yard safety pass. That only lasted for a few years because it suddenly became illegal."

He also elaborated on Allen's blitz packages, which included "grounding" receivers at the line of scrimmage, another move that would be illegal today: "Our cornerbacks, when certain blitzes were called, would line up head-on on the receivers and take them down at the line of scrimmage, either with a roll block or staying with them and not letting them get downfield. When we did that, we'd come with a safety blitz with Richie Petitbon or an all-out blitz with linebackers Bill George or Joe Fortunato or Larry Morris blitzing from all over the place.

"Whatever you did, it had to be perfect. Like if [cornerback] Bennie McRae came up on a wideout, his job was to take him out. He had to do so because if he missed, the receiver is down the field, and 6 points go against you. Bennie practiced that stuff day and night. Go back and look at the films from the '63 season. Nobody knew what the heck we were doing."

O'Bradovich, one of Allen's so-called diamonds in the rough, was tailor made to be a Bear. After starring as an all-state fullback at Proviso Township High School in Maywood, Illinois, just outside of Chicago, he played offensive end for two seasons at the University of Illinois. He dropped out of college after his junior year and played in the Canadian Football League in 1961 for the British Columbia Lions and the Calgary Stampeders. The Bears drafted him in the seventh round in '62.

"George Allen was in contact with me and asked if other teams were interested in me like the 49ers," O'Bradovich remembered. "He wanted to know if they had contacted me. But lo and behold, the Bears drafted me in the seventh round. So I left Canada and went to Chicago and made the team that first year in 1962."

The Bears found themselves a tough, relentless, and speedy defensive end in the 6-foot-2, 255-pound O'Bradovich, who was a load for blockers and often took on several at a time in his bid to create trouble for quarterbacks and ball carriers. Like Doug Atkins, he was a terror as a pass rusher. His motor never stopped, and he gave it his all for sixty minutes. "OB," as he was known, was also a wild, temperamental, and unpredictable player who was prone to on-the-field outbursts in his ten-year career from 1962 to 1971.

In an outstanding 1962 rookie season, O'Bradovich started thirteen of fourteen games, recovered a league-high five fumbles, and made sixty-two tackles. A virus sidelined him for the first eight weeks of the '63 campaign. But he returned to the lineup to face the Rams on November 10, replacing Bob Kilcullen, who had filled in admirably but lacked his natural ability as a pass rusher.

The Bears mustered only two field goals against the Rams, but it was enough for a 6–0 win, Chicago's only shutout of the season. The Rams weren't in a giving mood that day, in large part because of their imposing defensive front four of Rosey Grier, Deacon Jones, Merlin Olsen, and Lamar Lundy. Allen thought that front four, which averaged 6 feet 6 in height and 276 pounds in weight, was the most talented line the Bears would face all year.

"That front wall has the ability to get after people," Allen said at the time. "I am amazed at their size and quickness. Early in the season they were underachieving, but they appear to be coming into their own."[18]

Allen became well acquainted with that line after relocating to Southern California later in the '60s. In the '63 season, his 8-1 Bears faced a titanic clash against the 8-1 Packers at Wrigley Field, with first place in the Western Conference on the line. Interest in the game skyrocketed, with more than one hundred TV stations set to broadcast it and brokers selling tickets at then-astronomical fees of fifty to sixty-five dollars for seats worth about five bucks. President John F. Kennedy, an avid football fan, was invited to attend, but he declined.[19] The Packers hadn't lost since falling to Chicago in the season opener. This time, it wasn't even close. The Bears coasted to a 26–7 victory. Chicago's "majestic defense," as *Washington Post* sportswriter Dave Brady put it, held the Packers scoreless for fifty-five minutes and limited them to 71 yards rushing and 178 passing.[20] Packers quarterback Bart Starr missed the game due to a broken throwing hand. His backups, John Roach and Zeke Bratkowski, looked inept with a total of 5 interceptions.

The Bears now led Green Bay by a full game, and with four left, the Western Conference championship was theirs to lose. While they prepared for their upcoming game against the Steelers, earth-shattering news came on Friday, November 22: President Kennedy had been assassinated during a trip to Dallas.

None of the Bears wanted to play that Sunday.[21] But NFL commissioner Pete Rozelle decided that the games would proceed as scheduled, a decision he later called the greatest mistake of his thirty-year tenure. No NFL games aired that day on television, only on radio. The AFL canceled its games, and many college football games were postponed.

"Everybody thought the assassination of the president was terrible," recalled George Felix Allen, who was eleven at the time. "That day, my father wasn't at home because he was at practice preparing for the Steelers game, and he was gone that Saturday through Sunday in Pittsburgh. We had to listen to the game on the radio. Everyone was just in a very somber, sad mood."[22]

The Bears tied the Steelers that day, 17–17, and then went on to tie the Vikings by the same score before beating the 49ers, 27–7. The conference race came down to the final Sunday, with 10-1-2 Chicago a half game ahead of the 10-2-1 Packers. The Packers beat the 49ers, but the Bears punched their ticket to the championship game with a 21–17 victory over the Lions. In hosting the 11-3 New York Giants, winners of the Eastern Conference, the Bears would be vying for their eighth championship in franchise history.

The Bears' defense had been a juggernaut, a 1963 version of the "Monsters of the Midway." The Allen-coached unit led the NFL in ten of nineteen statistical categories and placed second in eight others.[23] The defense allowed a league-low 144 points (10.3 per game), 62 fewer than the next team, the Packers. Other major defensive firsts included interceptions (36), total yards (3,176), rushing yards (1,442), passing yards (1,734), pass completions (164), and ball-control plays (runs and passes, 801). Plus, the emphasis on stopping the run and the hiring of line coach Joe Stydahar paid off. The defense allowed 3.5 yards per carry, more than a yard less than in 1962.

Chicago notched a team record thirty-six interceptions, of which twenty-nine were credited to the foursome of Richie Petitbon, Rosey Taylor, Dave Whitsell, and Bennie McRae, arguably the best defensive backfield in the league. Taylor, the man Allen found by asking Grambling coach Eddie Robinson if he had "any good defensive backs" and whom he had signed as a free agent, intercepted a league-high nine passes, a Bears single-season record. (The Giants' Dick Lynch also picked off nine in 1963.)

Remarkably, Taylor had a hand in six touchdowns. He returned an interception 30 yards for a score, two of his other interceptions set up touchdowns, and three of his fumble recoveries set up scoring plays. He epitomized the huge benefits of ball hawking, which Allen preached. Of the Bears' fifty-two scoring situations (touchdowns, field goals, and a safety), the defense set up twenty-eight through fumble recoveries and interceptions. Four of the interceptions were returned for touchdowns.[24] In the days before the championship game, Taylor praised Allen for making his defensive players ball conscious and "pounding" it into them that "it's anybody's ball as soon as it goes up in the air."[25]

The defensive backfield thrived off the dominance of the NFL's finest linebacker trio—Bill George, Larry Morris, and Joe Fortunato—as well as the relentless harassment of quarterbacks by the Bears' exceptionally large defensive line. The gargantuan Doug Atkins, a consensus first-team All-Pro and the best pass rusher in the league, anchored the line. Sacks were not an official statistic until 1982. But team publicists described the 6-foot-8, 270-pound Atkins as a "towering figure on the Bears' great defense" in 1963, when the eleventh-year pro constantly terrorized quarterbacks and tackled one in the end zone for a safety. He also intercepted a pass.[26]

George Allen loved what Atkins brought to the game, and the defensive end gravitated to him in turn. A country boy from Tennessee, Atkins possessed freakish athletic ability that he parlayed into an incredible package of size, speed, and power. He originally went to the University of Tennessee on a basketball scholarship, before legendary Volunteers football coach General Robert Neyland recruited him. He earned All-American honors on the gridiron. He also possessed world-class high-jumping ability and once cleared the bar at six feet, six inches. Offensive linemen often found it futile to block the mountain-sized man because he could beat them multiple ways, whether by applying a bull rush, eluding them with his quick feet, or leapfrogging them. Moreover, no opponent wanted to make him mad. Word around the league was that as tough as Atkins was, he was even tougher when angered.[27]

Atkins was also a colorful character and an outspoken free spirit. His carefree approach in practice infuriated George Halas, and the two frequently clashed. In his 1979 autobiography, Halas wrote that Browns coach Paul Brown traded Atkins to the Bears after the '54 season because the defensive end "resented discipline of any kind." Halas also told of an argument he once had with Atkins after a fan telephoned to say that Atkins was plastered in a bar: "I drove over. Doug saw me enter and shouted a tumultuous river of profanities. I walked up to him and countered with a barrage that for volume and variety made his assault a peaceful brook compared to my Niagara. Doug put down his glass and came to camp." Halas and Atkins eventually came to respect one another—to an extent.[28] Atkins demanded a trade after the '66 season and played his last three years with the expansion New Orleans Saints, retiring at age thirty-nine.

How strong was Doug Atkins? Bruce Allen found out firsthand. During a fishing tournament in Tennessee in 1985, Atkins, in his mid-fifties at the time, playfully tossed him out of a boat. "I'm sitting in a boat, and I felt something like a forklift pick me up," Bruce remembered. "I got thrown into the freezing damn water. I got up and thought, 'Who in the hell?' It was Doug Atkins. He picked me up like I'm a 12-pound dummy and threw me six feet into the water to welcome me to Tennessee. I was probably 175 pounds. He still had the strength to do that."[29]

In Atkins's seventeen-year career, which included twelve with the Bears (1955–66), he won two championships, one with the Browns in 1954 and the other with Chicago in 1963. A four-time All-Pro and eight-time Pro Bowl player, he retired after appearing in 205 games, a record at the time for a defensive lineman. He was inducted into the Hall of Fame in 1982 and the College Football Hall of Fame in 1985. Halas called him the greatest defensive end in NFL history.[30]

Chicago's 1963 defense carried the team's unspectacular offense, nicknamed the "eleven sticks of dynamite" because of the fear it would explode at any time for all the wrong reasons.[31] But the defense stuck to its ball-control theme, maintaining possession on runs or passes 901 times, second only to the Giants' 914.[32] Tight end Mike Ditka caught fifty-nine passes and eight touchdowns and was a consensus first-team All-Pro. He also made the Pro Bowl. Quarterback Bill Wade established himself as one of the league's top-ranked passers and made the Pro Bowl, as did fullback Joe Marconi, who rushed for 406 yards.

"The players on defense used to kid us on offense," running back Ronnie Bull said in looking back. "We'd go on the field, and they'd say, 'Hold them for four downs.' But when we needed to score, we came through."[33]

But could the league's best defense stop the league's best offense in the championship game? The machine-like Giants tallied NFL-high stats in points (448), yards (5,024), and touchdowns (51). Their thirty-seven-year-old quarterback, Y. A. Tittle, posted NFL-high stats in completion percentage (60.2), touchdown passes (36), and passer rating (104.8), among others, and was named NFL Most Valuable Player, a first-team All-Pro, and a Pro Bowl starter. The present-day Hall of Famer, whose 36 touchdowns stood as an NFL single-season record until Miami's Dan Marino passed for 48 in 1984, had a smorgasbord of receivers to target, among them flanker Frank Gifford, split end Del Shofner, and tight end Joe Walton.

Tittle would be seeking the first NFL Championship of his then-sixteen-year career and the Giants their fifth since entering the league in 1925. Most recently, they had beaten Chicago by 40 points in 1956, the start of a glory period in which they appeared in six championship games in an eight-season span, winning once.

In the early years of that stretch, the Giants were known for a menacing defense led by such stars as middle linebacker Sam Huff, safety Emlen Tunnell, and defensive linemen Dick Modzelewski, Andy Robustelli, Rosey Grier, and Jim Katcavage. In the mid- to late 1950s, the Giants also had two assistant coaches, Vince Lombardi (offensive coordinator) and Tom Landry (defensive coordinator), who advanced to become two of the greatest NFL head coaches ever. Years later, both men would be head coaching rivals of Allen, with Lombardi leading the Packers and Landry, the Cowboys.

But a prolific offense defined the '63 Giants, and Allen hunkered down to prepare his defense for the formidable task ahead. He called for applying maximum pressure on Tittle in the pocket and denying him the ability to connect on the bomb by double-teaming Shofner and Gifford. He also aimed to shut down the screen pass, one of the Giants' key weapons. In one practice, the Bears' taxi squad quarterback repeatedly threw every one of the screen passes in New York's arsenal. Plus, Allen and Chicago's coaching staff created a four-hundred-foot film reel of eight of the Giants' games, guaranteeing hours and hours of studying.[34]

There was nothing fancy about the mind-set of the Bears' defense. "Get Tittle, knock him on his ass," O'Bradovich recalled. "That was basically it. You get Y. A. Tittle, and it's all over with—game, set, and match." He noted that a lot of the Giants' production on offense came via screen plays and "lates," when the quarterback drops back to pass, the backs set up like they're going to block, and the quarterback drops the ball into their belly—similar to a draw play. "That's what George Allen wanted stopped, the screen passes and the lates, because that was the heart of their offense," O'Bradovich said. "They ran it to perfection."[35]

The Giants were slight favorites. But in a conversation with New York reporters, Allen sounded extremely confident that his Bears could handle the NFL's top offense. "I said, 'Let me tell you something: The Giants haven't faced a defense like the Bears. Put that down and underline it,'" Allen, reminiscing about the game, told the *Los Angeles Times* in 1985. "When Halas saw that in the paper, he said, 'Oh, you shouldn't have said that. You're giving 'em ammunition.'"[36]

Allen couldn't have scripted a better game plan. Before a packed crowd of 45,801 at Wrigley Field on December 29, 1963, the Bears exhibited a masterful defensive performance in a 14–10 win over the Giants. On a bitterly cold day with the temperature at 4 degrees and the wind chill at –11, the defense strangled Tittle and company and compensated for a Bears offense that rushed for 93 yards and lost two fumbles. Tittle completed only 11 of 29 passes for 147 yards and threw five interceptions, two of them on screen passes that turned the tide in the Bears' favor. His favorite target, Shofner, didn't catch a pass and let a potential touchdown, one that would have put the Giants up, 14–0, go off his fingertips. The Bears also recovered a fumble, and a defensive formation they hadn't used all year called "fifty-one Mickey" resulted in two big sacks by Larry Morris.[37]

It's fair to note that Tittle was hobbling for half the game, after Morris hit him in the left knee as he released a pass late in the second quarter. Tittle left the game briefly, took pain-killing shots, and returned for the third period with a heavily taped knee. Throwing mostly off his back foot and with his passes lacking their usual zip, he tossed four interceptions in the second half, although Giants coach Allie Sherman refused to use injuries as an excuse for the loss.[38]

With the Giants nursing a 7–0 first-quarter lead, Tittle faked a screen pass to his right and threw to the left for Phil King in the flat. But Morris jumped the pass, picked it off, and ran 61 yards to the Giants' 5-yard line, setting up Wade's 2-yard sneak for a touchdown. Morris would be named the game's most valuable player. Later, with the Giants holding a 10–7 third-quarter lead, Tittle lofted a short pass to his right for Joe Morrison. O'Bradovich read it perfectly, staying back and pulling the ball down with one hand, and ran to the Giants' 14. A few plays later, Wade sneaked over the goal line from the 1. The extra point gave the Bears a 14–10 lead.

"We practiced that play all week," O'Bradovich said in retrospect. "We tried to know how the offensive tackle and the quarterback are going to set up and how many steps back the quarterback is going to take. Is he going to try to suck you in so you might take an inside rush? We knew that was coming."[39]

Chicago's defense held on from there, intercepting two more passes, both in the end zone, to stop fourth-quarter drives. First, it was Bennie McRae. Then Petitbon cradled Tittle's desperation pass after it floated into the end zone with less than ten seconds to play.

Champions for the first time since 1946, the Bears and their fans began celebrating. An exuberant Halas, with his sixth NFL Championship in hand, was hugged and congratulated on the sideline. But only one Bears coach received a victory ride on his players' shoulders—the man widely regarded as the true genius behind the team's success in the regular season and the championship game: George Allen.

Allen received more accolades in the steamy and noisy Bears locker room, a scene of bedlam. George Connor, a great Bears two-way lineman and linebacker from 1948 to 1955, was trying to conduct interviews for NBC, which broadcast the game, when Fortunato interrupted him: "I want to make a short speech. I want to announce, as one of the co-captains, that the game ball goes to the man who played such a great part in our fine defense—coach George Allen." Fortunato tossed the ball to Allen.[40]

Then, with NBC's cameras rolling and a national TV audience looking on with a combination of amazement and amusement, the players congregated to serenade the defensive wizard with their traditional victory song. Nasty Bears lineman-end Ed Sprinkle had conceived of the song in a previous era to honor a player or coach: "Hooray for George, hooray at last, hooray for George, he's a horse's ass!" In his 1979 autobiography, Halas tried to explain that the song was meant for him, but it clearly wasn't.[41]

"It was a wonderful victory for coach Halas, and it was a great thing for coach Allen," Bill George said in the locker room. "He helped us develop a great defense. Nobody will ever know all the work that went into this championship.

"Our objective was to protect against the screen. And in so doing, we contained the Giants to the outside also. And of course, we were watching against the long bomb. We knew Tittle threw that well. We were waiting for it. We were willing to let them gain a little bit on the ground as long as they didn't wreck us with a long touchdown pass."[42]

Allen also chimed in: "We double-teamed Del Shofner and Frank Gifford most of the day, and although their draw play hurt us some, we were more concerned about the Tittle bomb. Shofner didn't have a completion, so I guess the defense did its job well."[43]

O'Bradovich had no doubt who had engineered the championship victory: "In my mind, everything goes to George Allen. We scored two touchdowns, both on quarterback sneaks. Our offense didn't move that well. That defense proved without a doubt that you can win a world championship with defense."[44]

Chicago's '63 championship season transformed the forty-six-year-old Allen into the hottest coaching name in the league. "Fame Taps Mr. Allen," the Associated Press announced.[45] In the weeks following the championship game, he received inquiries from NFL teams, including a head coaching offer from the Eagles, and from an American Football League team. But he didn't bite, hoping a head coaching slot would open up at some point with the Bears.[46]

Halas, who was named NFL Coach of the Year, wasn't going anywhere—at least for now. Following the win over the Giants, he told reporters there "isn't much danger of me retiring at the present."[47] But was it time for the "grand old man of the NFL" to step down and hand the head coaching job to Allen, who seemed like the logical successor to Halas?

"No, I wouldn't say that at all," Mike Ditka said in looking back. "Coach Halas was the owner of the team. He had a right to do what he wanted to do. There's no question about that. By not doing that, though, that's why we lost Coach Allen. He went on to become a very successful coach with the Rams and Redskins. But no, Mr. Halas made all the calls. It wasn't like we were going to have a committee meeting on this, and the coaches would all get involved. He made the decisions. And it worked out pretty good for us."[48]

But in O'Bradovich's view, Halas needed to give the reins to his disciple and ride off into the sunset. The defensive tackle saw more championships on the horizon with Allen as head coach: "When we won the world championship in 1963, everybody thought Halas was going to retire. We're going to send him out as a world champ at his age. Let him retire. He's got all the money in the world, he owns the Chicago Bears, and he started the league. And he was going to go bye-bye and hand it over to George Allen. That was probably the biggest disappointment that I can remember back in those days. You look back to the 1960s, and when George Allen left for the Los Angeles Rams [in 1966], that was a sad day in Bear history as far as I'm concerned."[49]

More than two decades passed before the Bears were again champions. Led again by a ferocious defense on par with the '63 contingent as one of the greatest ever, the Bears lost just once in 1985 and routed the New England Patriots in Super Bowl XX, 46–10. But until reaching that summit, the franchise encountered a stream of mediocrity, starting with the remaining four years of the Halas regime: 5-9 in 1964, 9-5 in 1965, 5-7-2 in 1966, 7-6-1 in 1967.

At the time, though, Bears players and coaches basked in the glow of the '63 championship season and hoped for a repeat. While they prepared for the 1964 campaign at training camp, two pieces of shocking news surfaced, one of which would derail the season. A few weeks into camp, Allen learned from Etty that her father, Felix Lumbroso, had been accidentally shot at a hotel in the French resort town of Evian. Thirteen-year-old George Felix Allen was visiting his grandparents, Felix Lumbroso and Eugenie "Jenny" Lumbroso, when the incident happened. Felix was walking out of the hotel when his grandson, a few feet behind him, heard a loud bang.

"My reaction was, 'That's a firecracker,'" George Felix Allen remembered. "I turned around, and my grandfather is groaning in pain, and he falls to the ground. I said, 'Gee, what has happened to Popop?' I kneeled down to look at him and opened up his shirt to see what happened. As I did that, I saw this guy running the other way in a hallway in the hotel."

Lumbroso had been shot in his stomach area by the man who ran away, a young desk clerk who was spinning a handgun around when it discharged. He was arrested a few hours later and claimed the shooting was unintentional. The wound left Lumbroso, who was seventy-nine at the time, in critical condition. He was hospitalized in Evian, although several weeks would pass before word reached Etty.

The bloody incident occurred in mid-July. But Jenny Lumbroso didn't want Etty to know about it because she didn't want her to worry. On one of several letters she sent to Etty while her father was in the hospital, however, George Felix Allen surreptitiously wrote between the lines that the shooting had occurred. His crestfallen mother immediately told George and flew to Evian with their three-year-old daughter, Jennifer. Bruce stayed at Bears training camp, and Greg lived with a local family.[50]

In *Papa Bear: The Life and Legacy of George Halas*, Etty recounted how the Bears' owner, a devout Catholic and communicant who regularly attended mass, stepped up to support the Allen family during that trying time: "Mr. Halas told George, 'If Etty needs any money to go, I'd be happy to loan her whatever she needs for the trip.' We didn't have much money at all. That touched me so much. Mr. Halas had masses every day for my father. It was so wonderful of him to do that. I always had a lot of respect for him, and George did, too. We really loved the Bears."[51]

Felix Lumbroso was hospitalized for more than a month. He recovered, although the bullet wound slowed him down for the remaining thirteen years of his life. In the nearly three decades he knew George Allen, he and his wife held a strong emotional bond with their son-in-law.

"They liked his drive, his spirit, the way he treated their daughter," George Felix Allen said. "All of the characteristics that you'd want in a son-in-law, they saw in him. My father had flown all the way to Tunisia to ask for [Etty's] hand in marriage, and flying to Tunisia in the early 1950s wasn't easy. It's probably not easy these days, either. But it was much more difficult then. And I know my father really respected and loved them and my mother's sister, Lillian. There was mutual love and mutual respect between all of them. They were very close."[52]

Several weeks after Felix Lumbroso was shot, George Allen and the rest of the Bears organization were jolted by another tragedy. Two popular and talented players on the team, running back Willie Galimore and end Bo Farrington, were killed in an auto accident on the night of July 27, 1964. Their car skidded out of control on a dangerous turn near the Bears' training camp and crashed. They died instantly.

The coaching staff and players dedicated the '64 season to Galimore and Farrington. But the loss of Galimore left the team without a breakaway running threat. Allen, still in charge of player personnel duties, tried to compensate by trading for the versatile Jon Arnett from the Rams. In '64 Arnett rushed for 400 yards, caught twenty-five passes for 225 yards, and produced more than 500 yards on kick returns. But his arrival wasn't enough to prevent the Bears, demoralized from the loss of Galimore and Farrington, from struggling. They lost seven of their first nine games, including a 52–0 disaster to the Colts, and finished in sixth place in the Western Division at 5-9.

But one sequence during the '64 season sparked big headlines, with Allen leading a series of acquisitions that would serve as his parting gift to the Bears. In the first round of the 1965 draft on November 28, 1964, the Bears had three picks, their own at four and two others, three and six, from trades Allen had made with the Steelers and Redskins. With Allen as the team's top eye for talent, the Bears chose Illinois linebacker Dick Butkus with the third pick and Kansas running back Gale Sayers with the fourth—acquisitions that will forever leave football historians and enthusiasts in awe. Today Butkus is widely regarded as the greatest middle linebacker ever and Sayers as one of the most electrifying players ever to don an NFL uniform. Not surprisingly, both were selected for the NFL Films "NFL 100 Greatest" all-time team. Plus, their Hall of Fame induction marks the only time that two players from the same team who were selected with back-to-back picks would be enshrined—both on their first ballot, no less.

"How the Bears got Butkus and Sayers with the third and fourth picks, that's something Oliver Stone might want to do a movie about," Dan Pompei, a longtime Chicago sportswriter and coauthor of the *Chicago Bears Centennial Scrapbook*, said in reference to the famed film director. "On a list of the greatest all-time football players, it would be impossible to have Butkus and Sayers out of the top twenty. They would probably be in the top ten for a lot of people, maybe even higher than that. To accomplish what the Bears accomplished, both in knowing the talent and being able to get Butkus and Sayers, was improbable and incredible."

In Pompei's view, Allen was the primary architect in the Bears' quest to land the sensational duo. "There's no question George Allen was running the draft at the time. He was the guy who put everything in order. Obviously, George Halas had final say, but he trusted Allen implicitly at the time."[53]

The acquisition of Butkus and Sayers came at the height of the NFL's cold war with the AFL and marked one of the NFL's greatest wins in the interleague battle. At the time, the NFL was still under attack from the AFL, which was using all kinds of clandestine maneuvers to get the best college players.

To protect its interests, the NFL retaliated with "Operation Handholding" in the mid-1960s, assigning people to hide college players from the AFL, which used the same tactic. Both leagues hired lawyers, politicians, former coaches, and other professionals for the "babysitting" role.[54] Chicago businessman Vern Buol had been supervising Butkus, and NFL great Buddy Young had kept watch on Sayers.

Who was Vern Buol?

Buol was the vice president of High Grade Food Products, a large business on Fulton Street in Chicago that made Ball Park Franks and German bratwurst, among other products. He grew in prominence by actively supporting candidates in state and local politics and crossed paths with people in the Bears' front office, namely George Halas and his son, team president George Halas Jr. "He got a relationship in place by making himself available in his desire to become more involved with the Chicago Bears," said Jim Buol, Vern's oldest son. "He was an avid fan forever. He offered to scout for them at games at Northwestern University in Chicago and at other major colleges."

Through his ties to the Bears, Vern Buol also came to know George Allen. The two first met at Bears training camp during Allen's first full season, 1959, when the young assistant coach escorted Vern and his son, Jim, on a visit to the camp. Their friendship grew from there, and their families became tight. Allen was named the godfather of Vern Buol's youngest son, Chris.

"My brother and sister and I grew up with the Allens and would often be at their home," Jim Buol said. "When they moved out to other parts of the country, my mom and dad would visit with them. After George died [in 1990], my mother maintained a relationship with Etty Allen. So for my father, it was a close, lifetime friendship."[55]

George Felix Allen recalled that "Vern Buol was a good family friend in the Bears years and beyond. We'd have dinners together with him and his wife. Vern would kindly give us Ball Park Franks from his company when we lived in Chicago."[56]

Vern Buol and George Allen were almost the same age but had striking personality differences. Buol leaned toward the flamboyant side and was much more outgoing. He was known to curse from time to time. Allen was completely vanilla in how he expressed himself, a characteristic that his close friend admired. "I have extremely fond memories of my dad and George together," said Kim Buol, Vern's daughter. "They loved one another very much. My dad was always so impressed with how Mr. Allen would be a gentleman. When other coaches would be going crazy, he stayed under control. He was a gentle soul. My dad loved that about him."[57]

Both men spent time in the service in World War II—Allen in the navy's V-12 College Training Program and Buol in the European theater. Buol was a true war hero. He was a navigator in the army air corps when enemy fire struck his B-24 bomber in the skies over Hungary in September 1944. He parachuted out, broke his ankle upon landing, and was captured by German soldiers, marking the start of a terrifying chapter in his life. He ended up in a POW camp in East Prussia, part of what is now Poland, and was ordered to take part in the "Black March," a series of German-led marches to the west that began in February 1945. Some six thousand Americans were on those marches, during which many of the men died of sickness, hunger, and exhaustion. Others were killed by their guards.[58]

Buol survived the prison camp and earned military honors for his bravery and service, including the Air Medal, which is awarded for acts of heroism or meritorious achievement in military flight.[59]

Jim Buol said it was his understanding that NFL commissioner Pete Rozelle, whom his father knew very well, had assigned Vern Buol to babysit Butkus. But in Jim's view, George Allen had a say in it, too, considering the assistant's close ties to his father: "I'm quite certain that their relationship after that first trip down to Rensselaer began to grow, and when it came time to do it, I'm absolutely certain that Allen had input in it."[60]

The following year, Buol kept watch on Jim Grabowski, a coveted college running back whom the Packers were eyeing in the '66 draft. The Bears had recommended Buol to the Packers for the role, as the war with the AFL had forced NFL teams to adopt an "enemy of my enemy is my friend" sort of approach. The Packers and the AFL's Miami Dolphins took Grabowski with first-round picks, but he signed with Green Bay.[61]

In the 1965 draft, the Bears were determined to nab Butkus, a Chicago native of Lithuanian ancestry who was as Chicago hard-nosed and old school as they come. At Illinois he amassed tackles, fumble recoveries, and interceptions to become the best linebacker in the nation. He was named to many All-American teams and finished third in Heisman Trophy balloting as a junior, a remarkable feat for a defensive player. Today the Butkus Award goes annually to the best linebacker in the country.

Butkus first met Buol at the Waldorf-Astoria Hotel in New York City on the night before the draft. Buol stayed with Butkus that evening, even tagging along with him and Bill Taylor, an assistant football coach at Illinois, for a night on the town, including a stop at the famous Latin Quarter nightclub. The Bears had already made Butkus an offer and were trying to prevent him from being lured away by AFL teams, including the Denver Broncos and the New York Jets.

Today, Butkus is convinced that Allen assigned Buol to keep watch on him: "That's because every Friday during my rookie year, the three of us had lunch together. So they were tight. The wives were close. I didn't know Vern from Adam. He was a big Northwestern guy."[62]

Would it have mattered if Buol hadn't babysat him? Maybe not. Butkus's attorney, Arthur Morse, urged him to accept the Bears' $204,000 offer over the Broncos' $400,000 deal, arguing that the latter was inflated with phony perks.[63] Denver took him in the second round of the AFL draft. But Butkus was eager to play in the more established NFL and wear the orange and black of his hometown team.

Like Butkus, Sayers was intent on playing in the NFL, following a college career at Kansas, where "The Kansas Comet" set a Big 8 conference rushing record with 2,675 yards. Speedy and elusive, he was courted by the Chiefs and its wealthy owner, Lamar Hunt, prompting the NFL front office to assign Buddy Young, a Colts public relations executive and scout, to watch him and protect the older league's interests. Young, who became the NFL's first Black front office executive when he was hired as an assistant to the commissioner in 1965, began babysitting Sayers a few days before draft day, when the Bears and Chiefs both picked him in the first round. Young said he "practically lived" with Sayers for more than a week until he signed with the Bears on December 1, 1964.[64]

Today, Butkus is unaware if Allen played a role in tapping Young to babysit Sayers, who, like the PR executive, was Black. "Let's just say, I wouldn't put it past him," he said.[65]

Butkus and Sayers made instant impacts as rookies. Butkus posted career highs in fumble recoveries (7) and interceptions (5) out of his career tallies of 27 and 22, respectively. At the same time, he displayed a ferocity rarely seen in football and set the tone for his distinction as the meanest man in the game. From the moment he stepped on the field, the 6-foot-3, 245-pound middle linebacker terrorized ball carriers, who quivered in his presence. He tried to punish them and take their heads off. Many players suffered when crossing his path.

Butkus and Allen developed an immediate chemistry after Butkus arrived as a rookie. He believes Allen prepared him for the NFL better than anybody else, helping fuel an inner passion for the game. Allen also gave Butkus a leadership role in just his first season.

"He was just an amazing guy," Butkus remembered. "I think we hit it off because he was nothing but football. We had lunch together my rookie year every Friday. We'd go to this German joint in Chicago called Golden Ox. It was just amazing, talking football all the time. He also had that ability to find talent. He really liked veteran players who wouldn't make any mistakes. That was the key with George Allen. My rookie year we'd go over and over and over stuff. The idea was to never make a mistake twice. He was really good at picking veteran players. He had a lot of older players on his teams, but they got the job done.

"As a defensive player, I thought, 'I'm playing for a guy who really knows what the heck's going on.' That's why I paid attention and hit it off with him. He just lived and died football. He studied all the time and figured out ways to capitalize on mistakes by other teams."[66]

In Sayers, the Bears had a rare talent and their top offensive attraction since Red Grange, aka the "Galloping Ghost," in the 1920s and 1930s. In 1965 Sayers, aka "Mr. Versatility," rushed for 867 yards (5.2 average) and 14 touchdowns and caught 29 passes for 507 yards and 6 touchdowns. He returned 16 punts (14.9 average) with a touchdown and 21 kickoffs (31.4 average) with a touchdown. He set an NFL single-season record of 22 touchdowns and a rookie single-season mark of 2,272 all-purpose yards.

Both Butkus and Sayers earned Pro Bowl and consensus first-team All-Pro honors, with Sayers edging his teammate in NFL Rookie of the Year voting. But hideous knee injuries short-circuited their illustrious careers. In 1977 Sayers was inducted into the Hall of Fame at age thirty-four and remains the youngest person to receive that distinction. Butkus earned his gold jacket two years later.

Some of Allen's other '65 draft acquisitions, several of whom signed with AFL teams, made that draft even more extraordinary. With the sixth pick in the first round, the Bears took Tennessee defensive lineman Steve DeLong, winner of the Outland Trophy for the nation's best interior lineman. He signed instead with the AFL's San Diego Chargers, who picked him in the first round of the AFL draft. DeLong then embarked on a solid eight-year career with a Pro Bowl appearance in 1969, when he set a Chargers record with seventeen sacks.[67] The other picks included Syracuse fullback Jim Nance, who signed with the AFL's Boston Patriots and produced two 1,000-yard rushing seasons in his eight-year career, and Michigan State wide receiver Dick Gordon, who signed with the Bears and received two-time Pro Bowl honors and one first-team All-Pro honor in ten seasons.

For George Allen, losing DeLong to the AFL "stuck in his craw" more than any of his other Bears draft picks who had signed with the new league. That was Bruce Allen's view in retrospect. With DeLong added to the mix, Bruce said, "you're talking about a draft that's just insane."[68] Were it not for Halas and his miserly ways, it appears DeLong would have been a Bear.

"He was just about ready to sign with us but looked up and said, 'I'd like to have a car,'" George Allen said years later. "Halas said, 'What kind?' and DeLong answered, 'Nothing fancy; maybe a Chevy or a Ford or a Plymouth.' Halas coughed the way he used to and said, 'Well, I know where we can get a used car.' That was the end of DeLong."[69]

Because of Allen's ability to spot college talent that rose to stardom in the NFL—namely Ditka, Butkus, Sayers, and Ronnie Bull—he was in a league of his own. That's what Jim Dooley, a sure-handed Bears receiver in the 1950s and a colleague of Allen in the mid-1960s as a Bears assistant coach, seemed to believe. Dooley also compared him to Al Davis, who as AFL commissioner forced the merger with the NFL that took shape in 1970 and who then, as principal owner and general manager, built the Raiders into three-time Super Bowl champions. Allen and Davis were both mavericks who bucked the establishment.

"[Allen] may have been the greatest general manager ever," Dooley said. "As a coach and general manager, a personnel man, he was like Al Davis. He didn't have ownership, but he acted in the same way. He knew how to use it. Sometimes, it was legal. Sometimes, it was not. But he knew how to do it."[70]

Allen made one other memorable acquisition in 1965: Wake Forest free agent fullback Brian Piccolo, who led the nation in scoring (111 points), rushing yards (1,044), and carries (252) in 1964. After playing mostly a backup role to Sayers in the coming seasons, he died in June 1970 from an aggressive form of testicular cancer that spread to his chest. He was immortalized in the 1971 TV movie *Brian's Song*, which brought to life his close friendship with Sayers.

Brian's Song hit home for George Allen because Allen had once been a centerpiece of the Bears' family. In one scene, Halas (played by Jack Warden) is leading a meeting to inform Sayers (Billy Dee Williams) that he's being assigned to room with Piccolo (James Caan) when both players were rookies in 1965. The movie portrayed them as the first interracial roommates in the NFL, although in real life they started rooming together at least a year later. Also shown in the meeting were Bears cornerback J. C. Caroline (Bernie Casey) and soon-to-be Bears executive Ed McCaskey (David Huddleston). Interestingly, Casey starred at wide receiver for two seasons under Allen in Los Angeles before launching a successful acting career.

Allen thought the movie was fantastic. "It was not only his players, it's his team, Coach Halas, Gale Sayers," Bruce Allen said. "He liked the emotion that the movie showed. I remember him telling NFL Films founder Ed Sabol that *Brian's Song* teaches the right lessons about football: the camaraderie, the support, and all of that. He thought it spoke beautifully about the game. Now, a lot of the movie was fictional, as most movies are. But the theme wasn't fictional, including what one teammate means to another."[71]

In 1965 the Bears rebounded from a lackluster season to finish 9-5 and in third place in the Western Division. Halas, who won his three-hundredth game that year, was named NFL Coach of the Year for the second time in three seasons, rejuvenating his coaching career. At season's end, Allen crafted a white paper that laid out bold ideas for the team to show even further improvement, but Halas essentially ignored it.[72]

Allen was becoming impatient. Still a hot name on the NFL coaching circuit, he was more eager than ever to land a head coaching job. Halas had informally told him that at some point he would replace him as the Bears' head coach. But there was nothing definitive from Halas, who turned seventy in February 1965, about his plans to step down. Allen, who in June 1965 signed a three-year contract extension at $19,000 a year, was becoming frustrated as his coaching clock was ticking. Soon to turn forty-eight years old, he wasn't young for a man who wanted to enter the head coaching ranks.

"From what I understand, George Halas had told my father that he would eventually succeed him as coach of the Bears," said Jennifer Allen, George Allen's daughter. "He probably should have gotten that promise in writing. But my father wasn't a businessman. He didn't read his contracts. He just wanted to coach. That was his sole focus: coaching."[73]

Just as the regular season ended, a job opened on the West Coast. On December 23, 1965, the Rams fired head coach Harland Svare after he went 14-31-2 over three and a half seasons, including 4-10 in 1965. The Associated Press reported that Southern California coach John McKay was a prospect to replace Svare, along with Redskins assistant George

Wilson, a former Lions head coach; former Steelers coach Buddy Parker; and Allen.[74] Legendary Browns coach Paul Brown was also reportedly being considered for the job.

This was Allen's opportunity to make the leap to a head coaching job. While in New Orleans to sign Florida offensive lineman Randy Jackson, who was playing in the Sugar Bowl, he called Rams general manager Johnny Sanders on December 28 to relay his interest in the job.[75] Sanders asked Rams owner Dan Reeves, who suggested Allen first get permission from Halas to talk about the opening. The same day, Allen called Halas. In *The Future Is Now*, Allen said he told Halas that "an opportunity presented itself . . . which does not come along every day. I said I would appreciate his cooperation if I accepted. He said he would think it over." Halas, also quoted in *The Future Is Now*, told Allen it was "okay to talk to Reeves but also to inform Reeves that he was not available. And I told Allen the reason why he was not available. Most everyone expected the Bears to have a good football team in 1966, and I did not want our organization disturbed, as it would dilute our chances."[76]

Eventually the Rams narrowed the search to three candidates. Reeves assigned a different team official to act as a supporter for each one in a meeting. Rams publicist Jack Teele argued in favor of Allen. "I'd seen his success with the defense in Chicago and the admiration of the players," Teele said in a 2013 interview. "As an outsider, I didn't know how that admiration was achieved. But I assumed it was because of his coaching prowess and his ability to get along with players and teach defense. I was the most convincing of the arguers in that meeting. That, I think, led to the hiring of George Allen."[77]

Reeves offered the position to Allen on January 4.[78] The Rams' owner was impressed that as an assistant coach Allen had been awarded the game ball after the Bears won the '63 championship game.[79] Allen subsequently penned a thoughtful and eloquently worded resignation letter to Halas. The letter highlighted Allen's appreciation for the positive impact the Bears' legend had made on him, but at the same time Allen made it clear he had no option but to seize the Rams' coaching offer:

> Dear Coach Halas,
>
> No man has ever owed more to another than I do to you for all you have done for me. No one has ever had a more agonizing experi-

ence in arriving at a decision than I have had in bringing myself to this final act of resignation.

The opportunity which has been offered to me to become head coach of the Los Angeles Rams is one I feel I must accept. The job of realizing this ambition is marred only by the regret of leaving a team, and an association with you, which has given me the most rewarding years of my life.

In accepting the challenge to take over the Rams, I do so with deep humility, knowing that my opportunity has come about only because of my personal growth which has occurred under your leadership during the past eight years.

It is more than difficult to even imagine myself in competition with the Bears. Yet, I shall attempt to compete with you and with the other NFL teams with the same spirit which you have most exemplified.

Most sincerely,
George H. Allen[80]

Unfortunately for Allen, the letter made Halas no more sympathetic to the efforts of one of his loyal lieutenants—and the man who played so prominent a role in the '63 championship season—to advance his career. Instead, what ensued was one of the most bizarre feuds in NFL history, one that threatened to shake the foundation of the league. Halas and the Bears tried to prevent Allen—who had two years left on his contract—from getting the Rams job. The crusty old man was irate and didn't parse words in a statement to media:

"I am shocked that the Los Angeles Rams and their president, Dan Reeves, would attempt to pirate our coaching staff. It is widely accepted that the Bears could be an outstanding team in 1966, and we feel strongly that anything that would disturb our organization would dilute our chances. It would be unfair to the other coaches, the players and the fans.

"Within the framework of that thinking, the Rams were told Allen's legal and binding contract with the Bears had two years to go, and we expect him to fulfill the terms of his agreement. In seven and a half years with the Bears, George Allen has been an integral part of our coaching staff.

"In all my years of pro football, the Bears never before encountered such a flagrant case of tampering with a coach under contract to us. The Rams' utter disregard and contempt for legal obligations present a serious challenge not only to the Bears but to the entire structure of the National Football League.

"All of this is reminiscent of Reeves' tactics of three or four years ago when he attempted to hire Vince Lombardi away from the Packers. It is unfortunate that Allen can be misled through specious representation by the Rams and flout the terms of a legal two-year contract. Distasteful though any altercation is, the Bears must take whatever steps are needed to protect our best interest."[81]

Reeves could have asked NFL commissioner Pete Rozelle for permission to hire Allen. But he bypassed Rozelle, who had once worked for Reeves as the Rams' publicity director and general manager, and publicly voiced his frustrations while announcing Allen's hiring on January 10. In addition to head coaching duties, the five-year, $40,000-a-year job with fringe benefits gave Allen full control of player personnel. At a press conference that day with a dapper-looking Allen by his side, Reeves sounded incredulous about Halas's obstinacy, proclaiming, "I can't believe George Halas will stand in his way."[82]

"Last Christmas, George Allen called one of our staff men, Johnny Sanders," Reeves said, "and asked if the Rams might be interested in him as a head coach. Sanders called me the following Monday after Christmas, and I instructed him to tell George Allen to ask George Halas for permission to talk to us. Mr. Halas gave him this permission.

"Later, Halas rescinded this permission, and his objection was quite strong. Mr. Halas said he didn't want me to take Mr. Allen, or if you prefer, Mr. Allen to take me."[83]

This wasn't the first time Halas had stiff-armed one of his assistants who had tried to take a head coaching position with another team. In 1951 the Redskins showed interest in hiring Bears assistant Heartley "Hunk" Anderson as head coach. But Halas refused to release Anderson unless the Redskins traded Pro Bowl tackle Paul Lipscomb in return. The deal fell through, and then-NFL commissioner Bert Bell said Anderson had to honor the final year of his Bears contract.[84]

However, Halas allowed assistant coach Chuck Mather to speak after the 1965 season with any team that might be interested in him to fill a head coaching vacancy.[85] Mather ended up staying with the Bears as a scout.[86] Another Bears assistant, Abe Gibron, reportedly turned down a head coaching offer from the AFL's Miami Dolphins in 1966.[87]

But Halas showed Allen no leniency. To undercut his attempt to take the Rams job, Halas sued him in the circuit court of Cook County (Chicago) for breach of contract. He asked that a permanent injunction be issued to force him to complete the last two years of his Bears contract. The lawsuit alleged that Allen, in his seven seasons with the Bears, had obtained possession of team strategies and scouting reports and that the release of such information could be detrimental to the organization.

In the Allen household, one minute George, Etty, and the kids were ecstatic about the head coaching opportunity. The next, the family was scrambling for cover when the injunction papers reached their doorstep in Deerfield, Illinois.

"We were told, 'Do not accept service of this lawsuit,'" George Felix Allen recalled. "So we'd be in our house with all the lights turned off. The server would come to the door, and we wouldn't open the door for the papers. He'd sit out there in his car on the road in front of our house. We'd have to keep all the lights off, so he didn't think anybody was home. We'd look out the windows seeing that he's still in his car smoking a cigarette. We were kind of trapped in our own home. This wasn't frightening, but it added drama to what should have been a happy event.

"Generally speaking, you don't like losing a prized assistant coach. But it's an unwritten rule or an understanding that if an assistant has an opportunity to be a head coach . . . 95 percent of all coaches hope to become a head coach. Most don't want to stay a defensive coordinator or offensive coordinator or quarterbacks coach or defensive line coach forever."[88]

In New York, Rozelle said he saw "no cause" to interfere in the controversy. But he sounded like he sided with the Allen camp: "It has been traditional with the NFL and throughout sports that assistant coaches are permitted to take advantage of opportunities for advancement. It is hoped that the matter can be amicably resolved by the two clubs."[89]

Meanwhile, Bears standout defensive end Doug Atkins announced that he was quitting football because of Halas's treatment of Allen and his own inability to get along with the Bears' owner. "Halas has become too unreasonable," Atkins said after playing in the Pro Bowl. "He's impossible to deal with. I always got along great with Allen, and he did a fine job of handling the Bears' defenders. I'm in good shape and could play a few years more, but because of present conditions I intend to quit." Ultimately, Atkins, who had just finished his thirteenth season in the league, spent another year with the Bears and ended his career by playing three seasons with the Saints.[90]

The court proceedings before Judge Cornelius Harrington kicked off on January 12, 1966. Allen testified that after talking to the Rams' Johnny Sanders, he received oral permission from Halas to speak with Reeves about the job. He said it wasn't until he accepted the offer on January 4 that Halas withdrew the permission. Allen said Halas also told him eight or nine men were being considered for the Rams job and that "I didn't have much of a chance." Allen also acknowledged that he told Halas before accepting Reeves's offer that he'd stay with the Bears if they matched the Rams' handsome deal, which was more than twice what Halas paid him.[91]

The Bears' lawsuit centered on a clause in Allen's contract stating that he had "special, exceptional and unique knowledge, skill and ability as a football coach, the loss of which to the Club cannot be estimated with certainty, and cannot be fairly or adequately compensated by damages."[92] The Bears thus felt they had the right to seek a permanent injunction to prevent him from taking his talents to another team. In his testimony, Allen denied having any "unique" talents as a football coach, noting that every year "an average of 50 head coaches change jobs."[93] He admitted, though, that he hadn't read his contract.[94] One clause in that contract specified that he needed written consent from the Bears before accepting a coaching job with another NFL team.[95]

Allen's lawyer, Albert Jenner, who was a member of the Warren Commission that investigated the assassination of President Kennedy and who later served as a special counsel during the impeachment proceedings against President Nixon in the '70s, cited the "unique knowledge" clause and its impact on the injunction in calling Allen's contract illegal. He told Judge Harrington that the contract left Allen in no position to bargain and that Halas was trying to stop Allen from "bettering himself."[96]

After a six-day break, the court case resumed on January 18. Jenner and Halas's lawyer, Charles Short, engaged in a brief exchange before Judge Harrington issued his ruling: Allen's contract with the Bears was binding. On the basis of evidence presented in the hearing, Harrington accused Allen of breaching the contract by not having written permission to negotiate with the Rams and by verbally accepting the job. But before the judge could continue, Halas rose and asked permission to address the court. Jenner objected, and Short told Halas to sit down. But Halas approached the bench, took an oath, and addressed Harrington: "Your honor, I am most pleased with your decision upholding the validity of the contract. Your important ruling will uphold the integrity between National

Football League clubs and the sanctity of contracts. Validity was the issue here and will prevent the breakdown of organized football and all sports. George Allen was a minor issue here."[97]

Then came a dramatic twist that stunned the packed courtroom. Like an arbitrator of justice, Halas said he was dropping the lawsuit, avoiding what would have likely been an intense cross-examination by Jenner. Halas felt he had made his point on a technicality. From the defendant's table, an elated Allen walked over to Halas to shake hands. Still resentful despite the court ruling, Halas looked his former protégé straight in the eye and scolded him: "George, a few of those statements you made on the stand, I did not like. They weren't true, George." Halas then told Allen to call him and "bring in those books," a reference to the Bears' defensive manuals and texts that had been a source of contention.[98]

"I returned the books several days ago," Allen told the *Los Angeles Times* with a chuckle.[99]

Nearby, a reporter asked Halas if he would ever consider Allen to be the Bears' head coach. His response: "Well, I'll tell you, my boy, he won't be."[100]

In a news conference, Halas held nothing back in airing his side of the story, which he said "began in subterfuge and ended in chicanery."[101] In moving step-by-step through his version of the contentious process, he blasted Rozelle, Reeves, and Allen, accusing Reeves and Allen of "conniving" to break the contract. He explained that when Rozelle "made that ill-advised statement in which he advocated substituting a silly tradition for a legal document . . . we were more determined than ever to go through with the lawsuit."[102] Halas also charged Allen with offering to remain with the Bears after he'd accepted the Rams' deal if certain conditions were met, that is, if the Bears would match the Rams' $40,000 contract offer, if Halas would guarantee him the head coaching job when he retired, if Allen could be released for three to four years to coach the Rams, before returning to the Bears as head coach, and if Halas would give him an option to buy 5 percent of the Bears' stock.[103]

In his autobiography, Halas repeated his allegations that Allen had made the three- to four-year return and 5 percent stock option suggestions. He called the former "ridiculous" and the latter "even more ridiculous."[104]

Allen admitted that he'd agree to stay in Chicago if the Bears matched the Rams' offer or if Halas guaranteed in writing that he'd take over after the old man retired.[105] Beyond that, Allen never publicly confirmed the other quid pro quos that Halas laid out. Today, the Allen children adamantly deny that their father would go to such lengths to stay with the Bears. They say it's inconceivable that he wouldn't fulfill the five-year term of his Rams contract or that he requested the 5 percent stock option. "The only somewhat realistic truth I can confirm is that Papa Bear truly did want my father to stay with the Bears," George Felix Allen reasoned. "My father revered and appreciated George Halas, who made unenforceable promises to him that he would become head coach of the Bears when [Halas] stepped down in three or four years."[106]

So who really prevailed in the battle of the titans? The newspaper *Chicago's American* ruled it a tie: "Halas Wins—but So Does Allen."[107] In truth, Halas made himself look like a petulant child in the eyes of many by staging his weekslong crusade against Allen, who kept his composure and behaved like a Boy Scout. Perhaps Halas just felt slighted that Allen had initially contacted the Rams without approaching him first—going behind his back, so to speak—and was seeking some form of retribution. "Had [Allen] approached him and said, 'Coach, I know you want me to stay and coach, but I've got an opportunity over here,' he probably would have let him go," NFL historian Joe Horrigan surmised. "But it's when you try to leave and take matters into your own hands, sort of like, 'You didn't deal with me on this.'"[108]

Halas's decision to seek the court injunction was simply a "gesture to save face," Dick Butkus said in retrospect: "Why would he go to court or prevent George from making a move upward? If it's not going to happen here with the Bears, let me go, and if someone else wants me as head coach, fine, let me go. And he puts up this stand with the court and sues him. Suddenly, he walks away from the case. Come on."

Halas and Allen, Butkus added, should have worked something out that allowed Allen to ultimately take over: "Allen should have been hired eventually as head coach. But I don't know if he should have replaced him right at that point. That was one of the mistakes Halas made by not hiring him."[109]

Ed O'Bradovich insisted that Halas should have immediately handed the head coaching job to Allen instead of taking him to court. "Of all of his manipulations with coaches and players and the league over the years, he couldn't figure this one out," O'Bradovich said in hindsight. "He couldn't figure out he had a coach who was twenty years ahead of everybody else in the National Football League. Allen never should have left. Talk about a hollow feeling. It should have been a battle royal every year with Green Bay, and who's going to get it done. But it wasn't."[110]

By dropping the case, Halas prevented it from becoming a legal precedent that could block assistants not only in the NFL but in other sports, too, from becoming head coaches. But his outright refusal to tap into Allen's head coaching potential did the franchise no favors. After going 5-7-2 in 1966 and 7-6-1 in 1967, the Bears icon retired at age seventy-three on May 27, 1968. He named longtime assistant and Bears defensive coach Jim Dooley as his successor. The Bears then fell into an abyss, posting some of the worst seasons in team history, including 1-13 in 1969, 3-11 in 1973, and a couple of 4-10s. In the sixteen seasons between the time Allen left and when Mike Ditka arrived in 1982 and worked the Bears into Super Bowl form, they recorded a .403 winning percentage and two playoff appearances, both first-round exits. The coaches during that period were mediocre at best: Dooley (.379), Abe Gibron (.274), Jack Pardee (.476), and Neill Armstrong (.469).

Allen's departure "was a move the Bears really didn't recover from for years and years until the 1980s," said Dan Pompei, coauthor of the *Chicago Bears Centennial Scrapbook*. "They just fell into the worst period in their history when Halas got old. He struggled to hire people who could do what he used to do and what Allen did well. The team just couldn't win for many, many years."[111]

It had been a turbulent few weeks. But Allen was now free to begin a new chapter in his coaching career. First up, he contacted Reeves to sign the contract and embarked on organizing his coaching staff. Pete Rozelle, who faced his share of pressure during the Halas-Allen feud, shared his thoughts with Allen in a letter dated January 26, 1966:

> Dear George,
>
> I hope by now you and the family have had some opportunity to relax and recover from the problems of the past few weeks. It must have been a trying period.
>
> However, it is a matter of the past, and you have earned the opportunity now before you.
>
> Best personal wishes to you, Etty, and the children.
>
> Regards,
> Pete[112]

The cantankerous Halas would not part with his bitterness. In a sign of the grudge he would hold against Allen for years to come, he disparaged the rookie coach at a league meeting shortly after the two parted ways. He called Allen a schemer and a cheat and lectured on what he considered his shortcomings as a leader of men, a character builder, and a human being. Taking it all in, Vince Lombardi leaned over to Dan Reeves and whispered, "Sounds like you got yourself a helluva coach, Dan."[113]

Reeves, Lombardi, Halas, and the rest of the NFL would soon find out.

7

Erasing a "Country Club" Image

The storm clouds had passed—at least for now—as George Allen returned to Southern California, where he had coached Whittier's football team for six seasons in the 1950s. Following his release by the Bears, Allen, Etty, and the kids—George, Greg, Bruce, and Jennifer—stayed at their home in Deerfield, Illinois, before moving in March 1966 to the Los Angeles area. The family lived for a short time at a motel in the San Fernando Valley, where the Rams practiced, and moved into a rental home in Palos Verdes near the Pacific coast around the start of the '66 season.

In the Rams, Allen inherited a mess of a franchise. With seven straight losing seasons under three different head coaches and a .287 winning percentage and two last-place Western Division finishes during that span, the Rams had become a laughingstock of the league. They were the type of team an opponent would treat as a scrimmage before playing a much tougher game.

A series of dubious personnel moves had fueled the team's freefall. Shortly after the '59 draft, Rams coach Sid Gillman, who employed Allen on his staff in 1957, and the team's young general manager, Pete Rozelle, had dealt eight players and a draft choice to the Chicago Cardinals in exchange for fleet-footed running back and future Hall of Famer Ollie Matson, who had averaged more than 500 yards rushing in five first-team All-Pro seasons. Four of the new Rams acquired at the time were starters: defensive tackles Frank Fuller and Art Hauser, defensive end Glenn Holtzman, and offensive tackle Ken Panfil.

Matson fell way short of the hype. He averaged 304 yards rushing over the next four seasons, before being traded to the Detroit Lions. The Rams made regretful decisions to part ways with a host of other players whose names read like a Who's Who of the NFL's all-time best, including some who starred on championship teams: defensive end Andy Robustelli (Giants, '56), defensive tackle Gene "Big Daddy" Lipscomb (Baltimore Colts, '58, '59), quarterback Norm Van Brocklin and safety Don Burroughs (Eagles, '60), defensive back Jesse Whittenton (Packers, '61, '62), linebacker Larry Morris (Bears, '63), and defensive tackle Billy Ray Smith Sr. (Baltimore Colts, '70). Other Rams excelled elsewhere, such as cornerback Dick "Night Train" Lane, defensive end and kicker Lou Michaels, and wide receiver Jimmy Orr. Robustelli, Van Brocklin, and Lane are now in the Hall of Fame.

"I think that kind of knocked the wind out of us, losing all those ball players," said Ed Meador, a Rams safety from 1959 to 1970 and one of Allen's most valuable players.[1]

Another trade could have also been embarrassing, but it ended up producing one of the best NFL quarterbacks of the '60s. In a deal involving the Bears and Giants, the Rams traded quarterback Billy Wade, receiver Del Shofner, and guard John Guzik and obtained defensive back Lindon Crow, quarterback Zeke Bratkowski, and a first-round draft pick. Wade went on to quarterback the Bears' '63 championship team and threw for nearly 20,000 career yards, and Shofner terrorized the league as a Giants split end. The Rams used their draft pick, the second selection in the '62 draft, to take North Carolina State's Roman Gabriel. The 6-foot-4, 220-pound quarterback played with the Rams for two-thirds of his sixteen-season career. He started the seventy regular-season and two postseason games of the Allen era, establishing himself as one of the league's finest quarterbacks.

Gillman's successor, former Rams star quarterback Bob Waterfield, fared much worse than his predecessor and tallied a 9-24-1 record. He was fired eight games into the '62 season. His replacement, thirty-two-year-old Rams defensive line coach Harland Svare, produced a 14-31-3 mark that ended with a 4-10 season in the basement of the Western Conference in 1965. The season would have looked worse had the Rams not won three of their last four games.

Allen welcomed the task of lifting the Rams out of their malaise and promised to change what he saw as the team's "country club" image.[2] He inherited outstanding players, especially on defense, with a line averaging 6 feet 5 inches, 270 pounds, in ends Deacon Jones and Lamar Lundy and tackles Merlin Olsen and Rosey Grier, otherwise known as the "Fearsome Foursome." Front-office executive Elroy Hirsch acquired and signed many of those talented players. But existing talent isn't everything, and Allen faced a steep challenge to meet his ultimate priority: transforming the Rams into a winner. In his quest to do so, however, he clashed with the person who had presided over the Rams' ineptitude and who signed his paychecks: owner Dan Reeves. The two men had contrasting personalities and differed dramatically on how to run a football team, resulting in a crack in their relationship as wide as the San Andreas Fault.

For a while, everything was copacetic when Allen took the reins in his NFL head coaching debut. In addition to his coaching duties, his five-year, $40,000 contract allowed him to make trades, approve draft picks, and decide on the final roster. Reeves retained the final say on draft picks.

Who was Dan Reeves? Born in a mansion on Fifth Avenue in New York City to Irish immigrants in 1912, he inherited his family's successful grocery store chain and bought a seat on the New York Stock Exchange. In 1941 he purchased an NFL team, the Cleveland Rams, for $135,000.[3] He won his first NFL Championship in 1945, when the Bob Waterfield–quarterbacked Rams beat the Redskins, 15–14. Shortly after and despite fierce opposition from some NFL owners, he moved the Rams to Los Angeles, becoming the first established professional sports franchise to call the West Coast its home. That same year, 1946, two expansion teams also settled on the West Coast—the Los Angeles Dons and the San Francisco 49ers of the newly established All-American Football Conference (AAFC). (In 1926 an NFL team called the Los Angeles Buccaneers played all of its games on the road.) The Rams' move paved the way for other successful sports migrations to the West Coast in the coming years, including basketball's Lakers and Warriors and baseball's Dodgers and Giants.

Reeves wanted to play in the hundred-thousand-seat Los Angeles Memorial Coliseum. But before the team could use the publicly owned stadium, city officials demanded that the Rams sign a Black player. No Black players had been signed in the NFL since 1933 due to an unwritten agreement among the owners. Reeves complied with the mandate and broke the color barrier in '46 by signing two former UCLA stars, running back Kenny Washington and end Woody Strode, both of whom played with the Hollywood Bears of the Pacific Coast Professional Football League. Their signings came a year before Major League Baseball integrated with the signing of Jackie Robinson, a UCLA football teammate of Washington and Strode.

Reeves made other major contributions to football. He experimented with televising Rams games when the medium was in its infancy, helping to lay the groundwork for today's modern TV policies. Key to developing the NFL draft, he was also the first owner to employ a full-time scouting staff. "Reeves was a pioneer in the school of scouts in the NFL and was greatly ahead of a major portion of the league in scouting the small schools," said Jack Teele, the Rams' publicity director for much of the 1960s before his elevation to the front office.[4] Reeves also signed more Black players than any other NFL team in the 1940s and 1950s, names such as Paul Younger, Dan Towler, and defensive back Woodley Lewis, in addition to Washington and Strode.[5] In 1967 he was enshrined in the Hall of Fame, which calls him "one of the game's greatest innovators."[6]

George Allen was the tenth head coach Reeves had hired since buying the Rams in 1941, further evidence of why he had acquired the reputation of being a "firing owner."[7] He issued some of his pink slips at a bizarre time. He fired Clark Shaughnessy shortly after the Rams won the Western Division in 1949 but lost in the NFL championship game. He pressured Joe Stydahar to resign following a season-opening loss in 1952, after Stydahar had coached the Rams to the NFL Championship the year before. When Stydahar's successor, Rams assistant Hamp Pool, agreed to become the team's fifth head coach since the move to Los Angeles, the *Los Angeles Times* warned that he was entering into "a graveyard of coaches." With his revolving-door coaching policy in mind, Reeves also had a sobering message for Pool: "Something probably will happen to you within the next couple of years, and your reputation in the sports world will suffer," the *Times* quoted Reeves as saying.[8]

Reeves's trigger-happy ways were no mystery to Allen, who was nevertheless eager to resurrect a floundering franchise. His first priority was to organize his coaching staff, retaining only one who'd served under Svare: defensive line coach Jack Patera. His new assistants included offensive ends coach Howard Schnellenberger, the offensive coordinator for Alabama's national championship teams in '61, '64, and '65; offensive backfield coach Ted Marchibroda, who had played quarterback for the Steelers and had been a member of the Redskins staff the past five years; and special assistant Joe Sullivan, who was assigned to watch film, scout players, and prepare game plans for opponents after working in the same capacity with the Bears for eight seasons.[9]

With his coaching staff intact, Allen organized a special introduction session for Rams rookies in early April, mostly to see what kind of shape they were in. The timing of the surprising session so early in the off-season was unusual if not unprecedented. "No April Fool! Rams Hold Spring

Practice—for 24 Rookie Players," the *Los Angeles Times* headline stated.[10] Bruce Allen, a Rams ball boy during his father's coaching days in LA, said the session marked the beginning of NFL minicamps, an annual off-season occurrence today.

"He got criticized for starting something new," Bruce said. "Everything he got criticized for is usually because he was the first one to do it, such as Redskin Park [in 1971]. He also brought in the veterans at different times during the off-season because he wanted to meet them and know their condition."[11]

All along, Allen subscribed to an approach that he never wavered from as an NFL coach: acquiring clever, seasoned veterans who could help him win immediately, something he accomplished mostly by trading draft picks and established players who failed to meet his needs. He openly favored "graybeards" and "bald heads," theorizing that a team doesn't draft players to win a championship at the end of the season. "When the team has been losing this long, the public has no patience with more losing," he said early in his rookie season. "You have to win instantly. And secondly, I am personally not geared to waiting. I don't want to go through the ulcer and agony years of building."[12] In short, according to Allen, "I'm thinking of 1966, not 1969 or 1970. We want to win now. Let the other years take care of themselves."[13]

Allen immediately revamped the linebacker position and signed three former first-team All-Pros in a span of eight days. He acquired Maxie Baughan in a trade with the Eagles and lured two other veterans out of retirement: Jack Pardee and Bill George. In 1963 doctors discovered a malignant melanoma on Pardee's arm and removed it. He played in '64 but sat out the '65 season while serving as an assistant at his alma mater, Texas A&M, then returned to play for Allen. George, the most senior of the three and the "quarterback" of Allen's ferocious defense that carried the Bears to the '63 championship, was in his fifteenth season. Eventually, Allen had a starting linebacker trio with about three decades of experience: Pardee on the left, George in the middle, and Baughan on the right. They replaced three rookies who started much of the '65 season: Tony Guillory, Doug Woodlief, and Fred Brown.

"The day George Allen was hired," Guillory remembered, "I told our defensive line coach, Jack Patera, 'With George Allen, we're going to be out of [a starting job] because of his reputation for favoring older players.'

Young players didn't have very much of a chance. You can look at the draft. He just traded to make everything happen."[14]

Allen added more layers of experience by trading for three-time pro Bowl linebacker Myron Pottios (Steelers); two-time Pro Bowl cornerback Irv Cross (Eagles); running back Tom Moore (Packers), a Pro Bowler in 1962; and ninth-year Bears defensive lineman Earl Leggett. "It almost looked like he took the Pro Bowl teams and picked guys who were available, because almost everybody he brought in was a Pro Bowl player," Cross recalled.[15] Allen was especially giddy about the trade for Cross, calling him the "best right defensive halfback in pro football." The addition of Cross gave the Rams one of the NFL's best right-side defenses, which also included end Lamar Lundy, linebacker Maxie Baughan, and three-time Pro Bowl safety Ed Meador. Fifth-year player Chuck Lamson, the other safety, and second-year cornerback Clancy Williams rounded out the secondary.[16]

Cross, fresh off his two Pro Bowl seasons, was thrilled to depart from an Eagles team that had finished 5-9 in 1965: "I thought I went to heaven. I was really excited to play for George. I was a real student of the game. I loved every aspect of it. I thought at one time I'd become a coach myself. I loved working for George. He was a very detail-oriented coach. We had nice long productive meetings, and on the field we executed what we wanted to do. He had a system of communication that is the best I'd ever seen. He worked his tail off, and he had the ability to put guys in positions where they could be effective."[17]

By the time Allen's full stamp was on the roster, the Rams were one of the most experienced teams in the NFL. They averaged 4.9 years per man, trailing only Green Bay (5.6), Baltimore (5.5), and Chicago (5.2).

The moves shored up a defense that in '65 allowed the sixth-most points (328) and fourth-most touchdowns (41) in the fourteen-team league. It was especially porous against the pass, yielding the highest per-game completion percentage (58.7) and the seventh-most passing yards (2,614), while intercepting a league-low 11 passes. But the unit was stingy against the run, allowing the least yards rushing (1,409) and fewest average yards per rush (3.4).

The Fearsome Foursome keyed the defense's dominance against the run and stood as the best front four in the NFL.

But the line couldn't do it all. Allen plugged the gaps by wheeling and dealing on the trade market and giving up a slew of draft picks, a tactic he often deployed as a head coach and the way he earned the moniker "Trader George." But his veteran-based philosophy was antithetical to the thinking of Reeves, a strong proponent of drafting players and building for the future by stockpiling first- and second-round draft choices. Doing so enabled him to keep player salaries down and made a veteran think twice about asking for more money when he knew a lower-paid rookie was challenging him for his position.[18]

Essentially, Reeves was unprepared for such a strong-minded, control-oriented coach who dictated many of the player personnel moves and had no apparent concern about the team's finances. Allen reportedly ran up a $3,000 phone bill in his first month on the job.[19] Reeves, also the team's general manager by title, resented how Allen bypassed him and Elroy Hirsch on personnel matters. He accused Allen of not consulting management on the details of some of his trades, as well as of renegotiating the terms of Pardee's contract without informing the front office.

Allen's decision to sidestep management so Pardee could earn a lot more money drew admiration from his players and fortified his reputation as a "player coach."[20] That reputation had first surfaced in his days with the Bears, but the move infuriated Reeves.

"George had a problem with management," Jack Teele, a Reeves loyalist, said in hindsight. "It was evidenced in Los Angeles with Dan Reeves and in Washington with [Redskins president] Edward Bennett Williams. It was a method of motivating the players. 'It's us against them, fellas. Management isn't for us, the owner isn't for us; it's just you and me, guys.' That's the way he motivated, and it was successful for him. He won."[21]

George Felix Allen disagreed that an "us against them" approach is why his father, a genius at fostering team unity, began clashing with Reeves: "My father did care about the players. There's no question about that. He loved his players as people and wanted to get the best he could for them. He understood their backgrounds and families. My father knew what kind of players, what kind of talent he needed to have a winning team. His objective was winning. That's what coaches are measured by in sports."[22]

Allen and Reeves clashed several other times before his first season. Allen found the Rams' in-season training facility in the San Fernando Valley to be subpar for building a winning team, and he shared his dismay with Reeves. The facility had no weight room; players had to join a health club to lift weights.[23] An upgrade would come at a price for Reeves, but Allen felt it had to be made. From the smog-infested San Fernando Valley not far from Hollywood, the Rams moved about fifty miles south, to Blair Field in Long Beach, a stadium used mainly for baseball. It was a marked improvement over the prior facility, with better grass fields and a room reserved for the Rams players and outfitted with weights, a universal machine, and a sauna.

Allen always battled for the most comfortable training facilities for his players. "Without question, he was that way," Ted Marchibroda said in a 2013 interview. "He was always doing something to improve the ball club. I remember in Los Angeles there was a [new] machine to help the players. It was a whole series of machines. He was one of the first to have them. When he came to Washington, he started Redskin Park. He built it all from scratch."[24]

In a bid to maintain secrecy, Allen called for canvas to be put across the left-field fence at Blair Field and plywood strips to be nailed to the gates to seal off areas so nobody could see in and scout his practices.[25] He didn't want opponents or reporters to gather potential intelligence about the Rams and their game preparation techniques. He also hired a retired Long Beach police officer, Ed "Double O" Boynton, to patrol the grounds for possible spies. At times, Boynton drove Allen to and from practice, allowing the Rams' coach to study his playbook instead of spending time driving.

"There was a lot of room [at Blair Field] to have multiple things going on at the same time," Irv Cross explained. "They hadn't had that before. But George thought it was necessary to have that kind of a setup and have privacy during practice. It developed a certain kind of environment for the team. When you walked into that stadium, or when you walked in the gates to go to the locker room, you knew it was business from that point on. You had some jokesters. But practice was a serious thing. He worked the daylights out of us."[26]

Allen also improvised when it came to traveling to opposing cities. The Rams tied the Steelers at 1-6 for the league's worst road record in 1965 and won only ten of forty-eight road games in their prior seven nonwinning seasons. Allen thus arranged for his players to fly charter and stay in nicer hotels in the suburbs, away from potential distractions in downtown areas. He added a touch of Allen-style creativity in the process, but doing so didn't endear him to Reeves or NFL commissioner Pete Rozelle.

"The players used to party on the road and stay in the city," Allen once said. "So I told them, 'Anybody who I find in his room at 2 o'clock in the afternoon in bed alone will get a $25 bonus.' I called that the 'Siesta Bonus.'

I did that maybe the first three or four road games, and the league complained. I got a call from Rozelle and Reeves: 'You can't do that anymore, it's against the league rules.' I said, 'Listen, all I'm doing is trying to get them to stay in and prepare to play a good team and win.' No one had ever tried that before."[27]

The Rams players experienced a culture shock by the start of training camp on July 2 at Chapman College in Orange, California. Allen had posted motivational signs all over the locker room, hoping the messages would light a fire under his players. They were "little sayings that you might find pasted on a grammar school wall," Deacon Jones said in presenting Allen for Hall of Fame induction in 2002, calling them "one liners that seemed ridiculous."[28]

> "Is what I am doing—or about to do—getting us closer to our goal, winning?"
>
> "What you do during the rest of the year determines how you play during the regular season."
>
> "Ask yourself: What do you really want to accomplish?"
>
> "Try not to do too many things at once; know what you want, the #1 thing today and tomorrow. Persevere and get it done. Too often we make things more complicated than they really are."
>
> "If not us, who? If not now, when?"[29]

Allen also placed a large poster on the wall headlined "PROFILE OF A CHAMPION," under which he listed the attributes "Ambition, Coachableness, Aggression, and Leadership." On the bottom half of the poster, he described the "PROFILE OF AN ALSO-RAN" and cited a series of bad personal habits, including "No Drive, Know-It-All, Mouse, Follower, Watcher, and Corner-Cutter."[30]

It was just Allen's straightforward way of indoctrinating his players in the thought process that leads a team to having a leg up on the competition. "The first thing I want to do out there is instill a winning attitude," he said soon after the Rams hired him. "That's right. They've been losing too long. Listen, the Rams have outstanding personnel—some of the best in the league."[31]

The players and coaches saw a driven man who put in eighteen-hour work days while applying the fierce commitment to coaching that he had acquired from workaholics like George Halas and Sid Gillman. His assistants were working double shifts by the time the season started. "He was one of the first guys in the NFL to work as hard as he did," Marchibroda said. "We wouldn't leave until 10:00, 10:30 every night during the season and would come in early in the morning. I worked with him for nine years, and we worked as hard the ninth year as we did the first year. He left no stones unturned."[32]

Allen wanted a similar level of commitment from his players. But they needed to believe in him first. Rosey Grier realized how difficult that could be. Starting in 1955, the talented defensive tackle played seven seasons with the Giants, appearing in five NFL championship games and winning once. But after being traded to the Rams following the '62 season, he saw a vast difference from the winning atmosphere he was accustomed to in New York. He believed a selfishness permeated the Rams' locker room that fueled a toxic environment.

"When I came to the Rams, they were the most disorganized group of ball players I had ever seen in my life," Grier remembered. "A lot of ballplayers were looking for their own paychecks, how they can make more money for themselves. Forget about you, it's about me. How many times am I going to carry the ball, how many runs am I going to run, how many catches am I going to make, why are you not throwing me the ball? They didn't know what it took to win."

Furthermore, he said, "Black players didn't like Black players, and white players didn't like white players. Forget about getting along together. When I came to the Giants, I had an attitude that we love one another. Initially, when I told my teammates in LA that we win because we love one another, the guys didn't want to hear that."[33]

Roman Gabriel, too, saw an indifference among the players, an attitude that inhibited cohesiveness. "There were different factions," he recalled. "It wasn't just one group like forty guys for forty guys. They had been coached that way."[34]

Both men were impressed with Allen's initiative to resurrect the team. Gabriel remembered remarks Allen made that resonated with his players: "George came with a lot of respect because we all knew what he had done with the Bears running their defense. The first thing he told us is that 'you don't have to like me but [you] have to respect me, because all you've got to do is study my history.' The other thing that rang home is when he said, 'You guys have had a lot of problems for a long time. I'm ready to change that because a problem is a challenge waiting to be solved.' He also said, 'I'll know the first names of all of you because I want to know who you are, and I don't want to have to call you by number. I want to show you that I respect you, too.' About halfway through our first training camp, he knew everybody's first name."

Added Grier, "He didn't come in patty-caking. He showed the players the kinds of things he wanted to do and began to work them on the field to obtain that kind of play. They understood right off the bat that this guy came to win. He didn't come to play. Let's get our act together. Then, he got it together, and the team began to turn around. He got rid of a lot of the ball players that were troublemakers in a sense and weren't part of the growing need to come together."[35]

Allen's first training camp was demanding. Back in the day when players didn't train year-round and held other jobs in the off-season, he wanted his troops ready for the regular-season grind. He called for long, repetitive practices with several sessions per day in hot Southern California conditions, hoping to breed a mental toughness. Everyone saw his obsession with details. But no matter how innocuous something seemed, he believed it had to be covered. To him, even less visible components of the game like special teams could decide an outcome. Many of his meetings dragged on, too.

"George worked us so god darn hard," Gabriel recalled. "We were in pads three and a half hours a day on the practice field. That was probably the only complaint that we ever had. Near the end of the year when you were worn out, we were still out there three and a half hours in pads. George's whole thing was if you didn't practice with a great attitude—if you didn't act like you were having fun and practicing hard—we started practice all over again."[36]

In the eyes of Bruce Allen, the team's 1966 training camp and regular-season practices resembled a military boot camp: "His first year in LA, he worked them hard—harder than Coach Halas had ever worked his team. He really ran a tough ship from the beginning. He had a couple of three-a-days. He felt they needed everything to wake up and get going. It was brutal."[37]

To Deacon Jones, Allen's long, methodical practices were a "bitch."[38] Jones was itching to take his frustrations out on someone, so why not the coach's son? "Deacon would tape me up and leave me under the damn showers in between practices," Bruce recalled. "He was like, 'If we run those striders [sprints] again, I'll get you.' So we'd run the striders, and he'd put me in cold water in between the practices. It was torture, like Marine training."[39]

Determined to get his players in peak physical condition, Allen assigned each of them a maximum weight. Anyone coming in above that was required to pay $100 per pound.[40] He also put a few players on a strict diet. The Fearsome Foursome got the message. Grier dropped from 300-plus pounds to 287, Olsen from 284 to 278, Jones from 275 to 265, and Lundy from 276 to 255—for a total loss of 54 pounds. Mal Florence of the *Los Angeles Times* said it looked like they had "taken a television cram course from Jack LaLanne," the exercise pioneer and fitness promoter who hosted a popular television show at the time.[41]

In addition, offensive tackle Charlie Cowan lost twenty-five pounds, receiver Jack Snow dropped twelve, and guard Joe Scibelli shed ten. Some of the players said they felt weak after taking off so much weight, but Allen persisted. "I've been driving them hard," he admitted. For those overweight, he created a "fat man's" table in the dining room so they could eat anything—as long as the meal consisted of lettuce, cottage cheese, and raw carrots, among other low-calorie foods.[42] Allen's conditioning plan must have made an impact. In 1966 the Rams outscored the opposition in the fourth period, 64–48, after being outscored, 126–76, in the final quarter in 1965.

"The players who didn't make their weight were humiliated because they had to sit at the fat man's table," Bruce remarked. "Poor Roger Brown," he said of the gargantuan defensive tackle who joined the Rams in 1967. "He sat at that table. For my evening runs, he'd say, 'Go get me a pizza. I need something to eat.'"[43]

No one got a free ride through training camp, not even the team's first-round draft pick: Michigan All-American offensive lineman Tom Mack, who had arranged to marry his girlfriend on Saturday, July 2, the day rookies were to report for camp. Allen intervened when he learned about the couple's plans to take an extended honeymoon to Acapulco, Mexico.

"That's when he told me it's going to be kind of a short honeymoon because training camp opens the same day," Mack recalled. "He said he'd give me until Monday to get to training camp. I said, 'Wow, that's a big change.' So I ended up not really having a honeymoon, other than a couple of days nearby in Santa Barbara. Since then, my wife and I have never been to Acapulco."[44]

It's a good thing Mack reported on time. Too small to play tackle in the

NFL, the 6-foot-3, 245-pounder developed into a superstar at guard and a Hall of Famer. He was also an iron man. Starting in his rookie season, he appeared in 184 straight games in his thirteen-year career, now the third-longest streak in Rams history behind Jack Youngblood and Merlin Olsen.[45]

Shortly before the exhibition schedule kicked off on August 6 against the Browns, the Rams scrimmaged the Dallas Cowboys. A few years before Allen arrived in Los Angeles, the Cowboys had begun holding training camp at California Lutheran College in Thousand Oaks, about seventy miles north of Chapman College. Cowboys general manager Tex Schramm, who had held the same title with the Rams in the 1950s, was familiar with Southern California and scouted Cal Lutheran as a base.[46] Given the teams' proximity, Schramm, Cowboys coach Tom Landry, and Allen launched in '66 what would become an annual ritual: an intersquad scrimmage followed by an exhibition game. The Cowboys, who entered the NFL in 1960, had become one of the NFL's premier teams, reaching the NFL championship game in '66 and '67.

During the '66 scrimmage, the Rams' passing offense faced the Cowboys' passing defense, and vice versa. The same held for the rushing game. At the time, Allen and Landry both described the four-way scrimmage as a first in the NFL.[47]

"They'd come to our place for a one-day practice, and the next week we'd go to theirs," Irv Cross said in looking back. "We liked that because they were a pretty good team, and it gave us an opportunity to see how good they really were. They were doing the same thing, seeing what our strengths and weaknesses were. George thought it was a good idea to stop beating up your own teammates and start beating up somebody else. So [he thought], 'Let's see if we can get another team to come in here.'"[48]

Meanwhile, Allen tried to settle a quarterback controversy that had been smoldering for several years. Third-year Ram Bill Munson had taken most of the team's snaps since the Rams drafted him in the first round in 1964. But a knee injury sidelined him late in the '65 season. Gabriel stepped in and quarterbacked the Rams to three wins in the last four games, including upsets of the Packers, who tied the Colts for first place in the Western Division, and the Eastern Division–champion Browns. He just missed leading the Rams to an upset of the Colts, too.

Allen wanted to give Gabriel a solid chance to start in '66. But at one point, it was unclear how long the fifth-year quarterback would even be wearing a Rams uniform. Uncertain about his future as a starter in LA, he signed a four-year, $400,000 contract in May 1966 with the Oakland Raiders.[49] That Bay Area team had chosen him with the first pick in the AFL's 1962 draft. The deal, which would take effect in 1967, included a $100,000 signing bonus. Around the same time, he signed a two-year contract extension with the Rams that nearly doubled his salary, to about $40,000, and provided a $5,000 signing bonus and a $100,000 retirement plan.[50] Raiders general manager Al Davis reportedly went after Gabriel to retaliate for the New York Giants signing Buffalo Bills kicker Pete Gogolak while the interleague war was still raging.[51]

When he heard he was about to lose his strong-armed quarterback, Allen flew to Gabriel's house in North Carolina to persuade him to stay with the Rams. "He said, 'I know they're offering you a big bonus,'" Gabriel said in a 2019 interview. "'But I believe you can play here because I remember in the second half of one of our games [in Chicago] you came in and almost beat us. You're going to want to be in LA because a lot of people here don't know if you can play or not. You don't want to leave here and have them think you're not able to play. But I'll tell you what. I guarantee that if you're the best guy we've got, you'll be the starter.'"

Gabriel never cashed Oakland's $100,000 bonus check. He acknowledged it sounds "crazy" that he discarded the Raiders' much more lucrative offer. "But I trusted Coach, and he was true to his word," he said.[52]

Gabriel, not Munson, took most of the snaps in the Rams' 3-2 preseason, which included wins over Cleveland, St. Louis, and San Francisco and losses to Dallas and Minnesota. Allen named Gabriel the starter for the season opener against the expansion Atlanta Falcons, relegating Munson to a backup role for the next two seasons before he was traded.

In Allen's mind, the choice of Gabriel over Munson wasn't even close. "Bill was a good backup and a solid veteran at the time," Bruce Allen said. "But my dad saw Roman's work ethic and desire and athletic ability. Roman could run. You may only remember his days with the Eagles [in the 1970s], when it didn't look like he could run. But Roman was a good athlete, strong, powerful. [Vikings quarterback] Joe Kapp could run. But Roman was even bigger than Joe and tougher. My father just saw him as the leader to be. His desire to be great and his work ethic fit the bill for what he wanted."

Allen's benching of Munson didn't sit well with Reeves. But "my dad didn't care what Reeves thought," Bruce said. "He just thought it was so clear that Roman was the right leader for the team."[53]

George Allen left no doubt that Gabriel would be the starter, which was "very much the George kind of thing to do," Tom Mack said in reflecting back. "He'd decide who he was going with and make a commitment to that guy. He made it public enough so that Roman knew he was No. 1 unless he screwed up and that Munson understood he wasn't going to get the chance to play again. That was very hard on Munson, because he thought he was the quarterback."[54]

Preseason reports designated the defending NFL champion Packers, the Colts, and the Bears as the teams to watch out for in the Western Conference. But Gabriel was confident the Rams were no longer a league doormat. Mal Florence of the *Los Angeles Times*, in paraphrasing Gabriel, wrote, "Let this serve as a warning to the bullies of the National Football League. No longer will they be allowed to kick sand in the collective faces of the Rams and treat the boys like 97-pound weaklings."[55]

Allen, his players, and the rest of the NFL had an opportunity to contend not only for the NFL Championship but also for interleague bragging rights. Under an agreement announced on June 8, 1966, the NFL and AFL would compete at a neutral site in a world championship game that would kick off after the 1966 season. That game, eventually named the "Super Bowl," grew exponentially in popularity and appeal to become the spectacle it is today.

George Allen would ultimately see his day in the Super Bowl sun.

8

An Addiction to Winning

After working for eight months to plant the seeds for a franchise turnaround, George Allen opened his first season in LA on a winning note with a hard-fought 19–14 victory over the Falcons. But postgame controversy made larger headlines. Falcons assistant coach and former Rams great Tom Fears accused Allen of pumping Bob Jencks, a just-released Falcons kicker, for information. Fears charged that Allen had changed his defensive game plan based on information Jencks had shared with him. Jencks had played for the Bears for two seasons while Allen was their defensive coordinator. But Allen insisted the accusation was false: "If we had known what they were doing, we would have done better. Jencks did visit with us, but he spent time with Bill George, a former teammate. That's all I want to say about it."[1]

This was one of several times Allen was suspected in his head coaching career of trying to find cracks in the rules or circumvent them altogether. "I can recall a few times when a team put a player on waivers about a week before the Redskins would be playing that team, and George would sign him," said Steve Guback, the Redskins' beat reporter for the *Washington Star* during Allen's stint in the nation's capital. "The only apparent reason he would get him was to pump him for information. That enhanced his reputation of trying to be within the rules but yet sort of bending them."[2] Allen was linked to a number of other shady practices, including spying on teams, namely the Dallas Cowboys. The NFL fined him for such infractions as trading the same draft picks and not informing referees he was activating a player. The media thus dubbed him the "Flim Flam Man," a reference to his image as a con man.

Did Allen acquire any of those tactics from George Halas? Word around the league was that Halas would do anything it took to win, even if that meant spying on other teams. A 1958 article in the *Los Angeles Times* explored whether the Bears intercepted calls made by Rams coaches from the press box down to the field during Chicago's 31–10 win against the Rams in 1958. Rams assistant Bill Swiacki said he believed someone from the Bears had listened in on the calls.[3] Halas hired Allen as a consultant for that game, as well as the Rams-Bears clash two weeks later.

In the days preceding the Rams-Bears game in week two of the '66 season, Mal Florence of the *Los Angeles Times* reported that Halas was long suspected of dispatching his "henchmen" to spy on Rams practices and that Halas and Allen were taking countermeasures to prevent spying.[4] For now, Allen would get the better of his mentor in a reunion of the two men who had battled it out in a legal setting a few months earlier. Despite fumbling the ball seven times and spotting the Bears 10 points, the Rams exited with a 31–17 win at the Los Angeles Coliseum. Twice Allen tried to shake hands with Halas, who not surprisingly refused to reciprocate.[5]

After the game, Allen met up with a number of the players he had coached in Chicago, including Bennie McRae, Dave Whitsell, Richie Petitbon, Rosey Taylor, and Dick Butkus. "That was a great win, coach," Butkus told Allen.[6]

The Rams, off to a roaring start, had not opened 2-0 since 1955, a season that ended in a championship game appearance. But the 2-0 Packers handed them their first defeat, 24–13. Green Bay took a 17–0 lead, while its defense held the Rams to a single first down in the first half and sacked Gabriel seven times. Afterward, Sid Ziff of the *Los Angeles Times* took the Rams to task for what he viewed as their boring, ultraconservative approach, saying they were still "fighting an infantry war" while the rest of the league was airing it out. "They can change Ram coaches and change their personnel," Ziff wrote. "But the Rams are stuck with the same old game plan. They have got to stuff that ball down somebody's throat. The Ram offense Sunday was the poorest excuse for an unimaginative attack since Gen. Grant fought the Battle of the Wilderness. There was no deception, no cunning, no surprises."[7]

Allen took the blame for sticking to the run. In a team meeting, he slammed his fist on a table to emphasize a point and broke his hand in three places; it was not the first time he had injured himself in the line of duty.[8] He also predicted that the Rams would beat the Packers when they clashed again in the Los Angeles Coliseum in December. He said the Western Conference is "so tough and well-balanced" that a 10-4 record should be good enough for first place.[9]

The Rams rebounded by topping the 49ers, 34–3, and the Lions, 14–7, to hit the 4-1 mark for a first-place conference tie with Green Bay. Their defense was on fire, with sixteen takeaways in the last three games, including six in the win over the Lions. Allen had long preached ball hawking. "If the Rams continue to pilfer the ball from the opposition the way they have in the last three games," Jeff Prugh of the *Los Angeles Times* quipped, "they might even wind up pulling off the biggest steal the NFL has seen in years—the Western Conference title."[10]

The 4-1 start would have been unlikely without Allen's unwavering devotion to his job. He was channeling almost every waking minute into winning, whether by running long practices or watching game films or negotiating with other teams on potential trades. He felt no need to relax, and the time he once used for leisurely activities like gardening was no longer an option. He arrived at practice first and left after everyone else. This came at the expense of spending time at home with Etty and the kids. But Allen was confident his family understood why he was so dedicated to coaching.

Since the start of training camp, "I've probably eaten eight or nine meals at home with my family," he said during the 1966 season. "They know how I am, and I appreciate the fact that [Etty] doesn't interfere. She knows that during the football season, she isn't going to see much of me. We try to make up for it in the off-season. But we haven't been doing a very good job there, either."[11]

Allen never spent much time eating during the season. He worried that chewing on food would distract him from his coaching duties, hence his reason for tearing off the ends of bread. He also saved time by consuming peanut butter and jelly sandwiches and ice cream. Just before the '66 season, actress Lee Meriwether, the 1955 Miss America who played Catwoman in the 1966 film *Batman*, brought him a season's supply of vanilla ice cream.[12] It's no wonder that one of Allen's nicknames was "Ice Cream." To help guard against stomach ulcers created by the nerve-racking nature of the job, he drank a lot of milk. Once in a while, he'd have his favorite alcoholic drink, a blackberry brandy, or he'd split a beer with Etty.

But with a conference championship in sight, the Rams dropped four straight games, to fall to 4-5. The Rams' offense had virtually disappeared, scoring only three touchdowns during the four-game slide, which ended with a 21–13 loss to the 49ers on a muddy, sloppy field at San Francisco's Kezar Stadium. After the game, Deacon Jones said the field was like a "hog pen."[13] Allen echoed that remark two years later in one of his conflicts with Reeves. The losing streak also included a 17–10 loss to the Bears, after which Halas denied wanting to gain revenge against his protégé but nevertheless stated, "The Rams are nothing special, but it is a pleasure to beat them."[14]

Midway through the losing streak, the Rams welcomed a special guest to their practice facility at Blair Field. Former radio sportscaster and actor Ronald Reagan, the Republican candidate for governor of California, attended the team's workouts on October 28 with his son just eleven days before the gubernatorial election pitting Reagan against incumbent Democratic governor Pat Brown. When Reagan arrived, Allen halted practice and greeted his guest, saying, "This is a great honor. We hope that you bring us good luck, and that we bring you good luck."[15] Reagan addressed the players, telling them of his most iconic performance in Hollywood—his starring role as Notre Dame star halfback George Gipp in the 1940 film *Knute Rockne: All-American.*

Thus began a lasting friendship between two men of nearly the same age with perfectly combed hair, similar facial features, a strong work ethic, and midwestern and Irish Catholic roots. "They were so similar in looks and mannerisms," George Felix Allen said of his father and Reagan. "They looked like they could be cousins or brothers. They got along perfectly."[16]

Reagan handily won the election and served as California's governor from 1967 to 1975. Five years later, he was elected president of the United States, serving two terms in the White House. He long used his *Knute Rockne* line "just win one for the Gipper" as his political rallying cry.

On a four-game losing streak, the '66 Rams returned to the win column by beating the Giants, 55–14, tallying an NFL-record thirty-eight first downs and 572 yards rushing against a dreadful defense that yielded a league-high 501 points by season's end. Allen later said it was not his intention to embarrass his friend, Giants coach Allie Sherman. "But because of all the humiliation we'd gone through, the offense was hungry for points," he told reporters. "You'd have to feel what the team and the coaches have gone through these last four weeks, with everybody laughing at them and making fun of them."[17]

The victory kicked off a four-game win streak that included a 23–7 win over the Colts, who finished in second place in the Western Conference at 9-5, and ended with a 23–3 win over the Lions. The 8-5 Rams were now assured of their first winning season since 1958, with second place in the Western Conference and a berth in the Playoff Bowl, the winner of which would earn third place in the league, still on the line.

The win over Baltimore marked the Rams' last road game of the season. From then on, they were nearly indestructible away from home in the last four years of the Allen regime in LA (1967–70), going a jaw-dropping 24-5. He regularly reminded his troops that they were "kings of the road," playing on the title and lyrics of the country music hit "King of the Road."[18]

Beating Baltimore marked Allen's first victory over Colts coach Don Shula—Allen's fiercest coaching rival during his stint in LA.

A hard-nosed defensive back who had played for the Browns, Colts, and Redskins in the 1950s, Shula moved from college coaching to the NFL in 1960 as Detroit's defensive coordinator. When hired by the Colts in 1963, he was then, at age thirty-three, the youngest head coach in NFL history.[19] He instantly made his mark, with a cumulative regular-season record of 30-11-1 over the next three seasons—the third-best NFL winning percentage in that span (.732). His Colts fell to the Browns in the 1964 NFL championship game. In 1965 the Colts and Packers tied for first place in the Western Conference at 10-3-1, but Green Bay edged Baltimore in a playoff game and beat the Browns for the NFL Championship.

In his first three seasons, Shula had the pleasure of battling Vince Lombardi for supremacy in the Western Conference. But Allen's arrival in '66 meant Shula also had to contend with Allen's Rams. The Colts and Rams met two times in 1966, and a league realignment in 1967 left Shula and Allen colliding twice a year in the new Coastal Division, with Lombardi in the Central Division.

"It was like a war against the Rams," Bill Curry, a Colts center at the time, said in retrospect. "It was an incredibly fierce rivalry. It was that Coastal Division thing. We played them home and home. You knew you were going to be sore for a week after those games. But it was fun to play a great team like that."[20]

All along, Shula was wary of his divisional foe. "George was a great coach, very thorough, very well prepared," he said in a 2001 interview. "Just a very meticulous guy. He burned the midnight oil.

"When he was coaching on the West Coast, he would call me, and it would always be real late at night for me, but it was still early for him. I'd be sleeping. So the next morning, I'd call him back when I was up, and I knew he was still asleep. 'Did I wake you up, George?' We had a lot of phone conversations and went out a couple of times socially."[21]

Allen and Shula held a mutual respect. Two men with midwestern roots—Allen from Michigan and Shula from Ohio—they enjoyed each other's company when hanging out together. They once staged an arm-wrestling match at the Washington Touchdown Club in March 1973, two months after Shula's Dolphins defeated Allen's Redskins in Super Bowl VII, 14–7.

"Don Shula is the only other rival coach I remember my parents ever dining and socializing with," Jennifer Allen said. "My parents were fond of his wife, Dorothy. We all dined together during a visit to Florida. I remember Shula's open-hearted laughter and the way he enjoyed eating ribs. As a kid, I was stunned, as I somehow assumed all coaches only consumed peanut butter sandwiches and milk, like my father."[22]

The two coaches met twice a year for four seasons, from 1966 to 1969, after which Shula left to coach the Dolphins. Allen and Shula met only twice more after that, with Allen finishing 4-5-1 overall against Shula in head-to-head competition.

To qualify for the playoffs in '66, the Rams had to beat the 11-2 Packers, who had already clinched first place in the Western Conference, in the regular-season finale at the Los Angeles Coliseum. The Packers doused any Rams Super Bowl hopes with a 27–23 victory before 72,416 fans, the largest Rams home crowd of the season. "It's a sad way to end the season," Allen said.[23]

The Packers went on to beat the Cowboys in the NFL championship game to qualify for Super Bowl I at the Los Angeles Coliseum on January 15, 1967. Their opponent was the AFL's Kansas City Chiefs, and none other than George Allen was there to help his NFL rival, Lombardi, prevent a titanic upset by the Chiefs. NFL teams had only scant access to AFL game footage from the period before the merger agreement. But Allen managed to evaluate all the Chiefs' players and mailed to Lombardi all of that information—which included height, weight, speed in the 40-yard dash, and strengths and weaknesses—a few days before the Super Bowl:

> Dear Vince:
>
> Enclosed find information that we discussed. Please treat this in the strictest of confidence.
>
> If you have any questions, please feel welcome to call.
>
> Good luck and keep the pressure on.
>
> Sincerely,
> George Allen
> Head Coach[24]

The Packers bullied the Chiefs that day, 35–10, to protect the NFL's reputation as a league superior to the AFL and Lombardi's image as the gold standard of coaches. Allen was a long way from that elite level. But in '66, he'd orchestrated the greatest single-season turnaround in the NFL since Lombardi's first season in Green Bay in 1959, when the Packers improved to 7-5 after going 1-10 in 1958. With the Rams' leap from 4-10 to 8-6 for third place in the Western Conference, Allen earned votes for 1966 NFL Coach of the Year, behind the Cowboys' Tom Landry.

But Allen was named coach of the Western Conference Pro Bowl team. Five Rams—defensive linemen Deacon Jones and Merlin Olsen, linebacker Maxie Baughan, safety Ed Meador, and kicker Bruce Gossett—played for the Western Conference squad, which lost to the East, 20–10. Jones and Olsen were also consensus first-team All-Pros.

True to form, Allen took the Pro Bowl as seriously as any other game. At a luncheon for the seventy Pro Bowlers in Los Angeles, site of the game, emcee Frank Bull asked the West's starting quarterback, Johnny Unitas, how he was getting along with Allen: "Just fine. He's an extremely thorough coach. I think the playbook we have for this one game is bigger than the one we had at Baltimore for the entire season." A teammate of Unitas, Bears running back Gale Sayers, spoke of the loss of the former Bears assistant: "He's a great coach. I didn't have much contact with him while he was with the Bears. But I know one thing. When he left us, the Rams went to third, and we went to fifth [in the Western Conference]."[25]

Decades later, Bears middle linebacker Dick Butkus remembered a conversation he had with Jones and Olsen that year at the Pro Bowl: "I said, 'How do you like George?' They said, 'Oh, man, he's okay, but boy our practices are long.' I'm like, you guys had a winning season, how long could they be?' I'm thinking, 'That's George. He's making sure there are no mistakes to be made.' And they were complaining that maybe they had a little extra time on the field. But they won. I couldn't understand that. He turned them right around."[26]

Under Allen, the Rams' defense matured to become the NFL's best unit in '66, finishing first against the rush in yards per attempt (3.2) and allowing just 212 points, the fewest by the Rams in more than two decades of play.[27] The team placed third in interceptions (26) and in fumble recoveries (20).[28]

Allen's transformation of the Fearsome Foursome into an even more potent weapon impacted the success of the defense. As good as the line had been in '65, he unleashed it to go more after the quarterback instead of concentrating on the run. The pass rush, known as "heat," aimed to destroy the pocket. "We recognized, one, that we were good, and that we could play great together," Rosey Grier said in retrospect. "But we had to have a coach that had the same faith in us and would let us use our skills and talents to go after the quarterback. We messed up enough of the run that it was always very difficult for the quarterback to have a great, great game. They did have some great games, and there were some great runners out there. But we aimed for the quarterback as we got off the ball. Our whole point was getting in the backfield."[29]

The line resembled a "dream team" in the eyes of Irv Cross: "George let them go. He devised a system where they would be effective in the way they played and the style they wanted to play."[30]

The Paul Bunyanesque front four of 6-foot-6, 255-pound Lamar Lundy, 6-foot-5, 295-pound Rosey Grier, 6-foot-5, 275-pound Merlin Olsen, and 6-foot-5, 260-pound Deacon Jones was enormous for its day, outweighing their contemporaries at the same positions by about 20 pounds per man and dwarfing offensive linemen. "I had never been in a huddle where the guys were as tall as those guys were," Cross said. "I'll never forget. They always stood upright at the line of scrimmage. They never got down on the ground. That way, they could see the offense coming out of the huddle easier and intimidate the offensive linemen. They were generally taller than the guys they were playing against."[31]

"The four rush men, as we call them, put a lot of pressure on the quarterbacks," Allen said at the time. "That's one of the reasons we're winning. As far as four men go, this is the finest unit I've seen."[32]

Center Bill Curry went nose to nose with the Fearsome Foursome starting in his 1965 rookie season with the Packers and quickly learned how formidable they were. He remembered being "annihilated" by that front four in a 21–10 loss to the Rams late in the '65 season. "When Merlin Olsen, Rosey Grier, Lamar Lundy, and Deacon Jones decided to strap it on and come after the quarterback, nobody in the world could block those guys," Curry said.[33]

In Jones and Olsen, who manned the left side of the line, Allen was blessed with arguably the greatest players ever at their position. Both earned many first-team All-Pro and Pro Bowl honors, both were named to the NFL's all-decade team of the 1960s, both were first-ballot Hall of Fame inductees, and both were tapped for the NFL Films "NFL 100

Greatest" team that was announced in 2019 to coincide with the league's one-hundredth season.

Jones took the lead in making life miserable for quarterbacks. His career sack total rivals the top figures in NFL history, although sacks didn't become an official statistic until 1982. He debated NFL statisticians for many years about the credibility of his sack total, arguing for it to be official in the NFL record books. But the league resisted, saying sack statistics were sketchy at the time he played. An unofficial tally by pro football historian John Turney found that Jones posted 173.5 sacks in his fourteen-year career, which would put him third today behind Bruce Smith (200) and Reggie White (198).[34]

At least the man known as the "Secretary of Defense" could take credit for coining the term "sack" to acknowledge when defensive players tackle quarterbacks behind the line of scrimmage. "When I entered the game, there was no way of identifying what the linemen did, so I tried to find a term that fit what I was trying to describe," Jones said in a 2000 interview. "To me, you put all offensive linemen in a damn burlap bag, take a baseball bat, and beat on the bag. The word 'sack' came out of that. By putting some notoriety and flamboyancy in there . . . like a quarterback throws the football, a running back runs the football . . . it helped defensive linemen rise on the pay scale."[35]

Born David Jones and raised in Eatonville, Florida, a small, all-Black community that borders Orlando, Deacon Jones grew up in extreme segregation and poverty with parents who had fourteen children, six of whom died at birth. His father, Ishmael Jones, did whatever he could to make money, working as a carpenter, a laborer, a handyman, or a fruit picker in the fields.[36] David worked with his father, pitching watermelons from field to truck and picking oranges from trees, both of which were exhausting types of work. All the while, Ishmael instilled a strong work ethic in his son, plus discipline and toughness.

A strong athletic kid, Jones stood about 6 feet 4, 225 pounds by the time he began playing college football. He starred at defensive tackle at South Carolina State and later Mississippi Vocational College (now Mississippi Valley State), two historically Black colleges. Both schools received limited attention at the time from pro scouts, and Jones was uncertain if he'd be drafted in the NFL. But the Rams took a chance on him in the fourteenth round in 1961. Three games into the season, he began starting at defensive end, where the coaches felt his speed could best be exploited, and kicked off his ascension to an elite level.

Jones played with a rage rarely before seen, aiming to tear the head off every quarterback he faced—almost all of whom were white. There was a reason he felt that way. Growing up in the Deep South in the '40s and '50s, he was subjected to Jim Crow laws that enforced racial segregation, such as restrooms designated for "colored" people only. "I came from a Black college situation, from segregation, never having played against a white player until I came into the pros," Jones said in a 2001 NFL Films documentary. "I was the most frustrated individual you ever met in your life during that period because I was dealing with tokenism. I was dealing with quotas. I hated white people for a long time."[37]

Allen's predecessor with the Rams, Harland Svare, fueled Jones's frustration. Svare forced him to adopt techniques that he felt were awkward, such as changing his stance and coming off the ball on another foot. "Deacon tried and tried to do it, but this was just off-balance for him," said Elizabeth Jones, Deacon's wife of three decades, until his death in 2013.

Allen took a different approach. He realized how talented Jones was with incredible speed and burst and basically "let him run free," Elizabeth Jones explained. "George took him aside. He had personal conversations with him. He built him up in terms of his abilities and put a lot of confidence in him. Eventually, Deacon was named a team captain." Allen also helped rid the superstar of much of his animosity toward white people.[38]

All the while, Jones developed enormous respect for the man and came to see him not only as a coach but as a friend, too. In 1983 Jones married Elizabeth Pinto, a white Jewish woman. "[Five] years after I came into the NFL, I met George Allen," Deacon said in the documentary *Winning Is Living, Losing Is Dying: The George Allen Story*. "He brought about the only even playing field I ever had. I ended up having a coach who I give 100 percent credit for developing my career. All the things I was really upset about . . . my life just switched like that."[39]

Said Elizabeth Jones, "George treated him like a man. Just because he was Black certainly to George didn't mean that he couldn't be a team leader or that he had to have quarterback credentials. That wasn't George at all. He didn't care what color you were. As long as you played and you won."[40] According to Jennifer Allen, her father saw Deacon Jones as a tremendous leader on and off the field and a role model who could show young people the potential for success when people work hard and dedicate themselves to the task at hand, two "characteristics my dad held high."[41]

Jones's fourteen-year NFL career ended in 1974 with a season under Allen in Washington. But their friendship endured. For his 1980 Hall of Fame induction, Jones asked Allen to present him for enshrinement. The Allen family reciprocated by asking Jones to present the coach at his posthumous induction in 2002 and to be a pallbearer at Allen's funeral in January 1991. Jennifer Allen named her second son Deacon, after Deacon Jones.

George Allen had less of an affinity for the other future Hall of Famer, Merlin Olsen, a powerful man with quick feet who wreaked his own form of havoc. "Merlin was a great player who always had great off-the-field opportunities and interests," Bruce Allen recalled. "Deacon's passion for being great at football always inspired Dad."[42]

Olsen and Jones elevated each other's game, with Jones coming off the edge to take aim at the quarterback and Olsen stuffing the run and collapsing the pocket. Cowboys Hall of Fame defensive tackle Bob Lilly, as good as he was, watched game film of Olsen. "Merlin played the run well," Lilly said in a 2020 interview. "He was also a good pass rusher. But Deacon was so good that I heard Merlin tell him one time when we were in the Pro Bowl and were all on the same team, 'Deacon, I told you, I take care of the run, and you rush the passer.' They sort of played that way. Together, they were a great team."[43]

Olsen had tremendous respect for Allen's ability to reverse the Rams' fortunes and make them a playoff contender. "He did the most important thing for my team when I was there," Olsen said in a 2003 interview. "He turned us from a losing team into a winning team. He was a players' coach, and he certainly wasn't aloof. He was the kind of guy you could talk to."[44]

Grier and Lundy also contributed to the chemistry of the front four. Grier, who played his first seven seasons with the Giants, had superb moves and footwork, was a first-team All-Pro in 1956, and earned two trips to the Pro Bowl. But the Giants traded him in '63 to the Rams for defensive tackle John LoVetere and a draft pick.

Lundy, the tallest of the foursome, excelled in basketball and football at Purdue University. Drafted by the Rams in '57, he played his thirteen-year career in Los Angeles, first at tight end before switching to defensive end in his fourth season. He wasn't as fast or as strong as Jones. But he had long arms and great range.

While glamorizing the defensive line position, Jones, Olsen, Lundy, and

Grier evolved into celebrities off the field. They formed a Motown-style group modeled after the sensational singing foursome the Temptations. Grier, an accomplished singer and actor, led the group, which performed in 1965 on *Shindig!*, an American musical variety television series. Grier sang "Since You've Been Gone," as Olsen, Lundy, and Jones danced onstage with multiple choreographed moves. The same year, Grier sang "On Broadway" on *Hullabaloo*, a TV series similar to *Shindig!*

After going full blast in his first season as the Rams' coach, George Allen found time to relax with Etty. But Allen's definition of relaxation was somewhat distorted. He and Etty went to Honolulu for the NFL convention and crossed paths on the beach with *Los Angeles Times* sportswriter Mal Florence, who was in Hawaii at the same time. In a column written by his colleague, Sid Ziff, Florence shared his conversation with Allen: "I saw him coming out of the water one day. 'How do you do, I asked him casually.' You know, Allen is so statistically minded that he even had kept track of the waves he had ridden in. He told me, 'I caught twelve waves, Mal. I fell off four times, but the board nosed over twice, and that does not count. So I actually caught ten out of twelve.'"[45]

Back on the mainland, Allen added a new face to his assistant coaching staff. Former Vikings defensive coordinator Marion Campbell replaced Jack Patera as the defensive line coach. Allen also worked to retool the Rams' offense, which finished near the middle of the fifteen-team NFL in most categories in '66. Sixth-year running back Dick Bass rushed for a team-record 1,090 yards (4.4-yard average) and caught 31 passes, and newly acquired halfback Tom Moore caught 60 passes, an NFL record for running backs, for 433 yards and 3 touchdowns. Roman Gabriel, about to blossom into one of the league's top quarterbacks, set all-time team records in completions (217) and attempts (397).

In 1967, when entering the first NFL-AFL common draft, a by-product of the interleague merger, it was clear Allen's trading had zapped the Rams of draft choices. They had just ten picks in the seventeen-round draft—the least of any team—and only four in the first ten rounds.[46] On draft day, Allen traded his No. 1 pick and Pro Bowl tight end Marlin McKeever to the Vikings in exchange for three-time Pro Bowl running back Tommy Mason, tight end Hal Bedsole, and a second-round pick that the Rams used to take running back Willie Ellison.[47] The acquisition of Mason made Moore, who rushed for only 2.6 yards a carry, expendable. In July Allen traded him to Atlanta for a wide receiver with sprinter speed, Bernie Casey, who had averaged nearly fifty catches in his six NFL seasons. Casey gave the Rams a receiver who could consistently stretch the field, a weapon they lacked. He also eliminated the constant double teams that wide receiver Jack Snow was drawing.

"I feel Casey will help us tremendously," Allen said at the time. "He has excellent size and speed, and he's experienced. He will give us another all-the-way threat, which we need."[48]

The newcomers congregated with established Rams at a new summer training camp site. In a switch prompted by Allen, the Rams moved from Chapman College to California State University in Fullerton, about ten miles away. The main reason for the move was that the Fullerton campus had two adjacent full-sized practice fields, plus a huge area for blocking sleds, a large training room, and air-conditioned dorms. Allen described the new site as "comparable [to] or better than any in the NFL."[49] The move came just a year after Allen had called for the relocation to Blair Field as the Rams' in-season training site, a decision that had irked Dan Reeves. The owner didn't like the move to Fullerton either. But Allen was taking it upon himself to do what he felt would establish a championship team.

In addition to Allen's lavish spending on player salaries and his push for new training sites and equipment, his call for new bikes bothered Reeves. To supplement his players' conditioning, he arranged for every player in training camp to ride bikes to expedite their trips to meetings, practice fields, and the dining hall.[50]

In *The Future Is Now*, an unnamed Rams official elaborated on the toys that Allen obtained in his spending spree to improve the team: "He brought up things we never dreamed we needed. We had so many contraptions at training camp, we called it 'Disneyland North.' Over the years, we tested every kind of blocking dummy imaginable. Once, we had a tackling dummy known as 'Joe the Bartender.' It was like a big balloon, weighted at the bottom, and about seven feet tall, his arms outstretched, and something like a helmet on his head. He'd be the simulated receiver. A coach would throw the ball at him, and he'd bounce right back up. He only lasted a couple of sessions."[51]

With the 1967 season around the corner, the Rams were positioned to dominate. At least that's what Allen thought. He predicted that if the defense held opponents to less than 200 points and if the offense improved by at least 10 percent, the Rams could go all the way.[52] The confident coach even referenced Chinese culture, accurately telling his players that "according to the Chinese New Year, this is the year of the Ram."[53]

With Allen treating the exhibition season in his customary way—like the regular season—his Rams finished 6-0. He wanted his teams to have momentum heading into the regular season, so he went all out with his starters even in games that didn't count in the standings.

"You don't see that at all now," guard Tom Mack said in a 2020 interview. "Most of the kids today, when they start the season, it's the first time they've hit anybody. With George, you had three weeks of hard practice, then you had six exhibition games. Basically, the starters started and played most of those games."[54]

One of the six wins was costly. Against the Chiefs, Rosey Grier tore his Achilles tendon in the first half and crumpled to the turf. Playing for Grier, the Rams recovered from a 24–13 halftime deficit by outscoring the Chiefs, 31–0.

To replace Grier, Allen acted fast. He had defensive tackles in the newly acquired Dave Cahill and rookie Diron Talbert. But in his mind, it wasn't enough. He went for it all and traded three high draft picks to the Lions, including the Rams' top pick in '68, for two-time first-team All-Pro defensive tackle Roger Brown.

To be able to so quickly fill the vacancy left by Grier with a player of such high caliber, it was obvious Allen had done his homework on Brown. It even seemed he had the defensive tackle on speed dial. The thirty-year-old Brown, who had been to five straight Pro Bowls, was a fixture on the Lions' defensive line that also featured tackle Alex Karras and ends Darris McCord and Sam Williams. The line, widely considered the NFL's best front four before the Rams' Fearsome Foursome, gained fame for a devastating ten-sack performance in a 26–14 win over the Packers on Thanksgiving Day in 1962. Brown had six sacks that day, including a safety of Packers quarterback Bart Starr.

"We couldn't believe Allen was able to get him," cornerback Irv Cross said. "Roger was a pretty darn good player, and here he was in Los Angeles. We didn't lose anything with the kind of talent that we had."[55]

Allen didn't rule out a return by Grier. "That would give us the three finest defensive tackles in football," he said about Grier, Brown, and Merlin Olsen. "We would have a 'Fearsome Fivesome.'"[56]

At 6 feet 5 and more than 300 pounds, Brown was as big as Grier. He was excited to head west and play for Allen and the Rams. "George was one hell of a coach, and I think everybody who played back then would have loved to have played for him," Brown said in a 2019 interview. "The Lions needed a quarterback, and they put me on the block, and George grabbed me, and I was happy. Going to LA to play for Coach Allen was awesome, and to play with Deacon and Merlin and Lamar, that was also awesome. I was standing in the doorway waiting to be received."[57]

Acquiring Brown was one of Allen's greatest trades. With him in the lineup in place of Grier, the Rams didn't miss a beat in the new sixteen-team, four-division NFL: Capital, Century, Coastal, and Central. The Rams, Colts, 49ers, and Falcons made up the Coastal Division.

The Rams won their first three games: 27–13 over the expansion New Orleans Saints, 39–3 over the Vikings, and 35–13 over the Cowboys. At 3-0, they sat in a first-place tie in the Coastal Division with the Colts. Allen's retooled offense was on fire against the Cowboys before 75,229 fans at the Cotton Bowl in Dallas, with drives of 90, 72, 93, and 40 yards. The Rams rushed for 221 yards with nearly a 6-yard average against a normally stout run defense.[58]

In an interview prior to the Cowboys game, Allen reiterated that his Rams were capable of winning the NFL Championship. He also responded to a question on whether Dan Reeves had given him "carte blanche" to run the team the way he wanted: "Yes, Dan's been tremendous in all these trades we've made and in the new facilities we have today at Long Beach. The Rams used to practice in the [San Fernando] valley in a recreation park with an old, broken-down locker room. I wanted to move our offices from the valley, and I wanted a new practice field and training camp. We have all that. All our progress has been possible because Dan has gone along."[59]

But news surfaced that infuriated Reeves: Cowboys president Tex Schramm accused the Rams of spying on his team's practices in the days preceding the game. Schramm told reporters the same car was seen outside the Cowboys' practice facility on Wednesday and Thursday. He said the car sped away when a staff member went to check it out, adding that the Cowboys determined by the license plate number it was a rented vehicle assigned to a J. R. Sanders, LA Rams, at 7813 Beverly Boulevard in Los Angeles, the team's former address. (They moved to Chico Boulevard in 1967.) Johnny Sanders and Norm Pollum, two Rams scouts, were the primary suspects in the case.

Allen dismissed the accusation as "ridiculous." He explained that Sanders and Pollum scouted college football games, although he admitted that

Pollum had submitted a pregame report on the Cowboys. "What could we learn [by spying]?" Allen asked rhetorically. "We've already played them in [the] preseason. They have our game films, and we have theirs." Reeves, hiding his alarm over the accusation, said sarcastically that the Rams already knew that Cowboys receiver Bob Hayes ran the 100-yard dash in 9.1 seconds and that quarterback Don Meredith was right-handed. Allen shared his own suspicion, saying a guy had been seen in the trees next to the Rams' practice site taking notes on the eve of the team's departure for Dallas. He said the players had chased the man away.[60]

In those days, the Cowboys' 3.5-acre practice site backed up to Interstate 635, the loop around Dallas. The site was about 100 yards from a motel, where a big camera was set up to secretly snap photos of Cowboys practices, Bob Lilly remembered. He and his teammates suspected that the camera had ties to George Allen's coaching days with the Rams and Redskins. "I don't know if anybody ever shot a picture with it," Lilly said. "But it intimidated Coach [Tom] Landry. We ended up going to the Cotton Bowl. Then the helicopters started flying over, buzzing us. It got to where we went to some indoor practice field. It was kind of like a huge barn."

Lilly noted further that spying probably existed in different forms throughout the league at the time: "We heard about it, but as players we didn't know. All we knew was the only coach that seemed to do it overtly was George Allen. We knew whenever we played the Rams or Redskins that somebody was going to be in the motel or would be flying a helicopter over us, hovering, and they always had cameras inside. One of our scouts went to the Rams. Once, we caught him in a car outside our practice field. He may have been in a pickup truck [and] standing on a ladder or something. He was watching our practice."[61]

Irv Cross added a bit of clarity: "George didn't call it spying. He called it 'getting information.'"[62]

This came as the Cowboys were rising to elite status, only a few years after entering the league in 1960. In '66 they finished 10-3-1, won the Eastern Conference, and lost to the Packers in the NFL championship game. In '67 they won the Eastern Division at 9-5, beat Cleveland in the opening round of the playoffs, and lost to the Packers again in the NFL championship game. Tex Schramm's accusation also marked an early sign of the antagonistic feelings the Cowboys and Allen had for one another. The hostilities reached a boiling point after Allen arrived in the nation's capital in 1971 and inflamed a Redskins-Cowboys rivalry that was born in the '60s.

Bruce Allen thought the Cowboys regularly received favoritism from NFL commissioner Pete Rozelle, who knew Schramm well from the days when they were colleagues in the Rams' front office in the 1950s: "When my father got to LA in '66, the Cowboys were just starting to be a good franchise," he said. "Even though Schramm and Rozelle were both former Rams, the Cowboys got the benefit of the doubt on everything, including rules manipulation and things of that nature. But at the same time, you had to beat the Cowboys because they were a good team. My father studied everything they did in order to come up with the formula to beat them."[63]

Regardless of Schramm's allegation, the Rams were off to a red-hot 3-0 start in 1967. But they fell in week four to the 49ers at the Los Angeles Coliseum, 27–24. The Rams trailed at halftime, 20–0, but charged back to take a 24–20 fourth-quarter lead, before yielding a late game-winning touchdown.

The *Los Angeles Times* reported afterward that Allen was showing the "strain" of losing his first game in ten outings in '67, a stretch that included six exhibition games. Coaching the Rams was taking a noticeable toll on him, with his skimpy eating habits dropping him to about 170 pounds, 15 below his normal weight. Etty was an amazing French cook, but he preferred maintaining a bland diet. "I had a cup of coffee and a piece of toast this morning," he said during the '67 season. "I didn't eat lunch. Didn't have time. And I'm not hungry now."[64]

Like his first season in Los Angeles, Allen was spending a lot of time away from the family's rental home in Palos Verdes, which was thirty minutes from the team's practice facility in Long Beach. During the week, he'd sometimes sleep in a Long Beach motel so he didn't have to commute. Etty and Jennifer spent limited time with him from July to January.[65]

Eventually, Etty came to accept her husband's need for spending so many hours at work. "Sometimes, I would get upset because I had so much on my hands raising the children," she said in an interview with the *Los Angeles Times*. "But I think I've matured. I think I've come to accept it. I understand his responsibility to his job.

"George is very thoughtful, even though he is preoccupied with football. He used to bring flowers home to me, and he still does. Not all the time, but once in a while. He'll come in holding them behind his back. It's very touching."

With the Allens living a few blocks from the Pacific Ocean, George occasionally relaxed by taking walks along the beach with Etty and watching the waves. But those moments were fleeting during the football season. "He doesn't even give himself a chance to relax," Etty told the *Times*. "He's very intense. Very, very serious."[66]

The media picked up on his obsession with football. "Allen has dynamic, push, zeal," Bill Jauss of the *Chicago Daily News* wrote during the '67 season. "He has a tendency to ignore eating, sleep, recreation, his wife, and his four children to endlessly diagram plays or to study flickering films."[67]

In his 1970 biography of Deacon Jones, *Life in the Pit*, author Bill Libby also reflected on Allen's passion for the game: "A straight soul, who seldom drank anything stronger than milk and never used profanity, he was devoted to his family. But he would not let his devotion interfere with his work. He neglected everything else and concentrated on football."[68]

Unlike Etty and Jennifer, Allen's three sons—George, Greg, and Bruce—often enjoyed a front-row seat to their father's football life. George began attending Bears training camp when he was eight and was on the sidelines for many Bears games, and he and Bruce were always on the sidelines for Rams and Redskins games. Greg and Bruce spent a lot of time at Rams and Redskins training camps, and Bruce was a ball boy for the Rams and Redskins while his father coached those teams.

"There could not have been a better place for us boys to be than with our father and all those diverse football characters at training camp," George Felix Allen said. "My perspective from viewing and experiencing grueling hot training camps, many practices, and endless film study sessions was that my father's stressful intensity and all-consuming desire to look for ways to help the team win were normal. I could understand why my father would be exhausted at home when he could somewhat relax."

Putting things in perspective, George Felix Allen explained that the entire family rallied around the man of the house in support of his coaching endeavors: "Football was a unifying activity that brought our family closer together than if our father was a lawyer, doctor, or professor. Football was like a family business for us. We were always united in purpose, physically and mentally, on game day. We were 'all in' for whatever team my father was coaching."[69]

Following the 1967 loss to the 49ers, the Rams tied the Colts (24–24) and the Redskins (28–28), coming from behind in both games. Allen wasn't enthused about settling for ties, with his 3-1-2 Rams trailing in the Coastal Division behind the 5-1 49ers and the 4-0-2 Colts. But the Rams reeled off six straight wins to keep themselves in contention for the division title. The 9-1-2 team would have to beat the Packers and Colts in the last two games—no small feat—to win the division and make the playoffs. Both games were at the Los Angeles Coliseum.

Although the 9-2-1 Packers had already captured the Central Division title, Allen began preparing for the defending Super Bowl champions right after beating the Falcons to cap the six-game win streak. He subjected his troops to tougher-than-usual workouts. A typical one lasted two and a half hours, with wind sprints and relentless hitting among the linemen. "This is why we're in such good shape," Allen told reporters. "We do more running than anybody else. Roger Brown never ran so much in seven years in Detroit."[70] The intense endurance training paid off in '67, when the Rams outscored their opponents in the fourth quarter, 140–48.

The only thing at stake for Green Bay was knowing whether they would play the Colts or Rams in the opening round of the playoffs. But no one believed Lombardi would let his players roll over for this one. He knew he faced a stiff test against a coach and a team on a fast ascent. In the days preceding the game, the Packers acclimated themselves to Southern California temperatures by practicing in Santa Barbara. "Green Bay will be tough," Allen told the press. "They're the world champions. They never let up, even when they've clinched their divisional title."[71]

In the Saturday afternoon game, the Packers took a 24–20 lead in the fourth quarter. When a Rams drive stalled and the Packers regained possession late in the period, thousands of Rams fans streamed for the exits, knowing a loss meant the Colts were in the playoffs. The Rams called a time-out after each Packers play and forced a punt from Green Bay's 41-yard line with fifty-four seconds to play, setting the stage for the most electrifying moment in Allen's five seasons in Los Angeles.

Green Bay's left-footed punter, Donny Anderson, lined up around the 25. Nine Rams positioned on the line prepared to apply a bull rush in hopes of blocking the kick. Allen needed a big play from his special teams, which had made two mistakes that day, something uncharacteristic of his cherished units. In the first quarter, the Packers blocked a field goal and capitalized with a 30-yard scoring pass. In the third quarter, the Rams kicked off to the most dangerous return man in the league, speedy Travis Williams, whose 104-yard return for a touchdown tied the game at 17.

Tony Guillory, a 6-foot-4 substitute linebacker with a huge arm span and tremendous speed, lined up over the center. Although he was one of Allen's special team standouts, not many football fans outside of Los Angeles knew of him. A starting linebacker as a rookie in 1965, he had missed the '66 season because of a knee injury. In '67 Allen relegated him to special teams, preferring instead to start veteran linebackers Jack Pardee, Myron Pottios, and Maxie Baughan. Guillory wasn't happy, but he still played hard, which Allen asked of all his special teamers. In an outstanding season in '67, he blocked a punt, harassed another punter into running on fourth down to set up a Rams score, and excelled in other areas. Allen named him a special team co-captain in '68.

"When I came back from the knee injury, and it looked like I would be on special teams, I just made an all-out effort every time," Guillory said in retrospect. "I was one of the headhunters on the kickoff and punt coverage teams."[72]

Guillory was set to make the biggest play of his four-year NFL career. With a good jump on the ball, he maneuvered past the center and into the backfield, thinking the Packers' up-man, Tommy Crutcher, would block him and leave room for one of the edge rushers to come in free. But Crutcher, apparently distracted by others in the oncoming rush, missed Guillory, who dove and smothered Anderson's kick with his left wrist. Ram Claude Crabb picked up the ball and returned it to the 5 with forty-four seconds left. Two plays later, Gabriel connected with a wide-open Bernie Casey in the end zone for a 27–24 win.[73]

The crowd erupted, and pandemonium set in on the Rams' sideline, with many fans and players in shock over the unbelievable turn of events. Crabb and other Rams hoisted Allen on their shoulders for a ride off the field, with Allen's face displaying a mixture of tears and joy. Allen later said it was the first time he had ever cried at a game.[74] Jennifer remembers the scene well: "I had never seen my dad cry. He was laughing and crying at the same time. To me, seeing that as a six-year-old child—it was so confusing and yet also so moving. It clearly reflects how he emotionally put himself out there for the game and for his players. One of his players once told me that after a loss, the team felt bad because it had let my father down. The players felt bad because they knew how intensely and how personally he would take responsibility for the defeat. This win against the Packers was huge. He wanted to laugh, and he wanted to cry. Football is like that. It's a roller coaster."[75]

In his postgame press conference, Allen explained his thinking in trying to block the punt, which earned Guillory a game ball: "We've worked on that blocked punt play since last July and spent a little time each week sharpening it up. But we don't use it much because you always run the risk of getting a 15-yard penalty for running into the kicker. This time, it was a desperation move. The penalty wouldn't have meant anything, but blocking the kick did. [We] put everybody in the gaps in their line and come in with more men than they've got blockers. It was no time to give up. As long as there was time on the clock, we figured we had a chance. This was the opportunity of a lifetime, and we could not pass it up."[76]

So consumed by the thrilling win, he was at a loss when asked about the upcoming game against the Colts: "Baltimore? I don't know about Baltimore. I'm going to drink a glass of milk, and then I'm going to get dressed and have a slow glass of blackberry brandy, and then I'll start to think about Baltimore."[77]

When Allen woke up Sunday morning, an important detail from the Packers game—the Rams' biggest win in more than a decade—had eluded him. "I'm just unwinding now," he told the *Los Angeles Times* late Sunday afternoon. "I took a sleeping pill and retired early Saturday night. Honestly, when I got up, I couldn't remember whether we had won or lost."[78]

To Jennifer Allen, this inner turmoil speaks to the toll the game of football took on her father. "The emotional, psychological drain was so much that he couldn't remember if they won or they lost first thing in the morning," she said. "I think that pretty much sums up his life in football—that even when his teams won, it was exhausting."[79]

The Rams' fate would be decided on the last weekend of the '67 season. Who would win the Coastal Division? In the 11-0-2 Colts, the only undefeated NFL team, the 10-1-2 Rams faced a dangerous offense led by quarterback Johnny Unitas, the NFL's most valuable player, along with tight end John Mackey and flanker Willie Richardson—all consensus first-team All-Pros. Baltimore's defense was on par with the Rams' defense as the best in the NFL. Because the first Rams-Colts clash ended in a tie, the winner would go to the playoffs based on the rule that the team scoring the most points in the game gets the nod.

With the stakes so high, the Associated Press called the game a "little

Super Bowl" that had "captured the imagination of pro football fans."[80] Arthur Daley of the *New York Times* also hyped the rematch:

"It promises to be a spectacle of such irresistible appeal that it may elicit the highest television ratings of all football offerings to date. The fantastic comeback of the Rams against the Packers was such powerful drama that it acted as a build-up for another expected thriller.

"Few teams ever treated Bart Starr as disrespectfully as the Rams did. The big defenders harried the Packer quarterback with such venom that he was continually running for his life. But can they give the same rude treatment to Johnny Unitas?"[81]

The Rams, led by the Fearsome Foursome, answered that question unequivocally before a sellout crowd of 77,277 at the LA Coliseum. In a 34–10 Rams win, Unitas spent much of the game on the seat of his pants and rushing his throws. Facing unrelenting pressure, he was sacked seven times and threw two interceptions, after taking only eighteen sacks in the previous thirteen games. Roman Gabriel, writing the script of the best season of his then seven-year career, followed a 20-of-36, 227-yard, 3-touchdown performance against the Packers with his greatest game as the Rams' quarterback to date: 18 of 22, 257 yards, 3 touchdown passes. The Rams' eighth straight win tied a team record set in 1952.[82]

"The Rams really whipped us that day," then-Colts center Bill Curry said. "It was the only game we lost all year."[83]

At game's end, Allen took another victory ride on his players' shoulders, having posted his most monumental win in five seasons as the Rams' coach. The 11-1-2 Rams were Coastal Division champions and set for postseason play for the first time since 1955, while the 11-1-2 Colts were done for the season, an unthinkable scenario today, when teams with losing records win divisions and host playoff games. The win set up another Rams-Packers clash in a first-round playoff game on Saturday, December 23. Even though the Rams had a better record than 9-4-1 Green Bay, the Packers would host the game because of the preset arrangement in which, unlike today, the home team for each NFL playoff game was determined by a yearly divisional or conference rotation.

The Packers would face the best Rams team that Allen assembled in his five seasons in LA. Fueled by a much-improved offense, the Rams led the league in scoring with 398 points, more than 100 above their 1966 total, and in points allowed with 196, 16 less than in '66. Both marks met the team goals that Allen had laid out before the season to win the title: holding opponents under 200 points and a 10 percent improvement by the offense.[84]

Rams-Packers, of course, meant another battle of wits between two of the league's premier coaches: Allen and Lombardi. This wasn't a new coaching rivalry. Allen and Lombardi were combatants going back to Allen's days with the Bears.

The fifty-year-old Allen and the fifty-four-year-old Lombardi were similar in many ways. They openly proclaimed that winning took a back seat to nothing. Lombardi famously quipped, "Winning isn't everything, but it's the only thing. In our business, there is no second place. Either you're first, or you're last." He considered every game a "do or die proposition." Likewise, Allen lived to win football games and was visibly distraught when his teams lost. He compared losing to "death," saying a "loser is dead, whether he knows it or not." The two perfectionists coached teams that rarely committed game-deciding mistakes; they stressed simplicity in ball execution that was achieved by repetition in practice; they relied on quick and flexible defenses; and they were brilliant motivators who were adept at inspiring their players, albeit with different methods. The soft-spoken, patient Allen never berated a player in front of his peers. With a master's degree in education, he felt it was more productive to communicate like a teacher and explain something in a measured tone. The temperamental Lombardi was a more in-your-face coach who treated everyone like "dogs," an assessment offered by one of his Hall of Fame players, defensive tackle Henry Jordan.

In an article Lombardi wrote for *Look* magazine just before the '67 season, he told of how he tried to teach his players to "hate" the opponent, a philosophy he learned from his idol, Colonel Earl "Red" Blaik, Army's much-revered coach.[85] When asked about Lombardi's belief in "hate," Allen offered a definition suited to the sport: "You hate what the man is as a football player and what he stands for . . . you don't actually hate him as a human being."[86]

Defensive tackle Rosey Grier spent one season with Allen in Los Angeles and had played for the Giants in the '50s, when Lombardi was their offensive coordinator: "I got to play under Vince Lombardi, and I got to play under George Allen. Vinnie Lombardi was more of an intimidator. He taught you the game, but he was also a threat."[87]

Allen had enormous respect and admiration for Lombardi, whose name carries a singular mystique to this day. The two maintained a cordial relationship whenever they were together at off-season events. "I know my mother would always say how much she liked Coach Lombardi," George Felix Allen remembered. "It was possibly because of the Italian connection. My father would always try to learn some facet from Lombardi to improve his Rams or any team."[88]

By 1967 Lombardi was bidding for his fifth NFL Championship and second Super Bowl title. But Allen's Rams appeared to be catching the Packers at a perfect time. After winning the Central Division, Green Bay had lost two straight games, 27–24 to the Rams and 24–17 to the Steelers, although Lombardi sat some key players against the Steelers, including Bart Starr. The Packers were also battling a number of injuries that had left Lombardi with only three reasonably healthy running backs. "We're in real bad shape all right," Lombardi told reporters. "This is the worst shape we've been in for a playoff game since I've been here."[89]

This sounds a bit like Lombardi was masking his strategy. On a frigid day at Milwaukee County Stadium, the Packers ran the ball forty-five times—twice as many as they passed—for 169 yards and three touchdowns en route to a 28–7 victory. Although the Rams had one of the league's top rushing defenses, Lombardi said they were vulnerable against the run because of their tendency to go "all out" on the pass rush.[90] Starr complemented the running game with his steady passing hand: 17 of 23, 222 yards, 1 touchdown. The Packers went on to beat the Cowboys in the NFL championship game and the Raiders in Super Bowl II to earn Lombardi his fifth and final championship.

Following the win over LA, Packers guard Jerry Kramer said his team wanted the game more than the Rams did.[91] But Merlin Olsen reasoned that the Rams may have been worn out from back-to-back weeks of pressure-packed regular-season games against the Packers and Colts. Add the fact that Olsen and his teammates had chased the undefeated Colts all season in the Coastal Division, and it's understandable that the Rams could have been mentally sapped. Allen refused to make excuses. "It has been a great season, but you are only as good as your last performance," he said.[92]

A few days later, Allen echoed Olsen's assessment that the emotional drain had taken its toll on the team: "The thing that really hurt us in that [playoff] game is that you can have just so many emotional outbursts in a season. In the Coastal Division, we had a crucial game almost every week.

After we beat Green Bay and Baltimore, I think there was, perhaps, a slight letdown, which is only normal. I don't think any team in football could have beaten Green Bay, Baltimore, and then Green Bay again, back to back."[93]

In retrospect, Roman Gabriel speculated that the outcome of the Rams-Packers playoff game might have been different if the Rams had hosted the game, which would be the case if it were played today. "You would like to think it could have been," he said. "Who knows? I would have loved to have had a home playoff game in LA."[94]

The Rams' season wasn't over, with Allen's troops set to compete in the Playoff Bowl, which pitted the losers of the two first-round playoff games. Many players and coaches detested the Playoff Bowl, which meant nothing in the standings. It was mocked as the "Losers' Bowl" and the "Toilet Bowl." Lombardi called it a "hinky-dink" game.[95]

Not surprisingly, Allen the perfectionist took it seriously, putting his players through two-a-day practices in preparation for the Browns, who had lost to the Cowboys in the other first-round playoff game. He didn't think they should be on vacation in tropical Miami, the regular site of the Playoff Bowl. Some of his players thought he'd lost it. "The strain finally got to old George," they said. "Poor devil has blown his computer system." But Allen eventually loosened the reins. He canceled evening meetings and extended curfew a few hours so his players, a few of whom had brought their wives, could enjoy Miami's nightlife.[96]

The Rams routed the Browns, 30–6. Gabriel capped his stellar '67 campaign by completing 17 of 30 passes for 223 yards and 2 touchdowns and was named the game's most valuable player. Deacon Jones, the game's outstanding defensive player, led a pass rush that posted five sacks.[97]

The win climaxed a remarkable season. Over the course of five months and twenty-two football games, including six exhibition games, the Rams went 18-2-2. They won all seven regular-season road games, lending legitimacy to Allen's policy of keeping his players far from busy, urban areas the night before road games so as to avoid distractions and keep the focus on football. The coaching and widespread talent on the team had a lot to do with that road record, too. "Our 1967 season was the best year we had [under Allen]," said Gabriel, one of nearly a dozen Rams who made the Pro Bowl. "We had Green Bay and Baltimore in our last two games, and Baltimore was undefeated until we beat them that last game. We ended up 11-1-2, Baltimore 11-1-2, and Baltimore didn't get in the playoffs. I'm just thankful we made it. That's one of the things you always look back on."[98]

Allen received his due in 1967. He was honored as Coach of the Year by United Press International based on a vote by the nation's sportswriters; by *The Sporting News*, which polled all sixteen NFL coaches; and by the Washington Touchdown Club. An Associated Press panel of sports media voted Allen and Don Shula co-recipients of Coach of the Year honors, in a poll conducted before the Rams demolished the Colts in the last regular-season game.[99]

The 1968 season would mark another outstanding year for the Rams on Allen's watch, with a crazy sequence that no one in their right mind could have ever envisioned.

9

"Merry Christmas, You're Fired"

By any measurement, the 1967 season was a banner year for Roman Gabriel. By the end he was in the conversation as one of the NFL's top quarterbacks. Johnny Unitas, Bart Starr, and Washington's Sonny Jurgensen were considered the best in the game. Gabriel, New York's Fran Tarkenton, Dallas's Don Meredith, Philadelphia's Norm Snead, and the 49ers' John Brodie occupied the next level. Gabriel had made a dramatic leap from 10 touchdowns and 16 interceptions in '66 to 25 and 13, respectively, in '67. The 25 touchdowns, the most in his sixteen seasons, marked a Rams single-season record. His 2,779 passing yards were the second-highest season total in his career. He posted the third-highest passer rating among quarterbacks who started at least ten games (85.2). In addition to being selected for his first Pro Bowl, he was named the Rams' most valuable player.[1] Plus, he had validated Allen's decision to start him over Bill Munson, having won twenty-two games in thirty-three starts since the 1965 season.

With his powerful right arm, Gabriel could fire the ball into a receiver's gut or lay it softly in his hands as he stretched the field. He wasn't a running quarterback per se but showed flashes of mobility. With his iron-like 6-foot-4, 220-pound frame—a prototypical size for today's quarterbacks—he could take a pounding in the pocket and was a load to bring down. "I remember hitting Roman Gabriel a few times when he was throwing a pass. It was like hitting a tree," Cowboys defensive tackle Bob Lilly remembered. "That was mainly because of his strength and his body. When we hit him, it wasn't like hitting an ordinary quarterback. Most of them would just go down. But Roman would just stand there. He was that strong."[2]

Like his Rams teammates Deacon Jones, Merlin Olsen, and Rosey Grier, Gabriel made the most of living near Hollywood. Of Filipino descent and handsome, he had a brief career in television and film. He made his television debut in the popular sitcom *Gilligan's Island* in '64 and his movie debut in '68 as a prison guard in the comedy *Skidoo*. In the highlight of his acting career, he played a Native American adopted son of the iconic

John Wayne in the '69 movie *The Undefeated*. In later years, he appeared on the TV shows *Wonder Woman* with Lynda Carter and *Ironside* with Raymond Burr.

In addition to Gabriel's rapid rise, the wins multiplied in '67 because of vast improvement by the team's receiving corps. Rams receivers caught 23 touchdown passes, compared with 7 in '66. Bernie Casey, the speedy, big-bodied receiver Allen traded for before the '67 season, posted team highs in receptions (53), receiving yards (871), and touchdowns (8). His biggest catch was the last-second, game-winning touchdown in the dramatic win over the Packers. Casey was also a fearless blocker. "Bernie has to be one of the best trades ever," Rams assistant Howard Schnellenberger told the *Los Angeles Times* after the '67 season. "Everyone knows what he did for our passing game. But his blocking grade of 78% was a big improvement over the work we got at that spot in 1966."[3]

Although 1967 had been a historic year for Rams owner Dan Reeves, who was inducted into the Hall of Fame, he didn't seem to appreciate Allen's success: "Winning makes life more pleasant, but it makes it more difficult. In football, you're allowed twenty-four hours after a win to enjoy it. Then it becomes time to worry about the next game. In a way, when you're winning, there is more pressure on you, if you're going down to the wire every week, every minute, every play. Of course, it's not the sort of pressure you really object to. But after a while, it gets to you."[4]

Furthermore, Reeves just couldn't stomach some of Allen's decisions, including his benching of Munson in favor of Gabriel before the '66 season. Munson told the *Los Angeles Times* around the start of the '67 season that he would play out his option that year instead of signing the new contract Reeves had tendered. Reeves, who invested a first-round pick in the gifted quarterback in 1964, did not want him to play out his option. "We want Munson on the Rams," Reeves said at the time. "We need Munson."[5]

After backing up Gabriel for a second straight season, Munson decided in April 1968 he would no longer play for the Rams.[6] Allen responded by trading him and a third-round pick to the Lions for twelfth-year quarterback Milt Plum, who had thrown for more than 17,000 yards, punter and receiver Pat Studstill, running back Tommy Watkins, and Detroit's first pick in the '69 draft. Allen hoped that Watkins, who had returned three punts for touchdowns in his career, could be the "sleeper" in the deal.[7] Gabriel started all forty-three games in the final three years of Allen's tenure in Los Angeles. Munson played twelve more seasons in his mostly pedestrian career.

When Plum arrived, the Rams already had another new quarterback on the roster: Heisman Trophy–winner Gary Beban out of UCLA. The 6-foot, 190-pound Beban, who led the Bruins to a 23-5-2 record as a starter and a Rose Bowl win, was known as "The Great One." As a senior, he passed for 1,359 yards and 8 touchdowns and rushed for 11 more scores, edging out USC running back O. J. Simpson for the Heisman Trophy.

The Rams drafted Beban early in the second round of the '68 draft, despite Allen's warning not to pick him. Allen's instincts told him Beban lacked the skill set to be an NFL quarterback. But Reeves insisted on selecting him, arguing that he'd draw more fans to the Los Angeles Coliseum. "Reeves thought it would be a good marketing move," Bruce Allen explained. "When the Rams took him, Reeves told Dad, 'Plenty of teams wanted him. You're wrong, and I'm right.' Every now and then, Reeves would voice an opinion, and it wasn't based on research or film. The best example was Beban."[8]

Beban never signed a contract with the Rams. On June 14, 1968, the day of his wedding, Allen gave him a gift by shipping him to the Redskins for a No. 1 pick in the '69 draft.[9] "That trade pissed off Reeves," Bruce recalled. "He said, 'Gary's going to be a great player. You gave away our future.' My dad said, 'He will not even be a quarterback.'"[10]

George Allen hit a bull's-eye by trading Beban, who lasted two seasons after signing a three-year, no-cut contract with Washington worth at least $200,000.[11] He threw only one pass as a quarterback and played sparingly at running back, receiver, and defensive back. Redskins minority owner Jack Kent Cooke and team president Edward Bennett Williams had agreed on the idea to acquire the Heisman Trophy winner, Williams explained in *The Future Is Now*: "Poor Gary, he just couldn't cut it, I don't know why. George doesn't talk about it. He probably doesn't want to embarrass me."[12] With the Redskins' pick, No. 8 in 1969, the Rams drafted Florida running back Larry Smith. He played six seasons—five for the Rams and one for the Redskins—amassing more than 2,000 yards rushing and more than 1,100 receiving.

Separately, Allen tried to persuade Redskins coach Otto Graham to trade All-Pro wide receiver Charley Taylor, now a Hall of Famer. Allen offered the Rams' first- and second-round draft picks in 1968, running back

Willie Ellison, and either Doug Woodlief or Tony Guillory, both backup linebackers.[13] This time, Williams intervened and said no.[14]

By the time training camp was set to kick off in '68, most players weren't reporting. After negotiations with the owners over better player salaries and long-term benefits had stalled, the NFL Players Association voted to strike. The players wanted a larger percentage of the television revenue flowing into the league. The owners countered by declaring a lockout to mark the NFL's first work stoppage.

Allen didn't want his players to be rusty heading into the first exhibition game against the Browns. Without consulting Reeves, he organized informal practices for the players at local parks and gave them a script to follow. The coaches couldn't attend. "They were sort of like lockout, strike practices," said Bruce Allen, who was uncertain if his father was the only coach doing it at the time. "I would go there and take roll for practice. He didn't like some of my reports, but I said it is what it is. Deacon [Jones] was playing corner. He said, 'No, you can't let him do that.' I'm like, 'Deacon's not going to listen to me, I promise.'"[15]

A twelve-day work stoppage led to the league's first collective bargaining agreement but minimal concessions from the owners. The players reported for a condensed training camp, although three superstars—Deacon Jones, defensive tackle Merlin Olsen, and wide receiver Jack Snow—were still holding out for bigger contracts. Another original member of the Fearsome Foursome also was a no-show. Allen hoped to have defensive tackle Rosey Grier back in '68, after he had missed most of the prior season with a torn Achilles tendon. But Grier decided to retire from football. An erudite man with myriad talents that he applied in his fascinating career as an actor, writer, singer, and minister, he had moved on in life with the goal of trying to make a difference in society.

Grier had been influenced by a man who campaigned for the presidency on a platform of racial, social, and economic justice and fierce opposition to the raging Vietnam War: U.S. senator Robert F. Kennedy of New York. A Democrat and the brother of President John F. Kennedy, assassinated in 1963, Robert Kennedy had served as attorney general in his brother's administration and for a year under President Lyndon Johnson. He was strongly committed to the ongoing civil rights movement, which fought racial segregation and challenged many forms of racial discrimination.

The movement reached a zenith with the signing of the Civil Rights Act in 1964 and the Voting Rights Act in 1965.

Kennedy's message of hope resonated with Grier, who took it upon himself to be a bodyguard for the 1968 presidential hopeful. Two other Rams teammates, Deacon Jones and Lamar Lundy, also protected Kennedy on the campaign trail. Of the three, only the 300-pound Grier was by Kennedy's side in the late hours of June 4, 1968, at the Ambassador Hotel in Los Angeles, where Kennedy gave a victory speech to more than one thousand people after winning the crucial California primary. He thanked all of his campaign workers, including Grier: "And to Rosey Grier . . . who said that he'd take care of anybody who didn't vote for me."[16]

Minutes later, shots rang out. A Jordanian-Palestinian man upset with Kennedy's support for Israel fired at him as he was exiting the hotel, hitting him in the head and shoulder. Several other bystanders were shot and wounded.[17] Grier, who was not far behind, subdued the shooter, 5-foot-5, 120-pound Sirhan Sirhan, and helped yank the gun from him before he was able to fire at anyone else. Doctors operated on the forty-two-year-old Kennedy for nearly four hours, but he succumbed to his wounds. His death shook the country's psyche.

"It became personal to us that somebody we knew was involved in taking down Sirhan Sirhan after the shooting of Bobby Kennedy," George Felix Allen remembered. "I knew of nobody who wasn't upset about it. For Rosey Grier and others who were involved in the campaign, it was a defining part of their lives."[18]

The assassination of Kennedy came two months after the leader of the civil rights movement, Martin Luther King Jr., was gunned down by an outspoken racist, James Earl Ray. King had steered a national fight for civil rights that was intended to bridge the racial divide in a peaceful way. But the fight sometimes turned violent, with scenes of police using water cannon and other means to subdue the marchers and opponents of the movement shouting down the protesters. Racially charged riots erupted in U.S. cities in the 1960s. In 1965 in the Los Angeles neighborhood of Watts, six days of savage violence sparked by the arrest of two brothers and their mother, all Black, resulted in $40 million in property damage, more than thirty deaths, more than one thousand injuries, and about four thousand arrests. Riots and unrest were reported in more than one hundred cities following King's death in '68, with Washington DC, Baltimore, and Chicago suffering massive amounts of destruction.

Did these circumstances lead to racial tension among the Rams during Allen's tenure? Two Black players, Grier and Cross, and Roman Gabriel, who was part Filipino, denied in separate interviews that any racial friction existed on the team. "We didn't sense anything," said Cross, a Ram from 1966 to 1968. "We had great relationships with each other, guys from different parts of the country, from the Deep South and other places, that were our teammates. We just treated each other that way. We had some Black guys who had white roommates. But nobody made a big deal of it. That was just your roommate. I didn't stay in Los Angeles for a whole year. I was only there during the season and would go back to Philly in the off-season. So I didn't see the whole picture. But the Watts riots were a big deal, and other cities, Philly, New York, were torched as part of the civil rights issue. But our team was close. We never had any issues at all that I remember."[19]

Tom Mack noticed that the racial tensions had sort of a positive effect on the team: "As those riots persisted into the late 1960s, all of us probably got a little tense and more standoffish. But at the same time, we also worked a lot harder to convince each other that 'I don't have any problem with you, and you don't have any problem with me that I know of.'"[20]

To George Allen, the color of a player's skin made no difference in how he judged someone. Like many of his coaching peers, he considered sports a meritocracy, and his critique of a player focused on learning "what does this man bring to my team, and how can he make my team better," Grier said. But Allen wasn't totally colorblind, Grier added, noting that the coach tapped Lamar Lundy, one of the most senior and respected Rams, to speak to other Black players about concerns the coaches might have and other issues. Grier remembered that Lundy once talked to him about his playing ability. "[Allen] felt that a ball player that understood the background of the other ball players should talk to them, rather than send Merlin Olsen to speak to one of the Black ball players," Grier explained. "Merlin was a great guy and got along great with everyone. He could speak to anyone with dignity and pride. But George Allen chose Lamar Lundy instead."[21]

In a move that strengthened team camaraderie, Gabriel recalled, Allen organized a team dinner every Monday after a Rams victory. Many of those dinners were at Allen's favorite hangout in Los Angeles, the Italian restaurant Matteo's. "We were able to communicate and stay together that way," Gabriel said, adding that the players were welcome to bring their wives and girlfriends.[22]

The assassinations and deadly riots contributed to the tragic story line of the 1960s, one of the most turbulent decades in American history and a time when it seemed that the country was unraveling. Not since the Civil War had the United States been so divided. U.S. forces became bogged down in the Vietnam War, and hundreds of thousands of Americans marched against their country's continued involvement in the conflict. Many of those protesting were part of a "counterculture" synonymous with hippies, peaceniks, drugs, sex, rock and roll, and psychedelic clothing. The movement gained prominence as a national voice against the establishment and for bucking authority.

George Allen's style of life and his standards of self-discipline and respect for elders conflicted with the tenets of the counterculture revolution. He even preferred clean-cut players to those with long sideburns and goatees, although he would sign them if they could play. "The hippies and the counterculture and the drug users surely did not fit into his way of thinking," George Felix Allen said. "He didn't want us drinking or smoking cigarettes. LSD and all of that did not fit into my father's way of life."[23]

Allen's favorite musicians were not people like Jimi Hendrix and Janis Joplin, two of the greatest singers of the '60s, or rock bands like the Doors and the Beatles. Instead, he preferred Frank Sinatra, famed trumpeters Pete Fountain, Al Hirt, and Louis Armstrong, and the Count Basie Orchestra. New Orleans jazz and swing bands suited his taste for a style of music more soothing to the ear. One of his favorite movies was the G-rated 1965 classic *The Sound of Music*, the heartwarming story of an Austrian postulant who brought love and music into the lives of a retired naval officer and his seven children during World War II.

On the field, Merlin Olsen ended his holdout a few days past the end of the '68 strike, and Jones and Snow reported just in time for the kickoff of the Rams' exhibition opener against the Browns. A 4-2 preseason included blowout losses of 42–10 to the Cowboys and 35–13 to the AFL's San Diego Chargers. Still, Allen considered his team prepared to make a bid for the championship, with thirty-six of the forty players back from the '67 team.[24]

This time, Allen would not have to outduel a coach he deeply respected: Vince Lombardi. The man who had built the Packers' dynasty resigned shortly after winning Super Bowl II, claiming his responsibilities as coach and general manager had become too much for one person to handle. He decided to focus only on general manager duties. His exit seemingly gave

Allen and coaches such as Baltimore's Don Shula and the Cowboys' Tom Landry a clearer path to the title.

In typical Allen fashion, the Rams stormed out to win their first six games and held a one-game lead over the 5-1 Colts heading into their showdown in Baltimore. By then, Allen's unforgiving defense had held opponents to 11 points and 187 yards per game behind the play of such stars as Deacon Jones. The one-man wrecking ball toyed with offenses in a twenty-four-sack season.[25] That season, Jones earned his fourth straight consensus first-team All-Pro distinction. Overall, the '68 Rams yielded the fewest yards (3,118) since the fourteen-game season began in 1961.

Allen had beaten Shula in two of their past three meetings, with the other game a tie. This time, the Colts controlled the Rams from start to finish and won, 27–10.

Two more wins plus a tie left the 8-1-1 Rams a half game behind the 9-1 Colts. Then came fireworks. After a 20–20 tie with the 49ers in San Francisco's Kezar Stadium, Deacon Jones and Merlin Olsen blasted the condition of the playing field, saying the soggy, muddy surface was unfit for a football game. Jones had once called the same field a "hog pen." The next day, Allen used harsher language. To him, the field was a "disgrace to the league" and the "worst I've seen" in two decades as a head coach. He also referenced a segment of society that he abhorred: "The end zones are like quicksand—and the way they're painted, they ought to sell them to the hippies. We lost two touchdowns there. Bernie Casey sank in the quicksand and fell over. Jack Snow was inbounds on his catch—but there's so much paint on those hippie end zones that the officials couldn't tell. I blame the painters, not them. Are we in the paint business or football?"[26]

Dan Reeves was seething. He told the *Los Angeles Times* those comments sounded like an "alibi" that he "resented." Allen responded by saying he and his coaches had never "alibied or made excuses," adding, however, that "as much money as we spend in this league, we should give the players the best in playing conditions."[27] Their feud intensified after the next game, a last-second 24–21 win over the Giants at the Los Angeles Coliseum. In the locker room, Reeves asked provocatively, "George, how was the field today?" Allen, who refused to shake hands with the owner, replied, "Dan, you had no right to criticize me in the paper. You embarrassed me and my family. Here I am working sixteen to eighteen hours a day, trying to build our team into a winner, and you make a fool out of me." When Allen started walking away, Reeves ordered him back, to no avail.[28] Their nasty exchange likely foretold what was in store in about a month.

With three games to play, the 9-1-1 Rams still stood a half game behind the 10-1 Colts in the Coastal Division. Allen was confident his team could craft another roaring finish like that of 1967. He predicted a sweep of the Vikings, Bears, and Colts that would lift the Rams to the division title.[29]

In Minneapolis, where the Rams won only once in four games during the Allen era, they routed the Vikings, 31–3. The night before the game, a few players, including Deacon Jones, were reeling from the flu. But Allen summoned the energy they needed to pull off the convincing win. However, a deflating 17–16 loss to the Bears, coupled with a Colts victory, ended the Rams' title hopes. The Rams were gaffe prone against the Bears, yielding an 88-yard kickoff return, fumbling inside Chicago's 10-yard line, missing a 35-yard field goal in the final quarter, and earning a slew of penalties. But a maddening oversight by the officials may have cost them the game and the division title.

Trailing by a point with thirty seconds left, the Rams had a first down on Chicago's 32. Gabriel threw an incomplete pass, but a holding call against the Rams resulted in a 21-yard penalty that the Bears accepted. Instead of signaling first down, however, the yard marker advanced to second. Gabriel threw three incompletions, and the Bears escaped with the win. The next day, NFL commissioner Pete Rozelle suspended the officiating crew that worked the game, saying it had "erred" by missing the down.[30]

In a somber postgame locker room, an emotionally exhausted Allen refrained from criticizing the officials and explained that the loss rested on his troops suffering too many self-inflicted wounds: "We have no excuses, no alibis. We've drained ourselves dry—three years of working, and everything is down the drain. We have an axiom here that nobody can beat the Rams; the Rams lose because they beat themselves. The headline of this game is, 'Too many mistakes.'"[31]

With nothing to play for but pride, the Rams fell to the Colts in the season-ending game, 28–24. But Allen being Allen, he didn't take the meaningless loss lightly. *Los Angeles Times* sports columnist Charles Maher described him as a man in "torment" during his postgame press conference. "He answered all the questions, but his words were labored," Maher wrote. "It was like trying to interview a guy who had just been shot in the stomach."

Allen, on his way out of the stadium, further spilled his frustrations to

Maher. He agonizingly told of how he hadn't had a normal meal since the loss to the Bears and that his fixation on football since training camp in seven-day, eighty-hour work weeks was preventing him from spending valuable time with his wife and kids. He also spoke of having trouble sleeping: "It's been that way ever since the gosh-darn Bear game. This is one of the things Vince Lombardi told me got to him the most when he was coaching. He just couldn't sleep. He said it took him till Tuesday to get unwound, but by that time a coach has to start getting wound up again.

"A coach has got to be realistic. But when you've lost your last two games by a total of five points, it can't help but leave you emotionally drained.

"So many people are content to be paper on the wall. It's not the money that interests me. Money means nothing. The only thing that counts if you're a coach is to be able to feel you've accomplished a lot with the team. And I thought we were going all the way this year."[32]

With the 10-3-1 season over, at least the stressed-out coach could get accustomed to his family's fancy new home. After renting a house in Palos Verdes for about two years, the Allens moved in November 1968 into a home on a hill perched above a canyon overlooking the Pacific Ocean and Santa Monica Bay in Palos Verdes Estates. Etty Allen had found the property. After crisscrossing the Southern California area looking for a lot that suited her demanding tastes, she convinced a local builder to sell her the undeveloped property. She then designed just about every inch of the five-thousand-square-foot, $150,000 home with the builder, who was also an architect. "She loved that home," Jennifer Allen said. "She designed it in a Mediterranean style, echoes of her home in Tunisia. She put her soul into it."[33]

The location was breathtaking. Looking out past the Los Angeles Basin on a clear day, one could see all the way to the California town of Oxnard, about sixty miles north. The snowcapped San Gabriel Mountains were off to the side. George Allen's thirty-two fruit trees surrounded the home. Forty-five acres of parkland sat at the bottom of the canyon. "It was so beautiful," Jennifer said. "You could see so far."

The Allen family owned the home throughout George Allen's coaching days in Washington and beyond—a total of more than four decades. He died there on New Year's Eve 1990, and Etty passed away there on January 2, 2013, after which the home was sold. "Through all of the turmoil of life in the NFL and my dad's coaching in the United States Football League and everything, that house was always an anchor in our life," Jennifer said.

George Allen fielded an unexpected call at the new home at 8:00 a.m. on December 26, 1968. It was Dan Reeves, who told Allen what he had wanted to say for a while—that he was being fired. Allen didn't see it coming. Why in the world, he thought, would an owner dismiss a coach who had won 74 percent of his games with a 29-10-3 record and one playoff appearance over three years—a coach who had brilliantly transformed a fledgling franchise into one of the league's powerhouses?

Allen took the call in the master bedroom. The children, downstairs in the family room, saw the breaking news on television. They, too, were stunned. "We all said, 'What?!'" George Felix Allen recalled. "We were screaming up to our parents saying, 'Hey, it's on TV. What's this? The reports are saying he got fired.' Whenever they got the call, they didn't want to tell us as they tried to figure out, 'How do we break this to the kids?' Then they very soberly confirmed it. My mother said she'd write a book called 'Merry Christmas, You're Fired.'" (In 1982 George Allen wrote a book with that very title.)

Of his father, George Felix Allen said, "He was calm about it. Matter of fact, there were so many phone calls going back and forth with different people. There wasn't any anger about it. He was probably trying to figure out, 'Now what?'"[34]

The same day, Reeves essentially blamed himself for the firing. He said in a statement that it was "probably more my fault than his" and attributed it to a "personality conflict." Reeves also said Allen, who was making an estimated $50,000 a year, would be compensated for the last two years of his contract.[35] Strangely enough, the owner also promised Allen a $20,000 addition to his 1968 salary.[36] Reeves had "no idea" who would succeed Allen, he added.[37]

Allen described Reeves's call in a conversation with reporters: "He began rambling, and he rambled on and on. He told me I was a great coach, and that I could get a job any place, and that I shouldn't worry about money. He would take care of me. But he said that he was unhappy, and I had to go. I told him we should meet each other in person and talk this thing over. But he said his mind was made up. And basically, that's about all there was to it."[38]

There was a lot more to it. On top of the fact that Allen and Reeves were polar opposites in their beliefs of how to run an NFL team, the two had distinct personalities and priorities. Allen was a deadly serious person who rarely smiled and focused only on winning football games. He put his heart and soul into his job and could not care less about having fun. One of his nicknames was the "Green Arrow" because he was straight and true, and his favorite drink was milk. As Mel Durslag of the *Los Angeles Herald Examiner* once put it, "Allen is not Reeves' kind of cat."[39]

In contrast, Reeves loved to party and have a good time. A heavy drinker, he'd gather with his buddies late at night and into the early morning hours. "Listen, a guy who goes out after a loss and parties is a two-time loser," Allen once said. "First, he's a loser for losing, and second, he's a loser for thinking he doesn't look like a loser by partying it up."[40]

Reeves also condoned other people drinking on the job, based on a story that Allen once told journalist Steve Guback: "The Rams' scouting staff ran the draft with twenty-five-pound kegs of ice and beer right next to the table on the floor. That's how those guys [operated]. They'd stay up all night drinking. Then they'd drink beer to sober up. Scouts slept on the floor in Dan Reeves's home, drunk."[41]

Reeves's inability to establish a chemistry with Allen was one thing. The owner was also angry about a series of decisions and actions by the coach. These included Allen negotiating the terms of Jack Pardee's '66 contract without consulting the front office; the selection of Roman Gabriel over Bill Munson as the starting quarterback; the trade of Heisman Trophy–winning quarterback Gary Beban; the charges that the Rams had spied on other teams; Allen's extravagant spending on player salaries and bonuses; the move to new training camp and in-season training sites, among other necessities Allen thought would help the team win; and, what was likely the coup de grâce, the Allen-Reeves dispute over the condition of Kezar Stadium's field in '68. At one point, Reeves accused Allen of trying to establish complete autonomy in the front office.[42]

Asked years later if Allen ran up a huge phone bill trying to make trades with other teams, then-Rams official Jack Teele, who was very close with Reeves, shared a slightly different story: "Some of the assistant coaches told me that half the time he was [on the phone] with a shoe manufacturer trying to get an endorsement deal or with somebody else. They said it wasn't on trades as much as we all thought. 'Let me endorse your show, and how much will you pay me,' that kind of thing. I can't vouch for that. But that was what some of the assistant coaches told me. Yes, he was on the phone a lot, there's no doubt about that."[43]

What about the fact that Allen had turned the franchise into a big-time winner with booming attendance figures and season-ticket applications?

Didn't Reeves, who was known to say he enjoyed losing with other coaches more than winning with Allen, appreciate that? "I think so," Teele said. "But you must remember the players he did it with. Merlin Olsen, drafted by Dan Reeves. Deacon Jones, drafted by Dan Reeves. Lamar Lundy, drafted by Dan Reeves. The offensive linemen, Joe Scibelli, Charlie Cowan. Scibelli was a tenth-round [Rams] draft choice. I could go on and on and on. So if it was George's coaching, it was Reeves's drafting. George wanted the thought to be that it was only his trades that did it. I don't agree with that."

To George Felix Allen, Teele's point is not entirely accurate. Yes, the younger Allen said, the Rams possessed a solid crop of talent upon the arrival of his father, who cultivated that talent in a way his predecessors had not. He brought a formula for motivating and coaching those players into winners, while trading for a stream of other skilled and experienced players, many of whom knew what it took to succeed. "It's not as if the Rams were a talentless team," George Felix Allen said. "The Rams were an underperforming team. My father got players like Myron Pottios and Bernie Casey and kept everyone playing up to their full potential. A lot of it was just instilling an attitude that we can be winners, as opposed to accepting average or below-average play."[44]

Sportswriter Doug Krikorian, who joined the staff of the *Los Angeles Herald Examiner* in 1968, reasoned that Reeves's dislike for Allen stemmed from jealousy. In an interview, he insinuated that Reeves resented the fact that Allen wasn't one of the guys who would go out and drink with him, unlike his friends such as Teele and Bob Waterfield, who coached the Rams in 1960 and 1961 and for eight games in 1962.

"A lot of people were jealous of George," Krikorian said. "He was an eccentric guy. When you're like that and not part of, shall we say, the 'in crowd' . . . Reeves was a drinker, an alcoholic. Waterfield would get drunk. That's why Reeves hired him. Waterfield and Reeves would hang out at a bar on Ventura Boulevard.

"George didn't bow to them. He was all football. He was a teetotaler. I never saw George drink. Maybe a glass of wine. He liked ice cream. He was a health addict."[45]

At the time, *Los Angeles Times* columnist John Hall wrote that Reeves had decided to dismiss Allen before the end of the '67 season but was dissuaded from doing it on the grounds of his remarkable coaching record.[46] His official move to fire the coach shook the area like a Southern California earthquake and evolved into a public relations nightmare for Reeves. Veteran Rams players angry about the firing publicly vented their frustration the same day Allen was let go and threatened not to play for the Rams in 1969. Roman Gabriel grumbled that this was the third time in his career a Rams coach had been fired, the others being Waterfield and Harland Svare. He also took a swipe at Reeves.

"If George Allen goes to another team and wants me to play for him, I might make it known that I want to be traded," Gabriel told United Press International. "And if the Rams don't trade me, then I might sit down and think about how much allegiance I owe to this club. Now that [a firing has] happened a third time, I'm not convinced that it has anything to do with coaching ability."

Referring to Allen, Gabriel added, "He was for the players all the time. He got better training facilities and lots of other things just to make the players happy because that's what's important. You can't win without a happy team."[47]

Another Ram chosen for the Pro Bowl, offensive tackle Charlie Cowan, said there would be at least "28 empty spots" on the Rams' roster due to the firing, including his own spot. He noted that such players as Maxie Baughan, Jack Pardee, Deacon Jones, Tommy Mason, Ed Meador, and Gabriel would also not return to the Rams in '69. Eventually, almost every Rams player expressed support for Allen. "Reeves will have a young team next year," Cowan said. "I think that all the players with five or more years [of] experience will want to leave Los Angeles. We don't want to come back and play for a loser, and Dan Reeves told some of the players that he would just as soon settle for a 7-7 season." Meador, for his part, didn't know if a personality conflict should be the basis for firing a coach. "Perhaps you should put up with whatever it is for the benefit of the players," he said at the time.[48]

The next day, in another chapter of the soap opera, Allen and a dozen of his veteran Rams staged an emotional press conference the coach had scheduled at the Sheraton-West Hotel in Los Angeles—the same hotel where Reeves had announced Allen's hiring in January 1966. In an unprecedented scene and another surreal event in the coaching life of George Allen—less than three years after Bears owner George Halas took him to court to challenge his hiring by the Rams—the players flanked Allen to show unwavering support for their wounded leader. It looked like an employee rebellion against management.

Standing before scores of reporters, photographers, and TV cameras,

Allen gave his version of his acrimonious relationship with Reeves. Choked with emotion at times, he wore sunglasses to hide his tears.

"Mr. Reeves said a personality clash was involved," Allen said. "I won't go into the other situations, but I'll mention two. When I signed with the Rams, [equipment manager] Bill Granholm told me to look at the Ram training facilities in [the] San Fernando Valley. They were horrible. I wouldn't train the Russians there. So we made our in-season camp in Long Beach.

"Our preseason camp at Chapman College was terrible, too, so I made the switch to Fullerton Junior College.

"This cost a little bit more money, but everything I did was for the Rams—to improve the team.

"I saw Dan Reeves only once in the last seven months, and that was after the New York Giant game last month. In the three seasons I've been with the Rams, Reeves and I had only a dozen conferences at most. I made decisions on my own—maybe he didn't like them all—but somebody had to make them." (Reeves was away most of the '68 season while undergoing treatment at a New York clinic for Hodgkin's disease, a blood cancer.)

Sucking up his pride, Allen added that he'd like to smooth things over with Reeves if given the opportunity, noting that he had worked very hard to mold the Rams into a championship-caliber team. He didn't want to see that go to waste. He also said that when Reeves brought him on board, the owner told him he'd be the last coach he would ever hire.[49]

At the press conference, Deacon Jones, Ed Meador, Jack Pardee, Maxie Baughan, Dick Bass, and Lamar Lundy threatened to retire, while Gabriel reiterated that he would request a trade if Allen wasn't reinstated as coach.[50]

Jones and Meador issued some of the most emotional pleas for Reeves to reconsider his decision. "The last time you'll see number seventy-five play is in the Pro Bowl game if Allen doesn't come back," Jones said. "We've played under extreme conditions this year, flu and a lot of injuries. But we wouldn't quit this year because we owed this man [George Allen] something. Dan Reeves has the right to fire, but we're part of the club. He should consider us and our families—this is our livelihood—before he pulls the rug out from under you."

Meador, a defensive co-captain, said that when Reeves called him to say he was firing Allen, he had a warning for the owner: "I told him, 'Dan, you'd better get a plane for Cuba. You won't be welcome in Los Angeles. All my life, I wanted to play on a championship team, but it doesn't look like it if Allen doesn't return. At my age [thirty-one], it's best that I step down and let a rookie take over the free safety position for the Rams."[51]

Bruce Allen remembered how much his father was blown away by the player support at the press conference. "When he saw the outpouring of respect and love, even from guys who he didn't know had bought in, in this unprecedented display of unity, which is one of Dad's famous needs for a team, as well as teamwork and togetherness, it was overwhelming to him. That's where his tears came from. He was just so honored because he'd rather get the love from a player than a Medal of Freedom."[52]

George Burman, a Rams offensive lineman and long snapper at the time, said in retrospect that the players' near-unanimous support for Allen wasn't rooted in the fact that they loved him. "It was primarily that we had a good chance with George," Burman explained. "Things were going well, and some of those players had been through tough years and changes in coaches. They knew how that can fail miserably."[53]

Meador, who led a players committee that demanded to meet with Reeves, was spot on.[54] Not only were the players revolting against the owner, but the fans were up in arms, too, in a city where the firing had become the talk of town. The switchboards at Rams headquarters and at media such as the *Los Angeles Times* lit up like Christmas trees with calls from irate fans, who also picketed in front of the team's offices on Pico Boulevard.[55] Protesters held signs that expressed their disdain for Reeves: "NO ALLEN! NO FANS!"; "SHAME"; and "RAM FANS FIRE DAN REEVES—PERSONALITY CONFLICT."[56] Plus, a business associate of Meador, Ray Noxel, formed a citizens committee to protest the firing. Noxel created a petition that listed some 7,500 signatures of fans supporting Allen. He said he'd try to buy Reeves's controlling 51 percent interest in the team if Allen was not rehired, with Reeves reportedly considering a sale of the franchise.[57] The citizens committee reported receiving 2,500 letters, wires, and postcards demanding Allen's return to the Rams.[58]

Media were opining that the embattled owner had backed himself into a corner. Jim Murray of the *Los Angeles Times*, in a column headlined "Did Allen Lock Reeves Out of His Own House?" wrote, "For Dan, George was like the governess you hired to take care of your kids, and you come home one day to find she's locked you out, or turned them against you."[59] Mel Durslag of the *Herald Examiner* referred to how Reeves had embarrassed Allen in the press about his comments on the shoddy field conditions at Kezar Stadium. He wrote that if Reeves ever pulled a "stunt" like that on

Lombardi, who was reportedly being considered to replace Allen, or on "Paul Brown or Sid Gillman or Woody Hayes or Tommy Prothro, or on any number of other coaches," then "God help him."[60]

In addition to Lombardi, Rams assistants Ray Prochaska and Tom Catlin were reportedly strong candidates to replace Allen.[61] The names of two elite college coaches—Southern California's John McKay and Notre Dame's Ara Parseghian—also circulated in the press. Lombardi, who spent the '68 season as the Packers' general manager, was eager to return to coaching. But in Bruce Allen's opinion, Lombardi under no circumstances would have agreed to coach the Rams given Reeves's quick-trigger history of firing coaches, including someone like George Allen, who had made the Rams a championship-caliber team. Allen was the eleventh coach Reeves had parted ways with since buying the Rams in 1941. "The job that Dad did with the turnaround was really recognized by the coaches as amazing," Bruce said. "It was an unbelievable turnaround."

Furthermore, "Lombardi's not going to go from a place where he had complete authority to having somebody else do a draft for him, especially someone who's not working every day," Bruce said of Reeves. "You can make fun of some of the things that [Cowboys president] Tex Schramm did back in that era. But he did work it every day. Dan Reeves didn't work it every day. I can't imagine that marriage with Lombardi."[62]

George Allen had his own set of offers. Who wouldn't want a coach with his credentials? The *Los Angeles Times* reported that Buffalo Bills owner Ralph Wilson said he was interested in talking to Allen about coaching or managing his team.[63] Allen was good friends with Wilson. Bruce Allen remembered that the Packers "offered the world," with a deal that included a stake in a beer distributorship. "For the day and age, it would have been better than what he ended up getting from the Redskins in 1971," Bruce said.[64]

Then there was the Redskins, who had just fired Otto Graham after three lackluster seasons and were seeking a new coach. In his 1989 conversation with Steve Guback, Allen explained that Redskins minority owner Jack Kent Cooke, who also owned the National Basketball Association's Los Angeles Lakers and the National Hockey League's Los Angeles Kings, pursued him before the Redskins hired Lombardi in February 1969.[65]

Who was Jack Kent Cooke? A Canadian businessman who sold encyclopedias door to door during the Great Depression, he raised enough capital to invest in radio stations and newspapers and reached millionaire status by age thirty. He expanded his business empire through the sports industry. In 1951 he bought the Toronto Maple Leafs, a Minor League Baseball team that won four International League pennants. *The Sporting News* once named him Minor League Executive of the Year. After gaining U.S. citizenship in 1960 and moving to Los Angeles, he bought a percentage of the Redskins and gradually increased his stock in the team.

Cooke's main sports concentration was on the West Coast. He paid $5.2 million for the Lakers in 1965, then the highest price ever for an NBA team, and bought the Kings a year later when the NHL expanded with six new franchises. He insisted that both teams play in a modern sports palace, and, despite resistance from city officials, he privately financed a $16 million arena with Roman features that he called the Forum. Known as "The House That Jack Built" and "The Fabulous Forum," the Inglewood, California, venue opened in 1967.

Cooke and Allen became close friends. Cooke gave Allen, a huge hockey fan, and his family tickets to Lakers and Kings games at the Forum.

The Allens also visited Cooke and his family at their thirteen-thousand-acre cattle ranch in the foothills of the Sierra Nevada in California. The ranch featured a lodge, separate cottages for Cooke's sons, Ralph and John, a tennis court, and a pool. Cooke named the ranch Raljon after his sons. George Felix Allen remembered riding horses with John as they counted and moved cattle on the ranch. He once rode Cooke's horse Maximillion, a Tennessee walker. "It was by far my smoothest ride herding cattle," he said.

"Jack Kent Cooke was a lion of a man," George Felix Allen added. "Strong and brilliant in voice and eloquence, he was a gentleman who was extraordinarily well read and would inject quotes from Mark Twain to Winston Churchill to Julius Caesar. He's another example of someone similar to my father in a different sense. He started off selling encyclopedias during the Great Depression and was a visionary leader. Just a very unique, strong-willed person who shared my father's drive for success. He appreciated folks who came up from the bottom and worked hard and made their way close to the top. Mr. Cooke and my father got along very well, sharing perspectives on motivation and the organization of talent, teams, and life."[66]

Their work ethic was remarkably similar. Cooke was a fan of the saying, "The harder I work, the luckier I get." Allen, of course, knew all about the benefits of hard work. *Los Angeles Times* sportswriter Bill Libby shared this anecdote about their friendship in a 1971 article: "Jack was entranced by

George's devotion to duty. He noted that Allen once gave Cooke a rug as a gift, then grew distracted by how much the pattern on the rug reminded him of a football play. This, Cooke concluded, was a straight, serious, sincere man who wanted only to win games, which was the way it should be."[67]

Reeves and Cooke were once close, too. But their relationship deteriorated after Reeves lost a battle with Cooke to buy the Kings in '66. Reeves, who owned a Minor League hockey team, the Los Angeles Blades, once appeared to be the front-runner to acquire the Kings, but Cooke unexpectedly seized the franchise rights.[68] Consequently, Cooke's friendship with Allen didn't sit well with Reeves. In a *Los Angeles Times* article, Libby wrote that when Reeves considered selling the Rams in the early months of 1969, Cooke warned the prospective buyer that Reeves would back out of the deal, especially if he thought ownership would eventually pass to Cooke. The prospective buyer, believed to be architect Charles Luckman, raised about $20 million, the estimated value of the franchise. Reeves rejected the bid.[69]

In his conversation with Guback, Allen recounted his meeting with Cooke to become the Redskins' coach: "He came to my home with his wife, Jean. I was out of work for one week in 1968. I said, 'Jack, I've signed a five-year contract here, and I'd like to finish it. We've come so far with this team. I'd like to try to turn it around.' He said, 'Reeves will fire you again.' I said, 'I don't care about that. I want to fulfill this. These players stuck up for me.' I turned [the offer] down, and Jack was a little bit upset with me. You don't like to turn Jack Cooke down. He doesn't like that, either."[70]

The *Los Angeles Times* reported that Allen refused two "incredible" offers, one in the NFL and the other in the AFL. "We have reliable information from the city concerned that one club offered him two jobs, coach and general manager, at $85,000 a year," an unnamed veteran Rams player told the *Times*. "He would have had full control, which is what he wants, of course, and what you need to run a pro club today. And when [the team] read that he owns a $150,000 home, they called back and offered him a rent-free $150,000 house. I couldn't have blamed him if he'd gone. It takes quite a man to come back to us just on a principle."[71]

Allen also had an opportunity to coach at his alma mater, the University of Michigan. He told Guback that Michigan athletic director Don Canham offered him a $40,000 annual salary, help in finding a new home, and the support of a strong alumni base. "I said I'd be flattered," Allen said in response to Canham's offer. "I never thought that opportunity would come to me. Don told me to get away from that pro sport where one guy like Dan Reeves can control your destiny. If you have a personality conflict with him, he can fire you. He said, 'Come back to Ann Arbor. It's a great place to live. You can have a tremendous career right here. It's one of the best jobs in the country.'"

Allen refused that offer, too. "I said, 'Don, I've been thinking this over, and I haven't coached in college since 1956. I think I'm a pro coach, although I know I could do a good job at Michigan. Very few coaches ever lose there. You have such a great tradition and great facilities.' I said, 'I'm going to stick with the Rams. I know I'm going to get fired again, [but] I'll finish my contract, which has two years left. No matter what I do, Reeves will fire me.'"[72]

Allen instead recommended Bo Schembechler, a successful head coach at Miami University in Ohio, for the Michigan job. Schembechler proved worthy, compiling a 194-48-5 record at Michigan from 1969 to 1989, with two Rose Bowl wins and thirteen seasons when the Wolverines won or shared the Big 10 conference title.

With Allen's fate still in doubt, the Republican politician whom he had met during his coaching days at Whittier, Richard Nixon, took it upon himself to cheer him up in a letter dated January 3, 1969. Nixon, who lost to John F. Kennedy in the 1960 presidential election and to Pat Brown in the 1962 California gubernatorial election, had resurrected his political career. Several weeks removed from beating Democrat Hubert Humphrey in the '68 presidential election, he was set to be sworn in as the thirty-seventh U.S. president. He was certain Allen would have a similar comeback and return to the coaching ranks.

> Dear George:
>
> I don't know what the controversy between you and Dan Reeves involves, but from where I sit the Rams' loss will be some other team's gain.
>
> You have had remarkable success in your coaching career because of your ability to inspire your players to make that extra effort.
>
> I wish you the very best in whatever assignment you may undertake in the future, whether with the Rams or some other club.
>
> With kindest regards,
> Dick Nixon

Allen wrote back saying he was preparing to coach the West squad in the Pro Bowl in Los Angeles on January 19. He noted that he and Etty would be traveling that evening to Washington DC to attend Nixon's inauguration and "know we will see you there." He reminded the president-elect that "the tougher the job, the greater the reward."[73]

Meanwhile, Rams team doctor Jules V. (J.V.) Rasinski was busy helping Allen regain his job. Allen knew that Rasinski and Reeves were close. So he asked the doctor, a good friend of his, if he could convince Reeves to rehire him. Rasinski had to be persistent with the stubborn owner.

"I remember calling Reeves," Rasinski said in a 2019 interview. "He said, 'No, no, I'm sick of this crap. I don't want him anymore.' Actually, what happened is he was just jealous. He thought it was his team, but George was getting all the comments in the press because they were winning.

"So I called him two days later. I said, 'George is waiting to come back. He wants to come back. He'd work for nothing.' George didn't tell me that. I told that to Reeves, who said, 'No, no, I'm through with him, we're all through.'

"So the day before New Year's, I called him once more. I told Dan, 'I know you drink a lot. I know what happened. You were probably drunk when you fired him. But people are so happy that the Rams had a record of 10-3-1 last season. They're much better than in the past. Do you want to be remembered not as the owner of the Rams but the guy who fired the best coach in football when [you were] drunk?' So he called me back about an hour later and said, 'You're right. I don't want that recognition. Set up a meeting.'"

Rasinski strategized with Allen on reacquiring his job. "I said, 'When we go to Dan's house on New Year's Day—you know Dan drinks and his partners with the Rams drink with him—they're going to ask you if you'd like a drink. They know you're a teetotaler and don't drink. I want you to ask for a double blackberry brandy. Don't say I want a lemonade. Show them you're part of them, too.' So Dan said, 'What would you like to drink?' George said, 'I want a double blackberry brandy.' Well, they both started laughing so hard that it broke the ice. They talked for a while, and he hired him back."[74]

Reeves and Allen met once more, on Saturday, January 4. Reeves called for the meeting after Etty Allen, who spoke out freely about the controversy, told a Chicago radio station that Reeves wanted to rehire her husband but that he wanted more security as a condition for returning. Reports said Allen was seeking an indemnity clause that would require Reeves to "pay off" Allen if he were to be fired a second time.[75]

Finally, after twelve days of drama, Reeves caved in to the mounting pressure. On January 6, he announced in a press conference at the Century Plaza Hotel in Los Angeles that he was rehiring Allen. Allen spoke first, saying that in meetings between him and Reeves in recent days, it was clear that "we have each unintentionally hurt each other." However, he said the discussions were beneficial in establishing a line of communication.

"I am, therefore, very happy to be returning as Dan's coach," Allen said. "Aside from my family, my sole interest for the past three years has been the Rams, and I want very much to return to my players and finish the task to which I dedicated myself. I owe this to the players and the fans who have been so loyal to me."[76]

Allen also noted that because he and Reeves had resolved their differences, he planned to leave the press conference. Reeves extended his hand, and Allen slowly reciprocated. "The handshake seemed to pack all the sincerity of a marital vow by Zsa Zsa Gabor," Bud Furillo wrote in the *Herald Examiner*, referring to the actress and socialite who by then had been married five times and would wed nine times overall.[77]

Reeves stepped to the podium, saying Allen's "intense loyalty and devotion" sparked his decision to bring him back.[78] The Rams' owner went on to say, "A week ago tonight, Dr. Rasinski called me. He told me that George said there was nothing he would rather do than return to the Rams. I said, 'Doctor, if a man has that kind of dedication, maybe I should reconsider.'"[79]

Reeves said he guaranteed Allen the two remaining years on his contract and that two other coaches were under consideration—believed to be McKay and Lombardi—when he reappointed Allen. Reeves added that the players' bid to convince him to retain Allen was commendable but that he couldn't let them think they were responsible for his decision to rehire Allen. "As much as I admire them, football players shouldn't have any say whatever on whether a coach goes or stays," he said.[80]

Separately, Allen told Bud Furillo, "Boy, I got out of this because I came back, I didn't ask for anything, I kept the same contract, no extension of the contract, everything the same. [Rams vice president] Bob Reynolds said,

'George, I tell you, I've never seen anything like that, for a guy to come back and keep his word like that.' Because I was in the driver's seat, see, I could say, 'Hey, listen, I want a $40,000 raise, I want four more years.'"[81]

On January 6, 1969, Reeves officially re-signed Allen to a contract carrying the same terms as their original deal, climaxing another wild and dramatic period in Allen's coaching career.

10

A Bear and a Moose

Although Dan Reeves had rehired George Allen as coach of the Rams and the two gave a public display of renewed harmony, it seemed inevitable that Allen's days with the Rams were numbered. Anything short of a Super Bowl win was probably not going to persuade Reeves to extend Allen's five-year contract past the 1970 season. Neither man ever warmed to the other. They were just two people with diametrically opposite personalities who were on separate tracks in life and couldn't get past their feelings of mutual distrust. Deep down, they resented one another.

Rams offensive lineman and long snapper George Burman was convinced that Allen's return marked the "beginning of the end" for him. "Everybody knew that eventually George had to go, and that it would likely be at the end of his five-year contract," Burman said in the early 1970s. "It was like playing for a guy who was virtually gone. You didn't know exactly what to do. It bothered me. It bothered everybody."[1]

Asked about Burman's remarks in a 2020 interview, Rams guard Tom Mack replied, "I didn't feel that way at all. In my mind, you played one game at a time. We actually had two really good years [1969 and 1970]."[2]

Although he was anticipating the worst, Allen for the time being took steps to reconcile with his boss. In a letter to Reeves dated January 11, 1969, he called him the best owner in the league.

> Dear Dan:
>
> This is the first real opportunity that I have had to thank you for all you have done for me since I arrived in Los Angeles twenty-three months ago. Please accept my apology for not writing this sooner but I have devoted all of my time trying to field a winning team.
>
> Dan, I appreciate your support when we were losing in 1966 and your encouragement and help during the court trial. In addition, the many rapid changes that were made during the past two years were sometimes not to your way of thinking, but you went along for the good of the cause.

I think we have a solid team that can remain a top contender for the next two years, provided we have everyone pulling together on the same end of the rope. It will be tougher in [1969], but I'm sure we can do it.

Dan, I know just about every owner in the league, with the exception of [the Atlanta Falcons'] Rankin Smith, and I sincerely believe that I am working for and working with the best man in the NFL.

Personal Regards.

Most Sincerely,
George[3]

Los Angeles mayor Sam Yorty was among those thrilled to have Allen back. He declared January 19, 1969, "George Allen Day" in Los Angeles and presented him with a proclamation that day during the Pro Bowl at the Los Angeles Coliseum, where Allen coached the West team to a 10–7 win over the East.[4]

Although the rehiring meant that Don Shula's Colts would have to play Allen's Rams twice in one season, the Baltimore coach also liked that Allen had returned—if for nothing other than the competition. "I'm glad to see George Allen back," Shula told the *Los Angeles Times*. "I'm glad for him, I mean, not us. He's one of the best coaches around."[5]

With that, Allen began his off-season knowing the rift between himself and his boss had been put to rest. The confrontation had taken on a life of its own, with compelling elements ranging from the player rebellion, the emotional Allen-ordered press conference, the fan protests, and the rehiring of a coach less than two weeks after he was fired. That a team doctor helped mend the divide was noteworthy in itself.

The Rams had hired Dr. Jules Rasinski as their chief physician before the 1967 season. Allen had encouraged Rasinski, a family practice doctor who held the same role with baseball's California Angels, to accept the position. Rasinski said he would do so on one condition. "No amphetamines, no drugs, no pills, nothing like that," the doctor remembered saying at the time. "So [Allen] stuck with me and didn't permit the use of illegal substances."[6]

By the 1960s, amphetamines and other types of stimulants and "pep pills" had become commonplace in the locker rooms of American team sports. The Associated Press reported that NFL teams provided stimulants through team doctors and trainers in the '60s. Burman told the Associated Press in 1973 that amphetamines were available through the Rams during his first three years on the team (1965–67) but not after that.[7] Even after the league cracked down on the team-administered use of amphetamines, they seemed to be available to players through a source known as "Dr. Feelgood." As Rasinski said, "I'm sure every team had its own Dr. Feelgood," and furthermore, "some coaches said if you don't take the pills and play with the pills, I'm going to cut you."[8]

Some of the Rams players, Bruce Allen remembered, thought Rasinski was "square because he was so prudish, even with pain medications. He wasn't only concerned with the use of amphetamines. It was street drugs, as well." Bruce said it was rumored that the Rams didn't field winning teams for so long before his father's arrival in '66 partly because too many players used recreational drugs, such as marijuana, that hindered their ability to excel. "They were unfocused, and they were a partying team," he said. "They owned the streets of LA, and they ran the streets pretty well."

Bruce also recalled that Allen and Rasinski collaborated to launch one of the first drug education programs for NFL players. "Dad brought in speakers to teach the Ram players the downfall of drugs," Bruce noted. "I remember Pete Rozelle got mad at him because he brought in drug professionals and told the players, 'You're not allowed to do drugs. I'll drug test you.' Rozelle hated that and asked him why he was doing that. 'Because these guys have been going out and partying too much. That's why.' And [Rozelle] said, 'We don't want the public to know our players have been doing drugs.' Dad said, 'I don't give a damn. The public knows they've been doing it. The public's the one who told me [the Rams] have a drug problem.'"[9]

Rasinski also organized visits by drug safety experts. "When I started with the Rams in 1967," he said, "I had four agents from the U.S. Drug Enforcement Agency come out to training camp at Cal State Fullerton. They talked to the players about drugs, amphetamines, marijuana, all that stuff. They talked about marijuana being in cookies, brownies, and other places. I never permitted anything like that. That was all part of my beliefs. They could get it from some Dr. Feelgood who would try to ingratiate himself with the players, but not through me."

Off the field, Rasinski took excellent care of Allen, administering a complete end-of-the-season physical that included cardio tests on a treadmill. Despite the physical and mental toll a football season can take on a coach's body, Allen found the time to run laps and do calisthenics almost every day. "For his age, he was in very good shape," Rasinski said. "He ate well and exercised." Allen was fifty-three by the time he left the Rams after the 1970 season, although he looked much younger because he was so fit.[10]

Allen and Rasinski bonded so well that their families congregated at nearby Lake Elsinore and at each other's homes. In 1970 the two men went on a fishing trip to Alaska with George Felix Allen that marked his high school graduation present. The trip became an adventure. The trio flew two hours from Anchorage on a small pontoon plane to a glacier-fed inland lake. They tied the plane to a tree next to a cabin that had no electricity or plumbing. The three vacationers and the pilot were the only known people in the remote location at this time.

One day Rasinski and the Allens ventured out in a boat powered by a small outboard motor, intending to catch grayling trout in an area where very clear water flowed into a river. After a day of exploring and fishing, they turned and headed back toward the cabin but encountered a fierce, windy rainstorm that swept across the lake and sent dangerous waves over the side of the boat. Rather than battle the elements to reach the cabin several miles away on the other side of the lake, the three men beached the boat on a jut of rocky land. After propping the boat on fallen tree roots to serve as shelter until the rainstorm subsided, they noticed fish heads lying about, presumably from bear feasting. So they took turns keeping watch for bears with their .44 Magnum handgun. "We were lucky we didn't come onto that piece of land when the bears were eating," George Felix Allen recalled. "Nor did the bears return hungry during the hours we were stranded there."

Eventually, the wet trio got back in their boat and returned to the cabin. Upon arriving, they saw their tour guide fast asleep. Rasinski was livid because the guide had made no effort to find them while they were gone. "We were thinking, 'Which one of us is going to let him have it because he never came to look for us?'" he remembered. "So he said, 'Gee, you guys were out there a long time.' I said, 'I'd like to kick him in the ass.' We couldn't do anything to him because he was our pilot. He had to fly us out. The three of us were very fortunate we weren't killed. Wouldn't that have been a real headline!"

Separately, the three men saw a dead animal that looked like a moose. They presumed by bear tracks that a big mother bear and her cub had devoured it. "I saw this big mound of brown stuff steaming," Rasinski said. "I'm like, 'Gee, what the hell is that? It can't be a bear.' I got closer. It was a moose. The only thing left was a horn and skin. Everything was eaten, even the meat off the hide. You knew it wasn't long since the animal had been killed and eaten apart." The trio considered tracking the bear through the tundra and killing it but decided not to because of the difficulty of navigating the challenging terrain and because, as George Felix Allen observed on the trip, the "last thing you want to do is be anywhere near a mother bear with a cub," he said.[11]

After Allen accepted the Redskins' head coaching position in January 1971, he asked Rasinski to be Washington's team doctor. He even wrote Rasinski a letter of recommendation. But Rasinski opted not to go to DC because he didn't want to uproot his family. He remained with the Rams until 1973 and with the Angels until 1995.

In the months following his clash with Reeves, Allen vacationed in Mexico and Hawaii. He also went with his family and their dog, Hilda, to picturesque and pristine Kings Canyon National Park, known for its enormous sequoia trees, in California's Sierra Nevada. At the time, Allen served on a sports advisory committee for the retail chain Montgomery Ward, which sponsored and videotaped the trip for a commercial titled "It's a Different World." Allen narrated the commercial, which shows the Allen family hiking, playing volleyball, setting up a campfire, and erecting a tent. That's where video can be deceiving. "In the commercial, putting up the tent took three seconds," Jennifer Allen remembered. "It really took about seven hours: put piece A into B, but where's B? That's when I realized my dad was not a mechanic."[12]

It was no secret that George Allen drank a lot of milk to calm his ulcers. Thus, the Allens also starred in television commercials for Adohr Farms when the dairy company began making plastic milk containers. "My father had to say it so many times . . . 'Pure-Pak plastic cartons, try it and see,'" George Felix Allen recalled. George Allen also served as spokesperson for a local dairy that sponsored his weekly pregame radio show. In turn, the dairy delivered gallons of milk to the doorstep of his home in Palos Verdes Estates.[13]

Although he had been rehired and was eager to return to work, nobody heard much from Allen in the 1969 off season. A deafening silence emanated from his Long Beach office. He even intimated that his major trading days were over, according to Mal Florence of the *Los Angeles Times*, until news broke in May 1969 of his latest blockbuster deal. "Trader George" sent three quality players to the Eagles—offensive tackle Joe Carollo, guard Don Chuy, and cornerback Irv Cross—for arguably the best offensive tackle in the game, 6-foot-5, 295-pound Bob Brown, and defensive back Jim Nettles.[14] Brown lived up to his billing, earning Pro Bowl and first-team, All-Pro honors in each of his two seasons with the Rams. He also made the NFL 1960s All-Decade team and was inducted into the Hall of Fame in 2004.

Allen also focused on rebuilding two areas of the team decimated by injuries in '68: the offensive backfield and the receiving corps. One of the hobbling receivers was big-play threat Bernie Casey, who had missed most of the last four games of the season due to injury. Prior to the draft in January 1969, he gave Allen mixed messages on whether he'd return for his ninth season or retire and pursue his interests in acting and the arts.[15] In '67 the speedy Casey caught a team-high fifty-three passes and was instrumental in the Rams winning the Coastal Division. His reception total dipped to twenty-nine in '68.

Casey opted to retire in his prime at age twenty-nine. In a storied acting career, he appeared in dozens of films, including *Brian's Song*. Casey also became an accomplished painter whose work was widely exhibited, as well as a published poet.[16]

Casey's departure and the Rams' inability to find a replacement with similar big-play ability may have doomed their chances of winning a championship in 1969. The talented Jack Snow, who caught 29 passes for 500 yards and 3 touchdowns in '68, couldn't do it all by himself. It also hurt that around the start of training camp, Allen made perhaps his worst trade in LA. He acquired Eagles fullback Israel "Izzy" Lang in exchange for rookie defensive end John Zook and second-year wide receiver Harold Jackson. While Lang gained 1 yard rushing in 1969, his last season in the NFL, the 5-foot-10, 160-pound Jackson ended up being the one who got away. In 1969 he caught 65 passes for the Eagles, with league receiving highs of 1,116 yards and 79.7 yards per game. He made his first of five Pro Bowls in a sixteen-year career that included 579 catches, 79 touchdowns, and 10,372 receiving yards.

A twelfth-round pick in 1968 out of Jackson State, Jackson possessed "rocket speed," recalled Irv Cross, who served as an Eagles player-coach in '69 before retiring: "George would use him in practice just to have somebody with speed we could work against. When I left the Rams and went to coach with the Eagles, I told our personnel department, 'Get this guy. He's a great player.' We got him for peanuts. George didn't like him because he was so small. But the guy was greased lightning."[17]

In retrospect, Jackson felt Allen gave up on him only because of his lack of experience: "At the time, George didn't believe a whole lot in rookies. He was strictly a veteran football coach. You had to have some time under your belt when you played under George Allen."[18]

The Rams needed someone who could compensate for the loss of Casey at right flanker. It was hoped that rookie wide receiver Jim Seymour, one of three Rams first-round draft picks that year, would provide instant help. But the two-time All-American from Notre Dame joined the army and was lost for the season. Allen traded a draft choice for Packers flanker Claudis James, who instead retired, and he unsuccessfully tried to lure ten-year veteran Red Phillips, a former Rams and Vikings receiver, out of retirement. Pat Studstill, who also played receiver, was slowed by an injury.

Suddenly, the Rams were terribly thin at wide receiver. "Jack Snow, Wendell Tucker and a healthy Studstill give us good wide receivers but we still don't have the depth needed to win a championship," Allen said in the preseason.[19]

Eventually, Allen tapped the 5-foot-11, 185-pound Tucker, a third-year man, as Casey's replacement. Tucker had been an immediate sensation after Casey injured his thigh in the tenth game of the '68 season. He caught just seven passes, but four went for touchdowns, including a 60-yarder, the Rams' longest completion of the season. "My dad didn't dislike Harold Jackson," Bruce Allen said in looking back. "At least I never heard him say that. I think Harold had better speed, but Wendell was shiftier."[20]

Tucker posted 38 catches with 629 yards and 7 touchdowns in 1969, plus an NFL-long of 93 yards. But he wasn't a Bernie Casey–type, big-play threat whom opponents constantly feared.

"Bernie was a real, real addition to the team when he came," Mack said in retrospect. "Jack Snow was the wide end that we played. But Bernie was the running back that we'd use on the other side at wide receiver. The guy we ended up using was Wendell Tucker. He certainly wasn't Bernie. So did that hurt us? Yeah. You always get change, unfortunately. But they didn't go and get a top-of-the-line wide receiver when we lost him. I'm sure that hurt us when you look back on it."[21]

On the coaching front, Allen added two new men to his staff: Steelers assistant and five-time All-Pro LaVern "Torgy" Torgeson, who replaced

Marion Campbell as defensive line coach, and Stanford backfield coach and former San Jose State quarterback Dick Vermeil, who would oversee special teams. An assistant coach for special teams?

Leave it to George Allen, who emphasized special teams like no other coach in that era, to hire one of the first special team assistants ever. (That same season, the Eagles hired Marv Levy to coach their kicking units.) Upon becoming the Rams' coach in '66, Allen tried to legitimize his special teams. He immediately named running back Les Josephson the Rams' first-ever special team captain,[22] and he began prepping his kicking units to produce pivotal plays. They responded by making an art of blocking punts, including Tony Guillory's famous block in the 27–24 shocker over the Packers in 1967, and two in one game against the Bears in '68. But Allen felt his special teams could be even more impactful in altering the flow of a game.

In his search for a special teams coach, Allen asked a good friend, Stanford University track coach Payton Jordan, if he knew of anyone who fit the profile of the coach he was seeking. Jordan coached the U.S. track and field team, which at the '68 Olympics in Mexico City won a record twenty-four medals, including twelve golds.[23] Jordan recommended Vermeil, who soon learned about the detail-oriented nature of his new position.

"George told me during the interview that following the '68 season he had his staff grade all of the Rams' punt and kickoff coverage teams," Vermeil remembered. "He found out that there were players on each coverage team that had never made a tackle at any time during the season. He also told me he had lost a game because of a kickoff return and missed a playoff spot. This convinced him that he had to have a coach doing nothing other than organizing, preparing, motivating, and grading his special team players.

"George was always looking for an edge. He was a fanatic in terms of detail. He felt there were details not being taken care of within the kicking game and that the only way to do it would be to hire a special teams coach."[24]

Following a 5-1 exhibition season, the Rams traveled to Baltimore for the start of the NFL's fiftieth season. They were battling injuries, especially on defense with newly acquired safety Richie Petitbon, one of Allen's defensive stars in Chicago; linebackers Maxie Baughan and Myron Pottios; and linemen Deacon Jones and Merlin Olsen. Fourth-year defensive end

Gregg Schumacher, in for longtime starter Lamar Lundy, didn't even make the trip. A number of players on offense were hurting, too.

In '67 and '68, the Rams and Colts engaged in season-long races for the Coastal Division championship. In fact, since 1966 they had rarely lost to any other teams except each other. All signs pointed to a repeat sprint in '69, with the Colts pegged as the consensus preseason favorite to return to the Super Bowl, where they had been embarrassed by the Joe Namath–led heavy underdog Jets a few months prior.

Having finished 6-0 in the '69 preseason, the Colts appeared to be at least a touchdown better than the Rams. Not surprisingly, Allen called it a must-win situation. "There's a lot of pressure on the loser," he told reporters. "The team that loses can't afford to lose more than one game the rest of the way.

"If we win, we'd be on fire. Nothing could stop us."[25]

Allen was prophetic. A 27–20 Rams win kicked off an eleven-game win streak. Trailing 17–10 in the third quarter, they scored 17 unanswered points. Roman Gabriel established an early tempo for what evolved into the best season of his sixteen-year career. He completed 20 of 33 passes for 268 yards, with 3 touchdowns and no interceptions. His last scoring toss, a 16-yarder to Tucker, gave the Rams a 27–17 lead in the final quarter.

Allen sounded ecstatic in the postgame locker room, tossing in a few exaggerations in the process: "This is the greatest victory ever by the Rams since I have been coach. First, this game definitely disproved the claim we are too old. Our fellows are not over the hill. This was a tremendous achievement against odds. I don't think many folks back in Los Angeles thought we could come to Baltimore and win over Unitas. Everybody on our team had a hand in this. We fought, scratched, and clawed against odds and early bad breaks."[26]

The game also set the tone for Baltimore's 1969 season. The Colts played with a hangover from the massive upset to the Jets, finishing 8-5-1 and missing the playoffs. It was the last season in Baltimore for Allen's top coaching rival at the time, Don Shula, who accepted an offer to become coach, general manager, and a stockholder of the Miami Dolphins.[27]

In 1969 the Rams didn't lose again for two and a half months. Following a 24–23 victory over the Cowboys before nearly eighty thousand fans at the Los Angeles Coliseum, the 10-0 Rams stood firmly in first place in the Coastal Division. One more win meant they'd lock up the division title for the second time in Allen's four seasons in LA. They would also become the first NFL team since the '53 Cleveland Browns to win their first eleven games.

The eleventh win would need to come against the much-improved 5-3-2 Redskins in the nation's capital. After thirteen straight nonwinning seasons and long stretches of doormat status, the Redskins were proving to be a better team under first-year coach Vince Lombardi. The five-time NFL champion and two-time Super Bowl winner, restless in his general manager post in Green Bay in '68, had returned to coaching. Lured by a lucrative offer that included a $110,000 annual salary, the role of executive vice president that guaranteed him control over the draft and trades, and 5 percent of the Redskins' stock, Lombardi ended his coaching hiatus. Before stepping down from the Packers, Lombardi beat Allen three out of four times in head-to-head competition, including a 1967 playoff game.

The '69 game also featured the top two quarterbacks in the game, Roman Gabriel and Sonny Jurgensen, both graduates of New Hanover High School in Wilmington, North Carolina. As good as Gabriel had been the previous two seasons, he elevated his game to elite status in '69: a league-high twenty-four touchdowns and a league-low seven interceptions. His touchdown total was one short of his career high. At one point, Gabriel threw 206 passes without an interception, the second-best mark in NFL history.[28] A consensus first-team All-Pro, he was named the NFL's most valuable player by the Associated Press, United Press International, *The Sporting News*, and other organizations.

Allen drew up a plan to hound Jurgensen, one of the NFL's most prolific quarterbacks of that era. The Rams' defense responded appropriately. Leading the charge were the front four of Deacon Jones and Merlin Olsen, with Roger Brown and Coy Bacon alternating at right tackle and Lamar Lundy and Diron Talbert alternating at right end.[29] They produced an assortment of blitzes, while Jurgensen took 6 sacks, for 52 yards in losses, and threw 2 interceptions. Gabriel completed 16 of 29 passes for 128 yards and 2 touchdowns, including a 1-yarder to tight end Bob Klein that was set up by one of Allen's signature plays: a blocked punt.

Final score: Rams 24, Redskins 13.

"Eleven in a row—wouldn't you say that was a pretty good season?" Allen asked rhetorically in his postgame comments. The Rams' front four, he added, "put on one of their better rushes today. I wouldn't trade them for any line in professional football. We dogged Jurgy more than we expected to because it was so effective. Most of the time, we had him rushing his passes, didn't you think?"[30]

In beating the Redskins and wrapping up the Coastal Division title, the 11-0 Rams would face the Central Division champion Vikings for the Western Conference title. The two teams were destined to meet in the first round of the playoffs, but as in 1967, league rules mandated that the Central Division winner would host the playoff game.

Although there was nothing in the standings to play for, Allen felt something was at stake: the chance of being the first team in the fourteen-game era to go undefeated in the regular season and the first NFL team to do it since the 11-0 Bears in 1942. He had no plans to rest his starters. "With the possibility of an undefeated season, he was still going to keep the pedal to the metal," Bruce Allen said in hindsight.[31] Gabriel and his teammates thought the same way. "Not many teams have ever had a chance to win fourteen regular-season games, and we want to be the first in history to do it," Gabriel said at the time.[32]

The Vikings, on a ten-game win streak of their own, quashed that goal with a 20–13 win in the LA Coliseum, after which Allen accused his team of playing without emotion.[33] He subsequently eased the pressure on his squad, which entered a freefall with losses of 28–0 to the Lions and 13–7 to the Colts. A *Los Angeles Times* headline spoke to the alarming nature of the three-game collapse: "Rams Continue Mad Retreat into Playoffs, Fall to Colts."[34]

"That's the first time [Allen] really let up on us," Gabriel, one of six Rams to make the Pro Bowl that year, recalled. "As a result, we got our butts kicked."[35]

But it was back to business for the playoffs. Unlike the '67 trip to Green Bay, Allen wanted his players to settle in Minnesota nearly a week early to get used to the bitterly cold temperatures. The Rams began simulating play in the northern climes about five days before the game, practicing on a snow-covered field lined with bright orange paint. "George's idiosyncrasies," Gabriel explained. "He stated that every day could be Ram weather, so to acclimate, we went there a week in advance. We practiced outside during the week in the snow. If we had the sun, we practiced indoors. This helped us acclimate to the weather that was expected for game time."[36]

But Rams players weren't home to celebrate Christmas with their families. "We had one of our kids already," Tom Mack said. "So you obviously are not thrilled that you're away from your family. But at the same time,

[Allen] wanted to be sure that we were accustomed to the weather and the conditions. That's why he said we were going to go up early."[37]

The temperature at game time ranged from the low to mid-twenties, with the field in relatively good playing condition. The two heavyweight teams battled it out in an incredibly physical and bloody game. The first half belonged to the Rams, who took a 7–0 lead on a short flip from Gabriel to tight end Bob Klein. Another short touchdown pass to tight end Billy Truax gave the Rams a 17–7 halftime lead. But the momentum shifted in the second half. Several questionable calls went against the Rams, the most penalized team in the league, including a pass interference on cornerback Jim Nettles and a piling-on penalty on linebacker Jack Pardee on a Vikings touchdown drive that closed the gap to 3 points in the fourth quarter, 17–14. Another scoring march gave the Vikings a 21–20 lead. Three plays later, Vikings defensive end Carl Eller sacked Gabriel for a safety to increase the lead to 3.

On their final possession, Gabriel's dink-and-dunk completions moved the Rams to the Vikings' 44 with thirty-nine seconds to play. The Rams needed only a few yards to get in field goal position. Gabriel tried another short pass, but the ball hit defensive tackle Alan Page in the chest. He caught it on the deflection and rumbled down the sidelines before Gabriel knocked him out of bounds.

The Rams' locker room was like a morgue. Everyone sat in total silence wondering how the season had slipped away after an 11-0 start. For the second time in three seasons, Allen and his Rams had failed to advance beyond the first round of the playoffs. "What hurts is that everything was right on the button," he told reporters. "We were mentally and physically prepared for the game. We were sure we'd win.

"Yes, the Vikings were the better team, but only three points better. I can't single out any one reason why we lost the game. It was this play and that play, but it added up to the big thing. We played hard, and we played well, but we didn't win."[38]

A half century later, Mack echoed Allen's thoughts that the Rams were superconfident heading into the game: "I can honestly tell you we believed we were going to win that game. It was a very, very close game. The damn thing went back and forth. We actually beat the hell out of them. But you can argue that one way or the other. It was a very painful loss. Of course, I had that experience a lot, unfortunately. We always managed to lose to the damn Vikings. We'd come up with a different way to do it each time."[39] In the coming years, Mack's Rams lost to the Vikings three more times in the playoffs, including twice in the NFC Championship Game, and won once.

Just like two years earlier, the Rams had one more game—the meaningless Playoff Bowl in Miami—on January 3, 1970. Facing a Cowboys team that Cleveland had thumped the week before in the playoffs, the Rams routed Dallas, 31–0—Allen's first shutout in his four seasons in LA. Gabriel capped his MVP season by throwing 4 touchdown passes in 12 of 17 passing for 224 yards and was named offensive player of the game. Deacon Jones earned defensive player of the game honors.

In 1970 the NFL split into two thirteen-team conferences, the National Football Conference and the American Football Conference, with three divisions and four playoff teams—the three division winners and a wild card team—in each conference. The Rams, 49ers, Falcons, and Saints made up the NFC West.

Just before the season began, *Sports Illustrated* published an article on Allen and his expected fate titled "You Win! You're Fired!" The phrase played on the illogical thinking of firing a coach who sported a four-year record of 40-13-3 with a .755 regular-season winning percentage and two playoff appearances. Only the Cowboys' Tom Landry (.778) and Baltimore's Don Shula (.774) were better during that span.

In the article, author Alfred Wright noted that Dan Reeves couldn't relate to a man of Allen's unyielding dedication to football. "In the closely knit fraternity of football owners and their chums, Allen is regarded as a pariah for having painted their friend Danny into such an uncomfortable corner," Wright wrote. "They mutter about how Reeves has had to rescue Allen from illegal trades he made with imaginary draft choices. It is in this context that Allen now enters the fifth and final year of his contract with the Rams."[40]

Bruce Allen said his father may have thought he was a lame-duck coach when Reeves rehired him, but he never shared that sentiment with anyone else: "At the same time, I don't know if my dad would have stayed. He never got over the disloyalty from Reeves to fire him in the first place."[41]

Then again, it wouldn't be surprising if the procession of other coaches Reeves sent to the trash heap felt the same way about his lack of support.

"I think Dan Reeves had a bad relationship with everybody he was ever associated with," Richie Petitbon said in a 2017 interview. "I didn't know him. But I know that he and most of his coaches never got along. I'm sure that was definitely a problem with George. George had to have control of everything, and I don't think Reeves was that type of owner. That was just a natural bad relationship.

"I don't know what the problem was. But it was a big mistake on [Reeves's] part to let George go. I thought we had a great team in Los Angeles."[42]

Interestingly, one person in Allen's inner circle connected with Reeves on a personal level: Etty Allen. "My mom once told me about a dinner party where she sat beside Reeves," Jennifer Allen remembered. "At some point, they began discussing my mother's favorite language, Latin. My mother was fluent in five languages, and she said she enjoyed the Latin banter with him, as well as the incongruous nature of the two of them exchanging Latin phrases at an NFL dinner party."[43]

More than halfway into the 1970 season, whether the 5-3-1 Rams would qualify for their third playoff appearance in the Allen era was in question. But they reeled off three straight wins, the last of which—34–16 over the Saints—left them tied with the 49ers for first place in the NFC West at 8-3-1. But in a meeting that Allen dubbed a "championship game,"[44] the Lions upended the Rams, 28–23, leaving his 8-4-1 squad a full game behind the 49ers.

In the final week, the Rams visited the 9-4 Giants, winners of nine of their last ten games. With a 31–3 domination at Yankee Stadium, the Rams prevented the Giants from going to the playoffs. But later that day, the 49ers clinched the NFC West with a 38–7 win over the Raiders. The Rams also had a shot at the NFC's wild card spot, which the Lions secured by beating the Packers.

With the 1970 season over, Allen's coaching clock continued to tick. Charles Maher of the *Los Angeles Times* joked about the expected firing. "As you know, Ram president Dan Reeves phones his coach every other Christmas season to extend holiday greetings and fire him," Maher wrote. "Using a new pre-recording technique, I have made a tape of a conversation Reeves and coach George Allen will have some time before the end of the year.

"Reeves: Happy holidays, George. You're canned.

"Allen: Dan, you old son of a gun. Leave it to you to come up with the perfect gift. Who else would think of giving his coach the gate for Christmas?"[45]

Reeves, who lived in New York at the time so he could be treated at a clinic for Hodgkin's disease, called Allen for real on December 30 to tell him he was letting his contract expire at year's end—this, although Allen was the most successful long-term coach in Rams history, with a five-year regular season record of 49-17-4 (.742) and two playoff appearances. Reeves said his decision simply came down to their contrasting philosophies on how to run a football team. "It is unrealistic to continue," the owner told the Associated Press. "I have discussed this with our stockholders, and they are in full accord with this action."[46]

Allen quickly arranged a press conference at a park in front of the Beverly Hills Hotel in Los Angeles. "It was a cold conversation, no gratitude, no appreciation," Allen told reporters. "There was no thanks for what I've done. After this experience, I wouldn't take a position unless the general managership went with it."[47]

This time, there was no player rebellion. Unlike the loyalty Rams players had shown their coach after he was fired the first time, in '68, none of them came to this press conference. "There wasn't a huge uproar the second time around," remembered Mack, who added that Reeves would have had a much harder time firing Allen if he had won an NFL Championship or the Super Bowl.[48]

Reeves promised a new coach within a week, with many of the same names from the '68 firing surfacing in the media as possible candidates: Rams assistants Tom Catlin and Ray Prochaska, Notre Dame's Ara Parseghian, USC's John McKay, and former Rams receiver Tom Fears, who was fired as the Saints' head coach during the 1970 season.[49]

A week after dismissing Allen, Reeves replaced him with one of the nation's premier college coaches, UCLA's Tommy Prothro. The soft-spoken Tennessean, a good friend of Allen, had compiled a 104-55-5 record (.654) in sixteen seasons as a college coach, his first ten at Oregon State and his last six at UCLA. His teams had appeared in three Rose Bowls, winning once in 1966 with UCLA quarterback and 1968 Rams draft pick Gary Beban under center. Prothro, who signed a five-year, $90,000-plus-per-year deal with LA, said he had received feelers from the Rams as early as the fall of 1970.[50] He had no NFL head coaching experience.

Ironically, Allen's oldest son, George Felix Allen, played quarterback on UCLA's freshman football team in 1970, after starring at Palos Verdes High School. The younger Allen respected and admired Prothro, remembering him as a "character and a really interesting man with a lot of experience and wisdom. He was a big guy who had a presence about him."[51]

But Prothro wasn't in George Allen's league as a pro coach. He lasted two seasons: 8-5-1 in 1971 and 6-7-1 in 1972. The Rams missed the playoffs both seasons, losing six of their last eight games in '72, the year Allen took the Redskins to the Super Bowl. As the saying goes, be careful what you wish for. "Prothro was funnier than Allen," Mack said years later. "I remember we were in first place in the division in 1972 with a game and a half lead and six games to play. We lost five of the last six. It was just terrible. He told the guys in his southern drawl, 'Well, I think if I come back I'll be tougher and nastier,' whatever his definition of that meant. Someone said, 'Don't worry, you're not coming back.' He was a strange guy."[52]

Allen was not without job offers from the moment Reeves fired him. The Eagles, Packers, and Houston Oilers called, as did the Redskins. Jack Kent Cooke, Allen's friend and a 25 percent owner of the Redskins, told the *Los Angeles Times* that Allen would be a primary candidate if interim coach Bill Austin wasn't retained.[53] The Redskins, deflated by the death of Vince Lombardi to colon cancer just before the 1970 season, returned to a sub-.500 level under Austin in 1970 at 6-8. Ara Parseghian and Texas coach Darrell Royal also surfaced in the media as coaching prospects.[54]

"Why not?" Cooke said of selecting Allen. "He may be the best football coach in America. He's as dedicated and sincere a man as I've ever run across."[55]

With influence from Cooke, Redskins president Edward Bennett Williams lured Allen to the nation's capital, incentivizing the deal in a manner similar to how he attracted Lombardi. Hours after firing Austin, Williams made Allen the highest-paid coach in NFL history with a seven-year, $125,000-a-year contract. He also gave Allen the personnel control he wanted as a general manager who could draft, sign, cut, and trade players and negotiate their contracts.

Allen didn't come cheap. But for a franchise accustomed to mediocrity, he proved to be worth the price.

11

Mr. Allen Goes to Washington

Under George Allen's five-year reign as head coach, the Los Angeles Rams went from suffering seven straight sub-.500 seasons to being one of the NFL's most dominant teams. Allen loved the thrill of resurrecting teams with a history of losing. That challenge also stood before him with the Washington Redskins, who had an even longer stretch of futility: four winning seasons and no playoff appearances in the quarter century since the end of World War II. Other than an unspectacular 7-5-2 mark in their only season under Vince Lombardi in 1969, the team's last winning season dated all the way back to 1955.

Allen was enthusiastic to say the least when his number was called to revive the Redskins and turn them around. He was elated to be in a situation with a unified front office—compared with the factions that existed in LA—and to have the additional title of general manager, which would allow him to avoid the conflicts he ran into with Rams owner Dan Reeves. He was also excited to work for his good friend Jack Kent Cooke, who owned 25 percent of the Redskins and became the majority owner in 1974. Allen and Cooke had long discussed their perspectives about players, motivation, and organization, as well as sports, business, and life.[1]

"My father got him the job," said John Kent Cooke, one of Jack's sons. "When Dan Reeves fired George [in 1970], and the Redskins weren't doing well, Dad said there's only one guy to get. That's George Allen."[2]

Allen also liked Washington president and minority stockholder Edward Bennett Williams, who had gained a strong admiration for Allen after first encountering him at a league meeting in Hawaii in '67. Williams ran the team's daily operations because NFL cross-ownership rules barred Cooke from doing so due to his financial interests in the NBA's Lakers and the NHL's Kings. Cooke let Williams vote his shares.

Williams introduced Allen to the media on January 6, 1971, calling him the finest football coach in the business. "We have had a losing syndrome for fifteen seasons with one exception," Williams said. "The fans are impatient. I think we are obliged to get the best possible coach and personnel. I think we have taken a dramatic step in signing George Allen. I am saying unequivocally, unqualifiedly, and unambiguously that this is the last coach I will ever hire."

Williams and Cooke offered Allen a contract that resembled the one they had given to Lombardi. It made Allen the highest-paid coach in NFL history with a seven-year deal that included a $125,000 annual salary and various benefits that brought the deal's value up to $1 million. The only people Allen would report to were Williams and the team's board of directors. The lengthy list of fringe benefits included a $25,000 signing bonus, additional bonuses for reaching the playoffs and the Super Bowl, an expense account, and a personal car and chauffeur.[3]

The team also gave Allen the option to buy 5 percent of the franchise as a key inducement to get him to sign with Washington rather than one of the other teams bidding for his services.[4] The *Washington Post* reported that any stock option was outside of Allen's contract and involved shares other than the fifty the Redskins planned to buy back from Lombardi's estate.[5] Unlike Lombardi, though, Allen never bought into the team. "My father needed help in financing that payment and could not get it," George Felix Allen said in retrospect.[6] The Redskins were worth about $10 million at the time, so Allen had to pay $500,000 to buy a 5 percent share.

Allen chose the Redskins over the Eagles, Packers, Oilers, and a few other teams for other reasons, too. With three kids yet to complete high school, he wanted to bring his family to a marquee area for academics: the Washington metropolitan region. He also liked the countryside and natural beauty of northern Virginia and was interested in acquiring a farm. Janelia Farm near Ashburn, Virginia, caught his eye. But he kept looking.

Williams recommended that the Allen family settle in Potomac, Maryland, a wealthy DC suburb where Lombardi had lived when he was coach and where Williams also lived. Instead, the Allens rented a townhouse in a small luxury community on the other side of the Potomac River in McLean, Virginia, called Merrywood on the Potomac. They later bought a five-acre property in nearby Great Falls, Virginia. Just like she did with the family's home in Palos Verdes Estates in California, Etty Allen visualized the design of the new house and presented the details to an architect and a builder. The new red brick home resembled a French country chateau. "She designed and selected every material, from the mortar to the brick to the fireplace stones," George Felix Allen recalled. "She even hand-painted the tiles that lined the kitchen stove."[7]

The Allens were now part of a franchise with a storied history. The Redskins had amassed a remarkable 76-33-5 record (.697 winning percentage) in the NFL's formative years from 1936 to 1945. That ten-season span featured six NFL championship game appearances and two league titles.

But the post–World War II period was vastly different. Mostly mediocre to dreadful, the Redskins won 39 percent of their games and had twelve different coaches from 1946 until 1970. The 1960 and 1961 seasons epitomized their woes. They finished 1-9-2 in 1960 and 1-12-1 in 1961, the franchise's worst years ever, and went winless in twenty-three straight games. Most opponents with the Redskins on their schedule could pencil in a *W*.

The main culprit behind the team's precipitous fall was Redskins founder and owner George Preston Marshall. His decision-making, micromanaging, and iron-fisted approach, as well as his problematic racial policy, brought the team to its knees. Black players had been prevented from playing in the NFL from 1933 to 1945 due to an unwritten rule that Marshall championed.[8] The West Virginia native insisted on signing only white players. The Redskins were the southernmost NFL team through the '30s, '40s, and '50s, with Marshall sensing that signing a Black player would alienate his large southern fan base. "No n——'s ever going to work for me," he once said.[9] His discriminatory policy handcuffed the franchise. While other teams acquired Black players who emerged as stars, the Redskins descended into a quagmire.

By 1960 the renowned DC-based trial attorney Edward Bennett Williams was eager to invest in a sports team. He focused on the Redskins and eyed the 25 percent block of stock held by Redskins broadcaster Harry Wismer.[10]

But Williams refused to buy into the team unless Marshall abandoned his destructive racial policy. He told the obstinate owner he couldn't be part of an organization that was the "last bastion of discrimination." Marshall also faced pressure from the Kennedy administration and Secretary of the Interior Stewart Udall, who threatened to revoke his lease to play at the brand-new and federally owned DC stadium. Marshall heeded the ultimatum. Late in the '61 season, he arranged a trade for Browns running back Bobby Mitchell and three other Black players. Jack Kent Cooke and New York attorney Bill Shea, who ended up buying Wismer's 25 percent share, took credit for influencing Marshall to meet Udall's demand.[11]

Williams subsequently bought 5 percent of the Redskins for $75,000 in March 1962. More than a year later, a seriously ill Marshall handed control of the team's operations to three Redskins stockholders, including Williams, who took full control in April 1965.

Williams immediately tried to improve the Redskins' standing as one of the NFL's lowest-paid teams. He hired a new head coach after the '65 season, Cleveland Browns great Otto Graham, and compensated him with a top-of-the-line salary: $60,000 a year over five years. But Graham was fired after a 17-22-3 record in his first three seasons.

Graham's successor, Lombardi, taught the Redskins how to win in a 7-5-2 season in '69. Williams worshipped the legendary coach. The two men, both devout Catholics, attended mass together and held strong political leanings as Democrats with close ties to the Kennedy family. The 1968 Republican presidential candidate, Richard Nixon, was so intrigued by Lombardi due to his charisma, leadership qualities, and old-school philosophies that he considered him a possible vice-presidential running mate until finding out that he was a Democrat.[12]

Lombardi's death at age fifty-seven just before the 1970 season hit Williams hard. A pallbearer at his funeral at St. Patrick's Cathedral in New York City on September 6, 1970, Williams lionized the much-revered coach: "He had a covenant with greatness, more than any man I've ever known. He was committed to excellence in everything he attempted. Our country has lost one of its great men. The world of sport has lost its first citizen. The Redskins have lost their leader. I personally have lost a beloved friend."

One of Lombardi's assistants, Bill Austin, coached the Redskins on an interim basis to a 6-8 record in 1970. Cooke and Williams had surreptitiously phoned Allen during the 1970 season, which was a form of tampering with a contract.[13] After the season they went full throttle after Allen, the No. 1 NFL coach without a job. The Packers, Oilers, and Eagles also made bids for the coach with a .742 winning percentage, two playoff appearances, and an NFL Coach of the Year distinction over five seasons in LA.

"[In 1971] I think I would have gone with Green Bay, although I really liked [Eagles owner] Leonard Tose," Allen said years later. "I thought the Redskins had pretty good offensive personnel. They had the worst defense in the league. They couldn't rush the passer, and I felt we could restore the defense. I was general manager and vice president, plus I had an option to buy 5 percent of the team, which I didn't have with any of the others. Then there was my friendship with Jack. I respected Jack."[14]

Green Bay also went all out to get Allen following the 1970 season, Williams said in *The Future Is Now*: "There were five teams in all after him. But I felt we had the inside track because of George's friendship with both Jack and me. Both of us felt, without question, that he was the man to get. I had become convinced the first time I met him that he was going to be 'the' coach of the NFL one day, and I said so to several people. I mean, look at his dedication. He works while other people in sports sleep."[15]

Allen asked one of his Rams assistants, Ted Marchibroda, about the opening in Washington. Marchibroda had been an assistant coach in Washington for five seasons before serving as the offensive backfield coach throughout Allen's stint in LA. "I said, 'George, that's a great job to have,'" Marchibroda said in a 2013 interview. "It's a great city, there's a great tradition there. He ended up taking the Washington job. I don't think there was any question he was happy during all of the years that he was there."[16]

When Lombardi was hired two years earlier, an awestruck DC press went so far as to dub Saint Vince's arrival "the second coming." A strong sense of optimism accompanied Allen's arrival, too. President Nixon called to congratulate him and said 1971 would be a "very good year" for the Redskins.[17] If true, "Washington fans will be beholden to Mr. Dan Reeves, the owner of the Los Angeles Rams," Francis Stann of the *Evening Star* wrote. "Coach Allen gave him five straight years of winning teams—best in the Rams' history—and for his efforts Allen was fired by Reeves twice."[18]

Washington's personnel situation resembled that of the Rams when Allen arrived in LA in '66. Like the Rams, who had possessed a solid crop of talented defensive players led by the Fearsome Foursome, the Redskins featured their own set of stars but mostly on the opposite side of the ball. They included two future Hall of Famers in quarterback Sonny Jurgensen, who had thrown for nearly 30,000 yards in his fourteen-year career, and wide receiver Charley Taylor, the team's all-time reception leader at that point, with 396 catches.[19] Allen also inherited Jerry Smith, one of the most feared receiving tight ends in the '60s; Larry Brown, who rushed for a team record 1,025 yards in 1970, his second season in the NFL; and a solid offensive line led by Len Hauss, one of the best centers of that era. But as had been the case with the Rams, the Redskins needed a coach who could exploit that talent and find complementary pieces.

Under the direction of Jurgensen's golden right arm, the Redskins displayed one of the most explosive passing attacks in NFL history in the mid- to late '60s. The four-way threat of Jurgensen, Taylor, Smith, and flanker Bobby Mitchell was so dangerous that in one season, 1967, Jurgensen finished first in the NFL in passing, and Taylor, Smith, and Mitchell placed first, second, and fourth in receptions, respectively. Fans anxious to see the fireworks display filled up fifty-thousand-seat District of Columbia Stadium (later RFK Stadium), launching a string of home sellouts that lasted for decades.

Jurgensen played his first seven NFL seasons in Philadelphia. But the Eagles, in one of the most lopsided trades in NFL history, sent him and defensive back Jimmy Carr to Washington for quarterback Norm Snead and defensive back Claude Crabb in April 1964. Critics questioned why the Redskins traded the twenty-four-year-old Snead for the twenty-nine-year-old Jurgensen, or young for old. But while Sonny remained one of the game's elite passers, Snead was an above average quarterback at best.

Jurgensen was an artistic passer, and it's been said that nobody threw a prettier, softer football or could throw harder when he needed to. It was hard to drop one of his passes. He played eleven seasons in DC, solidifying his standing as one of the greatest pure passers in NFL history. He entered the Hall of Fame in 1983.

"We were scared to death of Sonny," said Cowboys Hall of Fame defensive tackle Bob Lilly, whose defense was picked apart by Jurgensen in some classic games in the '60s. "You never could trap him; he threw the ball too quickly. He could think real fast. He couldn't run real fast, so we didn't have to worry about that. But he didn't wait around to let the ball go. When we got off the ground to see where the ball was, usually one of the Redskins had it somewhere downfield."

Allen was thrilled to coach Jurgensen. He had faced the redhead twice in LA, including a '67 game when Jurgensen tormented the vaunted Rams defense with 334 yards passing, four touchdowns, and no interceptions.

But as Allen would discover, Jurgensen was no choir boy. He had a reputation as a free spirit and a happy-go-lucky playboy who missed curfews. "The trouble is that I'm red-haired and people notice me wherever I go," the man who drove a Mercedes 239SL sports car with the license plate SJ-9 once said. "If I'm at a party or having dinner out somewhere, somebody recognizes me, and the next thing you know the story is around that I was out having a ball." His protruding belly was also a cause for concern, and he sometimes showed a stubborn, ornery, and detached streak. With the

Redskins at 5-8 in '68, Otto Graham asked him at halftime of the season-ending game if he could play after sitting out the first half with a back injury. He refused to go in, later telling reporters a doctor had advised him not to play unless it was "really necessary."[20]

Despite being on vacation for long stretches prior to Allen's arrival, the Redskins' defense wasn't exactly rudderless. The unit featured excellent players in outside linebacker Chris Hanburger, now a Hall of Famer; safety Brig Owens; and cornerbacks Mike Bass and Pat Fischer. Defensive tackles Bill Brundige and Manny Sistrunk were solid, too. But in 1970, the defense gave up 314 points, the sixth-highest figure in the league. In one game, the Giants overcame a 19-point deficit by scoring three fourth-quarter touchdowns in a 35–33 victory. The 1970 defense was especially porous against the run, yielding 2,068 yards to finish twenty-fifth among the twenty-six teams.

"The Redskins have good offensive material, but they were last in the league in defense," Allen said at the time. "That's an area we'll have to build up. One good thing is that they have all of their draft choices."[21]

Those draft choices weren't around for long. In the days following his hiring, Allen spent hours on the phone at the team's DC headquarters trying to land cagey, battle-tested veterans mostly by trading draft picks, the same formula he had used in Los Angeles, where he had made some fifty trades. He aimed to live up to his promise of delivering a winning team in '71 by acquiring experienced players much less prone to making mistakes than rookies. When asked about the possibility that he was mortgaging the future, Allen declared, "I'm concerned about now. The future is now!"[22]

In his first trade, Allen dealt a reserve linebacker and Washington's fourth- and eighth-round picks in the '71 draft for Saints quarterback Billy Kilmer, a good passer and an exceptional tactician. A ten-year veteran, Kilmer had played for the Saints for four seasons after they entered the NFL as an expansion team in '67, and he threw for nearly 7,500 yards during his stint in New Orleans. The Saints and Rams played each other three times during that period. "I never beat him," Kilmer said of Allen, "but I moved the ball against him. For some reason, he liked something about me."

Although Kilmer often threw wobbly balls, Allen liked the fact that he was a leader who played with a competitive fire. Once a Heisman Trophy finalist at UCLA, where he starred at tailback as a passer, runner, and punter in the single-wing, Kilmer shattered his right leg in a car accident late in the '62 season while playing for the 49ers. The team doctor said his football career was likely over, even hinting at possible amputation. "He didn't make any bones about it," Kilmer said, oblivious to any pun. "He was 90% sure I would never play again." But the feisty Kilmer refused to surrender, undergoing multiple operations and rehabbing his way back. Much of his mobility was sapped when he returned to the 49ers in '64.

Allen in no way hoped to trigger a quarterback controversy between Jurgensen and Kilmer. He just wanted a seasoned backup to Jurgensen, who would be thirty-seven by the start of the '71 season. In Washington, Jurgensen had never enjoyed the support of a dominant defense. But Allen was determined to give him one. He envisioned No. 9 as the man who would reciprocate by giving him what had been elusive: a playoff run and an NFL Championship.

"Sonny was 100% going to be the starter that season," Bruce Allen, a team ball boy at the time, said in hindsight. "We played against him with the Rams. My dad was fascinated by Sonny. But he's a veteran, and Dad makes the Kilmer trade just to make sure if something happens with Sonny, we had a veteran to win."[23]

Of Allen's one hundred–plus trades as an NFL coach, the Kilmer deal would prove to be one of his finest, although Kilmer initially didn't want to play in Washington. "I told George right away that I wanted to be traded, that I didn't want to play behind Sonny Jurgensen," Kilmer remembered. "That was like water over the duck's back. He didn't even listen to me. He said, 'You're going to be part of a winning organization. We're going to win here right away.'"

Then-Redskins equipment manager Tommy McVean remembered a conversation he had with Kilmer soon after the trade: "I said, 'It's great having you here to back up Sonny. Sonny's no spring chicken, and it's good to have a backup quarterback that knows what's going on.' Kilmer grabbed me by the throat and said, 'Let me tell you something, you little son of a bitch. I didn't come here to back up anybody. I came here to play.' I looked at him and said I was just kidding. Anybody that had been around Sonny in football knew that he was a special guy. Johnny Unitas may have thrown the ball a little like Sonny, but nobody could throw the ball perfectly like Sonny did."[24]

A few days later, Allen put his stamp on the organization and signaled that he was calling the shots, not Edward Bennett Williams or Sonny Jurgensen or anyone else. On January 28, 1971—NFL draft day—Allen pulled off one of the biggest trades in league history. He shipped linebacker Marlin McKeever, plus the Redskins' first- and third-round draft choices in 1971, as well as their third, fourth, fifth, sixth, and seventh picks in 1972—seven in all—for six players from his former team: the Rams' starting linebacker corps of Jack Pardee, Myron Pottios, and Maxie Baughan, defensive tackle Diron Talbert, guard John Wilbur, and special teams star Jeff Jordan, plus a fifth-round draft choice. Baughan had already retired and could barely walk because of a foot injury. But Allen, being Allen, still wanted the seven-time All-Pro for his football smarts.

Allen was on the phone until 4:00 a.m. that morning negotiating the trade with Rams coach Tommy Prothro and their assistant general manager, John Sanders.[25] He also wanted another creaky but wily Rams veteran: four-time Pro Bowl strong safety Richie Petitbon. But that would have to wait a few months.

Six established players in return for one. Williams called the trade the "biggest heist" since Allen tried to acquire Charley Taylor in a '68 trade.[26] Critics, however, accused Allen of mortgaging the future by discarding so many draft choices. "I talked so long on the phone trying to get what I wanted that my ear got so sore I had to put the receiver on the other side and then put it back again to the other ear," Allen said in *The Future Is Now*. "I know I stayed up until four in the morning making the god-danged trade. I know that because the guy on the other end of the line said, 'Boy, oh, boy, what the heck time is it there? Boy, it's getting late here.'"[27]

Allen thought the trade upgraded the Redskins' defense at least 25 percent and that it was worth at least two wins that would put the team in playoff contention. "If we improve our defense," Allen told Steve Guback of the *Evening Star* a few days after the trade, "Sonny Jurgensen can pitch us to a division title. You can't win without defense."[28]

President Nixon expressed similar thoughts in a telegram to Allen: "Great trade. I am betting on the Skins for a championship in '71 or '72."

Allen continued remaking the team in his vision, parting ways with about twenty players and dealing draft choices like a deck of cards in return for solid veterans. He focused mostly on upgrading the defense and special teams—two aspects of the game that often put his traditionally unexciting, mistake-free offense in position to score. He acquired three defensive ends: Verlon Biggs, a three-time all-AFL selection with the Jets; teammate Jimmie Jones; and another AFL star, Ron McDole of the Bills. To improve the team's dismal punt return average of less than 2 yards in

1970, he obtained San Diego's Leslie "Speedy" Duncan, who'd tallied more than 5,000 career yards in punt and kickoff returns.

A few months into Allen's new job, his top nemesis in LA, Rams owner Dan Reeves, died at age fifty-eight after suffering from Hodgkin's disease. Prior to his death, Reeves and Allen engaged in one last war of words. In a February 1971 article in the *Los Angeles Times*, a seething Allen unloaded his resentment on the Rams' owner. Bill Libby, who wrote the column, noted that as Allen spoke, he became angrier, and his voice began to shake.

"We did not win the championship, but I am convinced we could have done so if we'd had the support of Mr. Reeves," Allen told Libby. "He is, after all, not only the owner, but the general manager. He refused me a free hand in the operation of the club, which any coach, Vince Lombardi, Paul Brown, any coach must have to succeed. If it isn't given to him, a coach must be strong enough to just take that authority on his own. I did. But I operated in an atmosphere of hatred. Our whole team did. Reeves hated me. Hating me, he hates the team. He sought to split us so we'd come apart. Somehow, I held the pieces together.

"I do not believe that any man in the history of sports has had to overcome as much as I have to accomplish as much as I have."[29]

Reeves responded by accusing Allen of a slew of infractions. They included lying, violating the NFL constitution, not consulting management on the details of some trades, making excessive payments, arranging a player's contract without notifying the Rams' front office, and trying to leave the Rams for another NFL coaching job before the 1970 season.[30] When asked why it took him so long to voice these allegations, Reeves said, "I am doing this now so the Ram players and fans will know the facts. I am hurt by the damage caused the Rams by these false charges. I cannot sit silently while all of us are attacked . . . while our chances of winning are undermined." NFL commissioner Pete Rozelle, who had at one time worked for Reeves, ordered Allen and Reeves to end their public criticism of one another. No fines were assessed.[31]

Allen had also infuriated Reeves by moving the Rams' training site from the San Fernando Valley to the much better but more costly practice facility in Long Beach. Similarly, once he arrived in Washington, Allen wanted a new practice site in a more secluded area. In fact, he made it one of his top priorities.

Allen was aghast at how the Redskins trained. From the end of training camp, they worked out on a field adjacent to RFK Stadium along the Anacostia River. The players carried their uniforms and gear to and from the field. There was security, but onlookers could sometimes watch training sessions. Redskin Brig Owens, then entering his sixth season, said teams paid residents of a nearby apartment complex to let coaches come in so they could spy on practices.[32] Plus, the Redskins sometimes traveled to sandlot and high school practice fields because their regular field was under water, frozen, or otherwise unplayable. When Allen's Rams had played the Redskins in DC in 1969, he told Lombardi it was unfathomable how the Redskins prepared for games in such a bush-league environment. Even the meeting rooms at the team's downtown Washington office were in poor condition.

Offensive tackle Terry Hermeling recalled that in 1970, his rookie season, the Redskins practiced at RFK Stadium after the baseball season ended, a major reason the turf was chewed up by game time. He also said the players had no weightlifting equipment. "I was totally surprised we had no weights because I was into that," Hermeling said. "When I first came to training camp in 1970, I was shocked at how little work the older veterans did to get in shape for football."[33]

Allen thought the Redskins deserved much better. "It was a losing environment," Bruce Allen reasoned. "Dad hated the team's offices being downtown. He thought that was a distraction. He vowed to change it."[34]

Allen envisioned a year-round training facility with practice fields, spacious lockers, and weightlifting and meeting rooms. The facility's location was critical. He wanted the players away from the hustle and bustle of Washington so that nothing could distract them as they prepared for games. In *The Future Is Now*, Allen described the intensity of his search for potential DC-area sites:

"We checked out Episcopal and a lot of other boys' schools. We checked out one of the racetracks. We checked out military installations. We checked [the University of Maryland]. We checked all the golf courses, minor league baseball parks, recreation facilities, schools that dropped football, like Catholic University, junior colleges. There's some reform school in Maryland, and we checked that out. We checked a Jewish boys' school that had good facilitics, but thcy'd be there the same time as football.

"We even had Governor [Marvin] Mandel of Maryland working on it. I met the governor at a banquet, and I told him, 'I got a project for you.'

He assigned somebody especially to look for us. He had a map, and he was going all around the Beltway trying to find us a site in Maryland."[35]

The Redskins' board of directors initially voted down the idea. "They said maybe next year," Allen told the *Washington Post* in 1988. "I said, 'I thought you guys wanted to win. You've had only one winning season in fifteen years, and that was 7-5-2 under Lombardi.' I told them next year was too late, and that's how we came up with the slogan, 'The future is now.'"[36]

Williams didn't offer wholehearted support either. "This isn't criticism of him," Bruce Allen said of Williams. "I think he liked the idea of seeing the players downtown. When he had a chance, he could go over to practice. Going out to practice near Dulles Airport wasn't something convenient for him. But he didn't stop my dad from doing it."[37]

Allen secured a permit for an undeveloped plot in a remote, forested area in Chantilly, Virginia, about thirty miles south of downtown DC, with the Blue Ridge Mountains on the horizon. He especially liked the fact that the seven-acre site in an area called Dulles Industrial Aerospace Park was just five miles from Dulles Airport. He believed his players could practice, shower, and be at the airport in a few minutes for a chartered flight to an away game. He even arranged with hotel executive Bill Marriott Jr. for a new wing to be added at the Dulles Airport Marriott that only Redskins players would use the night before home games.[38]

Allen announced his discovery at a press conference on May 12, 1971, saying the complex would cost about $500,000. "It is a wooded area, almost a forest," he said. "We will have seclusion . . . privacy to have good practices. We have finally got a permanent home." At a groundbreaking ceremony a few weeks later, Virginia governor Linwood Holton dubbed the team the "Virginia Redskins."[39]

But not everyone, namely local political officials, believed Allen could get a new facility going by the start of the season. "It was like, 'You can't build something like that,'" Bruce recalled. "'You can't buy or acquire a permit and do everything you have to do. You can't get that done by this season.' That's the worst thing you could ever tell my dad. He called the governor. He did everything. The construction crew worked around the clock to pop that building up in no time. He wanted the players when they reported to feel the difference between going downtown and the new site. They didn't really have a permanent spot. He wished he had done it bigger before the shovels went in the dirt."[40]

"Redskin Park," which opened a few weeks before the '71 season, was bold and futuristic by NFL standards and outdistanced the training complexes of every other team. "The Redskin players will no longer be a bunch of gypsies," Allen said at the time. "Redskin Park is like everything else we do, have done, and will continue to do. It will help us win. We are not interested in anything that won't help us win."

The new facility met Allen's goal of establishing everything under one roof. In addition to a full-length grass practice field and a full-length artificial turf surface, the site included a two-story, 22,500-square-foot building with every amenity a football team would want: large and small meeting rooms, carpeted locker rooms, training rooms, weight rooms, equipment storage rooms, and film rooms; a whirlpool, sauna, handball courts, and a basketball court; and offices for a doctor and a dentist. Each coach and scout had a private office with his own projector. A seventy-car parking lot sat in front of the building. The structure "contained more treasures than King Tut's tomb," Bill Gildea and Kenneth Turan wrote in *The Future Is Now*.[41] Etty Allen contributed her architectural design skills by making sure, for one, that the stairs were the correct depth.

"George knew he had to have a practice field away from the city so our minds would be directed at football," Billy Kilmer said in hindsight. "There was nothing out there at the time. It was just farm fields and practice fields. The nearest bar was about five miles away. We were isolated. But it was a fine facility."

Steve Guback: "I remember when I saw it for the first time. Kids were riding horses out there. It was nature and the law."

To maintain privacy, Allen closed all practices to the public and surrounded the grounds with a fence. Tall trees, functioning as another sort of security blanket, flanked the fields. Allen, always one with a love for nature and the outdoors, assigned someone to identify the trees, which took on such names as "Pignut Hickory" and "Virginia Pine." Other parts of the perimeter were called "Bears Britches" and "Rattlesnake Grass." He also recruited retired California police officer Ed "Double O" Boynton to patrol the grounds for spies and trespassers. Boynton had held the same role with Allen's Rams.

Kenneth Turan, who reported on the Redskins for the *Washington Post* from 1969 to 1972, remembered that everything felt very "high-powered" under Allen, "like this is the way we're doing things now. In and of itself [Redskin Park] didn't seem particularly high-tech. But just the notion of it and the location seemed like something different."[42]

Allen enjoyed his first true look at his new team in training camp at Dickinson College in Carlisle, Pennsylvania, the Redskins' summer training site since '63. Allen looked forward to training camp, a time of unbridled optimism when he could teach and mold players according to his vision. "My father loved the concentration and intensity of training camp, with players working hard and competing to make the team," George Felix Allen explained. "He liked determining the roster, the team camaraderie, and the minimal distractions, while getting his players in shape for the season."[43]

Speaking in a school auditorium, Allen kicked off camp by telling his players, "Today starts a new era as far as the Washington Redskins are concerned. Men, I think we're going to have a great season, and are we going to surprise some people."[44] Such positive vibes, as well as the bold moves Allen made to upgrade the roster, resonated within the organization. "When he came, you felt a winning atmosphere came with him," Charley Taylor said decades later. "He understood people very well, and he had a way of relating to the game of life. Those two things go hand in hand, and we had a complete team. He surrounded himself with people who love to play the game and preached that you win as a team and lose as a team."

An NFL Films crew followed Allen through camp, acquiring footage that was later packaged into a 2001 documentary titled *Three Cheers for the Redskins*. Allen's idiosyncrasies were front and center.

"I think maybe we'll cut one or two guys this week," he told reporters. "We're going to have an all-veteran team. There would be no rookies playing regularly for us, and that's the way it should be.

"There's a guy," Allen said in pointing to running back Tommy Mason, one of the newly acquired Rams. "He's not too old. What is he, thirty-four? One of the youngest guys on the team."[45]

In one of the practice sessions, return specialist Speedy Duncan accidentally slammed into Allen while running full speed and sent him sprawling. An X-ray showed a fractured rib.[46] The incident resembled times in Los Angeles when the preoccupied coach collided with much-larger players while they were in action.

"He's young and strong, he'll be okay," Duncan said.[47]

Allen injected humor into the accident, comparing it to when he broke his hand while slamming it down in anger after the Rams lost a game early in the 1966 season, his first year with the Rams.[48] "We won eight games that year," he said. "This could be a good omen. A broken rib ought to be worth ten games at least."[49]

Unlike Duncan, safety Brig Owens was an established Redskin. Traded to the team in '66 after spending his rookie season on the Cowboys' taxi squad, he had risen to become a valuable defensive back. He intercepted twenty-three passes from 1966 to 1970 and held the all-time Redskins record with thirty-six when he retired after the '77 season. He wasn't shocked to see all of the new faces, nor was he fazed by Allen's tedious three-hour practices that involved limited hitting but prepared players to react instinctively by game time.

"We had already heard about George," Owens said in retrospect. "Word travels among NFL players. We knew he liked to have long practices. We knew he specialized in defense, and he liked older players. Guys would tell us, 'Make sure you're in good shape and be prepared to stand around a lot. You probably won't be working as hard, but you're going to be doing a lot of standing in longer practices. With Lombardi's practices, we never went more than ninety minutes.

"Both coaches were great players' coaches. But they had different styles of coaching. Lombardi kept you under a lot of pressure. If you could handle his pressure, the games would be easy. If you couldn't handle his pressure, he'd get rid of you. It didn't make any difference whether you were a No. 1 draft choice, a Heisman Trophy winner, or whatever. George Allen was more softspoken but didn't tolerate mistakes."[50]

Someone at camp, reported Dave Brady of the *Washington Post*, observed that Allen refused to "jump down the players' throats when they do something wrong."

"I do not believe in it," Allen said at the time. "It is not my style to be yelling and screaming. I say if you make a mistake, forget it. I just get a player aside and talk to him like I am talking to you now. I do not believe in tearing down. I believe in building up [confidence]. Especially rookies . . . rookies make mistakes. That is why I like veterans."[51]

Another talented defensive back, pint-sized yet ferocious cornerback Pat Fischer, whose nickname was "Mouse," remembered that he and other pre-Allen Redskins were confused by all the new faces. At the time, Fischer, starting his fourth season in Washington after playing his first seven in St. Louis, had a tally of thirty-five interceptions, three Pro Bowl appearances, and two first-team All-Pro seasons.

"We didn't know whether he was going to bring in many more new players," Fischer said of Allen. "But it didn't take too long to make the adjustment, and all those old people that he brought in, actually I knew them all. I'd played against them already for eight or nine years. So we matched up personality-wise and experience-wise. The success George had was based on those people gelling, at least interacting with each other in a very positive way and liking each other."[52]

Allen continued fortifying the team, obtaining Petitbon, who had played his first seven seasons in Chicago and his last two for Allen in LA, and Colts wide receiver Roy Jefferson, a two-time Pro Bowler. For Jefferson, Allen shipped two draft picks and rookie receiver Cotton Speyrer, the Redskins' only choice in the first five rounds in '71. Jefferson, a sure-handed receiver with graceful strides, averaged forty-one catches in his first six years in the league with the Steelers, recording first-team, All-Pro honors in '69. Even so, he was traded to Baltimore, catching forty-four balls in a season that ended with the Colts' win over the Cowboys in Super Bowl V. He later requested a trade because he disliked Colts owner Carroll Rosenbloom, who down the road became a destructive figure in the life of George Allen.

"Carroll Rosenbloom had lied to me about renegotiating my contract," Jefferson said in hindsight. "I was adamant about not wanting to play for him. It was just principle. It had nothing to do with the team. I loved the team, I loved the coach, the players. It was Carroll Rosenbloom. He promised before the [1970] season to renegotiate my contract, then had selective amnesia at the end of the season. It's not like I dreamed that up. I like what George Allen had going on with the Redskins."[53]

Jefferson's arrival signaled that Allen would get his players anything they needed, even when that player was someone whom they playfully thought resembled a "pimp."[54] With ostentatious clothing in vogue, Jefferson wore pink, orange, and lavender jumpsuits, bell-bottom pants, colorful velvet hats, and a bag over his shoulder that looked like a purse. He became the Redskins' fashion king in the "mod" style.

Allen also did not care about the image that Ron McDole projected. He traded third- and fourth-round picks to Buffalo for McDole, who had played eight seasons with the Bills, starring on their '65 AFL championship team as a first-team All-Pro.

McDole, whose weight rose to more than three hundred pounds in Buffalo, looked nothing like your average defensive lineman. That's because of his rotund physique. But he possessed quick feet and incredible instincts when the ball was in the air. He intercepted six passes with the Bills and six more in the coming years with the Redskins, which were amazing numbers for a defensive lineman. In DC he became known as "The Dancing Bear."

"My weight didn't bother me as long as I could get the job done," he said. "With George, I had to weigh in at a certain weight every week, or I got fined. But I never got fined. George didn't really care what you looked like, as long as you got the job done. He said he never did have much luck with guys who looked like Greek Gods. I was in the right place."

Defensive tackle Bill Brundige was shocked the first time he saw McDole: "We're in the locker room, and all he's wearing is a jockstrap. You can hardly see the jockstrap because of all the fat around him. He came from Buffalo in the winter and was just about as damn white as a polar bear. And I'm looking at this guy, whose fat is dripping over the sides of his jockstrap and who's pale as a ghost, and I thought, 'This is the great Ron McDole, this is the guy coming in here? My God. George Allen is out of his mind.'"

In Buffalo, McDole had fallen out of favor with Bills coach John Rauch, who was eager to trade him. Allen "bothered Buffalo to death to get me," McDole remembered. "Bills owner Ralph Wilson said George called [him] at three in the morning. He said he drove [him] nuts so much. Then [Wilson] said we were going down the skids and that we had to build a whole new team. He said [he] just felt with all the good years that I gave him, the least he could do is send me somewhere where I can play."[55]

McDole was one of nineteen newly arrived veterans on Allen's revamped roster, which included ten former Rams, quickly dubbed the "Ramskins." Since his hiring, Allen had swapped seven players and twenty-four draft picks. The roster, which featured nearly a dozen new starters, mostly on defense, was now stocked with "battle-blooded veterans," according to one reporter. Eleven players on the '71 roster were thirty or older, and none of the team's eleven draft picks made the active roster, although three ended up on the taxi squad. Allen's geriatric group, which he called "old geezers" and "graybeards," evoked the words on the iconic inscription on the Statue of Liberty but with a twist: "Give Me Your Old, Your Tired, Your Weak, Your Infirm."

"George Allen brought in a bunch of old, tough, sons of bitches," said offensive tackle George Starke, a '71 eleventh-round Redskins draft pick who was cut and later played in DC from '73 to '84. "He didn't like young guys. He liked old tough guys, the Pat Fischers, Diron Talberts, Myron Pottios, Jack Pardees."

In rebuilding the team, Allen also provided a home for castoffs—veterans who were at odds with their former teams, like Jefferson, McDole, and Verlon Biggs. Biggs, who played for the Jets without a contract in 1970, demanded a higher salary, but the Jets refused to comply. That suited Allen, who traded the Redskins' top draft choice in '72 and a midround pick in '73 for the star defensive end.[56] Allen didn't care if other teams had given up on these players. That fact actually inspired him. He felt they all had something to prove and would play key roles for the Redskins. Of the twenty-two Redskins who started the last game of the '71 season against the 49ers, about two-thirds were drafted by other teams.

"Allen has overhauled the Redskins' scene more than anybody since [Redskins founder] George Marshall marched the whole club down here from Boston in 1937," Steve Guback of the *Evening Star* wrote.

Allen also remade his coaching staff, bringing in four men who had assisted him with the Rams: Ted Marchibroda (offensive coordinator), LaVern "Torgy" Torgeson (defensive coordinator), Marv Levy (special teams), and Boyd Dowler (receivers). He tapped Charley Winner, who had most recently served five years as the Cardinals' head coach, to coach the defensive backs and retained offensive line coach Mike McCormack from the previous Redskins staff. He brought Joe Sullivan, his longtime advisor in LA, to handle the assistant general manager duties.[57]

Allen believed he needed to retain one coach from the prior regime. "When I came to the Redskins, I cleaned house, and the first time I went to the Rams, I cleaned house," he explained. "But I usually tried to keep one person on the staff who I thought was a pretty good coach and knew something and could give me advice and guide me along the way on something that I might make a wrong decision on. So I kept Mike McCormack with the Redskins. Many times, you're better off doing that instead of cleaning house completely."[58]

In finalizing his '71 roster, Allen cut several players, among the last of whom was running back Dave Kopay, who performed well in the preseason with 70 yards rushing.[59] He also had a 3.2-yard-per-carry average, which was second behind Larry Brown's average, and eight catches.[60] Known for his hard-nosed play, the 6-foot, 220-pound Kopay showed versatility on special teams in two seasons with the Redskins—'69 and '70—and captained that unit.

Kopay was also gay, as was his Redskins teammate Jerry Smith. Both refused to publicly reveal their sexuality for fear of retribution, although in 1975 Kopay became the first known pro athlete to do so, following a nine-year NFL career. In his 1977 autobiography, *The David Kopay Story: An Extraordinary Self-Revelation*, Kopay expressed anger and bitterness toward Allen for being cut. He noted that Allen congratulated him after he caught 2 touchdown passes in an exhibition loss to the Colts and told him "he wanted to give me plenty of playing time from there on in to get ready for the regular season." A few weeks later, one of Allen's assistants told him he was being cut. Kopay said his sexual identity did not motivate Allen to release him: "I don't think [me] being cut had anything to do with [me] being homosexual, because I don't think [George] Allen or any of the other coaches knew about it," he wrote in his autobiography.[61]

Washington split its first four exhibition games, with a 17–13 win over Denver lifting them to .500. The Redskins gained only 94 yards against the Broncos, perhaps not surprising given that four Redskins, including starting quarterback Sonny Jurgensen, a veteran of the night life, and running back Larry Brown had missed two bed checks the night before, the last one at midnight. Quarterback Billy Kilmer and fullback Charley Harraway were also suspected of staying out all night. An unenthused Allen showed no favoritism, fining each one $500.[62]

The following week, Allen and the Redskins suffered a monumental setback in a 27–10 loss to the Dolphins. After throwing an interception, Jurgensen tried to make a tackle and ended up fracturing a bone in his left shoulder. He underwent surgery and was said to be out at least six weeks. Although Jurgensen had looked rusty and could no longer throw the long ball like he once did, Allen called the injury a "severe blow."[63]

Bill Kilmer was now the Redskins' man under center. In the last exhibition game, he had completed 15 of 24 passes for 175 yards and 2 touchdowns to rally his troops to a 17–17 tie with the Bengals. The Redskins finished 2-3-1, not the kind of hot preseason George Allen usually experienced with his teams. The more worrisome question, however, was whether the Redskins' future was still "now," as Allen had proclaimed, with Kilmer at quarterback instead of Jurgensen. He tempered his expectation of a nine- or ten-win season to no more than eight victories.[64]

Based on that prediction, the '71 Redskins would end up surprising not only Allen but the rest of the league, too.

12

Waking a Sleeping Giant

By September 1971 the time had arrived for George Allen to set his Redskins reconstruction plan in motion. But his boss, Edward Bennett Williams, was not exactly thrilled with the way Allen had carried out the plan, especially by trading a slew of draft choices and offering hefty salary increases to lure players to DC. Such disdain for Allen's monetary decisions sounded familiar to how Dan Reeves reacted to Allen's spending in LA.

Allen never hesitated to spend if he thought it would satisfy his bottom line: winning. The half-a-million-dollar investment he made with Redskin Park—a figure approved by Williams and the Redskins' board—helped establish his reputation as a free spender. So did the increase in player salaries under Allen by an estimated $300,000 in one season. "We traded for dissatisfied veterans and built almost our whole front defense that way," Williams said in *The Future Is Now*. "That cost money."[1]

Williams's aversion to Allen's rebuilding strategy was palpable at the Redskins' annual Welcome Home Luncheon, which always followed the team's return from training camp. In his state of the team address at the Washington Hilton Hotel before a sellout crowd of 2,100 Redskins fanatics, Williams disguised his discontent with jokes, such as "When coach Allen came to Washington, we agreed we wanted to win at any cost, and that he had an unlimited budget. He has already exceeded it."[2]

The highlight of the '71 schedule was a Monday night game in Los Angeles, where Allen would confront his old team. But that wasn't until December. As the regular season began, the Redskins faced a daunting early stretch with NFC East opponents on the road in the first three weeks: the Cardinals, Giants, and Cowboys. Allen told his players that Cowboys president Tex Schramm, a former colleague of NFL commissioner Pete Rozelle, had encouraged the league to stack the Redskins' schedule in hopes of derailing the Allen era early, according to Bruce Allen. He remembered, however, that "Dad said, 'We're going to show the league and Tex Schramm who the Redskins are.'"[3] The Redskins had also opened the 1969 season, Lombardi's year at the helm, with three straight away games. But at the time, only one opponent, New Orleans, was in the same division.

After three games, the '71 Redskins were 3-0.

In St. Louis, one of the aging Ramskins, safety Richie Petitbon, intercepted a career-high three passes, one of which set up the Redskins' first touchdown and another that sealed a 24–17 win. Washington's tenacious defense forced seven turnovers, including a fumble that linebacker Chris Hanburger returned 16 yards for a touchdown. The win improved Allen's opening-day coaching record to 6-0 and sparked a loud celebration in the locker room led by an animated coach who was showing his boyish enthusiasm. "Let's have three cheers for the Redskins," he told his players, who responded with a "hip, hip, hooray—hip, hip, hooray—hip, hip, hooray!"

"You know what you did, you beat them in their own backyard," Allen told his troops. "You came from behind. And we showed we've got some character. Next week, we get those goddamn Giants."[4]

One of the players in that mass of cheering humanity, Brig Owens, said in retrospect, "He was just getting us going. He was great at motivating players." When running back Calvin Hill played for the Cowboys, Owens noted, "he'd be looking at us across the field, and we'd be jumping up and down like college players. He always wondered what George was telling us and why those grown men were jumping up and down like college kids. So after Calvin came here [in '76], and George got us in a huddle, he said he himself would be jumping up and down. He bought into it."[5]

Against the Cardinals, quarterback Billy Kilmer completed only 6 passes in Allen's ball-control offense. But he connected on 23 of 32 for 309 yards and 2 touchdowns, both to Charley Taylor, in a 30–3 rout of the Giants. One of Kilmer's scoring passes, a 71-yarder, came on a play-action pass, the offense's new secret weapon. The Redskins totaled 427 yards and held the Giants to 156, with the defense's rebuilt front four making life miserable for Giants scrambling quarterback Fran Tarkenton and his backup, Randy Johnson. The win kicked off an incredible streak of eleven straight wins over the Giants under Allen.

Afterward, Allen told the press why it was so meaningful that Kilmer, linebacker Jack Pardee, and defensive end Verlon Biggs received game balls: the greatest moment in sports is "when you've got a victory, and you give away game balls."[6]

While writing about the game, *Evening Star* sportswriter Steve Guback gave birth to a moniker that will forever remain synonymous with the

Allen-era Redskins. Guback was on deadline with his story when a fan called. "He said [to] write something nice about the Redskins and all of those old guys," Guback said decades later. "I instantly thought of a movie called *The Lavender Hill Mob*." The classic 1951 British film is about a group of older, comically inept criminals who try to carry out a plan to steal gold bullion from a bank. "All those things sort of went off in my mind. Right then, I just referred to them as the 'Over the Hill Gang.'"[7]

Was Allen's 2-0 gang for real? They answered that question unequivocally at the dawning of one of the NFL's fiercest rivalries ever: the Washington Redskins and Dallas Cowboys. The two teams had carried on a rivalry in the mid-1960s, engaging in wild battles resembling shootouts at the OK Corral: 34–31 Redskins, 31–30 Cowboys, 34–31 Redskins, 17–14 Cowboys, 27–20 Redskins. In four of those five games, the winning points came in the final two minutes.

Allen intensified the rivalry several-fold. Knowing that Dallas was an elite franchise and the team to beat in the NFC, he whipped his players into a fury by stressing his dislike for the Cowboys, who the previous year had finished 10-4 and lost to Baltimore by 3 points in Super Bowl V.

"He made sure to instill as much hatred in us toward that team as he could," Redskins offensive tackle Terry Hermeling said in looking back. "He never disparaged anyone in the organization. He just disparaged the Cowboy name and the way the organization ran things. He tried to portray them in a way that they got favoritism from the league in the scheduling and whatever else you could think of. We often played the Cowboys in Dallas late in the season when it meant something. He believed the league scheduled it that way thinking it would always come down to a later game in who would win the division and be in the playoffs."[8] In five of Allen's seven years in DC, the Redskins played the Cowboys on the road in the final weeks of the season.

In the days prior to the game, Washington signed waived Cowboys quarterback Steve Goepel, most likely to pump him for information. "I did talk to him about what the Cowboys were trying to do this year," Redskins director of player personnel Tim Temerario told the *Washington Post*. "All teams do that. But we did not talk about anything specific."[9] Tom Landry, for his part, denied asking Pat Richter, a Redskins tight end from 1963 to 1970 who was with the Cowboys in the '71 preseason, anything about Washington.[10]

Norm Miller of the *New York Daily News* shed light on the Allen-Goepel encounter by paraphrasing safety and receiver Richmond Flowers, who played for the Cowboys at the time. "The kid got to Washington but never left the airport," Miller wrote. "Seems the Skins had a game coming up against the Cowboys, and Allen wanted info. He pumped the kid QB, then cut him in the airport lobby."[11]

The Cowboys, winners of six straight games against the Redskins, were 10-point favorites. They had won fifteen of their last sixteen games, with Super Bowl V marking their only loss. Plus, their offense had racked up a total of 91 points in wins over their first two '71 opponents, the Bills and Eagles.

Before seventy thousand fans in the rain-soaked Cotton Bowl, the Redskins sprinted to a 14–0 first-half lead on fullback Charley Harraway's 57-yard gallop and Bill Kilmer's 50-yard play-action pass to Roy Jefferson. They maintained the lead with a defense that controlled the Cowboys' high-powered offense and held the NFC's top rushing team to 82 yards in a 20–16 win.

Washington's locker room was a sea of jubilation led by the gleeful Allen. "Men, I know this is an overworked word, but it was a great, great victory, a complete team victory," he said. "Nobody gave us a chance, but we thought we could win if we played our game and didn't make mistakes."

The excitement level remained steady on the trip home, although the plane didn't. "That plane was rocking the whole way," remembered Bruce Allen, who was on the flight. "I don't think there was any food on it. It was probably just beer. The enthusiasm was incredible. At one point, the pilot announced, 'You have a great welcoming coming back. Your fans are waiting for you. We'll have more information when we get closer.' No one really understood. Some guys were thinking, 'Does that mean my wife's at the airport, and we're not going out as a team?' When he parked the plane, and you saw it, it was really stunning."[12]

Some ten thousand frenzied fans starving for a winner had flocked to Dulles Airport to greet the only undefeated and untied team in the NFL. It was like the waking of a sleeping giant. The Redskins' band played the team's fight song, "Hail to the Redskins," with signs of appreciation everywhere. As people tried to reach the celebration, traffic backed up more than ten miles to the Capital Beltway. Bruce Allen thought the scene was "breathtaking." The pilot, he explained, parked the plane away from its normal spot because the fans had come onto part of the tarmac. He couldn't imagine a similar scene today because of the security measures in place to guard against a terrorist attack.[13]

"The people were jam-packed," Kilmer remembered. "I knew then that we'd unlocked something here that's unbelievable and that I'd never seen being in the league for ten years. We got the fans enthused and really brought them alive. It just kept snowballing."[14]

After only three games, Allen was the talk of the town. In the local media, an *Evening Star* headline asked, "What Hath George Allen Wrought?"[15] The win over Dallas, *Washington Post* sports columnist Shirley Povich wrote, "elevates George Allen to an estate just short of canonization in coaching ranks for his feat of turning those career losers, the Redskins, around in such rapid fashion."[16]

While Allen was being exalted, the word "Redskins" became an in thing, according to Steve Gilmartin, the team's radio play-by-play voice from '64 to '73. "The big push was 1971," he said. "That was the year people started to believe, 'Yeah, we can win.' People were ranking the Redskins, church, and family one-two-three in importance, not necessarily in that order."[17]

Although Lombardi's Redskins went 7-5-2 in 1969, Gilmartin thought Allen's Redskins carried a different swagger: "For the first time, they firmly believed they could win. When Vince was there for that one season, some of the veterans bought into it. But they didn't feel as though they were going to be contenders. They figured they were going to be respectable. When they looked at the talent that the Dallas Cowboys had and knew they'd have to play them twice in one season, they realistically said, 'We're not going to beat the Cowboys, the Cowboys are going to beat us.' In 1971 they became a very confident football team."

By acquiring a procession of new players in '71 who made an immediate impact, Allen did what Lombardi thought wasn't possible in 1969. "I remember Lombardi once told me, 'You can't do that today,'" Gilmartin said. "Of course, Allen came in two years later and did exactly that. He picked up all these guys. They may have had some mileage on them, but they could still play. They say, 'He gave away the store.' But he didn't really. He still had a fairly good foundation there with some draft choices. Allen didn't like young players; he didn't trust them."

At the time, the Redskins were the only pro sports team in the nation's capital. The Washington Senators, the city's long-floundering baseball club, moved to Arlington, Texas, just as Allen began his first season in

DC. That team's only World Series victory came in 1924, and they had last appeared in the Fall Classic in 1933. A basketball team, the Washington Capitals of the American Basketball Association, had moved to southern Virginia in 1970. The NBA's Baltimore Bullets relocated to the DC suburbs in 1973 and remained a championship-caliber squad known as the Capital Bullets and then the Washington Bullets. An NHL expansion team, the Washington Capitals, began playing in 1974 but was horrendous on the ice.

In 1971 the only other local sports team that sparked curiosity was the University of Maryland men's basketball squad. Maryland's colorful coach, Charles G. "Lefty" Driesell, boasted in 1969 that his team had the "potential to be the UCLA of the East," a reference to the basketball dynasty of the UCLA Bruins.[18] Under Driesell, Maryland never won a national championship but developed into one of the country's most talented teams.

DC mayor Walter Washington recognized the Redskins' unique role in the nation's capital. "You're the only thing we have left," he said during a visit to Redskin Park on October 5, 1971, two days after the win over Dallas and five days before the home opener against the Houston Oilers. "It's a great thing for the city. It gets everyone fired up, gives them something to talk about and gets their minds off everything else."[19]

Allen often quoted the mayor on how much the team meant to DC. "My father really enjoyed Walter Washington," George Felix Allen said. "He was an enthusiastic leader and friend, and my father loved saying how Mayor Washington said the Redskins winning united everyone in the city."[20]

Since training camp, Allen had spoken about how special it would be for his players to get a pregame standing ovation when they first took the field. He wanted the fans, as Bruce Allen put it, to "appreciate and love their team." The welcome reception at Dulles was "one of the early messages about how we're going to be respected, not only in the NFL but here in DC," Bruce said. "'You'll see guys. You'll always get a standing ovation the same way the president gets a standing ovation when he walks into a room.' The enormous turnout at Dulles solidified his message to the team."[21]

Prior to the Oilers game, a record RFK Stadium crowd of 53,041 stood and applauded for five minutes as Redskins players were introduced one by one. Banners hung all around the stadium, including "Hail to the Over the Hill Gang" and "Like a Fine Wine, the Redskins Have Come of Age."

The Redskins disposed of the pesky Oilers, 22–13, as one of Allen's veteran acquisitions, defensive end Ron McDole, intercepted a pass and returned it 18 yards for Washington's only touchdown. The next week, one of the oldest Ramskins, Jack Pardee, intercepted three passes and forced a fumble in a 20–0 shutout of the Cardinals at RFK. The crowd responded by chanting "Par-DEE, Par-DEE, Par-DEE."

"I played in Los Angeles for more than a decade and loved it out there, but the fans could care less about the Rams," Pardee said in a 2013 interview. "There'd be 100,000 people in the Los Angeles Coliseum, and you couldn't hear a sound. But at RFK Stadium, the fans were going crazy. People loved the Redskins."

At the time, Pardee was thinking of someday coaching. Considered an extension of Allen on the field, he soaked up Allen's wealth of knowledge and, ironically, succeeded him as Redskins coach in 1978. "George was a good teacher," he said. "We'd go over scouting reports and did film work that I'd never been involved with before. We spent extra time in the classroom to cut down on the time on the field. I wanted to learn more about what he was doing. I really wanted to get [that] experience from who I considered the best."[22]

The Redskins' fifth win coincided with a Dallas loss, leaving Washington two games ahead of the Cowboys in the NFC East. The 1971 Redskins were the first team in franchise history to open a season with five wins since the 1940 Redskins, who had crafted a 7-0 mark. Allen, the talk of the NFL, was pictured on the cover of *Newsweek* magazine, which ran an article titled "Pro Football's Red-Hot Redskins." Another article, "Ice Cream Man Cometh: George Allen, Coach of the Redskins," a reference to his proclivity for ice cream, appeared in *Sports Illustrated*.

Redskins mania was everywhere. The nation's capital, so accustomed to political divisiveness, was captivated by Allen's Redskins, with Republicans and Democrats rooting for the once-dreadful franchise in an unusual show of bipartisanship. Home sellouts remained intact at RFK Stadium, which became the place to be on a Sunday afternoon—especially for U.S. lawmakers working right up the street on Capitol Hill, members of Nixon's Cabinet, and other politicians. Duke Zeibert's restaurant, a regular hangout for well-known and powerful figures, including Redskins owners Jack Kent Cooke and Edward Bennett Williams, became the go-to destination for Allen and his family after a victory.

"All of these politicians are interested in getting on the bandwagon and being seen," Allen told Williams in a phone call midway through the season. "[Maine senator Edmund] Muskie's been coming to every game now. He hasn't gone in the past. They all want tickets. The governor of Virginia brought in eight last week, and the Kennedys are coming and [Montana senator] Mike Mansfield is coming and [so is Secretary of State Henry] Kissinger."[23]

In the opinion of *Los Angeles Times* Washington bureau chief Robert J. Donovan, "George Allen's conquest of the capital is more complete than that of the British in 1812. Come to think of it, they only burned the White House, whereas he sat in formal splendor Tuesday night at President Nixon's state dinner for the prime minister of Australia. Practically unknown in Washington a year ago, Allen has become the envy of resident statesmen."[24]

But just like that, the 5-0 Redskins experienced two simultaneous setbacks, a 27–20 loss to the Chiefs in Kansas City and the loss of Charley Taylor, the team's leading receiver. A fractured ankle sidelined Taylor for the season, marking a major setback.

Allen quickly sought a replacement for one of the most dangerous receivers in the league. "I just stayed on the phone," he told the press. "I contacted all twelve clubs in our conference. Green Bay had no receivers, the Dutchman [Falcons coach Norm Van Brocklin] had no receivers, the Saints had no receivers." Allen claimed the Cowboys' Richmond Flowers off waivers but quickly traded him and two midrange draft picks to the Giants for Clifton McNeil, a big-play threat who could stretch the field. McNeil led the league with seventy-one catches playing in San Francisco in '68 and tallied a team-high fifty with the Giants in '70.

Allen's fast acquisition of McNeil resembled how he had worked his magic to obtain one of the best defensive tackles in the game, Roger Brown, the day after Rosey Grier ruptured his Achilles tendon on the eve of the '67 season. In finding McNeil, Allen defied critics who thought he was out of quality draft picks. "I'll tell you, Allen's amazing," Kilmer told reporters. "The key to his success is that he's on top of everything. Maybe nobody knew McNeil would be available, but he somehow did."[25]

The Redskins rebounded with a 24–14 win over the Saints to improve to 6-1. But without Taylor and tight end Jerry Smith, who was sidelined with a groin injury, the offense ground to a halt, scoring a single touchdown over fourteen quarters. In a 7–7 tie with the Eagles, Allen's newest acquisition, McNeil, caught a 32-yard scoring pass from Kilmer to tie the game at 7–7 in the fourth quarter. The Redskins still had the NFC's best record at 6-1-1.

But in a 16–15 loss to Chicago, perennial All-Pro Bears middle linebacker Dick Butkus, an Allen draft pick in '65, dove into the end zone to catch the winning point on a botched extra point attempt. Then came a 13–0 drubbing at the hands of the Cowboys at RFK, dropping the Redskins to 6-3-1 and a half game behind Dallas in the division.

With the Redskins posting only one win since their 5-0 start, Allen's good friend and the team's No. 1 fan, Richard Nixon, sensed their need for resuscitation. The White House called Allen and asked if the president could visit Redskin Park to give the players a pep talk.[26] The idea seemed logical. The Redskins would hear from the most astute football mind to ever reside at 1600 Pennsylvania Avenue.

Allen knew of Nixon's keen interest in football from the day they first met at an NCAA function in the early 1950s. Living in DC for most of that decade as the U.S. vice president, Nixon was no stranger to the Redskins. He presented star defensive end Gene Brito the keys to a new car at DC's Griffith Stadium in 1958. The following season, he was present for one of the greatest upsets in team history, a 27–24 win over the defending-champion Colts, who repeated as NFL champions in '59. He bolted to the locker room afterward to congratulate the coaches and players. "I have never seen a game to surpass this one," he told the Associated Press.

The following year, Nixon's political career hit a wall. In 1960 he lost in one of the closest presidential elections in U.S. history to Massachusetts senator John F. Kennedy. Two years later, he suffered another crushing defeat in his home state in the California gubernatorial election.

The consensus was that Nixon was done. He even signaled the end in a press conference in Los Angeles on November 7, 1962. With his resentment for the media long building for what he considered liberal bias in media coverage of him and his campaigns, he lashed out at the press with some one hundred reporters looking on. "You will now write it, you will interpret it, that's your right," he said with bitterness. "But as I leave you, I want you to know, just think how much you're going to be missing. You don't have Nixon to kick around anymore because, gentlemen, this is my last press conference."

That turned out not to be true, for Nixon crafted one of the most remarkable comebacks in U.S. political history. Displaying grit and determination—characteristics that were not lost on George Allen—he bucked those who thought he was washed up. He went on to defeat Democrat Hubert Humphrey and third-party candidate George Wallace in the '68 presidential election.

In a speech at the Pro Football Hall of Fame in 1971, Nixon credited his football coach at Whittier College, Wallace "Chief" Newman, with instilling in him the wisdom that a person who experiences a setback must be resilient and fight on.

"He didn't feel sorry for you when you got knocked down," Nixon said. "And he had a different definition of being a good loser. He said, 'You know what a good loser is? It's somebody who hates to lose and who gets up and comes back and fights again.' I think perhaps as I look back at those who shaped my own life, and there are a great deal of similarities between the game of football and the game of politics, that I learned a great deal from the football coach who not only taught his players how to win but who also taught them that when you lose, you don't quit. That when you lose, you fight harder the next time."[27]

Allen loved the bulldog spirit in Nixon. "One of the things I admire in the president is not that he came back and won but came back after being beaten twice," Allen said in *The Future Is Now*. "The determination to come back shows he is a competitor, and that is why he likes football. He is a very dedicated man. I really appreciate dedication. That's really what I look for most in my football players. We have players with less ability but more dedication, and dedication often makes the difference."[28]

Nixon entered the White House after the election of 1968, a year of national upheaval with racially charged riots in major cities and wide divisions over the raging Vietnam War. Nixon and Allen, also a Republican, corresponded mostly about football matters but at times delved into topics of national interest, such as the Vietnam War. In letters to Nixon, Allen supported the president's 1970 decision to commit U.S. troops, in combination with South Vietnamese units, to an intervention in Cambodia to fight North Vietnamese forces, as well as Nixon's escalation of bombing in North Vietnam in May 1972.[29] Many Democratic lawmakers on Capitol Hill, including the party's two leading presidential candidates, Senators George McGovern and Hubert Humphrey, denounced that intensification of the war effort.[30]

Shortly after Allen told Nixon that he liked his decision to authorize the escalation and "to hell with the second guessers," Nixon wrote back saying how he deeply appreciated Allen's "support for the measures I announced on May 8 to bring the fighting in Vietnam to an end."[31]

When Allen became the Redskins' coach in January 1971, his friendship with Nixon entered a new chapter. Only five years apart in age, the two maintained contact via phone calls and letters, with the president offering Allen congratulations, encouragement, and words of wisdom. Case in point: after the Redskins fell to Kansas City following a 5-0 start, Nixon sent Allen a handwritten note:

> Dear George,
>
> I saw the game on TV yesterday. A truly great team must prove that it can be great in defeat, as well as in victory. The Redskins proved they were a great team yesterday.[32]

Allen framed the letter, which Nixon signed "RMN," and hung it in his office at Redskin Park and later in his home in Palos Verdes Estates, California.[33]

In 1971 Nixon also began inviting Allen to the White House, although the coach mostly declined Nixon's offers to attend White House events, including a dinner in his honor. "Etty used to get mad at me because we turned down so many opportunities," Allen once said.[34] He felt that going to the White House would impede his efforts to give the same 110 percent commitment to football that he demanded from his players.

"They were very close friends," George Felix Allen said of his father and Nixon. "My father loved presidents and generals and other people who'd committed their lives to helping society. In his view, having a winning football team made for a better society. It made his players better citizens."[35]

With Allen in DC, Nixon caught broadcasts of as many Redskins games as he could. He arranged for an open-phone radio hookup to hear the play-by-play of Washington's 20–16 win over the Cowboys in 1971 at his retreat in Key Biscayne, Florida.[36] He also circumvented the NFL's blackout rule that prevented the broadcast of home games within a seventy-five-mile radius of the host city. From his retreat in Camp David, Maryland, about seventy-five miles north of DC, he watched two '71 games on twin TVs—the Redskins' 13–0 loss to the Cowboys on a Baltimore station and the Colts' 17–14 loss to the host Dolphins on another channel.[37]

Nixon hated the blackout rule, especially because people in the Washington area, including himself, couldn't watch Redskins home games on TV just as they were becoming great under Allen. In October 1972 his administration announced support for legislation that would prevent pro sports leagues from imposing blackouts of home games.[38] Rozelle rejected the idea, but Congress passed compromise legislation that prohibited the NFL from blocking local telecasts of home games sold out seventy-two hours in advance.[39] Nixon signed the bill into law just before the start of the '73 season. The policy exists to this day.

With the '71 Redskins in need of inspiration, Allen agreed to Nixon's request to address his 6-3-1 squad. On a blustery day, November 23, 1971, the gates swung open at Redskin Park, as the president, his Secret Service entourage, the White House press corps, and other reporters advanced like an ocean wave onto the main practice field, where the players were doing calisthenics. Allen suspended practice and waved his players over to see their surprise guest.

"We didn't know what was happening," Roy Jefferson said in an interview decades later. "I can see him right now coming into the park over by the gate. He didn't come through the office. At least forty to fifty people came through that gate."[40]

Terry Hermeling was also surprised: "They pulled up in a limo, with Secret Service agents coming in. You could see them surrounding the field. And you kind of go, 'What's going on?' All of a sudden, here comes the president of the United States."[41]

For ninety minutes, Nixon greeted the players and joked, shook hands, and posed for pictures: "Bill Kilmer, UCLA. My wife used to watch you." The president, a graduate of Duke University law school, teased another Duke graduate, Sonny Jurgensen: "Old red, from Duke, you're a little after my time but just a little."[42] Nixon told the injury-riddled squad that it possessed the spirit needed in sports and politics to "come back and win" after a setback, a scenario the president was all too familiar with. He also told the players to ignore the booing that rained down on them at RFK during the loss to Dallas. "I've heard a few boos myself in my lifetime," he said. "This whole city is proud of you."[43] The president predicted that the Redskins would win three of their last four games "if not all four" to earn a playoff spot.[44]

Allen called Nixon's visit "the lift we needed" for the upcoming game against the surging Eagles in Philadelphia. "It was one of the greatest honors I've ever had," Allen told reporters. "With all the problems he has, it is remarkable he could take time out to visit us."[45]

"I wasn't a Nixon fan, nor did I vote for him," said Jefferson, who campaigned for the '72 Democratic presidential nominee, George McGovern.[46]

"Not a lot of the guys voted for him. But everybody was excited that the president came to our facility. Anybody who didn't like him didn't show that they didn't like him."[47]

Not exactly. Redskins guard Ray Schoenke, a staunch Democrat who served as national chair of the group Athletes for George McGovern, was unamused by Nixon's visit. He shared that sentiment with Allen and asked him to arrange for McGovern to also visit Redskin Park. The coach agreed, but the visit never materialized.[48]

"I was a social activist as a player," Schoenke said in a 2014 interview. "I was very involved in politics. I was very much against the Vietnam War in the 1960s, and I wasn't afraid to say that. I wasn't against wars; I was just against that war. When Nixon came out to practice, I criticized him, and my coaches just went crazy. They said, 'How dare you? He's the president of the United States. You've got to have more respect.' I said, 'Well, there's a war going on.' I should have put another hat on, and I didn't. Allen was just furious at me, but I wasn't afraid to say something.

"Out of that whole episode, I told Allen I'd never play again unless he gave me a guaranteed contract. He gave that to me, and I had that every year in the final years of my career. Because he stepped up for me, I stepped up for him, and out of that I had one of the most cherished relationships I ever had with a coach. We talked endlessly about team practice, spirit, game plans, who should lead, and who should talk in the locker room. It was really neat."[49]

Toward the end of his visit, Nixon called a play that had produced nice yardage for the Redskins in 1971: a screen pass to Charley Harraway. After conferring with Nixon, Kilmer tossed the ball to Harraway, who ran unimpeded into the end zone.[50] Interestingly, Nixon also suggested a reverse to Jefferson, a play the Redskins planned to include in their playbook.

Was that a coincidence? Then-Redskins special teams coach Marv Levy explained that the reverse wasn't Nixon's original idea, noting that Allen fed it to him before his Redskin Park visit to make him seem football savvy. "Before Nixon came, Allen told him, 'Why don't you suggest that we install this tricky reverse to Jefferson?'" Levy remembered. "So Nixon told the players, 'You know what you guys ought to do? You should put in this reverse play to Roy Jefferson here.' He pointed right at him. George said, 'Yeah. That's a good idea.' The only two people who knew about that play to my knowledge were George and the president. So we put it in the next day."[51]

The Redskins made good on Nixon's prediction, winning three of their last four games. First came two straight victories over NFC East opponents: 20–13 over the Eagles in Philly and 23–7 over the Giants at RFK. Allen started Jurgensen against the Eagles, but he suffered another shoulder injury. Kilmer stepped in and threw a 28-yard score to Jefferson, the offense's first touchdown in three games.

Kilmer started against the Giants, against whom the oft-injured Larry Brown returned to his old form, gaining 129 yards on twenty-five carries. Washington's defense intercepted five passes.

The win set the stage for one of the most monumental and pressure-packed games of Allen's coaching career. With the best second-place record in the NFC, the 8-3-1 Redskins would clinch a wild card berth with a win over the 7-4-1 Rams in Los Angeles. A Rams win would put them in the playoffs; a loss would cripple their playoff chances.

Another huge subplot was Allen's return to Los Angeles. Still angry from two firings and the way Rams owner Dan Reeves had treated him, Allen wanted nothing more than to humiliate his former team. The game was also a homecoming for twelve former Rams turned Redskins who talked incessantly about showing up the team that had discarded them. Plus, five Redskins assistant coaches had once coached in LA.

Allen described the game, which was appropriately dubbed the "George Allen Bowl," as another civil war. "I guess there's never been a time in the NFL when so many good football players were friends one year and enemies the next," he told reporters.[52] In a war of words, Allen also said his defense would shut down the Rams' "gadget" offense, while Redskins defensive tackle Diron Talbert, one of the Ramskins, declared that the Rams would make enough mistakes for Washington to win. Rams defensive end Deacon Jones, one of the Fearsome Foursome from Allen's days in LA, said his Rams would "blow" the Redskins off the field.

Then there was Roman Gabriel, Allen's starting quarterback through his five-year stint in LA. Soon after the new NFL schedule showed in May 1971 that Allen would be returning to Los Angeles to play the Rams in December, Gabriel warned that Allen "is liable to leave the [Los Angeles] coliseum with a football in his mouth." In comments in the *Los Angeles Herald Examiner*, Gabriel accused Allen of failing to follow through on an offer to bring him to Washington at the same time he was acquiring the Ramskins. "I learned from someone else that he said I had too many problems," Gabriel said at the time. "He didn't want to take a chance with me."[53] Gabriel toned down his remarks in the days preceding the game, saying he respected Allen as a coach.[54]

Adding to the drama, the clash would be televised under the lights on ABC's new phenomenon called Monday Night Football. Then in its second season, Monday Night Football marked the first prime-time pro sports telecast. Critics, including affiliates and potential advertisers, argued that pro football could not compete with other prime-time shows. But ABC Sports president Roone Arledge envisioned the series as a form of mass entertainment that would appeal to not only diehard football fans but also casual onlookers. To him, the show mattered more than the game.

Arledge changed the way the NFL was viewed on television. He introduced the three-person broadcast booth with the loquacious, controversial, and urbane Howard Cosell, a former lawyer; jokester and former Cowboys quarterback Don Meredith; and folksy play-by-play man Keith Jackson. In 1971 Arledge replaced Jackson with Frank Gifford, thinking he would contrast perfectly with the often-combative Cosell. The banter between the New Yorker Cosell and the country-boy Meredith also made the broadcasts entertaining.

The new and bold broadcast became must-see TV, with Allen's Redskins leading the way in appearances. During his seven seasons in DC from '71 to '77, the team played in twelve Monday night games, the most of any team during that period, winning ten times.

"George would press the fact that the nation is watching us," Brig Owens said of Monday night games. "He thought everyone around the country wants to see what the Redskins are going to do. So he made it really extra special."

The atmosphere was electric on a chilly night in Los Angeles on December 13, 1971. "I remember before playing that game, you could cut the tension in the locker room with a knife," said Kilmer, who had spent a night in jail a few days prior after an altercation at a DC-area restaurant resulted in a charge of public drunkenness. A sellout crowd of 80,402 waited to witness the clash at the Los Angeles Coliseum, and a record Monday night audience of 66 million watched on TV. The Rams were favored by a touchdown.[55] "We were really charged up for the game," Talbert recalled. "You can imagine, all of us being let go, traded. The Redskins needed that win to make it all work for them."

Among those in the coliseum that night were Etty Allen and the kids: George, Greg, Bruce, and Jennifer. George and Bruce watched from the sideline. "We all came back for that game," George said. "It was a big game, and whoever won would make the playoffs. It was really something. The Redskins had some fans there. I think they liked my father. The place was packed. It was Monday Night Football, which was a really, really big deal in those days. Plus, it was such a pivotal, consequential game."[56]

Howard Cosell interviewed Allen before the game.

Cosell: "George, this one has been billed as a civil war. What about that characterization from your point of view?"

Allen: "Well, Howard, it's a big game for the Redskins because a win would put us in the playoffs. At the start of the season, nobody gave us a chance, especially after we lost Sonny Jurgensen."

Cosell: "Well, that's a short way of ducking the question. The truth is you're coming back to Los Angeles, and this game is desperately important for you."

Allen: "Well, it's a big game. It's perhaps the biggest game of my coaching career. We're not as strong as the Rams . . . we have a few injuries. We have some players who'll be playing about 70 percent."[57]

The game began not to Allen's liking. On the Redskins' first possession, Rams safety Kermit Alexander intercepted Kilmer's pass over the middle and raced 82 yards into the end zone.

The Redskins retaliated. Jefferson caught a slightly underthrown bomb from Kilmer on the inside of two defenders and ran into the end zone to finish a 70-yard scoring play that tied the game at 7–7. The play energized everyone on the Redskins' sidelines, where players were in a vocal, trash-talking mood. They took aim at Rams wide receiver Lance Rentzel, yelling "no pants Lance" when he lined up close to them.[58] In April 1971 Rentzel, then with the Cowboys, had pleaded guilty to exposing himself to a ten-year-old girl and received probation.[59] The Cowboys traded him to the Rams.

After an exchange of field goals, the Redskins broke the game open. Kilmer threw a 32-yard scoring pass to Clifton McNeil for a 17–10 Redskins lead two minutes before halftime. The Rams fumbled the ensuing kickoff, and Redskin Ted Vactor recovered the ball on the 8. A penalty moved it to the 2. But Brown failed to punch it through on three straight runs. Kilmer called time to confer with the coaches on the sideline.

"My policy is usually to go for three points," the conservative-minded Allen said to Kilmer. "How close are we to a touchdown?"

Kilmer: "An inch."

Allen: "We're going to go for the goddamn fourth-down play."

Offensive line coach Mike McCormack told Kilmer to call twenty-nine M-Boss, an off-tackle run by Larry Brown, and to "tell Charley [Harraway] he's got to block Kermit [Alexander]."

Brown, running to the right, cut outside of Harraway's crushing block on Alexander and slipped untouched into the end zone, putting the Redskins up at halftime, 24–10.

"Nice block, Charley baby," Allen told a grinning Harraway as he reached the sideline. "You made it. You made it."[60]

The Redskins padded the lead early in the second half. Cornerback Mike Bass picked off a pass in Rams territory. Kilmer completed a 37-yard throw to McNeil, then fired a 5-yard scoring pass to Jefferson for a 31–10 cushion, signaling a possible rout. The Rams closed the gap to 7 late in the game and had one last chance with thirty-five seconds left. But Speedy Duncan intercepted Gabriel's pass and returned it 46 yards for a touchdown to seal the 38–24 win. That play climaxed a miserable night for Gabriel, who fell short of his goal of embarrassing Allen. He completed 17 of 44 passes for 219 yards, with a touchdown and 2 interceptions.

Washington's locker room was euphoric, as the coaches and players rejoiced in clinching a wild card spot, the Redskins' first postseason appearance since 1945. Allen received a game ball, as did Kilmer (14 of 19, 246 yards, 3 touchdowns passes, 1 interception), Jefferson (8 catches, 137 yards, 2 touchdown catches), Duncan, and Tom Skinner, the team chaplain. The ecstatic Allen led his customary "hip-hip-hooray" cheer after a Redskins win and told his players, "This is a great, great victory. It's the best win of our lives. Men, let's just go on from here." They responded with a tribute that their coach knew all too well:

Hooray for George,
Hooray at last,
Hooray for George,
He's a horse's ass.[61]

"It was 15 minutes of crazy bedlam in the locker room, and George was leading it all, jumping up and down," Jefferson remembered. "He looked like a toy that you'd just wound up, jumping and clapping. It was truly exciting." In Talbert's opinion, "it was a victory we would not be denied. We whipped them from top to bottom the whole game."[62]

Jack Kent Cooke maneuvered through the wild celebration to congratulate his victorious coach. Allen also took a congratulatory call from President Nixon, who was across the globe meeting with French president Georges Pompidou in the Azores, an archipelago in the mid-Atlantic.[63] Allen told reporters this was a bigger win for him than when his Bears beat the Giants in the '63 NFL championship game.[64]

"He was in heaven," George Felix Allen said of his father after the Redskins beat the Rams. "He had a lot of victories with the Bears, obviously the championship game in '63. He had some great wins with the Rams, whether it was blocking Donny Anderson's punt at the end of the game [in 1967] to beat the Packers or the games against the Colts with Johnny Unitas. With the Redskins, he had a lot of them. But this was everything from vindication to revenge to exhilaration. You've beaten your former team that fired you twice.

"For my father, this is what made it all the more sweet: he traded for so many Ram players. The coaching staff, too. A lot of coaches who were with the Rams were now with the Redskins. So it wasn't just my father versus Tommy Prothro, who was really not the issue in the game. It was more the Rams organization and the players. And the players who were on the Redskins, former Rams, were playing against their former teammates. All of that was added on: motivation, drama, intensity, an 'I'll show you' type of revenge."[65]

With no chance to win the NFC East, the Redskins fell 20–13 to playoff-bound Cleveland in the season finale to finish 9-4-1. It was the most Redskins victories since the 1942 season, when they posted a 10-1 mark before capturing the NFL Championship. That same day, the Rams beat Pittsburgh to finish 8-5-1. But the 49ers topped the Lions to clinch the NFC West at 9-5, eliminate the Rams from the playoffs, and earn the right to host the Redskins in the first round of the playoffs. The Associated Press, *Pro Football Weekly*, and *The Sporting News* named Allen NFL Coach of the Year. United Press International named him NFC Coach of the Year.

Less than two weeks after flying to Los Angeles, the Redskins again had to travel to the West Coast. In San Francisco, they would face the NFL's third-ranked offense in total yards and the sixth-ranked defense in yards allowed. Allen, who held a 6-3-1 record against the 49ers from his days in Los Angeles, thought that despite losing twice to the Rams in '71, the 49ers were a better team than LA. "We're going to have to play one of our best games to beat them," he said.[66] The key to beating San Francisco, he stressed, would be to avoid mental errors.

San Francisco committed the first big mistake in the wet, windy conditions at Candlestick Park. Redskin Jon Jaqua blocked a punt and fell on it at the 49ers' 28, setting up Kilmer's short scoring pass to Jerry Smith. After an exchange of field goals, the Redskins threatened again late in the first half. Ted Vactor returned a punt 47 yards to the 49ers' 12 with about thirty seconds to play.

The Redskins then tried the play that Nixon suggested during his practice visit to Redskin Park—a reverse to Jefferson. Kilmer faked a handoff to Larry Brown and gave the ball to Jefferson as he came on an end around. Not fooled, San Francisco's Pro Bowl–bound defensive end Cedrick Hardman met Jefferson and dropped him for a 9-yard loss. The Redskins were forced to try a field goal. But George Burman, one of Allen's Ramskins, delivered a low snap, and Curt Knight's kick was blocked. Instead of taking valuable momentum into the locker room, the Redskins exited with nothing.

Another Redskins gamble backfired after Duncan returned the second-half kickoff 66 yards. Allen opted to go for it on fourth-and-inches from the 11, but Brown was stopped for a 2-yard loss. A field goal would have given the Redskins a 10-point lead over the 49ers with their sluggish offense. "It was just inches," Allen said later. "The percentages were in our favor to pick it up."

That was a major turning point. Three plays later, 49ers quarterback John Brodie hit receiver Gene Washington on a 78-yard touchdown pass, and Kilmer threw an interception that set up another San Francisco touchdown late in the third quarter.

Knight's field goal created a 17–13 game. But another huge error by the normally superaccurate Burman spelled doom for the Redskins. His snap skidded on the slick AstroTurf, traveling through the legs of punter Mike Bragg and into the end zone. The 49ers recovered the ball for a touchdown to go up 24–13 with a little more than three minutes left. After Brown caught a 16-yard scoring pass, the Redskins regained possession and moved close to midfield with the clock ticking down. But the 49ers sacked Kilmer as time expired, for a 24–20 win.

The loss dropped Allen's playoff coaching record to 0-3 and fueled criticism of his inability to advance teams in the postseason. He attributed the defeat to what he had warned about before the game. "I'm only going to say this once," he abruptly told reporters. "I'm very proud of our football team. We had a great season. We overcame a great deal of adversity to get this far. We made too many mistakes, and they didn't make any, that's why we lost. I said before the team making the fewest mistakes would win."

What about the reverse to Jefferson that backfired at the end of the first half? That play would have gone down in history as just a strange call by Kilmer, who chose his own plays and mirrored Allen's conservative thinking on offense. Kilmer could have opted for a much safer play to advance the ball toward the goal line.

However, the day after the game Redskins defensive tackle Bill Brundige made a remark guaranteeing that the origins of the reverse would live on forever. In hosting the *Redskins Report* on DC TV station WDCA, he said Nixon had called Allen in the days leading up to the game and said he'd like to see a flanker reverse with Jefferson.[67] In an interview years later, Brundige noted that Allen had relayed the president's wish in a team meeting the night before the game.[68]

Kilmer and Allen were strategizing in the coach's office when Nixon called. Kilmer was on the receiving end. "He said, 'Billy, it would be good if you ran a reverse sometime,'" Kilmer recalled. "I said, 'Yes, Mr. President, that'd be fine.' That was it. He didn't tell me we ought to do it inside the 15 or outside the 50. He said a gadget play might work well against the 49ers."

Kilmer added that he never would have called a reverse so close to the opponent's goal line, "because I got down there by running it, especially with Larry [Brown], and throwing it a little. I know a lineman brought that play in from the sidelines." He assumed that Allen or offensive coordinator Ted Marchibroda had called the play.[69]

In a 2013 interview, Marchibroda admitted that the reverse was his idea, his thinking being that a good time to run it would be inside the 20-yard line. But the play call was not based on Nixon's suggestion, Marchibroda noted. "We felt when looking at the film that that was a good time," he said. "We felt a reverse would work at that particular time."[70] Allen never confirmed nor denied the president's involvement in the play, calling it more of a "fairy tale" than anything else.[71]

"Nixon's play" has taken on a life of its own, serving as a topic of conversation more than a half century later and a key reason the lives of Richard Nixon and George Allen are intertwined to this day. Someone who is not a Redskins fan or a football enthusiast, for that matter, may still be inclined to discuss the play. Why did Nixon call it? Did he phone it in to the coaches during the game? Why was it run at that exact time? Why did Allen even agree to run a play that the president called? Seen in a negative light by many because of a presidential legacy tarnished by his 1974 resignation amid the Watergate scandal, Nixon is often the butt of ridicule because the play was an utter failure. His decision in this case was just on par with the controversial moves that led to the collapse of his presidency, his critics surmise.

Nixon suggested other plays, too. In a phone call with Dolphins coach Don Shula prior to Super Bowl VI, he told Shula that a down-and-in pass pattern to All-Pro receiver Paul Warfield would work well against the Cowboys. Nixon showed no imagination this time. That play had been a staple of Miami's offense all season.[72] Smothered by the Cowboys' defense, Warfield was a nonfactor in the Super Bowl.

Allen watched that day as the team he most detested, Dallas, beat the Dolphins, 24–3, and as his rival NFC East coach, Tom Landry, rid himself of his own inability to win the big one. Landry had previously lost twice in the NFL championship game and once in the Super Bowl.

Allen would have to wait, although early signs pointed to 1972 as being a special Redskins year. Virtually an entire defense that placed as one of the top NFL units in '71 was intact. That year, the Redskins intercepted a league-high 29 passes and yielded 13.6 points, 100 rushing yards, and 152 passing yards per game.

What's more, key players on offense were back and healthy, namely Brown, Jurgensen, Taylor, and Smith. The latter three had missed large chunks of the '71 season with injuries. The receiving trio of Taylor, Smith, and Jefferson promised to provide tremendous aerial striking power. On special teams, Allen would again have the services of Curt Knight, who made the Pro Bowl after converting a league-high twenty-nine field goals in '71.

Allen refused to overhype his team. "Right now, we're only as good as our last game," he told reporters at training camp, "and we lost that last one to San Francisco in the playoffs. What we did the rest of last year is history. Our success will be determined not by how well we play or defenses or [the] kicking game, but how well we work together as a forty-man team. Togetherness, that's the phrase."[73]

The coach's disdain for rookies, coupled with his wheeling and dealing of draft choices, left the Redskins with no picks in the first seven rounds of the '72 draft. That didn't seem to matter to Allen, who considered his draft picks to be veterans acquired for draft choices. But Pete Rozelle didn't care for how Allen traded some of his picks. The NFL commissioner fined Allen $5,000 and forced him to relinquish draft choices for reckless deals he had made before the '71 season. In a sign of the lack of ethics that tarnished his career, Allen traded the same second-round pick to the Jets for Verlon Biggs and later to the Rams for Richie Petitbon. He traded the same third-round pick to the Bills for Ron McDole and to the Chargers for Speedy Duncan. Consequently, the NFL forced the Redskins to give up two picks to the Rams (round six in 1973 and round one in 1974) and three to the Chargers (rounds three, four, and five in '73).[74]

"We wanted to impress on him how important this matter of sloppy bookkeeping of draft choices was, whether intentional or unintentional, because it involved competitive conditions," Rozelle said at an NFL executive committee meeting. "The owners had a deep concern because the acquisition of Petitbon and Duncan could have affected title races. I understand Petitbon had at least one big game and Duncan brought them from last to first in punt returns. If the Redskins had not had the draft choices to pay for them in trades, they might not have had them as players to help them improve."

Furthermore, Rozelle said Allen had made similar trades in Los Angeles but that no fines were necessary because Allen had worked out immediate settlements with the teams. In '72 the Redskins were also penalized for asking a former player for details about the team they were about to play—the tactic of pumping a player for information that Allen exploited.[75]

The *Washington Daily News*, in an article headlined "Flim-flam Man Burned," reported that some NFL owners labeled Allen a "con man" because he had deceived the Rams and Chargers. But contrary to rumors, Rozelle said none of the owners wanted Allen kicked out of the league, according to the *Daily News*.[76]

Bruce Allen explained that his father traded the same picks because of an administrative error by the league. At the time, he said, teams sent the terms of trades to the NFL via a TWX (Teletypewriter eXchange Service) telegram and that the league was responsible for confirming the terms of the trade. "My father had a board in his conference room that showed which choices the Redskins possessed," Bruce said. "The board hadn't been updated. Therefore, he made the trades thinking he had the picks. The league should have told both teams of the clerical error at the time of the trades."[77]

By the start of training camp in Carlisle, Pennsylvania, Allen was refreshed and tanned after a vacation in California. But he wasn't about to let his players relax: twenty-seven straight days of brutal two-a-day practices in the heat and humidity. Terry Hermeling, then in his first season as a starting offensive tackle, sounded incredulous about Allen's decision to put his players through such a grueling stretch. "They were three hours long, morning and afternoon, without a letup," he recalled. "That has to be a record. Twenty-seven straight days of two-a-day practices and night meetings without a day off."[78]

Two team captains, Diron Talbert and Len Hauss, agreed to lead a revolt that involved giving Allen the silent treatment during a Friday morning practice. "Allen would start practice by walking around, clapping, getting everyone pumped up," Hermeling recalled. "Talbert and Hauss came to everybody and said, 'Silence when he starts clapping and jumping around. We want silence.' We started out with jumping jacks and did our warm-ups and broke into groups. We gave him the silent treatment. He got the message. I'll never forget, nobody made any gestures as we went through the practice. We just stayed as quiet as we could. After the practice, he pulled everybody together and basically acknowledged our silence and gave us the weekend off. Everybody went absolutely crazy and just hauled ass screaming and yelling to the locker room."

The celebration was premature. According to Hermeling, Allen instructed his security guard, Ed "Double O" Boynton, to get the players out of the locker room because they needed to run wind sprints. "That was just absolutely nuts," Hermeling said. "But that's the kind of guy he was. He was very meticulous with detail. [Afterward], we all took off and went to DC for the weekend and had a great time."

One of the most compelling stories in training camp involved the top two Redskins quarterbacks: Kilmer and Jurgensen. Allen rewarded Kilmer for his bravura 1971 performance by essentially tapping him as the starter entering camp. Kilmer had rescued the Redskins after Jurgensen separated his shoulder in the preseason. He started eight of the team's nine wins and threw for thirteen touchdowns and more than 2,200 yards, with a 54 percent completion rate, to finish as one of the NFC's top quarterbacks.

Thus, no true competition existed for the starting role. But all eyes were on Sonny and Billy as they split playing time in the exhibition games, with Kilmer playing the first half of all six games and Jurgensen nearly all of the second. Jurgensen completed a greater percentage of his passes than Kilmer, but both threw for six touchdowns. Most important, in Allen's eyes, was that Kilmer did nothing to justify losing the starting role. He departed at halftime with the Redskins in the lead in five of the six games.

Allen believed he had the best one-two quarterback combo in the league, one reason the '72 season looked so promising in DC. But he declared himself a "one quarterback man," meaning he had no plans of rotating quarterbacks like Tom Landry did in Dallas with Craig Morton and Roger Staubach. Kilmer was undoubtedly his man. "There's something about him," Allen said with the regular season just days away. "I don't know if it's charisma or whatever. It's a fierce determination to lead and an ability to win. Those are great qualities."[79]

It was odd to see a healthy Sonny Jurgensen, a Redskins icon and the NFC's all-time active passing leader, warm the bench.[80] After Allen told reporters Jurgensen needed to "work" to make the team,[81] he showed greater self-discipline than in past years, dropping his weight below two hundred for the first time since '66 and refusing to stay out late and consume alcoholic drinks. *Sports Illustrated* ran an article on the slimmed-down Jurgensen headlined "When You're No. 2, You Diet."[82] Allen's decision to pick Billy over Sonny marked the genesis of a Redskins quarterback controversy that intensified in the coming weeks.

In '72 the Redskins also looked different in uniform design: maroon helmets instead of gold, with a new logo of an American Indian warrior. The logo replaced the *R* that Vince Lombardi had pushed for to resemble the *G* on the Packers' gold helmets. A prominent Native American, Walter "Blackie" Wetzel, envisioned the new logo. A fierce advocate for Native peoples and once the tribal chairman for the Blackfeet Nation in Montana, one of the largest Native reservations in the country, as well as president of the influential National Congress of American Indians, Wetzel worked with Presidents John F. Kennedy and Lyndon Johnson and many lawmakers to promote the welfare of Indian communities.[83] During his time in the nation's capital, he became a true Redskins fan.[84] In 1971 he approached Allen about replacing the *R* on the helmet. "From what I understand, Wetzel said, 'We don't like the *R* on the helmet,'" George Felix Allen explained. "So my father said, 'If you don't like the *R*, what would you like? Make a suggestion.' So he went back to Montana and met with his council and other tribes."[85]

Wetzel presented photos of Native Americans in full headdress, including one of former Blackfeet chief John Two Guns White Calf, who projected the look of a warrior and is often cited as the model for the U.S. Indian head buffalo nickel that was minted in 1913. Allen and the Redskins most admired the image of Two Guns White Calf, which, starting in 1972, adorned Redskins helmets for nearly half a century. (Under pressure from critics who argued that the team's name was a slur toward Native Americans, owner Dan Snyder retired the name and longtime logo in 2020. The team is now known as the Commanders.)

Allen appreciated the proud tradition of Native Americans. He took an interest in Native American history during his first college coaching stint at Morningside in Iowa (1948–50) and came to revere one leader more than any other: Chief Red Cloud. Red Cloud led the Oglala Sioux from the 1860s until his death in 1909 on the Pine Ridge Reservation in South Dakota. He opposed white westward expansion and is best remembered for leading a two-year battle against U.S. government soldiers in the 1860s, a battle aimed at protecting Indian land in Montana and Wyoming. One of the most historic phases of that battle, which became known as Red Cloud's War, was the 1866 Fetterman massacre in Wyoming. Red Cloud combined forces with Crazy Horse, a fellow Oglala, and some two thousand of their warriors ambushed and slaughtered eighty-one U.S. soldiers in the U.S. Army's worst defeat in the West until the Battle of Little Bighorn in 1876.

In his office at Redskin Park, George Allen displayed a plaque inscribed with Red Cloud's appeal to the Great Spirit, which is sometimes called Wakan Tanka, the Supreme Being and creator of the Lakota Sioux: "Great Spirit, grant that I may not criticize my neighbor until I have walked a mile in his moccasins."[86]

Allen named a philanthropy after Chief Red Cloud. In 1965, while serving as the Bears' defensive coordinator, he co-founded the Red Cloud Athletic Fund with Bears linebacker Bill George and Detroit Tigers pitcher Dizzy Trout.[87] This came after he had witnessed the despair on Pine Ridge, one of the most impoverished reservations in the country. A coach on the reservation, Gus Nimitz, had asked him for discarded Bears equipment. Allen responded by taking new athletic equipment from Montgomery Ward to the reservation but was "distressed when he observed that the youngsters did not even have moccasins," Dave Brady of the *Washington Post* wrote in 1971.[88] Allen sat on Montgomery Ward's sports advisory board at the time.

Profits from an annual banquet hosted by the Chicago-based Red Cloud Athletic Club went toward providing athletic equipment and building a gym for kids on the Pine Ridge Reservation. Over the next decade, the banquet raised more than $500,000 for athletic equipment and other aid to Indian youth. The Oglala Sioux tribe reciprocated by naming Allen an honorary chief.

When coaching the Redskins, Allen collaborated with the Touchdown Club in DC to start a similar effort that would raise college scholarship funds for Indian youth. The first scholarship was presented in 1974 to a teenager on the Pine Ridge Reservation so he could attend Yankton College in South Dakota.[89] Allen also arranged at the end of every season for the Redskins to send used sweatshirts, shoes, and other clothing to that reservation.[90]

Joe Huske was a two-time president of the Red Cloud Athletic Club and a chair of its board of directors. He said once Allen became associated with the Red Cloud fund, the group put on the biggest sports banquet of the year in Chicago. "We used to get eight hundred to a thousand people just like that," he recalled. "We could get anything. When Oakland won the Super Bowl [in the '76 season], we asked Allen to make a phone call. He had a ball signed by the Raiders delivered to my office for us to raffle off. We'd get $2,000 for the ball. That's a lot of money to raise just for a lousy football."

Huske also spoke glowingly about the extraordinary contributions that Allen made for needy American Indian children. "Boy, what he did for those Indian kids," he said. "That's real poverty. I grew up on the South Side of Chicago. That's poverty, too. But nothing like the reservation. The kids on the reservation had a chance because they had no chance before. When the state board says you can't play football or basketball, that you're not up to code . . . he didn't like that. He'd say, 'Joe, take care of that.' And I'd do it."[91]

Upon approaching the Redskins in 1971, Walter "Blackie" Wetzel "undoubtedly" knew of Allen's efforts to help American Indians, especially those on the Pine Ridge Reservation, according to George Felix Allen. "I know my father had an affinity and admiration for Native Americans and wanted to help them so they could have better opportunities in life," he said.[92] In a 1976 speech marking America's two-hundredth birthday, Allen called for American Indians to have their own state, "not as a place to keep him apart from us, but as a place in which he can reconstitute his great nations and from which he can stand in dignity."[93]

The Redskins entered the '72 season as one of the league's oldest teams. Unlike the three-game NFC East road trip to open the '71 season, they would kick off with only one game in hostile territory before returning home. The Minnesota Vikings, fresh off an 11-3 season and a first-round playoff loss to the Cowboys, would host the Redskins in a nationally televised Monday night clash.

About a week before the game, Allen put a little-known special teams player named Bill Malinchak on waivers. Malinchak, a wide receiver, had missed the last exhibition game against the Steelers but went unclaimed. So Allen brought him back, put him on the taxi squad, and activated him a few days before the season opener.[94] That sequence would normally fall under the radar, except when a special teams mastermind named George Allen is calling the shots.

Just like in Los Angeles, Allen was light-years beyond his NFL coaching brethren in his emphasis on special teams. Nobody knew that better than Marv Levy, his Redskins special teams coach at the time. To craft his final roster, Allen relied on a formula that determined who could contribute on special teams, according to Levy: "Say we had six wide receivers, if we were going to keep four, George would ask the receivers coach, 'Who are the best three?' The coach would name them, and George would turn to me and ask, 'Marv, who's the best special teamer?' He did that at every position. So the final keep at all the positions was a special teamer. There was no one until George who kept so many players on the roster because of their special teams abilities. No one."[95]

Malinchak was one of those players. "George worked so hard," Malinchak said in retrospect. "He went all day, all night studying the team that we're playing and looking for the smallest little detail that he could implement to win the game."[96]

Less than three minutes into the game, Malinchak charged in off the edge, blocked Mike Eischeid's punt, scooped up the loose ball, and ran 16 yards into the end zone. After the Redskins took a 17–14 lead in the fourth quarter, Malinchak again made the highlight reels by recovering a fumble deep in Vikings territory. That set up Charley Harraway's 9-yard scoring run that sealed the 24–21 Redskins victory.

It was a classic special teams performance by a George Allen–coached team. In addition to Malinchak's pivotal plays, Ted Vactor blocked a 43-yard field goal. Special teams had a hand in 17 points.

The Redskins improved to 2-0 with a 24–10 win over the Cardinals at

RFK. Larry Brown, who rushed for 105 yards against the Vikings, piled up 148 to become Washington's all-time leading running back with 3,214 yards. Jerry Smith caught two touchdown passes. Special teams produced another big play—a blocked field goal that Mike Bass picked up and returned for a score. The defense intercepted two passes, both of which led to touchdowns.

But Redskins supporters were getting restless. They found Allen's reliance on defense and special teams, coupled with a run-oriented offense that made the fewest mistakes possible, to be unexciting. Against the Cardinals, some of the fifty-three thousand fans at RFK booed Kilmer for his pedestrian passing approach and shouted, "WE WANT SONNY!" They remembered Jurgensen from his prolific passing days of the '60s and thought he would lead the team to aerial-dominated wins now that he had the support of a stingy defense.

"The Redskins are a boring team to watch," *Evening Star* columnist Tom Dowling wrote. "Not just wearisome or mildly dull, but debilitatingly and crashingly boring, like a three-hour Sunday afternoon sermon on the importance of plotting good works in attaining the blessings of Life Hereafter, the celestial Super Bowl itself."[97]

Kilmer played a solid game the next week at New England, completing 14 of 30 passes for 213 yards and 3 touchdowns, with an interception. But shortly after a 24–23 loss to the heavy underdog Patriots, he was out of a job.

The final minutes were wild. Curt Knight kicked a 33-yard field goal to tie the game at 24 with just under two minutes left. But the Patriots were called for roughing the kicker, and Allen opted to take the first down, wiping the points off the board. After the Redskins went 1 yard in three plays, Knight missed a 27-yard field goal with 1:22 left, but it wasn't over.

New England ran the ball three times with little success. That one-time reject Malinchak, who made a science out of blocking punts under Allen, then stormed through to block another one. The ball rolled into the end zone, where Malinchak tried to control it as his momentum carried him out of bounds. The referee ruled he didn't have possession in the end zone and signaled a safety, making the score 24–23 with fifty-seven seconds left. After a free kick, the Redskins took the ball on the Patriots' 48 and positioned Knight for a 50-yard field goal try. His kick was wide.

Apparent missed calls compounded the maddening loss. *Washington Post* images from the CBS telecast showed that Malinchak appeared to be in bounds when he fell on the ball and that Roy Jefferson had both feet down in the end zone on a 25-yard touchdown reception with 1:48 left, although officials ruled that he caught the ball out of bounds.[98] The Redskins also had themselves to blame, allowing the Patriots to recover from a 14–0 first-half deficit.

"I don't recall ever losing a more frustrating game," Allen said. "I went for the win rather than the tie. I'd do the same again. We had our opportunities, but we didn't take advantage. Minnesota was a team victory. Today was a team loss."

Suddenly, spoiled fans accustomed to winning under Allen took their ire out mostly on him and Kilmer, who missed 7 of 8 passes in the last two minutes against the Patriots. Never mind that the Redskins were tied with Dallas for first place in the NFC East at 2-1. "George Allen is a Mickey Mouse coach," one Redskins supporter grumbled. "To me, all those Redskins got old at the same time in the last quarter," another disgruntled fan opined.[99]

The loss to New England marked the start of a bitter two-week feud between Allen and the press. The day after the game, he chastised the media for pregame coverage that called the Patriots "patsies" and that cited fan discontent for his conservative approach on offense. His disgust for the press swelled.[100] Reports circulated suggesting that Jurgensen was leading most first-team practice drills that week at Redskin Park in preparation for the upcoming game against the Eagles. Journalists went into overdrive with speculation of a quarterback switch, and reporters peppered Allen with questions about whether a change was imminent. Allen thought those reports were way over the top. "Personnel changes are strategy, and I refuse to have anyone writing about strategy at my practices," he told reporters. "You're helping the enemy. The players and coaches are fed up with this."

Allen then laid down his rules with the media: "This is my team, and I say you can't write about [us] playing a new guard or linebacker. This is strategy." He warned that any reporter revealing information about the quarterback position or other "matters of strategy and personnel changes" would be barred from practice.[101] The next day, Friday, October 6, he closed practice drills to all media. At one point, a TV camera operator tried to record a workout from atop a nearby warehouse, but a Redskins security guard ordered him to stop filming.

In a postpractice briefing, Allen sharpened his media mandates. He said reporters should come to him first if they wanted to write something about a personnel change. "[Sportswriters] should want to help the Redskins," he said.[102] In Los Angeles, Allen once rewarded sportswriters with game balls because he believed that their reporting helped the Rams win a game.[103]

The *Washington Post* and its afternoon competition, the *Evening Star*, rejected Allen's terms for media coverage at Redskin Park. The *Post* refused to accept Allen's policy that prohibited reporters from attending practice on Thursday and Friday, as well as his demand that anything he divulged during the week on personnel moves or strategy must be kept off the record until Sunday. Any journalist not accepting those conditions would be barred from attending Redskins practices. *Post* sports editor James Clayton said Allen's policy was unacceptable because it would give him "complete control over all news about the team, control he could exercise by simply placing information off the record."[104]

Allen decided to reach a truce with the press. He issued a new policy that said all Redskins practices would be open to the media, except for rare closed sessions. He also said personnel moves that "carry no tactical significance" would be announced "as a matter of policy" and that everything he told reporters would be on the record. "The press has its job to do, and we have ours," he said in a statement. "And while our goals may come into conflict now and then, there is no reason why we cannot operate in general harmony."[105]

Meanwhile, a player very familiar to Redskins fans, old No. 9, was back in the starting lineup against the Eagles. Looking rusty, Jurgensen threw three interceptions in a scoreless first half when many fickle spectators hooted and jeered. But in the third quarter, he completed a 25-yard pass to Smith and a 35-yarder to Jefferson on a drive that ended with Brown's 2-yard touchdown run. He later connected with Jefferson on a 36-yard scoring pass in a 14–0 Redskin victory. Jurgensen completed all 7 of his passes in the second half and went 14 of 24 overall for 237 yards. The Redskins held the Eagles to 60 yards rushing and posted four second-half sacks, treating Jurgensen to the stellar defensive support he had often lacked before Allen's arrival.

With that, the first true Redskins quarterback controversy of the modern era shifted into high gear: Sonny versus Billy. The rivalry captivated the DC area as fans took sides and displayed "I LIKE SONNY!" or "I LIKE BILLY!" bumper stickers on their cars. From '71 until Jurgensen's last season, '74, the two quarterbacks alternated starting roles and subbed for one another when injuries sidelined their aging bodies. Both men carried a fierce desire to play. But they never let the duel become acrimonious, instead supporting each other on the field and hanging out away from the game in a friendship that endured long past their retirement from pro football.

Although Jurgensen was the fan favorite according to a 1972 opinion poll by a local TV station, Kilmer was Allen's preferred choice because of his conservative, ball-control, no-risk approach. He was like an on-the-field extension of Allen, who also admired his positive attitude. "Billy said we can beat anybody we play, we've got a good team, we're playing in the nation's capital, and we've got great facilities and coaching," Allen told Steve Guback in 1989.[106] In contrast, the coach was no fan of Jurgensen's eagerness to freelance and air it out. Like Kilmer, he also called his own plays.

"Billy followed direction better," Bruce Allen explained. "Sonny thought he could squeeze a ball into anything, and he probably still does. But the time of possession and things of that nature mattered. We had our own analytics department back then that kept track of the number of rushing attempts, time of possession, and other statistics. Sonny really didn't give a hoot about some of those things. I say that lovingly about Sonny. Sonny and I are good friends."[107]

Almost from the moment they began working together in the '71 off-season, Allen and Jurgensen clashed in terms of offensive philosophy. Jurgensen was accustomed to passing the ball in hopes of striking a receiver for a big gain or a touchdown. But Allen often preferred setting up for a field goal in similar scenarios and letting his defense win the game.

"I had just played for the best coach of all time in Lombardi, and that made it tough for him," Jurgensen said in thinking back. "George Allen wanted to win defensively. He said, 'If we don't make mistakes offensively, we can win.' That wasn't the way I had played before he came. He changed our offense. He wouldn't let us do whatever we were doing under Lombardi [in '69]. He changed the keys in the passing scheme, which didn't make sense to me. I said, 'Why are we throwing here when this linebacker is over here, and we've got the tight end, Jerry Smith, standing there wide open?' He said, 'You're not going along with the program, you're supposed to throw here.' It was always that way and, offensively, it hurt us. Everything was just different as far as I was concerned."

Terry Hermeling saw important qualities in both quarterbacks: "I'm not taking anything away from Billy, but Sonny was a player, a special guy, probably the best pure passer I've ever seen. But Billy had a way of motivating his teammates around him. He wasn't as talented as Sonny, but he was every bit the leader Sonny was. Billy led by example, too. He was a gritty guy. He never, ever said a word to anybody if someone missed a block or if something bad happened. He just kept going. He was a special guy."[108]

The next week, the Redskins' defense turned in another demonstrative performance in a 33–3 rout of the Cardinals. The defense held St. Louis to 151 yards and forced four turnovers that, along with another blocked punt, helped set up 23 points. Jurgensen hit his first 6 passes and completed 13 of 18 overall for 203 yards; Brown had his fourth-straight 100-yard rushing game; and Knight converted all four of his field goals.

The victory set up a showdown at RFK between the top two NFC East teams: the 4-1 Redskins and 4-1 Cowboys. Allen billed the matchup as a "championship" outing with "Super Bowl" written on it. The Redskins trailed midway through the third quarter, 20–7, but Jurgensen came to life. Recording key completions, he led two 80-yard touchdown drives that ended with runs of 34 yards by Brown and 13 by Harraway in a 24–20 Redskins win. Brown, the team's workhorse, was unstoppable. He rushed for nearly 100 yards on twenty-six carries and caught seven passes for another 100 yards. He was named NFL Offensive Player of the Week.

Brown was in the process of carving out the finest season of his eight-year career. By year's end, he had accumulated a career-high 1,216 rushing yards and 473 on the receiving end, earning the distinction of NFL Most Valuable Player.

Allen was blessed to have a running back as gritty and hard-nosed as Brown. Playing at about 190 pounds—light for a halfback—he wasn't speedy. But he was fearless while carrying the ball and ran as if every step meant something special to him. He took a beating in the process, with defenders often sending his body spinning in the air as he fought for additional yards. Every football player sacrifices his body, but Brown redefined what that truly meant. In addition to extraordinary toughness, Allen saw in Brown an exemplary work ethic and strong leadership characteristics. He regularly commended Brown for the way he prepared himself for games.[109]

Brown, an eighth-round pick out of Kansas State in '69, gained more than 5,000 yards in his first five seasons, then only the second player in NFL history to have done so besides perhaps the greatest running back of all time, Jim Brown. He idolized Jim Brown while growing up in Pittsburgh's rough Hill District, the birthplace of his fearless running style.

"I grew up in a pretty bad neighborhood, so I told people that I used to run home like that every night," he said in a 2014 interview. "I guess I also got that style from watching Jim Brown. He was the type of guy who never went out of bounds, and he was tough to bring down. I felt that my running style would create a situation where an opponent would have to think about whether he wanted to tackle me or not. If he thought about it, that was to my advantage."[110]

The day the Redskins beat Dallas, a banner at RFK read, "Four More Years of Nixon and Sonny," a reference to the upcoming 1972 presidential election. Nixon and Allen spoke by phone after the game, a call that became part of the roughly 3,700 hours of Nixon's wide-ranging and secretly recorded White House conversations between 1971 and 1973. Although the seventy-five-mile blackout rule was still in effect, Nixon said he was able to watch the game at the White House on a special closed-circuit hookup. He congratulated Allen on the enormous victory and praised Jurgensen, Brown, and Harraway for their clutch performances. "I'll tell you, Mr. President, our team has so much togetherness," Allen said. "I know that sounds corny. But we've got kind of a family, and everybody is happy for the other guy's success. The fans today were fantastic. The ground down there was trembling."

Allen and Nixon agreed that the win was huge for the Washington area. Regarding his scorn for the media, the president added that the victory "must have made all those damn press people [angry]. I hope you told all of them to go to hell."

Allen then told Nixon that his family would be welcome to join Etty Allen at a Redskins game in her box at RFK. The president replied that he'd attend a game after Election Day. "Otherwise, it's going to look as if we're trying to exploit the team, and I'd better not do that," Nixon said.[111]

With his time so limited, Allen didn't openly campaign for Nixon to win his second term in the White House. But he was one of more than four hundred coaches and players from the NFL, NBA, NHL, Major League Baseball, and other sports who backed the organization Athletes for the President.[112] On a poster signed by his supporters in the group, Nixon thanked the Redskins' coach: "To George Allen, with appreciation and best wishes from one of your fans, Richard Nixon."[113]

On November 7, 1972, Nixon won his second term with a landslide victory over George McGovern. He took every state in the country except for Massachusetts and the District of Columbia. The triumph came ten years to the day since he had declared his political career over after losing in the '62 California gubernatorial election. It also occurred nearly five months after five men were arrested in a break-in at the Democratic Party's national headquarters at the Watergate apartment complex in DC. The break-in sparked a scandal that led to the downfall of Nixon's presidency, but that was a bit down the road.

For the time being, the Redskins traveled to New York to face the 4-2 Giants, who were tied with Dallas for second place in the division after winning four straight. In the first quarter, Jurgensen completed a 13-yard pass to Jefferson. Jurgensen was not touched on the play, but his leg gave way. The thirty-eight-year-old walked gingerly off the field, as Kilmer again took charge. He completed 8 of 16 passes for 114 yards, with 2 touchdowns and an interception, in a hard-fought 23–16 victory that lifted the Redskins to 6-1. Brown was sensational, tallying a Redskins-record 191 rushing yards and 42 yards in catches. He was again named NFL Offensive Player of the Week.

As for Jurgensen, who had torn his Achilles tendon, his season was over. The ball now rested solely with Kilmer. Protected by an offensive line that allowed only eleven sacks that year, he resembled an All-Pro in leading the Redskins to five more victories to clinch the NFC East title.

The stretch included another victory over the Giants in which players threw punches and opposing assistant coaches slugged it out afterward. Giants head coach Alex Webster wasn't involved in the postgame brawl, but he was livid because Allen called a time-out with twenty-four seconds left and the Redskins ahead, 20–13, with the ball on the Giants' 4. The thought was that Brown needed only 1 yard to reach 1,000, but someone on the Redskins was statistically off. Brown ran for a touchdown but remained 5 yards shy of 1,000.

After the game, Allen exited the field quickly. "Allen didn't even say hello before the game and ran away from me when I went over to shake his hand afterwards," Webster told reporters. "We wouldn't care less, really. Why is he that way? It's just his personality, I guess. You guys know him better than I do."

Allen then told the press he meant nothing personal: "I didn't see Alex. I'm sorry he feels that way because I like him. At the end of the game, I was more concerned with getting everybody off the field without any more fights."[114]

Another win was telling. In a game billed as a possible preview to a playoff matchup, the Redskins knocked off the Central Division–leading

Packers, 21–16. They followed with their ninth straight victory, 23–7 over the Eagles, to improve to 11-1, the most regular-season wins in franchise history. The win also clinched the NFC East for the Redskins, thereby dethroning the two-time division champion Cowboys. For the first time in his head coaching career, Allen would have a playoff game at home. "This is just one step," he told the press. "Last year, our goal was to make the playoffs. This year, our goal was to win the Eastern Division title and go on from there."[115]

With two games left and nothing at stake, Allen rested some of his key starters. His top priority was preventing further injury to the engine of his offense, Larry Brown, who was hobbling on a bruised knee and heel after carrying the ball 285 times. The Redskins dropped those two games, 34–24 to Dallas and 24–17 to Buffalo. They trailed the Cowboys by 25 points at one point and committed a slew of uncharacteristic mistakes against the Bills. Although the losses meant nothing in the standings, Allen did not take them lightly. "Losing is like death," he stated after the loss to the Bills.[116]

But there's no denying that 1972 had been a banner year for Allen and his troops. The defense yielded an NFC-low 218 points and recorded 35 sacks and 33 turnovers in Allen's ball-hawking system. Linebacker Chris Hanburger was named NFC Defensive Player of the Year after intercepting a career-high 4 passes. Allen's cherished special teams tormented opponents, blocking 5 field goals and 4 punts. The run-first offense, with the intrepid Larry Brown leading the charge, scored 336 points, second in the NFC. Kilmer posted a career year. He completed 120 of 225 throws for 1,648 yards, with a league-high 19 touchdown passes, and made the Pro Bowl for the only time in his sixteen-year career.

Kilmer had an array of receiving weapons in Charley Taylor (team highs of 49 receptions and 673 yards, plus 7 touchdowns) and Roy Jefferson (35-550-3), two of the toughest and strongest wide receivers in the game, along with Brown (32-473-4) coming out of the backfield. Jerry Smith caught 21 passes, less than a third of his career high of 67 in 1967. But 7 went for touchdowns, earning him the nickname "Home Run."

By the time Smith retired after the '77 season, he had established himself as one of the best tight ends in NFL history, with 421 catches for 5,496 yards and 60 touchdowns, the latter figure an NFL record that stood for about a quarter century. Playing at 6 feet 3, 208 pounds, he lacked the size of other dominant tight ends of his era, such as 230-pounders Mike Ditka, John Mackey, and Jackie Smith. But he made up for it with an uncanny ability to read defenses and find openings in the secondary, with soft hands, and with his pattern of making acrobatic catches while laying out his body. He used his fierce competitive streak even to challenge teammates in practice.

"Every day, every play, it was a fight," said Hall of Fame safety Kenny Houston, a Redskin from 1973 to 1980. "I've never seen a guy as competitive as Jerry Smith. He didn't have a lot of size, but he had a lot of moves. He could hold a pattern longer than a lot of other tight ends, meaning he had an ability with his body to make you think he was doing something else, then he would break away from you. So he was very good to work against. Covering a guy like him helped me become a better safety."

During his time in the NFL, Jerry Smith never publicly disclosed that he was gay. For a pro athlete to do so in that era of a much less tolerant society would likely have led to ridicule and possibly football career suicide. It was only his death from AIDS in 1986 that brought his sexuality into the open.

George Felix Allen "strongly suspects" that his father knew Smith was gay. But as in the case of race or religion, Smith's sexual identity made no difference in how George Allen felt about him as a football player. "What mattered the most to my father was that Jerry Smith could stretch out to get open on the football field and had great hands, reliably catching many clutch passes, and a consistently positive attitude," he said. "He was well liked on the team, and every quarterback relied on him. All my father cared about was the character and the quality of a player to help your team win."[117]

In a 2020 interview, Billy Kilmer said Allen never mentioned anything to him about Smith being gay, and he never heard him say anything about it to anyone else. "It never came up around there," said Kilmer, one of Allen's closest player confidants. "In fact, I didn't realize he was gay until after I retired."[118]

When Smith was dying from AIDS, with his weight down to 150 pounds,[119] a Western Union telegram arrived for him at Holy Cross Hospital in Silver Spring, Maryland, on August 27, 1986. It was from the man who had been his head coach for more than half of his thirteen-year NFL career: George Allen.

> Dear Jerry:
>
> If anybody can lick this thing, you can. You not only were [the] best tight end the Redskins ever had, you also were the toughest. Like we've always said, no matter how many setbacks you've had,

keep fighting. I want you ready for my next team. That one will be called the Over The Hill Gang.

Warmest personal regards,
George Allen, CHRMN PRES COUNC ON PHYS FIT AND SPORTS
US Department of Health and Human Services[120]

That same year, 1986, the Redskins tapped Allen to pick an all-time Redskins team of twenty-two players to celebrate the fiftieth anniversary of the franchise's move from Boston to DC in 1937. "I'd like to say the easiest position for me to pick of all 22 is tight end Jerry Smith," Allen told the *Washington Post*. "Jerry will be my all-time Redskins tight end."[121]

A healthy Jerry Smith was one reason Allen felt confident about his squad heading into the playoffs in 1972.[122] Washington's opponent at RFK on Sunday, December 24, was one that had visited DC less than a month prior: the Packers.

The 10-4 Packers, winners of the NFC Central Division, looked much like the Redskins, with an offense predicated on the run and one of the NFL's best defenses. Their running game featured 220-pound backs John Brockington and MacArthur Lane, a powerful duo sometimes compared to the Rams' famed "Bull Elephant" backfield of the 1950s. They rushed for 1,848 yards in the regular season, with Brockington topping the 1,000-yard mark, and gained 118 in the regular-season loss to the Redskins, including 70 by Lane. But the Packers' passing game was terrible. Second-year man Scott Hunter completed only 43 percent of his throws, with 1,252 yards, six touchdowns, and nine interceptions.

The lights went on in Allen's imaginative defensive mind, as he plotted a way for his stingy defense to stop Green Bay's rushing attack. He would not disappoint.

1. Allen, in his midteens at the time, with his younger sister, Virginia, and their dog, Oiley. Courtesy of the Allen family.

1936

101
121

2. (*opposite top*) Allen (*seated, second from right*) played end on the Lake Shore High School football team in St. Clair Shores, Michigan. The powerhouse won seventeen of eighteen games in the mid-1930s. Allen admired his "outstanding" coach, Carlton Worden (*in suit, far right*), describing him as an excellent teacher, well organized, and self-disciplined. Courtesy of the Allen family.

3. (*opposite bottom*) Allen with his two favorite players in his first college coaching stint, at Morningside: halfback Connie Callahan (*left*) and end Leon "Shorty" Shortenhaus (*right*). Both were first-team all-conference, and Callahan remains one of the greatest offensive players in Morningside's history. Allen and Shortenhaus became good friends and kept in touch in the ensuing decades. Courtesy of Morningside College.

4. (*above*) Allen and some of the coaches he served with on the Chicago Bears' staff from 1959 to 1965: (*left to right*) his mentor, George "Papa Bear" Halas; Luke Johnsos; Clark Shaughnessy; Phil Handler; Chuck Mather; and John "Paddy" Driscoll. Mather encouraged Halas to hire Allen as the Bears' head talent scout. Allen replaced Shaughnessy as the team's defensive coordinator in 1962. Courtesy of the Allen family.

5. "In my mind, everything goes to George Allen." So said Bears defensive tackle Ed O'Bradovich of the architect of Chicago's 1963 NFL Championship season. Allen, who that season coached one of the stingiest defenses in NFL history, took a victory ride following the 14–10 championship game win over the Giants. He later received a game ball. Courtesy of the Allen family.

6. The Allen family at their Southern California home in Palos Verdes Estates in the late 1960s: (*standing, left to right*) Bruce, George Felix Allen, George Allen, and Greg. Seated are Jennifer (*far left*), Etty, and Hilda, the family dog and a calming influence on the often-restless coach. Courtesy of the Allen family.

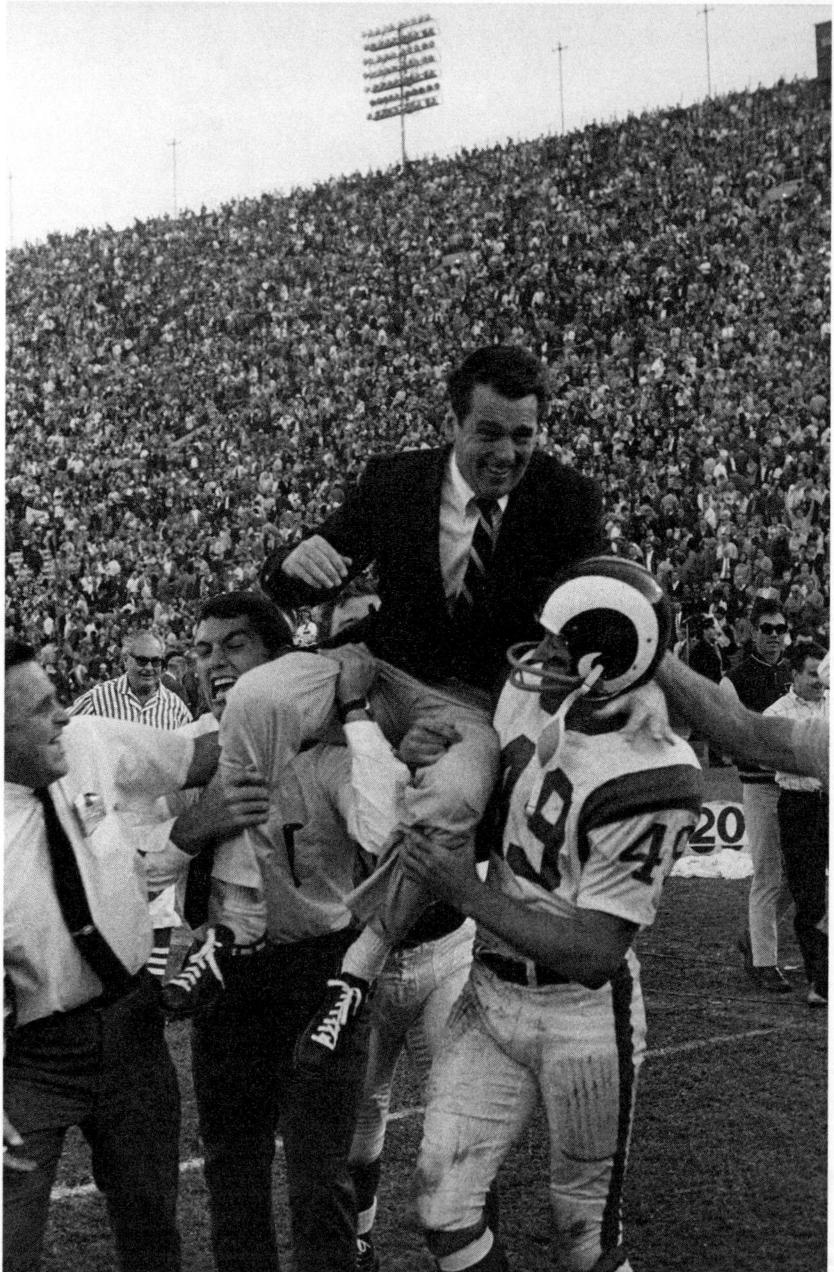
49
20

7. (*opposite*) With his face showing both tears and joy, Allen takes a victory ride following one of his most dramatic wins. With the Rams staring defeat in the face against the Packers in 1967, Tony Guillory blocked a Green Bay punt, setting up a touchdown with seconds remaining that clinched the 27–24 win. The next week, the Rams crushed the Colts to finish 11-1-2, capture the Coastal Division, and qualify for the playoffs. Bettmann via Getty Images.

8. (*above*) In an unprecedented scene in the NFL, Allen and a dozen of his veteran Rams players staged an emotional press conference at the Sheraton-West Hotel in Los Angeles, shortly after team owner Dan Reeves fired him following the 1968 season. The players threatened to quit if Reeves didn't bring him back, saying they didn't want to play for a "loser." Nearly two weeks later, Reeves acquiesced to the players' demands and rehired Allen. Bettmann via Getty Images.

9. "Redskin Park is like everything else we do, have done, and will continue to do. It will help us win." So said Allen in reference to the new practice facility that opened before the 1971 season. In addition to two full-length practice fields, the state-of-the-art facility featured a building with every amenity a football team would want in its pursuit of victory. Courtesy of the Washington Commanders.

10. (*opposite top*) Redskins fans longing for a winner realized their wish in 1971, when a 9-4-1 finish sent them to the playoffs for the first time in a quarter century. After the Redskins upset the Cowboys to improve to 3-0, thousands of fans swarmed the tarmac at Dulles Airport in northern Virginia to greet Allen and the players after their plane arrived from Dallas. Reprinted with permission of the DC Public Library, Star Collection © Washington Post.

11. (*opposite bottom*) Allen, taking questions from Dick Stockton of CBS Sports, is all smiles after beating the Packers, 16–3, in the opening round of the 1972 NFC playoffs, Allen's first postseason win in four tries as an NFL coach. Consolidated News Photos (photo by Arnie Sachs/CNP/Getty Images).

CHROMACOLOR

12. In his crowning moment as an NFL coach, Allen takes a victory ride following the Redskins' 26–3 demolition of the Cowboys in the 1972 NFC Championship Game at RFK Stadium. Two weeks later, the Dolphins capped their 17-0 season with a 14-7 win over the Redskins in Super Bowl VII. Allen's Redskins never again made it past the first round of the playoffs. Bettmann via Getty Images.

13. "Trader George" may have pulled off his best trade ever before the 1973 season, when he dealt five Redskins for Houston Oilers All-Pro safety Ken Houston. Houston didn't disappoint, making the Pro Bowl in each of his next five seasons under Allen en route to a Hall of Fame induction and a spot on the NFL Films "NFL 100 Greatest" all-time team. Consolidated News Photos (photo by Arnie Sachs/CNP/Getty Images).

14. Don Shula was one of Allen's top three NFL coaching rivals, posting a 5-4-1 edge in head-to-head competition. At the same time, the two maintained a mutual respect for one another. Courtesy of the Allen family.

15. (*opposite top*) Allen harbored deep suspicions about the press, fearing those "pesky" (as he called them) reporters would ask for information that opponents could use as "intelligence" or that might foment disunity on his teams. He was ahead of his time in his guarded approach with the media. Consolidated News Photos (photo by Arnie Sachs/CNP/Getty Images).

16. (*opposite bottom*) Like a mad scientist, Allen conceived of clever ways to outsmart opponent after opponent. Today, he's third in all-time winning percentage—behind John Madden and Vince Lombardi—for NFL coaches with at least one hundred career victories. Consolidated News Photos (photo by Arnie Sachs/CNP/Getty Images).

17. (*above*) Allen with the two most powerful men associated with the Redskins, owners Edward Bennett Williams (*left*) and Jack Kent Cooke, following a 35–17 win over the Jets in 1972. Both men were instrumental in Allen's hiring in Washington in 1971, and both soured on him over time before his departure from DC in January 1978. Courtesy of the Jack Kent Cooke Foundation.

18. Allen enlightens Richard Nixon during the president's surprise visit to Redskin Park on November 23, 1971. Sporting similar personalities, values, and beliefs, Allen and Nixon mirrored each other in multiple ways. The two football-loving buddies also maintained a disdain for the media, with Allen earning the moniker "Nixon with a whistle." Courtesy of the Allen family.

19. (*opposite top*) Allen never missed an opportunity to find someone who could contribute to his football team. Such was the case at a White House event in 1977, when he asked President Gerald Ford if Egyptian president Anwar Sadat knew of any athletes in Egypt who could play in the NFL. Sadat, immersed in historic peace talks with Israel, replied that he might be able to find a kicker. Photo by Ricardo Thomas. Courtesy of the Allen family.

20. (*opposite bottom*) In 1980 Allen campaigned for his friend Ronald Reagan during Reagan's bid for the presidency. Allen led a pro-Reagan bus tour that began in Westchester County just north of New York City and traveled 150 miles up the Hudson River to Albany. Reagan dominated incumbent Jimmy Carter that year to earn the first of his two terms in the White House. Courtesy of the Allen family.

21. Rams owner Carroll Rosenbloom and Allen were all smiles on February 1, 1978, when Allen was introduced for the second time as the team's new coach. The *Long Beach Independent* even referred to them as "the newlyweds." They "divorced" seven months later, when Rosenbloom fired Allen after two exhibition games. AP Photo.

22. While out of coaching following his departure from the NFL in 1978, Allen, pictured here in 1980, kept himself in shape with a rigid exercise program that included jogging, sprinting up hills, weightlifting, calisthenics, and hitting the punching bag. Reprinted with permission of the DC Public Library, Star Collection © Washington Post.

23. On February 2, 1982, about ten months after a bullet pierced his chest in an assassination attempt and to the alarm of his staff, President Reagan lifted two twenty-pound chrome-plated dumbbell weights that Allen gave him as a gift on behalf of the President's Council on Physical Fitness and Sports. Allen, appointed by Reagan, chaired the council from 1981 to 1987. Courtesy of the Ronald Reagan Presidential Library.

24. On the opening day of USFL play, March 6, 1983, Allen returned to RFK Stadium, where his Chicago Blitz defeated the Washington Federals, 28–7. Here, Allen confers with safety Eddie Brown, a two-time Redskins Pro Bowler and one of several NFL players Allen recruited to play for the Blitz. Consolidated News Photos (photo by Arnie Sachs/CNP/Getty Images).

25. (*opposite bottom*) In August 1989 Allen returned to Morningside at the request of Shorty Shortenhaus and Coach Dave Dolch to work with the football team and provide a spark heading into the season. Morningside, losers of fifteen straight games, began the season 2-0, which helped inspire Allen to return to coaching: "It showed me how much I missed it and how much I enjoyed it." He agreed to coach Long Beach State a few months later. Courtesy of Morningside College.

26. (*above*) Allen shocked the sports world by announcing in December 1989 his acceptance of the head coaching job at Long Beach State, one of the worst of the 106 Division 1-A programs and a school that nearly dropped football in the mid-1980s. "I took this job because it's so tough and different," he explained. "I'm a teacher, and I've carried that all through life." In his last year of coaching, Allen led the Long Beach State 49ers to a 6-5 mark, his twenty-first winning season in twenty-four years as a head coach. Courtesy of University Archives, California State University, Long Beach.

27. On August 3, 2002, Allen received his due with induction into the Pro Football Hall of Fame. His son, George Felix Allen (*second from left*), represented him at the ceremony. Also inducted that day were (*left to right*) tight end Dave Casper, receiver John Stallworth, defensive lineman Dan Hampton, and quarterback Jim Kelly. AP Photo / Ron Schwane.

13

His Crowning Moment

In the days preceding the Redskins-Packers playoff clash, one of the big questions circulating around town was whether George Allen would be able to revive his team following back-to-back losses after an 11-1 start. In 1969 his 11-0 Rams lost three straight games heading into the playoffs and fell to the Vikings in the first round.

Allen voiced confidence in his '72 contingent. In his view, they were better off than before facing the 49ers in the opening round in '71. "We're in better shape physically and mentally, and we will be playing at home," he told reporters. "I think we have a lot to look forward to."[1]

Realistically, Allen was well aware that without shutting down Green Bay's two powerful backs—John Brockington and MacArthur Lane—the Redskins would be in for a long day. He sketched out a risky maneuver that called for pulling his middle linebacker, Myron Pottios, and inserting 265-pound tackle Manny Sistrunk over the center to create a five-man front. The goal would not only be to stop the running game but to dare the Packers' mediocre quarterback, Scott Hunter, to pass. Sistrunk had been mostly a forgotten man, replaced as the starting left tackle early in the season by Bill Brundige. Redskins would also rotate in and out on defense to confuse Hunter.

The strategy suffocated Green Bay's offense. The five-man front, called the "quarter defense," was key to limiting the Packers to 65 rushing yards, 56 for Lane and 9 for Brockington. Sistrunk and the rest of the defensive line—ends Ron McDole and Verlon Biggs and tackles Brundige and Diron Talbert—created a wall with the aid of linebackers Pottios, Jack Pardee, Chris Hanburger, and Harold McLinton. Hunter, under constant pressure in the pocket, completed 12 of 24 passes for 150 yards, with an interception. He was sacked twice for 17 yards in losses.

The end result: a 16–3 Redskins win.

The Packers took the lead with a second-quarter field goal. But Redskin Herb Mul-Key returned the ensuing kickoff 42 yards to provide a spark. Who was Mul-Key? A former navy serviceman who had no pro or college experience, he had attended Allen's free agent tryout camp before the '72 season and raised eyebrows with his 4.35 speed in the 40-yard dash, a sizzling pace at the time. The Redskins signed him.

Just one player every three years. That's all Allen wanted for his free agent camps to be considered a success. He found a gem in the 5-foot-10, 180-pound Mul-Key, who made one of the most phenomenal debuts in NFL history in the late-season loss to Dallas. He amassed 271 yards: 173 on kickoff returns, 60 on the ground, and 38 in receptions. In the loss to Buffalo, he tallied 123 of the Redskins' 171 yards. He played three seasons in DC and is regarded as one of the greatest long-shot success stories in Redskins history.

After Mul-Key's kickoff return against the Packers, the Redskins drove 60 yards in six plays for a touchdown. Kilmer, who earlier had been woozy from a vicious elbow to the jaw, hit Jefferson with a picture-perfect 32-yard strike for the go-ahead score. Knight did the rest with three field goals in the Redskins' first postseason victory in thirty years.

Allen needed this win badly to offset a nagging image. His Rams teams had bowed out in the first round of the playoffs in '67 and '69, and his Redskins did the same in '71. He also needed to prove that his reliance on aging veterans would not zap his Redskins of the stamina and endurance needed for peak performance this late in the season.

Following the win, Allen addressed reporters while sipping his favorite drink: milk. "Jack Pardee called a great game," he said, "and you can underline the word great. We have a responsibility to the nation's capital. Winning is like being reborn. We had forty-seven guys reborn today. All you guys were reborn."[2]

In the raucous locker room, team captain Len Hauss gave a game ball to Allen: "Here's a ball for a guy that works real, real hard. And he's been in a lot of these games before. But it took a lot of castoffs, a bunch of Redskins, and a hell of a good group of guys to get him his [first] one." The coach led the cheers among a pack of giddy grown men and reminded them that their work wasn't done: "Men, great win. We beat them at their own game. You outhit them. Now we bring those goddamn Cowboys next!"[3]

In an NFC Championship Game collision at RFK on New Year's Eve, the Redskins would host their fiercest rival. At stake was a date with the AFC champion Miami Dolphins in Super Bowl VII at the Los Angeles Coliseum. Dallas, the NFC's wild card team at 10-4, advanced to the championship by nipping the 49ers in the opening round of the playoffs, 30–28.

Since Allen's arrival in DC, the Redskins-Cowboys rivalry had risen meteorically on the intensity meter. The two teams had come to loathe one another. But that mutual feeling of animosity took on the "heat of a Corsican vendetta," as United Press International phrased it, in the aftermath of the Cowboys' 34–24 win over the Redskins on December 9.[4]

Perhaps thinking that his Redskins might face the Cowboys in the playoffs, Allen took the lead in stoking the flames. Following the game, he accused Dallas of making "illegal, vicious" crack-back blocks, including one that receiver Lance Alworth aimed at Jack Pardee's knees with the intent of inflicting serious harm. The Cowboys refuted the charge and called out Charley Taylor for his blindside block that sidelined star linebacker Chuck Howley for the rest of the season with a knee injury.

The mudslinging had just begun. "This one is going to be emotional," Allen predicted as his Redskins began practicing for the game. "No holds barred."

Then came the Cowboys' much-anticipated decision on who would start at quarterback: the traditional pocket passer Craig Morton or the scrambler Roger Staubach. After Staubach separated his shoulder in the preseason, Morton started every game, including the playoff against the 49ers. But with Dallas trailing by 15 points in the fourth quarter, Coach Tom Landry tapped Staubach, who had quarterbacked the Cowboys to their Super Bowl win over Miami the year before but threw only twenty passes in the '72 regular season. Staubach, who became known as "Captain Comeback," threw two touchdown passes in the last ninety seconds to lift Dallas to the 2-point win over the 49ers.

At first, Landry was tight-lipped on his starter, most likely with the goal of confusing the Redskins. It was one of several psychological ploys he used that week. Allen said he expected Staubach to get the nod.[5] But Diron Talbert, Allen's point man for getting under the Cowboys' skin, said Morton should start and issued a warning if Landry decided otherwise: "There's no way they can start Staubach. Morton has been No. 1 all year and has brought the Cowboys this far. If Landry doesn't start him, all those guys will start wondering about their jobs. It could break the team apart."[6] By Thursday of that week, Landry had announced plans to start Staubach, who created chaos with his scrambling ability.

On paper, the two teams were evenly matched, meaning the one that made the fewest mistakes would likely win. Allen simplified his message in a pregame huddle just before his players took the field: "Just remember this. Forty men together can't lose."

Responding in unison, the Redskins destroyed the defending Super Bowl champions, 26–3, and earned the franchise that had struggled for so many years a once-unfathomable achievement: a trip to the Super Bowl. In the colossal win before a boisterous sellout crowd of 53,129 at RFK, all three phases of the Redskins clicked: offense, defense, and special teams. Allen praised his squad for giving a "near-perfect" performance: "I said all along, give me a bunch of older men who have taken care of themselves, and I can go all the way. A lot of people wrote us off as too old, too slow, and too heavy. Nobody wanted them. I just want to say they're a great group. The 'Over the Hill Gang' is a beautiful name."

The offense piled up 316 yards, led by Billy Kilmer, who played the game of his life with 14 of 18 passing for 194 yards and 2 touchdown passes. The self-proclaimed "wobbly" passer threw two tight spirals for touchdowns to Taylor, including a gorgeous bomb that he caught in stride and took into the end zone to give the Redskins a commanding 17–3 lead in the fourth quarter.

A swarming defense kept Staubach in check, sacking him three times for 25 yards in losses, and held the Cowboys to 169 yards overall. After converting his three field goal attempts against the Packers, Curt Knight went 4 for 4 in the NFC Championship Game, including 39-, 46-, and 45-yarders that padded the lead in the final period. With the win well in hand, video cameras caught Redskins reserve quarterback and field goal holder Sam Wyche, a recipient of Allen's animus for the Cowboys, wishing them well: "Die, you dogs, die. Die, you yellow dogs."

"We were in the same division, and they were the icon, the darling," Wyche said when asked why he used such creative phrasing. "Probably the Green Bay Packers, the Dallas Cowboys, the Oakland Raiders—those were the teams that came to mind back then. They sold the most jerseys in the sporting goods stores. George wanted the Redskins to take over the title of the best team, the most popular team, the most watched team in football. He wanted the nation's capital to be the football capital of the NFL."[7]

With a few minutes to play, police encircled the field, and the public address announcer warned of consequences if anyone tried to slip through.[8] It didn't matter. Thousands of people stormed the field when the final gun sounded, as Redskins players hoisted Allen onto their shoulders for a victory ride. They carried him through a sea of delirious fans, some of whom were able to touch or shake hands with the man who had just coached a perfect game. It would be seen as the crowning moment in the twelve-year NFL coaching career of George Herbert Allen.

The euphoria spilled into the streets of the nation's capital and its surrounding areas on a surprisingly balmy New Year's Eve. Densely packed crowds of people relished a moment that was long overdue. "In the midst of contentious divisiveness about the Vietnam War and other protests, people of all races, ethnicities, and political persuasions were united under the banner of the burgundy and gold," George Felix Allen recalled. "It was a pleasure driving in my Ford F-150 with the windows down yelling through Washington with throngs of happy, spontaneously partying people hailing, singing, and honking in the streets."

He and the rest of the Allen family had dinner at the Shoreham Hotel in DC before attending a black-tie New Year's Eve party that quickly morphed into a Redskins victory celebration. "In the big hotel ballroom, everyone vigorously sang along as a band loudly performed 'Hail to the Redskins' and 'California here I come, right back where I started from,'" George Felix Allen said. "It was truly a day and night of tearful exuberance and jubilation."[9]

Around 2:00 a.m., the Allens returned to their home in Great Falls, Virginia, grateful for a chance to unwind after a night of revelry. But time was limited. Shortly after they entered the house, the phone rang. The White House called to invite the family to come to see President Nixon that morning.[10]

Basking in the glory of his monumental feat, George Allen visited the president on a bright, sunny New Year's Day—January 1, 1973—in the Rose Garden at the White House. Joining him were Etty, their four children, and Etty's parents, Felix and Eugenie Lumbroso.

Nixon, who watched the NFC and AFC Championship Games at his retreat in Camp David, Maryland, and Allen discussed the win over the Cowboys and the Redskins' upcoming opponent in Super Bowl VII, the 16-0 Miami Dolphins.[11] Would the president pull for the team in his backyard or the one that played near his retreat in Key Biscayne, Florida? "I always root for the home team, and my home now is in Washington," Nixon told Allen.[12]

At one point, Nixon pulled from his desk drawer a football signed by

Rams players. He proceeded to share an esoteric detail about one of the players, to the amazement of his guests.

"My dad had given him that ball," George Felix Allen remembered. "He pointed out a Rams special teams player named Tony Guillory and remembered that he went to Lamar Tech, a little school in Texas. It's one thing to remember Roman Gabriel or Deacon Jones. But to remember a special teamer and the relatively obscure college he went to showed what a football fan he was."[13]

That day, Allen gave his assistant coaches their first day off since training camp began on July 5.[14] But that was it for anything resembling relaxation in the two weeks of preparation for the Super Bowl in Los Angeles, two years after Rams owner Dan Reeves had fired him for the second and final time. After Reeves died in April 1971, more than a year passed until the Rams gained new ownership. Chicago businessman Robert Irsay bought the team for nearly $20 million, then swapped franchises with Colts owner Carroll Rosenbloom before the '72 season in one of the more creative deals in sports history. But Reeves's loyalists, such as Jack Teele, were still in the front office. That Allen's Redskins stood on the cusp of an NFL Championship—in Los Angeles, no less—had to be disconcerting to those who had failed to grasp the magnitude of his feats in LA, where he was "kicked out like a vagrant," as Mel Durslag of the *Los Angeles Herald Examiner* wrote after the Redskins qualified for Super Bowl VII.[15]

The Redskins and Dolphins presented perhaps the most evenly matched Super Bowl to date. Both were run-oriented teams, the Redskins with 1,216-yard halfback Larry Brown and 567-yard fullback Charley Harraway, and the Dolphins with a trio that helped set an all-time NFL rushing record of 2,960 yards: Larry Csonka (1,117), Mercury Morris (1,000), and Jim Kiick (521). Both teams also had powerful defenses. The Redskins yielded the fewest points in the NFC (218) and Miami the fewest in the NFL (171).

In addition, the teams featured arguably the two finest coaches in the game. Allen and Miami's Don Shula, named NFL Coach of the Year by the Associated Press, were renewing their once-heated rivalry. They had not met in regular-season play since 1969, when Allen coached the Rams and Shula the Colts in the old NFL Western Conference. Shula held a 4-3-1 edge over Allen, not including Washington's 27–24 win over the Dolphins in the '72 preseason—Miami's last loss of any kind.

Oddsmakers pegged the Redskins as slight favorites over a 16-0 Dolphins squad vying to become the NFL's first unbeaten and untied team since the formation of the league's championship game in 1933.[16] Jimmy "The Greek" Snyder, for one, liked the Redskins because their defense didn't allow a touchdown against the Packers and Cowboys, while the Dolphins looked like anything but world beaters in topping Cleveland and Pittsburgh in the playoffs by a total of 10 points.[17] In addition, Miami defeated no playoff-bound teams in the regular season. The Redskins beat Dallas and Green Bay.

But the Dolphins had been to the Super Bowl before, losing to Dallas in Super Bowl VI. So Shula and his players were used to the distractions of Super Bowl week. Along with the Cowboys, the Chiefs and Colts also won on their second try. But Shula needed to beat the Redskins to shake the image that he couldn't win the "big one." In addition to Super Bowl VI, he had coached the Colts in their shocking upset loss to the Jets in Super Bowl III. His Colts also fell to Cleveland in the NFL title game in 1964. In essence, his coaching legacy was on the line.

Carroll Rosenbloom owned the Colts when the 18-point underdog Jets beat Baltimore in Super Bowl III. Still harboring resentment toward Shula for losing that game, he was convinced the Super Bowl pressure would catch up to him and that the Redskins would win. "I've seen him freeze up in the big ones," Rosenbloom said during Super Bowl week.[18]

Both teams arrived in the Los Angeles area on Sunday, January 7. A modest crowd of supporters greeted Allen and the Redskins after their plane touched down at Los Angeles International Airport. "It's great to be back," Allen said. "It's great to bring back a winner."[19]

The NFL required both coaches to hold a series of press conferences during the week. Early on, Allen was in a "relaxed, almost expansive mood" during a breakfast interview with the DC media, the *Washington Post* reported.[20] At one point, he explained to reporters why he had to know the position of the sun when the game kicked off at 12:30 p.m. local time. Known for leaving nothing to chance, he hired an expert to chart the sun at that exact time a few days before the game. The expert brought back a few diagrams.

"I did it because we never played that early there when I was with the Rams," Allen said at a press conference at Anaheim Stadium, where the Redskins practiced. "I wanted to see what it was like because we have had some trouble fielding punts here at the Big A."[21]

Allen's demeanor soured as the week progressed. Always a nervous wreck in the days before games, he took his skittishness to a pre–Super Bowl extreme. He came across as ornery, petulant, and impatient in the presence of reporters, voicing disgust that print and broadcast media personnel, about 1,400 of whom had descended on Los Angeles for the game, demanded so much of his and his players' time.[22] He called it a "circus atmosphere" and repeatedly complained of distractions. He once said partly in jest that his players' wives should avoid their husbands until after the Super Bowl: "I love those wives but only after the game. I wish they'd stop in Chicago and stay there. They have the rest of their lives to be together, but there's only one Super Bowl." Allen called for the wives and other family members to stay in a hotel near the Los Angeles International Airport, about forty miles from where his players stayed in Santa Ana.[23]

Shula, on the other hand, acted like he was used to the chaos that typifies Super Bowl week. He sounded relaxed, even joking at times with the press, and showed no sign that his reputation as a big-game coach was on the line. "Allen has made a statement that he has never lost a game in the rain," Shula said at one point. "If it rains on Sunday, we are going to forfeit."[24]

Two days before the game, the two coaches took part in an NFL-mandated press conference in Newport Beach. After Shula, "wearing a sunny smile and a sport shirt opened at the neck," addressed the media, the Associated Press noted Allen stepped to the microphone with his "dark eyebrows furrowed in a look of irritation, his lips tight and his jaw hardened."[25]

"This is the first time in 23 years as a head coach I have missed a meeting with my team," Allen growled. "I hope you fellows don't ask me the same questions today that you've been asking me all week."[26]

Allen complained that the media feast was cutting into his prep time. "Yesterday, we had thirty-one players in interviews for one and a half hours, and we had our worst practice of the week. This press conference could have been held yesterday. We'd like to have one day with the team where we don't have any distractions." He added that the Dolphins had a number of advantages, one being that it would be hard for the Redskins to regain their emotional high from the NFC Championship Game win over the Cowboys.[27]

"You sound like a loser," Steve Perkins, a reporter for the Cowboys' team newspaper, said in response.[28] "I don't think like one," Allen retorted.[29]

Len Shapiro, a *Washington Post* reporter who covered Super Bowl week and the game, remembered that Allen was "very negative. He didn't like all the distractions at the Super Bowl. 'I'm at this press conference. I should be working with my team.' There were demands made on these guys to show up for press conferences. He was just not a happy camper."

Allen's players, Shapiro added, were unhappy with him.[30] One player, speaking anonymously, told *Sports Illustrated* that "we should have left him in Washington."[31] His insistence that his players focus entirely on game preparation and avoid any of the LA-area attractions rubbed many of them the wrong way. He was in an irritable mood at a press conference when he scolded some of his players, albeit not by name, for wanting to go to restaurants instead of concentrating on the game.[32]

Players became restless. The *Washington Post* reported that some were missing from the team's hotel, the Saddleback Inn in Santa Ana, on Tuesday night of Super Bowl week, and that reserve offensive tackle Jim Snowden was caught trying to sneak out a window of the hotel. According to the *Post*, Allen wanted to fine Snowden and send him home but refrained from doing so upon learning that several starters were among the missing players.[33]

Allen touted the Dolphins as the finest team he had ever faced as an NFL coach.[34] To win, he was convinced the Redskins needed to slow down Shula's rushing trifecta of Csonka, Morris, and Kiick. But Miami also had a talented quarterback who could strike through the air: Bob Griese. Griese had fractured his ankle in the fifth game of the season, opening the door for veteran Earl Morrall, who won ten games as a starter before Shula benched him with the AFC Championship Game against the Steelers tied at 7 at halftime. Griese quarterbacked the rest of the Dolphins' 21–17 win, and Shula tapped him to start in the Super Bowl.

Griese, a Hall of Famer, completed only 8 of 11 passes for 88 yards, among the lowest totals ever by a starting and winning Super Bowl quarterback. But one of his completions, a 28-yard touchdown pass to receiver Howard Twilley, gave the Dolphins a 7–0 first-quarter lead. A 19-yarder to tight end Jim Mandich set up Kiick's short run just before halftime for a 14–0 game. The margin could have been larger, but a penalty negated Griese's 47-yard scoring pass to receiver Paul Warfield.

Meanwhile, before 85,462 fans at the Los Angeles Coliseum and 75 million television viewers, both Super Bowl records, the Redskins lacked the sizzle from their playoff wins over the Packers and Cowboys and ended up on the wrong end of a series of freakish plays.

Washington hoped to gain the first break with the Dolphins in punt formation early in the game. Knowing that center Howard Kindig lifted the ball up prior to snapping it, the Redskins planned to hit Kindig's hand to misdirect it and create a turnover. Allen explained the strategy to officials before the game, according to Bruce Allen: "Dad said if you slap it when it's in the air, that's legal because he's lifting it straight up. They agreed."[35]

Redskin Harold McLinton interfered with the snap and recovered the ball on Miami's 27. But the Redskins were penalized for illegal procedure, and the Dolphins retained possession. "Harold did such a good job that the ball hit the side of Kindig's thigh and fell underneath him," Redskins defensive end Ron McDole recalled. "Normally, it goes as a bad snap, and nobody knows what happened."[36]

Later in the quarter, the Dolphins sidestepped another landmine. Miami's Dick Anderson, surrounded by a sea of Redskins, recovered a fumbled punt by his own man at the Dolphins' 37. By halftime, Kilmer had passed for only 12 yards with two interceptions, and Brown and Harraway had only 49 yards rushing. The Redskins needed resuscitation, so Allen gave one of his typical exhortations just before the start of the second half: "Every damn guy in here now. Everybody listen to this. We've got thirty minutes to live."[37]

But Washington's bad fortunes continued in the second half. Charley Taylor was open for a moment at the goal line, but he stumbled as Kilmer's pass sailed just over his head. Later, with the ball on the Dolphins' 10, Kilmer's throw to a wide-open Jerry Smith in the end zone hit the crossbar, which was then directly above the goal line. "Hitting the crossbar is impossible," Bruce Allen said. "Billy tried the next year in training camp. Everybody was laughing. 'Go ahead, Billy. Hit it.' But he couldn't."[38]

Miami's Jake Scott intercepted Kilmer's next pass in the end zone and returned it 55 yards to around midfield. The Dolphins moved to the Redskins' 35 with time running out, and Dolphins kicker Garo Yepremian set up for a 42-yard field goal to ice the game. But his low kick hit the helmet of Dolphins lineman Bob Heinz. Yepremian scooped up the ball and made a feeble attempt to throw a pass, batting it upward like a volleyball. Redskins cornerback Mike Bass caught it and sprinted 49 yards down the sideline for a score. The conversion made it 14–7 with 2:07 left.

Finally, some life for the Redskins, who regained possession with 1:14 to play on their own 30. But they went nowhere in four plays, and Miami ran out the clock. This time, with his first NFL Championship in hand and his Dolphins finishing an unblemished 17-0-0, Shula enjoyed a postgame victory ride on his players' shoulders. Allen, so close but yet so far from an NFL title following a game that the Dolphins had controlled essentially from start to finish, made a slow, dejected exit. Redskin Terry Hermeling crossed paths with Allen as they walked off the field. "I congratulated him on a great season," Hermeling remembered. "He just had a blank stare on his face. He didn't care whether we had a great season or not. The ultimate was winning the Super Bowl. As I look back on it now, he was dead right."

Did Allen contribute to the loss by refusing to let his players unwind in the days prior? Hermeling recalled how Allen put his team through a grind in practice during the two-week break: "George worked us so hard. We went through a normal in-season practice the week after the Cowboys game. Then we flew to Los Angeles, and he did the same thing the next week in LA. That's where the letdown came from. I don't think he realized how much his hard practices would affect our performance in the game."[39]

According to Redskins safety Brig Owens, such a rigid approach backfired on the team, which went from playing its best game of the year, in the NFC championship blowout of Dallas, to its worst game, in the Super Bowl: "The guys never really had a chance to relax. We had a group of guys who were pretty wild. You can't corral the types of guys we had and keep them in meetings. So we went into the game flat."

In Larry Brown's opinion, the outcome might have been different had there been no Super Bowl week. "After we destroyed Dallas in the NFC Championship Game, I was ready to play the Super Bowl the next Sunday. You've got this week in between, and all kinds of things are going on. There were a lot of distractions, and before you know it, the game becomes secondary."[40]

Yes, the Dallas game. In the aftermath of the loss to the Dolphins, Allen and many of his players felt that they had played their real Super Bowl in the NFC Championship Game.[41] They were "on top of the world," as McDole put it, following such a decisive win over their most despised rival. In their minds, the two weeks leading up to the game broke any sense of momentum.

Following a night when he had an opportunity to come to grips with the Super Bowl loss and realize that his Redskins had crafted a spectacular season, Allen sounded more at ease as he and his team prepared to fly back to Washington.

"We played two perfect games to best Green Bay and Dallas," he told the *Washington Post*. "Normally, that should have been enough. But we needed a third. We didn't get it. The two-week wait may have been a distraction, and I'm convinced it helps to have gone through [Super Bowl] week once before.

"I know we'll be back. This is just the beginning."[42]

14

Cruising with George Allen

In the bowels of the Los Angeles Coliseum, with despondency written all over the faces of Redskins coaches and players in a hot and crowded locker room, one of the first people to console George Allen about the Super Bowl loss to the Dolphins was his good friend Jack Kent Cooke, the Redskins' controlling shareholder.

"You've had a wonderful season, George. This was a hell of an achievement, getting this far. It seems as though fate has a way of taking over. I'm just so sorry for you and the club.

"You know, at the end, I still thought you would tie it. Well, don't you be ashamed of a thing."[1]

Allen, being Allen, would never accept defeat. It just wasn't in his DNA. But falling to a team that finished 17-0 in no way tainted his distinction as one of the NFL's preeminent head coaches. In seven seasons, he had won an astonishing 71 percent of his games and had pulled off what few of his peers would ever accomplish: taking a team to the Super Bowl. It's as if he were making winning look easy. The Allen mystique had taken hold in the nation's capital, where the Redskins stood as an NFL power.

Following the tumultuous lead-up to the Super Bowl and the nerve-racking game, Allen tried relaxing by taking a Caribbean cruise with Etty and their daughter, Jennifer. Almost every year in the off-season during his seven-year stint in DC, the three went on a two-week cruise that left from Florida en route to Venezuela with stops in between. Proceeds from the cruises went to Project HOPE, an international health care organization. Other times, the trio went to Hawaii for league meetings.

On the cruises, George, Etty, and Jennifer never sailed past the island of Barbados, which is 530 miles from the Venezuelan capital, Caracas. Allen would get antsy, with his conscience reminding him that he should be devoting his vacation time to improving his football team. The family cut the trip short each time, flying home from Barbados. Jennifer Allen remembered how uneasy her father felt: "Invariably after a week on these cruises, my dad would say, 'We've got to get a plane. I've got to get back to Redskin Park.' There were no phones. He couldn't stand just being on a boat without phones. He'd realize immediately that he needed to meet the captain because the captain had a phone. Once, when we were in Haiti, he was anxious to find a phone. I believe he had to talk to [Redskins running back] John Riggins. My mom tried to explain to him, 'George, we're in Haiti.' But he kept pushing and asking and finally found a phone in Haiti's capital, Port-au-Prince."[2]

In her professional life, Jennifer Allen has established herself as a national journalist and a published author of books, including a memoir of growing up the daughter of a legendary football coach, *Fifth Quarter: The Scrimmage of a Football Coach's Daughter*. She has also been an on-air reporter for the NFL Network and NFL Films. In an interview for the NFL Network, she realized that her father wasn't unique in the panic that overwhelmed him on vacations when he couldn't focus on his top priority: football.

"For one NFL Network feature, I decided to do a round-table interview with a handful of coach's wives," she said. "All of their husbands were hard-driving coaches, winners, each one. I tossed up the question of what goes on in the off-season, family vacations, and so on, and then asked if any of them had ever gone on a cruise with the coach. They all jumped in and began talking over each other about how cruises drove their husbands nuts because they can just circle the decks so much. Their husbands get jittery, 'Why am I on this boat? Why am I on this island without a phone?' To them, there really wasn't an off-season."

Despite finding the cruises so stressful, Allen tried to make the most of them. In the Bahamas, he once spotted a few guys playing basketball, with his one-track mind telling him they might be pro football prospects. "They were playing basketball on dirt, so obviously they had athletic ability," Bruce Allen recalled. "My dad timed them in the 40. They ran a 4.8-second in the 40 barefooted. It was a good time considering you're barefooted. So we brought one of them to a tryout. But his speed didn't translate. Dad thought he could be a safety. He was a tall guy, too."[3]

In the weeks following the Super Bowl loss, the Redskins' coaching staff underwent a major transformation. Five of Allen's assistants departed, three of them landing head coaching gigs: special teams coach Marv Levy (Canadian Football League's Montreal Alouettes), offensive line coach Mike

McCormack (Philadelphia Eagles), and defensive backs coach Charley Winner (New York Jets). Such is the price of success.

While the exit of Levy, McCormack, and Winner was understandable because they all received promotions, the departure of assistant general manager Joe Sullivan and receivers coach Boyd Dowler raised eyebrows because they left without announced jobs. Sullivan's departure was the most shocking because he had long been Allen's closest coaching confidant. He had worked beside Allen for seven seasons when both were assistants in Chicago and under him during his five-year reign in LA and his first two seasons in DC—fourteen in all. But about two weeks after the Super Bowl, Sullivan abruptly announced he was leaving and going out on his own for "personal reasons." He said he didn't want to "shut the game out completely," however.

"I'm not head coaching caliber," he told the *Washington Post*. "If I stayed in the game, I'd be interested in a front-office or an administrative position. There's no bitterness, nothing like that. I've been with George Allen for fourteen years, and I have to move on."[4]

A few weeks later, the St. Louis Cardinals signed Sullivan for the newly created position of director of operations, which gave him much more authority and responsibility than he had before. Curiously, Allen had initially refused to endorse Sullivan's departure for the Cardinals. The *St. Louis Globe-Democrat* reported that with rumors swirling after the Super Bowl that Sullivan intended to quit, Cardinals president Bill Bidwell had asked Allen for permission to talk to Sullivan but that Allen told Bidwell he didn't think Sullivan would want to leave after being associated with him for fourteen years.

Such resistance irked Sullivan, who told the *Globe-Democrat* that "Allen did to me what Allen protested that George Halas once did to him [in] Chicago."[5] He was referring to the Halas-orchestrated full-court press, including litigation, to prevent Allen from leaving his position as a Bears assistant for the Rams' head coaching job in January 1966.

It appears that Allen just didn't want to lose Sullivan, who was known as Allen's alter ego and someone who could read his mind after working with him for nearly fifteen years. Sullivan spent so much time with Allen on football-related matters that his wife reportedly told him, "You have got to make up your mind whether you want to be married to George or to me."[6] Bruce Allen said his father always had a good relationship with Sullivan.[7]

"I suspect that, like all football coaches and staff, they spent more waking hours with their football jobs than with their spouse," George Felix Allen said. "And you know how many hours my father worked. Heck, if my father was home, he was on the phone with someone. Often, that person might be Joe Sullivan late at night or any time."[8]

Rumors had it that Sullivan was Allen's go-to guy for executing the coach's espionage missions. Allen was regarded as the NFL's master spy, an infamous tag that originated in his days in LA. Many around the league believed he called for clandestine measures to watch other team's practices. Larry Merchant of the *New York Post* once wrote that Allen "presumably hires his assistants straight out of the CIA."[9]

Some teams took precautions. In the days leading up to the Redskins' 1972 game against the New York Jets, the Jets reportedly didn't practice at their home field, Shea Stadium, in order to prevent bystanders from looking on. Instead, they used the football field at nearby Rikers Island, home to a large jail complex. "Let's see Allen sneak somebody in there," Jets coach Weeb Ewbank said.[10]

At times, Sullivan would disappear from Redskin Park for a few days. His whereabouts were a mystery to most of the team. But was he really Allen's chief spy? "That was so blown out of proportion," said Tommy McVean, the team's equipment manager at the time. "I never knew about him going anywhere to spy on anybody. One time, he went on a trip and came back, and then we signed [running back] Moses Denson. So he probably went to negotiate something on Denson. Joe was there every day at practice. He was George's No. 1 guy."[11]

Redskins linebacker Chris Hanburger felt similarly about Sullivan: "I don't know how he could do it because he was always with us. If we were getting ready to play the Eagles, he wasn't in Philadelphia spying on them that week to the best of my knowledge. Every week, he was at Redskin Park with us."

But opposing coaches were paranoid, thinking that Allen truly did have spies watching their practices. "I think so," Hanburger said. "I could be totally wrong. But it was out there. Whether he did or didn't have spies, I just don't know. I have no idea if he did anything like that."[12]

Allen filled the void of his departed assistants with such names as Bill Austin (offensive line), the Redskins' interim head coach in 1970; Paul Lanham (special teams); and Dick Bielski (receivers). He also named the just-retired Jack Pardee, who had made his mark as one of the NFL's best linebackers in his fifteen-year career, to coach the linebackers. Allen handed Pardee's role as the defense's signal-caller to Hanburger, who was entering his ninth season.

Allen's complex defense consisted of as many as 300 defensive alignments and 150 audibles.[13] He thus needed smart players who were well schooled in the game and not prone to making mistakes. Enter Hanburger, a four-time first-team All-Pro and nine-time Pro Bowler in his fourteen seasons, as well as future Hall of Famer. Nicknamed "The Hammer" and "The Hangman," he was known for making forearm tackles above the jaw line that nearly decapitated ball carriers.

"Coach Allen had us very well prepared for games defensively," Hanburger said in retrospect. "We had a tremendous number of defenses. We had a ton of audibles that we could call. Each player knew what every player did in each defense. Even though you'd go into the game with a certain number of defenses to use against certain players and formations, you could audible to something we didn't practice, and everybody still knew what to do. He was an innovator when it came to defenses.

"We never had defensive preparation like he brought to the Redskins. We didn't have special teams emphasized so much until he got there. It was just the way he was. Players took film home to study. Back then, we had 16-millimeter film. I had a projector and a screen in my basement. I'd haul film back during the week."[14]

In addition to the return of Hanburger and nearly every player from a squad with one of the league's best offenses and defenses in 1972, Allen stockpiled more talent. In his first big off-season move, he traded five players to the Houston Oilers for a player he called the "best strong safety in all of football": two-time AFL All-Star and three-time Pro Bowler Ken Houston. The Redskins also obtained a "fifth- or sixth-round" draft choice in the deal, according to Allen.

"It's tougher to find a great deep back than a linebacker," Allen said after the trade. "This will free Brig [Owens] to play either safety. And he could end up playing regularly because of [free safety] Rosey Taylor's age and shoulder. It all fits into place."[15]

A few days later, Allen traded an undisclosed draft pick to the Oilers for 6-foot-5, 240-pound tight end Alvin Reed, a two-time AFL All-Star. He then traded a second-round pick to the Packers for outside linebacker Dave Robinson, a consensus first-team All-Pro in '67 and a star on Vince Lombardi's championship teams, and persuaded him not to retire after a decade in the NFL. His arrival helped offset the impact of Pardee's departure from the roster.[16]

Trader George made his most shocking deal during training camp. With Larry Brown holding out, Allen acquired controversial Chargers running back Duane Thomas for a first-round draft choice in '75 and a second in '76. Thomas rushed for 1,596 yards in his first two seasons in the league with Dallas, but the Cowboys traded the moody and enigmatic player to San Diego, where he missed every down in '72. Allen took a chance on him, as he had with other disgruntled players.

Despite these personnel upgrades, Allen appeared nervous and restless in training camp, similar to his irritability in the days leading up to Super Bowl VII. In his dorm room in Adams Hall at Dickinson College in Carlisle, Pennsylvania, a reporter watched as he flicked the light switch on and off while scribbling down offensive and defensive formations. He expressed concern about his players' state of mind.

"I've had more problems this year as a coach than I've ever had in the past," Allen told Steve Guback of the *Washington Star*. "If we're thinking about anything but football, we're all going to be in for a rude awakening."

Guback wrote that such anxiety was nothing new for Allen: "By nature, Allen is an early alarmist. He fretted greatly during training camp. There were unexpected early difficulties which prevented the team from establishing a quick, decisive tempo. Allen himself had a continuing battle with the flu, which sapped his energy."[17]

In reality, the Redskins seemed primed for another deep run in the playoffs by virtue of sporting one of the most talented teams in franchise history—at least on paper. Essentially, the same well-balanced squad that had posted an 11-3 regular-season mark in '72 and crushed Green Bay and Dallas to vault to the Super Bowl was back. By opening day, the roster consisted of some twenty players who had earned Pro Bowl honors. Many preseason polls predicted the Redskins would repeat as NFC champions.

Allen called his '73 Redskins a "championship-caliber team," but he stopped short of predicting a trip to the Super Bowl.[18] Like his remarks after Super Bowl VII, though, he guaranteed they would return to the grand stage of pro football at some point.

"[DC] Mayor Walter Washington has said that the '72 Redskins were the best thing to happen to his city in years," Allen said in a preseason article he penned for *Sports Illustrated*. "That's quite an accomplishment and one that I'm proud of. We were a unifying force for the city; we gave the people something to cheer for. We took a city that was known for last place and united it. Blacks and whites, Marylanders, Virginians and Washingtonians, Democrats and Republicans, they all were pulling together for the same thing.

"We felt a tremendous obligation to the nation's capital since we were the only professional team here. I know we'll get back to the Super Bowl sometime. It could be this season, and it could be next. Nobody can predict that; there are too many intangibles. But I know we'll be back there again. I'm positive we'll be back."[19]

With the '73 season around the corner, Allen announced that Billy Kilmer would again start over Sonny Jurgensen, who had recovered from the Achilles tendon injury that sidelined him for the last half of the '72 season. "Kilmer is number one," Allen said. "There's no question about that. He took us to the playoffs two straight years and to the Super Bowl last season. We're pleased with Sonny's progress and expect him to be 100 percent. You need two good quarterbacks to go all the way. Miami proved it last season."

After a 5-1 preseason, the Redskins won five of their first six games. They opened with a 38–0 rout of the Chargers at RFK Stadium, making Allen 8-0 as a head coach on opening day. The defense intercepted four passes, three by new Chargers quarterback Johnny Unitas, scored two touchdowns, and recorded eight sacks, part of a team record-setting year of fifty-three sacks.

Not a bad way to start.

Kilmer completed 14 of 22 passes for 161 yards and a touchdown in more than two quarters of play the next week against the Cardinals and their new head coach, Don Coryell, Allen's successor at Whittier in 1957. But just days after announcing Kilmer as the starter, Allen suddenly went to his bullpen—Jurgensen—with the Redskins trailing, 17–10. The Cardinals went on to a 34–24 victory, with Allen naming Jurgensen the starter for the upcoming game against the Eagles, a 28–7 Redskins victory. The two aging, injury-plagued quarterbacks, dubbed "hobble and wobble," played musical chairs the rest of the season.

The win over Philly set up a showdown between the 2-1 Redskins and the 3-0 Cowboys, holders of first place in the NFC East. Before 54,314 fans at RFK and millions more watching the Monday night game on television, the Redskins relied mostly on a methodical offensive attack, as Allen waited for his defense to strike. It happened. With two and a half minutes to play, safety Brig Owens picked off quarterback Craig Morton's poorly thrown pass and returned it 26 yards for a touchdown to put the Redskins up, 14–7. Shortly thereafter, Allen's '73 off-season acquisition, Ken Houston, produced one of the most spectacular plays in Redskins history. The thrill of the moment was magnified because those lovable Cowboys were on the receiving end of Houston's heroics.

On fourth-and-goal on the Redskins' 4 and the clock running down, Morton dumped a pass off to fullback Walt Garrison at the 1, where Houston grabbed him from behind around the waist. An eerie silence gripped the stadium. But the crowd erupted into a deafening roar as Houston bulldogged Garrison to the ground well short of the goal line. Ironically, the powerful Garrison was an off-season rodeo cowboy who specialized in bulldogging steers.

After beating the Cowboys on such an electric night when Allen tallied another win over his most despised foe, the coach smiled while sipping a glass of milk. "This was one of the great ones of all time," he told reporters. "Every play in the game was like a civil war. Every play we gave a little more blood. Every play meant the game."[20]

Furthermore, he said, "I don't think I've had a team that showed any more character. I'm so proud of the Redskins. What a game for the nation to see. Underline character and spell it with capital letters. We beat a good football team and played sixty minutes of outstanding football."[21]

To Houston, the play served as the defining moment of a fourteen-year career that earned him Hall of Fame enshrinement and a spot on the NFL Films "NFL 100 Greatest" team announced in 2019, the league's one-hundredth season. When parsing his words, one can assume his career might have been less celebrated had he not played five seasons for Allen. During that stretch, he made the Pro Bowl each year and earned a consensus first-team All-Pro honor.

"You don't really understand what you learn from George Allen until you get out of the game and you have something to compare it to," Houston explained. "He always put you in the right defense. You did a lot of studying. He also taught you a lot of life lessons that you didn't even understand he was teaching you until you left the game. In the five years I played for George Allen, I never heard him say a curse word. His strongest word was 'geeez.' He had a way of showing you he was disappointed. But he never was that kind of coach. He always cared about his players. He was a great innovator because he taught me strategies and things I didn't know."[22]

Tied with Dallas for first in the NFC East at 3-1, the Redskins reeled off wins over the Giants and Cardinals, then lost two in a row, including a Monday night encounter with the Steelers in Pittsburgh. They remained tied with the Cowboys atop the division at 5-3.

Suddenly, a player unwavering in his loyalty to Allen made shocking comments, causing one of those distractions that annoyed the football-obsessed coach. In an interview with the *Washington Post*, Redskins long snapper and ten-year veteran George Burman estimated that one-third of the Redskins' players, including himself, used amphetamines prior to games. He softened the blow by saying the one-third figure was about the same throughout the league and that no teams openly dispensed amphetamines, meaning they were obtained privately. Burman also said amphetamine use is "an age-related thing" in that veteran players who had used them over the years continued to take them. Use of the drugs was more prevalent in his earlier years, especially when he played for the Bears in '64 and '65 and later for the Allen-coached Rams from '66 to '70, he noted.[23]

Burman met with NFL officials, including Commissioner Pete Rozelle, to discuss his remarks. They coincided with the league's new policy that various stimulants and other pills could no longer be distributed by team doctors.

The *New York Times* went further, reporting that sources close to the Redskins believed that up to 60 percent of the players used amphetamines during the team's march to the Super Bowl in '72. Speaking of 1973, a starter on the Redskins' defense told the *Times*, "Nothing has changed. Everybody is just as dapped as before." "Dapped" was short for Daprisal, one of the two amphetamines believed to have been used by Redskins players in 1972, according to the report.[24]

The allegations painted an unflattering picture of how Allen was running the team. He angrily denied that the Redskins had a drug problem and said he wanted it made "absolutely certain" that supporting the illegal use of amphetamines was the last thing on his mind. "If anyone advocates something like that, they'll be sued," he said. "I don't even smoke."[25]

Burman's revelation was troubling in itself. That it came from a player who called himself a "fan" of Allen, who had drafted Burman in 1964 and took him from Chicago to LA and then to Washington as one of the Ramskins, made the charge even more astonishing. The two met to talk it over. Burman said Allen told him not to "worry about it."[26]

Meanwhile, Allen and his good friend, President Nixon, were back discussing football matters. The two spoke after the victories over Dallas and St. Louis. "The president phoned to say that he enjoyed the game," Allen said after the Cardinals game. "He was concerned about Bill Kilmer's injury. The president wanted me to congratulate Mike Bass on his two pass interceptions. We just talked football. We didn't talk about his problems. He knows how I feel."[27]

Nixon's "problems" were tied to a scandal called "Watergate" that was exploding into one of the biggest U.S. political controversies the country had faced. It stemmed from a break-in at the Democratic National Committee headquarters, located in the Watergate office and apartment complex in DC, in the early morning hours of June 17, 1972. The plan was to bug the office and steal information from the committee. Five people were arrested on the spot, including James McCord, chief of security for the Nixon reelection campaign.

Watergate did not hurt Nixon's bid to earn a second term, but the scandal would metastasize into a full-scale investigation of him and his administration. In May 1973 a Senate select committee investigating the break-in began holding hearings. Its vice-chair, Howard Baker of Tennessee, one of three Republicans on the panel, famously asked, "What did the president know, and when did he know it?" The committee learned of Nixon's knowledge of his campaign's criminal activity and subsequent efforts to create a cover-up through riveting testimony from people like White House lawyer John Dean, who said he told Nixon at one point that a "cancer was growing on the presidency, and that if the cancer was not removed, the president himself would be killed by it." In separate testimony, Dean implicated Nixon and other White House officials as central figures in the Watergate cover-up.

The investigation also exposed the Nixon campaign's espionage and sabotage against those who opposed him. Dean told the select committee of the president's "enemies list,"[28] the purpose of which was to use the power of the federal government to "screw" those opposed to the president. The updated list of nearly six hundred people included the names of politicians, entertainers, labor leaders, educators, Democratic Party donors, and journalists. Bob Woodward and Carl Bernstein, the two young *Washington Post* reporters who broke stories on the Watergate scandal in a way that ushered in a new era of investigative journalism, were on the list.

As the *Post* and other media intensified their coverage of Watergate, the much-maligned president made clear in his secret recordings how much he abhorred journalists: "Never forget. The press is the enemy. The press is the enemy. The press is the enemy. Write that on the blackboard a hundred times and never forget it."[29]

Nixon continued to profess his innocence and tried to make Watergate go away. But the walls closed in on him. In October 1973 he agreed under pressure to release a series of tapes of his key conversations in the White House. "In all of my years of public life, I have never obstructed justice," he said at a press conference on November 17, 1973. "And I think, too, that I can say that I welcome this kind of examination, because people have got to know whether or not their president's a crook. Well, I'm not a crook. I've earned everything I've got."[30]

The same could not be said for Nixon's vice president, Spiro Agnew. He resigned in October 1973 after being convicted on an income tax evasion charge related to his term as governor of Maryland.

Did Nixon pick George Allen as his new vice president? Not quite. But he did select someone who had played football at Allen's alma mater, Michigan. Nixon tapped Representative Gerald Ford, the House minority leader and former center and linebacker on Michigan's undefeated national championship teams in '32 and '33.[31]

Although Nixon's tapes included conversations with Allen about the Redskins, no records exist of the president consulting his favorite coach on how he should respond to the Watergate crisis, especially regarding the waves of press coverage on the break-in and Nixon's alleged culpability in the crime. The two buddies both had acrimonious relationships with the press, but "it would be really hard for me to imagine that the president would ask my father, 'How should I handle this situation?'" George Felix Allen said. "I could not imagine him seeking anybody but his very closest advisors on that."[32]

Just like Nixon, Allen was again sparring with those pesky reporters. The peace treaty that Allen had negotiated with the media in '72 was a thing of the past. He simply believed there was too much press coverage and hoped the journalists would just disappear. This, mind you, was in the day when no more than ten reporters would appear at Redskin Park for a weekday practice, unlike the current stampede of twenty to twenty-five in the major media market of Washington DC.

In '73, following a four-game winning streak, the 9-3 Redskins stood atop the NFC East with a one-game lead over the 8-4 Cowboys heading into the next-to-last game against Dallas at Texas Stadium. The Cowboys rolled to a 27–7 victory, creating a tie for the division lead.

The two rivals won their season-ending games. But Dallas claimed the division title by virtue of topping the Redskins by 13 points in head-to-head competition. The 10-4 Redskins settled for a wild card spot and a trip to Bloomington, Minnesota, to face the 12-2 Vikings, winners of the NFC Central.

Final score: 27–20 Vikings.

For the fourth time in eight years, a George Allen team was eliminated in the first round of the playoffs. It was also the second time Allen had lost in the first round to fellow NFL coaching luminary Bud Grant, whose Vikings had also defeated Allen's Rams in 1969.

The Redskins led the Vikings, 13–10, early in the fourth period. But Vikings receiver John Gilliam caught two touchdown passes in a span of sixty-five seconds to give Minnesota an insurmountable lead. Allen's extension on the field, Kilmer, played gallantly. After spending several days in the hospital before the game due to an intestinal blockage and relying on intravenous feeding while there, he completed 13 of 24 passes for 159 yards with 1 touchdown, a 28-yarder to Roy Jefferson in the fourth period that cut the Vikings' lead to 24–20. Kilmer also threw a costly interception that set up Gilliam's second touchdown reception.

Was the loss attributable to bad luck? Safety and punt returner Speedy Duncan was thrust into action at cornerback, which he hadn't played in four years,[33] after Pat Fischer broke two ribs in the second quarter. Gilliam, an All-Pro, burned Duncan on both of his touchdown catches. Ted Vactor normally would have filled that role, but he broke an arm late in the season.

The bottom line is that the Redskins came up well short of those lofty preseason expectations. The way Allen had fortified his accomplished roster made a return to the Super Bowl a must in the eyes of many.

"When we lost in Super Bowl VII, everyone on that team believed that the next year we're coming back and winning it," defensive tackle Bill Brundige remembered. "Nobody dreamed that that was the only Super Bowl we'd play in."

The '73 season was chaotic from the start. Larry Brown, the powerful engine of the Redskins' offense in '72, was a training camp holdout wanting more money. Upon reporting two days after Allen acquired Duane Thomas, Brown was out of shape and struggled through an injury-riddled season, with career lows in rushing yards (860) and yards per carry (3.2).

Thomas, for whom Allen traded two top-five draft picks, was a dud with 95 yards rushing. He was also a problem off the field, nearly exchanging blows with a teammate. Allen repeatedly fined him for showing up late for meetings and practices.[34]

Toss in the uncertainty about which banged-up quarterback would start—Kilmer or Jurgensen—plus a long line of injuries to other key players and a defense caught out of position on a number of pivotal plays without Jack Pardee's clever signal calling. George Burman's drug-related accusation at midseason knocked Allen and his team for a loop. And were the players starting to tire of his rah-rah motivational approach?

"Last year, the troops unquestionably followed their leader all the way to the Super Bowl, hip hip hooraying all the way because it was so wonderful and new," wrote Len Shapiro, Redskins beat writer for the *Washington Post*. "This year, several players asked why."[35]

Less than two days after the playoff loss, Allen the workaholic was back at Redskin Park preparing for the '74 season, placing calls and talking to his players. He frowned on other coaches who failed to show the same level of focus. "You know, I made a call to another team this morning, and their office was closed," he told the *Post*. "And that team lost a lot of football games this year. Is it any wonder why?"[36]

Sounds like typical George Allen: never one to waste a minute that he could apply to winning football games. Obsessed he was, but his formula worked.

15

"Two Major Egos Clashing"

Edward Bennett Williams had a ferocious competitive streak and did little to hide it. The famous trial attorney and Redskins team president was fond of proclaiming his love for "contest living," in which every effort in trial law and sports is marked by a victory or defeat for everyone to see.

"In contest living, sometimes when you're at your very best you lose," he told the *Washington Post* in 1974. "Sometimes, when you're rotten, you win. Very few people are perceptive enough to know if you're very, very good or very, very bad. The world looks at wins and losses.

"When I go to court and win a case . . . I always say, 'What could we have done better? Where were we weak?'"[1]

Williams never took a case he didn't think he could win, and he prepared meticulously to achieve victory. His goal was to "know the facts of the case better than his client who lived them and certainly better than the opposition," said Brendan Sullivan, who worked alongside Williams for nearly two decades at his prestigious DC law firm, Williams & Connolly.

"No one worked harder than Ed," said Sullivan, a protégé of Williams. "No one thought harder than he did. I've never seen anything like it before or since. He worked until he dropped. That's the way he would prepare for a trial. He worked as though his life depended upon it. Of course, the client's life often did depend upon it. He was an insatiably hard worker."[2]

Such characteristics mirrored those of George Allen, a workaholic and perfectionist who, like Williams, strove to know his opponents better than they knew themselves. In that respect, Williams and Allen were programmed the same way. The two single-minded men, three years apart in age, gave every possible ounce of energy to excel in their professions. Their industriousness was a by-product of the Great Depression, when they worked as teenagers to support their families in homes where money was tight. Williams, an Irish Catholic, was the son of a floorwalker in a department store in Hartford, Connecticut, and pumped gas at a local station.[3] Allen, who was partly of Irish descent, planted potatoes and picked berries in a field. His father, an auto worker and a chauffeur, was out of work for some time.

When first meeting Allen at a league meeting in Hawaii after the '66 season, Williams became amazed by his work ethic and dedication to football.[4] "We talked," Williams said in *Sports Illustrated* in October 1971, "and the more we talked I began to realize that we had the same convictions: the same commitment to excellence, the same impatience with anyone who gets distracted, the same total immersion [into] the problem at hand. When I'm on a case, I become obsessed with it. That's the way Allen is about football. I felt like I was talking to myself."[5]

Williams also knew that, like himself, Allen agonized over defeats. "No one takes losing more personally than George," he once said. "Fortunately, George does not lose often."[6]

From a young age, Williams showed signs of legal brilliance. After graduating summa cum laude from Holy Cross College in Massachusetts, he finished near the top of his law school class at Georgetown University in Washington. He ascended in his profession to become perhaps the greatest criminal defense attorney of his time, a gifted orator who mesmerized juries and argued before the Supreme Court, with masterful skills at cross-examining and preparing a written brief.

"People like me would go to court for his summation during a criminal case," said Vince Promuto, a two-time Pro Bowl guard in the '60s and one of several Redskins whom Williams influenced to attend law school. "You couldn't get a seat in the courtroom. Everyone talks about [legendary American criminal lawyer] Clarence Darrow being a great attorney. Yet in my era with the Redskins, Williams was the Clarence Darrow of the country, for sure."

After hiring George Allen in January 1971, Williams took his seat on the Allen bandwagon. The team president bought into all of Allen's motivational clichés, such as "the future is now" and "winning is the science of being totally prepared." Williams was also giddy over Allen's immediate success. On the return flight from Dallas to DC after a 20–16 upset of the defending NFC champion Cowboys during the Redskins' 5-0 start in '71, an elated Williams stood in front of the plane and led his coaches and players in some country gospel music: "Gimme that, old time religion, Gimme that, old time religion, Gimme that, old time religion, it's good enough for me."[7]

"The relationship was good," Sullivan said. "It was new, and things were working well."[8]

Another protégé of Williams, Larry Lucchino, put it this way: "They were classic [type A personalities] and were on good terms as long as they were pointed in the same direction." Lucchino joined Williams's firm in 1974 and soon began doing legal work on the Redskins, becoming the team's general counsel in 1978.[9]

But Allen and Williams became incompatible over time. The alliance evolved into a philosophical struggle over how to run a pro football team and took a trajectory similar to Allen's descent into bitterness with Rams owner Dan Reeves.

Both men craved power and control. Williams, one of the most powerful figures in a city that's all about power, handed Allen what he wanted by giving him a complete grip on team operations as a general manager who could draft, sign, cut, and trade players and negotiate their contracts.

In Washington, Williams was tightly connected in political circles and a confidant to some of the most famous people in the city. He was comfortable schmoozing with everyone from Supreme Court justices to politicians to government officials to journalists to celebrities to pro athletes, whether it was at his favorite hangout in DC, Duke Zeibert's restaurant, at Toots Shor's restaurant in New York City, or in his owner's box at RFK Stadium. He just wasn't used to dealing with someone as iron-willed as George Allen.

"It just seemed like two major egos clashing," Lucchino said of Williams and Allen. "George was a full-court press who, from my understanding, just wanted as much control as possible, and Ed was the president of the team who was used to being in control of organizations and being the captain of his own ship. The room wasn't big enough for the two of them to fully occupy."

Lucchino also questioned whether Allen ever became comfortable with the governance structure that allowed Williams to maintain full control of the Redskins, despite owning a much smaller bloc than Allen's friend Jack Kent Cooke.[10] NFL cross-ownership rules prevented Cooke from controlling the Redskins because of his ownership of the NBA's Lakers and the NHL's Kings. (Cooke became the majority stockholder in 1974, with 85 percent of the team, but continued to give Williams 100 percent voting trust.)

"Ed was never the owner to Dad," Bruce Allen said. "Ed was the president of the team. Jack was always the owner. He respected the hell out of Ed because he was smart and knew the league and was able to maneuver in different worlds."[11]

Many of the disagreements between Allen and Williams were rooted in budgetary issues. Allen seethed when Williams mocked the coach's spending decisions, especially the financing of Redskin Park and the signing of veterans to pricey contracts, with his joke at the 1971 Welcome Home Luncheon that Allen had "exceeded" his "unlimited budget." To win and win fast, in other words staying true to his "the future is now" motto, Allen was convinced he needed to make sizable investments.

Hall of Fame middle linebacker Sam Huff, who had played for the Giants and Redskins before retiring after the '69 season, was at that Welcome Home Luncheon. He remembered Allen's reaction to Williams's comment: "Allen got right up to the microphone and lashed at him. He said, 'You want to win or not? You brought me in here to win. This is what it takes. Don't be counting the money.'"

When Williams made that comment, assistant coach Ted Marchibroda sensed a spike on the Williams-Allen tension meter. "Who owned the ball club?" Marchibroda asked rhetorically in a 2013 interview. "George knew who the owner was. Jack Kent Cooke. Maybe he had the okay to spend the money.

"I can't say where the breaking point was between the two. But he just didn't like that statement. I know that."[12]

Newly acquired fullback Mike Hull remembered that players cheered for Allen at the luncheon when Williams teased him about the budget. "Any complaints about the budget were simply further evidence of George's concern for his players, who were first and foremost on his mind," Hull said. "Nothing was too costly if it better prepared a player to make a big play and help win a ball game."[13]

During Allen's seven-year reign in DC, the team had one of the NFL's highest player payrolls, including a league-high $3.6 million in 1977, his last season in Washington.[14] That year, Allen also led the league in assistant coaches, having twelve, including a full-time strength and conditioning coach.[15]

Williams railed against the high player salaries, saying they were causing the team to lose money; the losses hit $340,463 in 1975,[16] $500,000 in 1976, and $750,000 in 1977.[17] Allen also signed a number of impactful players for pennies, such as running back and kick returner Herb Mul-Key from the team's free agent tryout camp (1972), plus kick returner Larry Jones (1974), running back Charlie Evans (1974), and safety and punt returner Eddie Brown (1975) off of waivers.

"We run an expensive operation," Williams said a few months after Allen took the Redskins to Super Bowl VII. "The coach's philosophy is to use tried and tested veterans. The philosophy is expensive, but successful. It accomplishes a purpose: winning. That's what our fans want."[18]

"The main thing is to win," Allen often told reporters. "If you win, nobody cares how much you spend."[19]

From the time he became head coach, Allen led efforts to increase the seating capacity of RFK Stadium, one of the smallest venues in the league, in hopes of generating more revenue and reducing the team's season ticket waiting list.[20] The list began multiplying during the pass-happy Sonny Jurgensen era in the '60s and reached nearly 9,400 by the mid-'70s. Allen found an architect to survey RFK to locate areas where more seats could be added, according to Bruce Allen.[21] During the Allen era, RFK expanded by about 4,000 seats, to 55,004, although the team didn't earn any revenue from concessions or parking at the DC-operated stadium.[22]

To help compensate for their financial losses, the Redskins raised ticket prices 15 percent, to the highest in the league during the Allen era. By 1974 their average ticket price of $9.33 far outdistanced the next team, the Colts ($8.55).[23] The Redskins were the primary beneficiary of tickets sold at RFK Stadium.

All along, Allen tried to keep Williams abreast of how he handled the expenses. Case in point: in a letter to the team president dated March 28, 1973, he provided an itemized list from equipment manager Tommy McVean of the cost savings in the equipment room. "We are always talking about spending money," Allen wrote.[24]

Williams was convinced that Allen was overspending to an extreme, no matter how many wins his coach racked up. In a memo dated February 3, 1975, he accused Allen of spending money needlessly and recklessly. "From your proposals made at the Board of Directors' meeting and your memorandum to Redskin personnel dated January 28, 1975," Williams wrote to Allen, "I have concern that you do not fully appreciate the gravity of our financial problems."[25]

Williams then suggested cuts in about a dozen categories of expenses, including player payroll, quarterbacks, assistant coaches, film, scouting, hotels, medical expenses, and equipment. He hoped the reductions would present an "immediate way to cut $500,000 of fat out of our budget. I know that when we get together, we can take another $250,000 out."

Williams said the biggest savings would be in player payroll: "For the past four years, we have been paying 57 or 58 full salaries to players against the league average of 50–51. If we cut down to the league average, we could save at least $200,000 a year. I see no reason why we cannot strive to keep our full salary roster at 47." In Allen's first four seasons, Williams added, the coach had kept "old retainers" on the roster who were getting paid full salaries but making "virtually no contribution." Among them were Maxie Baughan ('71, '74), Richie Petitbon ('72, '73), and Myron Pottios ('73), all of whom Allen had brought from the Rams.

Williams also gave Allen an ultimatum on the quarterback position. He insisted that both Sonny Jurgensen and Billy Kilmer could not remain on the roster, saying "we are obviously paying over $100,000 a year too much for quarterbacks." To Williams, it was one or the other. Jurgensen made a reported $180,000 in 1974 and averaged $150,000 during Allen's first four seasons. Kilmer made $125,000 in 1974.[26] Furthermore, Williams insisted that Allen make the promising Joe Theismann, a Heisman Trophy candidate and Canadian Football League star whom the Redskins acquired in March 1974, the starting quarterback in '75. Williams said all of the Redskins' owners wanted Theismann to be first string.

Plus, Williams urged Allen to eliminate his free agent tryout camps and the practice of putting players up at the Dulles Airport Marriott the night before home games. He said in four seasons only one signed player, Herb Mul-Key, had emerged from the camps and that ending use of the Marriott would save the Redskins $25,000. He also said receiving $22,000 in fines for a series of offenses in '74 could all be "ascribed to carelessness at the operational level."[27] In one case, the NFL fined the Redskins $10,000 in '74 for "tampering" with a player who was still the property of the St. Louis Cardinals. The league defined the infraction as a "competitive violation," which held a maximum fine of $25,000.[28]

Williams was no fan of Allen's unscrupulous personnel moves. In Allen's first two seasons in DC, Pete Rozelle fined him at least three times for breaking the rules, including a $5,000 whopper for trading draft picks he no longer possessed to the Chargers and Rams in 1971. Rozelle called that move "unprecedented" in the NFL and assessed the largest fine he could. The commissioner also said team owners "felt something drastic should have been done to punish Allen," with rumors swirling that some even wanted him out of the league because of his recklessness.[29] Williams intervened to save Allen from serious punishment. Privately, though, he was irate that his coach had the audacity to trade the same picks to different teams.[30]

In an April 1978 *Washington Post* article titled "The Final Plays," a take on the 1976 book *The Final Days* by *Post* reporters Bob Woodward and Carl Bernstein about Richard Nixon's last days in office, Len Shapiro and Nancy Scannell described how Williams felt about Allen's double draft dipping. "He had built a reputation in the legal and political circles of Washington and the nation as an honorable, ethical man," Shapiro and Scannell wrote. "And here was the coach he had hired charged with penny-ante chiseling."[31]

Added Larry Lucchino, "One of the secrets of Ed's litigation success was that he was a straight shooter. He was like, 'Show me the file, open the file, let everybody see it, and let's go from here.' So I suspect he was trying to run the Redskins with the same kind of openness and integrity. It became clear to me that George was a corner-cutter. I can say that based on the little information, little contact, I directly had with George."[32]

It complicated matters that Williams and Allen had virtually nothing in common in their personal lives. Unlike Lombardi, whom Williams idolized and even attended mass with, Williams and Allen spent little time together in non-Redskins circles. Williams's visits to Redskin Park became more and more infrequent, and he mocked Allen by calling him by his middle name, "Herbert."[33]

"Ed certainly recognized that George was an eccentric coach and laughed about some of the things George did to keep himself in shape," Lucchino said. "I remember one day George jogged down to the law office to meet with Ed as he was leaving. He and Ed were standing there, and George was stretching by leaning against the wall. Ed just thought that was very bizarre behavior."

Lucchino recalled further that Williams complained that Allen was difficult to communicate with and that the two pretty much had a "triangulated" relationship.[34]

"George Allen was nothing but football," said Peter Bennett Williams, son of the team president and a Redskins ball boy during the last three seasons of the Allen era. "If you started talking to him about politics, the weather, or anything else, in ten seconds you're talking about some football game."[35]

Interestingly, Williams's law firm represented the *Washington Post*, one of Allen's media adversaries, during the Watergate scandal that began in June 1972. Williams split time with Joseph Califano, who was general counsel to the Democratic National Committee when he became a partner in Williams's firm in '71, in legal matters related to the *Post*. Williams was treasurer of the Democratic National Committee from '74 to '77.

Nixon came to detest Williams and targeted him because of his firm's representation of the *Post*. A few months after the Watergate break-in, Nixon threatened Williams in a conversation with his chief of staff, H. R. Haldeman, and White House counsel John Dean: "I think we're going to fix the son of a bitch. Believe me. We are going to. We've got to, because he's a bad man."[36] The following year, Nixon asked his aide, Charles Colson, to figure out how to remove Williams as the Redskins' president, something that never took place.[37]

According to Williams's law firm colleague Brendan Sullivan, Nixon's threats amused the Redskins' president. "He framed the comments and put them in his office. Ed was not worried about anybody. No one was going to get Ed Williams."[38]

During Watergate, some political insiders even speculated that Williams was Deep Throat, the anonymous source who provided crucial information to Woodward and Bernstein and thus helped them break the Watergate story open, which ultimately led to Nixon's resignation. Williams's biographer, Evan Thomas, wrote that some concluded the Redskins' president could be the source because of his "connections and his vast store of inside knowledge."[39] Williams was not Deep Throat, who became known more than three decades later as Mark Felt, the FBI associate director during the Watergate era.[40]

Nixon, of course, was George Allen's good friend. Allen had supported him during his bid for reelection to the White House in '72, and the two often communicated about football-related topics. That Williams and his firm represented a major media outlet digging into the Nixon administration's role in the Watergate scandal did not trigger any awkwardness between Williams and Allen. "You've got to remember, back then, it wasn't like today," Peter Bennett Williams said. "Now, if a Democrat and a Republican are seen in the same room, they're going to shoot each other. 'Bipartisan' wasn't a dirty word back then."[41]

Allen respected the fact that Williams was a master of the law and brilliant at his craft, but he disliked Williams micromanaging his decisions about who to start at quarterback and threatening not to renew Allen's contract if he didn't comply.[42] Williams, whose nickname was "Panic Button," would call the coach's house late at night and tell him to start Sonny Jurgensen over Kilmer and Joe Theismann over Kilmer in later years. In the case of Jurgensen, Williams thought the team's lucrative investment in the prolific passer should be put to good use. He'd ask Allen, "George, we've got a half-million-dollar air force. When are you going to use it?"[43] Like many other Redskins fans, Williams preferred Jurgensen's tight spirals to Kilmer's wobbly passes.

Unlike Dan Reeves, who oversaw the Rams' scouting system and draft picks, Williams apparently considered the Redskins just a toy. Whatever he knew about football, no less the quarterback position, evolved from his fanaticism for the game. When coaching the Rams, Allen suckered him into trading a first-round Redskins draft pick for Heisman Trophy–winning rookie quarterback Gary Beban, who was a bust in his two-year NFL career.

"I knew Ed Williams," Kilmer said. "He'd get drunk and call George. Why didn't he call him in the daytime and tell him that? He didn't know anything about football. All he knew is what he saw as a fan. He didn't like me as a quarterback when I lost. When I won, he'd say I did a good job."[44]

Bruce Allen also knew about those late-night phone calls from Williams to the family's home in Great Falls, Virginia: "[Ed Williams] told him to start Sonny! Dad told me, 'It was a good call that confirmed his plan. Billy is the starter.'" Bruce emphasized that his father never buckled to Williams's demands about who to play: "He enjoyed doing what he wanted. He'd have preferred that Williams would have agreed with what he was going to do. But he was pretty stubborn that way. He was going to do what he thought was the right thing. It really didn't matter if he said it or a newspaper said it or whoever said it."[45]

Etty Allen also loathed Williams's ill-timed phone calls. "I remember my mom saying he called in the middle of the night," Jennifer Allen said. "She was really upset about it. I think some owners believe 'if you're my coach, and I hired you, you're required to deal with me 24/7. I'm paying you to deal with me.'"[46]

Williams voiced concerns to Allen beyond player personnel issues. He told the coach that Etty wasn't inviting the right people to sit in the Allen family's box at RFK Stadium, which bordered Williams's box, which was dominated by his Democratic buddies and other societal heavyweights.

Etty invited Democrats, too, such as Indiana senator Birch Bayh and Ethel Kennedy, the widow of Senator Robert F. Kennedy, but she also included Republicans, among them Secretary of State Henry Kissinger and Virginia governor Linwood Holton. Iran's ambassador to the United States, Ardeshir Zahedi, was also on her list, as well as obscure people without high social status, from diverse persuasions and backgrounds.

"She was inviting the milkman, the high school soccer coach, and other people who could never get a ticket to a Redskins game," Jennifer Allen recalled. "Next to [Etty] would be her father and mother and one high-powered person. My mom told my dad, 'Okay, Williams can have these seats.' So my dad told him, 'You can have the box, she'll sit in the stands.'"[47]

Like her husband, and despite being married to a famous football coach, Etty just wasn't enamored of people who possessed power, wealth, and fame. "Our mother wasn't partial to people she considered or who showed themselves to be snobby, pompous, elitist, sneaky, self-important, untrustworthy, dishonest, or boring," George Felix Allen said. "'Snobs' and 'snobby' were words she often used to describe some people. She'd invite people to the box based on their intensity, cheer, and personality rather than their political affiliation. That didn't matter to her. She wanted friendly people who would be loud and engrossed in the game. When I'd ask about some of her guests, she would say, 'He's very nice,' or 'I really liked talking with him,' or 'I like her spirit.'"[48]

It's important to note that Williams was no Boy Scout in his personal life. He engaged in heavy drinking, which led to drunken outbursts; according to Evan Thomas, one time he turned over a table and spilled drinks and food all over *Washington Star* sportswriter Morrie Siegel and his wife, *Washington Post* writer Myra McPherson.[49] He loved to indulge in liquor while schmoozing with his powerful friends and associates at Duke Zeibert's and other social settings. According to Brendan Sullivan, an avid squash partner of Williams, "Yes, Ed enjoyed a drink. Never saw him anywhere near intoxicated. When he was preparing for trial, he led the life of a monk, and all pleasures were suspended."[50]

In *The Man to See*, Thomas cites multiple circumstances when an inebriated Williams was no stranger to romantic escapades and extramarital affairs. Thomas called him an "incorrigible flirt."[51] Williams was married to Dorothy Guider from 1949 to 1959, before his marriage to Agnes Neill from 1960 until his death in 1988.

Williams passed away at the age of sixty-eight, after undergoing a half dozen operations, including cancer surgeries on his colon, lung, and liver. Allen's previous boss, Dan Reeves, died a decade younger, at fifty-eight, after battling Hodgkin's disease. He was also a big drinker who liked to party hard and another NFL owner with whom Allen had a contentious relationship.

Perhaps all of that was just a coincidence. Those circumstances, though, are too similar to ignore.

16

The Fourth Estate

George Allen didn't consider the press an enemy, but he harbored deep suspicions about print and broadcast media documenting the fate of his football teams. He maintained a tight-lipped posture with reporters for fear of something sensitive or negative slipping out that journalists could publicize. Such information, he believed, would give "intelligence" to opponents or foment disunity on his teams. He urged his players to be cautious, too, in how they responded to reporters and told them to say "no comment" to anything they felt was controversial. Nothing could be gained by answering such questions, he concluded.[1]

"Every time you're interviewed, there's some reporter asking an asinine question," he once said in a meeting with Redskins players. "No matter which way you answer it, you're wrong. So most of those guys are looking for a story, and if we don't feel like answering the question, we just say 'no comment.' But we don't want to give the opposition anything to use against us."[2]

Allen believed hometown journalists should be on board supporting his teams, instead of resorting to constant scrutiny and criticism. In his twisted way of thinking, he defined their role as cheerleaders and failed to comprehend why they would turn on their local team. "So, when you write about who should be quarterback, you're hurting the fans in Washington, you're hurting the football team," he told reporters after a game.[3]

Washington Post sportswriter Kenneth Turan coauthored the book *The Future Is Now*, which reviewed the Redskins' 1971 playoff season under Allen and elaborated on his eccentricities. In an interview, Turan said Allen's impassioned pleas for understanding from the press spoke to his tunnel vision that everyone should be on the same page: "He was a true believer. He believed in football and winning games. He believed in his ideas about football. He was very messianic. He wanted everyone to go along with him, including the reporters."

Regarding Allen's desire for the press to act like cheerleaders, Turan surmised, "I think it never crossed his mind like, 'Why wouldn't you be?'"[4]

Allen's relationship with the press was not as antagonistic when he coached the Rams from '66 to '70. With Los Angeles being a sports mecca—two baseball squads (Dodgers and Angels), a perennial NBA power (Lakers), a new NHL team (Kings), two college football powers (USC and UCLA), and the UCLA basketball dynasty, which won nine national titles from '64 to '73—the media zeroed in on more than just the Rams, although they were very successful under Allen.

The spotlight was much more intense in the nation's capital, where the Redskins were the only major pro team in town when Allen began his first season in 1971. In the pre-Watergate days of the early 1970s, the DC press corps was much smaller than it is today, and the daily media crush of the past quarter century on the city's NFL team did not exist. There were three daily newspapers—the *Washington Post*, the *Washington Star*, and the *Washington Daily News*—but fewer than ten reporters from print and broadcast media regularly covered practices at Redskin Park. Plus, there was of course no internet or social media.

Allen's sense of unease with the media intensified in this pressure-cooker scenario, and he came to hold the press in very low regard. Such paranoia earned him comparisons to his friend Richard Nixon. Reporters dubbed Allen "Nixon with a whistle" because, like the president, he believed the press was attacking him and his players in a game of "gotcha." The two friends were like the CIA, both withholding as much information as possible. The media mocked Redskin Park as "Camp Paranoia," "The Bunkers," and "Fort Allen." "Nixon was secretive, and George followed the same line," said Steve Guback, the lead Redskins beat writer at the time for the *Washington Star*.

"The *Washington Post* didn't like either of them," George Felix Allen said. "Neither seemed to handle the media very well. DC reporters would be analyzing every single thing. My father in his preparation would want to know what the other team was doing but wouldn't want anyone to know what he was doing. He'd say stuff like, 'That's a stupid question,' or 'You ought to write for the Style section.' To a sports reporter, that's quite an insult."[5]

In a 1973 column headlined "Reporters Occupy Top Spot on Allen's Enemies List," a not-so-subtle reference to Nixon's infamous enemies list, Shirley Povich of the *Washington Post* pointed to parallels in the disdain Allen and Nixon held for the press:

"Bothersome to Allen are the prying, pushy football writers who are continually trying to find out what in tarnation is going on with the Redskins. They have not been cooperative in Allen's effort to maintain for his athletes the monastic seclusion he says is good for them. At times, the reporters have, with a good second effort, been able to glimpse the forbidden practice field zones or isolate a Redskin athlete when an interview is granted, on those days when there is a crescent moon.

"Allen brought from Los Angeles, where he had a favorable press, his fascinating concept of the super football writer, one who was on Allen's team as a pompon typist, keeping Allen's secrets and leading the cheers. Almost after he established the Redskins' running game after his arrival in Washington, Allen established the distrust of the city's football writers. Especially when he told them, 'We'll have a winning football team, and that will make you better writers.'"[6]

Bruce Allen reasoned that his father was "just ahead of his time" in his guarded posture with the press: "If you listen to coaches today in all of sports, I don't think they disclose as much as the media would like."[7] Case in point: Bill Belichick. The famed New England Patriots coach is notorious for shutting down reporters' questions in his effort to reveal no sensitive information.

In a 1975 interview with the *Washington Star*, George Allen envisioned the standard he was setting for the future. "I believe in time that most coaches will follow the pattern that we've set. Some already have."

He went on to say that the press should be asked to abide by certain rules, including not being allowed on airplanes with players and in dorm rooms in training camp and being barred from certain practices and postgame locker room settings. "These to me are just the ABCs of coaching and winning," he said. "Anything that's going to be a distraction and prevent us from winning, I'm against."

Allen also told the *Star* he didn't consider the press an "enemy."[8] But he viewed the journalists who reported on the Redskins as "a bunch of raggedy ass communists out there trying to make trouble for him," said John Schulian, who covered the Redskins for the *Washington Post* from 1975 to 1977.[9]

"Ken Turan had long hair in those days, and George thought he was a communist," Schulian recalled. "A lot of us had long hair. [*Washington Star* columnist] David Israel had a big mop of hair, and he was always teeing off on George. My colleague, Len Shapiro, was very civilized. The guy who might have been in George's wheelhouse as a human being was

Steve Guback." While Allen chaired the President's Council on Physical Fitness and Sports under President Reagan in the 1980s, Guback served as the council's director of information.[10]

Len Shapiro, the lead Redskins beat reporter for the *Washington Post* from '73 to '78 as part of his forty-three-year career at that newspaper, was no stranger to fierce clashes with Allen. Ironically, as a member of the Hall of Fame selection committee, he later led a campaign that paved the way to Allen's enshrinement in Canton in 2002.

He remembered how excruciating Allen made life for those who covered the team: "We had our battles. I was twenty-six years old and had never covered a team like that. You literally had to fight for every piece of information. He didn't announce cuts. He didn't announce trades. You had to make twenty-five phone calls to find out who he had just eliminated from the roster. He made it very difficult."[11]

Furthermore, according to Shapiro, Allen allowed reporters to watch about a third of the practices but closed many of them when he was making positional changes, such as at quarterback with Bill Kilmer and Sonny Jurgensen. "That meant you could only go out in the beginning to watch them do calisthenics, and you couldn't even come out in the end until they were walking off the field," he said. Plus, filing stories on deadline was not a breeze. "After practice ended, George would run laps on the track around the grass field at Redskin Park before he came to see us," Shapiro recalled. "We're standing around. We're on deadline. It's 4:30, 5:00. I need to have a story written at 6:00, 6:15. It was not fun waiting for him."

One season, Shapiro noted, Allen decided he didn't want the media in the main building at Redskin Park because the press room overlooked the field. Reporters sometimes peeked out the window to watch practices. Allen thus arranged for them to write their stories in an on-site camper attached to a pickup truck, both owned by Redskin Diron Talbert. The camper, which sat next to one of the two practice fields, essentially became the press room.

Shapiro improvised to learn who was starting at quarterback. "If you went to the top bunk in the camper, you could lie on your stomach, look out the window, and see over the fence of the practice field what was happening out there," he remembered. "I saw out the window that Joe Theismann was working with the first team and was going to start over Kilmer. I wrote a story about it that appeared the next day, which of course infuriated Allen. You do what you've got to do to write your stories. The next time I went up to the top bunk, there was a post in the ground with a piece of wood, so it blocked the view from that window."

Shapiro also angered Allen by once writing that the Redskins had at least seventy players on the practice field, about two dozen more than the NFL allowed on a regular-season roster. Allen responded by threatening to bar him from Redskins practices if he ever wrote something like that again, although Shapiro said the NFL didn't fine Allen after the story was published. According to Shapiro, Allen even threatened to call *Washington Post* executive editor Ben Bradlee, a good friend of Edward Bennett Williams.

"I said, 'Here's ten cents, be my guest,'" Shapiro remembered. "He tried. Bradlee told him, 'If you want to throw Shapiro out of practice, we're just not going to send anybody. We won't write about you until game day.' Edward Bennett Williams told Allen, 'No, we're not going to ban anybody from the *Post*. They're going to be there.'

"Bradlee absolutely knew what we were dealing with," Shapiro added. "He was as supportive as you could possibly be to me and to our columnists."

Allen cleverly used Shapiro and others in the media as a motivating tool, drilling an "us against them" mentality into his players so they would see the reporters as the bad guys. For one, he posted newspaper clips in the locker room that he perceived as negative toward his team and players. "He used the press to light a fire under us," Billy Kilmer remembered. "He'd say, 'They don't respect you. They think you're a bunch of bums.' Things like that. I know he didn't care for the press at all, but he used them pretty good. He'd always try to intimidate and needle them, and something negative would come up about the Redskins. That would light a fire under us, usually when we played Dallas or some other big rival."[12]

Ace special teamer Mike Hull: "I can recall on numerous occasions, George waving a newspaper clipping in front of us, like a matador waving a red flag in front of a bull, pointing to the exact [provocative] words and reading it to us, always admonishing and warning us 'not to read the trash.' Somehow, those clips always ended up on the bulletin board."[13]

Shapiro encountered a few players who bought into Allen's "the press is evil" philosophy, including Kilmer, John Wilbur, and Diron Talbert. He found many others fine to approach for quotes, such as Ray Schoenke, Ken Houston, Mike Bragg, Sam Wyche, Larry Brown, Harold McLinton,

Charley Harraway, Terry Hermeling, Paul Laaveg, Rusty Tillman, and Mark Moseley.[14]

John Schulian started at the *Washington Post* just before the '75 season and backed up Shapiro on the Redskins beat. He had previously worked as a general assignment reporter at the *Evening Sun* in Baltimore and wrote a freelance article about a boxing promoter who ran a gym above a strip joint. That article, he said, appeared in *Sports Illustrated* and inspired *Post* sports editor George Solomon to call and offer him a job. "His first words to me were, 'How would you like to make George Allen's life miserable?'" Schulian recalled. "I said, 'Well, yeah, why not?'"

Allen, Schulian said, took "years" out of Shapiro's life: "It was not an easy job. Len was a great reporter. He was relentless. It was difficult. The atmosphere was difficult. You could not walk out of Redskin Park and not have thoughts."

Allen's idiosyncrasies gave Schulian plenty to think about: "He was nuts. Everything he did. The whole paranoia business with Ed 'Double O' Boynton. It was crazy. Eating ice cream so he didn't have to waste time chewing. It became funny. I don't think George Allen was evil. I'm sure he was capable of skullduggery. He traded draft choices he didn't have. He was just wacky. He was obsessive. I'm sure you can find movie directors who are obsessed. That's what they think about 365 days a year, twenty-four hours a day. There isn't any room for anything else."[15]

Around the same time Schulian came to the *Post*, the newspaper's afternoon competition, the *Washington Star*, recruited David Israel from the *Chicago Daily News* as a sports columnist. He and *Star* sportswriter Tom Dowling "were of a different breed than traditional sportswriters," Faye Haskins wrote in her 2019 book, *The Evening Star: The Rise and Fall of a Great Washington Newspaper*. "Readers either loved or loved to hate them but rarely ignored them."[16]

From the start, Israel showed Allen no mercy, blistering him with scathing commentary. Asked why he was so unyielding in his criticism, Israel appeared to be motivated by reasons beyond Allen's record on the field. "I don't believe there should be a disconnect between politics and sports," he said. "The fact that he was so directly tied to Nixon, who I abhorred, did not endear him to me. Especially back then when things were much more open in virtually every locker room, that 'us against the world' paranoia team building thing with professionals didn't really play for me."[17]

Israel unleashed his first barrage on Allen after the Redskins refused to renew Sonny Jurgensen's contract in May 1975, ending his eighteen-year Hall of Fame career. In a column that chided Allen for secretly telling Jurgensen about his release, Israel interpreted Allen's facial expressions at an ensuing press conference to mean something sinister: "George said it was the toughest decision he ever had to make in his coaching career, telling Sonny he was through. He thrust out his chin. His upper lip was stiff. There wasn't a hair out of place. George, you know, is the kind of man who can make tough decisions."[18]

In 1977 Israel labeled Allen a "con artist" after Williams announced that he and Allen had agreed to terms on a contract extension. In an article headlined "The Master of Psyche Finally Blew One," Israel insinuated that Allen would have been better off entering the '77 season as a lame duck coach, in part so he could use that designation to motivate his players by telling them that he was working just as hard as ever and that they should, too. Instead, "George took the money and ran," Israel wrote.[19]

Israel also vilified Allen at the end of the '77 season. In a sarcastic fictional letter addressed to Allen, whom he called "Coach Coach," Israel mocked him for missing the playoffs in the final week of the season. He also congratulated him on the "marvelous job you did this season to get that God-awful Washington Redskins team to finish with a terribly respectable 9-5 record" after spending "hours telling us what a rotten team you were saddled with." Israel was trying to say that Allen came up short with a team much better than the one he was downplaying.

In the same article, with the status of Allen's contract extension still in limbo, Israel wrote that "it comes as no surprise" that Williams "is now reluctant to keep you on the payroll. It comes as no surprise that he might be encouraging you to move on."[20]

This time, Allen had an influential defender: South Dakota senator George McGovern, the Democrat who had lost miserably to Nixon in the '72 presidential election. Although the rivals stood on opposite ends of the political spectrum, they had one thing in common: their love for the Redskins. McGovern penned a letter to Allen in response to Israel's column, saying it "deserves the prize as the most outrageous journalism of the year."[21] Next, in a letter to Israel that ran in the *Washington Star* on December 23, 1977, McGovern called the prose "wrong-headed, mean-spirited, and unjustified." The senator also said the Redskins, given their age and injuries, produced a "miraculously successful season" in '77 and that he hoped Allen would be back the following year.[22]

McGovern had company supporting Allen in the face of media attacks: Etty Allen. The coach's animated wife maintained a contempt for the press similar to that of her husband and often fired off colorful language to describe her feelings about journalists she believed were attacking him. According to her daughter, Etty once referred to reporters coming to the Allen family's home after the Rams fired him in 1968 as the "invasion of Normandy." Another time, Jennifer Allen recalled, the French-speaking Etty Allen told a reporter, "You Americans are so brutal! So different from the French. At least when a man is standing at the guillotine, we give him a cigarette before cutting off his head!"

"It's kind of incredible some of the things my mom said to the media," Jennifer said. "Washington would just love her now. She was a journalist's dream. She was so outspoken, honest, and direct."[23]

According to George Felix Allen, "Our vibrant mother was loyally protective of her husband and all of her children. Any reporters who were personally critical of my father or were ignorant about football were really persona non grata to her."[24]

Once, Kenneth Turan of the *Washington Post* thought Etty looked as if she was fuming at the press. "I was in an elevator with her just by chance after a game, going to the locker room," he remembered. "We had these big press passes around our neck. I remember her looking at us with great displeasure. She probably felt that we didn't understand her husband, that we were giving him a hard time he didn't deserve."[25]

The *Washington Star*'s David Israel, so prickly in his columns about George Allen, bore no ill will toward his wife: "She was a nice lady. I met her a couple of times. I'm sure she resented the hell out of me because I was tough on her husband, but she never let me feel that. She never said it. She was always pleasant."[26]

Years later, Israel's wife, Lindy DeKoven, reached out to Allen when he coached at Long Beach State. An executive and producer at NBC at the time, she asked him in 1990 to be one of the people in a surprise video montage saying something about her husband and wishing him a happy fortieth birthday. Allen agreed to do it.

Israel and DeKoven were vacationing in Hawaii when they saw on the news that Allen passed away on December 31, 1990. He was surprised by her reaction:

"My wife goes, 'Oh, no, I can't believe George Allen has died. That's so terrible.' I said, 'Why do you care about George Allen?' She said, 'I know you covered him and knew him.' She wouldn't have been that upset even if our neighbor died. She was so upset. Three months later, my birthday came around, and she showed the tape at a surprise party she had for me. She told me, 'Remember when I was all upset about George Allen? I was supposed to interview him the day after we got back from Hawaii.' I didn't even know she knew who George Allen was."

17

Motivation—George Allen Style

NFL Films released a documentary in 2008 on the top ten motivational coaches of all time. The fifth coach on that list was George Allen.

Every NFL coach has his own motivational style. Vince Lombardi, Jon Gruden, Bill Cowher, and Bill Parcells, who occupy the No. 1, 3, 6, and 7 spots on that list, respectively, had an acerbic, in-your-face style and relied on intimidation to strike a chord with their players. Marty Schottenheimer, occupying the No. 4 spot, was known for his fiery pre- and postgame speeches that sent many players through a wall for him: "There's a gleam. Let's get the gleam." Dick Vermeil, at No. 2, used emotion and tears to inspire his troops.

Allen was cerebral. He never cussed at or demeaned his players in front of others, taking more of a civil approach. Of all of his motivational skills, he may have been most proficient at promoting team unity toward a particular cause.

Guard John Wilbur, who played for Allen for five seasons—one in LA and four in DC—said long after retiring that he had earned a "doctorate in motivation" from Allen. Wilbur, who in reality held a master's degree in business administration, coached special teams at the University of Hawaii in the 1980s.[1]

"He was a humanist," Wilbur said. "He taught you to know about yourself and how to get the most out of yourself. With George Allen, you were the most important. He taught you how to find ways inside of yourself to commit yourself to the group effort."[2]

Dan Reeves, the Los Angeles Rams owner who fired Allen twice, praised him for his ability to communicate with his players.

"George has always been able to get the most out of football players," Reeves told the *Los Angeles Times* after the Rams went 8-6 under Allen in '66, his first season in LA. "One reason is that he takes time to work individually with players. He listens to their problems. When you have the regular work load of preparing for a game, it's hard to give that individual attention. But George does it. He becomes close to his players."[3]

One way Allen inspired his players was through meaningful phrases that he would say or post on locker room walls:

"Winning is the science of being totally prepared. There is no detail too small."

"Is what I am doing—or about to do—getting us closer to our goal, winning?"

"People of mediocre ability sometimes achieve outstanding success because they don't know when to quit. Most men succeed because they are determined to."

"If you're not being tested, you're not living. It's a test that challenges your character. The tougher the job, the greater the reward."

Allen also delivered pregame oratory, such as his words before the Redskins demolished the Cowboys 26–3 in the 1972 NFC Championship Game—"Forty men together can't lose"—and made remarks that stressed the importance of detail, organization, ambition, and industriousness: "Show me a person without goals, and I'll show you someone who's dead!"

With a master's degree in education, Allen enjoyed teaching the game of football. He was meticulous with details, covering everything in practice he felt would mean victory, even having players do certain drills to a repetitive, boring extent. He believed that trivial matters could reflect whether a team had what it took to win. For one, he wanted his players to break the huddle with emphasis so they would look like they exuded the necessary confidence to win a championship. He didn't tolerate uncleanliness, considering it a sign that teams weren't serious about winning. Case in point: prior to the Redskins' 17–6 win over the Packers in 1974 at Green Bay's Lambeau Field, he told Redskins safety Brig Owens that the Packers were sending the wrong vibe.

"He pointed out to me that there's trash around here, and that's a sign we're going to win because they don't pay attention to details," Owens recalled. "When we got to the team meeting, he repeated it again, saying 'we're going to win this game tomorrow because I saw paper around the stadium, and that means they don't pay attention to details.'"

Similarly, Allen once saw a Coke can outside Redskin Park. He found that unacceptable. "He brought that Coke can into a meeting and built it into his talk about sloppiness," Redskins special teams standout Bill Malinchak remembered. "He told us you must have pride in everything you do, and this might be a minor thing to you, but the guy that threw this will probably go offside. That guy will not work the extra little bit that we need for him to dedicate himself."[4]

Said linebacker Chris Hanburger, "He was so corny about a lot of things he said or did that you couldn't help get caught up in it. For example, we were going into the playoffs one year, and he was always one to get as much information on who we were going to play as he possibly could. He called up to one of the teams up north. We weren't playing them. He was trying to get extra film from them or something. He told us they weren't a winning team because when he called nobody was in their office. Let's face it. All he lived for was football."[5]

Allen was unorthodox in other ways, too. He did everything he could to instill a sense of hatred in his players toward their most bitter rival: the Dallas Cowboys. He took taekwondo lessons in the mid-1970s with legendary martial arts expert Grandmaster Jhoon Rhee, widely recognized as the "father of American taekwondo," and learned how to break boards with his hands and feet. He made it to the middle ranking of green belt.[6] To demonstrate this athletic skill, he called a Redskins team meeting to show what he would do to Cowboys coach Tom Landry if the two met at midfield. He wore a martial arts uniform in the demonstration, which Brig Owens remembered:

"George was showing us his stance. He hit a board and then another board, and he couldn't break the board. He hit it finally and split the board. A splinter went into his hand, and he was bleeding. Bubba Tyer, the trainer, rushed over to bandage it up. George said, 'I just want to show you, that's how I was preparing for Tom Landry.' It was just his way of saying, 'Get ready. If it came between the two of us, if we had to meet at the 50-yard line, I would be a little older, but I'd be in better shape.' It was all about preparation. If you work harder, and you're better prepared than your opponent, then you can win. George was a great motivator, one of the greatest motivators of all time."

A Redskins teammate of Owens, offensive tackle Terry Hermeling, also has vivid memories of how Allen played up his loathing of the Cowboys and their reputation as America's favorite team: "We were in Dallas, and we always had a team meeting on Saturday nights. Usually, he'd start off by talking. When we walked in, he turned the lights out and turned the Cowboys' highlight film on from the year before. Pretty much that was the end of the meeting. The next day, we kicked the crap out of them. He got us all built up into a feverish pitch. That's the way he operated during his coaching career."[7]

To connect with his players, Allen used other tricks. Once he became a head coach, he acquired a lot of older veterans who became the backbone of his teams. He convinced them they could still play and treated them better than any of their previous coaches. Some were on their third team when they signed with him, and he had a message for them when they arrived. "The first thing he would say is, 'Your other team gave up on you. They think you're too old,'" said Mike McCormack, an assistant coach under Allen in DC in '71 and '72.[8]

David Israel, a *Washington Star* sports columnist during Allen's last three years in DC, told of a conversation he once had with Billy Kilmer, the pugnacious quarterback who played seven seasons for Allen in DC. Kilmer was thirty-one and a veteran of nearly a decade when Allen traded for him in '71. The Redskins were his third team. "I said to him, 'George was not your kind of guy. Why were you guys so loyal to him?'" Israel recalled. "He said, 'Because he was the only person who would hire us. We were all at the end of our career, and he gave us all a second or third chance.'"[9]

Interestingly, many of the players who were established Redskins when Allen arrived in DC in '71 disliked playing for him at times, according to Steve Gilmartin, the Redskins' play-by-play voice from '69 to '73. But "Allen's imports would sing his praises forever, guys like Diron Talbert, Jack Pardee, Richie Petitbon. They thought Allen hung the moon. Some of the older Redskins didn't because they were more used to running the team themselves. That sounds crazy, but those guys kind of ran things."

Hall of Fame safety Kenny Houston was another Allen import: "George was a master motivator," Houston said. "We didn't have a guy who wasn't crippled, and we definitely had none who weren't old. But for some reason he could get those guys up for games. The whole defensive backfield together couldn't run a 10.4 [in the 100-yard dash], and I ran a 10 flat."[10]

Allen not only told his starters that the game rested on their shoulders. He said the same thing to nonstarters to get them psyched. Rusty Tillman, a fearless linebacker on kick coverage and a leader on special teams, was a recipient of such pregame talk.

"We'd sit in the back of the locker room and share thoughts," Tillman remembered. "When we were done, I just felt like I had to win the game, it was all up to me. It wasn't until I quit playing and started talking to some of the other guys that I learned it happened to everybody. He had a way of making every guy feel like they were the most important guy on the team."

Late in the 1976 season, Bill Malinchak suspended his career as a commodities broker on Wall Street to return to the Redskins upon Allen's request. Malinchak had played for Allen from '71 to '74, proving to be a deadly punt blocker. After returning, he blocked a punt in the final regular-season game in 1976, a win over the Cowboys that qualified the Redskins for the playoffs.

"He wanted your best," Malinchak said of Allen. "He asked a lot of you. He always gave you the best coaching, tried to get you the best facilities, and treated you like a man. At that time, there was a transition where not a lot of coaches had a lot of respect for their players. It was still that kind of chattel mentality among some of the coaches. He had a lot of respect for the players. It was a joy playing for him."[11]

In wanting to make his players feel like they were appreciated, Allen was all in for acknowledging those who stood out during a win. He gave out awards during the week, whether it was television sets, clock radios, or gift certificates, which were all a big deal in those days. Defensive end Ron McDole recalled that color television sets were stacked up on the practice field at Redskin Park after the '72 NFC Championship Game win over the Cowboys because Allen wanted to acknowledge that every player had contributed to the monumental victory. Plus, in recognition of the player who had a really physical game but barely played within the rules, Allen presented a cash prize and a plaque displaying a piece of barbed wire.[12]

To Bobby Mitchell, the Redskins' director of professional scouting during the Allen era, it made sense for a coach to give players such incentives at the time because nobody made tremendous money, relatively speaking. "You could do that and motivate the guys," Mitchell said years later. "That wouldn't motivate anybody today because money is so big. It was a totally different thing. Everybody in their era has to use what he has, and George Allen used what he had."[13]

Allen even welcomed one of his Redskins players, reserve quarterback Sam Wyche, into the effort toward providing awards to teammates, knowing that doing so would strengthen team camaraderie. At the time, Wyche owned a chain of sporting goods stores called Sam Wyche Sports World in his home state of South Carolina. He started a tradition by presenting a trophy the day after a win to the Redskins' assistant coach whose players gave an excellent performance. It was called the "horse's ass award," a take on the crude song Redskins players sang to Allen and others after a win.

"George went along with all of this," Wyche said in a 2019 interview. "He loved these kinds of things. That's where I guess he was a player's coach. He didn't want your mind to be all football. He wanted your mind on the team, and football would come naturally. But I would always say, 'Okay, guys, I know you're all excited. Here's the winner of this week's coach's "horse's ass award."' As soon as I said that, I'd pause: 'Now, George, we all know who the real horse's ass is. That's you.' He and everybody else would laugh. He knew I was going to say it. George enjoyed that. That was his personality. He was serious a lot with the media and in public speaking appearances. But he was right there with the same mind-set as the players. He wanted a little break the day after a game."[14]

After retiring in 1976, Wyche launched an NFL coaching career. He assisted Bill Walsh in San Francisco on offense for a four-season run that included a Super Bowl victory before head coaching in the NFL for twelve seasons, eight in Cincinnati. His Bengals reached Super Bowl XXIII, losing to Walsh's 49ers in the last minute, 20–16.

Wyche is considered a disciple of Walsh, who earned three Super Bowl rings and is in the Hall of Fame. He also learned a thing or two from Allen.

"He kind of kept everybody on their toes," Wyche remembered. "But at the same time, he opened the door for comments. I did steal that from him. A good coach is observant. George was very observant. If you're observing, you can learn from players. They can teach you what they've learned from a high school coach or a junior high school coach that could pay off in the pros. When I say be observant, I mean be specific with what you're observing."

Allen, Wyche said, was clever at getting into the psyche of his players: "What's the player going through right now in training camp? Some are not sure if they're going to make the team. They've got a totally different worry going on in their brain, versus someone like Sonny Jurgensen, who knew he was going to be on the team. Some of the guys were at the end of the roster. He could relate to that last guy just like he related to the guys who were going to be the eventual starters."

Allen also possessed a "boyish manner that led you to believe he really loved the game," according to Wyche. "He loved that job, and he couldn't hide it. Everybody knew it's going to be fun working with this guy. He doesn't have his sights on being the NFL commissioner. He's happy wherever he is."

Washington Star sportswriter Steve Guback, who covered the Redskins during the Allen era: "George was childish in a lot of ways. That stomping around on the field after a victory and that cheer with the horse's ass, all of that was high school stuff. But the players enjoyed it, and George enjoyed it and got a lot out of them with it."

To further promote player bonding and enable everyone to feel united as one, Allen encouraged and underwrote Friday night team parties, as well as other player gatherings. "He motivated us to do a lot of things together," Brig Owens recalled. "We were always together as a team."[15] Allen also welcomed the "5 O'clock Club," a group of players who gathered after practice in a shed at Redskin Park to drink beer and tell stories.

"George Allen was a very interesting cat," said Redskins offensive tackle George Starke. "He didn't drink or anything like that, but he knew team bonding was very important. The Redskins had a party every Friday. It was all this food, all this booze, and all these chicks. I'm sure George paid for it."

In another effort to keep his players happy, Allen allowed them to indulge in cake and ice cream on Thursdays at Redskin Park after every victory. Legendary DC restaurant owner Duke Zeibert started that tradition. He drove to Redskin Park four days after the '71 season-opening win over the Cardinals to deliver a large cake. "George Allen officiated the cutting ceremony," the *Washington Post* reported, "and 40 players, just in from a long workout, ate the cake and some 75 bricks of vanilla ice cream in about 10 minutes." As the Redskins built their five-game winning streak in the ensuing weeks, Zeibert delivered cakes that read "Beat Dallas," "Think Four," and "Get Five."[16]

It's safe to say that most of Allen's players loved playing for him and played hard for him. But he wore out his welcome with other players. To some, the chants of "hip hip hooray" and "three cheers" that he led in the locker room after a win lost their charm after a while. "To be perfectly honest, a lot of guys are sick of George," a Redskin said late in Allen's term in DC, according to journalists William Gildea and Kenneth Turan. "The rah-rah approach is getting old."[17]

Merlin Olsen, the Rams' defensive tackle who starred on the Fearsome Foursome during Allen's stint in LA, also soured on his colorful coach over time.

"Allen operates in a very pressurized atmosphere," Olsen said. "At the end of a season with George, I felt like I had been beaten by 1,000 war clubs. It's like you're on the inside of a giant bass drum.

"You can only go to the well so many times. The first time he says this is the most important game of your lives, you believe it. Maybe you'll believe it the second or third time, too. But the 20th time, you start to wonder. If you ask for the superior effort week after week, after a while you don't get it. Sure, that's probably a major reason we never won a championship."

Which takes us back to the list of the ten best NFL motivational coaches of all time. The fact that Allen never won a Super Bowl and captured only two NFL playoff victories leads some to ask why he's considered one of the greatest motivators. Shouldn't that honor be reserved for coaches who were most successful when the stakes were highest?

It's all for history to decide.

18

"He's All They Have"

It was the summer of 1974. As his team trained in Carlisle, Pennsylvania, for the upcoming season, his fourth in DC, George Allen looked on with sadness as his friend, Richard Nixon, was losing his grip on the highest office in the land. On July 24 the Supreme Court ruled unanimously for Nixon's secretly recorded White House tapes to be released, providing undeniable evidence of his complicity in the Watergate break-in and cover-up. In the face of certain impeachment by Congress, he became the first president to resign from office.

"I have never been a quitter," Nixon said in addressing the nation on August 8 from the Oval Office. "To leave office before my term is completed is abhorrent to every instinct in my body. But as president, I must put the interests of America first. "Therefore, I shall resign the presidency effective at noon tomorrow."

Vice President Gerald Ford, the Michigan football star from decades past, assumed the presidency. He occupied the White House for only two and a half years. During that time, Allen accepted Ford's invitations for White House state dinners honoring Egyptian president Anwar Sadat and Jordan's King Hussein. Allen, never one to miss a chance to improve his team, inquired of both leaders whether they knew of any local athletes who could play in the NFL.

"When I met Sadat, I asked President Ford, 'Can this man find a football player for us in Egypt?'" Allen told Steve Guback in their 1989 conversation. "So Sadat's looking at me, and I'm pointing my finger at him, and Ford's laughing. Sadat's answer was, 'I think I can find a kicker.' At the state dinner for King Hussein of Jordan, same thing, I asked him, 'Are there any football players in Jordan? Is there a big guy there that's fast and strong?' He said, 'We might be able to find a kicker.' So everything was based on having a victory before we went to any one of those things."[1]

Allen didn't enjoy the length of friendship with Ford that the coach had had with Richard Nixon and Ronald Reagan. But their ties to Michigan made for a "pleasant relationship," George Felix Allen said. "My parents spoke kindly of Gerald and Betty Ford," he remembered. "Too much for my liking, as I was a green political rookie and chairman of the Young Virginians for Reagan," he said, referring to Ronald Reagan's bid for the Republican presidential nomination in 1976. Ford won the nomination but lost to Jimmy Carter in the presidential election.[2]

On the day Nixon left office and boarded Marine One from the White House lawn, waving good-bye with his customary V sign, the Redskins played their second exhibition game. It was ugly. The Oilers blew them out, 48–3, before the smallest crowd ever to see a game at RFK Stadium, 14,768. A week earlier, they had lost to the Packers, 21–16, in what was then the smallest attendance in RFK history: 16,403.

Why such scant interest?

NFL veterans, using the slogan "No freedom, no football," were on strike ahead of training camp against the owners; the players sought a system that would give them a greater say in trades and allow them to switch teams when their contracts expired. The owners ridiculed the proposal, saying it amounted to "anarchy." After a forty-two-day strike, the players returned to work on August 10, with the owners meeting none of their demands.

During the strike, Allen took extreme measures to keep his veterans fresh and in shape, even bending the rules a bit.

"It always amazed me that we had a practice schedule," recalled George Starke, a Redskins offensive tackle who went on strike. "I know George was meeting behind the scenes with his generals, which was against league rules at the time, and giving them practice stuff to do so we had something to officially work with as a team. He wanted the team to stay together because at some point the strike was going to be over. Other coaches and owners were trying to split their teams because they were trying to get their players to come in. George knew those teams would not fare well when the strike was over."

With Billy Kilmer, Sonny Jurgensen, and Sam Wyche on strike, a rookie Redskins quarterback started in their first two exhibition games. Well, sort of a rookie: Joe Theismann.

To get Theismann, Allen had traded the Redskins' first-round draft pick in '76 to the Dolphins, who had drafted him in the fourth round in '71 following his star-studded career at Notre Dame. But instead of playing for Miami, Theismann bolted for the Canadian Football League's Toronto Argonauts, who gave him a $200,000 deal that included a $50,000 signing bonus, which was much more than Miami's offer.

In three seasons in the CFL, Theismann threw for 6,093 yards and used his scrambling ability to run for another 1,054, despite missing nearly an entire season with an ankle injury. In his first season, 1971, he was named rookie of the year and guided the Argonauts to the Grey Cup. He twice led his conference in passing. In 1974, however, the Dolphins still held his rights.

At Theismann's introductory news conference on March 1, 1974, Allen had to temper the enthusiasm of the young man, who had shown an athlete's cockiness since the days when he quarterbacked undefeated youth and high school teams in New Jersey. He grew up admiring another brash quarterback, the Jets' Joe Namath, changed the pronunciation of his name from "THEEZ-man" to "THIZE-man" to rhyme with "Heisman" when he was a leading contender for the coveted trophy during his senior season at Notre Dame, and wrote a book on quarterbacking before he threw his first pass in the NFL.

"Both Sonny and Billy are great quarterbacks, and I can learn a lot from them," Theismann said. "I will play here, I'm confident of that. But right now all I really want to do is compete for the job and help the Redskins win the championship."

"He may have to be patient," Allen said in response.

"Patience is a virtue," Theismann replied.[3]

The Redskins needed young blood at the quarterback position. Both Jurgensen and Kilmer had had surgery in the off-season and would be forty and thirty-five years old, respectively, by the start of the season.

Theismann, who didn't immediately inherit the starting role, evolved into an iconic name in Redskins lore, a megastar for part of the franchise's glory run in the 1980s and early '90s under Coach Joe Gibbs. So did another player Allen signed in '74. With kicker Curt Knight considering retirement, Allen brought four kickers into training camp to compete for the job: two soccer-style kickers and two who kicked straight on.[4]

A conventional-style kicker with a 6-foot, 205-pound frame and a booming right leg emerged from the pack: Mark Moseley.

Moseley scored 67 points for the Eagles as a rookie in 1970. But he was cut during training camp. He signed with the Oilers and scored 73 points that season but suffered an injury and was released after the first game in '72.

Moseley sat out the rest of that year, as well as the entire '73 season. He worked jobs in the Houston area that included selling real estate and installing septic tanks. While lifting weights and putting on twenty pounds, he wrote and called every team hoping to get a tryout. Only one person responded: George Allen. The coach with a nose for spotting great special teams players had seen Moseley convert two field goals in wet and sloppy conditions in a Redskins win over the Oilers at RFK in 1971.

"George called and asked if I was ready to come back in the league," Moseley recalled. "So I came here and beat out several other kickers for the job. He was always a very motivating guy. I remember the first time I walked out on the field with him, he put his arm around my shoulder and said, 'Mark, you're here because of what you did in the past against us. I know you can do it again. If you kick that way, you can beat these guys out, and the job will be yours.'"

Validating Allen's eye for special teams talent, Moseley led the Redskins in scoring over the next twelve seasons. Today he's the team's all-time leader in points (1,206). He was a master of the clutch kick, converting a flurry of field goals with the game on the line to put the dagger in opponents, including several during the Allen era in DC.

Other new players on the roster included two-time first-team All-Pro guard Walt Sweeney and running back Larry Smith, a first-round pick of Allen's Rams in '69. Allen traded multiple draft picks for both players, who replaced two Redskins starters lost to the newly formed World Football League: guard John Wilbur and fullback Charley Harraway.

Allen worked overtime to acquire another veteran in 1974: Chicago Bears middle linebacker Dick Butkus, perhaps the greatest ever to play his position. Since parting ways with Butkus after his rookie season in '65, Allen had tried repeatedly to trade for the menacing linebacker, with no success. During the '73 season, Butkus started nine games while battling chronic knee injuries and was not the force he once was. The five-time first-team All-Pro saw multiple doctors, who basically told him his career was over. He considered retirement.

But Allen didn't give up. With Butkus still under contract to the Bears, Allen "snuck me in town" after the '73 season so Redskins team doctor P. M. Palumbo Jr. could evaluate him, Butkus remembered. "This sticks in my mind to this day. George said, 'Doc, can he be ready for the playoffs next January?' He was such a stickler for having veterans that maybe he thought they can't do things as well physically that they did in the past but that they never would make a mistake. So he said, 'I want you to go to one more guy in Oklahoma. He did a procedure on Sonny Jurgensen, so I'd like to see what he says.'

"When I went down there, the guy took X-rays and turned off the machine and said, 'Dick, you're through unless you want to have your legs fused stiff.' So I called George back and told him the results: 'It's over, George.' His parting words were, 'Dick, be careful.' I said, 'I'll be all right with the Bears. I think I'm going to go into coaching and everything will be all right.' He just said, 'Be careful with the Bears.' And how right he was."

Butkus had just finished the first year of a four-year contract with the Bears. But Bears owner George Halas, who was tight with the dollar, had some ominous words for him. "Halas told me if I don't play, I'm not going to get paid. I had a no-cut contract," the veteran player said.[5] In a $1.6 million lawsuit, Butkus charged the Bears with breach of contract. He settled for $600,000 in 1976.[6]

On the field, the Redskins finished 2-4 in the team's most chaotic preseason since Allen began coaching the Redskins in '71—not the kind of sizzling start Allen-coached teams were used to. Facing them was what he called the toughest schedule in the league, with four '73 division champions, two Monday night games, and an eighteen-day stretch that included two games against both the Eagles and Cowboys. The last of the four was against Dallas on Thanksgiving Day.

With one of the oldest teams in the league still trying to get in shape following the strike, the Redskins seesawed through the first half of the season at 4-3. Jurgensen and Kilmer resumed their rotational starting roles, with Jurgensen pulling off one of the most spectacular wins in Redskins history.

The Dolphins, who had won their second straight Super Bowl in January 1974, led the Redskins, 17–13, with less than a minute left at RFK. But Jurgensen carved up Miami's defense and displayed his Hall of Fame skills in the process. He completed 6 of 7 passes on a 60-yard drive that ended with his 6-yard touchdown toss to Larry Smith, one of Allen's off-season acquisitions, for the winning points. Mark Moseley kicked 40- and 41-yard field goals, and Larry Jones, picked up by Allen for $100 off waivers, returned a kickoff 52 yards. The win marked the last time Allen went head-to-head with one of his fiercest coaching rivals, Don Shula. Shula posted a 5-4-1 edge over Allen, including Miami's win in Super Bowl VII.

Afterward, another player Allen signed a few weeks before the regular season—Fearsome Foursome cornerstone Deacon Jones—explained why a George Allen–coached team could never be counted out. The '74 season marked Jones's fourteenth in the NFL.

"That's the thing about George Allen's teams," Jones told reporters. "He surrounds himself with people who are tough and experienced. He teaches pride until it's baked in your mind. When it comes to squeakers, his old pros are going to win nine out of ten of them."[7]

By midseason, a wild card playoff spot appeared to be the best the 4-3 Redskins could hope for. They had lost twice to the Cardinals, who held first place in the NFC East, three games over Washington. Plus, such key players as Jurgensen and running back Larry Brown were bruised and battered.

Allen improvised. He moved tight end Jerry Smith farther outside the tackle to create more of a three-wide receiver formation and make the passing game a greater threat. Uncharacteristically, he also gave his players an extra day off from practice during the week. "I believe you should practice Tuesday through Saturday," he said. "And I started giving the team Saturdays off—we shortened our week so that we could finish up on Fridays. That worked for a while. That's the way coaching is—nothing works repeatedly. So then we changed that and gave them Tuesday off and practiced on Saturday. It was more important to have a mental lift than to be overly prepared and not leave it [the game] on the practice field."[8]

The Redskins blasted off, winning six of their last seven games. The air attack indeed opened up, with Jurgensen and Kilmer placing first and third in NFC passing stats, respectively. Jerry Smith caught forty-four passes, his highest total since '69, as part of a passing game that finished first in the league and compensated for a rushing attack that was No. 23 in rank.

After four straight wins, including a close 28–21 win over the Cowboys at RFK, the 8-3 Redskins had climbed back into the NFC East race and stood within a game of the 9-2 Cardinals. Next up was a Thanksgiving Day matchup at Texas Stadium against the 6-5 Cowboys, who were having a forgettable season. A win would clinch a wild card spot for the Redskins and cause Dallas to miss the playoffs for the first time since '65.

True to form, George Allen was psyched to face his archenemy and salivated at the prospect of torpedoing the Cowboys' season. He just couldn't stand anything about that team and its high-and-mighty belief in itself, which morphed in the late 1970s into the moniker of "America's Team." At one point, Cowboys linebacker D. D. Lewis proclaimed that the opening in the roof at Texas Stadium, where the Cowboys began playing in 1971, existed "so God can watch his favorite team play."[9] Cowboys general manager Tex Schramm added to the team's flamboyance by expanding the tradition of sideline cheerleaders into a glamorous choreographed squad of accomplished dancers that he envisioned as another form of entertainment. The Dallas Cowboys cheerleaders debuted in 1972.[10]

The Cowboys did not officially become "America's Team" until NFL Films produced a documentary by that name detailing the Cowboys' '78 season. That year, they appeared in their third Super Bowl over four seasons, losing to the Steelers for the second time in that stretch. They beat the Broncos in Super Bowl XII in the '77 season.

"They are the Notre Dame of professional football, a national team whose popularity extends from coast to coast," narrator John Facenda said in the documentary. "Their success and style has gained them a following across the United States. They appear on television so often that their faces are familiar to the public as presidents and movie stars. They are the Dallas Cowboys. America's team."[11]

Even before the Cowboys were dubbed "America's Team," Allen and his players thought the Redskins deserved that distinction because they played in the nation's capital. "We were the true America's team as far as George was concerned," said one of his lieutenants on the field, safety Brig Owens. Fellow safety Kenny Houston agreed: "We felt like they took our towels, basically."

"It was very easy to build a rivalry with them," Bruce Allen said of the Cowboys. "Dad believed they were standing in the way of what we wanted to accomplish. They were also trying to be something other than a football team."[12]

Much of Allen's focus was on beating the Cowboys, even to the point of trivial matters. He guaranteed that the Redskins would defeat Dallas if he could sink a piece of crumpled paper into a trash can or pull a weed and its roots out of the ground. He was wholly consumed with overcoming those blue-and-silver-uniformed guys with the shiny stars on their helmets. "I wish we would play Dallas in a fourteen-game schedule," he said in 1975. "I'd never have to worry about the team being up."[13]

By the 1970s, the Cowboys had acquired a very methodical, corporate-like image, which was an extension of their stone-faced, no-nonsense coach, Tom Landry. While the animated Allen displayed exuberance on the sidelines and kid-like antics in the locker room, the nattily dressed, fedora-wearing Landry showed little emotion. Allen, who had earned a green belt in taekwondo, had once chopped boards in a team meeting to motivate his players by showing that he was ready to battle Landry if the two met before a game. That would have been an epic showdown. Landry, who flew B-17 bombers over Europe during World War II, played one season for the New York Yankees in the All-America Football Conference and six seasons for the New York Giants as a defensive back, punter, and kick returner, earning Pro Bowl and first-team All-Pro honors.

Personalities aside, the Redskins-Cowboys rivalry descended into a showdown between two brilliant football minds who held a mutual respect for one another. Landry is often credited with introducing the 4-3 defense while serving as the Giants' defensive coordinator in the '50s. With the Cowboys in the '60s, he devised bold new schemes like the Flex defense, which became known as the Cowboys' "Doomsday" defense. The Flex, a variation of the 4-3, was predicated on confusing the offense by moving both tackles off the line of scrimmage in a zone-type defense against the run. In 1975 Landry became the first NFL coach to regularly use the shotgun formation, in which the quarterback takes the snap several yards behind the center in obvious passing situations.[14]

Allen built the Redskins-Cowboys rivalry into one of the fiercest in all of pro sports, an encounter on par with the drama of the Lakers-Celtics matchups in basketball and Red Sox–Yankees in baseball. He reveled in fanning the flames of the rivalry and introduced "Dallas week," when the intensity among Redskins coaches and players, and in the entire DC area, skyrocketed in the days preceding a Redskins-Cowboys game.

Ken Houston also wished he could have played the Cowboys every week. "The intensity of those games was unbelievable," he said in retrospect. "If you came out of that game, and you weren't bleeding or could barely walk, you hadn't played. They really felt like that. It started with Tom Landry and George Allen. They just really despised each other. It was brutal because the day training camp began, you started preparing to beat the Cowboys. That was it. That's what you did. I wish we could have played them fourteen games a year. That's how intense it was. We just loved to play them. It was always the perfect setting, Monday night, Thanksgiving Day, a 4 o'clock game, RFK. Those kinds of games still give you chill bumps."

Joe Theismann: "George's whole thing about playing the Cowboys was they were prima donnas, and we were bullies. Let's get them in a street fight, and we can kick their rear ends. It was all about us getting physical with the Cowboys. At the time, the Cowboys used the shotgun on offense and the Flex defense, and so much about them seemed cerebral. It wasn't that they were better than you, it was that they could outsmart you. We felt we needed to take it into the gutter."

As Theismann recalled, for Allen, who went 10-10 against Dallas in his coaching career, any loss to the Cowboys was "gut-wrenching." Theismann added, "He was just so fired up when it was Cowboys week. I don't know if he ever slept. You could call it almost an obsession to beat the Dallas Cowboys. It was great, great satisfaction when we did and great, great disappointment when we didn't."

The same way Allen yearned to defeat Landry, his top coaching rival in the '70s, Landry carried the same craving to beat Allen. Unlike Allen, he didn't share that sentiment with his players in meetings and during practice, but his hunger to conquer Allen was written all over him, recalled Cowboys receiver Drew Pearson, who in '74 was in his second NFL season. "What added more to the rivalry is that competitive feud between Coach Landry and George Allen," Pearson said. "Coach Landry really wanted to beat George Allen before the Redskins. There's no question that motivated him even more, not that he slacked off at any time. But we could feel the intensity level rise in all our preparation when we played the Redskins.

"We got as fired up as Coach Landry would get fired up. We could tell we were getting ready to play the Redskins. We could tell we were going to be competing against George Allen. I've always said you get up naturally for certain teams. Some games you have to force yourself, or you're dealing with injuries or whatever circumstances. I enjoyed playing at RFK more than I enjoyed playing the Redskins at Texas Stadium. Easy to get up for, the fans booing you, hazing you, and cheering the Redskins like they did."[15]

The first time the rivals clashed in mid-November, the Redskins roared to a 28–0 halftime lead. But as they turned conservative, Dallas rallied to close the gap to 7 and had a first and goal on the 7 with about four minutes left. Dallas advanced 1 yard in three plays. On fourth down, Pearson ran a quick slant route into the end zone, but a low pass bounced off his arm. After the game, Cowboys quarterback Roger Staubach was asked what his team would do differently when the Redskins and Cowboys played again in ten days on Thanksgiving, and he replied, according to the *Post*, "We'll beat them. That's what'll be different."[16]

Allen used that comment as fodder, placing it in meeting rooms and on bulletin boards at Redskin Park. "It didn't surprise me that Roger would say that," he said in the days preceding the game. "Of course, I'd rather not have my players say something like that. No sense giving them any ammunition."[17]

Staubach, who took over as the Cowboys' full-time starting quarterback in '73, was one of those players Allen loved to unnerve. He often tapped one of his most treasured veterans, outspoken defensive tackle Diron Talbert, to get under the skin of Staubach, a Naval Academy graduate and the 1963 Heisman Trophy winner. Staubach carried an innocent, unblemished image that, coupled with his stellar play in the '70s, earned him the title of "Captain America." Talbert, a Texas native, carried the torch for Allen by saying Staubach "wears skirts" and "can't read defenses," among other jabs.

"Those things kind of worked," Staubach said in hindsight. "George believed you distract the other team by saying things, and Landry wouldn't allow us to say anything."

With the Cowboys' midseason trade of veteran Craig Morton, the backup to Staubach was rookie Clint Longley, a small college All-American from Abilene Christian in Texas who had never thrown a pass in the NFL. The scouting report on Longley was unflattering: "Average setup and delivery, not exceptional quick release. Has a good arm but throws off balance and falls away a lot."[18] Talbert envisioned a dreamy scenario that few players would broadcast today. "If you knock [Staubach] out, you've got that rookie facing you," he told the press. "That's one of our goals. If we do that, it's great. He's all they have."

His wish came true. With the Redskins leading early in the third period, 16–3, linebacker Dave Robinson delivered a crushing hit that knocked Staubach out of the game. With the future Hall of Famer sidelined and his unproven replacement taking the snaps, it looked like the Redskins would coast to victory.

Longley put his strong right arm to work. He threw a 35-yard scoring pass to tight end Billy Joe DuPree and led a four-play, 64-yard drive that ended with a short touchdown run. The Redskins regained the lead, 23–17, on a 19-yard run by Duane Thomas, whom Allen had re-signed after his nonproductive '73 campaign, and seemed en route to a joyous Thanksgiving dinner after recovering a fumble with more than two minutes left. "We could smell the turkey," Redskins receiver Charley Taylor remembered.

But Dallas regained possession on its 40 with 1:45 to play. Six plays later, with the ball at midfield, the clock showed thirty-five seconds left. Some in the crowd of 63,243 had already headed for the exits.[19] In the huddle, Pearson told Longley he would line up to the left, close to the Redskins' sideline, turn in, and take off downfield. Before the snap, Pearson recognized a voice coming from the sideline. It was George Allen:

"'Dallas Cowboys, Tom Landry, Roger Staubach, Tex Schramm.' Oh yeah. Loud and clear. I think he wanted me to hear it. He thought they had the game won. The way that stadium was configured, you could hear a lot of the talking on the sidelines. It didn't get lost in the crowd noise like you think it would. I heard him distinctly."

Pearson expected cornerback Mike Bass to pick him up in man coverage. Instead, Bass lined up off the line of scrimmage to prevent Pearson from getting behind him and going deep down the sideline. The safety was expected to negate the inside route. As soon as he saw zone coverage, Pearson's eyes lit up like a Christmas tree.

"It was the perfect coverage for the route I told Clint I was going to run," Pearson said. "So when I come off the line of scrimmage, I'm just going to widen Mike Bass out. Now, he's out of the picture, and I weeded back in. Now, I'm almost man to man on [nickel back] Kenny Stone. God bless him. He was a good player, but he was no cover guy."[20]

Pearson faked like he was going over the middle, Stone bit, and Pearson raced past him staring at nothing but the end zone. Longley, nicknamed the "Mad Bomber" for his tendency to go for broke in practice, hit Pearson in stride inside the 5. He coasted into the end zone with twenty-eight seconds left. The conversion gave the Cowboys an improbable victory, 24–23.

Allen was beside himself in the quiet Redskins locker room. He told reporters he didn't have anything to say but called the game "probably the toughest loss we've ever had. We apparently had it won. We had our chances. We had double coverage down there. Our playoff chances. Excellent."[21] A loss to the Cowboys was bad enough, but it was especially galling to succumb to a rookie quarterback who became nothing but a one-game wonder. Longley returned to the bench and stayed there through the '75 season before being traded to San Diego, where he played one year as a backup and then retired from the NFL. One of his nine career games, though, was calamitous in the eyes of George Allen.

"It was the first time in my twenty-six years of coaching that we lost a game like that," Allen said a few days after the game. "Twice, Longley threw right into double coverage and got away with it. I talked with the players on the plane ride home. There were twenty different things we wished we could do over again.

"This type of defeat can stay with you a while and take something out of your team if you're not careful. These are the kind of games you remember if you live to be 100."[22]

Was it Allen's toughest single-game defeat ever? Bruce Allen said the Super Bowl VII loss to the Dolphins was worse.[23] Nevertheless, the sting of that second-half Thanksgiving collapse forever haunted George Allen and his family. "We still bring it up every Thanksgiving," Jennifer Allen said in 2021.[24] Pearson, a clutch, big-play receiver who caught nearly five hundred passes in his career and was enshrined in the Hall of Fame in 2021, remembered what Allen told him when former Redskins and Cowboys met in a charity flag football game in 1989. Allen said the zone defense in which the Redskins lined up on the winning touchdown pass was one of the "most regretful" decisions he ever made as a head coach, according to Pearson.

"He said that was one of the biggest mistakes he made by not changing that coverage or not going with the coverage he wanted to go with initially," Pearson said. "He said one of the coordinators told him to play that coverage. He wanted Bass on the line on me and Stone to pick me up deep. He thought that coverage may have worked better than the coverage we got."[25]

Because of that play, the Redskins needed to wait eleven days for another chance to clinch a wild card spot. A few days before that Monday night game in Los Angeles against the Rams, Kenny Stone unintentionally crossed paths with Allen at Redskin Park. Everyone knew how badly Stone felt after Pearson burned him on the winning touchdown pass. Allen tried instilling some positive reinforcement in the beleaguered safety.

"I was in the hallway making sure that I didn't run into Coach Allen," Stone remembered. "Lo and behold, I saw him one day. He asked me how I was doing. I told him I was okay. He goes, 'You know, Kenny, the only way you can overcome a play like that is to make a big play in the next game.' I played for enough coaches who wouldn't have handled it that way. He was a winner, and he knew how to motivate players. As a young player, it helped me. That's why guys like me loved to play for him."[26]

With the Redskins leading, 23–17, the clock ticking down, and the Rams in possession—the same scenario that existed in the Dallas game—quarterback Ron Jaworski threw a long pass that was intercepted with twelve seconds left by none other than Kenny Stone—his fourth of a team-high five interceptions that season. The win clinched Allen's fourth playoff appearance in four seasons in DC and marked the second time in two games that he had topped the team that discarded him, both before a Monday night TV audience at the Los Angeles Coliseum.

The 9-4 Redskins now sat tied for first in the NFC East with 9-4 St. Louis. A win over the Bears in the season finale, coupled with a Cardinals loss to the Giants, meant the Redskins would win the division, once a distant thought. Both Washington and St. Louis won, leaving the Redskins as the NFC wild card team facing another trip to LA to play the NFC West–winning Rams.

In a 42–0 dismantling of the Bears at RFK, the Redskins piled up 511 yards in the most overpowering display of offense in the Allen era. Kilmer sat while Jurgensen and Theismann split the two halves, throwing a touchdown apiece. Washington's defense, one of the best in the NFL in '74, posted four interceptions and four sacks and allowed a mere 126 yards. Even Deacon Jones, the perennial All-Pro playing the last game of his star-studded career, kicked an extra point to put the Redskins up, 42–0. How did that happen?

According to punter Mike Bragg, who subbed that day for injured kicker Mark Moseley, after the Redskins took a 35–0 lead in the fourth quarter, Jones lobbied Allen for the chance to kick the conversion if the Redskins scored again. "Coach thinks, 'Okay, the Bears are just going to run the clock out, and this won't even matter,'" Bragg said. "So [Allen] said, 'Yes, you can do it.'"

After the Redskins took a 41–0 lead, the moments before the kick were chaotic. "Deacon goes into the huddle, and I stay on the sideline because coach says, 'Let him kick it,'" Bragg remembered. "Sonny calls timeout. He comes to the sideline and says to Coach Allen, 'You really want to let him kick this?' Coach says, 'Yeah, I promised. Let's just get this over with.' Sonny said this is getting to be a three-ring circus. This is like rubbing salt in their wounds. He said he wouldn't hold for it. So Theismann goes in and holds."[27]

With the repositioning of the goalposts to the back of the end zone in '74, Jones attempted a 20-yard kick. It bounced off the right upright and over the crossbar.

So after an incredibly slow start for an Allen-coached team—a 2-4 preseason and a 4-3 mark in the first half of the season—the Redskins were twenty-eight seconds from going 7-0 in the second half. They were steamrolling into the playoffs. Maybe the forty-two-day summer strike played a role in the second-half surge. Due to the strike, the veteran players didn't have to grind through Allen's notoriously tedious training camps. In '74 it took them longer to find their stride in the regular season. But once they did, the Redskins became a team nobody wanted to face.

"This was not a young football team," Theismann said. "So not having all of that preseason, not having training camp, but really sort of using the early part of the season to get in shape and get things to where you wanted them allowed us to peak toward the end of the year."[28]

To *Washington Star* sportswriter Steve Guback, Allen's top-tier motivational skills also played a decisive role in the team's ascent. "If there was one thing Allen maintained all season long it was the Redskins' emotion and drive," Guback wrote on December 21, 1974, just before the playoffs began. "He called every game a 'championship game' and has his team believing it. His intensity at practice, his restlessness during a game, his exuberance after victory, infected the Redskins almost to the point where they seemed possessed. They played the way Allen wanted them to play, always fired up."[29]

Yet the team looked deflated in the playoffs, turning the ball over six times against the Rams in their sloppiest game of the year, a 19–10 loss. Kilmer started the game. But Allen benched him for Jurgensen, with the Rams ahead early in the fourth period, 13–10. Sonny came out firing before linebacker Isiah Robertson, whom the Rams had selected with a No. 1 pick that Allen traded in his 1971 purge of draft choices, picked off a pass and returned it 59 yards for a touchdown. Unlike the magic he had shown in the regular season, Jurgensen failed to rally the Redskins in his first and only career playoff appearance, throwing two more interceptions that sealed the team's fate.

For the third time in four seasons, Allen's Redskins were eliminated in the first round of the playoffs. In the locker room, an anonymous player vented to Guback on Allen's decision to start Kilmer: "I just hope you rip the S.O.B. for not starting Jurgensen. You could poll this team, and if they'd tell you what really was on their mind, it would have been 100% for Jurgensen. When he finally gets in, we're behind, we're backed up on our own nineteen, and he has to throw."[30]

Jurgensen or Kilmer, Sonny or Billy? That question had hovered over Allen's team for three full seasons. The 1975 off-season was no different, with the Redskins' quarterback position dominating the news. Would both of those ancient quarterbacks, with a combined thirty years of NFL experience, remain on the roster? If not, which one would Allen keep? It was a luxury to have both. In '74 Jurgensen placed first in the NFC with a 64.1 completion percentage. Kilmer was third, with a 58.5. And how did Theismann, the young, mobile quarterback who was itching to get on the field, factor into the equation? He completed 6 of 7 passes for 123 yards and a touchdown in the '74 season finale against the Bears, his best performance of the year.

Edward Bennett Williams, in a February 1975 memo to Allen that featured a list of suggestions for trimming the team's expenses, insisted that both Jurgensen and Kilmer could not remain on the roster. To Williams, who said "we are obviously paying over $100,000 a year too much for quarterbacks," it was one or the other. Jurgensen made a reported $180,000 in 1974 and averaged $150,000 during Allen's first four seasons. Kilmer made $125,000 in 1974.[31] All of the team's owners, Williams noted, believed Theismann should be the team's starting quarterback in '75.[32]

In addressing the quarterback quandary, Allen conveyed his affinity for Kilmer and said any belief he'd "had it in" for Jurgensen since becoming the Redskins' coach in '71 was "inaccurate."

"When I've used Sonny, he has done a good job," Allen said. "I think Sonny made more of a contribution last year and was with the program more than any other year. Billy Kilmer has been 100 percent with our football program. I have some loyalty—if anything, I'm sometimes too loyal to players and carry them beyond their playing time—and Billy has taken us to the playoffs four straight years. I just can't drop him. I think if Sonny had been healthy and had been able to contribute that wouldn't have been a problem. So it has been circumstances more than anything else." Allen also declared that he'd never been a "two quarterback" coach and that Kilmer was the team's "No. 1 quarterback."[33]

In a sign of the inevitable departure of one of his quarterbacks, Allen signed Randy Johnson, who had thrown for more than 7,500 yards in eight NFL seasons. Most recently, he had played one season for the Hawaiians of the World Football League and led them into the playoffs. Johnson was one of three possible backups to Jurgensen that Allen listed when he became the Redskins' head coach in January 1971. Another one was Kilmer.

Meanwhile, contract extension talks with Jurgensen that had begun about a year earlier dragged on. If unsigned by May 1, he would technically become a free agent. "I'm here every day, and I'll be here when Sonny has time to sit down and talk about his future," Allen said after signing Johnson.[34] Given the uncertainty about who would be staying and going, Kilmer asked Allen for a trade.

A few days before the deadline, Allen and Jurgensen met alone at the Dulles Airport Marriott. The coach told the eighteen-year veteran with more than 32,000 career passing yards, 255 touchdown passes, a 57.1 completion percentage, and an 82.8 passer rating that he was being phased out of the Redskins' quarterback rotation. The two had never seen eye-to-eye on offensive philosophy. Allen's decision brought their discord to a crescendo.

"That was a very sad moment," Jurgensen said in looking back. "I felt I could still contribute. I felt I would have enough intelligence to know when to get out.

"Billy had a desire to be traded at the time. But George was trying to talk Billy out of that. He said if we can't talk Billy into staying and coming back with us, then we would have you back. I said, 'That's no fun.' That was hurtful. It didn't sit well. It made me decide that if you don't think I can help you, then thank you very much."[35]

Jurgensen, who went 11-2 as a starter under Allen, compared with 41-49-5 in his previous seven seasons, tearfully announced his retirement at a press conference on May 1 at Duke Zeibert's restaurant in DC. Duke Zeibert presented him with a bottle of his favorite scotch. Sonny took questions from reporters, saying he understood Allen's decision but didn't appreciate how it was conducted. He also said he had received an offer to play in the World Football League but didn't think he would accept it.

Allen was a few blocks away at the time participating in a karate exhibition that benefited his American Indian scholarship fund.[36] The same day, he held his own press conference at Redskin Park.

"Money was a factor," Allen said. "But Sonny has been injured three of the four years I've been here. We have a young quarterback named Joe Theismann who has to be developed. We felt that Billy Kilmer could play fourteen games, and that Theismann would back him up.

"This is the toughest decision I've had to make in my coaching career."[37]

The night before, the Washington Bullets hosted the Boston Celtics in an NBA playoff game at the Capital Centre in Landover, Maryland. At halftime, Allen appeared on the video screen over the court and began plugging his upcoming karate exhibition. He was met with deafening boos from the more than nineteen thousand fans in attendance because of his perceived callousness in showing a beloved player the door.[38]

Sonny Jurgensen was a tremendous fan favorite then and in the ensuing years as he remained synonymous with the franchise. In 1975 he began doing sportscasting for local TV station WTOP and color analysis on NFL games for CBS. When commenting on the Redskins, he went full bore in criticizing Allen's decision-making, whether it was benching Billy Kilmer or taking points off the board after a penalty in exchange for a first down. Jurgensen even questioned Allen's motivational skills, one of his premier coaching talents.

But a year after his retirement, Jurgensen told the *Washington Post* that Allen had done him a "favor" by refusing to offer him a contract. "I'd had enough injuries," he said. "I'd played long enough. Yes, it was a blow to my ego, but it was the right time. I know that now. If I had tried to play another year, the TV possibilities might not have existed."[39]

In 1981, two years before his Hall of Fame induction, Jurgensen became a color analyst for the Redskins' radio network and maintained that role for nearly four decades. He was a pillar on the "Sonny, Sam, and Frank" trio that gained fame during the Redskins' glory years under Joe Gibbs in the 1980s and early '90s. In announcing his retirement before the 2019 season, he singled out special relationships he had built since becoming a Redskin more than fifty years earlier, in 1964, including coaches Bill McPeak, Otto Graham, Vince Lombardi, and Joe Gibbs; owners Edward Bennett Williams, Jack Kent Cooke, and Dan Snyder; and front-office executives Bobby Beathard and Bruce Allen.

Conspicuously absent from that list was George Allen.[40]

But was Allen fully to blame for Jurgensen's departure in 1975? In addition to Allen, offensive coordinator Ted Marchibroda harbored doubts about Sonny's ability to stay healthy and start over a "period of time."[41] Plus, Williams issued his ultimatum that, for economic reasons, Allen couldn't keep both Kilmer and Jurgensen on the roster. Bruce Allen described that as the "pressure point."[42] Thus, what precipitated Sonny's exit is open to interpretation.

Williams told the *Washington Post* that he supported Allen's decision "100%" to part ways with Jurgensen. He curiously noted that Jurgensen's salary did not factor into the decision but opined that Sonny could no longer play without a near certain risk of injuries.

"Joe DiMaggio retired," Williams said. "Every athlete reaches the point where he has to step down. It would have been dreadful if he played again in 1975 and got hurt. There is no question in my mind that if he did come back he would have gotten hurt."[43]

As for Kilmer, Allen reined in his gutsy leader. The Bears and 49ers were reportedly interested in him at one point, but trade talks never materialized.[44] Heading into the '75 season, Allen for the fifth straight year named Kilmer the starting quarterback, followed by Theismann and Johnson. "I went to George Allen because I knew there were some teams out there that wanted me," Kilmer remembered. "I knew he wasn't going to trade me, but at least I wanted him to know that I wanted to be. George liked me. He really saved my career, and I knew his feelings about me. I used it as a tool to find out how much he really liked me or respected me."

As if Jurgensen's fate were not enough to dominate the off-season news, Allen's pursuit of a colossal-sized man to block kicks and take up space on the defensive line—pro wrestler André the Giant—created its own set of headlines. The 7-foot-5, 450-pound behemoth had never played football, nor was it known if he had the instincts to play the game. Born in the French Alps and of Bulgarian descent, he didn't speak English. So why the interest other than his size and strength?

After the NFL draft in January, Allen said he'd like to sign an "unusual" player, perhaps someone seven feet tall. That's the story Redskins personnel director Tim Temerario told at a news conference at Duke Zeibert's restaurant in DC, just days before the start of training camp. With that in mind, Temerario tracked down and initiated talks with André's agent, Vince McMahon, who accompanied the pro wrestler to the press conference.

Allen had a history of making surprise acquisitions, although it soon became clear that this one was a long shot. Both sides expressed interest in cutting a deal, with McMahon saying it was "not impossible" that André the Giant would end up on the Redskins. "His box office appeal would double if he did," McMahon said. "He is an unbelievable athlete. I am sure that with proper coaching he could make it in pro football."[45]

Temerario said he spoke to Allen about whether André the Giant possessed the quickness and agility to be a defensive tackle or end. Temerario also doubted the wrestler's ability to commit enough time to the Redskins, given his year-long schedule that involved traveling from city to city for wrestling matches. "If he's willing, we could try him out today or tomorrow," Temerario said. "If he runs the forty in seven seconds, forget it."[46]

Other impediments were the language barrier and André's annual earnings of more than $200,000. Allen couldn't come close to matching that kind of money, especially for only a six-month commitment, although McMahon said his client wouldn't ask for an "unusually high purse" as long as he could play in Washington. "I have a soft spot for the Redskins," McMahon said. "I still have season tickets. For the Redskins, we'd make concessions. For any other team, no."[47]

But just like that, it was over. André the Giant bolted town for wrestling matches in Scranton, Pennsylvania, and New York City, never entertaining another thought of playing football.[48]

Were Allen and the team serious about signing him? "That was more of an off-season stunt than anything else," said *Washington Star* sportswriter Steve Guback, who reported on the press conference at Duke Zeibert's. "Andre couldn't play football for crying out loud. He didn't know how to rush a passer or shed a blocker. It made for a nice offseason story."

Bruce Allen didn't consider it a publicity stunt but a way to gain an edge on opponents. He said his father thought André would be a great field goal and extra point blocker, partly because of the goalpost repositioning from the goal line to the back of the end zone in '74. Because of that change, Bruce explained, kicks took off on a lower trajectory and were easier to block at the line of scrimmage.

"[André the Giant] was making so much money that he didn't want to do it," Bruce surmised.[49]

To Joe Theismann, who attended the press conference at Duke Zeibert's at Allen's request, the André the Giant story was a by-product of Allen's talent at marketing the name of his team. During his days in the Canadian Football League, Theismann saw André the Giant wrestle in Canada and became a friend.

"You have to put things into perspective," Theismann said. "Back in '74, you didn't have the 24/7, 365 media that you have today. You had three newspapers in town, maybe two, and not a lot of network TV. George wanted to make sure the Washington Redskin name was out there. He was extremely creative and a great marketer of the football team."[50]

Not long after, Allen acquired a defensive tackle who wasn't as big as André the Giant but still loomed incredibly large: 6-foot-7, 295-pound Dave Butz. Once the top draft choice of the St. Louis Cardinals in '73 and the fifth player chosen that year, he arrived in DC during the '75 exhibition season amid a shockwave of controversy. It was because George Allen the maverick decided to test the waters of free agency, a rarity at the time.

Butz had missed nearly the entire ’74 season due to a serious knee injury and played out his option to become a free agent. The Cardinals were unsuccessful in re-signing him, so Allen maneuvered in to sign him to a three-year, no-cut $200,000 contract, outbidding the Raiders in the process.[51]

Butz came at a steep price and not just because of his salary. Under the “Rozelle rule” for free agency, NFL commissioner Pete Rozelle would award a compensation package to the Cardinals if the two teams failed to reach an agreement. The Cardinals, perturbed that Allen had signed Butz before the two teams could agree on compensation, wanted Allen to pay dearly for acquiring a player that Cardinals director of operations Joe Sullivan, Allen’s former right-hand man with the Redskins and Rams, said had “unlimited potential” and could possibly be the best defensive lineman in the NFL.[52]

“My father’s first objective was getting Dave Butz signed,” Bruce Allen reasoned. “He wanted to make sure he got the player and the person. The draft compensation was in a range that he could deal with later.”[53]

Cardinals coach Don Coryell was skeptical that a deal could be reached. “There’s no way you can negotiate with a man like him,” Coryell told reporters in reference to Allen.[54] But after a few weeks of haggling, the Redskins and Cardinals agreed on compensation before Rozelle had to intervene. Allen gave the Cardinals his first-round picks in ’77 and ’78 and a second-rounder in ’79, the steepest package since the Saints signed tight end Dave Parks in ’68 and compensated the 49ers with defensive tackle Kevin Hardy, a No. 1 pick that year, and a No. 1 choice in ’69.[55] The Redskins received the Cardinals’ fifth- and fifteenth-round choices in ’76 and their sixth-round pick in ’77, in addition to the rights to Butz. One NFL general manager thought Allen had made a “terrible deal” for a relatively untested player fresh off a brutal knee injury.

“I’d only think about giving up that much for a very superior quarterback or middle linebacker or running back, someone who I knew would put us completely over the hill,” the general manager told the *Washington Post*. “If he plays, he’s got to be a dominant force, not just a so-so guy. If he’s good but not great, say like Bill Brundige, then it’s an awful deal. It will affect the franchise, because things like the Duane Thomas deal kill a team if they happen too often.”[56]

Allen paid two No. 1 draft choices for the talented and moody Thomas, one in ’75 and one in ’76. But Thomas rushed for only 442 yards and five touchdowns over the '73 and '74 seasons. After the Redskins refused to meet his $165,000 contract demand, he signed with a World Football League team.[57]

In the Butz trade, the Cardinals' picks turned out to be quarterback Steve Pisarkiewicz (1977), defensive back Ken Greene (1978), and linebacker Calvin Favron (1979).[58] Pisarkiewicz was a complete bust, Greene had a modest seven-year NFL career, and Favron played mostly on special teams over four seasons.

Interestingly, of all the players Allen coached over the years, he found Butz the hardest one to motivate when he first came to the team. But some Allen-style mentoring and inspiration garnered the approval of U.S. secretary of agriculture Earl Butz, Dave's uncle.

"I spent a lot of time with him," Allen said. "He came in at 309, 310 pounds and couldn't even run eight striders, or eight 40s. He was in such bad shape. He had been working in a bank as a teller, he had some sit-down job, and he came in late. He was behind everybody, and we had kind of a complicated defensive system. So he started making mistakes, and some of the defensive players got on him. I counted on him to help us because I knew he had a lot of ability. I believed in him and knew that in time he'd be an All-Pro. I told him that."[59]

Sure enough, Butz improved steadily under Allen and became one of the league's premier defensive linemen. He was named to the NFL's All-Decade Team of the 1980s (second team). In his greatest season, 1983, he earned Pro Bowl and first-team All-Pro honors, posting a career-high 11.5 sacks and forcing a team-high 5 fumbles, as the 14-2 Redskins marched to Super Bowl XVIII. That year he was named the NFL's Defensive Lineman of the Year. He started on two of the Redskins' Super Bowl–winning teams in the 1980s, XVII and XXII.

For Allen, the Butz transaction contributed to a hectic day of personnel moves. He also acquired offensive tackle Tim Stokes from the Rams for four Redskins draft picks and traded reserve cornerback Ted Vactor to the Bears for an undisclosed draft choice. In all, he parted ways with seven draft choices and picked up six, a flurry of single-day activity he had not engaged in since trading seven picks and a linebacker to the Rams on January 28, 1971, draft day.[60]

The Redskins opened with resounding wins at RFK over the Saints (41–3) and Giants (49–13). Then came a 26–10 loss to the Eagles, Allen's first in nine games against Philadelphia as the Redskins' coach. With Allen's mother, Loretta Hannigan Allen, looking on at Veterans Stadium, the Redskins committed six turnovers and allowed 395 yards against the 0-2 Eagles, the second most in Allen's stint in DC. He called the loss a "good whipping."[61]

Against the Eagles, the Redskins lost nickel back and special teams standout Ken Stone to a serious knee injury. He had already blocked a punt and a field goal that season. So Allen went to his extensive files and claimed second-year safety Eddie Brown, who had just been cut by the Browns, off waivers for $100. Allen called him a "replica of Kenny Stone." Brown was also impressed with his new coach when the two met for the first time.[62]

"He knew more about me than my mother," Brown remembered. "You think that's funny, but he had it laid out: 'This is what I expect out of you. This is what we want you to do.' I'd been in pro ball for two years. Nobody had a plan. It was sort of helter-skelter. Allen gave me a playbook that was about three inches thick. He said, 'Now, you just have to know this by Sunday.' That was about an inch and a half of it."[63]

Allen's extensive homework on Brown produced enormous returns—literally and figuratively. Brown's 13.46-yard punt return average in 1976 was the second-best mark in Redskins history. His 1,150 punt return yards were No. 1 in the Redskins' record books by the end of the '77 season.

Prior to those feats, Brown took part in perhaps the most thrilling and frustrating season in Redskins history: 1975. A year earlier the NFL had implemented a fifteen-minute overtime period for regular-season games tied at the end of regulation—a move that Allen had long opposed because of his belief that it didn't help the game that much.[64] In 1975 the Redskins played in three overtime games and two others that came down to the final play—all in a little more than a month. The resilience and intestinal fortitude of the Redskins' players were put to the test. So was Allen's patience with the referees.

The Redskins went 1-2 in the overtime games. They first knocked off the Cowboys at RFK to move into a first-place tie with Dallas in the NFC East at 5-2. After Bryant Salter blocked a 28-yard field goal try at the end of regulation to preserve a 24–24 tie, Kilmer sneaked over from the 1 in overtime for the winning score.

Two weeks later, with the 6-2 Redskins in St. Louis battling the 6-2 Cardinals for first place in the division, the Cardinals faced a fourth and goal from the 7 with twenty-five seconds left and the Redskins up, 17–10. Cardinals quarterback Jim Hart connected with receiver Mel Gray in the end zone, but cornerback Pat Fischer pounded Gray simultaneously and forced the ball out before Gray's feet hit the ground.

Confusion ensued. One official ruled touchdown. Another signaled incompletion. After about a ten-minute huddle, an official emerged raising his arms. The extra point tied the game, and St. Louis won on a field goal in overtime. It appeared Allen and the Redskins got robbed.

"Everyone on our sideline thought we won the game," Allen told reporters. "We were jumping up and down and congratulating each other. Then the officials have a powwow and decide to change their decision. We lost by delayed reflex. It's the first time I've ever seen that happen."[65]

In the minds of Allen and his players, the play became known as the "phantom catch." "Under no circumstances was Mel Gray's catch a completion, by the rules of 1975 or of today," Bruce Allen said, making a statement of fact.[66]

The next week, the Redskins saw a repeat at RFK when forty-eight-year-old George Blanda kicked a 27-yard field goal in overtime to give the Raiders a 26–23 win. The game may have ended in regulation if not for another bizarre call in the fourth period. The officials ruled that Ken Houston interfered with Raiders receiver Cliff Branch, although it appeared that Branch had rammed into Houston. The penalty call moved the Raiders 32 yards and set up a short field goal that gave Oakland a 23–16 lead. The Redskins tied the game at 23 with a little more than two minutes to play.

After the losses to the Cardinals and Raiders, Allen voiced his support for instant replay, a contentious issue from the time the NFL began regularly televising games in the late 1940s. He also advocated for instant replay because of a game-deciding call in the Redskins' loss to the Patriots in '72. Replays showed that Redskin Bill Malinchak, after blocking a punt with less than a minute to play, recovered and had possession of the ball before rolling out of the end zone. Instead of taking a 28–24 lead, the Redskins lost, 24–23, because of perhaps the most controversial safety call in NFL history. In 1976 the NFL began experimenting with instant replay and adopted limited use of it a decade later. It has existed in its current form for more than two decades, with a few tweaks along the way.[67]

"Dad was at the forefront of wanting instant replay to avoid mistakes by refs changing the outcome of a game," Bruce Allen said. "He demanded it in the 1980s in the United States Football League, which adopted it.

The NFL belatedly got around to his innovative way of thinking shortly thereafter. The league knew that the Gray completion and the pass interference penalty against Kenny Houston were both mistakes that cost the Redskins wins in 1975."[68]

At 6-4 and with his playoff hopes on life support, Allen said the Redskins would make the postseason. His players answered with a no-quit attitude by pulling off two straight wins on the last play of the next two games. In their third straight game against a 1975 division winner, the 10-0 Vikings, the Redskins squeaked out a 31–30 win. Defensive end Ron McDole, who made an art of blocking kicks in his eighteen-year career, deflected a 45-yard field goal try to preserve the win.

"It sure would be nice to get a game where we'll get ahead and stay ahead and be able to relax a little bit," Allen told reporters. "But each week I'm so proud of this football team. We've had the three overtimes and today, in which we showed as much character as any football team I've been associated with."[69]

One week later, Mark Moseley booted his first of many game-winning kicks for the team, a 39-yarder with two seconds left in a 30–27 victory over Atlanta. Now, a win over 8-4 Dallas at Texas Stadium would put the 8-4 Redskins in the playoffs. A loss, and they were done. The Cowboys administered a pounding with their largest margin of victory over Washington in the Allen era: 21 points. With a 23-point loss to the lowly Eagles in the season finale at RFK, the Redskins finished 8-6.

It had been a wild season. Amid all of the mentally exhausting finishes, the Redskins persevered. But two questionable calls were key to torpedoing their bid for a fifth playoff appearance in Allen's fifth season in DC. The season also marked the start of media speculation about Allen's contractual status and his future with the Redskins. Reports focused on whether he planned to leave after the '75 season for a new job, whether he intended to fulfill his seven-year contract through the '77 season, or if he wanted to extend it. In a wide-ranging interview with the *Washington Star* in the '75 off-season, Allen was asked whether he had thought about leaving the Redskins if an option to own stock in a team ever came up. He responded by putting a positive light on what were likely uncomfortable meetings with Edward Bennett Williams.

"I've been very happy here," Allen said. "Ed Williams has cooperated with me. He's been a good man to work for. I actually enjoy visiting with him because he's competitive. It would take a gold-plated offer to get me to leave. Naturally, every coach, though, wants ownership."

When asked if he owned stock in the Redskins, Allen said, "I expect to have it someday, put it that way."[70]

During the season, the *Washington Post* reported that Allen and his Los Angeles–based attorney, E. Gregory (Ed) Hookstratten, were seeking to launch contract extension talks with Williams. Columnist Ken Denlinger wrote that it was a "curious time" to begin negotiations on a contract that didn't expire for two and a half years. But he surmised that the desire to renegotiate may have stemmed from the five-year, $750,000 contract with other lucrative benefits that another Hookstratten client, John McKay, reportedly signed to coach the expansion Tampa Bay franchise. McKay, a four-time national champion at USC, had never coached a down in the NFL before signing with Tampa Bay.

Williams said no extension talks were imminent: "I think George Allen has done a superb job as coach of the Redskins. . . . I was delighted that he wants to talk about a new contract. But I am not in the process of negotiating a contract with him, and I am not going to address myself to this matter until at least 1976 or 1977."[71]

In a separate report, Allen said he was uncertain whether he'd even be interested in a contract extension if the issue came up.[72] But in trying to keep any sensitive negotiations private, he quashed rumors that he was considering an early departure after the '75 season. The New York Jets, the San Diego Chargers, and the expansion Seattle team had been mentioned as possible destinations for him.[73]

"I'm quite happy here, and I have two years remaining on my contract," Allen told the *Washington Star* in December 1975. "I'm not thinking about another team. My goal is to win and eventually win the championship and the Super Bowl. That hasn't changed. Nobody has talked to me about another team, and I haven't talked to anyone."[74]

Shortly after the season ended, Williams suppressed rumors that several other teams were considering Allen as their head coach, describing the talk as "a lot of hokum." He also stated unequivocally that Allen would coach the Redskins in '76 and reiterated what he said in '71: George Allen would be the last coach he'd ever hire. "George has no plans to go elsewhere, and we have no plans to get a new coach," Williams told the *Washington Post*.[75]

Williams also predicted a busy off-season of personnel decisions because of a new avenue for acquiring players.[76] He was referring to a court decision that declared the Rozelle rule, which established "fair and equitable" compensation when a team loses a free agent to another team, in violation of antitrust laws. Without the rule, NFL teams would supposedly be more inclined to sign free agents who had completed their contract-option seasons because no compensation was required through draft choices, players, or money. This unfettered free agency period lasted one season, 1976, and was a precursor to the modern era of free agency.

No team was more aggressive than the '76 Redskins in exploiting the free agent market. No other team, for that matter, really took advantage of it. Allen's propensity for trading draft picks for proven veterans had sapped the Redskins of valuable selections that he could use to draft or trade for players. They picked no earlier than the fifth round from '72 to '75 and eyed a similar scenario in the '76 draft.

Allen thus seized the opportunity. He first signed running back Calvin Hill, a two-time 1,000-yard rusher for the Cowboys who in '75 played in the World Football League, which folded that year. The 235-pound Hill, who signed for an estimated $135,000 a year, was the big runner Allen had sought to help strengthen a running attack that finished twentieth in the league and averaged only 3.9 yards a carry in '75. However, questions existed about Hill's stability because he had undergone two knee operations since entering the league in 1969.

Cowboys president Tex Schramm wasn't surprised at Allen's boldness in signing Hill. "George Allen has always been a pioneer in this area, hasn't he?" Schramm asked rhetorically.[77]

Shortly thereafter, Allen signed another former Cowboy in free agency, tight end Jean Fugett, one of more than forty players who had played out his option.[78] The 6-foot-3, 226-pound Fugett, who signed in the $70,000 to $90,000 range,[79] had posted career highs of thirty-eight catches and 488 receiving yards in 1975, his fourth year in the league. Allen envisioned him playing tight end, where he would eventually replace the aging Jerry Smith, and wide receiver.

But the big prize arrived in July: Jets fullback John Riggins. The 6-foot-2, 235-pound Riggins, a rare combination of size, speed, and power, posted his best season in '75, his fifth in the NFL, with 1,005 yards rushing and 363 receiving. He made the Pro Bowl for the first time.

Allen, who had long been seeking a big, bruising runner, signed Riggins to a fifteen-year, $1.5 million contract, an extraordinary deal at that time. It reportedly matched the $1.5 million contract another powerful free agent fullback, Larry Csonka, had negotiated with the Giants.[80] Once he became a Redskin, Riggins sounded relieved to no longer be on the Jets, who had adopted mostly a passing offense with Joe Namath at quarterback, thus limiting Riggins's carries. The Rams, Vikings, and Oilers had also been interested in signing Riggins, who said he didn't choose Washington because of the money.[81]

"I could have gotten more money from some other team," Riggins told *Sports Illustrated*. "But that wasn't my only consideration. I wanted to be with a contender and, more than that, with a coach who can handle veterans. That's been coach Allen's strength all along."[82]

By acquiring Riggins and Hill, Allen addressed a position where the Redskins had depth with talented halfback Mike Thomas. In '75 Thomas rushed for 919 yards and was named NFL Rookie of the Year. Another thousand-yard running back, Larry Brown, was back for his eighth year. But because of injuries his numbers had plummeted since his '72 NFL MVP season of 1,216 rushing yards. Brown gained only 56 in 1976 and retired after eight seasons. Today, the gritty running back refuses to blame Allen, who used him excessively for long stretches, for derailing his career.

"We both benefited from the way he used me in his offenses," Brown said in a 2014 interview. "The career span for a running back is about three and a half years. Based on that, I was able to make my mark and leave an indelible impression. Allen was very superstitious. He didn't like to make a lot of changes. That meant there was no substitution. The players he had a great deal of confidence in were the people he had on the field. My willingness to take on that responsibility was pretty good at that time. It was the right decision."[83]

As for Riggins, Allen envisioned him as part of a dual-threat backfield, not only as the blocking fullback that he was in New York. "He saw him as the future running back," Bruce Allen said. "Remember the era. [Green Bay's] Jim Taylor was a fullback, and Paul Hornung was the tailback. You could have a 700-yard back in those days at fullback and a 700-yard back at halfback."[84]

Allen's aggressive moves in free agency—which began with his surprise signing of Dave Butz—failed to endear him to many around the league. Pete Rozelle, Tex Schramm, and other league executives were so angered by how strongly he waded into free agency that they influenced decisions to blackball him from NFL head coaching jobs in later years, according to Bruce Allen.

"He did it because no one else was going to sign anyone," Bruce said. "Several teams tried to sign John Riggins, but it pissed off people. He signed Calvin and Jean from the Cowboys just to piss off the Cowboys, obviously. That was really to stick a pin in the Cowboys' eye. He would have done more, but he didn't have the economics to do so."[85]

Despite exhausting much of his available budget, Allen wasn't done remaking the roster. He traded safety Bryant Salter for Dolphins safety Jake Scott, the most valuable player in Miami's win over the Redskins in Super Bowl VII, and a No. 2 draft pick in '77.

He also traded their seventh- and eighth-round picks to the Chiefs for 6-foot-8, 265-pound defensive end John Matuszak.

Matuszak, the first overall pick in the '73 draft, came with a lot of baggage. His college career and his first three NFL seasons had been marred by conflicts with coaches and team officials. Plus, he was out of control away from the game. Police once allegedly found four grams of marijuana in his car, an amount categorized as a misdemeanor. Just before his trade to the Redskins, he was hospitalized because of low blood sugar. Drinking vodka after taking Valium, a tranquilizer, caused the illness, Allen said at the time.[86]

Matuszak's stay in DC lasted two weeks. Allen cut him. He played his next six seasons with the Raiders, winning two Super Bowls.

"The Tooz was born to be a Raider. He was a wild man," said John Schulian, a *Washington Post* sports reporter at the time. "They brought him in because when he put his mind to it, he was a wonderful football player. He was 6-8, 270 pounds, with about a 32-inch waist. He was the most incredible physical specimen I'd ever seen up to that point.

"It did not take a genius to know that Matuszak was not going to be George's kind of guy. He was going to try to run around and decapitate people. He was not under control. He was a force of nature. George probably wanted guys who would be in the places he wanted them to be."[87]

When it was all over, Allen's wheeling and dealing had rivaled the frenetic pace of 1971, his first off-season in DC. His plunge into signing players in free agency, plus other signings such as Jake Scott, who inked a deal worth $90,000 to $125,000, left the Redskins with reportedly the league's highest payroll: $4 million.[88]

Despite a 2-4 preseason, Allen was confident the investments would pay off. He eyed an appearance in Super Bowl XI in Pasadena, California. "If not now, when?" he asked. "We made more progress in the offseason than any team in football. It'll be a long while before anybody sees this type of acquisition again."[89]

Edward Bennett Williams bought into the hype and applied his share of pressure on Allen at the Redskins' Welcome Home Luncheon. "I want to make a new, bold promise," he told a sellout crowd at the Sheraton Park Hotel in DC. "I believe deeply and sincerely that we have the best team in Redskins history, and I believe that we are going to have the best season in Redskins history."[90]

Aside from the roster additions, the Redskins appeared positioned for a fantastic season. Six of the first eight games were at home, and the overall schedule was soft compared with the prior season. Only two opponents, Dallas and St. Louis, had finished with winning records in '75.

Allen led the 10-4 Redskins back to the playoffs as the NFC wild card entry. But the end was all too familiar: a 35–20 loss to the Vikings in Minnesota. For the fourth time in DC and the sixth time in his coaching career, Allen failed to get his team past the first round of the playoffs. Counting the loss in Super Bowl VII, his teams were now 0-7 in postseason games on the road.

At one point, it appeared the Redskins would miss the playoffs for the second straight season. A 12–9 field goal–filled loss to the Giants at the Meadowlands left the 6-4 squad two games behind the 8-2 Cardinals in the race for the NFC wild card berth. The Redskins were in position to win with the ball on the Giants' 7 and less than a minute left. But Joe Theismann threw an interception in the end zone, a week after tossing three touchdown passes—all to free agent acquisition Jean Fugett—in a win over the 49ers.

Allen was despondent after giving the Giants their first win of the season, calling the loss "a heck of a blow."[91] Those skeptical of Washington's chances of reaching the postseason and of Allen's coaching future didn't hold back, including the press.

The *Washington Star*: "After an Autopsy, the Redskins Can Be Buried."[92]

The *Washington Post*: "The String Has Almost Run Out for Yo-Yo Redskins—If Redskins Need a Change It's in the Coaching."

"The Redskins' logo this season ought to be a yo-yo," *Post* columnist

Ken Denlinger wrote. "Up and down, up and down they go, out of the playoffs two weeks ago, back in last week, and now surely out again today.

"The scoreboard fluttered only after seven successful swings of the legs by the smallest players on the field and stopped at Giants 12, Redskins 9. Then the Giants' hearts went aflutter. Could they at last be digging George Allen's professional grave?"[93]

Allen would have none of it. His troops reeled off wins over the Cardinals, Eagles, and Jets to enter the final Sunday at 9-4. The Redskins and Cardinals, both 9-4, were tied in the battle for the NFC wild card berth. To punch their ticket, the Redskins needed to win at Texas Stadium over the 11-2 Cowboys, who had already clinched the NFC East, unless St. Louis lost to the Giants. The Redskins held the tiebreaker over the Cardinals.

In the weeks preceding the game, Allen tried to revitalize a phase of the Redskins' special teams that once produced a series of big plays. The Redskins had not blocked a punt since the first game of the '75 season. So Allen improvised while down a player on the punt return unit due to injury. In a first for a man with a history of making audacious personnel decisions and most likely an unprecedented move in sports, he phoned master punt blocker Bill Malinchak, a broker on the New York Mercantile Exchange, a commodity futures exchange, and asked him to return to the Redskins for the stretch run. Malinchak had been cut twice by the Redskins and last suited up in the NFL in 1974, his fourth season playing for Allen.

Still, his allegiance was unbreakable when it came to Allen. A few hours after suspending his career as a broker in silver, copper, and gold futures, he was practicing with the Redskins' punt-blocking team. In the process, he took a sizable pay cut to jump from Wall Street to Redskin Park. "It wasn't even close," he said when asked about the difference.

"George for me was certainly the greatest coach I ever played for," Malinchak said years later. "He was such a player's coach. You've heard that term so many times, but he really was. He prepared ball players for games probably as good or better than anybody ever. I mean not only execution-wise, but mentally, too. He talked to each player individually, and when you went into a game, you felt like the game rested on your shoulders, whether you were a special teams player or whether your name was Billy Kilmer or Charley Taylor. It didn't matter. Every player felt like he needed to make a big play, and he made you feel that way about that game. That's a special quality. I had a huge amount of respect for him just because of his work ethic and his love for his players.

"If you wanted to play football, you'd want to play for George Allen."[94]

Allen felt that Malinchak had at least one more big play in him. He was prophetic. Late in the first quarter, Malinchak charged into the Cowboys' backfield with only the up back to outmaneuver and deflected a punt by Danny White. The block set up Mark Moseley's short field goal for a 3–0 Redskins lead.

In the third quarter, the Redskins trailed, 14–10, in a game that had become a must-win. The Cardinals had beaten the Giants earlier in the day, meaning "win and go to the playoffs" or "lose and go home." Late in the game, two of Allen's expensive free agents decided the outcome. With 4:34 to play, Calvin Hill swept around the right end on a 15-yard touchdown run to put the Redskins up, 20–14. After a turnover, John Riggins ran 3 yards for a score and a 27–14 Redskins edge that held. The other pricey free agent, tight end Jean Fugett, caught a 6-yard touchdown pass in the second quarter. Another new acquisition, cornerback Joe Lavender, intercepted a pass on the Cowboys' final drive.

As the seconds ticked off, reality set in that Allen had defied skeptics who buried him and his team when times were tough earlier in the season. On his way off the field and into the Redskins' locker room, he and some of his players ripped down a banner at Texas Stadium that read "LOSERS."

The win over Dallas qualified the Redskins to play the Central Division champion 11-2-1 Vikings. But the Redskins looked like they were in a different league. The Vikings scored two first-quarter touchdowns, led 21–3 at halftime and 35–3 in the third quarter, and coasted to a 35–20 win that did not reflect their sheer domination.

Washington's loss led to increased chatter about Allen's future in the nation's capital. He said he planned to honor the last season on his seven-year Redskins contract. What a season of uncertainty it would be.

19

The Beginning of the End

At some point, George Allen began harboring second thoughts about staying on as the Redskins' head coach. By all accounts, his adversarial relationship with Edward Bennett Williams served as the impetus for him not wanting to fulfill his seven-year contract. Williams's micromanaging of Allen and his public mocking of Allen's spending habits infuriated the accomplished NFL coach, who always claimed that, when making decisions, his only focus was on winning. Allen's ability to buy stock in the Redskins and retain his full duties as general manager, with control over the team's personnel and financial matters, also triggered clashes between the two men.

Allen may have concluded that he wanted out as early as January 1973. The day after losing Super Bowl VII, he reportedly called Rams owner Carroll Rosenbloom to express interest in the team's opening for a head coach.[1] The Rams ended up hiring Chuck Knox.

In 1976 Allen wrote two letters to Redskins majority stockholder Jack Kent Cooke—one just before the start of the season and one toward the end—notifying him that he planned to leave after the '76 season and would not stay for the last year of his contract. He said he would not be a "lame duck coach" and that he had been thinking of this for "some time."

"I appreciate all of the cooperation you both have given me, and the record we achieved here we can all be proud of," Allen wrote, with "you both" referring to Cooke and Williams. "At the present time, I have nothing else in mind and have not been contacted by another other club. But my experience and judgement tells me this is the best thing to do for the entire organization."[2]

Williams's reaction to those letters, one of which he was copied on, will never be known. But he left no doubt publicly that he expected Allen back for the '77 season and beyond. Two days after the '76 season ended with a playoff loss to the Vikings, Williams said he planned to begin negotiations right away to extend Allen's contract. He expressed no urgency to finalizing the extension but noted that he and the Redskins always wanted

Allen to stay on. He indicated that Allen was in line for a raise and that the extension would be multiyear.

At the same time, Williams sounded disappointed that the '76 Redskins had failed to meet his preseason expectation of producing the "best season in Redskins history." The loss to the Vikings marked their fourth exit in the first round of the playoffs since Allen took over in '71. "I expected a good season," Williams said. "We didn't get quite what we hoped, but 10-4 is nothing to be ashamed of."[3]

Progress on the contract extension was not to Allen's liking. In a letter to Williams in March '77, he described the handling of his contract negotiations over the past twenty months as a "disgrace" and reiterated that he might be inclined to step down and forgo the final year of his contract.[4] But after months of news reports that Williams, Allen, and the coach's attorney, Ed Hookstratten, were working on the extension, Williams announced it in July 1977. In a press conference, he said Allen would get a "very, very substantial" increase in salary and noted that he and Allen had agreed on extending the contract for the '78, '79, '80, and '81 seasons. Some reports described the increase to be up to double Allen's original salary of $125,000,[5] which would bring his salary in line with those of the highest-paid coaches in the league, including Philadelphia's Dick Vermeil, Tampa Bay's John McKay, and New England's Chuck Fairbanks.

Williams also indicated that a stock option clause was not included in the original '71 contract but that it came in a letter from Jack Kent Cooke. Williams added, though, that Allen might still be able to buy into the franchise. "If he wanted to buy the stock, I'd take it up with Jack, and we'd talk it over," he said.[6]

The announcement came as a relief, as Allen had voiced concerns about the difficulties of winning as a lame-duck coach.[7] He missed the press conference because of funeral services for his mother, Loretta Hannigan Allen, who passed away that week at age ninety-one. His oldest son, George Felix Allen, read his remarks:

"I'm pleased that this has been resolved before training camp opens. I think it's for the benefit of the entire Redskins organization. The tremendous effort of our players has made the last six years the most gratifying of my coaching career.

"Due to my family's fondness for the area and the fine friends we've made here, we now consider this our home. I appreciate the confidence Ed Williams has shown."[8]

To meet Williams's demand for the Redskins to improve on their 10-4 mark in 1976, Allen needed to again rely on an aging team. Fourteen players on the '77 roster were over thirty, with Billy Kilmer and Ron McDole (both thirty-eight) the most advanced in years. In the first year of a draft reduced from seventeen to twelve rounds, the Redskins picked only six players. All of their other picks had been traded away in transactions with other teams. Ultimately, four of the picks never played a down in the league. The one with the most longevity played three seasons.

But one 1977 rookie acquisition made his mark: Colgate all-conference safety Mark Murphy. The Redskins didn't think Murphy would be drafted but wanted to sign him anyway. So they "hid" him during the draft to gain exclusive access to him as a free agent. Allen called Murphy his "thirteenth-round draft choice." The superstitious coach believed that because of his success with two other Redskins thirteenth-round picks, wide receiver Frank Grant and defensive tackle Dennis Johnson, applying that tag to Murphy would yield similar results.

"There were about four or five of us they gambled wouldn't be drafted, and they put us up at a hotel out by Dulles Airport," Murphy remembered. "They drove us all around DC the second day of the draft. As soon as the draft ended, they brought us out to Redskin Park and said, 'You haven't been drafted. But we really like you, and we want to sign you as a free agent. Here's our offer. Take five minutes and think about it.'"

Murphy ended up playing eight seasons, all in DC, and intercepted twenty-seven passes. Another pillar on Joe Gibbs's early, dominant teams, he picked off a pass in the Redskins' win over Miami in Super Bowl XVII and intercepted a league-high nine during the Redskins' march to Super Bowl XVIII in '83. He earned Pro Bowl and first-team All-Pro honors that year.

In '77 Washington faced an easier schedule, against opponents with a combined 60-79-1 record the year before. But they suffered a few key injuries, including running back John Riggins, Allen's most expensive free agent acquisition in '76. Riggins missed six games with a right knee injury. The Redskins lost twice to the Giants and the eventual Super Bowl–champion Cowboys, both a first for Allen in DC, and finished 9-5, with Allen barely missing the playoffs for the second time as Washington's coach.

His defense was magnificent, allowing 189 points, the fourth-lowest total in the league and a Redskins record in the seventeen-year history of the fourteen-game season. The unit also recorded two shutouts and held two other teams to single-digit point totals. But the offense was nonexistent. The Redskins scored 196 points, the lowest total by far in the Allen regime and nearly 100 points below the prior year's total.

The Redskins stood 3-3 and 4-4, with playoff hopes fading and many in the media having written them off. But displaying their customary no-quit attitude under Allen while relying on a blocked kick, an intercepted pass, or a great return to generate a spark, they won five of their last six games, including the final three.

In the season finale, the Redskins hosted a 10-3 Rams team that had clinched the NFC West. With the Redskins leading 17–0 in the third period, the Rams battled back and had a chance to tie at the end but missed a 40-yard field goal, leaving the Redskins clinging to playoff hopes. The next day, the Bears beat the Giants on a field goal with nine seconds left in overtime to earn the NFC's wild card spot. The Redskins and Bears each finished with 9-5 records and 8-4 conference marks, the first possible tiebreaker. But the Bears outscored their NFC opponents by 48 points, the Redskins by only 4, giving Chicago the playoff spot.

Although the Redskins came up short, the *New York Daily News* named Allen NFC Coach of the Year for "getting the most out of every area of his team." Allen and Miami's Don Shula, who was the best AFC coach, were singled out for "keeping their rag-tag teams in playoff competition until the final games of the final weekend."[9]

After seven years in Washington (71-77), Allen had won 69 percent of his regular-season games, with a 67-30-1 record. That mark accounted for the third-best winning percentage in Redskins history and the fifth best in the NFL during that period, behind Shula, Minnesota's Bud Grant, Dallas's Tom Landry, and Pittsburgh's Chuck Noll. But Allen captured the NFC East only once, and his record in five playoff appearances left much to be desired at 2-5.

Why did Allen's Redskins lag behind the marquee teams of the 1970s—the Steelers, Cowboys, Dolphins, and Vikings—who combined for fourteen Super Bowl appearances and eight wins during the decade? After their Super Bowl VII appearance in the '72 season, the Redskins were a very good team but not a premier squad. For one, they had one of the oldest rosters in the league during the Allen era, including the third-oldest team in NFL history in '76.[10] Plus, Allen's wheeling and dealing for veteran players drained the team of quality draft picks, giving credence to the early warnings that he was mortgaging the future in exchange for winning immediately.

Of the twenty-eight NFL teams at the time, excluding the two 1976 expansion franchises (Seattle and Tampa Bay), Allen's Redskins drafted the fewest players (sixty-nine) in his seven seasons in DC. The Redskins picked only five players in the top five rounds. Their highest pick was a second rounder in 1971, Texas wide receiver Cotton Speyrer, whom Allen promptly traded for seventh-year receiver Roy Jefferson. Of the sixty-nine players drafted on Allen's watch, only sixteen played at least one game for the Redskins, although some were gems: running back Mike Thomas (fifth round, 1975), wide receiver Frank Grant (thirteenth round, 1972), and offensive tackle George Starke (eleventh round, 1971). Allen left the Redskins without a pick through the first eight rounds in 1978 and no picks from rounds two to six in 1979.[11]

Allen also traded valuable draft choices for players who failed to produce long-term results, among them running back Duane Thomas for a first-round pick in '75 and a second-rounder in '76, as well as safety Bryant Salter for a third-round pick in '76 and second- and fourth-rounders in '77.[12]

Then there was the Dave Butz acquisition. Allen parted ways with two first-round picks and a second-rounder for the promising defensive tackle, who was a disappointment at first and only became a dominant player long after Allen had departed.

However, some of Allen's veteran acquisitions produced excellent returns. Ron McDole, Diron Talbert, and Billy Kilmer, all of whom he acquired by trading multiple draft picks in '71, helped key the Redskins' Super Bowl run in '72 and stayed with him for his seven years in DC. Jefferson, who played six seasons for Allen before retiring, was also important in the Super Bowl season. Kenny Houston, obtained in '73, turned in five straight Pro Bowl seasons.

What if Allen had accepted a bad season or two in exchange for acquiring a high position in the draft and building his team by stockpiling young talent? That's what *Washington Post* sports columnist Ken Denlinger argued, saying Allen relied on "frequent patchwork,"[13] instead of taking a track similar to a team like the Steelers, who drafted nine Hall of Fame players from 1969 to 1974, a period that began with 2-11-1 and 1-13 seasons, to establish a base for a dynasty that captured four Super Bowls in the '70s. The big year was 1974, when the Steelers drafted future Hall of Famers Lynn Swann, Jack Lambert, John Stallworth, and Mike Webster and signed undrafted free agent Donnie Shell, whose bust is also in Canton. An infusion of youth, Denlinger surmised, might have provided the firepower the Redskins needed for a push through the playoffs.

"Through most of Allen's pro career, here and in Los Angeles, his teams have somehow managed to burn themselves out just when the champions are reaching back for another burst of energy," Denlinger wrote. "For backs-against-the-wall courage and drama, the Redskins are exquisite. But don't ask them to go the classic NFL distance.

"Probably, this is in large part due to Allen's notion of how to build a team. Perhaps the one flaw in an otherwise superior football mind is his inability to suffer for greatness, to dare to be bad."[14]

One could argue that the lack of an elite quarterback also factored into Allen's inability to get the Redskins Super Bowl rings. Sonny Jurgensen, perhaps the NFL's most prolific passer in the '60s, missed almost the entire '71 season and failed to stay consistently healthy the last three years of his career: '72 to '74. Billy Kilmer showed flashes of excellence and steady leadership as a game manager but was never mistaken for one of the league's top-tier quarterbacks. After Jurgensen departed, Kilmer started 70 percent of the Redskins' games in Allen's last three seasons, including a playoff game. It's too bad that Allen, when coaching the Redskins, didn't have Roman Gabriel in his prime. Playing under Allen in LA, Gabriel was one of the NFL's premier quarterbacks from '67 to '69, a stretch when the Rams won 80 percent of their regular-season games.

Joe Theismann, who started for the Redskins when Kilmer didn't, showed the potential to be a good quarterback, like when he threw three touchdown passes to Jean Fugett in a 1976 win. But he was inconsistent on the whole. He improved under Allen's successor, Jack Pardee, before becoming one of the best quarterbacks to ever wear the burgundy and gold under Joe Gibbs, who came to DC in '81. Theismann quarterbacked the Redskins to two Super Bowls, winning once, during the Gibbs era. He was named the NFL's most valuable player in 1983. In twelve NFL seasons, all as a Redskin, he tallied franchise records of 25,206 passing yards, 2,044 completions and 3,602 attempts, plus 160 touchdown passes.

Allen's reluctance to hand the full-time starting mantle to Theismann is worth examining. What if Allen had given him room to develop earlier in his career? Not only did Edward Bennett Williams insist that Theismann should start as early as the '75 season, his second in the league, but offensive coordinator Ted Marchibroda, a loyal assistant to Allen for ten seasons, also voiced support for Theismann to be the starter in '75.

"Joe has the ability, desire, and determination to be an excellent quarterback," Marchibroda wrote in a Redskins position evaluation paper in January 1975, just before he left to coach the Baltimore Colts. "Works hard and prepares himself very well, even though he knew he would not play a great deal. He has football experience beyond his years. He should be given the opportunity to start for the Redskins."[15]

Bobby Beathard was Miami's personnel director when the Dolphins traded Theismann to the Redskins in 1974. Beathard pushed for the trade after seeing Theismann star in the Canadian Football League. The Dolphins drafted Theismann with a fourth-round pick in 1971 (and still held his NFL rights) and had future Hall of Famer Bob Griese in his prime when they traded Theismann to Washington. "I went up to Canada to watch Joe play and then to meet with him," recalled Beathard, the Redskins' general manager through most of the Gibbs era. "I was convinced that he could be what he ended up being."[16]

Theismann, a scrambling quarterback in an era of pure pocket passers, would do anything to get on the field and returned punts in his first two seasons, averaging 10.5 yards one year. Allen gave him his first true taste of NFL quarterbacking when he started five games in 1976. After Kilmer started the first six games of the '77 season, including a loss to the Giants that left the Redskins 3-3, a perturbed Theismann made scathing remarks about Allen to a crowd of about two hundred at a Redskins sports dinner. He later apologized.

"I was raised to believe if you compete with a guy one on one you'll be evaluated equally and based on competition," Theismann said. "But don't think when I'm out there on that field I don't hear you. I hear you all the time, and it's you and my family I play for. I don't play for George Allen. I stopped playing for George Allen two years ago because I can't play for someone who treats me that way. I just can't respect that."[17]

At one point, Theismann asked Allen to trade him: "I told George, 'Look, obviously this is a very old football team, and I'm not an old person. Why don't you just trade me, and I'll come back in ten years when I'm of the age when you want people around here?'" Theismann recalled. "He didn't do it. Thankfully, no one would listen to me at that time."[18]

After Theismann went off on Allen at the sports dinner, Allen started him the next six games. The Redskins won four. Theismann tallied a 47 percent completion percentage, six touchdowns, eight interceptions, and a 59.2 passer rating during that stretch. Allen then benched him, tapping Kilmer to start the final two games with a wild card spot within reach.

Today Theismann is uncertain whether an immediate designation as the bona fide starter would have meant a faster career progression. All he knows is that not even a pry bar could separate Allen from his beloved veterans like Kilmer, "Mr. Blood and Guts."

"George would have done exactly what he wanted to do," Theismann surmised. "That was the impression I always had of him. He had a vision, he had a concept, he had a philosophy, and he was going to follow it, irrespective of recommendations from anyone. Billy managed the game well. George wanted to run the football. I believe the greatest victory that George could have ever received would have been 2–0 in a game where the offense didn't make a mistake and turn it over, and the defense won the game with a safety."

Meanwhile, Allen did not sign the four-year contract extension that Williams announced in July 1977. The question of how much authority Allen would retain factored into his reluctance to ink a deal, specifically whether he'd be able to trade for and cut players and negotiate their salaries without needing to ask for anyone's permission. The delay also involved a dispute between Allen and Williams over control of the team's financial operations, according to a *Washington Post* report midway through the '77 season. Allen had maintained almost total authority on spending decisions since the retirement of front office executive Dave Slattery after the '75 season, but Williams wanted to retain some of that control, the report said.[19]

The Redskins lost $500,000 in both '75 and '76, and they lost nearly $750,000 in '77 according to an estimate. Williams believed Allen's spending habits were putting the team in the red. But interest payments on a $6 million loan that Williams and Cooke took out to retire the remaining shares of stock from the estate of Redskins founder George Preston Marshall appeared to also contribute to the losses. The Redskins, for example, listed $830,000 in interest payments in '75.

There was also the matter of the stock option. In their April 1978 *Washington Post* exposé, "The Final Plays," Len Shapiro and Nancy Scannell documented how the negotiations on the contract extension played out. They noted that Jack Kent Cooke met with Allen in Las Vegas before the extension was announced in July 1977, with Ed Hookstratten joining the talks by phone. Hookstratten is quoted as saying that Cooke agreed on a continuation of the stock option, in addition to other incentives Allen wanted.[20]

But in truth, the extension included no opportunity for Allen to invest in the team. The fact that the original stock option offer supposedly came in a letter from Cooke to Allen and was not written into the '71 contract apparently gave Williams leverage to not honor it in the ensuing years and to leave it out of the extension. Nothing was legally binding, and Williams could, "theoretically, legally call all the shots," although Cooke owned a much greater percentage of the team, according to Larry Lucchino, Williams's colleague at his law firm, Williams & Connolly.[21]

In George Felix Allen's opinion, "The balking on the stock option provision was harmful in the overall relationship."[22]

Plus, Cooke, who had played such a key role in Allen's hiring in '71, never pushed for the stock option to be reinstated. That's largely because the NFL in October 1977 concluded a megadeal worth $576 million with the three major television networks. The pact boosted the value of NFL teams, with each one receiving an annual payment that rose from $2.1 million to more than $5 million. The Redskins were suddenly worth an estimated $22 million, compared to $10 million in 1971. The deal also involved an increase in the number of regular-season games to sixteen and an additional wild card playoff team in each conference—all starting in '78.

It was likely not just Williams who did not want Allen to have the opportunity to buy into the team. "I don't think Jack wanted the 5 percent [stock option] in the contract, either," Bruce Allen said. "It became a much more valuable 5 percent than when they recruited him, and Jack is a businessman. It transformed into a very valuable asset, and Jack had Ed be the bad guy. Ed said, 'I'll take the role.'"[23]

Cooke also began to question Allen's habit of withholding information from Williams, according to Cooke's son, John Kent Cooke: "Dad thought the world of George as a coach. He thought he was the best in the league. And in his day, he was. But he was very persnickety, and he kept things very secretive. He didn't tell Ed Williams what he was doing, and that was part of the problem. He didn't want anybody to know what he was doing because he didn't trust anybody in case it all leaked out."

In the younger Cooke's view, this had nothing to do with Allen's decisions to pay some players enormous salaries, which had to be approved by both Ed Williams and Jack Kent Cooke. "He just wouldn't talk," the latter's son said. "He wouldn't share things with people. He was a one kind of mind and that was football only, just football. That's all he cared about. And, of course, winning."[24]

But did Allen want to remain in Washington in the first place? He had claimed all along that he wasn't interested in any other head coaching opportunities, although his name had been linked to a series of vacancies since his arrival in DC. During the '77 season, Williams came to suspect that his coach was in contact with a team that looked like it might have a job opening after the season: the Los Angeles Rams. He accused Rams owner Carroll Rosenbloom of "tampering" with Allen, a charge that Rosenbloom called a "joke."[25] Hookstratten, who happened to be the Rams' general counsel and was very close to Rosenbloom, was one of several people in Rosenbloom's ear trying to get Allen the job, according to Hookstratten's son, Jon Hookstratten.[26]

"There was some concern about double negotiations going on," Larry Lucchino remembered.[27]

Allen also became suspicious of Williams. During the '77 season, the Allen family began hearing funny sounds when answering their home phone in Great Falls, Virginia, followed by a lull. They called the phone company, which dispatched a security team to investigate a possible wiretapping. The conclusion was the phone was tapped, with Williams among those suspected of carrying out the mischief to learn if Allen was speaking to other teams. Allen wanted to publicize the wiretapping.

"I said, 'I'm going to report this to the newspaper,'" Allen recalled in 1989. "'I'm going to call a press conference and tell everyone about it.' [A security person] said, 'Please don't do that because we'll never catch the person or people who are doing this.' I said, 'How do you know it's tapped?' He said a [telephone] pole in the front corner of our yard has a bug halfway up it. He said it has to be done by somebody who knows his work, a pro. He said, 'We think we can catch him. If you cooperate and don't tell anyone, we'd like to find out who it is.' Right away, I said, 'Maybe it's those damn Dallas Cowboys.' But Dallas or some other team wouldn't get enough [information] over the phone like that. Then I said maybe it's Ed Bennett Williams or somebody from the media.

"We told our kids about it, which was probably a mistake because when they got on the line they'd swear and make all types of crazy noises. Whoever heard that probably thought, 'Hey, they know we're listening.' About a week later, the security people came back and said the bug is gone. Somebody got tipped off."

The culprit behind the wiretapping was never determined, Allen said. He had also been concerned that his phone lines at Redskin Park were bugged, but an investigation of the facility turned up nothing conclusive.[28]

It was around this time that Allen allegedly showed interest in coaching his former team, the Rams. But this wasn't the first time he had done so while under contract with the Redskins. The morning after losing Super Bowl VII to Miami, he called Rosenbloom, who had just dismissed Tommy Prothro and was seeking a new coach. "I quickly reminded George that he had five years left on his Washington contract," Rosenbloom said. "George said he knew that, but he asked me to keep him in mind just the same."[29] Allen also reportedly sought permission to speak with Rosenbloom when the Lions were pursuing Rams coach Chuck Knox after the '76 season. Hookstratten even considered trying to get the Redskins to release Allen from the last year of his contract so he could accept the Rams job. Rams general manager Don Klosterman denied those stories.[30]

Knox's inability to reach the Super Bowl frustrated Rosenbloom to no end. Knox, in his first NFL head coaching stint, molded the Rams into a big-time winner after taking over in '73. In the five-season period from '73 to '77, he crafted a 54-15-1 regular-season record for a .783 winning percentage that tied Minnesota's Bud Grant for the best in the NFL during that stretch. The Rams won at least ten games in each of the five seasons and sported the stingiest defense in the league during that period. But similar to Allen, Knox's playoff record was disappointing: 3-5. His Rams reached three conference championship games but lost twice to the Vikings and once to the Cowboys.

Rosenbloom had nothing on his mind but Super Bowl after the '72 ownership swap that left him in control of the Rams and Robert Irsay in control of the Colts. Although he had a Super Bowl ring from Baltimore's win over Dallas in Super Bowl V, by 1977, when he turned seventy, he knew time was running out on him for his Rams to win the big one.

Rosenbloom liked Knox personally. But the coach's plodding, run-based offense that earned him the moniker "Ground Chuck" drove the owner crazy. Rosenbloom called that offensive style "dull."[31] A call Knox made in the NFC Championship Game against the Vikings on December 26, 1976, exemplified his conservative approach. On fourth down with the ball six inches from the goal line in the first quarter, he opted for a field goal. The Vikings blocked the kick and returned it 90 yards for a touchdown in a 24–3 Minnesota victory. Knox was blasted after the game. "You don't start championship football games by going for a field goal from the six-inch line of the other team," Jim Murray of the *Los Angeles Times* wrote. "The Rams won't be in the Super Bowl again this year because that's precisely what they did."[32]

Doug Krikorian, a Rams beat writer and columnist at the time for the *Los Angeles Herald Examiner*, said, "There was a lot of talent on those Rams teams. They should have been in at least two Super Bowls in the 1970s. The game plans by Knox were just dreadful. Opponents knew all the time what they would do."[33]

Following the '76 championship game loss to the Vikings, Rosenbloom was ready to let Knox walk. The *Oakland Press*, a newspaper in Michigan, reported that Rosenbloom and Lions owner William Clay Ford had arranged a deal in which Knox would take the Lions head coaching job. Rosenbloom denied that, but he said in a separate report he was willing to let Knox go "if he'd be happier in Detroit." Knox, who had negotiated a new five-year deal with the Rams in '76, ended up staying in Los Angeles.[34]

In 1977 the Rams won the NFC West for the fifth straight season. But in a by then familiar pattern, they faded in the first round of the playoffs to the Vikings at the Los Angeles Coliseum. Three thousand miles away, Williams and Allen restarted contract talks, but negotiations stalled again, mainly over the same sticking point: Allen's part ownership of the team. Allen said he wouldn't sign on the advice of Ed Hookstratten. Etty, who was so influential in his life, also instructed him not to sign because of the absence of the stock option. "Mom was a big believer and lecturer that you can't trust people who break their promises," Bruce Allen said. "Removing the stock option is an example of breaking a promise."[35]

But was Allen's refusal to sign the extension rooted in something other than the stock option? Was it simply because he wanted his old job in LA back? That's what some influential people around the league, including Williams and Cooke, were thinking.[36] The Rams would have had to compensate the Redskins with a first-round draft pick if they had signed Allen while he was still under contract in Washington,[37] meaning he might have been better off getting fired. Allen told the *Washington Star* his first preference was to stay in Washington but admitted that the Rams' top spot was a "very select job" and that LA is a "very desirable place."[38] The Allens still owned their beautiful oceanview home in the Los Angeles suburb of Palos Verdes Estates, a further incentive to return to the West Coast.

Jon Hookstratten is unaware if his father told Allen to refrain from signing the extension because of anticipation that the Rams would be seeking a new head coach after the season. "I don't know what could have been said between my father and George," he said in an interview. "But it's obvious that [Allen] was having significant problems with Edward Bennett Williams, who was another real volatile character and personality." He believes his father would have encouraged Allen to sign the extension because it was such a lucrative offer. "At that point, my dad would be looking at it and going, 'Okay, we've got a great financial deal here. Why not do it?'" he surmised.

The younger Hookstratten, echoing Bruce Allen, thinks the most plausible theory is that Allen, with backing from Etty, refused to sign the contract without the stock option. "Etty was a very strong personality," Hookstratten said, "and if the ability to buy a piece of the team wasn't in there, I think they would have had a real problem with that. I'm really emphasizing the two because I just remember that was the thing. It wasn't just him as the football coach. He's got his partner at home telling him, 'You're being cheated, you're being this, you're being that. This is something you should be receiving, especially when you had it before.'"[39]

George Allen also felt that Williams was trying to scale back his power as a general manager. "Some of the fine print bugs him," *Washington Post* sport columnist Shirley Povich wrote. "It says here that Williams is determined to clip his wings; that Allen can't have all the authority he seeks over the Redskin operations, or even as much as he's had the last seven seasons. Williams is telling Allen his blank check as the biggest-spending coach in the NFL is no more. . . . Williams wants his franchise back from a coach who was viewing it too much as his own."[40]

While the drama played out, Williams, sensing Allen might not return, made his own secretive inquiries with other coaches. Marv Levy, the Redskins' special teams coach under Allen in '71 and '72, subsequently coached the Canadian Football League's Montreal Alouettes, guiding them to the CFL championship in 1977. He remembered Williams speaking to him about the Redskins' head job, but, backed by an Allen recommendation, he signed as the Chiefs' head coach on December 20, 1977.

"Edward Bennett Williams said, 'Marv, we'd love for you to come and be the coach,' Levy recalled. "I told him that I'd just about committed to the Chiefs, and that's where I'll be going. I went to Kansas City because I knew the Redskins had traded away all of their draft choices for a long time."[41]

Allen was not considered for the Chiefs job,[42] but he had the nation's capital wondering if he was staying or leaving. Despite his inability to craft a playoff run aside from the '72 season, as well as his conservative approach on offense and his chief reliance on defense, many Redskins fans wanted him to stay. If nothing else, they remembered those excruciating days not long before, when the Redskins ranged from anemic to mediocre, as well as the franchise's revolving coaching door from past years. Nobody wanted to go back there. At the time, Allen was tied with Ray Flaherty as the team's longest-tenured coach (seven years) since the team played its first season in Boston in 1932. According to a *Washington Post* poll taken before the '77 season, more than 40 percent of respondents thought Allen had done an excellent or good job as coach, and 73 percent would keep him as coach if they were the team's owner.[43]

"I don't think the fans ever turned on Allen," Steve Guback said in retrospect. "They were winning, and when you're winning, people are enthusiastic. A lot of fans were willing to accept George's thinking because he'd been successful."

Weeks went by without a signing. But developments surfaced on the West Coast. On January 9, Carroll Rosenbloom disclosed that he had given Knox permission to speak to other teams about coaching opportunities and that Knox had agreed to allow Rosenbloom to search for another head coach.[44] Two days later, Knox left a Super Bowl–contending team and signed with Buffalo, which had finished 2-12 in '76 and 3-11 in '77. That left only one NFL team with a head coaching job open at the time: the Rams.[45]

On January 13 the *Washington Star*, citing a "highly placed" NFL source, reported that the delay in finalizing the contract involved the Redskins' reluctance to meet Allen's demand to buy 5 percent of the team at its 1969 value: $10 million. In the same article, the *Star* quoted Williams as saying Allen had been asking for "something else which he is not going to get," which presumably was his desire to invest in the team at its 1969 value.[46]

The next day, Williams and Allen met for several hours in Williams's office, with the team president giving Allen a final contract offer and an ultimatum: sign it by the end of the day, or the Redskins would be seeking a new head coach. Allen said he first wanted Hookstratten to review the document. When the weekend passed without a signing, Williams decided he'd had enough. With backing from Cooke, he told Allen he was ceasing contract talks and would be looking elsewhere for a coach. Upon Allen's request, Williams gave him permission to speak with other teams about coaching opportunities. He believed that Allen was Rosenbloom's top choice to be the Rams' next head coach.[47]

"I was not going to be hustled by Carroll Rosenbloom," Williams said at the time. "I know Allen wants that job, and I hope he gets it, but I couldn't wait any longer. I was not about to leave him with an unsigned contract while he waited to see what the Rams were going to do."[48]

Early that week, Allen reportedly flew to Los Angeles to meet with the Rams about their opening.[49] Williams, though, held out hope that Allen might still accept his terms and thus waited a few days before telling the press.[50] Then, on Thursday, January 19, the *Washington Star* and the *Washington Post* both plastered the news on the front page: George Allen had been fired. The blockbuster story accompanied front-page articles in both newspapers about a breakdown in historic Israeli-Egyptian peace talks and a farmers' strike that brought tractor trailers to the nation's capital and tied up traffic around the city. The firing came six months after Williams and Allen had agreed on a contract extension.

Williams explained to the media that Allen had exhausted his patience after half a year without signing and that it seemed apparent to him that the Redskins' coach was eyeing the Rams job. He said he had to act in the best interests of the team and announced plans to "restructure" the Redskins by hiring a head coach and a general manager—what had become the trend throughout the league. Allen had managed both roles in his seven-year term. "I want a coach who has Washington as his first choice," Williams said.[51]

When asked about his remark in 1971 that Allen would be the last coach he'd ever hire, Williams retorted, "Well, I was wrong."

In the *Washington Star* on January 19, Steve Guback had an exclusive interview with Allen. Guback had learned about the firing the previous day while speaking to Williams at a funeral for Chester Minter, the Redskins' longtime comptroller. Guback proceeded to phone Allen, who couldn't contain his revulsion for Williams.

"Nothing he does surprises me," Allen charged. "The only reason I haven't signed a contract is because of this one man. That's Williams. And I haven't applied [for] or approached anyone about a job at all. I've had all types of opportunities. I've always felt this would be my last coaching job.

I've given the Redskins, the organization, the players, and the community everything I have, my heart and soul, to the extent of losing my health. And this is what you get."

Guback asked Allen if Williams was seeking a loophole to fire him, and he replied, "It's quite obvious that he probably didn't want me to stay on and was looking for a way out." Allen said a stock option clause that allowed him to buy 5 percent of the team had always been in his '71 Redskins contract but that Williams had removed it from the extension.

Allen went on to spew vitriolic comments about his former boss—remarks that likely haunted him down the road in his bid to return to the NFL coaching ranks. The comments made Allen look like the villain and Williams the victim in their power struggle. "Devious" and "deceitful" were two of Allen's descriptions of the famous criminal trial lawyer:

"Listen, he's a cold-blooded fish. He uses people. That's what he is. He doesn't care about people. He only cares what he can get out of them. That'll be the same way with whoever else comes in here.

"The guy's a Jekyll and a Hyde. Anybody that deals with him, one day he calls you up, and he's ranting and raving, and the next day he's as meek as a kitten. Anybody that works with him knows that. I may call him. I may have some more to say. That's his training. He's an actor. Another thing I don't appreciate with this guy, I don't appreciate somebody calling me [at] 11 o'clock at night, waking me up, and getting me out of bed [to] tell me if you don't change quarterbacks, you're not going to get a new contract."

That's presumably why, Guback reported, Allen elevated Joe Theismann over Billy Kilmer when the Redskins fell to 3-3 in '77 after losing to the Giants for the second time. Later, with the Redskins in contention for a wild card spot and two games to play, Allen said he received a "sarcastic" phone call from Williams after re-inserting Kilmer in the starting lineup.

"All Ed does is paint a black picture," Allen said. "He always talks about big payrolls, old players, high ticket prices, and criticizes the offense. Every time he raised ticket prices, he said it was because of George Allen. We don't have the highest payroll in the league. That's another of his fabrications.

"I would never say these things. This is not my personality to say things about anybody. But when you get treated this way, then I'm going to attack."

Despite such loathing for Williams, Allen said he was "very close" to signing the contract. But he claimed he couldn't reach Ed Hookstratten because he was first in New Orleans at the Super Bowl, then went to Chicago to apparently speak with another of his clients, Bears coach Jack

Pardee. Allen said that if he could have reached Hookstratten, "I think I would have signed."[52]

Some in the media mocked Allen. *Washington Post* sportswriters William Gildea and Kenneth Turan, who had showered him with praise in *The Future Is Now* after he transformed the Redskins into a playoff team in '71, this time elaborated on what they deemed his faults. The belief in the Redskins' front office, they reasoned, was that Allen had taken the team as far as he could. "More than that, his trade-now, pay-later philosophy had quite conceivably built a bleak future—and at unprecedented expense," they wrote. "The concept of giving Allen an unlimited budget and having him, in Redskins president Edward Bennett Williams' once joking words, 'already exceed it' no longer seemed practical. After seven years, Williams felt the results no longer justified the expenditure."[53]

Allen antagonist David Israel of the *Washington Star* compared the coach's departure to the presidential collapse of his longtime friend Richard Nixon: "Like the Trickster he so admired, George Allen caused his own downfall with his massive insecurity and paranoia. For most of his career, Allen thrived on these qualities. He turned them into assets. But ultimately, it had to end."[54]

Bob Messenger of the *Greenwood Commonwealth* in Mississippi chided Allen for dragging his feet on Williams's contract offer: "Something is wrong when a coach who has never won an NFL championship wants to 'think over' a quarter-of-a-million dollar offer before signing on the dotted line. Who in their right mind can blame [Williams] for cutting Allen loose? More to the point, Allen has failed in seven years at the Skins helm to bring them to the pinnacle of professional football in this country. His method of pooh-poohing the college draft system in favor of a roster teeming with 35-year-old veterans has gotten him nowhere."[55]

Williams promised to move quickly to find a replacement. Candidates mentioned in the media included St. Louis coach Don Coryell, Stanford coach Bill Walsh, former Notre Dame coach Ara Parseghian, and three former Allen assistants: Pardee, Baltimore coach Ted Marchibroda, and Cincinnati assistant Mike McCormack. A few current Redskins assistants, including offensive coordinator Charlie Waller and defensive coordinator LaVern "Torgy" Torgeson, were also named.

The day Allen's firing went public, Pardee quit the Bears. He had a 20-22 record over three seasons, including a 9-5 mark and a playoff appearance in '77, the Bears' first since their '63 championship season. After one season as an assistant on Allen's staff in '73, he coached the Florida Blazers of the World Football League to the championship game in '74.

Pardee flew to Washington to meet with Williams, who had admired him going back to his playing days in DC in '71 and '72, and he emerged as the top choice to replace Allen.[56] A few days later, Williams signed him as the team's new coach. True to his word, Williams also hired the team's first official general manager in nearly two decades, Dolphins player personnel director Bobby Beathard, considered one of the most clever front-office minds in the game. Williams put Beathard in charge of the draft and player contracts and said Beathard and Pardee would have equal power on trades.[57]

The same time Pardee became Williams's number one candidate, Allen had emerged as the hottest name in the Rams' coaching search. Rams general manager Don Klosterman said Allen would "certainly be considered a top candidate by virtue of his history as a football coach."[58] Rosenbloom made it clear that Allen, if hired, would only be handling coaching duties. Allen said he would work for Rosenbloom in any capacity "because of the respect one winner has for another," sources close to Allen said at the time. They added that he would "welcome the chance" to work with Klosterman, as well as the owner's son (assistant to the president Steve Rosenbloom) and anyone else in the front office.[59]

Allen tried to remain optimistic while he anxiously awaited an answer from the Rams. "Dad was in great spirits thanks to the players and coaches," Bruce Allen said. "Every day and night, Redskin players and coaches were coming over laughing, eating, and drinking. Many friends in the area stopped by, too."[60]

Hiring Allen would mark a notable change for Rosenbloom. He had filled all four of his previous openings with NFL assistants, showing a keen eye for head coaching talent. Weeb Ewbank won two NFL Championships with the Colts and later a Super Bowl with the Jets, Don McCafferty won a Super Bowl with the Colts, and Don Shula made the Colts one of the league's preeminent teams in the '60s before winning two Super Bowls with the Dolphins. Chuck Knox took the Rams to the playoffs in each of his five seasons in LA and to three NFC Championship Games.

In addition to Allen, Cowboys offensive coordinator Dan Reeves was high on Rosenbloom's list of candidates. Media also named Don Coryell,

Bill Walsh, and Grambling's Eddie Robinson as possibilities, although Walsh withdrew from contention. Rams defensive coordinator Ray Malavasi was a long shot.

"Reeves has made a tremendous impression on Rosenbloom," a knowledgeable source told the *Los Angeles Herald Examiner*. "He really likes him. He also likes George Allen. He doesn't know what to do."

And Rosenbloom's thoughts? "This is the toughest decision I've ever had to make," he said. "There are just too many good candidates. It's like having the first pick in the draft and having five or six O. J. Simpsons available."[61]

Rosenbloom had taken a liking to Allen the time they first crossed paths, at an NFL meeting in Hawaii in the 1960s. "George interested him mostly as a personality," son Steve Rosenbloom said in retrospect. "But wherever George went he had a winning record. That's the common denominator. But of course, he and George weren't together, either. You can admire somebody from afar for various reasons. But it's different when you work together, just like a marriage."[62]

Not everyone aligned with the Rams, though, was thrilled with Allen possibly returning to coach the squad he had led to a 49-17-4 mark from '66 to '70. "If he's coming, I'm going," said linebacker Isiah Robertson.[63] He and Rams quarterback Pat Haden, who also never played under Allen in LA, approached Steve Rosenbloom at the Pro Bowl and said "they didn't want any part of Allen," according to a high-level NFL source quoted by the *Washington Star*.[64] The *Star* article also said some of the Rams who had played for Allen during his prior stint in LA were among those opposing his return and that Don Klosterman had lobbied against Allen. Guard Tom Mack, linebacker Jack Reynolds, center Rich Saul, and wide receiver Harold Jackson were the only current Rams who had previously spent time with Allen.

When asked about the report that said Allen's chances of becoming the Rams' head coach had diminished based on an "intensive lobbying campaign," Carroll Rosenbloom responded, "We [Ram executives] don't coach our players, and we don't expect our players to pick our coach."[65]

Rams defensive end Fred Dryer was also unenthusiastic about an Allen hiring. The Rams had assembled a good defense with such players as Dryer, defensive end Jack Youngblood, and linebackers Jack Reynolds and Isiah Robertson, whom the Rams drafted with the No. 1 pick that Allen traded when acquiring the Ramskins in '71. The '77 Rams defense allowed the second-fewest points in the league (146) and the fourth-fewest rushing yards. Dryer thus questioned the wisdom of hiring another defensive-minded coach. He felt the team's struggles in the playoffs against Minnesota and Dallas were rooted in their boring, unproductive offense and that the best coach by far to revive that unit was offensive mastermind Don Coryell. In five seasons in St. Louis (1973–77), Coryell revolutionized pro football with a daring, innovative passing attack that paved the way to NFC East titles in 1974 and 1975. His offense, which became known as "Air Coryell," was one of the best in the league during his five-year stint.

Shortly after the Rams lost to the Vikings on December 26, 1977, in the first round of the playoffs, Rosenbloom called Dryer into his office to ask him about Coryell. Dryer had played for Coryell at San Diego State (SDSU) in '67 and '68, when the Aztecs went a combined 19-1-1, won a small college national championship, and split another national title. He was well aware of Coryell's passing game wizardry, not only from his days at SDSU but also from the Rams' battles against the Cardinals' Coryell-coached offense. The Cardinals' Jim Hart was a good quarterback, but Coryell "turned him into an All-Pro just by coaching," Dryer said.

Dryer unequivocally told Rosenbloom to sign Coryell if he could get him. Coryell was still under contract to the Cardinals and would cost a No. 1 draft pick.

"He said, 'I hear he's an alcoholic,'" Dryer remembered. "I simply said, 'So is Don Klosterman, your general manager. So is half the coaching staff. So is [defensive coordinator] Ray Malavasi.' I told him Don Coryell is the guy you want. He'll score 50 points a game. It'll be so exciting. He's never had a defense like ours. Don't think for a minute that Don Coryell can't deliver offensively what Chuck Knox couldn't or what George Allen can. He looked at me and said, 'It's going to cost me a No. 1 draft choice if I sign Coryell.' I said, 'Pay it.' He said, 'I'm not giving up a No. 1 draft choice for any coach.'

"I said to him, 'You've got to be kidding me.' He said, 'No, I'm not kidding.' I said, 'You just cut off your nose to spite your face. The difference in this sport is leadership. You're complaining that Chuck is not giving you the proper leadership and [fielding] what should be a championship offense. So when it comes time to get another coach, you're going after a defensive coach in George Allen. He's not an offensive coach. He's a special team guy. He's a preparation guy. You have to understand that the difference in this league is coaching. Why do these teams win? Why does Dallas win and beat us in the playoffs? What about the Vikings? They have a terrific defense, but they're in Super Bowls because offensively they're good enough to compete and beat the rest of the field.'"[66]

The Cardinals later fired Coryell on February 10, 1978. He signed with San Diego a quarter of the way into the '78 season, taking the Chargers twice to the AFC Championship Game and four times to the playoffs.

Deep down, Dryer concluded, Rosenbloom wanted a coach he felt could overcome the Cowboys and Vikings. In the owner's mind, that was George Allen, whose Redskins had routed the Cowboys in the '72 NFC Championship Game but went 0-2 against the Vikings in the playoffs. Dryer also pointed out that Ed Hookstratten had offered to encourage Allen to return to LA.

According to Dryer, "Hookstratten told Rosenbloom, 'If you want me to work on George, I'll get him over here, and I'll appeal to George's sense of ego and say we made a mistake several years ago, and the Rams want you back now to lead us to the Super Bowl. You're going to inherit a tremendous defense and tremendous offensive talent. So we want you to consider coming back. We'll cut you a nice deal.' In the middle of all this, George's name started getting bandied around, and once it started getting bandied around, they closed George out real fast."[67]

Steve Rosenbloom, too, believed his father considered Allen the missing piece in the Rams' quest to reach the Super Bowl. The notion was that after five seasons of coming so close with Knox but never winning the NFC championship, Allen would be the one to vault the Rams to the league's premier event. The younger Rosenbloom said his father was willing to overlook Allen's antagonistic relationships with his previous NFL owner-bosses—Dan Reeves and Edward Bennett Williams—and his desire for total managerial control. The most important factor to him was that Allen was a proven winner who had captured nearly 70 percent of his NFL games.

"My father was a very strong-willed person, and it came down to being his way or the highway, so he wasn't worried about George, and he thought it was worth a shot," Steve Rosenbloom said in looking back. "To get so close to the Super Bowl in those [Knox] years, year after year, it was killing my father. We just couldn't climb that last step. The further you go, the more devastating the loss. I wouldn't say desperation was his thinking but 'what are we missing, here?' He was looking for something else to climb those last steps and hoping somebody like George might provide it."[68]

Similarly, Steve Rosenbloom noted that his father had signed thirteenth-year quarterback Joe Namath, creaky knees and all, as a free agent in '77, hoping he would lead the Rams to the Super Bowl. Namath spent much of the year in the training room, played in only four games, and retired after the season.

But when his name was called among the Rams' executives, Steve Rosenbloom did not support the hiring of Allen. For one, he disliked Allen's "the future is now" philosophy of trading draft picks for seasoned veterans who could help him win immediately. He said he and his father had relied on the draft going back to their ownership days in Baltimore as the primary tool for building a successful team. "We spent a lot of time and attention in that area," he said. "But George or any other coach couldn't just call another team and trade somebody and inform us. It didn't work that way. It would really go through Carroll. He would talk to several others, and we'd kick it around and say why it was good or not so good, and what do you think of this, and maybe we shouldn't do this. It wasn't a snap judgment. Winning is part of the program, but trying to disrupt the future of the team to win today would not be a good formula. George also had to be in charge of everything. That was another thing."

Jack Teele, the Rams' publicity director during much of Allen's first stint in LA, was a front-office official by the time Allen was a coaching candidate in '78. In 2013 he opined that Allen had too much of a problem with management in LA and DC.[69] Steve Rosenbloom said Teele also disapproved of Allen's return.

"Sure, because he had a front row seat," Rosenbloom said. "Some of us others didn't have a front row seat, and you could still get an idea that, 'Gee, this isn't going to work.' Two very strong personalities, both in charge, so to speak. It was one of those things almost doomed to failure. I guess there was still a possibility it could work, but people would have to change their way of doing and looking at things."[70]

Like Dryer, Steve Rosenbloom thought an "Air Coryell"-type offense would be the right medicine. "We needed a coach that wasn't running [an offense of] 3 yards and a cloud of dust," he said. "We had the talent to have a very good offense. It wasn't really taken advantage of. So we lost some games when we didn't play as well as we could have if we had opened up that offense. I thought Coryell would be a great coach. But for whatever reasons, George bubbled to the top."

On Tuesday, January 31, reports surfaced that the Rams had chosen a new coach. It was a man who once said an NFL head coach must have "complete control of the football program to win, and even then it's difficult."[71]

George Allen was returning to Los Angeles.

20

"Someone Has Cut Out My Heart"

"I'm home."[1]

His voice nearly cracking with emotion, George Allen uttered those words before 150 reporters at the Century Plaza Hotel in Los Angeles on February 1, 1978. Seven years after being fired by the Los Angeles Rams for the second time, Allen was back as head coach with that very same team.

"This morning when I had breakfast with Mrs. Allen, we both said this was like . . . like a dream come true. Here, we're back in LA . . . and happy."[2]

Why wouldn't he be? Not only was Allen still doing what he loved to do—coaching in the NFL—but he was free from the shadow of Edward Bennett Williams, whom he had come to resent more with each passing day. Plus, the Allen family still owned their Mediterranean-style home overlooking Santa Monica Bay and the Pacific Ocean in the swank LA suburb of Palos Verdes Estates, so the move back was seamless.

Rams owner Carroll Rosenbloom introduced Allen at the news conference, as journalists scribbled down notes and TV cameras focused on the two figures among media eager to report on the return of one of the winningest coaches in the league—and perhaps the most controversial. Rosenbloom and Allen had reached a deal the night before, although terms of the contract weren't finalized. Rosenbloom would only say that the two "agreed in principle on all points" of a "multiyear contract." The contract, the *Los Angeles Times* reported, was a three- to five-year agreement with a base salary of less than $200,000 with bonuses. It included no stock option.[3]

A photo caption in a Long Beach newspaper, *The Independent*, identified Allen and Rosenbloom, both looking happy while standing side by side, as "the newlyweds."[4] But judging from Rosenbloom's jokes, snarky remarks, and threats, their honeymoon appeared over before it started. The owner's curious comments sounded like he was keeping Allen on a short leash and maybe even having buyer's remorse. In one statement, he said, "We talked about a year-to-year contract. But we finally agreed on week-to-week."[5] In another: "I felt he was the guy for this particular job at this particular time. If he doesn't do it [get the Rams to the Super Bowl], he won't be here."[6]

Rosenbloom did not parse words when stressing that Allen was hired only as the head coach and not a general manager who could make the final call on player trades. With the coach-GM dual-responsibility scenario becoming an NFL thing of the past, such decisions would be made with Allen's consent by the Rams' front office of Carroll Rosenbloom; general manager Don Klosterman; assistant to the president Steve Rosenbloom, the owner's son; and administrative assistant Jack Teele—a holdover from the days of Rams owner Dan Reeves. Not having sole authority for trades would mark a seismic change for Allen. Heading into the 1977 season, "Trader George" had made 131 trades, 81 with the Redskins and the rest when he coached the Rams to a 49-17-4 record from '66 to '70.

"We'll make no trades that George doesn't want—any more than we made trades our other coaches didn't want," Carroll Rosenbloom said. "George will even play an active part in the draft—and that will be a new and refreshing experience for him."[7] Rosenbloom joked that maybe the Rams should send Allen to Berlitz, a well-established language education and leadership training company, to brush up on his drafting skills.

"He has a simple problem," Rosenbloom added. "All he has to do is coach and teach. We'll do everything else. The only other thing he has to worry about is taking us to the Super Bowl. Sure, he's got pressure on him to get there, and I don't want him to forget it for one waking moment. He won't forget it. I can tell you that."[8]

Allen, nattily dressed in a tan three-piece suit, said reaching the Super Bowl was his top priority but that all would not be lost if the Rams didn't get there in 1978.[9] He also said he'd be fine concentrating only on coaching.

"I relish the opportunity to just coach and teach," he said. "After having seven years of being vice president and general manager [in Washington], I really didn't have enough time for football. I'm amazed we did as well as we did the last seven years."[10]

Allen, a mastermind on defense and special teams, knew his mission also consisted of jazzing up the Rams' vanilla offense. His predecessor, Chuck Knox, was known for his heavy reliance on the run and lack of imagination on offense, a major reason Rosenbloom lost confidence in his ability to win in the playoffs and reach the Super Bowl.

"We will run a multiple offense, meaning one in which many different formations are used," Allen said. "I would have used it at Washington this year if we hadn't had so many players hurt. A multiple-set offense puts so much pressure on the defense that you almost have to use it."[11]

In a surprising twist, Allen extended an olive branch to those prying reporters with whom he had experienced so much friction over the years: "I've been portrayed as peculiar and different, and a myth has been painted about George Allen . . . that I don't cooperate with the press. I know the responsibility you have. I'll do everything I can to help you do your job. I would like to know you on an individual basis."[12]

The Rosenbloom-Allen pairing looked like an odd marriage and left many wondering whether two strong-minded men who craved control could coexist. On top of that, Rosenbloom was well aware of Allen's run-ins with other NFL owners. The current Rams owner had been a close and longtime friend of Reeves, who had fired Allen twice during his first coaching stint in LA.

Rosenbloom, one of the NFL's high-profile owners, also had a good rapport with another Allen foe: Edward Bennett Williams. Their friendship was evident in a letter Williams wrote to Rosenbloom on January 13, 1975, about three weeks after the Rams beat the Redskins in LA in the opening round of the playoffs and two weeks after the Rams lost to the Vikings in the NFC Championship Game: "Sorry I didn't see you when I was out there getting my licking," Williams wrote. "I know you'll be back meaner and more cantankerous than ever after this rest, that is—if it's possible for you to be more disagreeable."

Then, in another of his knocks on Allen's spending decisions, Williams wrote, "We had a great year. We haven't got the final big one, but I think George kept our losses under a million . . . which must entitle him to a bonus under that contract Eddie Hookstratten got for him."[13]

Yet, Rosenbloom ignored the Allen naysayers who were in his ear urging him not to hire the controversial coach, such as Steve Rosenbloom and Jack Teele, a Reeves loyalist who disliked Allen. Carroll Rosenbloom knew Allen was a proven winner with a hunger for reaching the Super Bowl that mirrored his own. In his mind, that's all that counted. "People keep saying I can't get along with George," Rosenbloom said at Allen's hiring. "Why not?"[14]

Like Reeves and Williams, Carroll Rosenbloom rose to prominence in another line of work before establishing a foothold in the NFL. Born in Baltimore in 1907, he was part of a family of nine children, six boys and three girls. The boys were raised to work in the successful clothing business run by their father, Solomon Rosenbloom, who had immigrated to the United States from Russia in the late nineteenth century. The business made denim work clothes and sportswear.

Rosenbloom lived for a time down the street from H. L. Mencken, the famous American journalist, satirist, and social critic.[15] The young Carroll attended the University of Pennsylvania, where at 5 feet 11, 170 pounds, he played halfback on the Quakers' football team in the 1920s. His backfield coach was a man named Bert Bell, who would one day be NFL commissioner.

After college, the ambitious Rosenbloom took on more responsibility in the family company and gained full control when his father died in 1942. By then, Carroll had become known as the "Overalls King of America," as Dan Moldea wrote in his 1989 book titled *Interference*, noting that Rosenbloom added to his fortune during World War II by cornering the market on battle fatigues and parachutes for American soldiers. The company grew to manufacture other garments, bought out clothing manufacturers, and came to employ nearly seven thousand workers after the war.[16]

Rosenbloom was realizing the wealth he had envisioned years before. "I always knew I'd be a millionaire," he told *Sports Illustrated* in 1965. "I believe that anyone who wants can make money. That's not very difficult. I can remember sitting on a park bench in front of our house in Baltimore, and my brother Ben said, 'What are you going to do?' 'I'll tell you one thing,' I said. 'When I'm 34, I'm going to retire.'"[17]

When Rosenbloom was in his midthirties, another job opportunity came calling. His old coach at Penn, Bert Bell, tried influencing him to join the NFL's fraternity of owners. Bell, the NFL commissioner from 1946 to 1959, knew well of Rosenbloom's wealth and business acumen. He asked him in '53 to buy a majority interest in the Baltimore Colts, a team being given a second chance after playing one season in 1950 and folding for financial reasons.

"Bert had a home near me in Margate, New Jersey," Rosenbloom told the *Los Angeles Times* in '78. "He kept telling me I ought to come into the league, and I kept saying I didn't have time. Finally, to get away from him, I took the family to my home in Palm Beach and shut off the phones. But one of my brothers flew down and said, 'Carroll, you're really in a hell of a jam. Bert Bell has told the press the only way Baltimore can keep the franchise is if you will come in as owner.'

"So Bert had me on the spot. If I didn't take the team, they'd 'hang the Jew bastard.' But I got the franchise for nothing, really. I put up $13,000 for my share of the stock."[18]

Rosenbloom promised the city of Baltimore a championship within five years. Meeting his goal, the Johnny Unitas–led Colts beat the New York Giants to win the NFL Championship in 1958 and repeated with a championship win over the Giants in 1959. After a few mediocre seasons, Rosenbloom fired coach Weeb Ewbank and in 1963 hired Don Shula, who won 75 percent of his regular-season games over the next seven seasons. But he was skunked, 27–0, by the Browns in the '64 NFL Championship, fell short in a '65 playoff loss to the Packers, and suffered a '67 season-ending loss to Allen's Rams that kept the 11-1-2 Colts out of the playoffs. In Shula's most dramatic loss, the AFL's Jets shocked the 17.5-point favorite Colts in Super Bowl III, 16–7, in what is considered the greatest upset in NFL history. Consequently, Shula acquired a reputation as a coach who couldn't win when the stakes were highest.

Rosenbloom carried his own dubious reputation. While in Baltimore, he showed an apparent shady side connected to his penchant for gambling. An NFL investigation cleared him of betting against the Colts in a 1953 game. But it's long been rumored that he bet on the Colts in their '58 championship game against the Giants. With the game tied at 17 and the Colts driving in the first overtime playoff in NFL history, Unitas opted for a touchdown instead of a field goal, which would not have beaten the spread. Fullback Alan Ameche slammed 1 yard into the end zone to give the Colts a 23–17 victory. Nothing conclusive has ever come to light regarding a Rosenbloom bet influencing Unitas's overtime decisions. But Dan Moldea wrote in *Interference* that, based on accounts from many figures in sports gambling, Rosenbloom bet $1 million on the Colts. Moldea, a well-respected investigative journalist, also quoted a convicted bookmaker turned government informant who said Rosenbloom, utilizing a Mafia gambling network, bet $1 million on the Colts in Super Bowl III.[19]

After Super Bowl III, Rosenbloom praised Shula in one breath and voiced bewilderment in another: Shula "is as fine a coach as there is in football. But something happens every year, so we must be doing something wrong. I know that management must put out one tremendous effort to come back. If we don't, somebody else should have the team."[20]

At odds with Rosenbloom, Shula departed after the '69 season to become coach, general manager, and a minority stockholder of the Miami Dolphins. Rosenbloom, who could be witty and charming but also mercurial, ruthless, and gruff, did his part to alienate Shula. He failed to comprehend why Shula lost so many pivotal games, once calling him a "loser of the big ones."[21]

In a 2008 interview with the *Baltimore Sun*, Shula said his relationship with Rosenbloom turned unpleasant after Super Bowl III: "I loved Baltimore—the people, the fans, and everything that Colts football stood for. But Rosenbloom's buddies never let him forget [the Super Bowl III loss to the Jets], and he never let me forget it. If we had won that game and continued to win, I certainly wouldn't have gone. I'd still be in Baltimore, eating crab cakes."[22]

Rosenbloom would also run short on patience with Allen. After signing with the Rams, Allen relocated to Los Angeles to set up his assistant coaching staff and make other arrangements in preparation for the '78 season. The rest of the family stayed in Virginia. Etty was arranging to sell the Allens' home in northern Virginia, where Jennifer was finishing her junior year at Langley High School and Greg was exploring postgraduate studies in psychology at George Mason University.[23] Bruce was a senior at the University of Richmond, where he had set school punting records on the football team. (The Colts drafted him in the twelfth round in 1978, but he didn't play in the NFL.) George Felix, who earned a law degree at the University of Virginia in 1977, was serving as a law clerk in Charlottesville.

"My parents wanted me to move to California after my clerkship ended in the spring of 1978," he recalled. "My father somehow got Carroll Rosenbloom to talk to me to bolster my parents' efforts to persuade me. Mr. Rosenbloom spoke to me by telephone about the reasons and the help he could provide if I moved to practice law in California." George visited cities in California but decided to stay in Virginia, "unpersuaded that California was the place for me."[24]

Soon after arriving in LA, Allen reunited with someone he had coached a quarter century earlier—Bill Harris, an end at Whittier during Allen's first four seasons at the school, '51 to '54. The Los Angeles–based Harris, who had majored in chemistry at Whittier and then risen to multimillionaire status through executive roles in development, contracting, and manufacturing companies, was good friends with Bud Furillo, the entertaining *Los Angeles Herald Examiner* sports columnist known as "The Steamer."

Furillo, the sports editor at the *Herald Examiner* during Allen's first stint in LA, also knew Allen well.

One day, Harris remembered, Furillo made a suggestion: "He said, 'Hey Bill, you played for George, why don't we all go out to dinner?' I said, 'Yeah, let's do it.' So he got a hold of George. We all went to a restaurant in LA. It was great reuniting with him."

Harris and Allen had kept in touch after parting ways in the 1950s. After reuniting in '78, they formed an almost inseparable bond, with Allen coming to see Harris as a loyal, caring, and generous friend. "We probably talked every day until he died," said Harris,[25] who became a part owner of the Chicago Blitz and Arizona Wranglers when Allen coached in the United States Football League in the 1980s. Harris was also a special advisor to the President's Council on Physical Fitness and Sports when Allen chaired that federal body under President Reagan in the 1980s. Beyond his collaborations with Allen, Harris committed himself to helping some of the most disenfranchised people in the world, including those in the East African country of Tanzania. He passed away in 2022.

Meanwhile, while everything was copacetic between Allen and Rosenbloom in the '78 off-season, Allen's messy divorce from the Redskins entered a new chapter. The drama stemmed from Allen's comments about his desire for some of his former players to play for him in LA, as well as unsettling remarks he made about a ghost from his past: Edward Bennett Williams. Plus, the Redskins fined Allen more than $14,000 for what they defined as unjustified expenses he racked up during his stint in DC.

At a press conference announcing the hiring of Redskins GM Bobby Beathard on February 24, 1978, Williams and new Redskins coach Jack Pardee warned Allen not to tamper with their players to persuade them to play for the Rams. Allen must understand "he has to deal with us before he can do anything with our players," Williams said. Pardee: "I just want to let everyone know that we will not stand for any tampering or interfering with our players."[26]

Their comments followed Allen's published remarks that he'd like to have certain players, namely quarterback Billy Kilmer and linebacker–special teams star Pete Wysocki. The thirty-eight-year-old Kilmer, a Redskin in all seven of Allen's years in DC, told the *Washington Post* "it's no secret" he'd like to reunite with Allen.[27]

Allen denied that he had spoken to any players about their joining him in LA, specifically Kilmer, whom he had seen at Kilmer's wedding in Las Vegas. He called such allegations "ridiculous."[28]

The tampering controversy surfaced again in July. Jim Murray of the *Los Angeles Times* reported that NFL commissioner Pete Rozelle had written a letter to Allen warning him that his public comments about Kilmer bordered on tampering. Allen again denied that he had "tampered" with Kilmer but aimed insults at Williams. "Ed Williams can't sign him," Allen told Murray from Rams training camp. "They do not get along. Of course, we would want Kilmer. But there is no way we can get him, and there has been no tampering."[29]

Kilmer, who signed a two-year contract extension with the Redskins, didn't think Allen should be singled out for tampering. Kilmer said he'd talked to "a lot of coaches" in the '78 off-season, including two of Allen's Redskins assistants turned head coaches, the Colts' Ted Marchibroda and the Chiefs' Marv Levy, as well as Raiders managing general partner Al Davis.[30]

Rozelle's letter packed an additional punch, noting that the NFL had fined Allen $3,000 for "continuation of direct and personal attacks" on Redskins staff in published articles. Murray's column indicated that Allen had described Redskins management as "suddenly self-righteous men" and had accused the team of tapping his phones. As for the man Allen had once called "a Jekyll and Hyde and a cold-blooded fish," Allen this time belittled Williams as "petty, mean, and vindictive."[31]

Williams refused to comment on Allen's latest remarks, which came in response to a $14,047.64 bill Allen received for unauthorized expenses he made while coaching the Redskins. The Redskins refused to detail the expenses, but the *Los Angeles Herald Examiner* reported that the payments included flowers for Allen's secretary, long-distance phone calls to his sons, car expenses, vitamins, oranges, and a pair of pajamas he bought at training camp.

"The big sports charged me $36 for three tickets for my son to [go to] a game in Atlanta," Allen told the *Herald Examiner*. "Mind you, I was vice president, general manager, and head coach of the club, and I got charged for tickets."

Allen was irate that the Redskins also charged him nearly $500 for repossession of two cars that the team had lent him for his use. He had given them to his sons George and Bruce. "When the Redskins fired me, they demanded the cars immediately," he told the *Herald Examiner*. "One boy was in Abingdon, Virginia and the other in Richmond at school. We told the club the cars would be returned by the end of the week. But instead, Williams sent people to get them right away—like repossession jobs.

"I bruised Williams' ego after I was fired, so he's apparently decided to get me."[32]

While the latest segment of the soap opera was playing out, the Rams were preparing to begin training camp at Cal State Fullerton, east of Los Angeles. The '78 season featured a decline in exhibition games from six to four but an increase in regular-season games from fourteen to sixteen, as well as an extra wild card playoff team in each conference.

Nearly sixty players—seventeen veterans and forty-one rookies—showed up for the first day of camp on July 9, with the rest expected to report on July 20 for two-a-day drills.[33] Allen had been unable to persuade Rams executives to trade with the Redskins for Kilmer or Wysocki, but the front office agreed to trade two offensive linemen and a series of draft choices.[34] In return they'd get one of Allen's other favorite Redskins: kick return specialist and safety Eddie Brown, who played in the Pro Bowl in '76 and '77.

Allen's staff of ten assistant coaches included four he brought from the Redskins and three holdovers from Chuck Knox's staff, one of whom was Ray Malavasi. Malavasi, the offensive coordinator and offensive line coach, had previously served as defensive coordinator under Knox. Widely credited with the success of the Rams' defense that keyed five straight NFC West championships and yielded the fewest points (830) and yards (16,908) in the league during that span, he had been mentioned in the press as a long shot to replace Knox.

"Rosenbloom wanted my dad to keep Malavasi on his staff," Bruce Allen remembered.[35]

In the coming weeks, Allen's history of vanquishing opponents in 71 percent of his regular-season games, with no losing seasons over a dozen years, remained an afterthought to those who opposed his hiring. "The behind-the-scene criticism heightened," recalled Doug Krikorian, a Rams beat writer and columnist at the time for the *Herald Examiner*. "You had people in the organization putting the knock on him." Krikorian and his *Herald Examiner* colleague, columnist Mel Durslag, were two of Allen's allies in the media. Both were longtime friends with Allen, since his Rams coaching days in the '60s.[36]

Plus, a cast of veterans led by linebacker Isiah Robertson, defensive tackle Larry Brooks, and defensive end Jack Youngblood—three star players—led an anti-Allen drumbeat in training camp that evolved into a revolt.[37] At the same time, Allen was fighting to be accepted on a team that had been very successful under his predecessor, Knox, and was stocked with talent on both sides of the ball. Many of the Rams players liked Knox and resented his departure. Those circumstances led to an untenable situation.

Some Rams players also refused to accept Allen's rigid practice schedule, which was aimed at injecting discipline into a team that was "lollygagging" under Knox, according to Krikorian, who said, "They won five straight division titles, but they didn't do anything."[38] Complaints surfaced that Allen was working the team too hard during his two-a-day practices. Unlike Knox's two-a-day practices of three and a half hours total—one and a half in the morning and two in the afternoon—Allen's consumed five and a half hours overall: two and a half in the morning and three in the afternoon. The additional reps in the brutal Southern California summer heat, humidity, and smog grated on some players, including a few quoted anonymously in a *Los Angeles Times* article headlined "Camp Allen, Not Ft. Knox."

"That's what happened to Allen's teams in Washington," one player said of the tedious practices. "By December, they had nothing left."

Another player said, "George just rams that accelerator down to the floor, like [race car champion] Mario Andretti. If the car lasts, it lasts. If not, he just throws it away and gets a new car. Sometimes, it doesn't seem like he cares about anything but his program and himself.

"Our team doctors have to fight for water breaks. George still operates on the reward system . . . that we have to *earn* water. My God, in this heat and smog you don't earn it, you *need* it. On most teams, the thinking is 1978. This camp is still 1946."[39]

Defensive end Fred Dryer, then in his tenth season of a thirteen-year, 103-sack career, warned Allen about the long practices and "reinventing the wheel" with the Rams' dominant defense, which produced five All-Pro players in '77: Youngblood, Brooks, Robertson, cornerback Monte Jackson, and free safety Bill Simpson. Dryer said Allen turned the offense over to his assistants on that side of the ball but that he planned to modify a few things on defense.

Dryer told Allen, "'George, let's not try to change everybody. We need a tweak here and a tweak there. Don't beat the crap out of this team. Let's move the pile down the road here. We're close. As a team, we're pretty good, and you know that because you played against us, and you beat us, and we've beaten you.' You've got players asking whether George is going to get rid of Ray Malavasi's great defense and put in his blitz packages every down. George's teams had all of these weak side linebacker blitzes and tackle twists, and all of this composition of defensive movement. Everybody respected George immensely. But George wasn't the owner or the general manager. He was coming to a team that honestly didn't need him."

At one point, Dryer recalled, Allen had a message for Malavasi: "George said, 'Hey, Ray, this is what we want to run.' Ray didn't like it. Ray said, 'I'm probably a better coach than you defensively.' So there was a lot of that. There was confrontation all the way. That was the leading issue in training camp, and it was not necessary."[40]

Eddie Brown, one of Allen's most loyal players in Washington, observed that many of the Rams players were not used to the length of Allen's practices. Under the previous coaching regime, "an hour and fifteen minutes was a long practice for them," he said. Under Allen, "we were out there for three hours on many occasions. He expected them to work a lot harder than they'd ever worked."

Brown recalled that, in response, some of the Rams players wanted Malavasi to be their head coach. "Oh sure," he said. "They had no say in George being hired, and Coach Malavasi was one of their best friends. Everybody loved coach Malavasi."

Malavasi, according to Brown, was tight with Isiah Robertson and many other players who liked him so much because he went easy on them. "He gave into them," Brown said. "Pretty much whatever they wanted to do he would let them do. He wasn't quite disciplined enough."[41]

Allen's strict water policy, which he began enforcing in his college coaching days as a way of building mental toughness, snowballed into another enormous controversy. The policy alarmed the Rams' medical staff, which feared dehydration and other potential health problems with the players practicing so long in such searing heat.

One of the team doctors, Toby Freedman, argued with Allen about his decision to limit access to water, according to Dryer. "Freedman said, 'You've got guys that are dehydrated, and that's causing some serious issues,'" Dryer remembered. "You can't mess around with that. Toby's the one that forced the issue with George about water. He said, 'I'm a doctor.' So that whole thing erupted. He just told George, 'You're crazy.'

"When you think back on all of this, how perverse the profession of football was, and the people who were entrusted with making decisions like that . . . coaches all over the place saying, 'We're going to punish you and then deny you water. Then you're going to run sprints until you pass out. At the training table, we're going to put out salt tablets for you.'"[42]

Guard Tom Mack, one of the few Rams who had played for Allen in his first go-around in LA, implored his teammates to understand the purpose of Allen's water restrictions. "I spent my time explaining to the guys playing offense over and over again that he was doing something that was strictly an issue of mental toughness," said Mack, an eleven-time Pro Bowler who was inducted into the Hall of Fame in 1999. "I told them if you put up with it, you're going to end up with a good team in the long term."[43]

Allen was wrong to deny his players water, Krikorian acknowledged, adding that he was just taking the same "old school" approach other NFL coaches had subscribed to over the years. "Toby Freedman, who was my doctor, didn't like George," Krikorian said. "It goes back to what they saw in George. They didn't want George there. He was a different kind of cat. You think George was the only one who didn't give the players water? How about Vince Lombardi? You think the Packers got water? I'm sure Lombardi's practices were harsher than George's."[44]

Allen's obsession with cleanliness and perfectionism also rubbed some players the wrong way. He disliked, for example, that the players would leave trash on the field and sit on their helmets on the sidelines during practice. In Allen's mind, both of those acts were signs of laziness.

"'If you're going to drink water in Dixie cups, you have to put them back in the trash can, you can't leave them on the field,'" Dryer remembered Allen saying. "'We've got to pick up the trash. One of the reasons you haven't won in the past is because you're not picking up trash.'

"I knew what George meant, and so did many of the carryover people. It wasn't like it was an all-out revolt. [But] saying putting trash cups on the field is one of the reasons you don't win—I don't think that's right."[45]

Mack told Allen that his message wasn't getting through to the players: "George was very much the way George always is. He'd lick his lips. 'We've just got to keep doing it. We'll just keep pecking away at it.' His approach was his approach, and that's what he did."[46]

"All I can do is what I know is successful," Allen said during training camp. "People who win over the long haul are those who have a program they stick to. Numerous coaches around the league are following my program to the letter, and they're very successful. If some of our players don't like my methods, if they don't like it here, there are twenty-seven other teams in the NFL."[47]

Amid the chaos of training camp, one of the vehement opponents of Allen's hiring, Steve Rosenbloom, took it upon himself to see a different side of the man known to care about only one thing: winning football games. One evening, the door to Allen's room at the University Village Apartments in Fullerton was open as Rosenbloom passed by. He walked in.

"I saw a window of George that probably most people don't see," Rosenbloom said in hindsight. "It was just him and me. We always got along anyway. But that was the first time I really got to spend so much time with him, and I thought it was very interesting that I could talk to George. Football hardly came up in the conversation. If it did, it was just a passing thing. I got to see George as George, without him being wrapped in football and winning and all that. I gave him the opportunity to get away from it in our conversation. It probably cleared his mind, because we didn't talk about football or the team or who was doing what."[48]

The imaginative offense that Allen promised in his introductory press conference in February was virtually nonexistent in the Rams' first two exhibition games. In a 14–7 loss to New England at home, the Patriots' starters shut out Allen's first team in the first half, 14–0. Rams starting quarterback Pat Haden threw for only 84 yards.

To make a point, Allen benched three of the four starters who had briefly walked out of training camp apparently for reasons unrelated to his lengthy practices.[49] All four had been fined $500 apiece for each day they missed.[50] Wide receiver Ron Jessie and cornerback Monte Jackson saw no action against the Patriots. Isiah Robertson, who opposed the hiring of Allen from day one, was relegated to playing with the Rams' second-string defense, rookies, and free agents in the second half. Offensive tackle Doug France started with the first team.

A few days after the New England game, Carroll Rosenbloom reportedly met in private with some veterans. "The players did a number on George," said one player who spoke to the press anonymously. "They complained like hell about his longer practices and his new system. They felt he was losing control of the team."[51]

With the Rams preparing for their second exhibition game, Allen asked Dryer and Youngblood if he could speak to them one day after practice. In an interview four decades later, Dryer flashed back to the conversation, saying the information Allen relayed to the two defensive linemen helped trigger his ultimate firing:

"The three of us are down in the far end zone. [Allen] says, 'I want both of you to know I traded Isiah Robertson to Green Bay this morning.' I said, 'What's that?' He said, 'Yeah. I traded Isiah to Green Bay this morning. We're going to tighten this defense up a little bit.' He said that's one of the positions where we've been weak. I looked at Jack, and Jack looked at me. Jack said to me, 'Can he do that?' It was one of the great moments he and I had together. I said, 'I don't think so.'

"Here's the beauty of that conundrum: somebody in Green Bay took his call and told him, 'Yeah, you've got a deal.' Those owners in Green Bay knew that George doesn't have the right to do that. All trades go through Don Klosterman. The league knows everybody. They knew Carroll and Klosterman. But the hilarity comes in when George . . . who was he talking to? I kept asking myself. Who was George talking to that said, 'Yeah, that's a deal'? And how fast did the Packers' ownership contact Carroll Rosenbloom and say, 'George just called up here and traded us Isiah Robertson'?

"We know the dynamic of George. We know what he likes to do. He's been doing it all his life. But suddenly now we've got a situation where George calls one of the teams up and says, 'I'm going to trade Isiah Robertson.' Of course, everybody knows you can't do that, George. It's Jack Youngblood's line to me, 'Can he do that?'"[52]

No trade was consummated—at least not then. The Rams shipped Robertson, who had a history of confrontation with management and teammates, to Buffalo just before the '79 season.

But did Allen really trade Robertson? It's unfathomable to Krikorian that Allen would try to make such a deal. First of all, he said, Allen couldn't arbitrarily trade a player without at least consulting Klosterman and others in the front office. Carroll Rosenbloom made it clear up front that he wasn't granted that type of power. Second, in Krikorian's eyes, Allen was too smart to believe he could do something as audacious as that.

As far as word getting back to the owner about Allen trying to trade Robertson, "There again, that's part of the knives in his back," Krikorian said. "There was a lot of that about George then. That corroborates that they wanted him out of there. They did not like him. That story supports the fantasy that he was a loon and losing it.

"I love Freddy [Dryer]. I was as close to him as anybody. He didn't like

George. He wanted his guy Coryell there. So I don't know whether this is revisionist history or fake news or whether I'm getting dementia. It's just ridiculous. Nobody was closer to that Rams team than me. I wrote seven stories a week on that goddamn team for seven years, and I don't remember that. I had every story there was."[53]

In their second exhibition game, the Rams looked lifeless in a 17–0 loss to the Chargers at the LA Coliseum. The offense produced 109 yards and never crossed midfield on its own, starting in Chargers territory after a short punt and a blocked punt. Rams receivers dropped six passes. Plus, several players, including Robertson, claimed they had the flu. Three of them were running backs who didn't dress for the game. Carroll and Steve Rosenbloom reportedly seethed while watching from the press box,[54] and the Rams were booed off the field at halftime and again at the end of the game.[55]

Afterward Allen told reporters he played everyone he wanted to—more than seventy players. He said when a team experiments like that, "you're going to make mistakes. We made too many. I told the players it's nothing that can't be corrected."[56]

One day later, Sunday, August 13, the Rosenblooms drove forty-five minutes from Bel Air to Cal State Fullerton to meet with Allen. The two, along with Klosterman, talked with Allen for about two hours. Carroll Rosenbloom decided he had seen enough and told Allen he was letting him go, marking the fourth time Allen had been fired by the same team.[57]

"It is my feeling that I made a serious error in judgment believing George Allen could ever work within our framework," the senior Rosenbloom said in a statement to the media. "It has been extremely difficult for him to adjust to his new situation. Unquestionably, he is a fine coach and administrator. His record speaks for itself. However, I am certain it is in the best interest of all concerned that we make the change at this time.

"It's probably my saddest decision because I'm very fond of George Allen."[58]

Given the power that the headstrong owner wielded in the front office, there's little doubt that he made the final call on Allen's firing. But to intercept any thoughts that the player unrest had influenced his decision, he remarked, "My players don't help me select my coach, so they have nothing to do with me firing my coach."[59]

Today Doug Krikorian disagrees: "Carroll was overwhelmed by all the people coming up to him and telling him what a bad guy [Allen] was.

He thought the team was going to fall apart. It wasn't going to fall apart. George would have got them going, believe me. But they didn't like him. He came in there and changed the culture totally."[60]

Shortly after the firing, Carroll Rosenbloom called a meeting to tell the players of his decision, believed to be the quickest dismissal of a head coach in NFL history. He said he had replaced Allen with Malavasi, who had accumulated twenty-three years in the coaching ranks and finished 4-8 in his only head coaching stint, with the AFL's Denver Broncos in 1966.

Around the same time, Allen told reporters that he was "shocked" by the firing. He felt he had the right mix of talent to win the Super Bowl in a three-year time span and failed to understand why the Rams' management had stripped him of that opportunity. One reporter asked why he thought he was let go.

"You'd have to ask Carroll Rosenbloom that question," he responded, still wearing his Rams warmup jacket. "I don't know. I only know one way to go, and that's to give it everything you have, work hard, be dedicated and committed to your job. I did it my way. It's been successful. I told him he was making a serious error in judgment." But, he said, "there's no question in my mind the team will come around." After all, he reminded the press, "we're playing over seventy guys each game. We had [the] flu, some bumps and bruises. It's the preseason. We're learning a new system."[61]

With regard to his future, Allen asked rhetorically, "Will I coach again? I know if I do it will be under a different situation than it was here. I just feel so empty right now. Like someone has cut out my heart."[62]

"I guess I made a serious mistake giving up a great job in Washington."[63]

The firing upset Rams players who supported Allen, such as guard Rich Saul and running back John Cappelletti. Saul, a holdover from Allen's first stint in LA and the twin brother of Redskins guard Ron Saul, who had also played for Allen, went to the coach's apartment at Cal State Fullerton to apologize to him.[64] Tom Mack remembered feeling "disappointed" that he was unable to convince his teammates to embrace Allen's message of mental toughness. "It was very hard to get them to understand that kind of thing because in their minds they're thinking they're basically a half inch away from the championship already," Mack said. "And if they get a guy that they like who happened to be Malavasi . . . so they go, 'Oh boy, we got our guy.'"[65] One Ram ecstatic over the Malavasi hiring was, not surprisingly, Isiah Robertson, who raised both of his arms and said, "Free at last." Previously, Robertson said August 13 would have been his last day as a Ram if a coaching change wasn't made.[66]

In the press, Malavasi said he didn't think Allen got a fair shake, noting that he was "as surprised as everyone else" about Rosenbloom's sudden decision.[67] But is that how he really felt? Allen's good friend Bill Harris sensed that Malavasi was an architect of the Allen firing. Harris said he lived in an apartment complex with several Rams players with whom he socialized, that he knew Malavasi, and that he was in constant touch with Allen.

"I knew Malavasi was in the middle of it with George," Harris said. "After practice, Malavasi would get on the phone and talk to [Carroll] Rosenbloom: 'Man, this guy's crazy, he's making us do this, he's working the guys too hard, etc., etc.' I think the players were all right with [Allen]. Malavasi was the guy."[68]

According to Bruce Allen, "Ray [Malavasi] wasn't used to the long hours of meetings and preparations and probably did exaggerate the players' discontent. Ray had a different personality than Dad's previous coaches. He wanted to go out every night. Dad wanted coaches to work every night."[69]

Harris said, "George thought everything was going all right because he was just being George. He liked discipline. He liked to work the guys hard. A lot of pro football players don't think they have to work that hard. He didn't believe that. He wanted them to work hard and long hours. I was in Hawaii on vacation when George called me and said, 'Well, he fired me today.' I said, 'What the heck's going on over there?'"[70]

In Bruce Allen's opinion, the rapid firing felt like a "setup" by Carroll Rosenbloom. He implied that Rosenbloom was in cahoots with Pete Rozelle, a disciple of Dan Reeves, to fire his father. "Everyone knew of my dad's eccentric qualities, his dedication, and his demand for total commitment from everybody around him," Bruce said. "That should not have been a surprise to anybody. You fired a coach who had won 71 percent of his games."[71]

Steve Rosenbloom said his father wasn't "vindictive" like that. Regarding Carroll Rosenbloom's comment at Allen's introductory press conference that Allen was on a "week-to-week" contract, Steve Rosenbloom said it was his father's way of simply bracing for the hiring to possibly go off the rails. "My father wasn't asleep at the switch," he said. "He wasn't under any illusions. 'Desperate' is not the word, but you have to understand that winning is everything. That's how it was for George. That's how it was for my father. But they were different people and had different ways. But he was willing to take a shot. My father knew the problems that George would bring, so none of it was a surprise."[72]

Where was Allen's longtime attorney, Ed Hookstratten, as this drama played out? Hookstratten, who was also the Rams' general counsel at the time, took management's side in the controversy, recalled his son, Jon Hookstratten: "From my perspective, it was as ugly as it could be because you've got our two worlds colliding. You've got the Carroll Rosenbloom world where we're very close to him, and you've got the George Allen world where my dad had worked with him all those pressure-packed years. It doesn't feel good to say it, but I think my dad chose sides. He chose Carroll Rosenbloom's side, and that was it."

Also according to Jon Hookstratten, Rozelle mandated shortly after the firing that Ed Hookstratten relinquish his double duties, which amounted to a conflict of interest. In the ensuing years, Ed Hookstratten transitioned to serving as an agent for many national sportscasters, athletes, and entertainment personalities. He had minimal contact with Allen.[73]

When trying to comprehend the bizarre nature of Allen's hiring and firing, namely how the odds seemed stacked against him from the beginning and also the swiftness of his dismissal, is it possible that he wasn't Carroll Rosenbloom's first choice to replace Chuck Knox? Did Rosenbloom envision hiring Allen so he could show Malavasi how to run an intense, no-nonsense training camp that would possibly inject the players with key ingredients they needed to play championship-caliber football—mental toughness and fourth-quarter endurance—before discarding him in favor of Malavasi? Today the Allen family dismisses that theory, saying their father was Rosenbloom's first choice all along.

"I definitely believe Rosenbloom wanted Dad's how-to-beat Dallas playbooks and coaching staff," Bruce said. "Dad was great at assembling coaching staffs. The Rams couldn't get by Dallas in those years. I remember Rosenbloom told him, 'You're the one who can beat Dallas. We have to beat Dallas.' Malavasi would have been a fallback candidate if Dad didn't take the job."[74]

According to Jennifer Allen, "Carroll Rosenbloom wasn't going to bring in a future Hall of Fame coach to mentor another coach. I don't know of any owner who would do that. All owners want to win immediately. Only a very few are patient enough to ride through the ups and downs."[75]

The day of the firing, unfortunately enough, moving vans arrived at the Allen family's house in Palos Verdes Estates with furniture and other items from their house in Virginia. George Allen was indeed "home." Without a coaching job, though, he was a man disconnected from his primary passion in life. He was determined to get it back.

21

Uncharted Waters

Less than a day after Carroll Rosenbloom fired George Allen, the Rams players practiced for the first time under their new head coach, Ray Malavasi. As expected, it was shorter than an Allen practice—two hours—and many of the same players who complained about Allen's demanding style not surprisingly felt a sense of relief.[1] Showing their true talent, the Rams dominated in the last two exhibition games: 26–7 over Seattle and 28–3 over Oakland.

Meanwhile, with the ashes rising from Rosenbloom's abrupt and dramatic purge of Allen, the accomplished sixty-one-year-old football coach sought answers as to why his career had suddenly fallen off the rails. "Do you think I got a fair chance . . . two preseason games?" he asked reporters.[2] Many in the media agreed with him, castigating Rosenbloom in the process: "Allen wasn't fired, he was lynched," read a headline in the *Sun-Telegram*, a Southern California newspaper.[3]

Shortly after the firing, *Los Angeles Herald Examiner* sportswriters Melvin Durslag and Doug Krikorian, along with the newspaper's editor, James Bellows, agreed to meet with Rosenbloom and his son, Rams front-office executive Steve Rosenbloom. The Rosenblooms were concerned that the newspaper's coverage of the Allen firing was too harsh. Durslag and Krikorian, friends of Allen, sympathized with him over his sudden dismissal.

"Both Melvin and I just ripped the holy hell out of [Carroll Rosenbloom] and his organization for firing George," Krikorian recalled. "I would just go on and on. They tried to silence us, and Bellows just told them to go to hell. What they did to George was ridiculous."[4]

Vern Buol, Allen's good friend and colleague from his days coaching the Chicago Bears, also took it upon himself to blast Carroll Rosenbloom. In a letter, he told Rosenbloom he had fired the greatest coach in pro football and that he agreed with those in the press who called the move dumb.

"It was a loss not only to the Rams but also to all professional football," Buol wrote.[5]

Perhaps Allen had sensed something was in the works months before the mid-August firing, based on a recollection from Steve Rosenbloom. With the Rams having migrated from training camp at Cal State Fullerton to their regular practice site at Blair Field in Long Beach after Allen's firing, Malavasi told Steve Rosenbloom that the phone in his office at Blair Field had been tapped. An electrician determined that the wires from Malavasi's office connected with the phone in Allen's office, allowing the then-head coach to push a button and listen to phone conversations. Malavasi was still a Rams assistant at the time.

The only explanation for why Allen would do such a thing is because of paranoia, Steve Rosenbloom surmised. Training camp ended a few days after Allen was fired, so he would have had to carry this out sometime before camp began.

"We just had to shake our heads and chuckle, really," Rosenbloom said. "But it was sort of George, too. Nobody was overly surprised. He had it set up so he could listen. I'm not saying that he listened. He wouldn't have been able to listen all the time. They all had offices there. It was a small building with nothing fancy. It would be easy to run some wires.

"Look, George couldn't have been any more surprised about his firing than Carroll. The handwriting was on the wall. I'm sure George thought it through. He knew Carroll pretty well, and you don't screw around like that. I'm not talking about the phone tapping, but all of the other stuff. Maybe George forgot he's not supposed to trade players without telling somebody."[6]

When told in 2022 of Malavasi's accusation, an incredulous Bruce Allen denied that his father had tapped the phones. Bruce said he never knew Malavasi had said something so "obviously wrong."[7]

Of his four firings as a pro head coach—Rams ('68 and '70), Redskins ('78), and Rams ('78)—George Allen found Rosenbloom's dismissal the hardest to take. Being let go just before the start of the regular season is "like being promised a big movie part and then being told just before the shooting starts that you are to be found dead in the opening scene," he wrote in his 1982 book, *Merry Christmas—You're Fired!*[8] As hard as it was for Allen to understand the Rams' motive for the firing, he needed to come to grips with his absence from NFL coaching for the first time in twenty years. "My problem is figuring out each morning how to pass the day," he said. "How many miles can a guy run? How long can he sit reading a book?"[9] Not since the window between his first Rams coaching stint in 1957 and his hiring as a Bears assistant in 1959 had he not been in pro football. At the same time, he brimmed with confidence that he would someday return to coach in the NFL. "None of us felt that this was the end," Jennifer Allen said. "If anything, he was even more directed and focused to return to coaching football."[10]

Allen tried to work out his financial situation with the Rams. In signing a three-year, $200,000 contract, he had agreed to a deferred schedule that called for at least a $50,000 monthly payment, with the balance coming annually.[11] In a letter to Carroll Rosenbloom dated August 19, 1978, he asked for monetary assistance.

"Since my dismissal, I have lost the TV show and radio show," Allen wrote. "One of the reasons I accepted a salary of $50,000 with the balance deferred was because of extra income to be derived from these shows. When I signed the contract, I sent you a note that I needed more cash flow. We have not sold our home in Virginia. We are supporting two homes, with two children in school, and trying to help George Jr. get started in his career. Do you have any suggestions regarding this matter?"[12]

In comments to *Los Angeles Times* sportswriter John Hall, Rosenbloom ripped Allen for making such requests: "We are paying him $200,000 for not working, and I got a letter from him demanding extra considerations for expenses because of the firing." Rosenbloom also elaborated on two major reasons he fired Allen: his refusal to listen to the team doctors about giving the players access to water in practice, and his insistence on dividing the coaching staff into three parts.

"George had his coaches who came over with him from the Redskins, the Knox coaches left over from the last staff, and the new coaches," Rosenbloom told the *Times*. "He didn't seem to trust anybody but the Redskin coaches. He was suspicious of the others. Sometimes, he had staff meetings with only the Redskin coaches, locking the others out in the cold. They simply were not told what was going on. It was tearing everybody apart, and it was only getting worse."

Regarding the water, Rosenbloom said seven players collapsed and required emergency treatment one afternoon because their body fluids plummeted to dangerous levels. "Building mental toughness is one thing, destroying an athlete's health is another," he said.[13]

Rosenbloom made his remarks a few days before the regular-season opener against the Eagles. He spoke of a huge turnaround in team attitude under Malavasi and said the Rams might have gone winless in '78 with Allen as their head coach.[14] In reality, the Rams charged out of the gate to win their first seven games, including double-digit victories over their two playoff nemeses from the 1970s, the Cowboys and Vikings.

Allen was in the television booth for the Rams' second game, a 10–0 win over the Falcons. The next week, he watched from the booth as the Redskins beat the Cardinals, 28–10. He'd signed a contract with CBS to be an NFL color analyst, a role he maintained for four seasons (1978–81). In the first three seasons, he teamed with play-by-play man Vin Scully. Following a CBS lineup switch, he teamed in '81 with play-by-play voice Lindsey Nelson, known for wearing multicolored sport jackets. A retired player was also in the booth at times, creating a three-person broadcasting team.

Bruce Allen said his father loved the friendship he built with Scully, best known for calling Los Angeles Dodgers baseball games for nearly seventy seasons, and the meaningful role he had in the booth, where his coaching instincts set in. Allen had no tolerance for ineptitude and could sense a losing coach as early as pregame preparations: "He would not go to a game just to go to a game," Bruce remembered. "He loved the coaching profession. He thought it was the greatest and most important profession. That's part of his thousand-percent focus on the job. In the production meetings, he'd talk to different coaches of the teams playing each other. It demoralized him to think, 'How is this guy, who has no idea what's going to happen to him in this game, the head coach, and I'm not a head coach?'"[15]

CBS told Allen he could be as critical as he wanted when commenting on a game. He mostly hesitated to call out other coaches on air, although he once criticized Malavasi.[16] "They would joke that two minutes of silence from George meant that some coach just messed up," Bruce said. He didn't know how to explain it other than Allen thinking, "'I had no idea why they were in that coverage. No idea why they did this. No idea why they did that.' But he didn't want to say why."[17]

No different than in his coaching days, Allen was relentless with preparation and details. Never would he call a game unprepared. "A broadcaster has to be descriptive, explicit, unbiased, and concise," he once said. "Whereas in coaching you must elaborate and repeat to get your point across. It's a different type of responsibility. When you make a decision on the field, it could cost you the championship."[18]

Allen expected the same focus and commitment from his broadcasting colleagues. Longtime pro football statistician Joe Band remembered a game when Allen worked with Hall of Fame running back Jim Brown, whom Allen had tried to lure out of retirement while coaching in LA and DC,[19] and refused to tolerate what he perceived as Brown's lack of preparation. "George got so angry at Brown because he was shooting off the hip," Band said. "He was saying things that were wrong, and George Allen was very meticulous. He studied. He was very thorough. He would prepare and prepare and prepare. In fact, he would over-prepare sometimes. These two almost went at it. I stepped in between them, and some other guy may have stepped in."[20]

Broadcasting enabled Allen to keep abreast of the other NFL teams. He watched game tape and took extensive notes to position himself for the day when a phone call would come with a coaching offer. "It was his way of analyzing all the games, strategies, and players," Bruce said. "He was really doing it to stay fresh and stay on course to come back and coach."[21]

Allen enjoyed being a color analyst. "However, I do miss the close association with my players," he told *Football News* in 1979. "After 29 years of coaching, you're bound to miss not [*sic*] being on the sidelines."[22]

Rams defensive end Fred Dryer, who retired after the '81 season, had conversations with Allen when his broadcast television crew requested to speak with players and coaches in preparation for Rams games. One comment Allen made is seared into his memory. "He said it was a big mistake leaving Washington," Dryer recalled. "He said he regretted it."

Dryer, who lived in Long Beach at the time, would occasionally go to the Allens' home in Palos Verdes Estates to see him. "I knew Etty and his sons and his daughter," he said. "Everybody was upset that it didn't work out. I pulled my punches a little bit with George in the aftermath. I didn't want to hurt him. I never told George about my conversation with Carroll Rosenbloom about Don Coryell. I never confided in him about that. It was a dead end road. Why do it?"[23]

Dryer's 1978 Rams finished 12-4 but lost to the Cowboys in the NFC Championship Game in a replay of years past. In '79 the Rams went 9-7, their fewest wins since '72. But they found a way to beat Dallas in the opening round, 21–19, before topping Tampa Bay in the NFC Championship Game, 9–0. In Super Bowl XIV, the Rams put up a valiant effort against the heavily favored Steelers but lost, 31–19.

Some of the Rams players who had disliked Allen's rigorous practices, including Jack Youngblood and Larry Brooks, gave him a lot of credit for the Rams reaching the Super Bowl that year, according to the recollections of safety Eddie Brown, who played three seasons for Allen in DC. "He taught them how to work harder and do things better," Brown said. "They said, 'In all reality, George has a lot of responsibility for this. He was here only a few months and for about four weeks of practice, but he really taught us what we need to be doing.'"[24]

The man who had hired Allen for the sole purpose of getting the Rams to the Super Bowl didn't see the game. While swimming in high waves by his Florida beach home in April 1979, Carroll Rosenbloom drowned. He was seventy-two. A coroner who autopsied his body called the drowning nothing other than an "unfortunate accident."[25] But Steve Rosenbloom maintains a suspicion that his father was murdered, saying he wasn't a good swimmer and would never have battled rough currents.[26] No one has ever been charged in his death.

Allen's replacement in LA, Malavasi, coached the Rams through the '82 season, finishing 44-41 over five seasons with three playoff appearances. But after missing the playoffs for the second straight season in '82, he was fired and replaced by USC coach John Robinson. In 1987 Malavasi died of a heart attack at age fifty-seven.

In the early years while Allen was out of coaching, at least a dozen NFL head coaching jobs opened and closed without him getting an offer. College possibilities also failed to materialize. In 1981 he spoke with Kentucky governor John Y. Brown Jr. about the possibility of replacing Fran Curci as the school's coach. Allen was friends with Governor Brown and his wife, CBS NFL commentator Phyllis George. But Curci maintained his job for another season.[27] Separately, according to the *Washington Post*, Allen was offered a job as both head coach and athletic director at the University of Illinois.[28]

New York fans undoubtedly wanted Allen and his sharp football mind for their pro teams. With the Giants and Jets both skidding toward 4-12 seasons in 1980, the *New York Post* ran a poll that asked fans who they most wanted as their coach. Sixty-one percent of Giants fans said Allen, with 12 percent for the next closest competitor, Super Bowl IV winner Hank Stram. Thirty-seven percent of Jets fans said Allen and 23 percent said Stram, again the closest competitor.[29] Allen had voiced interest in coaching the Giants late in the '78 season, before they hired Ray Perkins.[30]

Both the Giants and Jets retained their coaches after the 1980 season.

But a team very familiar to Allen had an opening: the Redskins. After a 6-10 season in 1980 and a 24-24 mark with no playoffs in the three seasons since Allen's departure, the Redskins fired Jack Pardee on January 5, 1981. A few days later, the *Washington Post* reported that the Redskins had informally contacted Allen midway through the 1980 season. The report said he was later mentioned as a replacement for Pardee but that the team had since dropped him from consideration.[31]

Bruce Allen explained that Jack Kent Cooke, who was instrumental in Allen's hiring in 1971 and who by 1980 had taken control of the team's daily operations from Edward Bennett Williams, led his father to believe he'd be selected for the position. But Redskins general manager Bobby Beathard, who was spearheading the search, wanted to go in a different direction. Beathard did not subscribe to Allen's philosophy of trading draft picks to build a team with veteran players, instead preferring to acquire younger players and mold them for the future.

"I just believed that the day of those older veterans . . . I don't think teams were willing to do that anymore," Beathard said in a 2013 interview. "Teams wanted to train younger guys the way they wanted them. George was really unique and amazingly successful at doing what he did. I watched what happened with his teams and thought, 'Boy, maybe George Allen is the only guy who could do this' or is willing to take a bunch of seasoned or older guys and get them playing together. He did a great job and gave away a lot to do it. He paid them a lot, and it worked for him. I didn't believe in that philosophy, nor would I have been successful at it. I don't think many people in the league believed in that philosophy at all."[32]

The days when coaches maintained complete control over personnel decisions—as Allen had with the Redskins—were also becoming a thing of the past.[33] Bruce Allen said his father would have wanted both coaching and general manager duties.

"You can understand [Beathard's] thinking at the time," Bruce said. "Bobby said, 'I don't want to go back. He won't like me, and I'll get fired. I won't fit in with him.' I hate to say it because I liked Jack Pardee as a player and as a person, but they struck out with Jack. They were looking for something and found it. Jack [Kent Cooke] felt bad about what happened between my father and Ed Williams, too."[34]

Beathard found "it" in an obscure Chargers offensive assistant named Joe Gibbs, who engineered the greatest era in the DC team's history. During his twelve-year reign (1981–92), the Redskins won three Super Bowls, finished first in the NFC East five times, and made the playoffs eight times. Their 140-65-0 record, which included a 16-5 postseason mark, equaled a .680 winning percentage, spelled dynasty, and led to Gibbs's Hall of Fame induction in 1996. During that period, only the 49ers posted a higher win percentage (.738).

However, the first month of Gibbs's DC tenure told a different story. The Redskins lost their first five games in 1981 each by double digits. Dissent was rampant in the nation's capital, with Gibbs thinking he was about to get fired.

John Kent Cooke, the owner's son, said his father was about to bring back George Allen. But the younger Cooke advised him against doing so. "I said, 'Dad, you can't do that because all hell is going to break loose,'" he recalled. "Not only in the media, which would be voicing what the fans were saying. But it also would be difficult for our relationship with Ed Williams because he and George Allen did not get along. To bring George back would have been an insult to Ed."

Jack Kent Cooke stayed the course with Gibbs as coach, who achieved his enormous success with several players who had first tasted winning on Allen's watch: quarterback Joe Theismann, kicker Mark Moseley, running back John Riggins, offensive tackle George Starke, guard Ron Saul, safety Mark Murphy, cornerback Joe Lavender, and defensive tackle Dave Butz. Riggins was the most famous of that cohort. He pulled off one of the most memorable single-game performances in Redskins history: a 166-yard rushing game in Super Bowl XVII, highlighted by his 43-yard fourth-down touchdown run that put the Redskins ahead for good in a 27–17 win over Miami. He finished with 11,352 career rushing yards and entered the Hall of Fame in 1992.

Does Allen deserve any credit for Gibbs's lofty achievements in DC? Not really, just as it wouldn't be right for Dan Reeves and the coaches who preceded Allen's stints in LA and Washington to take credit for his success, despite all of the superior talent he inherited, including Hall of Famers Deacon Jones and Merlin Olsen in LA and Charley Taylor, Sonny Jurgensen, and Chris Hanburger in Washington.

One other NFL head coach opening at the time deserves mention. After the '81 season, the Bears fired Neill Armstrong following his third losing season in four years. During the season, rumors surfaced that friends and associates of Bears owner George Halas were urging him to bring back

Allen.[35] Allen had been the architect of the roaring Bears defense that carried the team to the '63 NFL Championship.

But "Papa Bear" Halas never forgot the acrimony that accompanied Allen's departure for the Rams in 1966. "When you've been burned once, you think twice before you do something like that," Halas told the *Chicago Tribune* in October 1981. "I don't think I'd rehire him."[36]

Two weeks after Armstrong was fired, Allen reached out to Halas to express interest in the Bears' head coach opening.[37] Halas, however, remained unwavering in his contempt for the assistant coach who brought him his sixth and last NFL Championship.

"Coach Halas, being Coach Halas, who I respect the hell out of, just said, 'I'm going to hold a grudge,'" Bruce Allen recalled. "He didn't use those words. But he was like, 'No, I can't do it.' I know what he said was very complimentary. I love Coach Halas and what he did for the NFL. But he was like, 'I'm interested. I know you'd do great. But I don't think I can get over what we went through.'"[38]

Instead, Halas hired a Bears favorite whom Allen had drafted in 1961: Mike Ditka. Ditka had followed up his Hall of Fame playing career by serving as a Cowboys assistant coach from '73 to '81. During that time, he wrote a letter to Halas saying he'd like to someday return to Chicago to be the Bears' head coach. Halas took him up on his offer.

Ditka promised a Super Bowl trip within three seasons. He nearly delivered. His '85 Bears went 15-1 and devoured every team they faced in the postseason, including a 46–10 rout of the Patriots in Super Bowl XX. Just like the '63 team, Chicago's ferocious defense was largely credited with the dominance of that '85 team, specifically the nasty "46 defense" run by defensive coordinator Buddy Ryan that put eight men in the box and relentlessly pressured the quarterback. In a scene reminiscent of players carrying Allen off the field following the '63 championship game, Ryan received a victory ride—as did Ditka—after their Super Bowl XX win. In all, Ditka produced seven playoff teams in eleven seasons coaching in Chicago.

In a 2019 interview, Ditka said Allen's interest in the Bears' opening in 1982 did not worry him. Asked if he had adopted any of Allen's coaching techniques, including motivational strategies from the master motivator, he replied, "Everybody has to be themselves. I couldn't be Coach Allen. I couldn't be Buddy Ryan. I had to be me. Whether it's right, wrong, or otherwise, that's who I had to be. I had a definite idea of what I wanted to do with our football team."[39]

Thus, if one of his former teams like the Redskins or Bears didn't extend a contract to Allen and end his hiatus from the game, which one would? Some media sounded bewildered about why one of the winningest coaches in NFL history had yet to receive an offer.

In "The Best Coach in Exile," *Los Angeles Times* columnist Jim Murray wrote, "He lost a lousy couple of exhibition games and was called in and summarily fired. The National Labor Relations Board would not have let you do that to a car wash attendant. But a football coach has less rights than a shoeshine boy."[40]

Rams general manager Don Klosterman, who reportedly opposed Allen's hiring in 1978, told the *Los Angeles Times*, "It's hard for me to believe that with his record he's not coaching."[41]

John Schulian, who covered the Redskins for the *Washington Post* during Allen's days in DC, interviewed him for the *Chicago Sun-Times* in 1981. In a column headlined "Football on Allen's Mind . . . and Blackball on His Back?" Schulian called him the NFL's "most famous unemployed coach" and tried to strike a sympathetic tone regarding his absence from the league.

"George Allen will be back," Allen said to Schulian. "You can underline that and put it in caps. In fact, you'd better underline it twice. GEORGE ALLEN WILL BE BACK."[42]

Schulian gained the impression that Allen was somewhat desperate. "I don't think it was a financial desperation," he said in a 2020 interview. "It was just, 'What am I going to do with all of these empty days when I could be out there showing somebody how to disguise their blitz?'"

Allen didn't ask Schulian explicitly for help finding a job. But "when you stripped everything away, that's exactly what he was asking," Schulian said. "What do you hear? What do you know? There was something poignant about it. In the early '80s, he was calling sportswriters all over the country trying to see what the job situation was. He wanted to be part of a team. He wanted to be a coach again. I think a lot of us, myself included, really had a bit of a turnaround about George. We saw him as a far more human character than we ever had when he was a head coach."[43]

But was Allen really being blackballed? That would mean the owners had colluded to make sure no one hired him. Whether it was because of his insistence on both coaching and making personnel decisions, his confrontations with owners, or that he had shaken the NFL status quo with his expensive dive into free agency, no one was beating down the doors to hire him. Another theory is that teams no longer needed Allen to win games and lure fans because franchises were guaranteed at least $5.5 million a year in television money.[44] Still, it seemed bizarre that the owners refused to reach out to someone with his coaching acumen.

"Why would an NFL team not go after a guy like George Allen?" Len Shapiro, who had a hostile relationship with Allen as the *Washington Post* beat writer, asked rhetorically.

"He was a proven winner and was considered by most people the best defensive mind in the game at that point. Somebody should have hired him. I have no doubt in my mind that whether it was just an unwritten rule, we don't need this guy, it's not worth it, he's too much trouble. Plus, there had been trouble in Washington, obviously the controversy about him leaving there, more controversy when he left the Rams. I suspect most owners said, 'Who needs this. Let's get a younger guy. We don't need the problem.'"[45]

Today, Bruce Allen believes Pete Rozelle led efforts to blackball his father because he angered powerful people around the league with his costly free agent signings in the mid-'70s. But at the time, George Allen didn't think he was being blackballed. "I think blackballed is a very strong word," he told the *Milwaukee Journal Sentinel* in 1981. "The toughest thing about not coaching is seeing the way some NFL teams are playing. They're not playing very well."[46]

Perhaps Cleveland Browns owner Art Modell summed up the Allen question the best in his comments to the *New York Daily News* in 1982: "The problem with George is a lack of understanding of the prerogatives of ownership and the need to run an organization with financial discipline. It's always a divided camp in his organization. He'll win more than his share of games and win brilliantly, but at a price, alienating players from owners.

"There's always been a problem with him, and not just trading draft choices he didn't have, because that's been done before. It's just that he creates an adversarial relationship with ownership, and that's not good. That was his downfall. Word gets around."[47]

At least Allen was able to make up for lost time while he was out of coaching. He found himself busier than in the days when he worked nearly around the clock to prepare his teams for the next opponent. He traveled with Etty to Paris, Rome, Portugal, and Switzerland, and he fished in Alaska and the Mexican resort city of Cabo San Lucas. He attended the Kentucky Derby and the 1980 Winter Olympics in Lake Placid, New York, and presented his good friend Deacon Jones for the Hall of Fame in 1980. He also gave motivational speeches and authored the 1982 book *Merry Christmas—You're Fired!* The title stemmed from his firing by Dan Reeves the day after Christmas in '68. In the book, he offered advice on how to survive a job loss and on finding your next place of employment. In his rare leisure time, he enjoyed gardening and planting fruit trees outside his house.

Plus, in 1978, Allen served as national chair of the National Alliance of Business (NAB) youth summer jobs program. The position resembled his role as chair of the Nixon administration's summer employment program for youth, when Washington led the country for six years (1971–77) in generating summer jobs for kids.[48] On behalf of NAB, he traveled to cities nationwide trying to convince corporate executives to hire youth. He set a goal, for instance, of filling 270,000 jobs for unemployed kids in the summer of '79.

One of his stops that year was in Dallas. Mike Ditka, then a Cowboys assistant coach, introduced him at a luncheon, where he tried to persuade local business leaders to become involved.[49]

"Beyond his focus on football, the one cause he thoroughly immersed himself in was the NAB youth summer jobs program," George Felix Allen remembered. "He was much more than a name endorsing a worthy effort. He was a very active chair, calling the top executives of businesses and persuading them to commit to hiring specific numbers of young people each summer. He was so proud that in the years when he was chair, Washington DC was first in the number of youth jobs in the entire program. He posted a board with the numbers on his workout room wall at our home in California. That sign stayed on the wall until the home was sold after our mother's passing in 2013."[50]

Despite being friends with Nixon, Allen, a Republican with conservative beliefs, never campaigned for him while he ran for political office, nor had he openly supported any other political candidates. Consumed by the demands of coaching, he never had the time.

But now he did. In 1980 he campaigned for another man with high political aspirations: Ronald Reagan. Their friendship was born in the mid-1960s, when Reagan was running for governor of California and Allen coached the Rams. With Reagan vying for the presidency in 1980, Allen led a pro-Reagan bus tour that began in Westchester County just north of New York City and traveled 150 miles up the Hudson River to the capital,

Albany. Allen gave speeches on the tour in support of his Republican friend. In the 1980 election, Reagan toppled the incumbent, Democrat Jimmy Carter, to take hold of the White House. He was reelected in a landslide over Democrat Walter Mondale in '84.

Allen's daily itinerary also featured his legendary exercise routine. Having always believed in an active life, he maintained a one-and-a-half-hour workout highlighted by a five-mile jog through his neighborhood and around the track at a local high school. He added 101 sit-ups and 31 pushups—"I always like to do one more of everything than I promise myself I will," he often said to explain his exercising mind-set.[51] He also had a weightlifting circuit on his universal gym at home. Such devotion to exercise dropped his weight to 170 from a high of 190 and left him in his midsixties in better shape than many people much younger.

Allen built up his endurance to run long distance, too. One of his sons, Greg Allen, was awed by father's athleticism when the two did a triathlon together in '89, a year before George Allen died. "I was in my thirties, and he was seventy-two," Greg said. "There was nobody out there his age, and his run time still beat about half of the runners. He was always jogging and running up hills in Palos Verdes. He'd get out of bed and do fifty push-ups. He was a total physical fitness nut.

"He did 5K and 10K runs all the time. In Palos Verdes, they always had George Allen 5K and 10K March of Dimes annual runs. He worked with the March of Dimes to make those events happen. He wasn't just a poster board or celebrity they used to put a name on the event. He also ran it. He loved working out."[52]

Allen's name recognition and dedication to exercise made him a perfect pick to serve as chair of the President's Council on Physical Fitness and Sports (PCPFS). In July 1981, President Reagan appointed him to replace college basketball television commentator and former Marquette coach Al McGuire. The Supreme Court's Justice Byron "Whizzer" White, a University of Colorado star running back in the '30s and a two-time first-team All-Pro in the NFL, swore Allen into the position on September 22, 1981.[53] It was the only federal body with which Allen was ever involved. That same year, Reagan presented Allen with a presidential commendation in recognition of his professional feats. Allen also earned two such commendations from President Carter and one from President Nixon.[54]

Allen's original thirteen-member council included a former adversary:

Dallas Cowboys quarterback Roger Staubach. He tapped Southern California businessman Bill Harris, his good friend and Whittier player from decades earlier, to be a special advisor to the council.

"I was like his right-hand man," Harris said in a 2015 interview. "I traveled with him to all the meetings. He asked me to be on the council. I refused because I was so busy and didn't want to be tied down. So he said, 'You've got to be a special advisor.'"[55]

When accepting the PCPFS chair, an unpaid position, Allen had a message for Reagan: "I told the president I would not be an honorary leader. Rather, I wanted to take active leadership in setting and achieving real goals for physical fitness awareness throughout the country."[56] To do so, Allen laid out an ambitious plan to establish a series of new entities devoted to keeping Americans fit and healthy: the National Fitness Foundation, the U.S. Fitness Academy, the National Fitness Classic, National Fitness Testing Week, and various youth fitness forums. He also wanted every American to have a physical fitness card—gold, silver, or bronze, depending on their level of ability.

"He dove into that position with all of the energy that he had for everything else," Harris remembered. "He was putting in twelve-hour days trying to make something work. He was worried about physical fitness for kids because physical fitness classes were shutting down all across the nation. Many high schools no longer had physical education."[57]

Allen didn't want Americans—adults and kids—to lose their appreciation for exercise. He penned an inspirational essay while chairing the council: "A workout is 25 percent perspiration and 75 percent determination. Stated another way, it is one part physical exertion and three parts self-discipline." He also emphasized the following about exercise: A workout makes you better today than you were yesterday. It strengthens the body, relaxes the mind, and toughens the spirit. When you work out regularly, your problems diminish and your confidence grows; a workout is a personal triumph over laziness and procrastination. It is the badge of a winner—the mark of an organized, goal-oriented person who has taken charge of his or her destiny; and a workout is a wise use of time and an investment in excellence. It is a way of preparing for life's challenges and proving to yourself that you have what it takes to do what is necessary.[58]

Through his work on the council, Allen appreciated the chance to reunite with his friend Ronald Reagan, whom he admired for his smarts, humor, and classiness, among other characteristics. Over the years, Allen told of Reagan's request to visit the Rams' locker room with his son, Ron, after a 13–7 season-ending loss to the Colts at the Los Angeles Coliseum on December 21, 1969. Allen remembered asking a police officer, "'You mean he wants to come in even though we lost?' He said, 'Yeah.' I said, 'If he wants to come in, fine.' When he got in there, I had the team kneeling and giving thanks. We were saying our prayers."

Allen also noted that evangelist Billy Graham, a longtime friend of Reagan, referred to that visit in one of his sermons. "[Graham] said what a lesson for a young lad to see his heroes bowing down praying after a defeat and giving thanks," Allen told Steve Guback in 1989. "It's a lesson [Ron] remembered all his life."[59]

In February 1982 President Reagan hosted a reception for the President's Council on Physical Fitness and Sports in the East Room of the White House. George Allen attended the event with Etty and his son George. He also brought a gift for the president on behalf of the council: two twenty-pound chrome-plated dumbbell weights. The inscription on one dumbbell read, "TO RONALD REAGAN A GREAT LEADER AND A GREAT AMERICAN, FROM GEORGE ALLEN, CHAIRMAN, P.C.P.F.S. (PRESIDENT'S COUNCIL ON PHYSICAL FITNESS AND SPORTS) FEB. 2, 1982." The other one urged the president to "STAY STRONG." The weights sat in a velvet-lined mahogany and teakwood chest with brass fittings inlaid with the president's initials.[60] Members of the president's staff wanted Allen to keep the chest closed because they worried that Reagan would try to grab the weights while he was still recovering from injuries sustained in an assassination attempt ten months prior, right after he exited the Washington Hilton hotel in DC. The bullet just missed his heart, leaving him close to death. But he was back at work at the White House two weeks later.

"My father insisted to the staffers that President Reagan needed to open the chest so he could see the weights and the inscriptions on them," George Felix Allen recalled. "At the presentation, the fears of the president's protective staff were realized. My father opened the top of the chest with the attractive inscribed gift of weights for President Reagan to see. Exuberant with the gift, the president grabbed both dumbbells and lifted them over his head. The staffers standing next to me gasped, 'Oh, noooo!' His recovery was not at all impaired."[61]

As the president lifted the weights with a big grin on his face, Allen stood a few feet away with his mouth wide open in laughter. He had to be impressed with the ease at which Reagan, a few days from his seventy-first birthday, raised forty pounds of weight over his head. Reagan, always in good condition due to his devotion to exercise, whether it was horseback riding or chopping wood, took up an intense exercise program following the assassination attempt that put him in better physical condition than when he came to the White House.[62]

"He's in better shape than most of his Cabinet people, and some of them are thirty years younger," Allen told Guback, the PCPFS information officer during Allen's term. "I like people who want more out of life than just a job. The president has all the qualities to be the type of football player that I've always wanted on my team. He's competitive. He doesn't get discouraged. He stays in shape. He has innate leadership qualities. Either a guy's a leader or he isn't. He's a natural leader. He's tough. Every time I see him, we talk about his workouts and maybe a different exercise."[63]

Reagan, appreciating everything Allen was doing to keep Americans in shape, remarked at a separate White House PCPFS reception in 1984, "Attention to physical fitness is one of those things that says something about a nation and its people. It's an important indication of America's level of energy, competitiveness, and vigor."[64]

Despite such a prestigious role, Allen felt something was missing from his life—something that had driven him with a passion. In the back of his mind, he wanted to get back into football. He still watched game films to study NFL teams and players, and he received press releases and statistics from the teams. He missed getting his teams prepared each week for opponents, most notably the Dallas Cowboys.

"We beat those Cowboys in their own backyard," he said emphatically in the 1980s from the back patio of his house in Palos Verdes Estates, pointing to the final score of a 1976 season-ending game inscribed on a dumbbell weight. "Redskins 27. Cowboys 14. Made the playoffs."[65]

Besides coaching, owning a team also appealed to Allen, an opportunity that never materialized while he coached the Redskins because of his inability to exercise the stock option. But in the early months of '82, an ownership scenario surfaced north of the border.

In 1981 the Canadian Football League's Montreal Alouettes finished 3-13, despite the signing of high-profile NFL players such as Vince Ferragamo, the Rams' quarterback in their Super Bowl XIV loss to the Steelers, and wide receiver Billy "White Shoes" Johnson. Canadian businessman

Nelson Skalbania, who had purchased the Alouettes a year before, lost a reported $2.8 million in '81, a single-season CFL record. He filed for bankruptcy and sought investors to revive the fledgling franchise.

While raiding the NFL for players, Skalbania approached Allen with an offer to coach the team. Allen turned it down. But in March 1982, Skalbania offered Allen the role of team president along with 20 percent ownership and an option to become the majority owner by year's end. He believed Allen's name would restore credibility to the team and attract investors. Allen then accepted his offer. Soon after, Skalbania agreed to sell the entire franchise to an Allen-led group of investors and give them full control of the team in a few days.[66]

Allen's investors included Bill Harris and Chicago financier Tom King. Allen set up an office at Olympic Stadium in Montreal, hired his son Bruce as vice president of football operations, and tapped his French-speaking wife, Etty, to make promotional appearances. The Allens and their investors aimed to recapture the six thousand season ticket holders who didn't renew their packages after the '81 season.[67]

Allen had an ulterior motive for owning and revitalizing the Montreal franchise, considered possibly the most lucrative CFL team because of the city's large population and the size of the sixty-six-thousand-seat Olympic Stadium.[68] "This was the early '80s before the start of the USFL," George Felix Allen explained. "He believed the NFL could expand into Canada to Montreal or maybe Toronto. It had been only two decades since the NFL last played exhibition games against CFL teams. He also knew of the talent in the CFL in players like Joe Theismann," who played for the Toronto Argonauts before Allen acquired him for the Redskins in 1974. "So to him, this was an all-consuming matter."

But George Felix Allen, then a practicing lawyer, had a word of caution for his father: "My final advice was that with the laws of Canada and how much you have to have of Canadian ownership, the team is for sale because the owner is bankrupt. I said all you're doing is buying a bunch of lawsuits. You're just not going to get investors, nor why would you want to buy a team that has so much debt that you have to pay off?"[69]

Allen heeded his son's advice. He walked away from the deal after learning that Skalbania had not paid off his 1981 debts.[70] The franchise folded under Skalbania's ownership in May 1982 and has been rebranded several times since.

George Allen was now back in familiar territory: outside the football arena. No matter how busy he had been with his vast array of endeavors, he sensed a disconnect in his life. His absence from coaching was tearing him apart emotionally. "Coaching isn't my profession," he often said. "It's my life."

Bruce Allen: "He really thought that's what he was put on this earth to do. My dad loved and respected the coaching profession. If you took that away from him, it drove him crazy.

"When he chaired the President's Council on Physical Fitness and Sports, he traveled the world: Russia, Germany, China, Japan. He was promoting America and telling everyone to be physically fit. My mom thought what he was doing was fantastic. Officials in other countries welcomed him, and he attended state dinners around the world. One time, he was depressed when he came back. I said, 'What's wrong?' He said, 'Everyone's calling me "Mister."' I said, 'Out of respect?' He said, 'I want to be a coach. I don't want to be "Mister." I don't want to be the Honorable George Allen.' If a high dignitary in another country calls you 'Honorable' or 'Mister,' it is out of respect. But to Dad it was a demotion from coach. That's just who he was."[71]

22

A New League Comes Calling

In the early 1980s, the National Football League battled a perfect storm. Labor strife rooted in demands by the players' union for a much larger share of the NFL's gross revenues triggered a player strike that nearly wiped out the entire '82 season. Tarnished by more than two months of empty stadiums and nine weeks of canceled games, 1982 would go down as the most turbulent year in NFL history.

At the same time, a new twelve-team league with very wealthy owners and franchises in many major NFL markets was in the planning. The league's creators believed that with strong financial backing and well-funded franchises in big cities; two television deals, including one with ESPN, a rising network in cable television; and a spring-summer schedule, the new entity was prepared to take its place alongside the most popular sports league in the country.

It was called the United States Football League (USFL).

David Dixon, an American businessman and sports executive who had helped create the NFL's New Orleans Saints in 1967, founded the USFL. He had first envisioned a spring-summer football league in the '60s, but it failed to take hold. In 1980 he repackaged the idea while eyeing the growth of a new entertainment phenomenon—cable television—especially its sports programming. He believed the USFL could someday compete with the NFL in fan popularity.

Dixon traversed the country seeking investors to buy USFL franchises for about $6 million each.[1] He also sought proven football minds and personalities who might have an interest in coaching in the upstart league. One such person was George Allen, whom Dixon assured when the USFL was just a thought that the new league is "going to make it."[2]

"[Dixon] was talking to everybody around the country," said Steve Ehrhart, who served as legal counsel to the USFL's competition committee in the league's early days, before taking on other high-profile USFL roles. "He contacted a number of coaches who had had good careers in the NFL but were not actively coaching at the time. There was John Ralston, who had been the head coach of the Denver Broncos; Chuck Fairbanks, who had been the head coach of the New England Patriots; and George Allen. George always wanted to coach again, and so did Chuck Fairbanks."[3]

At the time, Ehrhart was trying to establish a set of rules for the USFL. As a sports agent, he had represented about one hundred NFL players in the 1970s but did not know Allen well. But Allen somehow knew details about Ehrhart, including that he had played quarterback in the 1960s at Colorado College, a Division 3 school. As Ehrhart recalled, "He knew I had played football in college. That was just his thoroughness and attention to detail. I didn't realize that he had a photographic kind of mind. He knew so much about me and had clearly done some research. That just stunned me. I was a small college player. I was no big star. I thought, 'Man, this guy is really sharp and really dedicated.' Of course, his work ethic was always phenomenal."

The concept of a spring-summer league piqued the interest of Allen, who was seeking ways to return to pro football. The USFL, he thought, would provide him a chance to not only coach but also to possibly own a share of a team, an opportunity that eluded him with the Redskins and that he withdrew from with the Montreal Alouettes.

The USFL announced its official formation on May 11, 1982, designating twelve teams to each play a twenty-game schedule starting in March 1983. The franchises would be in Boston; Birmingham, Alabama; Chicago; Denver; Detroit; Los Angeles; New York; Philadelphia; San Diego; San Francisco; Tampa; and Washington. The San Diego and San Francisco franchises relocated to Arizona and Oakland, respectively, before the league's opening kickoff.[4]

In the ensuing weeks, Allen received inquiries from three USFL teams wanting him to come on board. He didn't name them, but media reports indicated that two of them may have been the Chicago and Los Angeles franchises. "If I join any team as coach or general manager, I would have to have some liquidity in the ownership," he told the *New York Times*.[5] Allen's name also surfaced as a possible USFL commissioner, but ESPN president Chet Simmons was hired for that position.[6]

Allen broached the idea of co-owning a USFL team with his good friend Bill Harris. Harris remembered the conversation: "We're talking, and he said, 'Why don't we get into that new league? Bill, I'd like to do that.' That started a whole new phase of our life. He asked, 'Do you want to buy into the new league?' I said, 'If you want to, it would be a great place to start and get back into [football] again.'

"The next day, I called David Dixon and set up a deal. George had his number naturally. We went after the Chicago franchise."[7]

J. Walter Duncan, an Oklahoma oil entrepreneur who grew up in Chicago, was supposed to own the Chicago franchise. But after New York real estate magnate Donald Trump withdrew as the owner of the New York franchise, which became the New Jersey Generals, Dixon persuaded Duncan to take on ownership of the Generals.

That development opened the door for Allen and Harris to apply for ownership of the Chicago team, for which they had to post a letter of credit for $1.5 million,[8] prompting them to search for other investors. The letter of credit was like an insurance policy to compensate the league in case a franchise failed to pay its bills. With the letter, the league could see "you were substantial enough so you wouldn't fold in your first week," Harris said. "The World Football League folded [in the mid-1970s] because the owners weren't able to get through the early times."[9]

Allen then reached out to a friend, high-profile heart surgeon Dr. Ted Diethrich. Diethrich had tried for years to buy an NFL franchise and expressed interest in owning the USFL's team in Phoenix.[10] Allen and Diethrich first met in '76, when Diethrich came to Redskin Park to speak to the players about heart disease. The following year, Allen underwent a heart screening exam at Diethrich's Arizona Heart Institute and received a 102 percent physical fitness rating, a remarkable score for a man sixty years old.[11]

"We really didn't have to search for capital that much," Harris said. "Dr. Diethrich had a friendship with George and wanted to get into a football program. He had the money to do it. When [Allen] called, he said, 'Yeah, I'd like to be involved.'"[12]

"I got a phone call from George Allen," Diethrich recalled. "He said, 'They're going to start a new league in Chicago next week. Do you think you'd be interested in it?' He was very excited about it of course. We could have a lot of fun. Finally, we went to the meeting in Chicago. They didn't vote us in the first time around. But the fellows they voted into Chicago didn't pan out, and we did get the franchise. It was all really because of Coach Allen. I never went into this to make a lot of money. It was really for the enjoyment and the experience."[13]

Diethrich posted the $1.5 million letter of credit. He would be the Chicago franchise's majority stockholder and team president with a 60 percent ownership stake, while Harris would be the executive vice president and treasurer and Allen the chairman of the board and head coach. Allen owned a 10 percent share, but Diethrich and Harris handled all of the franchise's financial commitments.[14]

"To get George to coach, they offered him a percentage of the team," explained Stan White, a linebacker who had starred in the NFL for a decade before Allen recruited him to play in the USFL. "Bill Harris put up anything that George would have had to. George was one of the [owners] who signed my contract," White said.[15]

According to Bruce Allen, "Both Dr. Diethrich and Bill wanted him to be an owner. They thought it was better for the franchise. The goal for none of those three was what happened with USFL owners selling their interest in a year or two. They all had a longer-term outlook, believing the USFL could survive as a spring-summer league."[16]

The Chicago franchise became official on June 21, 1982.

"I'm anxious to get back," Allen said at a news conference. "It's going to be interesting and challenging to create a football team from scratch. We want this new team to unite Chicago like the Redskins united Washington in the '70s. America will support another professional football league."

Allen then went on to list a half dozen reasons why he thought the USFL would succeed, including the league's $18 million reserve fund. He also said the USFL would take an approach opposite that of the World Football League, which struck megadeals with a series of NFL stars, such as the Dolphins' Larry Csonka, Jim Kiick, and Paul Warfield, before going under after two seasons.[17]

"The World Football League put players first," Allen said. "We'll create our own league and our own stars. There are plenty of players. When I was with Washington, we cut enough players to stock another franchise."[18]

In reality, the odds seemed stacked against the USFL succeeding. Many people ridiculed the idea of spring-summer football and frowned on the ability of a new league to compete for fans against the behemoth NFL, which overtook Major League Baseball in the '60s as the nation's preeminent spectator sport and became a spectacle in the '70s.

But Allen loved the idea of a league that would challenge the NFL for big-name players, just like the American Football League did to the more established NFL in the '60s with clever and hardworking personnel minds like that of his friend Al Davis. Similar to the AFL, which created a bidding war with the NFL for college players, USFL teams were also well financed by wealthy owners.

"He was just ready," Harris said. "He jumped right in and got on the phone getting former NFL players and assistant coaches. In about two weeks, we were organized and had an office in Chicago."[19] The team would play at sixty-five-thousand-seat Soldier Field in Chicago, home of the Bears, and its practice facility was just outside the city at Maine North High School in suburban Des Plaines, which Allen called "Blitz Park" in a take on "Redskin Park." The school had closed in '81 because of declining enrollment.

To the USFL's Steve Ehrhart, who went on to become the league's executive director and the president, general manager, and part owner of the USFL's Memphis Showboats, Allen's hiring helped bring tremendous credibility to the USFL. He said Allen wanted to be in Chicago because of his NFL connections to the city. But Ehrhart didn't get the impression from speaking with Allen that he wanted to embarrass George Halas for bypassing him several months prior in favor of Mike Ditka.

"I would couch it more that George was just very motivated and very excited to be in football and to build something," Ehrhart said. "He was obviously trying to be recognized, but I think it was a much bigger picture. But there's no question he wanted to put the country on notice. I don't know if it was directed as much at the Bears but to the entire country to show that George was back. That was a lot of the attitude of the people in the league."[20]

Allen, who still chaired the President's Council on Physical Fitness and Sports, immediately became the face of the franchise. In setting up the front office, he named his twenty-five-year-old son Bruce to be the team's general manager. After coaching at Occidental College in LA in 1979, Bruce became head coach and general manager of the Los Angeles Thunderbolts in a California pro league and worked as a scout for the Oakland Raiders. The new franchise's first hire was former New England Patriots scout Mike McCarthy as the director of college scouting. The coaching staff included two of Allen's Redskins assistants, Charlie Waller and Paul Lanham. Tommy McVean, the Redskins' equipment manager during Allen's seven-year stint in DC, was back in the same role in Chicago.

George Allen went public to announce a team naming contest, saying the name should be "aggressive, short, and punchy" because Chicago is a "physical city." The contest drew more than twenty thousand submissions from fans in Illinois and nineteen other states, with team owners choosing "The Blitz."[21] "A blitz is a way of hitting the enemy with everything you have," Allen said.[22] He also designed the team's helmet logo.

The Allens were probably the most aggressive of anyone in the league in establishing their roster early on, according to Ehrhart. By then, Bruce had acquired much of his father's legendary work ethic, so the hundred-hour work weeks suited him just fine. "They made a hell of a team," Ehrhart said in amazement. "They were very accomplished, and they knew what they were doing." The duo also had the advantage of being one of the first USFL teams to have a front office, whereas the Michigan Panthers, for example, didn't hire a coach and general manager until the fall but ended up winning the USFL championship in the league's first season.[23]

George Allen was used to revitalization projects, such as when he took over two floundering franchises: the Rams in '66 and the Redskins in '71. This time, he started from scratch in a venture that differed drastically from his past experiences in the pros. For one, there was no videotape of USFL teams. That was alien to Allen, who had spent hours and hours studying game films to spot his opponent's strengths and weaknesses. For a time, even paper clips and envelopes were nowhere to be found.[24]

"When you are in a league that has no history, the minor problems become fascinating," Allen wrote in his 1990 book *Strategies for Winning*.[25] Despite those deficiencies, he welcomed the challenge that stood before him. "If you ask anyone in the USFL, it was a blast starting with absolutely nothing," Bruce said. "Being the underdog was intriguing to him. I also loved the concept of a start-up league, mavericks and rebels and all of that stuff."[26]

George Allen had full authority to build the team exactly the way he wanted. He and the Blitz not only signed the USFL's first player,[27] UCLA consensus All-American tight end Tim Wrightman, but they stole him from the NFL team right in their backyard. Wrightman, a 1982 draft pick of the Bears, signed with the Blitz in early August. He had been unable to negotiate with the Bears due to the expiration of a contract between the NFL and the players' union on July 15.[28] With the Blitz, he agreed to a reported two-year, $400,000 deal—a huge figure for a third-round NFL pick.

"This is a historic day," Allen said in announcing the signing of Wrightman. "He's the first major player signed by the league, the first with total credibility."[29]

Wrightman was not from one of the five schools assigned to the Blitz as part of the USFL's regional allocation system. To help fans identify with local college players and encourage them to sign with a team in their area, the league limited franchises to signing players from their region alone—except for those selected in the common draft. Notre Dame, Northwestern, Illinois, Northern Illinois, and Western Illinois were the colleges assigned to the Blitz.

The owner of the USFL's San Diego franchise, Bill Daniels, filed tampering charges against Allen, saying he had violated league rules by signing Wrightman. Blitz vice president Bill Harris acknowledged that San Diego had been awarded territorial negotiating rights to Wrightman. Harris added that he had "complete approval" from San Diego's general manager to negotiate for Wrightman by virtue of trading future player and draft considerations to the San Diego franchise.[30]

Allen's name also came up in connection with alleged tampering of other USFL players who were the regional property of teams.[31] The *Washington Post*, in an article headlined "USFL Déjà Vu: Is Allen Up to Old Tricks?" reported that some teams were pushing to have Allen fined.[32]

Ehrhart said the league fined Allen for tampering. But he refrained from characterizing Allen's personnel moves as unethical. At the time, he explained, all USFL teams were "scrambling on a full-speed basis" to determine how to get the league off the ground, with the reality that many teams—and to a greater extent player agents—tried to sign players outside of their regional zones. The USFL entering its first season was like the Wild West, he said.

What Allen did was "aggressive and supercompetitive," Ehrhart said. "Then layer over the supercompetitive label that he wanted to beat the tail off of every other team in the league. In the final analysis, he also wanted to make sure that we succeeded as a league."[33]

Regarding a quarterback, Allen preferred acquiring one with solid NFL experience, saying it could be his alter ego from his coaching days in DC, Billy Kilmer. Kilmer had been out of football for three seasons after passing for more than 20,000 yards in his sixteen-year career. "I might sign Billy if he gets a little more experience," Allen joked.[34]

The Blitz signed a quarterback who came close to Kilmer's experience: fourteen-year NFL veteran Greg Landry. With nearly 16,000 passing yards, a 54.6 completion percentage, and 97 touchdown passes, Landry was waived in July by the Colts, where he had played his last three seasons, following eleven in Detroit. He was close to retirement, but Allen and the Blitz revived his career in Chicago.

First, the Blitz had to cut a deal with the USFL's New England franchise, which owned the territorial rights to Landry because he had played at the University of Massachusetts. Not surprisingly, "Trader George" made the first trade in USFL history, dealing away the rights to four players to get Landry.[35]

"[Landry] said the only person in the USFL he would play for was George Allen," Dick Coury, coach and general manager of the New England franchise, said in August 1982. "I said fine, but he'll have to trade for him."[36]

Allen and his staff proceeded to form one of the most experienced teams in the league, corresponding with his preference for seasoned veterans less prone to making mental mistakes, especially on defense. The roster eventually had his fingerprints all over it, resembling a Chicago Blitz version of the "Over the Hill Gang." In the coming months, the team signed four more players with at least ten years of experience, including outside linebacker Stan White. In January 1983 White became the first active NFL player to sign with a USFL team.[37] He accepted a three-year, no-cut contract with a $200,000 annual salary, the highest on the team. But White, a seventeenth-round NFL pick in 1972, earned a little more than $1 million for the three-year period with bonuses included, although he only played two seasons in the USFL. After signing with the Blitz, he helped recruit Joe Ehrmann, his teammate with the Colts and Lions. In 1984 he assisted in recruiting safety Bruce Laird, a twelve-year NFL veteran and another of his Colts teammates.

Allen thought White was worth the investment. Not the "biggest, fastest, or strongest" player, as White described himself, he was a mentally sharp linebacker and Allen's kind of field general, a quarterback on defense in the mold of Redskins Jack Pardee and Chris Hanburger, who would call all the signals.[38] In eleven NFL seasons, his first eight with the Colts and his last three with the Lions, the iron man missed only four starts, excluding those in his rookie season. Today he's first in career interceptions for a linebacker (34) and is tied for the most by a linebacker in one season (8), according to NFL positional statistics maintained since 1960.

Plus, White had played in a George Allen system in the NFL, where Maxie Baughan, an Allen disciple, was the defensive coordinator during White's last five seasons in Baltimore and his three years in Detroit.

White, who earned a law degree from the University of Baltimore in 1978, served on the NFL Players Association's executive committee in '82, when the players carried out the first regular-season walkout in league history. His involvement in the union alienated the NFL and the Lions, who didn't offer him a new contract after the '82 season. "At that point, anybody who was involved in the union was looking to the USFL, because NFL teams knew the league wouldn't look kindly on us when we would go back," White recalled. "The year of the strike, Detroit drafted a linebacker in the first round, Jimmy Williams, basically to take my place."[39]

All of that was fine with Allen, who had a history of resuscitating the careers of players who had clashed with the management of their previous teams. Allen had become persona non grata with the NFL, so it seemed natural that he and White saw similarities in one another.

"George did that when he was in Washington," White said. "He took all of those players that had alienated other teams and put them together. I knew he didn't care about stuff like that and actually liked it, because he was able to get players that way. He had a lot of player reps on his team that were sort of let go and didn't feel wanted by the team that they were with. So there was a kinship between us."[40]

The '82 walkout began after the first two regular-season games. The players demanded a greater share of the television revenues, among other benefit increases. Few could have imagined it at the time, but there would be no football games for sixty-two days. The NFL finished the regular season by playing seven games, plus a four-game playoff format that included Super Bowl XVII.

"We actually thought the NFL's labor strife would be beneficial to the USFL, and it was," Bruce Allen said. "We hoped they would go on strike for the entire year."[41]

Although the NFL players' strike had the makings of the perfect gift, USFL teams were too busy building their rosters to relax in preparation for their first season. In addition to established players, the Blitz focused on unearthing hidden talent. Seeking the next Herb Mul-Key, the electrifying running back and kick returner who had raised eyebrows in a Redskins free agent tryout camp in '72, Allen called for nine tryout camps around the country, more than any other USFL team. The Blitz also organized special tryouts at Blitz Park and minicamps in Chicago, Houston, Washington, and Los Angeles.

"Have you ever heard of a guy named Herb Mul-Key?" Allen asked the long-shot prospects at his camp at Gallaudet College in Washington. "He came to a camp like this we had for the Redskins one year, made the team, and later went to the Pro Bowl."[42]

By year's end, the Blitz had evaluated more than 3,000 undrafted free agents of all shapes and sizes and placed 271 under contract.[43] A few made the team, including quarterback Tom Porras and cornerback Lance Shields. As a favor to the USFL teams that started much later in building their rosters, the Blitz placed on waivers any free agents who didn't make the final roster.

"George and Bruce were searching high and low," Steve Ehrhart recalled. "They said even if we only find one or two guys, it's worth it. They were having camps all over the place. They may have just thrown a big lasso around everybody. The other teams were jealous because they weren't organized enough."[44]

In *Strategies for Winning*, Allen told the story of a prospect who arrived an hour late for a Blitz tryout camp in Los Angeles. The player, Tom Porras, approached Allen on the practice field and asked if could still try out. Allen asked him how he got onto the field, given that the ten-foot-tall fence gate had been locked. Porass admitted climbing over the fence.

"If you wanted a [tryout] so badly that you climbed over that gosh darn fence," Allen told him, "I'll certainly give you one."

Porass wowed the coaches, made the team, and played three years in the USFL, his first two as a backup quarterback on Allen's teams. He later played ten seasons in the CFL.[45]

Another free agent prospect was Rick Telander. An All–Big 10 cornerback from Northwestern whom the Kansas City Chiefs drafted in 1971, Telander never made it in the NFL. But the Blitz were contacting everybody from the five schools in their territorial region who had been drafted by NFL teams since '71 to see if they wanted to try out.

When the Blitz called, Telander also happened to be a senior writer for *Sports Illustrated* magazine. At first he was uncertain whether the Blitz had an ulterior motive for inviting him to the camp. Perhaps, he thought, they wanted to gain free publicity, similar to how sports journalist George Plimpton chronicled his stint in the Detroit Lions' 1963 training camp in his book *Paper Lion*. Telander also had some reservations about Allen, such as his friendship with Richard Nixon. But he knew Allen loved aging veterans, so he decided to give it a shot.

"He thought young guys might be better athletes, but he had this thing about older guys," Telander said in a 2021 interview. "He was known for that. I wanted to see if I could ease my way in, and maybe George would have some sympathy [and think], 'You know, this guy, he's a crafty old veteran.'"

His flirtation with pro football lasted only five days. Telander, who was thirty-three at the time, pulled a muscle doing a standard backpedaling drill during a minicamp at Blitz Park in November 1982. He later quit the camp, telling himself, "Rick, this isn't going to happen."[46] He then documented his experience in a *Sports Illustrated* article titled, "A Final Farewell to Football." The article gave the Blitz and the USFL free national exposure after all, just as the team was heading into the league's inaugural season.

During the minicamp, Telander took a short plane flight with Allen and director of college scouting Mike McCarthy to the Logan Correctional Center in Lincoln, Illinois. Several months prior, the Blitz had received a letter requesting a tryout from a man serving a twelve-year sentence there for armed robbery. The inmate, 6-foot, 225-pound Michael Sifford, said he could play linebacker, bench-press 420 pounds, and run a 40-yard dash in 4.8 seconds. Voted most valuable player at another Illinois prison in '81, Sifford was eligible for parole in January, just before the USFL's first season.[47]

George Allen granted the tryout. As the Redskins' coach, he had tried out some inmates at the Lorton Reformatory in Virginia.[48] Now he gave Sifford a rigorous test: vertical jump, three-jump explosion, 195-pound bench press "burnout," 20-yard dash, 40-yard dash, the "jingle-jangle" for lateral quickness, the cone drill for endurance, position drills, and the "Wonderlic" test, an assessment used largely to measure cognitive ability.

Telander took notes:

Allen: "I'll be able to tell in two minutes if he can play."

Telander: "How?"

Allen: "How he moves his body. . . . We don't want to embarrass him."

Allen and McCarthy then resorted to sarcasm, with Allen asking, "I wonder if we have the rights to this prison."

McCarthy: "We have the rights to Red Grange and George Halas."

Halas and Grange, the Hall of Fame running back known as "The Galloping Ghost," were in the Blitz's territorial zone because they had both played their college ball at Illinois. At the time of Sifford's tryout, Grange was seventy-nine years old and Halas was eighty-seven.

The Blitz never invited Sifford to attend a tryout camp. But "it just cracked me up that he would even go to the prison," Telander said of Allen.[49]

Bruce Allen said his father, savvy when it came to promoting his team's name, had publicity on his mind when he agreed to the tryout, which received national media exposure: "Without a doubt. But when you say publicity, it's also the hope for a young man to get on the straight and narrow. It's a good gesture to do for your community, and it's a great gesture to help a young man."[50]

A few weeks later, the USFL held its first college draft, on January 4, 1983. The common draft, in which teams selected players from any school, consisted of twenty-four rounds. The territorial draft, which restricted teams to choosing from their local schools, included twenty-six rounds.

Not surprisingly, the Blitz made the first trade of the common draft. They exchanged draft positions with Arizona to gain the No. 2 pick and selected Ohio State running back Tim Spencer, one of the Buckeyes' all-time leading rushers (3,553 yards). Later in the first round, Chicago sent three draft choices to Boston to acquire the eleventh pick and chose Trumaine Johnson, who had amassed more than 4,000 yards at Grambling as a wing back, wide receiver, and kick returner. Many pro scouts considered Johnson a first-round NFL pick.[51] Those two rang up huge numbers in the USFL over the next two seasons and went on to productive NFL careers. Third-round pick Frank Minnifield out of Louisville started nearly all of the '84 season for Allen at cornerback and later became a four-time Pro Bowl player in the NFL.

The Blitz took a page from the AFL's playbook to acquire Spencer and Minnifield. They obtained guarantees from both players in December 1982 at the Holiday Bowl and the Blue-Gray Classic college all-star game, respectively, that they would sign with the USFL over the NFL.

Johnson signed with the Blitz as well because George Allen knew Grambling coach Eddie Robinson from years past. In '61 Allen, as the Bears' head talent scout, had visited Grambling to learn more about defensive tackle Ernie Ladd but ended up signing Rosey Taylor, a free agent defensive back whom Robinson recommended. Taylor went on to an NFL career that he ended with Allen's Redskins in 1972.

"When I went down there [to Grambling], Dad said, 'Make sure you see Coach Rob[inson], and tell him I say hi and that Rosey's doing well,'"

Bruce Allen recalled. "That was an endorsement you just couldn't buy. Coach Robinson did sign off. There was no way Grambling players would sign with the USFL unless Eddie Robinson gave it his blessing, and he did. I was sort of a messenger between those two."[52]

Allen's storied football history, popularity, and even his eating habits came in handy in other ways, too. Prior to the USFL's opening season, the *Chicago Sun-Times* contacted the Blitz to request the coach's participation in a story about ice cream for the newspaper's Sunday food section. Allen, of course, had long been known as "Ice Cream" because of his affinity for the easy-to-swallow food that allowed him to forgo chewing and concentrate on football. The Blitz, in search of ways to promote the team and sell tickets, snatched the opportunity. But not everything went smoothly, recalled Don Kojich, a public relations assistant for the Blitz:

"We agreed to carve out a half hour for the photo shoot. The photographer was there at 10:30 in the morning. It ends up a few things got in the way. Coach kept delaying it. I had to tell the photographer that we're going to get this done. Just bear with me. Finally, Coach came in. We gave him strawberry ice cream, but it started dripping on his pants. He wasn't happy about that, and he really wasn't happy about the photo shoot. But we finally got it done. When it came out on Sunday, we bought extra copies of the *Chicago Sun-Times*."[53]

On January 31, 1983, the Blitz opened training camp at Glendale Community College on the outskirts of Phoenix, close to Dr. Ted Diethrich's Arizona Heart Institute. Ninety players were auditioning for the forty-player active roster and a ten-player developmental squad.

"I really love this," Allen said at the time. "It's a tough job. It's the toughest job I've ever had. And the tougher the job, the better I like it."[54]

But Allen realized that his new league was still without basic necessities. "We don't even have towels and soap," he told *Advertising Age* magazine a few weeks before the start of the inaugural season. "We can't take anything for granted. I wake up two, three times a night thinking of things that have to be done."[55]

According to Bill Harris, "George was the type of guy who wanted to make everybody believe that everything was tough to do. He'd say crazy stuff like, 'We have maybe three footballs out there,' or 'I'm not sure how many we've got.' But it was a really great setup. We had a good operation, and our practice facilities at the high school were really nice. We could also practice at Soldier Field when we wanted to."[56]

Allen, meanwhile, revived Edward Bennett Williams's memorable 1971 quote, "I gave him an unlimited budget, and he exceeded it." With the freedom to build the team and no league-wide salary cap, Allen had authorized higher spending for players like Stan White, Tim Wrightman, Greg Landry, Tim Spencer, and Trumaine Johnson. Chicago was near the top of the USFL in salaries, while other teams, such as the Denver Gold, operated on tight budgets, according to Steve Ehrhart.[57] In terms of travel, hotel, and meals, Allen "insisted on treating all of us like we were NFL players on an NFL team and spending money like an NFL team," White remembered. "He wanted it to be a first-class organization."[58]

Allen stayed true to that philosophy with the media as well. "Even though we weren't the NFL, we were a professional football club," Kojich said. "We did things in a very first-class manner that first year in the money we spent. Even our press box food was catered at a certain level. Then we got to the second year, after we traded franchises [with Arizona], and we went from serving high-end food and great sandwiches to hot dogs and popcorn. I'm not kidding."[59]

By March the USFL was ready for its inaugural season, determined to put an entertaining product on the field. Every team would play eighteen regular-season games, with a home-and-home series against each of its division opponents. In a league with twelve franchises and three divisions—Atlantic, Central, Pacific—Chicago was one of four teams in the Central Division, along with the Birmingham Stallions, Michigan Panthers, and Tampa Bay Bandits. Each of the division winners and a wild card team would make the playoffs. There were no exhibition games.

Many in the media billed the Blitz as one of the league's premier teams, in part because Chicago sported more than a dozen former NFL players, led by the aging quintet of Greg Landry, Stan White, defensive linemen Joe Ehrmann and Junior Ah You, and middle linebacker Joe Federspiel. Rounding out the list were two-time Pro Bowl safety and kick returner Eddie Brown and defensive end Karl Lorch—two of Allen's Redskins players—as well as cornerback Virgil Livers, fullback Kevin Long, defensive end John Lee, safety Luther Bradley, flanker Lenny Willis, halfback Doug Dennison, and kicker Frank Corral. "If headlines were victories, the USFL's Chicago Blitz would have to be considered the pick for the new league's inaugural championship title," United Press International reported on February 10, 1983. "Under the leadership of media-conscious George

Allen, the Blitz have made most of the noise for the new league since its inception last year."[60] Stan White remembered that he and his teammates bought into the hype.[61]

But Chicago was not alone in making headline-grabbing moves. Other teams signed blue-chip college players certain to be first-round NFL draft picks—signings that increased parity in the league and added to its intrigue. The most dynamic rookie signing was Herschel Walker, a three-time All-American running back at Georgia and winner of the '82 Heisman Trophy. Others included North Carolina running back Kelvin Bryant (Philadelphia Stars) and Michigan wide receiver Anthony Carter (Michigan Panthers). Plus, the USFL recruited recognizable NFL names in its three-year history, including running back Joe Cribbs (Birmingham Stallions) and quarterbacks Brian Sipe (New Jersey Generals) and Doug Williams (Oklahoma/Arizona Outlaws).

Although the Blitz had the most accomplished NFL head coach in George Allen, three other former NFL head coaches with winning records joined the league: Chuck Fairbanks (New Jersey Generals), Red Miller (Denver Gold), and John Ralston (Oakland Invaders). Hugh Campbell (Los Angeles Express) and Ray Jauch (Washington Federals) had both won CFL championships.

A few days before the league opened on March 6, 1983, the Allens—George and Bruce—received a letter of encouragement from Leon "Shorty" Shortenhaus, one of George's most talented players in his first college coaching gig, at Morningside College in Sioux City, Iowa. The two had kept in touch over the years. Shortenhaus, the assistant director of admissions at Morningside at the time, told the Allens he looked forward to seeing the Blitz play at Soldier Field.

"All of us want to wish you the very best!" Shortenhaus wrote. "I read the article in *The Sporting News* about all the teams and noticed your tough schedule. We have faith in you and know you'll do a fine job."[62]

With excitement building in the days preceding the USFL's kickoff, anticipation was also rising in Allen's old stomping grounds in the nation's capital, where the Blitz would debut against the Washington Federals. Journalists prepared to descend on RFK Stadium to report on Allen's return to the city where he had coached the Redskins to five playoff appearances, including a trip to Super Bowl VII, and a 40-10-1 record at RFK.

"I don't know if it was more than we anticipated, but we anticipated there would be a lot of coverage," Kojich recalled. "A new league but also

George Allen, who had a lot of success with the Redskins. He was very revered and well known at that time."[63]

The Blitz disposed of the Federals, 28–7, before 38,010 rain-soaked fans. The next day, newspaper headlines reflected on Allen's return to DC along with Chicago's victory, with the *Washington Post* offering the headline "Allen's Exile Is Ended with Triumphant Return."[64]

Allen's postgame comments signaled that nothing about him had changed since he left Washington seven years earlier, namely his obsession with winning and his sideline mannerisms.

"Coming back here was a traumatic thing for me," he told reporters. "Winning, whether it's in the NFL or the United States Football League or playing tiddlywinks, is it. I've said it before: When you win you are reborn, and when you lose, you die a little."[65]

He added: "During the national anthem, during our workout here Saturday . . . it was all very emotional. I spent seven happy years here. I'm proud of what we accomplished, and what we did for the city. When the game started, I was raring to go, licking my tongue."[66]

But then the Blitz experienced two straight humbling losses, including a 30–29 shocker to the Arizona Wranglers in one of the greatest upsets in USFL history. Against a team that in '83 tied the Federals for the worst record in the league (4-14) and the most points allowed, and that scored the fewest points in the league, the Blitz blew a 17-point fourth-quarter lead.

Chicago won eight of its next ten games, including a 19–13 overtime victory over the Generals at Giants Stadium. In the days prior, Allen's longtime friend and the foremost football aficionado of all time in the White House, Richard Nixon, chimed in on the matchup between the 7-4 Blitz and the 3-8 Generals.

"I doubt if anyone could devise a defense to contain Herschel Walker," Nixon told the *New York Daily News*. "But if anyone can, it would be George Allen because he's a defensive genius."

In the same article, Allen called Nixon a "very intelligent sports fan" and extended an invitation to the former president, referring to Nixon's infamous play call that the Redskins ran in a '71 playoff loss to the 49ers: "The way we've been moving the ball lately, I wouldn't mind if President Nixon sent me over another play."[67]

Walker had a big day, rushing for 141 yards and two touchdowns. But his fumble set up a field goal that tied the game at 13 late in the fourth quarter. In overtime, Chicago's reserve quarterback, Tim Koegel, ran for the winning touchdown on a fake field goal. Koegel, who set up the play with a 38-yard pass to Trumaine Johnson, was in for Greg Landry, who suffered a season-ending ankle injury in the fourth period.[68] Subsequently, the Blitz traded offensive lineman Kari Yli-Renko for Generals starting quarterback and ten-year NFL veteran Bobby Scott, who rotated with Koegel the rest of the season.[69]

The next week, the Blitz improved to 9-4 with a 36–11 win over Arizona. But Allen was steaming after his team blew a 13-point lead over the Boston Breakers and lost, 21–15. The outcome left the Blitz and Breakers, both 9-5, tied for the only wild card playoff spot.[70]

On the flight home, Allen heard a Blitz player who sounded like he was content with the loss. Don Kojich saw what happened next. "Our reserve quarterback was in the back laughing about something," Kojich remembered. "Coach Allen got up, went to the back of the plane, and blew up at the guy. If we weren't at 40,000 feet, he might have thrown him out of the plane. He was upset and dressed him down and said, 'You're one play away from being in the game.' He probably should have been in the game, because our starting quarterback played with a concussion. With the concussion protocols of today, he definitely shouldn't have been in the game."[71]

After two Blitz wins in the next three weeks, Chicago's playoff fate came down to the last regular-season game, a 31–7 win over the Oakland Invaders that left the Blitz 12-6. The Michigan Panthers also finished 12-6, but they had swept Chicago in head-to-head competition in the regular season, giving the Panthers the Central Division title and the Blitz the wild card.

In the opening round of the playoffs, Chicago would face a Philadelphia Stars team that posted the league's best record, 15-3. At the league's request, the Blitz flew to Philadelphia a few days in advance to help hype the game in one of the country's largest media markets. Once there, a local TV reporter requested an interview with Allen, who was staying at a hotel near the airport with his players. Kojich told the reporter Allen was out near the airport on his daily jog. The reporter and his camera crew took off looking for Allen and caught up with him.

That evening, Kojich watched the eleven o'clock news to monitor press coverage of the championship game. The interview with Allen was part of the broadcast.[72]

"The subject of conversation varied," Kojich said. "However, things turned completely whacky when George began talking about conditioning.

He was explaining how he hoped our players would be in good enough condition to play four complete quarters without wilting in the heat and humidity [as had been our trademark that year], when just at that moment the reporter came upon a dead dog lying in the weeds. The dog was on its back with its legs up in the air. Rigor mortis looked like it had set in several days earlier.

"Without missing a beat, Coach Allen took note of the dog as he was jogging by and commented that there was a perfect example of somebody who wasn't in perfect condition to play football for him. Only George Allen, a physical fitness fanatic and chairman of the President's Council on Physical Fitness [and Sports], would come up with something like that. I laughed until my sides ached. It was a vintage George Allen performance."[73]

Before more than fifteen thousand fans at Philadelphia's Veterans Stadium on July 9, 1983, Allen and his troops, hoping to avenge a 7-point loss to the Stars a few weeks prior, took command of the playoff game and led with less than twelve minutes to play, 38–17. Allen, Stan White remembered, sounded confident at the time—perhaps a little too confident: "He just came up to me and was so excited because we had a 21-point lead, and we were playing so good on defense. I can still see him saying that. George's mantra was celebrate after victory. Don't do all the celebrating in the middle of a game when you make a tackle or score a touchdown."[74]

The celebration proved premature. Chicago's offense and top-ranked defense both faded in the heat, as the Stars scored 27 straight points, including Kelvin Bryant's 1-yard overtime dive into the end zone for a 44–38 win.

"All of a sudden, the offense was three and out, three and out, three and out, and we got a couple of penalties and pass interference calls," White explained. "They threw a flea-flicker back to the quarterback for a touchdown. It was really hot that day, and we were an older team, and we really ran out of gas in the fourth quarter. We were having to call time out, because we were on the field the whole time. That was the downside, I guess, of a veteran team on a very hot, miserable day like that. We just lost ourselves in the fourth quarter."[75]

Blitz owner Ted Diethrich, whom White called a "nervous Nellie," sounded incredulous over his team's implosion.[76] "All of a sudden, we got so damn conservative," Diethrich told the *Washington Post*. "I don't know why."[77]

Statistically, that season the Blitz scored a league-high 456 points, led by Tim Spencer and Kevin Long, who both rushed for more than 1,000 yards; Trumaine Johnson, who caught 81 passes for 1,322 yards; and Greg Landry, who passed for nearly 2,400 yards. On defense, Chicago yielded the second-fewest points in the league (271), with the front four of Joe Ehrmann, Junior Ah You, Kit Lathrop, and Karl Lorch combining for 39 sacks and Luther Bradley intercepting a league-high 12 passes.[78]

But Diethrich was unhappy with his team's record, with what he felt was a lack of media support, and with the skimpy attendance at home games at Soldier Field, where the Blitz averaged about eighteen thousand fans in the sixty-five-thousand-seat stadium.[79] They lost a reported $3 million in the USFL's first season.[80]

Plus, Diethrich didn't like flying to Phoenix to do his medical work during the week and returning to Chicago on the weekends. To relocate to his hometown, he orchestrated a deal perhaps crazier than the Rams-Colts ownership swap in '72. He and Bill Harris sold the Blitz to Milwaukee-based cardiovascular surgeon Dr. James F. Hoffman for $7 million.[81] They then bought the Arizona Wranglers for an identical amount. In Arizona, the Diethrich-Harris-Allen ownership structure remained the same, with Allen retaining the title of head coach and chairman of the board. Marv Levy, Allen's special teams coach in Washington in the early '70s and later the coach of the CFL's Montreal Alouettes and the Kansas City Chiefs, became Chicago's coach.

As part of the deal, the team names remained in their cities, but the coaches and players mostly switched. A handful of the players stayed in Chicago, and two stayed in Arizona, including quarterback Alan Risher, who threw for more than 2,600 yards in '83 and sparked the Wranglers' 30–29 comeback win over Chicago with a series of clutch throws.[82]

Allen understood why Diethrich relocated to Arizona. But he was no proponent of the franchise swap. "It's not that Dad saw himself as Superman," Bruce Allen said. "But he understood the big markets and the media contracts, and he knew the networks disliked the idea of George Allen leaving the third-biggest TV market at the time. Our TV ratings were excellent with the Blitz. It would have been better for the league if George Allen coached in a bigger TV market. Dad probably could have stayed in Chicago with the new owner. But he wasn't going to do that to Dr. Diethrich and Bill Harris."[83]

George Allen was also skeptical of the USFL's rapid expansion in '84. The league added six new franchises to bring the total to eighteen, and it created four divisions: Atlantic, Southern, Western, and Pacific. The Pacific Division consisted of the Wranglers, the Los Angeles Express, the Denver Gold, and the Oakland Invaders. An eight-team playoff format featured four division winners and four wild card teams.

"It was my father's advice that instead of expanding to eighteen teams, we go to ten teams or at least stay at twelve," Bruce said. "He believed we had to shore up these teams before we expand. But everybody saw a way to get their money back. There were losses in the league from $1 million to $3 million. The league sold six expansion teams at about $2 million apiece so everybody could get whole. That was the mistake. Too many people wanted to get their money back. Growing by 50 percent in one year is insane. If we had stayed at twelve or gone to ten, the league definitely would have succeeded."

Bruce noted that his father never saw the league as a fast way to make a buck. "When the vision was sold, that wasn't the idea of the USFL," he said. "Dad was a strong believer that spring football would have been successful."[84]

In Arizona one of Allen's new assistant coaches was a face from the past: Roman Gabriel, Allen's star quarterback with the Rams. Allen's decision not to bring him to DC in 1971 had angered Gabriel, but the two patched things up. Gabriel, an assistant with the USFL's Boston Breakers in '83, felt honored when Allen asked him to be his quarterback coach in Arizona. First, he had to withstand an interrogation.

"Coach called and said he wanted to meet me for dinner," Gabriel said in a 2019 interview. "He asked nine million questions, which I understood. After a while, I said, 'Coach, I realize if you don't hire me, you're going to use what I'm telling you about how I coach.' Luckily, he hired me."[85]

Like they did in Chicago, the Wranglers practiced in Phoenix on a beautifully maintained field at a vacant high school. Their offices and meeting rooms were also at the school. As backup quarterback to Greg Landry nearly the entire season, Alan Risher had limited contact with the defensive-minded Allen during practice and games in '84, the only season they were together. But he recalls snapshots of Allen's idiosyncrasies.

"George was very interesting," Risher said. "This happened all the time: he'd call a ten o'clock team meeting on the day of a regular practice. Everybody's in the meeting, and George is notoriously fifteen, twenty minutes late every meeting. He makes a grand entrance by himself, and he always started the meeting off with, 'Hey, I just got off the phone with President Reagan,' or 'Hey, I just got off the phone with Pete Rozelle,' or 'Hey, I just got off the phone with [USFL commissioner] Chet Simmons.' He was always name-dropping somebody that was huge in politics or football. He always had a story saying he was on the phone with some bigwig. It was funny as hell."

One day, as Risher walked from the locker room to the practice field, he heard Allen say his name. Risher didn't expect what happened next:

"I've got my helmet, my shoulder pads, and I'm walking by myself for whatever reason. Maybe we had some early drills for the QBs. He pops out of the office and says, 'Hey, Alan. Come here.' 'Yeah, Coach?' He goes, 'Hey, man, I've got to give you a copy of my book.' It was some type of fitness book that President Reagan had signed. I said, 'Okay, Coach. Thanks a lot.' So I take about six or seven steps heading toward the field. He goes, 'Hey, Alan, wait a minute, wait a minute, come here. I forgot to autograph that for you.' I remember that story like it was yesterday. I tell people about it all the time."[86]

On paper, Allen's Wranglers looked much better than the '83 team, who at 4-14 had tied for the league's worst record. After all, the Wranglers were now the Blitz in their second season. In a preseason radio campaign, Allen declared, "We aren't going to lose. I won't allow it."[87]

The Wranglers opened at home with a 35–7 whitewashing of Oakland in the seventy-thousand-seat Sun Devil Stadium at Arizona State University in Tempe. But as the season unfolded, inconsistent play and a slew of injuries left them at 4-6 following a 24–23 loss to San Antonio.

Allen called his players together for a team meeting. "I gave a little talk on what it takes to win," he once said. "I used to do the same thing when I was coach of the Los Angeles Rams or the Washington Redskins. We had more talent in those days, but the motivational factors were basically the same. In twelve years as a head coach in the National Football League, we never had a losing season."[88]

Allen and his staff also decided to adjust the practice schedule. During the day, the Phoenix-area temperatures sometimes rose to an excruciating 115 degrees, making for miserable conditions during Allen's repetition-heavy, three- to three-and-a-half-hour practices. Gabriel and offensive line coach Ray Wietecha thus approached Allen with a suggestion that practices begin at eight or nine in the evening so the players wouldn't have to battle such inferno-like temperatures.

"George's thing was you practice when you play, which makes a lot of sense," Gabriel said. "We were out there in full gear during the day, and guys were getting dehydrated and tired because it was so hot. Finally, we got the nerve to explain to him that somehow we've got to get out of the sun. George used to run a few miles every day and do push-ups and sit-ups. He got dehydrated.

"We came in after practice one day, and he was in the cold tub. He said, 'I'm going to call the guys together and tell them we're going to practice at night, so at least they won't see the heat.'"[89]

His decision was not universally welcomed. "That was a morale buster," Allen told Guback. "One of my players said, 'When am I ever going to see my children? They'll be going to school. I come home at night, and they're asleep. When are we going to be with our families?' Originally, I said maybe I'll let you vote on this, whatever you decide is okay with me. Then I could see there was division. At the end of a practice, I said we're going to practice at night from now on, period. Let's make the best of it."[90]

Allen's tedious practices remained. He afforded no leniency to his assistant coaches either, as Alan Risher learned from his quarterback coach, Roman Gabriel. "He worked his coaches to death," Risher said. "They wouldn't leave their offices until about midnight or until they were finished with their work. He was spying on them, making sure they were in their offices. Anybody who ever coached with him would say, 'Man, this is a crazy experience.'"

Improvisation was needed when the lights around the field went dark during practice one night. "There was some type of power outage," Risher remembered. "He made all the players get their cars and use the track around the football field as a parking lot. We parked our cars on the track with the lights on in order to finish the practice. The damn footballs were banging off everybody's head. It was funny, man."[91]

The season had become a head-scratcher for Allen, who couldn't comprehend why his hard work wasn't breeding more success. The strain took a toll on the sixty-seven-year-old coach, who said at one point that he had lost fifteen pounds and couldn't sleep.[92]

With the Wranglers at 4-6, a rallying cry began circulating through the locker room: nobody wanted the stigma of being on Allen's first losing team in his fourteen years as a pro head coach. The team's veteran leaders—Stan White, Greg Landry, Karl Lorch, Eddie Brown, and others—stepped forward to reinforce the fact that "this isn't going to happen," Bruce Allen recalled. "We talked about it in team meetings when Dad's not there: this will not happen."[93]

The mantra turned the season around.

"We just re-upped our commitment and started playing better football," White said. "Greg Landry started playing better at quarterback, and that always helps. Our defense started playing really good football. We had a couple of good games, got our confidence, and went on from there."[94]

The Wranglers won six of their last eight games, finishing 10-8 and earning a wild card playoff spot. Winning the last four was reminiscent of how Allen's Redskins won their final four games to earn the NFC's only wild card spot in '76. "The comeback in the second half of that [1984] season was very rewarding to Dad," Bruce said. "Very rewarding."[95]

"Isn't winning great?" Allen asked a reporter after a 36–0 rout of the Blitz, who finished 5-13 that season, in the next-to-last game. "I don't know what comes ahead of it. I really don't . . . especially when you work so hard to do it."[96]

In the season finale, the Wranglers defeated the Los Angeles Express, 35–10, marking the ninth time in his fourteen pro coaching seasons that a George Allen team qualified for the playoffs. In a divisional playoff game, the Wranglers would face the Western Division winners, the 13-5 Houston Gamblers, coached by his protégé and Redskins successor Jack Pardee.

To win this one, Allen and his staff needed to control Houston's prolific quarterback, 6-foot-3, 220-pound Jim Kelly, another college star who signed with the USFL in '84. Kelly, whom Bruce Allen had tried to recruit for the Blitz after he finished his college career at Miami, passed for USFL records of 5,219 yards and 44 touchdowns that season in an explosive pass-first run-and-shoot offense devised by Houston's offensive coordinator, Darrel "Mouse" Davis. Kelly's main targets were Richard Johnson and Ricky Sanders, the league's top two receivers, with 115 and 101 catches, respectively.

However, Houston allowed a whopping 82 sacks, and Allen saw a window. His advice for his defensive line, which posted league highs that year of 73 sacks and 558 yards in losses led by John Lee (league-high 20 sacks) and Karl Lorch (13), was basic: "Be patient. Keep the pressure on Kelly. Rush him. Get to the big, tough rookie before he can run or shoot."[97]

Before nearly thirty-three thousand fans at the Houston Astrodome, Allen turned in one of his greatest defensive masterpieces. Kelly was his usual productive self, with twenty-three completions for 301 yards. But he threw no touchdown passes, for the first time all season, and two interceptions. Heeding Allen's advice, Arizona's defensive front pressured Kelly relentlessly and sacked him six times. The Wranglers also stuck to their strategy of playing a soft zone to keep the ball in front of them and prevent Kelly from making backbreaking throws, in addition to disguising their pass coverages. Their defense held Houston to field goals on three long drives.

"When we played them earlier in the year, they beat us pretty badly [37–24]," Stan White said in hindsight. "We played our regular defenses, our man to man and different things, and they just smoked us. So in the playoff game, George has never liked this, but he did a bend but don't break. We played a lot of zone, took away all their big plays. Then when they got down into the plus-20, we would blitz and play man and gamble a little bit, because you had the end zone to back you up. There weren't big plays to give up. It's a little tougher to throw down there and run that offense down there. We were a lot softer, something George hated. But even if it was something he hated, he would do it if it helped him win the game."[98]

According to Bruce Allen, "Dad had a great way of not insulting you or making you feel bad. He'd say, 'We can't cover them in man, meaning they're much faster and quicker than we are.' He didn't call it 'rope a dope,' but we would invite them to our red zone. In the red zone, speed doesn't matter. As long as we don't allow a home run around midfield or any of that, then we have a chance. In the red zone is where we win. That's exactly what happened."[99]

The Gamblers led in the fourth quarter, 16–3. But Arizona, dominated at that point in total yards and time of possession, struck back with Tim Spencer's 20-yard touchdown run and Greg Landry's 11-yard scoring pass to Doug Dennison with less than two minutes remaining. Frank Corral's conversion gave the Wranglers a 17–16 victory and Allen's first playoff win in more than a decade.

In postgame comments, White poked fun at the run-and-shoot offense: "Yeah, the offense of the '80s. And the George Allen defense of the ages, the '60s, the '70s, and now the '80s."[100]

White and his teammates gave the game ball to Allen, who compared the win to the Redskins' 26–3 victory over the Cowboys in the '72 NFC Championship Game, Allen's crowning moment as a pro coach. "This ranks up there with the best of them," he said.[101]

After overcoming one talented quarterback, the Wranglers would face another in the Western Conference championship: Steve Young of the LA Express.

In 1984 Young wasn't as much of an aerial threat as Kelly, but he was more adept at scrambling. He ran for 515 yards despite missing the first six games for the 10-8 Express, who beat the defending USFL champion Michigan Panthers in the opening round of the playoffs, 27–21. That game went into a third overtime period, marking the longest pro football game ever. Young passed for 295 yards and two interceptions and ran for 44 more yards, including a crucial 2-point conversion at the end of regulation.

Young was also the $40 million man. In signing with the Express six games into the '84 season, he agreed to a $40 million annuity paid out over four decades, through 2022.[102] It was the most lucrative deal in the history of pro team sports at the time. Young, who starred in college at Brigham Young and finished as the runner-up in Heisman Trophy balloting in 1983, was another huge catch for the USFL, which outmaneuvered the NFL in '84 to acquire its second straight Heisman Trophy winner, Nebraska running back Mike Rozier.

With the Express's home field, the Los Angeles Coliseum, preparing for the '84 Summer Olympics, the Wranglers hosted the game at Sun Devil Stadium. That was just one quirk in the scheduling. League officials agreed to move the kickoff time from 12:30 p.m. to 8:30 p.m. so players could avoid the extreme daytime temperatures, which were still around 100 degrees at game time.

Young, who sat out LA's season-ending loss to the Wranglers, struggled against a defense that harassed him throughout the game and sacked him four times. He completed 7 of 23 passes for 126 yards, with 2 interceptions. To put the defensive pressure in perspective, he threw for just 51 yards before an inconsequential late touchdown drive.[103] "We made sure our guys stayed in their lanes because he was really a runner at that point," White remembered. "We didn't give him any big plays. Didn't give him a chance to scramble. We had spies on him, so George had a good game plan for him."[104]

The Wranglers bounced back from a 17–7 deficit by scoring 28 straight points against a defense that may have been dragging from its ninety-three-minute marathon the week before. A trick play that Arizona blew up sparked a major momentum swing. With Los Angeles leading 17–7, Express punter Jeff Partridge faked a punt on fourth down from his 35-yard line and passed the ball. The Wranglers knocked it down and scored four plays later to close the gap to 3. Allen and his staff learned of the play in the days preceding the game.

"We knew definitely they would throw it," Wranglers assistant head coach and special teams coach Paul Lanham, Allen's special teams coach for five seasons in DC, told reporters afterward. "They thought they had us fooled."[105]

A special teams star for Allen's Redskins, safety Eddie Brown, was perfectly positioned to deflect the pass. "We suspected that play all along," he said in retrospect. "They had different personnel in than they normally did. We were pretty sharp about picking that kind of stuff up. They had done it maybe twice before during the season."[106]

From there, Chicago's first draft pick in '83, Tim Spencer, ran for two touchdowns and caught a pass for a score. Mack Boatner ran for the other touchdown to give the Wranglers a 35–17 lead with minutes left in the game.

When the final gun sounded in Arizona's 35–23 victory, ABC play-by-play man Tim Brandt, who spent time on the Redskins' practice squad in '73 and launched his sportscasting career in DC in the mid-1970s, sang Allen's praises as the unassailable winner walked off the field amid a sea of players and fans reaching out to offer congratulations: "a native of Gross[e] Pointe [Shores], Michigan, whose storied football career spans four decades . . . the coach of the Arizona Wranglers, and the USFL Western Conference [champions].

"They talked about him earlier in the year saying his job was in jeopardy. I talked to George about that earlier this week. He said he couldn't think about that. He had to concentrate on winning football games. Concentrate on turning things around. He did that. His team won six of its last [eight] ball games. Came in here as the favorite and stopped a very talented, very young Los Angeles Express."[107]

After two victories that showcased Allen's defensive genius, the Wranglers faced a strong test in the USFL championship game against the Philadelphia Stars. The Stars finished with the league's best regular-season record, 16-2, and featured running back Kelvin Bryant, the USFL's second-leading rusher (1,406 yards). Former Redskins safety Brig Owens, one of Allen's field generals during his coaching days in DC and a starter in Allen's only Super Bowl appearance, offered words of advice to his former coach and quoted defensive tackle Diron Talbert, one of the Ramskins. "Congrats. You made it," Owens wrote in a Western Union telegram. "Take the next step to victory. Coach, don't kick any chairs, 'cause you may have to play injured. However, as Talby used to say, whatever it takes to win, do it."[108]

The Stars redeemed themselves after their loss to Michigan in the 1983 USFL championship game by inflicting a 23–3 rout of the Wranglers before fifty-two thousand fans at Tampa Stadium. Philadelphia controlled the game from the start, using a methodical approach led by Bryant's 115 rushing yards on twenty-nine carries, and maintained possession for 72 percent of the game.

When it was all over, Allen had failed to capitalize on another opportunity to win a league championship game. In postgame comments, he described the roller-coaster season as the "toughest year in my coaching career" and said he wouldn't want to endure another one like it for even "$20 million."[109] He said he needed a few months to decide if he wanted to return as coach.

About a month later, Allen announced his decision to continue coaching, telling the Associated Press, "I enjoy winning, and I enjoy the competition. To keep testing yourself, that's the challenge for me." Several weeks later, however, he informed Diethrich that he was resigning as coach but would stay with the team as part owner and chairman of the board. In an interview with the *Washington Post*, he admitted, "I doubt if I'll ever coach again."[110] In fourteen years as a pro head coach, George Herbert Allen had posted a 138-61-5 regular-season record (.693 winning percentage) and a 4-10 playoff mark (.286).

"This is a sad moment for me, but it is also a very proud time for me," Allen said in an official Wranglers statement. "This 1984 season was my most difficult assignment, but it was also the most rewarding. We ended up playing for the championship and came away with the silver medal. Now, I'd like to spend more time seeing this franchise through and staying active in policy areas that can help everyone involved in the organization maintain their winning profiles.

"Looking back over the years I have spent in the game of football, I am fortunate to have worked for George Halas, the founder of the National Football League, and people like Clark Shaughnessy and Sid Gillman. These men have taught me how to think about this game, and they have all played a part in the contributions I have been able to make during my years as a coach."

Allen also said he was anxious to spend more time traveling with his "beloved wife," Etty, and focusing on his duties as chairman of the President's Council on Physical Fitness and Sports.[111]

Allen named one of his loyal assistants going back to his days in DC as his successor: Paul Lanham. "This is a time of great mixed emotions for me," Lanham said to reporters. "How do you replace a legend?"

Allen told those reporters, "He won't falter. Paul will do a good job. He's an old friend and a colleague who's been with me since way back in my days with the Washington Redskins in the National Football League. I'll be here every day trying to make this franchise successful. I'm not leaving football. I'm just changing jobs."[112]

In a few weeks, though, Allen would be out of football. Ted Diethrich, who had lost millions of dollars in the first two USFL seasons,[113] agreed to merge with the USFL's Oklahoma Outlaws and retain a 25 percent clip of the team, which was rebranded as the Arizona Outlaws. He soon decided he wanted out altogether. So did George and Bruce Allen. The Allens might have been able to stay on with the Outlaws, Bruce remembered, but both said no. Longtime Arizona State coach Frank Kush resigned as head coach of the NFL's Indianapolis Colts to become Arizona's new head coach.

"Working with Dad was the best," Bruce said. "You knew what he wanted, and he knew what I wanted, so it was so good. We didn't have to talk as much as you think. How do you replace that? I wasn't ready to do that. Without a doubt, the USFL was the best years of my professional life."[114] Bruce went on to a career as a sports agent, before serving as a senior executive for the Oakland Raiders (1995–2003), earning the NFL Executive of the Year Award in the Raiders' 2002 AFC championship season. He was later general manager of the Tampa Bay Buccaneers (2004–8) and general manager, executive vice president, and president of the Washington Redskins (2010–19).

The USFL played a third season in 1985 with fourteen teams. The Baltimore Stars, formerly the Philadelphia Stars, beat Oakland for their second straight championship in what became the USFL's final game. A year later, a court ruled on a $1.3 billion antitrust suit the USFL brought against the NFL. Donald Trump, the brash and flamboyant real estate tycoon, was the initial catalyst behind the lawsuit, which also had backing from other USFL owners.[115] After buying the New Jersey Generals in September 1983, Trump said he favored the USFL eventually going head to head with the NFL by playing its games in the fall and winter. He was confident the upstart league would soon achieve parity with its more established rival.[116]

The lawsuit alleged that the NFL used monopolistic practices to control the business of football, saying a competitor could not succeed in the fall because of the NFL's contracts with the three main TV networks.[117] A jury found the NFL guilty of monopolizing pro football but awarded the USFL only $1 in damages, which is trebled in antitrust cases. The USFL was history.

Similar to his view of the league's rapid expansion after the '83 season, George Allen felt the USFL had made a rash decision in its bid to play in the fall. He believed that concept, if entertained at all, should have been explored six to eight years down the road, when the league would surely have a more solid financial footing.[118] The USFL's weakness was in the owners who too often "rained on their own parade," he wrote in *Strategies for Winning*.[119]

At least Allen got what he wanted out of the league.

"He proved once again that he could coach and win," Bruce Allen said. "He saw it more like that. It was more of a test to show everyone that 'my structure can win.' And it was a more difficult winning than if you took over a bad NFL team at the time and had to turn them around from losing to winning. You had to create everything. We had nothing. To win under those circumstances and then win in two different cities in the USFL was a heck of an accomplishment."[120]

23

"Are You Kidding?"

Upon resigning as head coach of the USFL's Arizona Wranglers after the 1984 season, George Allen vowed to dedicate more time to chairing the President's Council on Physical Fitness and Sports (PCPFS). When President Reagan appointed him to that prestigious post in September 1981, Allen had laid out an ambitious plan to make American adults and children fit and healthy.

During the '80s, a fitness boom in the United States fueled a wave of societal pastimes targeting health-conscious adults: aerobics, exercise clubs, Nautilus machines, personal trainers, racquetball and squash courts, and nutrition-oriented promotions. But schoolchildren seemed to miss the revolution. During that decade, various studies, including one by the PCPFS, found that kids had stagnated in school fitness programs and were more overweight compared with children from earlier decades. A study of nearly twenty thousand boys and girls included the alarming results that large percentages of kids couldn't run a mile in less than ten minutes and couldn't do even one pull-up.[1]

Allen was appalled. "The best-kept secret in the United States today is youth fitness, or lack of," he told the *Los Angeles Times* in 1986. "Kids have no endurance, no strength and very little flexibility.

"A lot of boys and girls today can't even run a mile in thirteen minutes. Think about it! Most adults can walk a mile in eleven minutes without straining."

The root of the problem, according to Allen and other fitness experts, was that schoolchildren were not receiving the proper support for exercise and nutrition largely because of reductions in school budgets.[2]

Allen's solution was an idea he conceived of early into his tenure as PCPFS chairman when he established the National Fitness Foundation. The Indianapolis-based nonprofit group aimed to generate enough private contributions to fund the construction of a $50 million national fitness academy. The academy would serve as a national training headquarters and research center for coaches and physical education instructors, who would pass on their knowledge and expertise to students in schools nationwide. Allen expected it to open before the end of President Reagan's second term in office.[3]

"The idea for the academy has been around, but nobody has had the drive or leadership to push it through," Allen said. "The academy is something that should have been done forty years ago."[4]

Allen tapped his good friend and special advisor to the PCPFS, Bill Harris, to chair the academy's site selection committee. Harris and his team spent a year studying about 360 possible sites, with Indianapolis, Houston, Miami, and Malibu, California, getting top consideration.[5] They finally settled on another Southern California location: a 175-acre site in the Laguna Hills area of Orange County.[6]

Allen announced the choice at a press conference at the Century Plaza Hotel in Los Angeles on February 13, 1985—the same hotel where Carroll Rosenbloom had introduced him as the Rams' new coach almost exactly seven years earlier. He sounded relieved that the search had come to a close.

As the *Orange County Register* reported, Allen said getting the project going "has been tougher than playing the Dallas Cowboys." He noted that "it has been my dream for probably five years. This is more important than football. If you don't have fitness, you don't have anything. I've been a coach all my life. Fitness is number one."[7]

Allen unveiled preliminary sketches of the academy at a banquet honoring First Lady Nancy Reagan in New York City on April 15, 1985. He envisioned a facility that resembled the vast sports academies in Europe, China, and Japan, with a gym, a fitness training department, a weight training center, a sports medicine clinic, classrooms, dorms, a library, and an amphitheater, among other amenities. It would also be a clearinghouse for literature on fitness, diet, health, and nutrition.

President Reagan voiced enthusiasm for the project in a letter to Allen in June 1985:

"Congratulations to all of you who are working so diligently to make the United States Fitness Academy a reality. The academy, the first of its kind in the country, will serve as a training and leadership center dedicated to the improvement of fitness for all Americans. I can think of no better or more inspiring goal.

"The ancient Greeks first preached that a sound mind and a strong body go together. Those words still ring true. The Academy will help make

America a happier, healthier, and more productive nation. We can be proud that this will be the legacy for us all."[8]

Despite the hype surrounding the academy as a premier U.S. site for training coaches and phys ed instructors, coupled with solid backing from the U.S. president, no permits were issued for constructing the facility. As months dragged on, local government officials expressed frustration with the foundation's lack of flexibility in meeting Orange County building requirements. To Allen, it was like battling through a lot of red tape.

"As a coach, I'm used to having people do things the way they should be done and no politics," he told the *Los Angeles Times* in January 1986. "As a football coach, I've always gotten things done on time and been successful. But when you get into politics, you're playing games."[9]

Allen organized fundraising banquets to help finance the academy. The banquets saluted prominent figures who had made significant contributions to America's health and fitness through their work at the national level. They included Nancy Reagan; former president Gerald Ford; entertainer Bob Hope; real estate entrepreneur Donald Trump; David A. "Sonny" Werblin, chairman of the Madison Square Garden Corporation and a former New York Jets owner; and veteran sportswriter Paul Zimmerman, who was with *Sports Illustrated* at the time.[10] In addition to the president, Bob Hope, Donald Trump, and NFL star Walter Payton were among those who endorsed the academy.[11]

"Those people all helped him in his quest to raise money, and they were great about helping," Bruce Allen said. "They knew my father was trying to help the youth in America."[12]

Allen came to know Trump through their involvement in the USFL. Even before Trump purchased the USFL's New Jersey Generals in September 1983, he attended some of the league's early organizational meetings and encountered Allen at places like Trump Tower, his skyscraper in Midtown Manhattan.

The two became friends. George and Etty Allen visited Trump on a number of occasions, including a trip in May 1986 to his new home, Mar-a-Lago, a historic mansion built in the 1920s by heiress Marjorie Merriweather Post in the resort town of Palm Beach, Florida.[13] Trump had purchased Mar-a-Lago for a reported $8 million. For decades, he teased the possibility of someday running for president.[14]

That same year, Allen penned a *USA Today* question-and-answer article titled "Too Often, Our Fitness Programs Are a Joke." The topic was "flabby kids." With Allen contributing his thoughts as an exercise fanatic and chair of the PCPFS, the article explored why America's youth had fallen behind in staying fit and healthy, for one, by not embracing the exercise boom pervading the country.

Shortly after the article appeared on August 14, 1986, Trump sent a copy to Allen and wrote: "George—a great article—keep up the fight. Best, Donald."[15]

Bruce Allen remembered those inspirational words when he sent Trump a note on August 2, 2015, a few weeks after Trump announced a run for the presidency. Bruce was the Redskins' president and general manager at the time.

> Donald:
>
> Twenty-nine years ago, you sent my father a great note. Today, he would send you the same message.
>
> "Keep up the fight."
>
> Good Luck,
> Bruce Allen

Trump responded, "Bruce. Still true. Have a great season. Best, Donald."[16]

Meanwhile, Allen's fitness academy gained no traction, and his quest to complete the imaginative project proved futile.

"Despite the support of some of America's most prominent corporate and athletic personalities, including President Reagan," Mark Landsbaum of the *Los Angeles Times* wrote in June 1988, "and despite a succession of high-profile fundraising events that have helped him bring in more than $2.7 million, nearly all of which has been spent, not a shovel of dirt has been turned at the south Orange County site chosen for the academy."[17]

The *Orange County Register* reported that a lack of fundraising support, missed deadlines, and tense relations with local officials, among other factors, doomed the project. Bob Mathias, a two-time Olympic gold medal decathlete and former member of Congress who for a time served as executive director of the National Fitness Foundation, said Allen came up short in pursuing potentially wealthy donors.

"He said he didn't have time for that," Mathias told the *Orange County Register*. "He worked on other projects . . . and as a result, nothing happened."[18]

Bruce Allen explained that his father faced too daunting a task to build the academy with private funds: "He didn't get any governmental financial support. The thought when he first proposed it was, 'Great idea, George. But we have no money for that.' 'What if I can raise it?' 'Okay, great, try.' It was too much of a heavy lift."[19]

About a year before the idea of the academy collapsed, Allen with "great regret" resigned as chairman of the President's Council on Physical Fitness and Sports.[20] President Reagan announced that Dick Kazmaier, the 1951 Heisman Trophy winner, would succeed him.

In his tenure from 1981 to 1987, Allen was easily the most active PCPFS chairman since the council's inception in 1956. "Whatever he was doing, he did it at 110 percent," George Felix Allen said. "He really enjoyed working for President Reagan on the council."[21] Allen's achievements included a youth testing exchange program with the Soviet Union and a youth fitness awareness media campaign.

"I take great pride in the many accomplishments of the council," Allen said upon his resignation. "The number of American adults who are exercising regularly has almost doubled in the last decade, and we have called attention to the need to improve the fitness of youth worldwide.

"I used to think that playing Dallas was a big deal, but the emphasis on physical fitness impacts on the lifestyles of millions. The strides we have taken to improve the fitness of our youth, which has been our number one priority over the last seven years, will have a dramatic and lasting effect on the future of this country."[22]

Despite stepping aside from the PCPFS and retiring efforts to build the academy, Allen remained active with the National Fitness Foundation. He took the lead in organizing and promoting the first World Congress in America on Fitness, Nutrition, and Sports for All, a five-day event in Chicago in May 1990 that included delegates from seventy-six countries, including twenty-five Third World nations. The event aimed to build a better understanding of fitness and nutrition and share ideas with Third World countries.

Allen planned the conference with the help of Soviet, Czechoslovakian, and West German officials. With the Cold War raging and President Reagan involved in nuclear arms limitation talks with the Soviets, Allen developed a fascination with the Soviet Union's government-mandated approach to engaging kids in fitness programs. As chair of the foundation, he arranged a swap with Soviet officials: some eighty-two thousand

American kids, ages six to sixteen, took the Soviet test for fitness, while thirty-five thousand Soviet kids took the American test.

"They passed our test hands down," Allen said of the Soviet kids. But the American youth were lacking in endurance and upper-body strength when they took the Soviet test, he learned.[23]

George Felix Allen had to remind his father that the Soviet system was impossible to replicate in the United States: "He was considering what we need to do to get American kids in better shape and compared us to the Soviets. He said, 'Here's what youth in Russia have to do. I said, 'Dad, it's the Soviet Union. They're communists. It's a dictatorship. These are good aspirational goals. But you can't have the government telling people they have to do a number of these things, the number of sit-ups and push-ups and pull-ups and running for miles under a certain time.'"[24]

At the same time, Allen never lost sight of his own rigorous fitness regimen: running, swimming, cycling, hitting the punching bag, lifting weights, 10Ks, bike-a-thons, and triathlons. Doing so would be antithetical to the George Allen way. Paul Fine, the son of longtime Redskins photographer Nate Fine, saw Allen's dedication firsthand.

Nate Fine was the Redskins' photographer for fifty-one years. From games and practices, he shot stacks of pictures and miles of video, gaining recognition as one of the best in a business where coaches were so dependent on game films to learn about themselves and opposing teams. Of course, George Allen, who dubbed Fine the "Cecil B. DeMille of football" after the legendary film director, was in a league of his own. "No other coach used film like he did," Paul Fine said in retrospect. "It was one of his weapons. Dad didn't even know how [Allen] had the time to look at the tons and tons of film that he shot."

Paul Fine said that after his father died of cancer in April 1988, Allen flew from Los Angeles to Washington DC, to pay his respects. Keeping to a tight schedule, he attended the funeral service, went out for a run, and left to catch a plane, all in a matter of two hours.

"We had the service at our house, and a lot of people were there, including former players and coaches," Fine said. "I went up to my bedroom, and he was in there changing clothes. I asked him what he was doing. He said, 'You know I run. I've got to run right now, and then I need to catch a plane.' I said, 'You know this meant so much to Dad.' He said, 'I wouldn't miss this for anything, but I need to get going.' So he ran for an hour and came back, put his clothes on, said good-bye to everybody, and he was off."[25]

Although Allen had been out of coaching since leaving the USFL in 1984, his mind never strayed from football and coaching. His notes from a 1986 planning calendar paint the picture of a man immersed in thought about his top passion in life:

> "I'm not saying I'm perfect. I have a lot of faults. I know myself. I know what it takes to get everyone together, working hard, preparing themselves to win."
>
> "Football is a game of conditioning (1), fundamentals (2), team play (3), and toughness (4). If you don't have raw talent, you must have great defense."
>
> "Winning is a George Allen tradition."
>
> "A successful coach is willing to do that which the unsuccessful [coach] is not willing to do."[26]

Allen kept abreast of developments in the NFL, with an eye on returning to coaching. Living in Palos Verdes Estates, he attended many Raiders home games when they played in Los Angeles in the '80s. He would go as a guest of Al Davis, the team's primary owner and general manager. The two, who first met in '63 when Allen was the Bears' head talent scout and Davis coached the Raiders, spoke regularly when Allen was out of coaching in the '80s. Tommy McVean, equipment manager for Allen's Redskins and his USFL teams, also maintained a close relationship with Allen in the ensuing years and ran a marathon with him in LA in the mid-'80s. "He'd be talking to Al Davis every day about football. They were close buddies," McVean said.[27]

Allen and Davis maintained a kinship of sorts, both having showed a rebellious side over the years and little inhibition for challenging the establishment. Plus, the credo that Davis laid out for his Raiders, a "commitment to excellence," was similar to the 110 percent effort that Allen, a perfectionist, expected from his players.

Bruce Allen, who knew Davis well from working as a Raiders senior executive from 1995 to 2003, put them in the "mutual respect club."

"They were different, and they would joke with each other about how different they were," Bruce said. "When we were at dinners together, I'd watch the two of them react to each other. I'm sure no one said some of the things to Al that Dad did and that no one said some of the things to Dad that Al did.

"They could be completely honest with each other. They gave their opinions on the 46-type blast, which is a defense, or a player or a coach or an owner or a media person or a political situation or a current event. They didn't agree on everything. It was like, 'Well, I see him as this, and you see him as that.' It was a great debate. Neither one would hold back. It was just an honest opinion, and both respected each other's opinion. I don't want to put words in Al's mouth, but he thought Dad was great at football."[28]

Did Davis ever consider hiring Allen as head coach? Davis felt strongly about the issue of civil rights. In the 1960s, he took steps to protect his Black players from discrimination, such as refusing to play an exhibition game in Alabama to protest the state's segregation laws. He hired Tom Flores, one of the NFL's first Latino coaches, in 1979, and then, in 1989, one of its first Black coaches, Art Shell, a legendary Raiders offensive tackle with two Super Bowl rings who entered the Hall of Fame in 1989. Shell was synonymous with the silver and black.

"First and foremost on Al's mind when hiring Art is that he was a Raider," Bruce Allen said. Upon hiring Shell, Davis spoke to George Allen about coaching the Raiders' defense, according to Bruce: "Dad said, 'What happens when you and I disagree on the quarterback?' Al said, 'You would concentrate only on the defense, so you wouldn't have the authority to ask me about the quarterback.' Dad wasn't going to be the defensive coordinator for Art Shell."[29]

But an opportunity of sorts surfaced at Allen's first head coaching stop, Morningside College in Sioux City, Iowa. Because of his friendship with Leon "Shorty" Shortenhaus, an all-conference end at Morningside when Allen coached there (1948–50) and later the school's associate director of admissions, Allen followed the football program. He also maintained close ties to the college, donating $5,000 a year to an academic scholarship in his name. Morningside awarded him an honorary doctor of laws degree in 1973.[30] By the end of the '88 season, the team had lost fifteen straight football games. Erv Mondt, who went 19-46-1 (.292 winning percentage) as Morningside's head coach from '83 to '88, departed after the '88 season.

The program needed a spark. Shortenhaus contacted Allen and suggested half-heartedly that he return to NCAA Division 2 Morningside as the head coach. "George said, 'You know, I might just take you up on that offer,'" Shortenhaus said at the time. "'Let me think it over.'"[31]

Realistically, Allen was not going to leave his home in Palos Verdes Estates for a job fifteen hundred miles away. But he was willing, at Shortenhaus's request, to be on the search committee for a new coach. Allen recommended Dave Dolch, who had guided Bowie State in Maryland to a 9-2-1 season and a spot in the NCAA Division 2 playoffs, after taking over a program in 1986 that had lost twenty straight games. During a meeting in Washington, Dolch told Allen that, if he accepted the job, "he'd like coach Allen to pay us a visit," according to Shortenhaus.[32]

With Dolch on board, Shortenhaus suggested that Allen return for at least a day.[33] "What they thought I'd do is come back and ride around in a car and accept a plaque and say a few words to the team before I go home," Allen said at the time. "I said, 'If I come back, I'm going to come back for two-a-days and really work with the team, try to raise money for the college, and go all out because I don't want to be associated with the team losing the opener.'

"I felt and knew I could help them. Every job I've ever had was a rebuilding job: Morningside, Whittier, Redskins, Rams, Chicago Blitz, Arizona Wranglers. They were all teams from scratch and had been down. I went to Morningside because they took a chance on me forty-one years ago. That was my first head coaching job. I met Etty there and got my start there. That's why I went back there."[34]

To repay Morningside for launching his career, Allen volunteered to coach for two weeks to prepare the Chiefs (formerly the Maroons) for their 1989 season opener against Northwestern College of Iowa. The Red Raiders had finished 12-1 in 1988, losing only to Sioux Falls in the NAIA Division 2 playoffs. NFL Films sent a crew to Sioux City to document Allen's return, which he described as a combination of "*Rocky*, *Hoosiers*, and *Field of Dreams*," referring to three of the most highly acclaimed sports drama movies of the twentieth century.[35]

To inject the program with a fresh attitude, Allen suggested that the school outfit members of the football team with baseball caps emblazoned with "110%." Focusing mainly on defense and special teams, he oversaw two-a-day practices the first week and after-class drills once school began. On one play, he was blindsided, knocked to the ground, and broke a finger. But he refused to put it in a splint, and the next day hit the pad on the reactor, which teaches quick footwork and handwork by players. The other coaches were impressed with how the seventy-two-year-old man refused to let the injury detract from his coaching duties.

In meetings with the players, Allen listed six things they needed to do to become winners. "The last point was you have to get three people to believe in you if you're going to win," he explained. "You guys don't have much confidence because you haven't won. One is your coach. He has confidence in you, or you wouldn't be here. Two, GA, I put my initials down. The third guy is you. You've got to believe in yourself. If you have those three, you're going to win."[36]

Aside from coaching, Allen took part in speaking engagements, TV and radio interviews, autograph and photo sessions, and a banquet in his honor. He also visited hospitalized survivors of United Airlines Flight 232, which crashed during an emergency landing at the Sioux City airport on July 19, 1989, killing 111 people with 185 survivors.[37]

In the season opener, Morningside turned in a vintage George Allen performance before seven thousand home fans. The Chiefs recovered three fumbles, intercepted two passes, and blocked a punt in a 31–13 win over Northwestern. They also stopped Northwestern twice on fourth down inside Morningside's 10. The offense produced some big plays, too.

After the game, Morningside's coaches and players met at midfield and asked Allen to say something. "I told them, 'Hit hard and watch the good things happen.' We always used to put that on the board with the Redskins. They all cheered, and I said, 'Let's have three cheers for Morningside: hip hip hooray, hip hip hooray, hip hip hooray.' They gave me a game ball."[38] Allen gave that ball to a boy in a coma from injuries suffered in the crash of Flight 232.[39]

Not only was Allen instrumental in ending Morningside's fifteen-game losing streak, but he learned something about himself from his return to Sioux City: his hunger to coach was alive and well. "It showed me how much I missed it and how much I enjoyed it," he told Steve Guback in 1989. "But I'll tell you what. It was different from pro coaching because those guys were so receptive and so hungry. The fact that we won the game and played so well made a big difference. This was one of the most rewarding things I ever did in my life."[40]

Following his appearance at Morningside, which won its second game but lost its last nine that season, Allen received two offers from other teams to coach in 1990 without naming them.[41] Perhaps one of the offers was from a college that seemed like the unlikeliest landing spot for a man with his coaching pedigree, a school that just a few years prior was close to disbanding its football program.

After a 6-5 season in 1986, Long Beach State just outside of LA nearly dropped football when school president Stephen Horn announced that the boosters needed to raise $300,000 in one month, a goal they barely met. The program remained solvent in the coming seasons,[42] but they needed to improvise to make money. In both 1988 and 1989, in twelve-game seasons, the Long Beach State 49ers played four home games in order to earn percentages of the gate receipts of the host schools. When playing at home, they drew an average of 2,650 fans—among the smallest Division 1 attendance figures, at off-campus Veterans Memorial Stadium, an antiquated venue known as "The Tomb" with a capacity of about 12,000 and stands on one side.[43] Long Beach City College owned the stadium.

The 49ers also struggled on the field. They went 11-24 from 1987 to 1989 under Coach Larry Reisbig, who resigned following a 4-8 campaign in 1989, with a 2-5 record in the Big West Conference. The '89 season included ugly losses of 63–10 to Hawaii, 52–10 to Oregon, and 52–0 to conference champion Fresno State.

With the program on shaky financial ground and only one winning season in the past six years, athletic director Corey Johnson took steps to find a dynamic football coach. He originally considered Allen to be on the search committee for a new coach, before Allen told him he could help revive the program. "He led them on, saying, 'Hey, I may want to do this, I think I can do this,'" Bruce Allen said in hindsight.[44] Johnson and university president Curtis McCray then tossed a Hail Mary. They asked Allen, one of the most prominent names in the football coaching business, to take the reins of the 49ers' program.

Bruce Allen, a Phoenix-based sports agent at the time, represented his father in negotiations with the school. One day George asked his son to fly in from Phoenix and join him for a meeting near the Long Beach airport. Bruce was floored when he learned that his father was considering the job:

"I said, 'What are we doing?' He said, 'Don't tell your mom.' I said, 'Are you going to tell me who we're going to meet?' I really thought this was like a real estate or an investment deal. Then the athletic director of Long Beach State comes in. We're in the coffee shop. They're talking about how money has to be raised for the school because they're going to drop football. I'm just listening. I have no idea what they're talking about. But obviously they know each other and have had a few conversations. I thought they wanted to use my dad for a fundraiser. Dad was saying, 'You can't drop football. It's too important to the kids.'

"The athletic director said, 'We want your dad to be the head coach.'

I replied, 'You want my father to be the head coach at Long Beach State? When's the last time you had a winning season?' The guy laughed. I look over at my dad. He's looking at me sort of like my son would look at me when I'd say, 'You didn't go to class.' It was like he tricked me into coming by not telling me what this was about. I said, 'Tell me more about this plan that you guys have come up with that obviously my mother has no idea about.' They said, 'You're here to look at some documents.' I said, 'I'm here to look at some documents? Are you kidding?'

"I remember saying, 'I have to talk to my dad. Excuse us.' I said [to him], 'Are you kidding? I'm shocked. How did this all start?' It was like your dad telling you all of a sudden, 'I'm dating someone other than your mom.' I asked him how long he'd been having these conversations. He's like, 'I think I can do it.' I'm like, 'Dad, Long Beach State? Do you want me to call a school like USC or UCLA? What about Arizona State or Arizona? Do you want to go to a big college? I'm sure they'll be interested.' He said, 'No, [Long Beach State is] going to drop football. We're going to save the program.' Corey Johnson just hit the right chords with Dad."[45]

Allen consulted several of his coaching peers on the Long Beach State opening. Hank Stram and three-time national champion Barry Switzer of Oklahoma, both of whom made guest appearances with Allen on the TV show *Coach* starring Craig T. Nelson in December 1989, advised him not to accept the position, as did Bo Schembechler, who won 80 percent of his games and two Rose Bowls while at Michigan from 1969 to 1989.[46]

Some of Allen's other friends encouraged him to go for it, among them actor Dabney Coleman and real estate developer Bill Harris.[47] Longtime Michigan athletic director Don Canham also supported his taking the job.[48]

Coleman, who gained stardom in the early 1980s with key supporting roles in such hit movies as *9 to 5*, *Tootsie*, and *WarGames*, met Allen for the first time at a restaurant in Los Angeles when he was out of coaching following his stint in the USFL. Coleman knew instantly that Allen belonged in coaching. He told him it didn't matter where he ended up, joking that he had to coach even if his destination was Division 3 Hampden-Sydney College in Virginia.

"All he talked about was football," Coleman said of his initial meeting with Allen. "That's all he thought about. I said, 'You've got to coach football again.' He said, 'I think about it every day.'"

After receiving the offer from Long Beach State, Allen asked Coleman what he should do. "I said, 'I think you should take it,'" Coleman recalled.

"He said, 'I think I will. But don't tell Etty I said that.' She didn't want him to coach anymore."[49]

With that, George Allen dove head-first into a job that he called "the toughest in America." Not concerned about the money, he agreed to a three-year contract at $100,000 per year. In addition to coaching, he pledged to help raise funds for the school's athletic foundation, with McCray expecting Allen to generate $1 million by the end of his second season, through private endowments.[50] A contract squabble nearly prevented Allen from taking the job, so the school agreed to pay him an extra $10,000 so he could get a driver to transport him twenty miles from his home in Palos Verdes Estates to Long Beach and back. Such proximity was a key reason he accepted the job.[51]

Allen's hiring injected the program with national exposure from media, mostly perplexed about why a man with such a successful coaching history—most of it in the pros—would accept a job that appeared to be beneath him and at Long Beach State to boot, one of the worst of the 106 Division 1 programs. In the biggest media event to date in the school's history, more than two hundred people, including journalists, athletic department personnel, excited 49ers boosters and fans, and friends and former players witnessed his introductory 49ers press conference at the Long Beach Airport Marriott on December 19, 1989.[52] *Sports Illustrated*, *The Sporting News*, ESPN, ABC, and CBS were among the national media in attendance.[53]

"I'm not a miracle worker," said Allen, sporting a 49ers baseball cap. "I took this job because it's so tough and different. I'm a teacher, and I've carried that all through life. The main reason I'm here is to get a struggling football program off the ground. It'll take a little time. I can't trade for a Billy Kilmer."[54]

He commented further that "to win, you have to get people who want more out of life than a paycheck. I didn't come here for the money. I can make more in two weeks of speaking engagements than I can by coaching here for a year or more."[55]

In typical George Allen style, he asked the crowd to give "three big hip, hip, hoorays" for the 49ers.[56]

Just like media and fans, Allen's decision to coach at Long Beach State shocked his family. Etty jokingly threatened to start smoking again and feared that his workaholic style might cause him to drop dead on the sidelines. His son, Greg, a psychologist, offered to give him free counseling sessions.[57] Bruce told him he must like misery. At first, Jennifer was also a bit confused by his decision. But today, she explains why her father, using his own logic, seized the opportunity.

"I was excited for my dad to return to coaching, especially at the college level. My dad was a teacher foremost, and when he began his work at Long Beach State, he was most inspired by the way he could encourage and mentor these athletes. The team didn't have a winning history. That was all the more enticing to him. As he would say, 'The greater the challenge, the greater the reward.' For him, the task was to be a teacher and guide for this team, and that in itself would lead to victory for these young men, be it on or off the field."[58]

The next chapter of George Allen's coaching career would present his most difficult challenge. But no matter how formidable the task or how crazy it sounded, he felt he needed to again meet his calling in life. He just needed to coach.

24

An "Almost Impossible" Task

The scene was forlorn, especially when considering George Allen's stature as one of the most accomplished football coaches in the business. His office in one of the old physical education buildings on Long Beach State's campus was drab, part of a small converted classroom with a couple of chairs for visitors and a few shelves for papers and books. The *Washington Post* described it as "slightly wider than Diron Talbert's wingspan and about as deep as four golf clubs laid end to end."[1] Allen thought it was smaller than his office from his first coaching stint four decades prior, at Morningside College. In reality, it was about the same size as everyone else's office on that corridor, except Allen had a connecting door to his secretary that made it seem a little more spacious. Plus, the office lacked air-conditioning, causing his loving wife, Etty, to envision the worst of what her septuagenarian husband might suffer in the sweltering Southern California summer temperatures.

"My wife, Etty, came by to visit me one day and went outside and broke down and cried," Allen told *Long Beach Press-Telegram* sports columnist Doug Krikorian in July 1990. "She worries too much about me. She calls me three, four times a day asking me how I feel. She thinks I'm going to suffer a severe heat stroke."[2]

That office was light years from the size, comfort, and amenities of Allen's executive suite at Redskin Park. But in a way, it spoke to how much he had sacrificed in prestige and ego just to coach one of the most woeful Division 1 football programs, as well as the lengths to which he was willing to go to satisfy his indefatigable desire to coach. But that's where he hunkered down in an attempt to lead the 49ers to football legitimacy, even at the age of seventy-two—perhaps the oldest person at the time to ever start coaching at the Division 1 level.[3]

Upon his arrival, several Long Beach State sports programs were making serious runs for national championships, including women's volleyball, women's basketball, softball, and baseball. But football was off the radar at one of the largest institutions in California's state university system; it had at the time a student body of 33,000. Students, residents in a city of 400,000, and the university's 125,000 alumni were finding other things to do on Saturdays than support a lowly football team at a school two miles from the Pacific Ocean and appropriately dubbed "The Beach." In 1989 the athletic department sold only 369 season tickets for its four home games at off-campus Veterans Memorial Stadium, where a total of 246 students showed up during the 4-8 season at the 12,000-seat venue.[4]

To make matters worse, school officials were not taking football seriously and were neglecting it in ways that any new coach would find maddening. Case in point: Long Beach State owned only eight footballs when Allen arrived. He immediately bought three dozen more.[5] Plus, there was no dedicated football meeting room; players gathered in the gym and in classrooms, and the old weightlifting and locker rooms were unsatisfactory for a Division 1 football program. In addition, the school's golf team sometimes used the football practice field as a driving range, leaving golf balls everywhere. Allen complained about that to athletic department authorities, who put a stop to it.[6]

But none of this should have surprised Allen, who knew what he was getting into upon embarking on this chapter in his legendary coaching career. In his mind, everything seemed "stacked" against him.[7] To him, it was an "almost impossible situation."[8] Speculation even surfaced that he would resign before his first game. But he insisted that the reason he took the job was because it would be so difficult.[9]

"I think he was just more frustrated above everything else, because he wanted to win," said Steve Janisch, a Long Beach State sports publicist who was assigned at Allen's request to follow the football team exclusively. "He wanted to establish a program. I don't want to say it was a pet project, but it was a source of pride for him that he was going to come in and try to build this program into something that was important. He understood the things that needed to be done. You've got to put money into it. You've got to have the facilities. Long Beach State just didn't have it at the time.

"But his eyes were wide open. He knew what the facilities were like. But he believed that he could help elevate things and get Long Beach State football to a level where it could compete. It was going to be a multiyear project."[10]

Still, this was Allen's first time on the college sidelines since his final season at Whittier in 1956. After a thirty-four-year layoff, could he prepare a group of teenagers and young adults for the grind of a football season and keep them focused and inspired? What's in it for a coach with the third-highest regular-season winning percentage in NFL history to take the reins of a college program that was on life support just a few years prior?

Those were some of the questions Ray Didinger of the *Philadelphia Daily News* asked when he swung by Long Beach State to interview Allen. This wasn't the first time Didinger had come in contact with the coach, as he had covered the Eagles in the eras of Mike McCormack (1973–75) and Dick Vermeil (1976–82). He remembered how "antsy" Allen was back then and how hard it was to keep his attention for more than five minutes.

"He was always so suspicious," Didinger said in looking back. "He always wanted to know who you were and who you worked for. If you worked for the paper in the city of the upcoming opponent, he wouldn't tell you anything because he was convinced you were a spy. He was absolutely convinced that whatever he told you, you were going to run back and tell the Eagles. That's total nonsense, but that's what he really believed."

When interviewing Allen at Long Beach State, Didinger didn't sense any of those phobias. He found the coach to be much more relaxed, and he felt humbled to be granted an hour-long, one-on-one interview. The two spoke in Allen's unspectacular office, which Didinger compared to a Division 3 setup. The wall was barren, he remembered, except for a picture of Allen with Richard Nixon during the president's visit to Redskin Park in 1971 and a photo of Allen being carried off the field after the Redskins beat the Cowboys in the '72 NFC Championship Game.

Didinger sensed no bitterness in Allen about not receiving any NFL head coaching offers since the Rams fired him after two exhibition games in '78: "If anything, he seemed quite energized. The opportunity to coach a program, regardless of where it was, sort of gave meaning and purpose to his life again. Whether it was coaching the Redskins or coaching Long Beach State, it was clear that he just needed to coach. He needed to have a scoreboard in his life. It just so happened that the scoreboard was there. It wasn't at RFK. It was at Long Beach State. There was a smaller crowd and a lesser program, and he wasn't going to get an invitation to the Rose Bowl. But that didn't matter. It was just the fact that there was a game to play that Saturday, and that was all he needed to get him out of bed in the morning.

"He was sort of adrift when he wasn't coaching. He had a lot of friends in football, and he knew a lot of guys who were friends that were coaching here and there. He would visit and consult with them. He continued to watch games and film. He always had his toe in the water for sure. But he needed to have a team of his own. He needed to have a program of his own. He would have welcomed almost any opportunity, but nobody came calling until Long Beach State did. The program was virtually dead, and [the school] figured this was one last attempt for relevancy. They said, 'George Allen. Why not.'"[11]

As for assistants, Allen inherited five from the previous staff, but he requested more slots to meet the NCAA maximum of nine at the time. He had liked big coaching staffs all the way back to his days in the NFL, so every position and every detail could be covered. Among the assistants he recruited was a man he knew well, Raiders' Hall of Fame cornerback Willie Brown (hired as defensive backs coach), and another he met through his son, Bruce: Harvey Hyde, former University of Nevada, Las Vegas (UNLV), head coach (hired as associate head coach and running backs coach). Allen also brought in Pete Kettela (receivers coach), who had coached with him in the USFL in '84.

The hiring of Brown surprised Allen's buddy, Raiders owner and general manager Al Davis. Brown had coached the Raiders' defensive backs from '79 to '88. Davis was preparing to bring him back in 1990, but Allen signed him first.[12]

Hyde, Allen's go-to guy for recruiting, had coached UNLV to a 26-19-1 record from '82 to '85, with a California Bowl win and Pacific Coast Conference Coach of the Year honors in 1984. The school fired him after the '85 season because some of his players encountered off-the-field troubles.[13]

Allen, too, had a hand in recruiting. But he often found it to be a maddening process, especially when trying to lure players to a low-level Division 1 football school with an unremarkable program. He once learned that the girlfriend of a potential recruit was about to give birth and went with Brown to a hospital to sign him. He caught up to the player, who told him his girlfriend was going to have a girl. "I tell him, great, she can be a cheerleader one day for Long Beach," Allen told the *Long Beach Press-Telegram*. "Unfortunately, the player chose to go elsewhere.

"The last time I recruited players was in 1956 at Whittier. I was recruiting against schools like Occidental and Redlands and Pomona. Now, I've been going head-to-head against schools like USC, UCLA, Washington State and Fresno State. Tough. Real tough. They all have stadiums, and the kids seem to like that."[14]

Plus, "Trader George" was unable to deploy the tactic he had used so successfully to fortify his teams in the pros: trading players. However, as outlandish as it sounded, he envisioned a regional draft in which each school could have up to forty picks and one player could be picked by as many as four schools.[15] Interestingly, his idea was similar in concept to the NCAA Transfer Portal launched in 2018, which allows football players to transfer from one school to another with maximum visibility, organization, and compliance, without being handcuffed by the restrictions of the past.

Allen had long supported freedom of player movement, siding with the players in their fight for free agency in the NFL. But under the watchful eye of the NCAA, with its byzantine rules that drove him batty, he couldn't replicate his maverick approach on the college level. "The rule I've followed is if it makes sense to do something, it must be a violation," he told the sports daily *The National* in February 1990.[16] Tommy McVean, his good friend and the equipment manager of his Redskins and USFL teams, remembered voicing a word of caution: "I said, 'Coach, as much as we pushed the envelope in the NFL, you know the NCAA is going to be watching you like a hawk.'"[17]

Allen's initial recruiting class included at least fifteen junior college transfers, one of whom was Chris Tsangaris, who started at middle linebacker for two seasons at Allan Hancock College in Santa Maria, California. At first, Tsangaris debated between transferring to Washington State in the Pac-10 and Long Beach State, both of which offered him a scholarship. He was leaning toward Washington State. But upon Allen's hiring in December 1989, he became intrigued with the opportunity to play for a defensive mastermind.

"One of my buddies signed at Long Beach State," Tsangaris recalled. "He was like, 'Before you start on your recruiting trips, come here so we can be together one more time.' So by the time I agreed to make my first visit to Long Beach so I could hang out with my buddy, they hired George Allen. Everything changed. I was like, 'Oh my God, I was just going up for a good time. Now I get to meet Coach Allen.'"[18]

Tsangaris became well acquainted with Allen at a meeting of the coach's first class of potential recruits. Allen, he remembered, asked all of the players in the room to name their No. 1 hero. While everyone mentioned their top football hero, Tsangaris, who is from Montreal and grew up addicted to hockey, shared the name of his childhood idol: Chris Nilan, who played in the NHL for thirteen seasons (1979–92), including ten with the Montreal Canadiens. Nilan was no scoring machine, with single-season career highs of 21 goals and 37 points. But Tsangaris admired him for his tough-guy image and propensity to fight. Nicknamed "Knuckles," he won a Stanley Cup with the Canadiens in '86.

Tsangaris was uncertain at first whether it was worth mentioning Nilan's name. "I'm asking myself why I should bring it up," he said. "To be honest, I'm not going to this school anyway. I have some other aspirations and bigger-name schools. But I just threw out the name of a random hockey player, a fourth liner, and said, 'Who cares, right.' The next thing I know, Coach Allen is slamming the table with both of his hands. He stood up and gave everybody in the room a full accounting of Chris Nilan's background, his role, and the importance of what he did. I'm just sitting there in shock thinking, 'How is this happening? How does he know everything I know about Chris Nilan?'"

Tsangaris committed to play for the 49ers. That season, he was Allen's defensive quarterback on the field, calling signals in the mold of Allen's field generals from the past like linebackers Bill George, Jack Pardee, Chris Hanburger, and Stan White.

Allen also took a special interest in a player who came to Long Beach State in 1987: receiver Mark Seay. Following the eighth game of his '88 sophomore season, Seay was shot by a suspected gang member at a kids' Halloween party in Los Angeles. As he shielded his two-year-old niece from the gunfire in a heroic act, a bullet pierced one of his kidneys and stopped about an inch from his heart.

Doctors removed his damaged kidney but left the bullet lodged about an inch from his heart. With thirty-one catches for 480 yards at the time, he sat out the final four games of the '88 season. He thought he was ready to return in 1989, thinking a flak jacket would protect his other kidney. But the university refused to let him play, believing the risk of injury to his remaining kidney was too great.

Seay took the school to court seeking an immediate injunction so he could play. He lost the hearing, although the judge said he could revisit it at some point. He was forced to take a medical redshirt in '89.

Allen's hiring in December 1989 made Seay even more enthusiastic about returning to play. "I thought, 'Man, I would love to play for Coach Allen,'" he recalled. "I knew of his background with the Rams and Redskins. The assistant coaches told me they were going to talk to Coach Allen on my behalf to see if they can get me back out there. I was happy about that."[19]

Allen came to see qualities in Seay beyond his talents as wide receiver.

He considered him a good human being and dedicated himself to allow the university to let him play again. Once, Seay remembered, Allen told him he would get him back on the field even if he had to go to the president of the United States.

"This was the first time since I got shot where I actually had somebody who really was going to be able to pull the trigger to get me back out there again," Seay said, no pun intended. "That's the first time I heard that in two years. I was so excited. I just knew it was going to happen. I felt in my soul that he was going to be the one to help me. I told him I believed he was a godsend for me because only Coach Allen could have brought me out of that situation."

Seay said Allen lobbied on his behalf at a meeting that included Long Beach State president Curtis McCray and athletic director Corey Johnson. In April 1990 the university agreed to an out-of-court settlement that allowed Seay to play if he cleared medical tests. He signed a waiver absolving the school of liability if he injured his functioning kidney.

Seay was chosen as a team captain that season.[20] He posted team highs of 48 catches and 771 receiving yards, with 4 touchdown receptions.[21] Following Long Beach State, he played five years in the NFL, with highs of 58 catches, 645 receiving yards, and 6 touchdowns in 1994, when his San Diego Chargers reached Super Bowl XXIX. In a 49–26 loss to the 49ers, Seay caught 7 passes and a 2-point conversion. None of that likely would have been possible without George Allen.

Meanwhile, in keeping with his responsibilities to help raise money for the 49ers' athletic department, Allen led a fundraiser that spoke volumes about his name power. Nearly 1,200 49ers enthusiasts attended a $100 a plate dinner in Long Beach under the wings of the Spruce Goose, the massive wooden flying boat built by Howard Hughes's aircraft company during World War II. The dinner raised $117,000 through gate receipts, with a sports memorabilia auction providing additional income.[22] Merle Makings, the Long Beach State athletic department's marketing director, helped drive the ticket sales. Allen knew Makings through the USFL's Arizona Wranglers and had lured him to Long Beach State.

"This is the biggest sports dinner in the history of Long Beach—1,200 people," Don Dyer, a longtime 49ers fundraiser, said at the event. "There's a certain mystique to George's name. It's going to be fascinating around here for as long as he stays."[23]

ESPN sports journalist and commentator Roy Firestone emceed the fundraiser. Guests included actors Walter Matthau and Dabney Coleman, actress Cathy Lee Crosby, Long Beach mayor Ernie Kell, and former Allen players Billy Kilmer, Larry Brown, Dave Butz, and Jeff Severson, who had played at Long Beach State, as well as Roman Gabriel, Deacon Jones, Tom Mack, and Dick Bass.

"He looks alive, excited again," Kilmer said, after posing for a photo with Allen.[24]

With a touch of sarcasm targeting Allen's propensity to trade for NFL veterans, Kilmer warned, "He's got to remember he can't trade freshmen for seniors in this league. The NCAA won't let him do it. And scholarships are not draft choices."[25]

The fundraiser exemplified how Allen was single-handedly raising the visibility of not only Long Beach State's football program but the school itself. He generated about $4 million in publicity for the university in the spring of 1990 alone, a figure based on the projected cost of ads about him, of a similar size or duration, that ran in print media or on television shows. That number was expected to approach $10 million by the start of the season.[26] If social media had existed at the time, those estimates would have been much higher.

"More so than the actual dollars, I think there was a great feeling for having Coach Allen at Long Beach State," Dan Radakovich, a Long Beach State assistant athletic director at the time, said in retrospect. "The things that he brought vaulted the public persona of the institution forward. He was a great football coach, and everybody wants to be successful. His ability to identify talent and recruit and bring players in to make the team more competitive was the biggest reason to bring him here. The fact that he was a celebrity around the country was also a real positive. At the time, it was hard to gather crowds for our home games. So having Coach Allen and some of the people that he brought in and his methodology of coaching created a lot of positive energy around the program."[27]

Hope was in the air when the 49ers gathered for spring practice, which marked Allen's first true look at his new team. His players caught a glimpse of him, too. While stretching, they witnessed a man doing 60-yard sprints on the nearby practice field. This wasn't some college track star. Allen turned seventy-three years old on April 29, although media noted that he was seventy-one or seventy-two. Another year older, yet the former chairman of the President's Council on Physical Fitness and Sports was maintaining his daily running schedule of three to five miles a day, which helped free him of the tremendous anxiety that accompanied the job.

Today, Pepper Jenkins, a second-team All–Big West Conference 49ers defensive end in 1989, can still picture Allen motoring down the field during spring practice: "We were out there for about an hour and fifteen minutes. He wasn't running like an old man. This guy was moving. We're like, 'Oh no. If he's running like that, what the hell do you think he's going to do to us?' We were all in our late teens and early twenties. It was just the message that sent to me. He was no talker. He was a doer. That was my impression of him. After he finished, he came over and talked to us. He explained what he was looking for and what he expected out of us."[28]

The master motivator was at it again, setting an example to inspire his young players. He wanted them to see that he drove himself hard. In a letter to the team, he asked thought-provoking questions similar to those he had presented to other players in the past:

> Do you have a drive for greatness?
> Do you have a desire to be successful?
> Do you want to be a champion?
> Do you have goals established for education?

"Everyone has the will to win . . . but the real winners have the will to prepare and win," Allen wrote. "The power of belief is the greatest source for human achievement. Develop these intangible characteristics that will help you become a believer."

> Believe in
> 1. yourself
> 2. teammates
> 3. coaches[29]

Signs with Allen's inspirational sayings were posted all over the athletic department:

> EVERYBODY TAKE CARE OF THEIR OWN JOB—GEORGE ALLEN
> HIT HARD AND WATCH THE GOOD THINGS HAPPEN—GEORGE ALLEN
> IS WHAT I AM DOING OR ABOUT TO DO GETTING ME CLOSER TO OUR OBJECTIVE . . . WINNING?—GEORGE ALLEN

Promoting a similar theme, Allen displayed a placard on his office desk that read, "Everything here is waiting for you to improve."[30] He tried to build a sense of identity among his players on defense with T-shirts proclaiming, "I play tenacious defense for George Allen."[31] He also designed a new helmet logo that resembled his Redskins helmet design from nearly two decades earlier. Instead of brown and gold helmets with a decal saying "49ers" on the side, the players would sport shiny black helmets with gold, black, and white stripes down the middle and three decals: "LB," "togetherness," and one for the city of Long Beach.

"There's nothing wrong with [the] 49ers," he told the *Long Beach Press-Telegram*. "But I think of the San Francisco 49ers. Long Beach means more to me. I want Long Beach to be proud of the team, and the players to be proud of Long Beach."[32]

Allen hoped his players, too, would pick up on the incredible pace he was keeping up to transform them into a winner. The nation's oldest Division 1 coach was putting in his standard twelve- to fourteen-hour days that sometimes lasted as late as midnight. With a singular focus on football, he sometimes forgot to eat. One of his secretaries, Julie Allen (no relation), left a jar of peanut butter on his desk after he skipped meals.[33] His other secretary, Patty Dalton, took calls from Etty reminding him to eat.[34]

Sports publicist Steve Janisch had a front-row view of Allen's industriousness. "I always had a pretty good work ethic," Janisch said. "But his work ethic was astronomical. He was there every day early in the morning, stayed until late at night. He was 100 percent focused. He expected everyone around him to kind of do the same thing, too, to be as dedicated and focused as he was. But he wasn't asking anyone to do anything that he wasn't doing himself. Most of us were all on board during that time. But they were long days. I guarantee you that. It was 24/7 once you're in the season, but he kind of demanded that and expected that from everyone else. I was more than happy to do it."[35]

With training camp a few weeks away, Allen took a trip down memory lane when he returned to the nation's capital to coach in a charity flag football game between retired players from the Redskins and Cowboys on June 23, 1990. The old faces were there, including Washington's Billy Kilmer, Diron Talbert, Dave Butz, and John Riggins, along with Cowboys players Roger Staubach, Harvey Martin, and Charlie Waters. Before more than ten thousand fans at RFK Stadium, Allen watched as an old adversary and a player he and Talbert loved to antagonize, Staubach, threw five touchdown passes and ran for another in a 42–22 Cowboys win. Allen was the only participant in the game still active in football.[36]

His main focus, of course, was on Long Beach State, where he had spearheaded a series of important upgrades to the football program since coming on board. The school spent $120,000 on improvements in equipment and facilities, with $70,000 coming from the Spruce Goose fundraising dinner.[37] The changes included revitalized weight and locker rooms, a new dedicated team meeting room, and an enclosed practice facility with a protective tarp. Allen also envisioned the construction of an on-campus twenty-five-thousand-seat stadium that he hoped would improve attendance figures and the recruitment of talented players.

"Building the stadium was an important objective," Bruce Allen said. "It would have had a sponsor's name on it. Dad met with various companies to pay for the cost."[38]

Once training camp kicked off on August 8, media requests to interview Allen accelerated. Outlets such as ESPN, CNN, the Financial News Network, and the Sports News Network all reported on his unconventional return to coaching, as did the *Washington Post*, the *Chicago Tribune*, the *Dallas Morning News*, and *Sports Illustrated*.

Janisch said Allen, never a fan of the media, complained at times about having to do so many interviews. But once the camera lights came on and reporters scribbled notes, he was great about it.

"He knew his stature was going to bring publicity, and that was important," Janisch said. "My job wasn't hard to get people because I had reporters calling me 24/7 to do interviews. Anyone and everyone was calling."[39]

Long Beach State's roster included eleven returning starters and thirty-one returning lettermen. The coaches were counting on senior Bobby San Jose to be the starting quarterback, but he became ineligible.[40] So Allen named 6-foot-3, 185-pound junior college transfer Todd Studer, who impressed in spring practice but had never thrown a pass in major college football. His top receivers included Mark Seay and Sean Foster, a first-team All–Big West player in '89. On defense, Allen moved Pepper Jenkins, a senior, to weak outside linebacker to make better use of his speed and quickness.[41]

Allen's assistant coaching staff included three former NFL players with Super Bowl rings: Willie Brown; two-time All-Pro defensive end Cedrick Hardman, who played ten seasons for the 49ers and two for the Raiders;

and Mike Davis, a teammate of Brown who played eight seasons for the Raiders and one for the Chargers. Hardman and Davis were volunteer coaches. With that trio, Allen hoped his players would learn from players who had reached the pinnacle of the sport. He also wanted recognizable names on his staff to raise the visibility of the program.

Allen's invitation to Hardman is worth noting. Hardman produced one of the most infamous plays in Allen's coaching history, tackling Redskins receiver Roy Jefferson on an end around for a 9-yard loss in a '71 playoff game and spoiling a chance for them to go up by two touchdowns right before halftime. The 49ers won the game, 24–20. That play will forever be linked to President Nixon, who told Allen before the game that he wanted to see a reverse to Jefferson.

Allen also invited a few of his old NFL players to speak to the team: Dick Butkus, Roman Gabriel, and two members of his Fearsome Foursome defensive line in LA, Deacon Jones and Rosey Grier. Chris Tsangaris and his teammates soaked in their presence: "Who else in the country got to be exposed to those legends?" Tsangaris asked rhetorically. "It was just unreal."[42]

According to Dan Radakovich, "There were some incredible opportunities for the student-athletes to meet and have face time with some great [NFL players] and other folks in the community because George had great relationships with them. It was really interesting to walk out to practice and see who might be there on a given day."[43]

In the eyes of Shayne Schroeder, the school's sports information director, Allen loved the young men he was coaching: "I think it rejuvenated him quite a bit, to be honest, because he had been out of coaching about six years. So he thought this was a great opportunity. I don't think he was doing it for a fortune, clearly. He already had that. I think he just wanted to be back in football and be a part of something."[44]

Although Allen was at least fifty years older than his players, his boyish personality and innocent, youthful enthusiasm likely helped them relate to their coach. "He was like a kid sometimes," Jenkins said. "You could just see the passion that he had for the game."[45]

Did the players gravitate to Allen right away? "Absolutely," Schroeder remembered. "I don't think they needed to be schooled on who he was, even though he was much older. That was very well known. He hired big-name people like Willie Brown and Cedrick Hardman, which added a little more excitement to the program. They were visible on campus. I don't think there was any jealousy from any other sports that this attention was going to football because [the other coaches] all realized that what's good for football is good for Long Beach State."[46]

But for Allen, something differed about working with this group that he hadn't experienced since he last coached at the college level thirty-four years prior. He was accustomed to coaching mature players out of college, not naïve teenagers and young men in their early twenties. That dynamic created a challenge in itself. "I'm not used to players wearing earrings," he told the Long Beach Rotary Club before the season started. "I'm not used to players with ponytails. And I'm not used to women trainers. I've gotten rid of the first two."[47]

Bruce Allen recalled that his father "didn't understand the way they thought at that age. Learning that environment was brand new to him. Boy, did he jump on that. He wanted that. He wanted to learn how they think.

"He would go to the classrooms to see who was in the classes. It was his way of authentically caring for these guys, and who you are, and what you're going to be in the future. These are Long Beach State guys. It's not USC or Alabama, where they're hoping for an NFL career. But they're going through college getting a free education. So he was like, 'Take advantage of this.' He'd ask the players why they didn't go to class. The kid would say this and this and Dad was like, 'I didn't get that. What does he mean by this?' I'd have to explain to him a seventeen-year-old's mind-set. Not that I was an expert at it, but we'd just laugh about it."[48]

A few days before the season opener against Clemson, the *Long Beach Press-Telegram* ran a photo headlined "Gen. Allen Hits the Beach," with Allen dressed in military fatigues like Gen. Douglas MacArthur, supreme commander of U.S. forces in the southwest Pacific during World War II, in front of three of his players. Allen wore sunglasses and had a MacArthur-like wooden pipe in his mouth.[49] The cover of Long Beach State's 1990 football media guide featured a grinning Allen with his thumbs up above a familiar motto: "The Future Is Now!"[50]

That season, the 49ers would host six home games at Veterans Memorial Stadium, the most since 1969. The university sold nearly nine hundred season tickets, almost three times as many as the previous year.

All optimism aside, Big West Conference coaches picked the 49ers to finish fifth in the eight-team league.[51] Plus, it had dawned on Allen that the challenge of righting the program would be more arduous than he anticipated. He thought that coaching at Long Beach State was one of the five toughest Division 1 jobs.

"It's like the toughest Division 1 job in the country," he told the McClatchy News Service. "We almost dropped football. We don't have the support of the students or community. Facilities are lacking. We don't have our own stadium. We don't have any depth in players."

In the McClatchy article, Allen was asked why he took the job under such circumstances: "Because everyone said it was an impossibility. When about five people told me it was impossible, that's when I got interested."[52]

Allen knew his 49ers didn't have a fighting chance against Clemson, the 10th-ranked team in the country. The Tigers finished 10-2 in 1989, beat West Virginia in the Gator Bowl, and returned about fifty lettermen, including fifteen starters. He compared the game to heavyweight boxing champ "Mike Tyson fighting an amateur."[53] Not joking but prophetic, Allen called the 49ers "58-point underdogs" to Clemson.[54]

Before a hostile crowd of seventy-two thousand mostly orange-clad fans in Clemson's "Death Valley," the Tigers barely beat the spread: 59–0. It was a bloodbath. The 49ers never crossed Clemson's 45-yard line, gained 57 yards, rushed for fewer than 16, and turned the ball over three times. Seven players scored for Clemson in its highest scoring output since 1981.

Long Beach State just did what many other lower-level college programs do for a big payday. But Allen had opposed playing Clemson in the first place, even if playing the Tigers meant Long Beach State's athletic department would earn $250,000 ($183,000 net). "I don't think these types of games help the winner or the loser," he said after the loss to Clemson. "I don't want to be involved in any more games where we're totally outmanned."[55]

Bruce Allen, who was at the game, said, "After the Clemson game, he was so mad at college football. He asked, 'Why are we doing this? Why do you send these guys out to fly across the country just to be embarrassed like this?' He said, 'Next year I'll raise you $250,000 at a banquet so you don't do that to these guys, because it's not fair.'"[56]

A 0-1 record became 0-2 with a 27–13 nonconference road loss to Utah State, which led 17–0 in the first half. Not since Allen's first season at Whittier, in 1951, when the Poets lost their first four games, had any of his teams started so badly. Enough with the inspirational slogans and the other tactics he had used to indoctrinate his players with a winning mind-set. This time, he felt he needed to do something that would strike a nerve. After the loss to Utah State, he walked in on his players while they were in a meeting room. Mark Seay remembered what transpired next:

"Most of the guys were talking, and we were getting louder and louder. When he walked in, everybody just kept talking. He went to the front of the meeting room and started writing on the chalkboard. He spelled out, 'There's no I in team.' He underlined 'I' and 'team.' Then everybody became so quiet you could hear a pin drop. He said, 'We lost the game. We're losers. We're losers, you see.' He said it with meaning, but at the same time he was very calm about it. But you could tell he was upset. He said, 'There's nothing good about losing. When you lose, you're not supposed to like it. You've got to hate it. It's a beautiful day outside, but when you lose, it's an ugly day. You have a beautiful wife at home. But when you lose, your wife is not that beautiful. You've got to hate losing!'

"That was the eye-opening introduction to looking at ourselves as a team and saying to ourselves that we lose because we've accepted losing, because we never took losing to that degree. That was the beginning stage of what we were not conscious about. We became conscious that day of being a loser. He allowed us to get to a place where we couldn't run anymore from where we were."[57]

Nothing changed in the win column, as the 49ers fell to 0-3 with a 38–20 nonconference road loss to San Diego State. This time, they surrendered a 21–0 lead but mounted a comeback to trail by 8 in the third quarter. But they came no closer.

San Diego State piled up 514 yards, following Utah State's 475 and Clemson's 418 for a total of 1,407 yards through the first three games—not exactly the stingy defense for which George Allen's teams were reputed. On offense, Todd Studer showed improvement against San Diego State with 268 passing yards and a touchdown, but the 49ers' running game was again nonexistent. They also lost the ball on a fumbled punt return for the second straight week to add to ten turnovers through the first three games.

With Long Beach State at 0-3, Seay recalled being "so embarrassed as a team and at the effort we were putting forth for Coach Allen. I was hurting because I wanted to make Coach Allen proud. I wanted us to make him proud. For the first time, we couldn't say it was the coaching. We had to look at ourselves."[58]

Seay did something uncharacteristic at halftime of the San Diego State game. "I lead between the lines," he said. "But I was forced to say something as a player. As one of the leaders on the team, I just felt like I owed it to Coach Allen to step up and speak out. I almost went into tears. I remember saying how blessed we are, and what an opportunity we have to go out and play as a team and play as one. If we do that, we can win this game. Then I went into talking about my own personal testimony that everyone could relate to because they remembered when that happened to me. I told them that I didn't think I was going to have the opportunity that I have now and how lucky we were to have this opportunity as people and as members of a team. But we need to play like it, and we're not playing like it."

In an outstanding effort that day, Seay caught eight passes for 128 yards. Out of breath with seconds remaining, he squatted down on the sidelines away from his teammates and stared at the ground, contemplating the demoralizing 0-3 start. The next thing, he saw some feet and felt a pat on the back.

"It was Coach Allen. He goes, 'You did good. You did good. You did good. We needed that. Now we're going to start winning.' I said, 'Huh?' But don't you know, we did. We started winning after that."

Seay didn't know whether Allen was referring to his halftime speech or his statistical output. But in their first home game, the 49ers delivered a solid all-around effort in a 28–7 conference win over Pacific before 5,366 fans at Veterans Memorial Stadium. Studer played his best game thus far, completing 18 of 29 passes for 296 yards and 3 touchdowns. The defense yielded 302 yards, far below the 469-yard average through the first three games, and 1 touchdown.

In an emotional locker room, Long Beach State center Joshua Schwager gave Allen the game ball. He handed it to Seay, who caught a team-high 5 passes for 64 yards. "He inspires me the way he plays with a handicap, and he inspires the team," Allen said of his top receiver.

On the victory, Allen said, "It seems like we've been waiting forty years to win this game. I just can't believe it. This is better than an NFL win. I'm going to have to pinch myself tomorrow to make sure it's real."[59]

The 49ers made it two straight with a 21–20 victory at home over Division 1-AA Boise State. Studer led a game-winning 80-yard drive that ended with a 10-yard scoring pass to one of his other talented receivers, Sean Foster. The extra point accounted for the winning margin. Now, riding a surge of momentum, the 2-3 49ers were favored in their next game, another conference outing at home. Granted, it was against a 0-4 New

Mexico State team with twenty-one straight losses. But Long Beach State took care of business with a 31–27 win.

With three straight victories for the first time since '85, the 49ers had improved to 3-3, 2-1 in the Big West Conference. Allen praised his players for not folding when they were winless. "Three in a row, holy Moses," he said. "I feel drained because I know we could have lost it."[60]

Studer provided a steady hand during the winning streak, averaging seventeen completions for 275 yards. His key target was Seay, the team's leading receiver after six games with twenty-five catches for 329 yards and a touchdown, the same pace he was on statistically when he was shot after eight games in '88. On defense, players like linebacker Pepper Jenkins; lineman Ed Lair, who posted a team-high ten sacks by season's end; free safety Shawn Wilbourn; and Chris Tsangaris stood out on an improved unit. Wilbourn, Jenkins, and Tsangaris were the team's leading tacklers in 1990.

During the week, the defense practiced against the scout team with talented players in running back Terrell Davis and quarterback Mike McCoy, both of whom were recruited by Allen's staff and later made their mark in the NFL. Davis rushed for 7,607 yards in a seven-year NFL career with Denver and won two Super Bowls, including Super Bowl XXXII when he rushed for 157 yards and three touchdowns in a 31–24 win over the Packers and earned MVP honors. He's in the Hall of Fame today. After a season at Long Beach State, McCoy transferred to Utah, where he threw for 7,409 yards and forty-nine touchdowns over three seasons. He has since coached in the NFL, including four seasons as head coach of the Chargers (2013–16).

Allen's optimism and upbeat demeanor keyed the 49ers' 1990 turnaround as well. "It was just his ten weeks of positive reinforcement," Tsangaris remembered. "The coolest thing is the ten goals he would establish. We would regularly go through those to start off the week's meetings. We recapped the last week and determined that we accomplished this or didn't accomplish that and how do we accomplish that. He was incredible at communicating that. We used those ten markers to judge ourselves and figured out what we needed to work on to make sure we got all ten. If we achieved all ten, we would be successful, and if we didn't get at least seven of the ten, there's no way we would win.

"It was objective based. If you get these markers taken care of, good things will happen. You buy into it. You're hit over the head with positive reinforcement and objective goals to meet, so eventually you start making that happen."[61]

The 6-foot-2, 240-pound Tsangaris came off the bench the first three games. But he moved into the starting lineup when senior Nick Pantuso suffered a pinched nerve in practice.[62] As a starter, he spent hours during the week in Allen's office preparing for the next opponent. To nobody's surprise, Allen's primary concentration during game week was on the defense. He came to rely on Tsangaris to lead his defensive strategies on game day.

Tsangaris witnessed the meticulousness with which Allen plotted for each opponent. "His whole angle was preparation, and literally knowing every inch of [an opponent's] game plan was huge for him," Tsangaris recalled. "But the way he had it programmed, and the way he presented it, was very systematic. It wasn't just overwhelming amounts of information. But literally the preparation he put into it with the middle linebacker calling the plays was unreal.

"I'm talking about [the ball] on their 30, left hash mark, this is what they're running. That was it. We just went from there, and 95 percent of the time he was correct. He was a mastermind at breaking down the other team's offense. By Wednesday and Thursday, you're really dialing things in and realizing this is what they're doing."

The strategizing in Allen's office was often interrupted by someone calling to speak with the popular football coach. Ronald Reagan, famed singer-actor Frank Sinatra, and many active and former NFL coaches and administrators were among those who called, Tsangaris remembered.

"I almost became numb to it," he said. "Imagine a twenty-two-year-old kid from Canada sitting there and not even paying attention to Frank Sinatra. That's how often they were happening. When they would call, [Allen] would be visibly upset and say, 'Dang it.' He just didn't want people to interrupt him while he was studying film. But he knew it would be important to take these calls, so he would stop and say, 'Quiet. Don't say anything.'"[63]

On the field, the 3-3 49ers eyed a serious test to improve their winning streak. They were returning to the road to face 3-2-1 conference foe San Jose State, which was only a few points shy of a 6-0 mark. Allen said the Spartans featured "Pac-10-caliber players and experience."[64]

Not since 1983 had Long Beach State won four straight games. It wasn't to be in 1990, as San Jose State romped to a 46–29 win. The Spartans piled up 614 yards. The following week, two-time defending conference champion Fresno State improved to 6-1-1 and 3-0-1 in the conference with a 28–16 win over the 49ers in Fresno, California.

With his 49ers at 3-5 and three games to play, Allen was eyeing his first losing season since his Whittier Poets finished 3-6-1 in 1954. Both Seay and Tsangaris believe they and their teammates were unaware it had been more than three decades since he had experienced a losing record.

"All we knew is that we wanted to become addicted to winning instead of losing," Seay said. "He turned us on to accept winning. Nothing else matters. Only winning matters. Because of the good Lord upstairs and who Coach Allen was and what he meant to the game and how that [transformed] into helping people, the young men on the team, God just made sure that we finished the deal to keep him as a winning coach and not a losing coach, because he didn't deserve it."[65]

Perhaps the 49ers received divine intervention in their final trio of games, all at Veterans Memorial Stadium. They opened with a 37–35 conference win over Cal State Fullerton. Sean Cheevers kicked three field goals, including the game winner, with six seconds left. Long Beach State was staring at defeat to a team that would finish last in the conference at 0-7. But Lair recovered a fumble with about two minutes left, and the 49ers drove 41 yards to set up Cheevers's 20-yard field goal.

Next up, Long Beach State needed another last-minute miracle against Division 2 Cal State Northridge. With the 49ers trailing, 24–17, Studer threw a 21-yard touchdown pass to Jeff Exum, the 49ers' second-leading receiver that year, with 1:17 to play. Never known as a gambler, Allen decided to go for the 2-point conversion to take the lead. A defensive back deflected Studer's pass, but it landed in Seay's arms for a 25–24 win.

"Long Beach State hasn't had a winning season in five years," Allen said when asked what compelled him to go for 2. "And this gives us a chance, especially the seniors, to go out winners.

"This was the first successful two-point play of my career. I hope it was the last one."[66]

Astonished by the job Allen was doing, Doug Krikorian of the *Long Beach Press-Telegram* urged the Los Angeles Rams—3-5 at the time en route to a 5-11 season—to fire head coach John Robinson after the season and give Allen the job: "Absurd? Maybe so, but Allen is showing once again this season with his remarkable work at Long Beach State—he somehow has squeezed four wins out of personnel that should be winless—that he still has the knack for resurrecting moribund teams even though he is in his 70s. In fact, George Allen just might have no coaching equal in the 20th century when it comes to pulling off such a trick, having once upon a time injected life into such terminal entities as the Rams and Washington Redskins."[67]

It had come down to this: a Big West Conference clash between 5-5 Long Beach State and 4-6 UNLV. Before 4,649 fans, Studer threw three touchdown passes and the 49ers rushed for 231 yards—their largest single-game total since 1984—in a 29–20 triumph. Long Beach State built a 15-point fourth-quarter lead, a luxury after playing so many games decided in the last minute. Allen's wife and daughter watched from the stands and his sons Bruce and Greg, from the sidelines. As the clock wound down, the crowd serenaded the 49ers' coach with chants of "George, George, George." When it was all over, he took a ride on his players' shoulders reminiscent of the '63 NFL championship game and the '72 NFC Championship Game. Once he hit the ground, his players gave him a victory bath by dumping a full ice bucket on his back.

"Ouch, that's cold," he said with a wide grin.[68]

George Allen did it. What he had described before the season as an "almost impossible" task—achieving a winning campaign—did not prove insurmountable.[69] He finished with a 6-5 mark, the 49ers' first plus-.500 season since 1986, and a 4-3 and fourth-place finish in the conference, all improvements over their 4-8 overall, 2-5 conference record in 1989. Remarkably, only one other Division 1 team, Alabama, started out 0-3 and ended up with a winning record.

Allen also succeeded to an extent in reviving fan interest in the program. The 49ers won all six of their games played at Veterans Memorial Stadium, where attendance averaged 4,696 fans, a 77 percent increase over the '89 season but still too skimpy for a 12,000-seat venue.

Famed *Los Angeles Times* sports columnist Jim Murray, who wrote of Allen's prodigious talents while he coached the Rams from '66 to '70, noted that Long Beach State's football team had Allen's fingerprints all over it: "When Clemson, a powerhouse in the South, beat his Long Beach team, 59–0, most Allen-watchers nodded their heads sagely. When he quickly lost to Utah State, 27–13, and San Diego State, 38–20, it was freely predicted the 'Goodbye, George' signs would soon be hung out in the rooters' section. Then the team began playing like a George Allen team—

smart, dogged, relentless football. Undiscovered ability has always been a hallmark of an Allen team."[70]

Allen was mentioned in the media as the possible Big West Conference coach of the year. But first-year San Jose State coach Terry Shea, whose 9-2-1 Spartans finished first in the conference at 7-0, received that honor. Ten Long Beach State players earned all-conference recognition, with Jenkins and Lair on the first team and Seay, Wilbourn, and Cheevers on the second team.

"These players never gave up," Allen said at a season-ending news conference. "They played sixty minutes and gave 110% right down to the wire. They didn't give up on the field, and they didn't give up on the sidelines. I think as they walk around campus they can be proud that they are winners."[71]

In an article he wrote shortly after the season for *Sports Illustrated*, "My Most Gratifying Year," Allen explained that he loved how his "time-tested coaching techniques" worked just as well in 1990 as they had in his first year of coaching, forty-two years earlier. He learned that his Long Beach State players needed the same things his Morningside players needed in 1948: discipline, organization, motivation, togetherness, and love.

"We had to start all over with fundamentals," Allen wrote. "My staff and I taught stance and starts, blocking and tackling, all the things you teach a Pop Warner team. By our last game, in which we beat UNLV 29–20, my Forty-Niners were playing almost like a George Allen team.

"What my staff did was to help a bunch of good guys who were drifting aimlessly. We gave them things they desperately needed to be human beings. They are bigger, faster and stronger today than they were a year ago, but none of that would matter if they didn't also have character, dedication and loyalty."

Allen also wrote that he told his players they should highlight the winning season on their résumés.[72]

"He tried to teach them that this is your job interview," Bruce Allen said. "You're going to go after you're done at Long Beach State for a job interview. How do you want to present yourself? One, you want to look your best. Two, you want to say that you are successful. The way to show you are successful is by putting on your résumé that Long Beach State has had a winning season. That was one of his coaching points."[73]

For Allen, whose own résumé now showed twenty-one winning seasons in twenty-four years of head coaching, the 1990 season had been an emotional and physical grind. In the ensuing weeks, he gave no indication that he planned to resign. George Felix Allen was under the impression that his father was uncertain about coaching another season at Long Beach State. He recalled him saying that the school needed to provide better facilities for the football program.[74]

Steve Janisch saw Allen shortly before Christmas. With the news that West Texas State had dropped its football program, Allen asked Janisch to gather as many details as he could on the school's best players in hopes of recruiting some of them. Janisch drove to Allen's home in Palos Verdes Estates to give him a roster, statistics, and other information.

"He took me around his house, because that's the first time I had ever been there," Janisch recalled. "He seemed in great spirits. He was already talking about next year and looking forward to it."[75]

Hula Bowl officials invited Allen to coach in the annual college All-Star game in Hawaii on January 19.[76] For the nearby Rose Bowl in Pasadena, Long Beach State allowed Iowa's football team to use the school's football practice field to prepare to play Washington on New Year's Day. Allen, long fond of people from Iowa because of his ties to Morningside, took the lead on hosting the Hawkeyes.

"I'd never met coach Allen before, but I couldn't have been more impressed with the man in his dealings with us," Iowa coach Hayden Fry told the *Los Angeles Times*. "He's definitely from the old school, the way he checks up on details and asks if there is anything we need."[77]

Actor and good friend Dabney Coleman, a staunch supporter of Long Beach State's football program and the featured speaker at the team's 1990 season-ending banquet, spoke to Allen a few days before the end of the year. He said Allen invited him and his girlfriend to go to Hawaii for the Hula Bowl. Coleman also recalled Allen saying something else: "I'm not feeling so good."[78] Allen mentioned the same thing to longtime friend Bill Harris.[79] He told the Associated Press on December 27 that he hadn't been completely healthy since the ice-water drenching following the last game of the season.[80]

After the dousing, Allen stayed on the field awhile, celebrating with his players and answering questions from reporters, with temperatures in the 50s and a biting wind. He later boarded the bus back to Long Beach

State in his wet clothes.[81] A few weeks later, when Allen was helping Iowa prepare for the Rose Bowl in relatively cold weather, Pepper Jenkins saw him not wearing a jacket.[82]

Allen developed a cold and bronchitis. His doctor prescribed medication and advised him to abstain from exercising. He complied. "He hated to miss a workout," Harris recalled. "The last time I spoke to him, he said, 'Bill, I can't even get a workout in. I'm feeling so lousy. It's terrible.'"[83] On the morning of December 31, Etty exercised at a local gym. Upon returning just after noon, she found her husband sprawled on the kitchen floor of their home in Palos Verdes Estates. She performed CPR and called her son, Greg, a psychologist. He came to the house, but it was too late.[84]

George Allen had suffered a fatal heart attack.

The Allen family was devastated. Shock was also the universal reaction among his friends and current and former players, as well as Long Beach State officials, members of the media, and many other people who knew him and of him. Granted, he was seventy-three years old, but he was also a fanatic with exercising and healthy living. How could such a self-disciplined man with a body better conditioned than many people half his age—a man who took part in marathons, triathlons, and bike-a-thons and who did daily sets of push-ups and sit-ups—suddenly die?

Chris Tsangaris thought Allen's death was like a "bad dream." As a senior, Tsangaris was going to have Dick Butkus, the greatest middle linebacker of all time, as his position coach in 1991. Just before Christmas, Butkus had agreed to Allen's request to be an assistant coach in '91, but he changed his mind when Allen died.[85] Tsangaris was watching the Rose Bowl when the news came across the screen.

"Unreal. This did not just happen," he remembered thinking.[86]

Tsangaris and his teammates felt like they had lost not only a coach but a man whom they had come to respect for his passion, enthusiasm, and determination. Terry Canavello, editor in chief of Long Beach State's school newspaper, the *Daily Forty-Niner*, wrote that under Allen, the "players learned to be winners even when, according to the pundits, they should have been second-class losers. Players who were 'only good enough' to come to Long Beach State discovered determination and began doing the impossible—winning football games in unbelievable come-from-behind victories."

Canavello admitted to being one of many skeptics of Allen when he arrived because he was "full of talk" about a winning season and a new stadium. But "those, like myself, who expected a prima donna star were quickly awed by the amount of time and energy Allen devoted to the program. Allen demonstrated in his life what made him a superstar and what kept him one."[87]

Washington Post sportswriter Len Shapiro was planning to host a New Year's Eve party at his house in Middleburg, Virginia, when a blurb came across the wire around 7:00 p.m. "Literally, some of us were putting our coats on to get out and celebrate the new year, except over the wire comes, 'George Allen, Dead,'" Shapiro remembered. "I took my coat off. My friend, Bill Gildea, took his coat off. [Sports editor] George Solomon took his coat off. We all went to work writing and editing and getting out the paper for the next edition."[88]

The *Los Angeles Times*, like many other media outlets, reported that Allen's poor health since the end of the season could have been linked to the ice-water bath.[89] But a private autopsy showed that Allen had died from a rare heart spasm brought on by arrhythmia, an irregular heartbeat, and that his death was not connected to the ice water or pneumonia. About a year prior, he had been diagnosed with atrial fibrillation (AFib), an abnormal heartbeat. But he refused to undergo surgery for a pacemaker at a doctor's suggestion, Jennifer Allen remembered her mother telling her.[90]

On Friday, January 4, Allen was buried in a private ceremony at Green Hills Memorial Park in Rancho Palos Verdes, a few miles from Palos Verdes Estates. Billy Kilmer, Deacon Jones, Bill Harris, and Allen's three sons served as pallbearers. Etty decided that her husband should wear a navy blue blazer, a red-and-blue striped tie, and khaki coaching pants—the combination he often wore on game day when coaching the Rams. The family placed a football and other items in his casket before laying him to rest.

Later that day, a public memorial service took place at the Rolling Hills Covenant Church in Palos Verdes Estates. Etty and the kids, George, Bruce, Greg, and Jennifer, wanted to make the service special by celebrating the life of a coach and teacher—not only a husband and father—who touched the lives of so many people. They wanted it to be an event that would have made George Allen proud. Hundreds of former players, friends, and family members, including two busloads of well-dressed Long Beach State football players, paid tribute to Allen.

To some, the service had the feel of a football game. "My mom and I went to the ladies room before the service was about to begin," Jennifer

Allen remarked. "We were looking in the mirror, and one of us said, 'I feel like I'm going to a Redskins game.' The other one said, 'So do I.'"[91]

The service, led by family friend and the Redskins' team chaplain in the 1970s, Tom Skinner, was two hours of laughter and tears. George, Bruce, and Greg all spoke with reverence about their father. Bruce said that after arriving at his parents' home following his father's death, he found a note that George Allen had written. The note said:

> Win a championship
> Have every player graduate who I've recruited
> Build a stadium [underlined several times]
> Take a tougher job

Raiders owner Al Davis said "Allen was a great man. I loved him."[92] Dabney Coleman described him as "pure, naïve, boyish, and above all, very, very simple."[93] Two of Allen's NFL quarterbacks, Billy Kilmer and Roman Gabriel, reflected on his traits as a perfectionist and motivator.

Kilmer said, "We all know where George is today. He has it organized. And George, save a spot for me. I want to be on that team."[94] And Gabriel recalled that "one of the favorite expressions of coach Allen was, 'When I run into a rock or a boulder, no matter how large or how small, I'll find a way to move it.' We listen to a lot of people, but we learn from a few. George Allen was one of the few."[95]

Allen's tombstone at Green Hills Memorial Park reads,

GEORGE H. ALLEN
April 29, 1918–Dec. 31, 1990
LOVING AND BELOVED
HUSBAND, FATHER AND COACH
RAIN OR SHINE
THE FUTURE IS NOW

Epilogue

THE ULTIMATE HONOR

Just days after George Allen's death, Long Beach State honored him by naming its football practice field after the man who had rejuvenated the football program. Willie Brown was chosen to replace him as head coach, but the 49ers descended to a 2-9 record in 1991, their lowest win total in a decade. A few weeks later, the school disbanded the program because of financial constraints brought on by a statewide budget crisis. To this day, the school, now known as Cal State Long Beach, does not have a football program.

Players scattered to other schools. Running back Terrell Davis transferred to Georgia, and quarterback Mike McCoy left for Utah. The school also lost a number of other promising players who had been recruited by Allen and his staff. The field named after Allen is now part of a thousand-seat stadium used by the women's soccer team. It's called George Allen Field.

Allen has been recognized in other ways, too, because of the special stamp he left on the coaching profession. He was inducted into the RFK Stadium Hall of Stars in 1985 and the Washington Touchdown Club Hall of Fame in 1990. Long Beach State and the two other colleges where he coached—Morningside and Whittier—have enshrined him in their own Halls of Fame. Whittier's weight room is called the George Allen Fitness Center. The Virginia Sports Hall of Fame and the Michigan Sports Hall of Fame inducted him in 1998 and 2012, respectively. The weight room at his alma mater, Lake Shore High School in St. Clair Shores, Michigan, is named in his honor.

For many years following the end of Allen's NFL coaching career in 1978, however, a glaring hole existed on his résumé—no accolade affirming that he had reached the pinnacle of his profession: the Pro Football Hall of Fame. His coaching feats justified that he deserved to follow the other NFL luminaries into the shrine in Canton, Ohio. Tops among his accomplishments was his regular-season winning percentage of .705, which stood third behind John Madden's (.750) and Vince Lombardi's (.728).

Today, with ties no longer part of the calculation, those three are ranked in the same order: Madden (.759), Lombardi (.739), and Allen (.712). Allen also coached twelve NFL seasons without ever having a losing record—a phenomenal achievement in itself.

Sportswriters who reported on Allen during his coaching days spoke out on his behalf. Steve Guback, who covered Allen's teams for the *Washington Star* and later served as his information officer with the President's Council on Physical Fitness and Sports, built a case for him in a 1987 letter to the *Baltimore Sun*'s Vito Stellino, a member of the Hall of Fame selection committee. Guback, in part, described Allen as the only coach in NFL history to never have a losing season in more than ten years of coaching. The following year, Allen was a finalist for the Hall of Fame, but he wasn't selected.

During Allen's 1990 season at Long Beach State, Douglas Looney of *Sports Illustrated* and Jim Murray of the *Los Angeles Times* sounded incredulous that his bust was not in Canton.

"Allen is one of the premier coaches in the history of the game, but he has never received his due," Looney wrote. "It's a joke that Allen is not one of the thirteen coaches in the Pro Football Hall of Fame." Allen's regular-season winning percentage, Looney noted, was better than those of three other coaches in the Hall of Fame at the time: Earl "Greasy" Neale (.596), Sid Gillman (.550), and Weeb Ewbank (.502).[1] Murray called it a "disgrace" that Allen wasn't in the Hall of Fame.[2]

Allen was a finalist again in 1998 and 1999, but the end result was no different. Someone had to take up the mantle. The *Washington Post*'s Len Shapiro, Washington's representative to the selection committee and one of Allen's top media adversaries during his coaching days in DC, stepped forward to help him earn his due. "I was the guy who had to make it happen," Shapiro reasoned.[3]

Shapiro had started lobbying for Allen after he died in 1990. But once Shapiro was named to the Hall of Fame's seniors committee in addition to his role on the regular selection committee, he spoke up even more, calling it a "travesty" that Allen wasn't yet in Canton. In 2001 Shapiro nominated Allen as the only senior candidate for the 2002 induction class and gave a speech on his behalf to his fellow committee members.

Asked why he felt so confident that Allen should be in, Shapiro explained, "He was a great innovator. He was one of the first guys to use the nickel defense and the dime defense. He was a defensive wiz. He was the guy who was responsible for the Bears winning the title in '63. They didn't carry Halas off the field, but they carried Allen off. He had a good career with the Rams, turned them into a winner. Came to Washington, turned around that team, although Vince Lombardi had started the process in '69. But Allen showed up two years later and within a year, they were in the Super Bowl."

What about his 2-7 record in the playoffs? "That's what his detractors would bring up. I think that may have been a factor when he was a regular candidate as opposed to a senior candidate."

The same year, 2001, NFL Films released a documentary that provided additional momentum for Allen's induction. *Winning Is Living, Losing Is Dying: The George Allen Story* chronicled how he left an indelible mark on the game as an ingenious football coach, a superb innovator and motivator, and a man whose primary devotion in life was to winning football games. All of Allen's family members spoke in the documentary, as did players from the Redskins, Rams, and Long Beach State. Journalists, including Len Shapiro and another antagonist of Allen when he coached the Redskins, David Israel of the *Washington Star*, told stories about his battles with the press, his quirky personality, and how deeply football was ingrained in his psyche.

In August 2001 the Hall of Fame's seniors committee named Allen its finalist for induction into the Class of 2002. That meant he automatically moved into the final seven candidates for the 2002 class. He needed at least 80 percent of the vote when the Hall of Fame's thirty-five-member board of selectors—sportswriters from around the country—cast their ballots on February 2, 2002, the day before Super Bowl XXXVI in New Orleans. His selection would not be a surprise, because the senior finalist is usually elected.

Even so, the Allen family was elated when news broke that day that George Herbert Allen had been elected to the Hall of Fame. Bruce Allen, a senior executive with the Oakland Raiders, wore his father's 1963 Chicago Bears championship ring while addressing reporters in a packed news conference at the Super Bowl media center. He relayed word about the induction to an aide to his brother, George, a U.S. senator from Virginia who was in New Orleans giving a political fundraising speech. In his distinguished political career, George Felix Allen served one term in the U.S. House of Representatives representing a Virginia district (1991–93), one term as Virginia's governor (1994–98), and one term as a U.S. senator from Virginia (2001–7).

During the speech, the aide walked in on George and gave him a thumbs-up that Bruce was on the other end of a cell phone call to share the big news. At that moment, fellow Republican and former congressional representative and vice-presidential candidate Jack Kemp, who quarterbacked at Occidental College while Allen coached at rival Whittier and had remained friends with Allen over the years, made a surprise appearance during the speech, along with San Francisco 49ers general manager and former UCLA football coach Terry Donahue.

"Providentially, Jack Kemp and Terry Donahue walked into the room just as I was getting the good news about my father's induction into the Hall of Fame," George Felix Allen said. "Jack and I hugged. We were both thinking how special this moment was. It was absolutely perfect in so many ways."[4]

On August 3, 2002, George Allen took his place among the pantheon of the greatest NFL coaches and players in a ceremony welcoming him and the rest of the new class—Jim Kelly, Dave Casper, Dan Hampton, and John Stallworth—on a sunny day before eighteen thousand people at Fawcett Stadium on the Hall of Fame's campus. Family, dozens of Allen's former players and coaches from the Rams and Redskins, and friends came to Canton to see the coaching legend receive his due. In previous years, the enshrinement ceremony took place on the steps of the hall's museum, but it was relocated to Fawcett Stadium in 2002 to accommodate the growing crowds showing up year after year.

In 1980 George Allen had presented Deacon Jones, the most feared member of Allen's Fearsome Foursome in Los Angeles, for induction into the Hall of Fame. In 2002 Jones returned the favor by presenting Allen. George Felix Allen represented his father for enshrinement.

Said Deacon Jones: "How sweet it is! Yeah, we knew it was going to happen sooner or later. Members of the board of directors of the Pro Football Hall of Fame, new inductees, and my partners in the back—fellow enshrines. The honorable senator from the great state of Virginia, Mr. Mayor, ladies, and gentleman—the future is now!

"Teamwork, hard work, pride, determination, and competitive spirit permeated the life and times of the man I am honored to present for induction to the greatest sports Hall of Fame of them all—coach George Allen.

"I stand here representing all of the players—both college, professional—

who were fortunate enough to play for coach George Allen. He was the consummate player coach, and he let the world know it. I want to personally thank the Allen family for giving me the opportunity to execute this task. I've been waiting a long time for this one.

"My experience with George Allen began in 1966 when he was hired to lead the Los Angeles Rams out of the depths of despair. I remember walking into the locker room that first morning and seeing little signs plastered all over the place. Little sayings that you might find pasted on a grammar school wall. One-liners that seemed ridiculous. The Rams had not had a winning season since 1958, and we needed a miracle worker not a schoolteacher. We all looked at each other and shrugged. But, then we met coach Allen. And that was exactly what we got—a miracle worker of the utmost degree.

"He drove us to make the most of ourselves, and he made us winners. Finishing the season with an 8-6 record. And we learned to love those little sayings of George Allen. How did he do it? Teamwork, hard work, pride, determination, and competitive spirit. Every stop he made, every level of football he coached he had a winning season using these five points that I believe make a champion. Eight and six was a good beginning, but we wanted more, and more we got. Through George Allen's leadership, forty men made a total commitment to our coach and to winning.

"Nineteen-sixty-seven, his second year with the veteran team, coach Allen led us [to an] 11-1-2 season, winning the Coastal Division championship. We won again in '68 and in '69. We won eleven straight games. In fact, George Allen is the only coach in the history of the NFL to have coached twelve years or better and never had a losing season. He taught us that the harder we work, the luckier we got. And, boy did we get lucky and stayed that way through his tenure. I recently reread a quote from George and I remember it like it was heard yesterday, 'I have told my team,' said coach, 'that God, family, and football are the three most important things in their lives. During the season, football comes first.'

"'And we all,' George said, 'should have some leisure. Leisure time is the five or six hours you sleep each night.' Yes, that exemplified George Allen and the ethics he required when you worked for him.

"The future was now for George Allen. 'Trader George' as he became known. He needed veteran players to understand his complex system so he traded every rookie who came his way. Much to the dismay [of] those in the league who were avidly touting the draft. And, when he left the Rams and went to the Washington Redskins, he took his 'Over-the-Hill Gang' with him and won again. But, he had to win, and he had to win now. And, he needed veterans to do it. George Allen's commitment to defense is well known in the world of football. But let it be known that special teams was one of the important parts of his football machine. Coach Allen was the first to hire a special teams coach and insist on open end practices. And, we practiced until we covered every plan and every eventuality, until we did it in our sleep during our leisure time.

"Often times, it's best to describe someone in their own words. And, I can find none better that exemplified coach George Allen than those words he said, 'In sports, the only measure of success is victory. We must sacrifice everything to this end. The man who can accept defeat and take his salary without feeling guilty is a thief.'

"I cannot think of a thing that money can buy that a loser can enjoy—fancy cars, clothes, parties, and pretty women are only window dressing. Winning is the true goal. Only the winner's alive. The loser's dead whether he knows it or not.

"Coach George Allen may have passed on but he's not dead. He's a man who never had a losing season. A man who was always true to his dream. Members of the board of directors of the Pro Football Hall of Fame—I, David 'Deacon' Jones, a 22-year-old member of this hallowed body—present for induction, my friend and the best damn coach my teammates and I ever had."

George Felix Allen spoke next: "Deacon. Deacon. Thank you for that powerful tribute. It means so much to us because you are an inspiration and the best darn defensive end who ever played the game! Bruce [Smith] is all right, he went to Virginia Tech but Deacon's better. And I want to also thank my father's trusted friends—Ed and Steve Sabol—for the insightful documentary which really allowed us to better understand you Deacon, and my father.

"To Mayor Watkins, distinguished guests, ladies and gentlemen, fans all, I know if my father were here today he would tell you all—'Gosh . . . This sure is a great day to be alive!' But, I feel that George Allen is with us all—in the living spirit of all those who have gathered to celebrate this pinnacle of football honors, joining with this great class of inductees and their presenters.

"My father would have celebrated with a typical glass of milk—maybe even allowed one blackberry brandy. But he would also say that this honor is a 'team victory!' He would give thanks to God and say 'this is a victory for all of the players, coaches, and staff who were on our teams.'

"First and foremost, I know he would be looking at my mother in appreciation for her loving support, all her good advice and encouragement, and that lucky game day rice pudding. Mom, through all the joy, uncertainty, superstitions, raising your four children, you were always his Steady Etty and his MVP. Even more, you were the love of his life.

"He'd be proud to see all his grandchildren here, and his children. Jennifer, the successful author; Greg, the thoughtful counselor; and Bruce, who followed our father's footsteps into football with his creative success with the Raider nation, working with Al Davis—the great Al Davis who has always been a thoughtful friend for all our family.

"George Allen, as a coach and father, believed that discipline, consistency and a fighting spirit were keys to success. Adherence to these principles are why my father was a winner in life and why all of his players and coaches still are.

"It wasn't easy being Coach George Allen, though, because the establishment did not always welcome his innovative ideas or methods of producing and assembling winning teams. Most importantly, though, he was a man who had the courage of his convictions. And, because of that courage, he was stronger, his teams were stronger, and the game is stronger. And, thanks to the sportswriters, like Len Shapiro. We today honor his lifetime of achievement.

"He first started off as a head coach in America's heartland at Morningside College in Sioux City with his two-man 'Shorty' Shortenhaus. Then on to the fiercely named 'Poets' of Whittier with another two-man, 'Bronco' Bill Harris, whose friendship with him over the decades never wavered.

"After working a season under Sid Gillman, my father was so grateful for the opportunity and experience to lead in Chicago with the 'Master,' the 'Creator' of the NFL—George 'Papa Bear' Halas. I remember well that 1963 NFL Championship Game on frozen Wrigley Field when the defense, the 'Monsters of the Midway'—with Atkins, Fortunato, Morris, George, Richie Petitbon, Rosey Taylor, Jones, McRae and O'Bradovich—all of those guys in a very tough game led them to a tenacious victory. And they gave my father the game ball and sang that infamous, ribald song.

"After eight years with the Bears, Dan Reeves hired my father on as head coach of the Rams, where a great turnaround was led by the Fearsome Foursome—Deacon, and Olsen, and Lundy, and [Rosey] Grier, and later

Roger Brown—as well as Jack Pardee, Baughan, Pottios, Cross, Meador, and solid offense with Dick Bass, Jack Snow, Tom Mack, and Roman Gabriel.

"The magnificent lion of a man, Jack Kent Cooke, brought him to Virginia as coach and general manager of the Redskins, where many of the family members came along, like Diron Talbert and John Wilbur from the Ramskins, to form the 'Over-the-Hill Gang.'

"Now, when challenged for his decisions and asked by, I recall, Warner Wolf, about the future prospects of a more senior lineup, my father replied, 'The future? This team hasn't been to the playoffs in over two decades and you're worried about the future? The Future Is Now!' And, indeed, it was, and they consistently won and made the playoffs.

"Those seven years with the Redskins were like Camelot and a winning tradition was born. The team—our extended family—really was forged during that time, with great leaders like Brig Owens, Hanburger, Bragg, Tillman, Charley Taylor, Fischer, Malinchak, Len Hauss, Jurgensen, and Larry Brown; and great new 'Skins' newcomers like Billy Kilmer, McDole, Ken Houston, Eddie Brown, Jefferson, Moseley, Theismann, Butz, and the always polite John Riggins.

"In the 1980s, George Allen chaired the President's Council on Physical Fitness and Sports for his long-time friend Ronald Reagan, and he also led the Blitz and the Wranglers to playoff successes, and drafted and recruited fellow honoree Jim Kelly into the USFL.

"At all times and at all hours, my father benefited from dedicated assistants such as the eloquent Marv Levy, Torgeson, Marchibroda, Waller, Vermeil, Lanham, Sullivan, Hickman and Casserly, and Bobby Mitchell. And keeping it all together were fantastic staff members like security by 'oo' Boynton, Shirley Krystek, John Jenkins, the cunning Tommy McVean, and relying on professionals like trainer Bubba Tyer and Drs. Rasinski, Palumbo and Knowlan to keep the players playing.

"In 1990, my father remarkably turned Long Beach State into a winner and in what turned out to be the last weeks of his life, he penned an article for *Sports Illustrated* about, what turned out to be, enduring values.

"'At a time when concepts like working together and being positive seem old-fashioned to some people,' he wrote, 'it's reassuring that those ideas still have value. I learned that players need the same things they needed in 1948—discipline, organization, conditioning, motivation, togetherness, love. No matter what a player did, I usually gave him another chance. It wouldn't have helped to kick players off the team, because then I wouldn't have had a chance to work with them.'

"George Allen loved his players, he loved his coaches, he loved the game.

"To my father, I hope you are enjoying this reunion, because many of the gang's all here to celebrate your contributions that you made during your inspiring life. Thank you for the blood and spirit that you gave to your family, and to the joy of life that you gave to all your winning teams and their fans. Coach Allen, you are with us all in our hearts, in our memories.

"Ladies and gentlemen, on behalf of my father—my family thanks you from the depths of our heart for this ultimate honor. You have made this a great day to be alive! Thank you all."[5]

With that, George Allen was immortalized with a bust in the Pro Football Hall of Fame. His legacy was set in stone.

Acknowledgments

This project followed a pattern in longevity identical to my first book, *The Redskins Encyclopedia*. It took me about seven years from the time I put pencil to paper for this biography to hit the shelves. I learned once again that writing a book is no easy task.

Along the way, so many people graciously gave their time for interviews and other research purposes. First off, I must extend my heartfelt thanks to the Allen family. George Allen's children—George, Greg, Bruce, and Jennifer—granted me interviews at my request, withstanding my persistence in the process, and gave me unfettered access to their photo archive and other images. Susan Allen, George Felix Allen's wife, was also an enormous help. The family also gave me permission to access George Allen's extensive collection of documents that they donated to the Pro Football Hall of Fame. That proved to be an invaluable resource. Archivist Jon Kendle and curator Jason Aikens went out of their way to assist me at the Hall of Fame.

Others who provided tremendous assistance included Joe Dmohowski, a librarian at Whittier College; Josh David Bennett, an archivist at Indiana University; and the always dependable John Labombarda from the Elias Sports Bureau in New York. Nobody is better than John at retrieving statistics on pro sports.

The Media School at Indiana University allowed me to access the vast collection of documents donated by Steve Guback, who was an Indiana graduate, the Redskins' beat reporter for the *Washington Star* during Allen's coaching days in DC, and Allen's information officer for the President's Council on Physical Fitness and Sports. Guback, who crafted a seventy-five-year career as a sportswriter before passing away in 2018, kindly allowed me to use first-person interviews he carried out with George Allen in the 1970s and 1980s. Those recordings proved to be another amazing resource, allowing me to flesh out the manuscript with George Allen's personal thoughts about his life and coaching career.

Lastly, I want to thank Monty Wood of the U.S. Census Bureau and my friend and high school classmate Sheri Kosman for their research assistance, as well as former Redskins assistant equipment manager Tom Heckler and my longtime literary attorney, Phil Hochberg, for their support and inspiration. Robert Taylor, my editor at the University of Nebraska Press, handled my manuscript with a wonderful touch of professionalism and sensitivity. UNP's team of editors also did an excellent job. Thank you to all.

Appendix A

ALL-TIME COACHING RECORD

College

YEAR	SCHOOL	RECORD	PERCENTAGE
1948	Morningside	3-6-0	.333
1949	Morningside	7-3-1	.700
1950	Morningside	7-2-1	.778
1951	Whittier	2-7-0	.222
1952	Whittier	9-1-0	.900
1953	Whittier	6-3-1	.667
1954	Whittier	3-6-1	.333
1955	Whittier	8-2-0	.800
1956	Whittier	4-3-3	.571
1990	Long Beach State	6-5-0	.545
Totals		55-38-7	.591

National Football League

YEAR	TEAM	RECORD	PERCENTAGE	POSTSEASON
1966	Los Angeles Rams	8-6-0	.571	0-0
1967	Los Angeles	11-1-2	.917	0-1
1968	Los Angeles	10-3-1	.769	0-0
1969	Los Angeles	11-3-0	.786	0-1
1970	Los Angeles	9-4-1	.692	0-0
1971	Washington Redskins	9-4-1	.692	0-1

1972	Washington	11-3-0	.786	2-1 (lost in Super Bowl VII)
1973	Washington	10-4-0	.714	0-1
1974	Washington	10-4-0	.714	0-1
1975	Washington	8-6-0	.571	0-0
1976	Washington	10-4-0	.714	0-1
1977	Washington	9-5-0	.643	0-0
Totals		116-47-5	.712	2-7

United States Football League

YEAR	TEAM	RECORD	PERCENTAGE	POSTSEASON
1983	Chicago Blitz	12-6-0	.667	0-1
1984	Arizona Wranglers	10-8-0	.556	2-1 (lost in USFL championship)
Totals		22-14-0	.611	2-2

Overall

	RECORD	PERCENTAGE
College	55-38-7	.591
Pro (including playoffs)	142-70-5	.670
Combined	197-108-12	.646

Appendix B

COACHING TREE

George Allen's assistants who became NFL head coaches:

Dick Vermeil (Rams 1969)
Eagles: 1976–82, 54-47, 3-4 playoffs (lost Super Bowl XV)
Rams: 1997–99, 22-26, 3-0 playoffs (won Super Bowl XXXIV)
Chiefs: 2001–5, 44-36, 0-1 playoffs
Pro Football Hall of Fame

Marv Levy (Redskins 1971–72)
Chiefs: 1978–82, 31-42
Bills: 1986–97, 112-70, 11-8 playoffs (lost Super Bowls XXV, XXVI, XXVII, XXVIII)
Pro Football Hall of Fame

Ted Marchibroda (Rams 1966–70, Redskins 1971–74)
Baltimore Colts: 1975–79, 41-33, 0-3 playoffs
Indianapolis Colts: 1992–95, 30-34, 2-1 playoffs
Baltimore Ravens: 1996–98, 16-31

Jack Pardee (Redskins 1973)
Bears: 1975–77, 20-22, 0-1 playoffs
Redskins: 1978–80, 24-24
Oilers: 1990–94, 43-41, 1-4 playoffs

Mike McCormack (Redskins 1971–72)
Eagles: 1973–75, 16-25
Colts: 1981–82, 9-23
Seahawks: 1982, 4-3

Joe Walton (Redskins 1974–77)
Jets: 1983–89, 53-57-1

Pete McCulley (Redskins 1977)
49ers: 1978, 1-8

Howard Schnellenberger (Rams 1966–69)
Colts: 1973–74, 4-13

Schnellenberger is remembered much more today for the fame he achieved in the college coaching ranks. In twenty-four seasons of college coaching (Miami, Louisville, Oklahoma, Florida Atlantic), he posted a 141-133-3 record and won all six of his bowl games. His most memorable season was when his Miami Hurricanes finished 11-1 in 1983, beating Nebraska in the Orange Bowl, 31–30, to claim the national championship.

Bill Belichick, winner of a record six Super Bowls as head coach of the New England Patriots and two more as the New York Giants' defensive coordinator, is not part of the Allen coaching tree. However, he learned Allen's defense while working in 1975 under Colts defensive coordinator Maxie Baughan, a linebacker who played four seasons for Allen in Los Angeles and followed him to DC as one of the Ramskins. "I learned a lot about the Redskins' defensive schemes and the techniques they employed, as well as the breakdowns they use to prepare the defense for the upcoming opponent," Belichick said in an interview. While focusing on special teams during a series of assistant coaching stops from '75 to '84, Belichick referenced Allen's book *George Allen's Guide to Special Teams*. He thinks Allen made a "huge impact" on the evolution of defense and special teams. "He was brilliant in both areas, and he passed his knowledge and system to those who worked for him, and they passed it on to others like me," Belichick said. "People who did that for me are Ted Marchibroda, Maxie Baughan, and Ralph Hawkins. They were great ambassadors of Coach Allen and his system."

Notes

Prologue

1. George Allen, "What It Takes to Win," unpublished paper, 1985, George Allen Collection, Pro Football Hall of Fame, Canton OH (hereafter cited as GAC).
2. Ken Denlinger, "This Morning: Fitting Images," *Washington Post*, January 19, 1978, D1.
3. Brig Owens, interview by author, June 22, 2020.
4. George Allen, "A Hundred Percent Is Not Enough," *Sports Illustrated*, July 9, 1973, 76.
5. G. Allen, "What It Takes to Win."
6. This quote from George Felix Allen and other quotes throughout the text whose sources are not specifically cited come from the author's previous work, *The Redskins Encyclopedia*.
7. William Gildea, "George Allen: He Never Stops," *Washington Post*, January 14, 1973, E4.
8. Bill Malinchak, interview by author, November 14, 2017.
9. Bruce Allen, interview by author, February 10, 2020.
10. "A Child Shall Lead Them," *Time*, November 27, 1972, 97.
11. Bob Verdi, "A Final 'Hello' from Coach Allen," *Chicago Tribune*, January 3, 1991, A1.
12. George Allen, unpublished interview by *Washington Star* sportswriter Steve Guback, 1975, Steve Guback Collection, Media School Archive, Indiana University, Bloomington (hereafter cited as SGC).

1. Humble Beginnings

1. G. Allen, *Strategies for Winning*, 25.
2. George Herbert Allen birth certificate, May 3, 1917, from Allen family records.
3. R. L. Polk 1917 Detroit city directory, 2334, via Bentley Library, University of Michigan, Ann Arbor.
4. Higbie Maxon Agney Realtors, "Historical Architecture of Grosse Pointe—the Lost Ford Estates [designed by Albert H. Spahr]" (blog post), April 17, 2018, https://www.higbiemaxon.com/blog/historical-architecture-of-grosse-pointe-the-lost-ford-estates-designed-by-albert-h-spahr.html.

5. Higbie Maxon Agney Realtors, "Historical Architecture of Grosse Pointe."
6. R. L. Polk 1920 Detroit city directory, n.p.
7. R. L. Polk 1920 Detroit city directory, n.p.
8. E. H. Houghton, letter of recommendation for Earl Allen on stationery of the Universal Book Stores in Detroit, January 20, 1920, GAC.
9. 1930 U.S. Census, via Bentley Library.
10. George Felix Allen, interview by author, March 15, 2018.
11. George Felix Allen interview, March 15, 2018.
12. Greg Allen, interview by author, June 12, 2013.
13. Jennifer Allen, interview by author, December 6, 2019.
14. Gildea and Turan, *Future Is Now*, 44.
15. J. Allen interview, December 6, 2019.
16. Gildea and Turan, *Future Is Now*, 45.
17. George Allen, article for *Sports Fans' Journal*, 1980s, 19 (scrapbook clipping), GAC. Subsequent quotes are from this article until noted otherwise.
18. J. Allen interview, December 6, 2019.
19. Jennifer Allen, interview by author, February 15, 2015.
20. Gildea and Turan, *Future Is Now*, 45.
21. *Aurora* yearbook, 1943, Michigan Normal College, GAC.
22. V-12 Program History, U.S. Navy Memorial, https://homepages.rootsweb.com/~uscnrotc/V-12/v12-his.htm.
23. George Allen résumé, 1957, GAC.
24. Alma College football encyclopedia, 1994, 78, GAC.
25. "Cat Chatter," *The Almanian*, three separate issues in 1943 and 1944, courtesy the archivist/librarian at Alma College, Alma MI.
26. Enrollment information from Department of Special Collections and University Archives, Marquette University Libraries, Marquette MI.
27. George Allen, Notice of Separation from the U.S. Naval Service, December 23, 1945, from Allen family records.
28. J. Allen interview, December 6, 2019.
29. U.S. Navy Hospital Corps School, Certificate of Graduation, August 31, 1945, and U.S. Navy Hospital Corps School, Certificate of Award, softball (undated), from Allen family records.
30. George Allen, recorded conversation with Steve Guback, 1989. Access to recorded conversations courtesy of Steve Guback. Subsequent quotes are from this recorded conversation until noted otherwise.
31. J. Allen interview, February 15, 2015.
32. "Sig Phis Set Scoring Mark: Chi Psi, Sig Chis Cop Cage League Crowns," *Michigan Daily*, March 6, 1947, 3.
33. Gildea and Turan, *Future Is Now*, 48.
34. G. Allen résumé, 1957.
35. G. Allen recorded conversation with Guback.

2. The Roots of His Genius

1. George Allen, "Pound for Pound as Good as the Big Guys: U-M's Unheralded 1947 Football Champions," *Sports Fans' Journal*, August 1987, 19.
2. Canham with Paladino, *From the Inside*, 199.
3. George Allen's handwritten notes from University of Michigan football practices, 1947, GAC.
4. "150-Pounders Face Stiff Test against OSU: Initial Win Pleases Wolverine Coaches," *Michigan Daily*, November 4, 1947, 5.
5. Wayne DeNeff, "It All Started Here for George Allen," *Ann Arbor News*, December 21, 1967.
6. G. Allen, *Strategies for Winning*, 125.
7. G. Allen, "A Study of Outstanding Football Coaches' Attitudes and Practices in Scouting." Subsequent quotations are from this master's thesis until noted otherwise.
8. Gildea and Turan, *Future Is Now*, 51–52.
9. G. Allen, *Strategies for Winning*, 31.
10. Canham with Paladino, *From the Inside*, 199.
11. G. Allen recorded conversation with Guback. Subsequent quotations are from this recorded conversation until noted otherwise.
12. G. Allen, *Strategies for Winning*, 32.
13. G. Allen recorded conversation with Guback.
14. G. Allen, *Strategies for Winning*, 32.
15. "Buckingham New Athletic Director: Les Davis Resigns to Take Radio Post," *The Morningsider* (Morningside College), September 1948, 1.
16. G. Allen, *Strategies for Winning*, 32.
17. "New Head Football Coach at Morningside," *The Morningsider*, May 1948, 1.
18. Gildea and Turan, *Future Is Now*, 55.

3. Heartland to Southern California

1. "Fame Taps Mr. Allen," *Christian Science Monitor* via the Associated Press, March 26, 1964, 12.
2. Dick Weikert, interview by author, June 5, 2013.
3. Gildea and Turan, *Future Is Now*, 54.
4. G. Allen recorded conversation with Guback.
5. G. Allen, letters to Connie Callahan and Bob Hooks, May 21, 1948, SGC.
6. Gildea and Turan, *Future Is Now*, 55.
7. "People," *Collegian Reporter* (Morningside College), September 29, 1948, 8.
8. George Felix Allen, interview by author, March 28, 2018.
9. "Over Midland," *Collegian Reporter*, September 29, 1948, 7.
10. "Maroons Drop Loop Tilt," *The Morningsider*, October 1948, 6.
11. *Burbank Leader*, July 26, 1989, B1–2 (scrapbook clipping), GAC.

12. "Summarizing the 1948 Football Season," *The Morningsider*, November 1948, 6. Subsequent quotations are from this article until noted otherwise.
13. Allen family members, interviews by author, 2018.
14. George Felix Allen, interview by author, April 9, 2018.
15. Etty Allen, letter to the Allen children, 2008, GAC.
16. Greg Allen, interview by author, June 12, 2013.
17. George Felix Allen interview, April 9, 2018.
18. "People," *Collegian Reporter*, January 18, 1951, 10.
19. George Felix Allen interview, April 9, 2018.
20. Greg Allen, interview by author, June 15, 2013.
21. *Sioux City Journal*, May 27, 1951, sec. 2, 3.
22. Etty Allen, interview by author, June 15, 2012.
23. George Felix Allen interview, March 28, 2018.
24. Davis, *Papa Bear*, 336.
25. "Just Couldn't Refuse California Grid Offer," *Sioux City Journal*, August 15, 1951 (scrapbook clipping), GAC.
26. "Football Practice to Start," *The Morningsider*, March 1949, 8.
27. Jim Fowler, interview by author, July 17, 2018.
28. "1949 Maroon Football Prospects," *The Morningsider*, September 1949, 7.
29. Fowler interview.
30. Weikert interview.
31. "Maroons Turn Back North Dakota University," *The Morningsider*, September 1949, 7.
32. The Official NCAA Football Guide (1950), 55–56, and the official NCAA statistics bureau, courtesy media relations staff at the NCAA.
33. George Allen "Best Player" submission, *Saturday Evening Post*, 1952 (scrapbook clipping), SGC.
34. "We Keep Him," *Collegian Reporter*, March 2, 1950, 8.
35. G. Allen recorded conversation with Guback.
36. "Head Football Coach George Allen and President Earl A. Roadman" (photo caption), *The Morningsider*, November 1950, 6.
37. "Just Couldn't Refuse California Grid Offer" (scrapbook clipping).
38. "Just Couldn't Refuse California Grid Offer" (scrapbook clipping).
39. "Morningside Begins New Fall Semester," *The Morningsider*, September 1950, 2.
40. "Just Couldn't Refuse California Grid Offer" (scrapbook clipping).
41. "Allen Named Poet Football Coach," *Quaker Campus* (Whittier College), September 14, 1951, 4.
42. Cooper and West, *Whittier*, 374.
43. Bill Harris, interview by author, April 9, 2015. Subsequent quotes are from this interview until noted otherwise.

44. "Mid-West vs. Coast Technique: Coach Allen Finds Mid-West 'Hungry,'" *Quaker Campus*, September 21, 1951, 4.
45. "2 Legends of Whittier: Coaches Inducted into College Hall of Fame," *Los Angeles Times*, March 16, 1989, 7.
46. "Poet Back: Herman Reed," *Quaker Campus*, November 17, 1950, 5.
47. Al Stoll, interview by author, November 10, 2018.
48. George Allen, "Are the Fans Ruining Football?" *Los Angeles Times*, November 11, 1951, 17.
49. George Allen personal profile, circa 1954, GAC.
50. Harris interview, April 9, 2015.
51. G. Allen, *Strategies for Winning*, 33.
52. G. Allen, *Strategies for Winning*, 33; "Football Clinic Held at Whittier," *Los Angeles Times*, August 6, 1953, C3.
53. "Whittier Football Coach Honored," *Los Angeles Times* via United Press, December 18, 1951, C3.
54. "Parallel Lives: Richard Nixon and George Allen in Washington," Richard Nixon Foundation, Richard Nixon Presidential Library and Museum, Yorba Linda CA, October 12, 2017, https://www.nixonfoundation.org/2017/10/parallel-lives-richard-nixon-george-allen-washington/.
55. Nixon, *RN*, 19.
56. Nixon, *RN*, 19.
57. Al Stoll, interview by author, December 7, 2018. Subsequent quotes are from this interview until noted otherwise.
58. "Footballers Shaping Up under Careful Eye of Coach Allen," *Quaker Campus*, May 16, 1952, 4.
59. Whittier 1952 football prospectus, GAC.
60. "50 Gridders Greet Allen," *Quaker Campus*, September 19, 1952, 8.
61. Unidentified scrapbook newspaper clipping, ca. 1960s, GAC.
62. "Poets Spoil Poly's Homecoming," *Whittier Daily News*, November 9, 1952 (scrapbook clipping), GAC.
63. "Poets Win Pigskin Game by Forfeit," *Los Angeles Times*, December 25, 1952, C3.
64. "Coach Allen Names Best Players in Past Six Years," *Quaker Campus*, February 1, 1957, 4.
65. Max Fields, interview by author, December 13, 2018.
66. Harris interview, April 9, 2015.
67. Norm Haack, interview by author, November 4, 2018.
68. Haack interview.
69. Harris interview, April 9, 2015.
70. Haack interview.
71. Stoll interview, December 7, 2018.
72. "Whittier's Allen Flies to Idaho for Job Confab," *Los Angeles Times*, February 2, 1954, C3.

73. "Whittier College Pigskin Preview," *Quaker Campus*, May 13, 1955, 6.
74. George Allen's 1955 preseason Whittier football notebooks, GAC.
75. "Sports Parade," *Los Angeles Times*, November 3, 1955, C1.
76. "Tigers Tamed: Poets Blast Oxy Offense," *Quaker Campus*, October 18, 1955, 6.
77. George Felix Allen, interview by author, December 19, 2019.
78. "Four Players Repeat on Little All-America," *Los Angeles Times* via the Associated Press, December 6, 1956, C2.
79. Wade Holland, "We're Satisfied!" *Quaker Campus*, November 11, 1955, 1, 5.
80. John McNichols, interview by author, January 31, 2019.
81. Steve Henson, "Testing His Last Legs: Ventura Semipro Team Has 60-Year-Old Player Who Just Can't Quit Football," *Los Angeles Times*, November 21, 1995, VYC1.
82. John McNichols, interview by author, February 7, 2019.
83. Paul Zimmerman, "Tay Brown Considered for WSC Job," *Los Angeles Times*, January 10, 1956, C2.
84. "Allen to Remain as Poet Coach," *Los Angeles Times*, January 14, 1956, B4.
85. "Allen Quits Job as Whittier Coach," *Los Angeles Times*, January 12, 1957, A2.
86. "Allen Gives Resignation: Desires Full-Time Coaching Position," *Quaker Campus*, January 10, 1957, 1.
87. William Barry Furlong, "Gillman Call Turning Point in Allen's Career," *Washington Post*, December 22, 1974, F1.
88. *Quaker Campus*, January 10, 1957, 1.
89. Howard Seelye, "Sandscript," *Palos Verdes News*, January 27, 1966, 4.
90. Anonymous source, interview by author, December 6, 2018. Subsequent quotes are from this source until noted otherwise.
91. McNichols interview, January 31, 2019. Subsequent quotes are from this source until noted otherwise.
92. Harris interview, April 9, 2015.
93. Gildea and Turan, *Future Is Now*, 59.
94. Fields interview.
95. McNichols interview, January 31, 2019.
96. Fields interview.
97. Pat Putnam, interview by author, December 17, 2018.
98. Fields interview.
99. John McNichols, interview by author, February 2, 2019.

4. At the Car Wash

1. Furlong, "Gillman Call Turning Point in Allen's Career," F1, F7.
2. "Rams Sign George Allen as Assistant Coach," Los Angeles Rams press release, April 19, 1957, GAC.
3. Gildea and Turan, *Future Is Now*, 61.
4. Sid Gillman to George Allen, June 28, 1956, GAC.

5. McNichols interview, January 31, 2019.
6. McNichols interview, January 31, 2019. Subsequent quotes are from this interview until noted otherwise.
7. Lyle Gillman, interview by author, February 10, 2019.
8. "Rams Sign Swiacki as End Coach," *Los Angeles Times*, February 26, 1958, C3.
9. Dick Hyland, "Elroy Hirsch Quits Football for TV Position," *Los Angeles Times*, January 15, 1958, C1.
10. Katzowitz, *Sid Gillman*, 245.
11. Bisheff, *Los Angeles Rams*, 42.
12. Kathryn Flynn, University of Michigan placement analyst, to George Allen, January 3, 1958, GAC.
13. Letterhead promos for "The Rams Car Wash," GAC.
14. George Felix Allen, interview by author, January 20, 2019. Subsequent quotes are from this interview until noted otherwise.
15. Agreement note between Coye Jensen of Power Plus Golf Clubs and George Allen, April 8, 1958, GAC.
16. George Felix Allen interview, January 20, 2019.
17. Voit Rubber Corporation, undated company promotion, GAC.
18. George Felix Allen, interview by author, March 22, 2020.
19. George Felix Allen, interview by author, January 21, 2019.
20. Davis, *Papa Bear*, 332.
21. Joe Horrigan, interview by author, March 15, 2019.
22. "Ex-Ram Aide Turns Up in Bear Camp," *Los Angeles Times*, October 20, 1958, C4.
23. Davis, *Papa Bear*, 335.
24. "Bears Sign George Allen," *Los Angeles Times*, December 23, 1958, C2.
25. Halas with Morgan and Veysey, *Halas by Halas*, 281.

5. Doing It George's Way

1. Davis, *Papa Bear*, 49.
2. Halas with Morgan and Veysey, *Halas by Halas*, 147.
3. Carroll et al., *Total Football II*, 370.
4. Davis, *Papa Bear*, 338.
5. William Barry Furlong, "This Morning: Redskins Owe Much to Halas' Blunders," *Washington Post*, December 15, 1974, C1.
6. "Wit and Wisdom of George Halas," *Chicago Tribune*, November 2, 1983, D_A2.
7. Davis, *Papa Bear*, 336.
8. George Felix Allen interview, March 22, 2020.
9. George Felix Allen, interview by author, May 20, 2019.
10. Horrigan interview.
11. George Felix Allen interview, May 20, 2019.

12. William Barry Furlong, "The Last Puritan," *Sports Illustrated*, January 31, 1966, 13.
13. Ed O'Bradovich, interview by author, March 3, 2019. Subsequent quotes are from this interview until noted otherwise.
14. George Felix Allen, interview by author, November 4, 2018.
15. Kevin Lamb, "NFL Draft: Looking Back . . . Bears' Allen Did Job the Old-Fashioned Way," *Chicago Sun-Times*, April 18, 1988, A4.
16. George Felix Allen interview, November 4, 2018.
17. Information on BLESTO from Halas with Morgan and Veysey, *Halas by Halas*, 206–7.
18. Cooper Rollow, "Bears Good Example of Draft Value," *Chicago Tribune*, December 5, 1963, H6.
19. Horrigan interview.
20. Horrigan interview.
21. Dave Steidel, "Billy Cannon, Part 1—The War Begins," *Tales from the American Football League*, January 23, 2013, http://talesfromtheamericanfootballleague.com/billy-cannon-part-1-the-war-begins/.
22. Curran, *$400,000 Quarterback*, 90.
23. George Von Benko, "Birth of the Super Bowl: NFL-AFL Merger Remembered," *Pittsburgh Sports Report*, January 2006, http://www.pittsburghsportsreport.com/2006-Issues/psr0601/06010101.html.
24. William Wallace, "Davis, New Commissioner, Opposes Merger with N.F.L.," *Los Angeles Times* via *New York Times*, April 29, 1966, 53.
25. "Davis Wants 'to Play with Best,' Signs Bear Pact," *Chicago Tribune*, January 3, 1960, A3.
26. Mike Ditka, interview by author, August 8, 2014.
27. George Strickler, "Halas Begins Overhaul Job on Bear Line, Signs Ditka," *Chicago Tribune*, January 12, 1961, D1; "Bears Sign 'Best College Player,' End Mike Ditka," *Baltimore Sun* via the Associated Press, January 12, 1961, S17.
28. Mike Ditka, interview by author, March 29, 2019.
29. Sam Huff, interview by author, August 5, 2014.
30. Ditka interview, March 29, 2019.
31. George Strickler, "Bears Sign Ron Bull, Top Draft Pick," *Chicago Tribune*, December 20, 1961, C1.
32. Ronnie Bull, interview by author, June 28, 2019.
33. Jack Olsen, "A Workhorse Texas Bull," *Sports Illustrated*, October 14, 1963, https://vault.si.com/vault/1963/10/14/a-workhorse-texas-bull.
34. Kevin Lamb, *Chicago Sun-Times*, April 18, 1988, A4.
35. Bull interview.
36. Olsen, "Workhorse Texas Bull."

37. Olsen, "Workhorse Texas Bull."
38. "Glueck Signed by Bears, but Mitchell Lost," *Chicago Tribune*, December 19, 1962, C4.
39. Bruce Allen, interview by author, February 12, 2020.
40. Cooper Rollow, "Meet Roosevelt Taylor, the Musical Bear, Who Rocks and Rolls His Foes," *Chicago Tribune*, July 26, 1964, B4.
41. Roosevelt Taylor, interview by author, June 29, 2019. Subsequent quotes are from this interview until noted otherwise.
42. B. Allen interview, February 12, 2020.
43. Charles Ross, interview by author, November 4, 2019.
44. William Conklin, "Rams Get Crow of Giants and Wade Goes to Bears," *New York Times*, January 29, 1961, S1.
45. Cooper Rollow, "Petitbon and Whitsell in Bears' Fold," *Chicago Tribune*, June 7, 1964, B4.
46. Halas with Morgan and Veysey, *Halas by Halas*, 253.
47. Richie Petitbon, interview by author, November 15, 2018.
48. Bull interview.
49. Joel Bussert, interview by author, July 7, 2019.
50. Davis, *Papa Bear*, 367.
51. "Fame Taps Mr. Allen," *Christian Science Monitor* via the Associated Press, March 26, 1964, 12.
52. Davis, *Papa Bear*, 364–69; Youmans and Youmans, *'63*, 4.
53. Bussert interview, July 7, 2019.
54. Davis, *Papa Bear*, 369.
55. Halas with Morgan and Veysey, *Halas by Halas*, 255.
56. Youmans and Youmans, *'63*, 2.
57. George Strickler, "Allen to Head Bear Defense," *Chicago Tribune*, February 13, 1963, B1.
58. Cooper Rollow, "Bears' Ron Bull Is N.F.L. Rookie of Year," *Chicago Tribune*, December 13, 1962, F4.
59. Rollow, "Bears' Ron Bull Is N.F.L. Rookie of Year," F4.
60. Horrigan interview.
61. Halas with Morgan and Veysey, *Halas by Halas*, 323.
62. Ditka interview, March 29, 2019.
63. O'Bradovich interview. Subsequent quotes are from this interview until noted otherwise.
64. George Strickler, "Giants Clinch Title; Beat Bears, 26–24," *Chicago Tribune*, December 3, 1962, C1.
65. B. Allen interview, February 12, 2020.
66. Bill Curry, interview by author, May 19, 2020.

6. "Allen Never Should Have Left"

1. "Allen to Head Bear Defense," *Chicago Tribune* via United Press International, February 13, 1963, B1.
2. George Strickler, "Bears Sign Stydahar as Defense Aid," *Chicago Tribune*, February 15, 1963, C1.
3. Bull interview.
4. Youmans and Youmans, *'63*, 1–2.
5. Cooper Rollow, "Bears' Defensive Line Overhauled by Stydahar," *Chicago Tribune*, August 28, 1963, C1.
6. "George Halas Cracks Whip over His 'Pampered' Bears," *Baltimore Sun* via the Associated Press, August 6, 1963, 20.
7. George Felix Allen interview, May 20, 2019.
8. Richie Petitbon, interview by author, August 25, 2019.
9. "George Halas Cracks Whip over His 'Pampered' Bears," 20.
10. "In Short: Packers Still 'Loaded'; Lombardi Confident," *Christian Science Monitor* via the Associated Press, September 10, 1963, 12.
11. Youmans and Youmans, *'63*, 155.
12. George Felix Allen interview, May 20, 2019.
13. Cooper Rollow, "Bears Win and Bedlam Reigns," *Chicago Tribune*, September 16, 1963, E1.
14. Rollow, "Bears Win and Bedlam Reigns," E1.
15. Gildea and Turan, *Future Is Now*, 63.
16. "Foe's Remark Helps Bears," *Baltimore Sun* via the Associated Press, February 16, 1964, A4.
17. O'Bradovich interview. Subsequent quotes are from this interview until noted otherwise.
18. Youmans and Youmans, *'63*, 147.
19. Davis, *Papa Bear*, 388.
20. Dave Brady, "Bears Slap Down Green Bay; Steelers Collar Redskins," *Washington Post*, November 18, 1963, A22.
21. Ditka interview.
22. George Felix Allen, interview by author, August 23, 2019.
23. Chicago Bears 1964 press guide, Pro Football Hall of Fame.
24. Chicago Bears 1964 press guide.
25. "Bears' Aerial Defense Seen Tough for Tittle," *Baltimore Sun* via the Associated Press, December 26, 1963, S37.
26. Chicago Bears 1964 press guide.
27. Doug Atkins tribute page, Pro Football Hall of Fame, accessed January 2023, https://www.profootballhof.com/players/doug-atkins/.
28. Halas with Morgan and Veysey, *Halas by Halas*, 316.
29. Bruce Allen, interview by author, March 28, 2020.

30. Doug Atkins tribute page, Pro Football Hall of Fame.
31. Richie Petitbon, interview by author, November 30, 2018.
32. Chicago Bears 1964 press guide.
33. Bull interview.
34. "George Allen Wistfully Remembers That Giants-Bears Game Play by Play," *Washington Times*, May 17, 1982, 7B.
35. O'Bradovich interview.
36. Rich Roberts, "Allen: 'Shades of 1963': Bears Did It with Tough Defense Once Before—and Won NFL Title," *Los Angeles Times*, January 6, 1985, C16.
37. Roberts, "Allen: 'Shades of 1963,'" C16.
38. "Sherman Defends Tittle's Play in Championship Game," *New York Times*, December 30, 1963, 25.
39. O'Bradovich interview.
40. Cooper Rollow, "Bears Are Awed . . . Then They Go Wild!" *Chicago Tribune*, December 30, 1963, B1.
41. Halas with Morgan and Veysey, *Halas by Halas*, 264.
42. Rollow, "Bears Are Awed . . . Then They Go Wild!," B1.
43. Cameron C. Snyder, "'We Were Lucky,' Quips Bears' End Doug Atkins," *Baltimore Sun*, December 30, 1963, S17.
44. O'Bradovich interview.
45. "Fame Taps Mr. Allen," *Christian Science Monitor* via the Associated Press, March 26, 1964, 12.
46. "Bears' Allen Is Approached on Eagle Job," *Chicago Tribune*, February 19, 1964, B1; "Fame Taps Mr. Allen," 12.
47. "Bears Give Allen Ball," *Baltimore Sun* via the Associated Press, December 30, 1963, S17.
48. Mike Ditka, interview by author, April 5, 2019.
49. O'Bradovich interview.
50. George Felix Allen, interview by author, September 21, 2019.
51. Davis, *Papa Bear*, 411.
52. George Felix Allen interview, September 21, 2019.
53. Dan Pompei, interview by author, October 9, 2019.
54. Rand, *300 Pounds of Attitude*, 211.
55. Jim Buol, Kim Buol, and Chris Buol, interview by author, September 30, 2019.
56. George Felix Allen interview, September 21, 2019.
57. Jim Buol, Kim Buol, and Chris Buol interview.
58. Justin Buol, "A Comprehensive History of the Buol Family," chap. 18 (2018), unpublished work in author's possession.
59. From Buol family records.
60. Jim Buol, interview by author, October 2, 2019.
61. Maraniss, *When Pride Still Mattered*, 383.

62. Dick Butkus, interview by author, September 11, 2019.
63. Butkus and Smith, *Butkus*, 119.
64. Cooper Rollow, "Bears Sign Sayers, No. 2 Draft Choice," *Chicago Tribune*, December 2, 1964, E1.
65. Butkus interview.
66. Butkus interview.
67. Rick Smith, *1981 San Diego Chargers Fact Book* (San Diego Chargers, 1981), 41.
68. B. Allen interview, February 12, 2020.
69. Tom Friend, "George Allen Gives Recruiting the Old College Try for 49ers," *The National* (sports daily), February 16, 1990 (scrapbook clipping), GAC.
70. Davis, *Papa Bear*, 33.
71. B. Allen interview, March 28, 2020.
72. Klawitter and Jones, *Headslap*, 308.
73. Jennifer Allen, interview by author, September 30, 2019.
74. "No Decision Reached on Successor," *Baltimore Sun* via the Associated Press, December 24, 1965, B1.
75. Halas with Morgan and Veysey, *Halas by Halas*, 281.
76. Gildea and Turan, *Future Is Now*, 65, 77.
77. Jack Teele, interview by author, June 8, 2013.
78. "Allen to Talk to Rams' Boss," *Chicago Tribune* via United Press International, January 10, 1966, E2.
79. Charles Maher, "George Allen Can Talk, Just Ask the Players," *Los Angeles Times*, December 20, 1966, B3.
80. Gildea and Turan, *Future Is Now*, 66–69; "Bears Ask Injunction to Stop Allen," *Chicago Tribune*, January 12, 1966; Bisheff, *Los Angeles Rams*, 165.
81. "Halas Blasts Reeves for 'Tampering,'" *Washington Post* via the Associated Press, January 11, 1966, B1; "Halas Blasts Rams for Signing Allen," *Chicago Tribune*, January 11, 1966, B1.
82. Davis, *Papa Bear*, 429; "Bears' Aide Hired; N.F.L. Feud Erupts," *Baltimore Sun* via the Associated Press, January 11, 1966, C1.
83. "Bears' Aide Hired; N.F.L. Feud Erupts," C1.
84. Furlong, "Last Puritan," 14.
85. *Chicago's American*, January 13, 1966; *Chicago Sun-Times*, January 15, 1966 (scrapbook clippings), both in GAC.
86. "Bears Name Mather Scout for Colleges," *Chicago Tribune*, February 6, 1966, B2.
87. "Allen Denies Having 'Unique' Talent, Says Pro Trade Secrets Nonexistent," *Washington Post* via news dispatches, January 13, 1966, D1.
88. George Felix Allen interview, September 21, 2019.
89. "Pot Simmers as Rozelle Ducks Feud; Halas Boils," *Chicago Tribune*, January 12, 1966, C1.
90. Gildea and Turan, *Future Is Now*, 80.

91. Gildea and Turan, *Future Is Now*, 71.
92. Contract between Chicago Bears Football Club, Inc., and George H. Allen, starting on March 31, 1965, and signed on June 22, 1965, GAC.
93. "Allen Denies Having 'Unique' Talent, Says Pro Trade Secrets Nonexistent," D1.
94. George Strickler, "Never Read My Bear Contract—Allen," *Chicago Tribune*, January 16, 1966, G1.
95. Contract between Chicago Bears and George H. Allen, signed on June 22, 1965.
96. Strickler, "Never Read My Bear Contract—Allen," G1.
97. Strickler, "Never Read My Bear Contract—Allen," G1; "Halas Wins but Releases George Allen," *Baltimore Sun* via the Associated Press, January 19, 1966, C1; Mal Florence, "Halas Drops Suit; Rams Get a Coach," *Los Angeles Times*, January 19, 1966, B1.
98. "Halas Wins but Releases George Allen," C1.
99. Florence, "Halas Drops Suit; Rams Get a Coach," B1.
100. Furlong, "Last Puritan," 14.
101. George Strickler, "Halas Tells His Side of Allen Case," *Chicago Tribune*, January 20, 1966, J1.
102. "Halas Says Allen Made Four Propositions to Stay with Bears after Taking Rams' Job," *Washington Post* via United Press International, January 20, 1966, F1; Strickler, "Halas Tells His Side of Allen Case," J1.
103. "Halas Charges 'Chicanery' by Rozelle, Reeves and Allen," *New York Times* via United Press International, January 20, 1966, 40.
104. Halas with Morgan and Veysey, *Halas by Halas*, 282.
105. Unidentified scrapbook clipping, GAC.
106. George Felix Allen and Jennifer Allen, interviews by author, October 14, 2019.
107. "Halas Wins—but So Does Allen," *Chicago's American*, January 18, 1966, A1.
108. Horrigan interview.
109. Butkus interview.
110. O'Bradovich interview.
111. Pompei interview.
112. Pete Rozelle to George Allen, January 26, 1966, GAC.
113. Dave Brady, "Biggest Man in Washington? George Allen!" *Washington Post*, November 14, 1971, E11; Bob Verdi, "A Final 'Hello' from Coach Allen," *Chicago Tribune*, January 3, 1991, A1.

7. Erasing a "Country Club" Image

1. Ed Meador, interview by author, April 6, 2019.
2. Mal Florence, "Rams Relaxed for Playoff Bowl," *Los Angeles Times*, January 7, 1968, 14.

3. Tom Reed, "How Moving a Franchise from Cleveland to L.A. Benefited the Browns and Fostered Social Change," Cleveland.com, February 3, 2014, https://www.cleveland.com/browns/2014/02/cleveland_rams_browns_move_to_los_angeles.html.
4. Teele interview.
5. Piascik, *Gridiron Gauntlet*, 9.
6. Dan Reeves tribute page, Pro Football Hall of Fame, accessed March 20, 2019, https://www.profootballhof.com/players/dan-reeves/.
7. Bisheff, *Los Angeles Rams*, 179.
8. Frank Finch, "Pool Succeeds Stydahar as Ram Coach; Joe Paid $11,900," *Los Angeles Times*, October 1, 1952, C1.
9. Los Angeles Rams 1966 press guide, Pro Football Hall of Fame.
10. Mal Florence, "No April Fool! Rams Hold Spring Practice—for 24 Rookie Players," *Los Angeles Times*, April 3, 1966, C4.
11. B. Allen interview, March 28, 2020.
12. Melvin Durslag, "How Tough Should a Coach Get?" *Los Angeles Herald Examiner*, October 12, 1966 (scrapbook clipping), GAC.
13. Gildea and Turan, *Future Is Now*, 83.
14. Tony Guillory, interview by author, November 11, 2019.
15. Irv Cross, interview by author, April 12, 2019.
16. Los Angeles Rams 1966 press guide.
17. Cross interview, April 12, 2019.
18. Klawitter and Jones, *Headslap*, 318.
19. Gildea and Turan, *Future Is Now*, 98.
20. Klawitter and Jones, *Headslap*, 319.
21. Teele interview.
22. George Felix Allen interview, September 21, 2019.
23. Roman Gabriel, interview by author, April 13, 2019.
24. Ted Marchibroda, interview by author, July 17, 2013.
25. Mal Florence, "Counter-Spy Measures Taken by Allen, Halas in Secret Drills," *Los Angeles Times*, September 14, 1966, B5.
26. Irv Cross, interview by author, April 8, 2019.
27. G. Allen recorded conversation with Guback.
28. Deacon Jones presenting George Allen for Hall of Fame induction, August 3, 2002, https://www.profootballhof.com/players/george-allen/.
29. Klawitter and Jones, *Headslap*, 311–12.
30. Klawitter and Jones, *Headslap*, 310–11.
31. "Allen Tells Plans for Rams," *Chicago Sun-Times*, January 20, 1966, 112 (scrapbook clipping), GAC.
32. Marchibroda interview, July 17, 2013.
33. Rosey Grier, interview by author, June 13, 2013.

34. Roman Gabriel, interview by author, April 12, 2019. Subsequent quotes are from this interview until noted otherwise.
35. Grier interview.
36. Gabriel interview, April 12, 2019.
37. B. Allen interview, February 12, 2020.
38. *Winning Is Living, Losing Is Dying: The George Allen Story* (NFL Films, 2001).
39. B. Allen interview, February 12, 2020.
40. Durslag, "How Tough Should a Coach Get?"
41. Mal Florence, "Grier Checks In at a Svelte 287," *Los Angeles Times*, July 18, 1966, B8.
42. Sid Ziff, "Starving at Orange," *Los Angeles Times*, August 4, 1966, B3.
43. B. Allen interview, February 12, 2020.
44. Tom Mack, interview by author, April 22, 2019.
45. Tom Mack bio, Pro Football Hall of Fame, accessed March 20, 2019, https://www.profootballhof.com/players/tom-mack/biography/.
46. Jim Carlisle, "Carlisle: Back in a Simpler Time, Cowboys Made Cal Lutheran Their Home," *Ventura County Star*, August 12, 2013, http://archive.vcstar.com/news/carlisle-back-in-a-simpler-time-cowboys-made-cal-lutheran-their-home-ep-292455311-351642611.html/.
47. "Rams, Cowboys in 4-Ring Circus," *Los Angeles Times*, July 29, 1966, C7.
48. Cross interview, April 8, 2019.
49. Mal Florence, "Gabriel Signs . . . and Signs," *Los Angeles Times*, May 27, 1966, C1.
50. Mal Florence, "Munson Realistic—He's Still No. 2," *Los Angeles Times*, May 12, 1967, C1.
51. Mal Florence, "Gabe Won't Deny Signing," *Los Angeles Times*, May 28, 1966, A2.
52. Gabriel interview, April 12, 2019.
53. B. Allen interview, February 12, 2020.
54. Tom Mack, interview by author, March 9, 2020.
55. Mal Florence, "Rams No Longer Patsies, Claims Gabriel," *Los Angeles Times*, September 8, 1966, C5.

8. An Addiction to Winning

1. Mal Florence, "Falcons Cry U.N.C.L.E. Following Rams' 19–14 Victory," *Los Angeles Times*, September 12, 1966, B1.
2. Steve Guback, interview by author, August 16, 2003.
3. "Cloak and Dagger: Rams Suspect Bears Overhear Strategy Phoned by Assistants," *Los Angeles Times*, October 20, 1958, C1.
4. Mal Florence, "Counter-Spy Measures Taken by Allen, Halas in Secret Drills," *Los Angeles Times*, September 14, 1966, B5.

5. "Bears' Halas Skips Allen Hand-Shake," Associated Press, September 18, 1966 (scrapbook clipping), GAC.
6. Bud Furillo, "George Allen—the Spellbinder," *Los Angeles Herald Examiner*, September 17, 1966 (scrapbook clipping), GAC.
7. Sid Ziff, "Rams' Horse-and-Buggy Game Can't Raise Gallop," *Los Angeles Times*, September 26, 1966, B1.
8. J. Allen, *Fifth Quarter*, 147.
9. Al Wolf, "Packers Will Lose 4 Games—Allen," *Los Angeles Times*, September 27, 1966, B5.
10. Jeff Prugh, "Rams Feel They Can Steal Title," *Los Angeles Times*, October 11, 1966, B1.
11. *Winning Is Living, Losing Is Dying*.
12. Hal Jensen, "Ice Cream Allen Hits Jackpot—a Season's Supply," *Los Angeles Herald Examiner*, August 12, 1966 (scrapbook clipping), GAC.
13. Charles Maher, "Jones Slings Mud at Kezar Gridiron: 'Like a Hog Pen,'" *Los Angeles Times*, November 7, 1966, B1.
14. "Ram-Bear Locker Room," *Los Angeles Times*, October 24, 1966, B7.
15. John Hall, "One for the Gipper," *Los Angeles Times*, October 29, 1966, A3.
16. George Felix Allen interview, December 19, 2019.
17. Charles Maher, "Rams Got 'Hungry' Because They Were Laughed At—Allen," *Los Angeles Times*, November 14, 1966, C1.
18. George Felix Allen, interview by author, June 5, 2020.
19. Don Shula bio, Pro Football Hall of Fame, accessed March 22, 2019, https://www.profootballhof.com/players/don-shula/.
20. Curry interview.
21. Don Shula, interview by author, March 15, 2001.
22. Jennifer Allen, interview by author, May 13, 2020.
23. Mal Florence, "Proud Packers Wreck Ram Bowl Hopes," *Los Angeles Times*, December 19, 1966, B1.
24. George Allen to Vince Lombardi, January 4, 1967, GAC.
25. John Hall, "Pro Bowl Luncheon Develops into 'Testimonial' for Allen," *Los Angeles Times*, January 18, 1967, C2.
26. Butkus interview.
27. Los Angeles Rams 1967 press guide, Pro Football Hall of Fame.
28. Jim Murray, "Don't Snicker at the Man in Sneakers—Yet," *Los Angeles Times*, August 20, 1967, H1.
29. Grier interview.
30. Cross interview, April 12, 2019.
31. Cross interview, April 12, 2019.
32. *The Fearsome Foursome: A Football Life* (NFL Films, 2012).
33. Curry interview.

34. Deacon Jones bio, Pro Football Hall of Fame, accessed March 21, 2019, https://www.profootballhof.com/news/deacon-jones-1938-2013/.
35. Deacon Jones, interview by author, July 15, 2000.
36. Libby, *Life in the Pit*, 17.
37. *Winning Is Living, Losing Is Dying.*
38. Elizabeth Jones, interview by author, December 11, 2019.
39. *Winning Is Living, Losing Is Dying.*
40. Elizabeth Jones interview.
41. J. Allen, interview by author, December 2, 2019.
42. B. Allen, interview by author, April 15, 2020.
43. Bob Lilly, interview by author, January 3, 2020.
44. Merlin Olsen, interview by author, August 2, 2003.
45. Sid Ziff, "Allen Took to the Surf," *Los Angeles Times*, March 3, 1967, C3.
46. Mal Florence, "Rams Face Slim Pickings in First Joint NFL-AFL Player Draft Today," *Los Angeles Times*, March 14, 1967, C4.
47. Mal Florence, "Rams Trade McKeever for Mason, Bedsole," *Los Angeles Times*, March 15, 1967, C1.
48. Mal Florence, "Rams Get Veteran End Casey, Trade Moore to Atlanta," *Los Angeles Times*, July 11, 1967, B1.
49. "Rams Summer Camp Moved to Fullerton," *Los Angeles Times*, April 1, 1967, A4.
50. Mal Florence, "Would You Believe Grier as a Cyclist?" *Los Angeles Times*, July 27, 1967, B5.
51. Gildea and Turan, *Future Is Now*, 98.
52. John Hall, "It Could Be Worse," *Los Angeles Times*, June 14, 1967, B3.
53. Al Larson, "Rams, You're Kiddin'!" *Independent Press-Telegram* (Long Beach CA), December 10, 1967, D1.
54. Mack interview, March 9, 2020.
55. Cross interview, April 12, 2019.
56. Mal Florence, "Lions' Roger Brown Traded to Rams for 3 Draft Picks," *Los Angeles Times*, September 8, 1967, B1.
57. Roger Brown, interview by author, April 6, 2019.
58. Mal Florence, "Rams' Offense Rips Dallas, 35–13," *Los Angeles Times*, October 2, 1967, A1.
59. *Los Angeles Herald Examiner*, October 1, 1967 (scrapbook clipping), GAC.
60. Mal Florence, "Cowboys Blow the Whistle on 'Spying' Rams," *Los Angeles Times*, September 30, 1967, A1.
61. Lilly interview.
62. Cross interview, April 8, 2019.
63. B. Allen, interview with the author, March 15, 2010.
64. Gildea and Turan, *Future Is Now*, 87.
65. Gildea and Turan, *Future Is Now*, 87.

66. Charles Maher, "Ram Coach's Wife Is a Devoted 'Widow,'" *Los Angeles Times*, October 13, 1967, B1.
67. Bill Jauss, "Lombardi vs. Allen: 2 Types of Dedication," *Chicago Daily News*, December 21, 1967 (scrapbook clipping), GAC.
68. Libby, *Life in the Pit*, 98–99.
69. George Felix Allen interview, June 5, 2020.
70. Gildea and Turan, *Future Is Now*, 87.
71. Mitch Chortkoff, "George Allen Began Early for Packers," *Los Angeles Herald Examiner*, December 4, 1967 (scrapbook clipping), GAC.
72. Guillory interview.
73. Bisheff, *Los Angeles Rams*, 96.
74. Mal Florence, "Allen's Uneasy Thought: 'Did We Win or Lose?'" *Los Angeles Times*, December 11, 1967, E1.
75. J. Allen interview, December 6, 2019.
76 . Bisheff, *Los Angeles Rams*, 99.
77. Tex Maule, "A Real Wowser for the Rams," *Sports Illustrated*, December 18, 1967, 17.
78. Florence, "Allen's Uneasy Thought," E1.
79. J. Allen interview, December 6, 2019.
80. "Colts-Rams Game Biggest of Season," *New York Times* via the Associated Press, December 17, 1967, 191.
81. Arthur Daley, "Sports of the Times: Last Roadblock Lucky Bounce the 610-Pound Crush," *New York Times*, December 15, 1967, 70.
82. Paul Zimmerman, "Gabriel, Defense, Wreck Colts, 34–10," *Los Angeles Times*, December 18, 1967, 1.
83. Curry interview.
84. Hall, "It Could Be Worse," B3.
85. Vince Lombardi, "Pro Football: A Game for Madmen," *Look Magazine*, September 5, 1967.
86. Bob Oates, "Lombardi Hates; Sid Loves, Allen Fears," *Los Angeles Herald Examiner*, August 23, 1967 (scrapbook clipping), GAC.
87. Grier interview.
88. George Felix Allen interview, December 19, 2019.
89. "Lombardi Sends Wounded Packers Limping through Their Paces," *Los Angeles Times* via United Press International, December 20, 1967, B8.
90. Paul Zimmerman, "Ram Front Four Human after All; Bye Bye Title," *Los Angeles Times*, December 24, 1967, G1.
91. "Old Pros' [*sic*] Desire the Difference," *Los Angeles Times*, December 24, 1967, G4.
92. Zimmerman, "Ram Front Four Human after All," G1.
93. Charles Maher, "Allen Works Hard to Win Stupor Bowl," *Los Angeles Times*, January 7, 1968, I4.

94. Roman Gabriel, interview by author, April 9, 2019.
95. Tim Rohan, "The Playoff Bowl: The Worst Kind of Garbage Time," *Sports Illustrated*, June 22, 2017, https://www.si.com/nfl/2017/06/22/nfl-playoff-bowl-garbage-time.
96. Maher, "Allen Works Hard to Win Stupor Bowl," 14.
97. Maher, "Allen Works Hard to Win Stupor Bowl," 14.
98. Gabriel interview, April 13, 2019.
99. Los Angeles Rams 1967 press guide.

9. "Merry Christmas, You're Fired"

1. Los Angeles Rams 1967 press guide.
2. Lilly interview.
3. "TD Production of Ram Receivers Shows Impressive Gain—Up 329%," *Los Angeles Times*, March 10, 1968, C12.
4. Bisheff, *Los Angeles Rams*, 167–68.
5. Mal Florence, "Munson Indicates He'll Play Out Ram Option," *Los Angeles Times*, September 19, 1967, C3.
6. "Munson Makes It Definite—He's Finished as Ram," *Los Angeles Times*, April 4, 1968, OC_B1.
7. "Rams Get Three Lions, No. 1 Draft for Munson," *Los Angeles Times*, May 2, 1968, D1.
8. B. Allen interview, February 12, 2020.
9. Bob Oates, "Rams Trade Beban to 'Skins for No. 1 Draft," *Los Angeles Times*, June 15, 1968, A1.
10. B. Allen interview, February 12, 2020.
11. Dave Brady, "Gary Beban Is Released by Redskins," *Washington Post*, November 8, 1970, C7.
12. Gildea and Turan, *Future Is Now*, 12.
13. Dave Brady, "Teammates, Foes Put Taylor Higher than Critics' Choices," *Washington Post*, December 21, 1969, 48.
14. Gildea and Turan, *Future Is Now*, 12–13.
15. B. Allen interview, February 12, 2020.
16. Dial Torgerson, "Kennedy Dies, Succumbs to Assassin's Bullet," *Los Angeles Times*, June 6, 1968, O1.
17. Torgerson, "Kennedy Dies, Succumbs to Assassin's Bullet," O1.
18. George Felix Allen interview, December 19, 2019.
19. Cross interview, April 12, 2019.
20. Mack interview, April 22, 2019.
21. Grier interview.
22. Gabriel interview, April 13, 2019.
23. George Felix Allen, interview by author, March 18, 2020.

24. Bob Oates, "Rams' Championship Aspirations May Hinge on Another 110% Effort," *Los Angeles Times*, September 10, 1968, E2.
25. Los Angeles Rams 1969 press guide, Pro Football Hall of Fame.
26. Bob Oates, "Deacon Accuses Crow of Illegal 'Cheap Shot,'" *Los Angeles Times*, November 19, 1968, D1.
27. Mal Florence, "Reeves Censures Allen for Criticism of Kezar," *Los Angeles Times*, November 20, 1968, 16B.
28. Bisheff, *Los Angeles Rams*, 168.
29. Bob Oates, "Allen Predicts Sweep for Title," *Los Angeles Times*, November 26, 1968, F1.
30. Mal Florence, "Rozelle Suspends Officials for 'Losing' Down," *Los Angeles Times*, December 10, 1968, C1.
31. Mal Florence, "Rams Lose a Down—and Shot at Title, 17–16," *Los Angeles Times*, December 9, 1968, E1.
32. Charles Maher, "An Empty Feeling," *Los Angeles Times*, December 17, 1968, H2.
33. J. Allen interview, December 6, 2019. Subsequent quotations are from this interview until noted otherwise.
34. George Felix Allen interview, December 19, 2019.
35. "Rams Owner Fires Coach George Allen," *Chicago Tribune* via United Press International, December 27, 1968, C1.
36. Bob Oates, "Allen: I'm Back Because My Players Stood Up for Me,'" *Los Angeles Times*, January 7, 1969, E1.
37. Mal Florence, "Rams Fire Allen in 'Personality Clash,'" *Los Angeles Times*, December 27, 1968, 1.
38. Bisheff, *Los Angeles Rams*, 169.
39. Melvin Durslag, "Who Is Reeves' Kind of Guy?" *Los Angeles Herald Examiner*, December 29, 1968, D-2.
40. J. Allen, *Fifth Quarter*, 3.
41. G. Allen recorded conversation with Guback.
42. Bisheff, *Los Angeles Rams*, 170.
43. Teele interview. Subsequent quotes are from this interview until noted otherwise.
44. George Felix Allen, interview by author, September 19, 2019.
45. Doug Krikorian, interview by author, August 27, 2021.
46. John Hall, "Winning Isn't All," *Los Angeles Times*, December 27, 1968, D3.
47. "Rams Owner Fires Coach George Allen," *Los Angeles Times* via United Press International, December 27, 1968, C1.
48. Mal Florence, "We Don't Want a Loser—Cowan," *Los Angeles Times*, December 27, 1968, D1.
49. Hank Hollingworth, "Allen: 'All I Did Was for the Rams,'" *Independent Press-Telegram*, December 28, 1968, C1.

50. "Rams Threaten to Retire," *Chicago's American* via the Associated Press, December 28, 1968 (scrapbook clipping), GAC.
51. Mal Florence, "Jones, Baughan, Bass to Quit If Rams Don't Keep Allen," *Los Angeles Times*, December 28, 1968, C1.
52. B. Allen interview, February 12, 2020.
53. George Burman, interview by author, October 25, 2015.
54. Gildea and Turan, *Future Is Now*, 101.
55. Bisheff, *Los Angeles Rams*, 169; "Group Formed to Support George Allen," *Los Angeles Times*, December 28, 1968, C3.
56. "George Lost His Job, but Not His Fans," *Los Angeles Herald Examiner*, December 30, 1968, D1 (scrapbook clipping), GAC.
57. "Group Formed to Support George Allen," C3; Bob Oates, "Reeves Rumored Ready to Sell Rams," *Los Angeles Times*, March 28, 1969, G3.
58. "Allen Boosters Say 2,500 Protest Firing," *Los Angeles Times*, December 31, 1968, D4.
59. Jim Murray, "Did Allen Lock Reeves Out of His Own House?" *Los Angeles Times*, December 31, 1968, D1.
60. Durslag, "Who Is Reeves' Kind of Guy?," D2.
61. "Allen Fired; Players Threaten Revolt," *Los Angeles Times*, December 27, 1968, D1.
62. B. Allen interview, February 12, 2020.
63. Florence, "Rams Fire Allen in 'Personality Clash,'" 1.
64. B. Allen interview, February 12, 2020.
65. G. Allen recorded conversation with Guback.
66. George Felix Allen interview, December 19, 2019.
67. Bill Libby, "George Allen's Farewell," *Los Angeles Times*, February 7, 1971, A28.
68. John Hall, "Trap That Jack Built," *Los Angeles Times*, May 22, 1968, B3.
69. Libby, "George Allen's Farewell," A28.
70. G. Allen recorded conversation with Guback.
71. Oates, "Allen: I'm Back Because My Players Stood Up for Me,'" E1.
72. G. Allen recorded conversation with Guback.
73. Letters from Richard Nixon to George Allen and from Allen to Nixon, GAC.
74. J. V. Rasinski, interview by author, December 8, 2019.
75. Mal Florence, "Allen Meets with Reeves; Situation Remains the Same," *Los Angeles Times*, January 5, 1969, D1.
76. Bisheff, *Los Angeles Rams*, 171.
77. Furillo article quoted in Bisheff, *Los Angeles Rams*, 171.
78. Mal Florence, "Reeves: 'Allen's Intense Loyalty, Devotion Sole Reason,'" *Los Angeles Times*, January 7, 1969, E1.
79. Bisheff, *Los Angeles Rams*, 171.
80. Florence, "Reeves: 'Allen's Intense Loyalty, Devotion Sole Reason,'" E1.

81. Furillo article quoted in Gildea and Turan, *Future Is Now*, 101–2.

10. A Bear and a Moose

1. Gildea and Turan, *Future Is Now*, 103.
2. Mack interview, March 9, 2020.
3. George Allen to Dan Reeves, January 11, 1969, GAC.
4. "A Day for Allen," *Los Angeles Times*, January 19, 1969, B7.
5. Bob Oates, "Shula Coaches 'Only on Sunday,'" *Los Angeles Times*, January 9, 1969, E1.
6. Rasinski interview.
7. "Ex-Gridder Says Pep Pills Used by Many Professional Players," *Times-Leader, Evening News, Record* via the Associated Press, November 15, 1973 (scrapbook clipping), GAC.
8. Rasinski interview.
9. B. Allen interview, February 12, 2020.
10. Rasinski interview.
11. Rasinski interview; George Felix Allen, interview by author, December 18, 2019.
12. Jennifer Allen, interview by author, December 8, 2019.
13. George Felix Allen interview, December 18, 2019.
14. Mal Florence, "Eagles' Bob Brown Traded to Rams," *Los Angeles Times*, May 13, 1969, OC_A1.
15. Bob Oates, "Casey Quits Rams to Pursue Career in Arts," *Los Angeles Times*, May 2, 1969, D1.
16. Mike Barnes, "Bernie Casey, Football Star Turned Actor, Poet and Painter, Dies at 78," *Hollywood Reporter*, September 20, 2017, https://www.hollywoodreporter.com/news/bernie-casey-dead-actor-nfl-910749.
17. Cross interview, April 12, 2019.
18. Harold Jackson, interview by author, March 24, 2020.
19. Mal Florence, "Rams' Top Draft Choice Seymour Lost for Season," *Los Angeles Times*, July 31, 1969, OC_B1.
20. B. Allen interview, March 28, 2020.
21. Mack interview, March 9, 2020.
22. Maher, "George Allen Can Talk, Just Ask the Players," B3.
23. Frank Litsky, "Payton Jordan, U.S. Track Team Coach, Is Dead at 91," *New York Times*, February 6, 2009, https://www.nytimes.com/2009/02/07/sports/othersports/07jordan.html.
24. Dick Vermeil, interview by author, May 1, 2018.
25. Mal Florence, "Past Haunts Allen as Crippled Rams Engage Colts," *Los Angeles Times*, September 21, 1969, C3.
26. Joe Hendrickson, "'Greatest Ram Victory'—Allen," *Pasadena Star-News*, September 22, 1969 (scrapbook clipping), GAC.

27. "Rozelle Upholds Baltimore Claim," *New York Times*, April 14, 1970, 64.
28. Los Angeles Rams 1970 press guide, Pro Football Hall of Fame.
29. Bob Oates, "Rams Contain Sonny, Clinch Coastal Title, 24–13," *Los Angeles Times*, December 1, 1969, C1.
30. Kenneth Turan, "Rams Front Four Hound Jurgensen in Demonstration of Their Respect," *Washington Post*, December 1, 1969, D1.
31. B. Allen interview, March 28, 2020.
32. Mal Florence, "The Next Ram Target: A Perfect 14-0 Season," *Los Angeles Times*, December 1, 1969, C1.
33. Mal Florence, "Allen Can't Abide Defeat," *Los Angeles Times*, December 8, 1969, F1.
34. "Rams Continue Mad Retreat into Playoffs, Fall to Colts," *Los Angeles Times*, December 22, 1969, D1.
35. Gabriel interview, April 13, 2019.
36. Gabriel interview, April 13, 2019.
37. Mack interview, March 9, 2020.
38. Mal Florence, "No Tears, Just Stunned Silence," *Los Angeles Times*, December 28, 1969, C1.
39. Mack interview, March 9, 2020.
40. Alfred Wright, "You Win! You're Fired," *Sports Illustrated*, September 7, 1970, https://vault.si.com/vault/1970/09/07/you-win-youre-fired.
41. B. Allen interview, March 28, 2020.
42. Richie Petitbon, interview by author, March 15, 2018.
43. J. Allen interview, December 8, 2019.
44. Bob Oates, "Rams-Lions a 'Championship Game'—Allen," *Los Angeles Times*, December 9, 1970, H1.
45. Charles Maher, "Dan and George," *Los Angeles Times*, December 23, 1970, F2.
46. Bob Myers, "Happy New Year, George, You're Fired," *San Bernardino Sun* via the Associated Press, December 31, 1970, sec. D.
47. Mal Florence, "Allen Sacked Again—Grounds: Incompatibility," *Los Angeles Times*, December 31, 1970, E1.
48. Mack interview, March 9, 2020.
49. Florence, "Allen Sacked Again," E1.
50. "Rams Sign Prothro to 5-Year Contract," *Los Angeles Times* via news dispatches, January 3, 1971, D1; Dwight Chapin, "Rams Land Prothro—for $90,000 Plus," *Los Angeles Times*, January 3, 1971, D1.
51. George Felix Allen interview, March 18, 2020.
52. Mack interview, March 9, 2020.
53. Florence, "Allen Sacked Again," E1.
54. Dave Brady, "Job Talk Centers on George Allen," *Washington Post*, December 26, 1970, C2.
55. Florence, "Allen Sacked Again," E1.

11. Mr. Allen Goes to Washington

1. George Felix Allen interview, December 18, 2019.
2. John Kent Cooke, interview by author, May 6, 2021.
3. "Allen's 14-Point Contract Said Richest Ever Offered," *Washington Post* via the Associated Press, January 30, 1971, C1.
4. George Felix Allen interview, December 18, 2019.
5. Dave Brady, "Club to Retire Stock Bought by Lombardi," *Washington Post*, April 18, 1971, D10.
6. George Felix Allen interview, December 18, 2019.
7. George Felix Allen interview, December 18, 2019.
8. O'Toole, *Fight for Old DC*, 21.
9. Thomas, *Man to See*, 168.
10. Thomas, *Man to See*, 167–68.
11. Dave Brady, "Shea Opines Running Redskins Becoming Too Much for Marshall," *Washington Post*, September 12, 1962, D2.
12. Maraniss, *When Pride Still Mattered*, 446.
13. G. Allen recorded conversation with Guback.
14. G. Allen recorded conversation with Guback.
15. Gildea and Turan, *Future Is Now*, 13–14.
16. Ted Marchibroda, interview by author, June 25, 2013.
17. "Nixon Phones Allen, Sees 'Good Year,'" *Washington Post* via United Press International, January 9, 1971, D1.
18. Francis Stann, "Reeves May Have Done Redskins Fans a Favor," *Evening Star* (Washington DC), January 10, 1971, F2.
19. Washington Redskins 1971 press guide, Pro Football Hall of Fame.
20. Ken Denlinger, "Theofiledes Surprised, Too," *Washington Post*, December 16, 1968, D2.
21. Mal Florence, "Allen Hired as New Coach, GM of Redskins," *Los Angeles Times*, January 7, 1971, E1.
22. Ken Denlinger, "Allen to Draft Defense First," *Washington Post*, January 21, 1971, D1.
23. B. Allen interview, March 28, 2020.
24. Tommy McVean, interview by author, September 15, 2017.
25. Dave Brady, "Redskins Stack Defense with Veteran Rams," *Washington Post*, January 29, 1971, D1.
26. Brady, "Redskins Stack Defense with Veteran Rams," D1.
27. Gildea and Turan, *Future Is Now*, 22.
28. Steve Guback, *Evening Star*, February 15, 1971 (scrapbook clipping), GAC.
29. Bill Libby, "George Allen's Farewell," *Los Angeles Times*, February 7, 1971, A28.
30. Mal Florence, "Allen Insists It Is Reeves Who Is Stretching the Truth," *Los Angeles Times*, February 16, 1971 (scrapbook clipping), GAC.

31. Mal Florence, "Reeves Breaks Silence, Answers Allen's Attack," *Los Angeles Times*, February 14, 1971, C1.
32. Owens interview.
33. Terry Hermeling, interview by author, July 5, 2020.
34. B. Allen interview, February 10, 2020.
35. Gildea and Turan, *Future Is Now*, 188–89.
36. Richard Justice, "Williams Practiced a Relentless Drive to Win," *Washington Post*, August 14, 1988, 45.
37. B. Allen interview, March 28, 2020.
38. B. Allen interview, March 28, 2020.
39. Dave Brady, "Redskins Lock Up Dulles Reservation," *Washington Post*, May 13, 1971, K4; Dave Brady, "Allen Late as Redskins Dig Virginia," *Washington Post*, June 3, 1971, D1.
40. B. Allen interview, March 28, 2020.
41. Gildea and Turan, *Future Is Now*, 187.
42. Ken Turan, interview by author, August 4, 2020.
43. George Felix Allen, interview by author, June 27, 2020.
44. *Three Cheers for the Redskins* (NFL Films, 2001).
45. *Three Cheers for the Redskins.*
46. Ken Denlinger, "Allen Suffers Broken Rib in Pass Drill," *Washington Post*, July 30, 1971, E1.
47. Steve Guback, *Evening Star*, July 30, 1971 (scrapbook clipping), SGC.
48. Denlinger, "Allen Suffers Broken Rib in Pass Drill," E1.
49. Guback, *Evening Star*, July 30, 1971.
50. Owens interview.
51. Dave Brady, "Moderation Is Key at Carlisle as Allen Directs Adult Redskins," *Washington Post*, July 16, 1971, D1.
52. Pat Fischer, interview by author, March 10, 2003.
53. Roy Jefferson, interview by author, July 31, 2020.
54. McDole with Morris, *Dancing Bear*, 119.
55. Ron McDole, interview by author, July 15, 2003.
56. William Gildea, "Verlon Biggs Signs to Play for Redskins," *Washington Post*, June 11, 1971, D1.
57. Washington Redskins 1971 press guide.
58. G. Allen recorded conversation with Guback.
59. William Gildea, "Redskins' Claim for Karras Voided," *Washington Post*, September 16, 1971, H1.
60. Kopay and Young, *David Kopay Story*, 177.
61. Kopay and Young, *David Kopay Story*, 177.
62. Dave Brady, "Redskins Burn Up Denver, Win with 94-Yard Attack," *Washington Post*, August 16, 1971, D1; Gildea and Turan, *Future Is Now*, 22.

63. Steve Guback, “Shoulder Surgery Shelves Jurgensen,” *Evening Star*, September 6, 1971, A1.
64. Dave Brady, “Allen Sees Team ‘Banding Together,’” *Washington Post*, September 10, 1971, D1.

12. Waking a Sleeping Giant

1. Gildea and Turan, *Future Is Now*, 144–45.
2. Bob Addie, “Deluxe Verbiage,” *Washington Post*, September 11, 1971, E1.
3. B. Allen interview, March 28, 2020.
4. *Three Cheers for the Redskins.*
5. Owens interview.
6. Steve Guback, “Kilmer Stars for Redskins,” *Evening Star*, September 27, 1971, D1.
7. Steve Guback, interview by author, August 23, 2003.
8. Hermeling interview.
9. Dave Brady, “Redskins Scouts Track an Interloper,” *Washington Post*, October 2, 1971, D3.
10. Ken Denlinger, “Redskins Scheduled to Face Cowboys’ Groovy Morton,” *Washington Post*, September 30, 1971, E3.
11. Norm Miller, “Allen’s ‘I Spy’ Tactics Have Giants Worried,” *New York Daily News*, October 28, 1972, 34.
12. B. Allen interview, March 28, 2020.
13. B. Allen interview, March 28, 2020.
14. Bill Kilmer, interview by author, November 6, 2020.
15. Steve Guback, “What Hath George Allen Wrought?” *Evening Star*, October 4, 1971, D1.
16. Shirley Povich, “This Morning with Shirley Povich,” *Washington Post*, October 3, 1971, D1.
17. Steve Gilmartin, interview by author, March 15, 2002. Subsequent quotes are from this interview until noted otherwise.
18. William Gildea, “Driesell Begins Groundwork on Creating ‘UCLA of East,’” *Washington Post*, March 20, 1969, 45.
19. “Mayor Visits Redskins,” *Washington Post*, October 6, 1971, C1.
20. George Felix Allen interview, March 18, 2020.
21. B. Allen interview, March 28, 2020.
22. Jack Pardee, interview by author, January 16, 2013.
23. *Three Cheers for the Redskins.*
24. Robert J. Donovan, “New Potomac Fever: Who Says Bipartisanship Is Dead in D.C.?” *Los Angeles Times*, November 4, 1971, E1.
25. Steve Guback, “George Allen Strikes Again: Enter McNeil and Exit Flowers,” *Evening Star*, October 27, 1971, D1.
26. G. Allen recorded conversation with Guback.

27. "President Richard Nixon Speaks at 1971 Hall of Fame Gold Jacket Dinner," YouTube, February 16, 2018, https://www.youtube.com/watch?v=OA3mTgI13PQ.
28. Gildea and Turan, *Future Is Now*, 261.
29. George Allen letters to Richard Nixon, undated (from 1970) and May 10, 1972, GAC.
30. Spencer Rich and Richard L. Lyons, "Democrats Lash Out, but GOP Rallies for Nixon," *Washington Post*, May 9, 1972, A11.
31. George Allen to Richard Nixon, May 10, 1972; Richard Nixon to George Allen, May 15, 1972, both in GAC.
32. Jennifer Allen, "Nixon's Tricks Not in the Redskins' Playbook," ESPN.com, accessed April 17, 2023, http://www.espn.com/page2/wash/s/allen/020308.html.
33. G. Allen recorded conversation with Guback.
34. G. Allen recorded conversation with Guback.
35. George Felix Allen, interview by author, September 10, 2002.
36. Gildea and Turan, *Future Is Now*, 261; John Underwood, "The Ice-Cream Man Cometh," *Sports Illustrated*, October 25, 1971, https://vault.si.com/vault/1971/10/25/the-icecream-man-cometh.
37. "Nixon Watches 2 Games at Once," *Washington Post* via the Associated Press, November 22, 1971, A3; Gildea and Turan, *Future Is Now*, 261.
38. "TV Blackout Ban Backed by Nixon," *New York Times* via United Press International, October 4, 1972, 58.
39. "House Geared Up to Lift TV Curtain for Opener," *Washington Post* via the Associated Press, September 12, 1973, E1.
40. Jefferson interview.
41. Hermeling interview.
42. Gildea and Turan, *Future Is Now*, 262.
43. Don Irwin, "Redskins Powwow with Big Chief on the Art of Winning," *Los Angeles Times*, November 24, 1971, A1.
44. "Nixon Pays Surprise Visit to Redskins, Gives Pep Talk," *New York Times* via the Associated Press, November 24, 1971, 41.
45. Paul Attner, "Redskin Visitor Sees a Better Day," *Washington Post*, November 24, 1971, D1.
46. Ken Denlinger, "Candidates Woo Athletes," *Washington Post*, October 14, 1973, C3.
47. Jefferson interview.
48. G. Allen recorded conversation with Guback.
49. Ray Schoenke, interview by author, October 16, 2014.
50. "President Richard Nixon Visits the Washington Redskins," YouTube, 1971, https://www.youtube.com/watch?v=aUT2r-hyODU&feature=youtu.be.
51. Marv Levy, interview by author, August 4, 2020.

52. Bob Oates, "Allen Views Ram-Redskin Confrontation as 'Another Civil War,'" *Los Angeles Times*, December 11, 1971, E1.
53. Bud Furillo, "Gabriel Finds Receiver; Aims for Allen's Mouth," *Los Angeles Herald Examiner*, May 6, 1971, C1.
54. Mal Florence, "Emotional Factor Makes Game One of High Points of Season," *Los Angeles Times*, December 7, 1971, D2.
55. Dave Brady and Paul Edwards, "To Kilmer, Arlington Is a Toddling Town," *Washington Post*, December 7, 1971, D1.
56. George Felix Allen interview, December 18, 2019.
57. 1971 NFL Monday Night Football, Washington at Los Angeles, YouTube, December 13, 1971, https://www.youtube.com/watch?v=_fYKmXFnnZs&t=4812s.
58. George Felix Allen interview, December 18, 2019.
59. "Rentzel Receives Probation: Landry Silent," *Washington Post*, April 9, 1971, D1.
60. 1971 Washington Redskins Team Season Highlights, "Three Cheers for the Redskins," YouTube, accessed April 17, 2023, https://www.youtube.com/watch?v=ENMnMc_7gDU&t=2719s.
61. 1971 Washington Redskins Team Season Highlights, "Three Cheers for the Redskins."
62. Gildea and Turan, *Future Is Now*, 292.
63. Gildea and Turan, *Future Is Now*, 292; G. Allen recorded conversation with Guback.
64. William Gildea, "George Allen Savors Biggest Victory," *Washington Post*, December 14, 1971, D1.
65. George Felix Allen interview, December 18, 2019.
66. Steve Hershey, "Redskins Wall of Consistency," *Evening Star*, December 22, 1971, C1.
67. "49ers Make Reversal of Nixon Policy," *Washington Post*, December 28, 1971, E1.
68. Bill Brundige, interview by author, January 17, 2002.
69. Bill Kilmer, interview by author, September 6, 2011.
70. Marchibroda interview, June 25, 2013.
71. G. Allen recorded conversation with Guback.
72. Dave Anderson, "Coach Nixon Sends in a Play to the Miami Dolphins," *New York Times*, January 4, 1972, 1; Shirley Povich, "This Morning with Shirley Povich," *Washington Post*, January 6, 1972, F1.
73. Steve Guback, "Allen Calls for 'Togetherness,'" *Evening Star*, July 15, 1972 (scrapbook clipping), GAC.
74. Steve Guback, "Allen Out More," *Evening Star*, April 13, 1972, C1; Dave Brady, "Allen Trades Cost $5,000," *Washington Post*, May 24, 1972, D1; Eric Lincoln, "Flim-flam Man Burned," *Washington Daily News*, May 24, 1972 (scrapbook clipping), GAC.

75. Brady, "Allen Trades Cost $5,000," D1.
76. Brady, "Allen Trades Cost $5,000," D1; Lincoln, "Flim-flam Man Burned."
77. Bruce Allen, interview by author, December 1, 2020.
78. Hermeling interview, July 5, 2020. Subsequent quotations are from this interview until noted otherwise.
79. George Solomon, "Kilmer Is Allen's Man, Starting Quarterback," *Washington Post*, September 7, 1972, K1.
80. Solomon, "Kilmer Is Allen's Man, Starting Quarterback," K1.
81. Steve Guback, "Message for Jurgensen," *Evening Star* (undated scrapbook clipping), GAC.
82. Ron Reid, "When You're No. 2, You Diet," *Sports Illustrated*, August 21, 1972, 20.
83. Shawn White Wolf, "Tribal Leader Rubbed Elbows with Elite," *Independent Record* (Helena MT), November 2, 2003, https://helenair.com/news/tribal-leader-rubbed-elbows-with-elite/article_cdd827b1-877b-5c63-b8fb-0a9d91d03383.html.
84. Lance Wetzel, interview by author, July 18, 2020.
85. George Felix Allen interview, August 23, 2019.
86. Dave Brady, "Redskins Boss Shows Sioux That He's No Indian Giver," *Washington Post*, March 28, 1971, C4.
87. Joe Huske, interview by author, January 11, 2020.
88. Brady, "Redskins Boss Shows Sioux That He's No Indian Giver," C4.
89. "Allen Heads Indian Fete Here," *Washington Post*, August 8, 1974, D8.
90. Tommy McVean, interview by author, September 7, 2020.
91. Huske interview.
92. George Felix Allen interview, December 18, 2019.
93. George Allen bicentennial speech, "Music '76!" June 16, 1976, GAC.
94. Steve Guback, "Malinchak Makes His Mark," *Evening Star*, September 19, 1972 (scrapbook clipping), GAC.
95. Marv Levy, interview by author, November 15, 2020.
96. Malinchak interview.
97. Tom Dowling, "Of Victory with Allen," *Evening Star*, September 26, 1972 (scrapbook clipping), GAC.
98. George Solomon, "Allen Relives Wild Finish," *Washington Post*, October 3, 1972, D1.
99. "Forgetting How to Lose," *Evening Star*, October 3, 1972 (scrapbook clipping), GAC.
100. Solomon, "Allen Relives Wild Finish," D1.
101. George Solomon, "Jurgensen Steps Up Drills, Speculation Irks Allen," *Washington Post*, October 6, 1972, D1.
102. George Solomon, "Redskins Practice Closed; Allen Mum on Strategy," *Washington Post*, October 7, 1972, E1.
103. Gildea and Turan, *Future Is Now*, 182.

104. "Post Rejects Allen's Conditions for Coverage," *Washington Post*, October 12, 1972, G1.
105. "Allen: New Press Policy," *Washington Post*, October 15, 1972, C10.
106. G. Allen recorded conversation with Guback.
107. B. Allen interview, March 28, 2020.
108. Hermeling interview.
109. George Felix Allen and Bruce Allen, interviews by author, November 30, 2020.
110. Larry Brown, interview by author, December 18, 2014.
111. Richard Nixon Tapes: Talks Football 1 (Coach George Allen), YouTube, October 22, 1972, https://www.youtube.com/watch?v=b0Z8ZwjXpW4.
112. Ken Denlinger, "Candidates Woo Athletes," *Washington Post*, October 14, 1972, C3.
113. "Athletes for the President" poster, 1972, courtesy of George Felix Allen.
114. Dick Heller, "Webster Shook over No Shake," *Evening Star*, November 13, 1972, C1.
115. Steve Guback, "The Redskins Qualify for Bigger Challenge," *Evening Star*, December 4, 1972 (scrapbook clipping), GAC.
116. Myra MacPherson, "What Does George Allen Prefer to Football?" *Washington Post*, December 24, 1972, F1.
117. George Felix Allen, interview by author, November 15, 2020.
118. Kilmer interview, November 6, 2020.
119. Gary Pomerantz, "Esteem Expressed for Smith," *Washington Post*, August 27, 1986, C1.
120. Western Union telegram from George Allen to Jerry Smith, August 27, 1986, GAC.
121. Pomerantz, "Esteem Expressed for Smith," C1.
122. David DuPree, "Allen: Better than in '71," *Washington Post*, December 19, 1972, D2.

13. His Crowning Moment

1. DuPree, "Allen: Better than in '71," D2.
2. William Gildea, "'All the Way, We're No. 1,'" *Washington Post*, December 25, 1972, E1.
3. Washington Redskins 1972 Vintage Highlights, YouTube, posted March 22, 2015, https://www.youtube.com/watch?v=L8QI8s4XdLo&t=479s.
4. "Grudge Game Sunday," *Chicago Daily Defender* via United Press International, December 27, 1972, 26. Subsequent quotes are from this article until noted otherwise.
5. Dave Anderson, "Allen Helps Landry Pick Quarterback," *New York Times*, December 28, 1972, 41.
6. Washington Redskins 1972 Vintage Highlights, YouTube. Subsequent quotations are from this video compilation until noted otherwise.

7. Sam Wyche, interview by author, July 12, 2019.
8. Michael Kernan, "The Horn-Tooting Hilarious Hoo-eee! of Victory," *Washington Post*, January 1, 1973, C1.
9. George Felix Allen, interview by author, October 25, 2020.
10. George Felix Allen interview, October 25, 2020; Bruce Allen, interview by author, October 25, 2020.
11. "Mrs. Nixon Suggests Wives Watch Football," *Baltimore Sun* via the Associated Press, January 2, 1973, A1.
12. David DuPree, "Allen Gives Staff Day Off, Celebrates with President," *Washington Post*, January 2, 1973, A1.
13. George Felix Allen interview, September 10, 2002.
14. DuPree, "Allen Gives Staff Day Off, Celebrates with President," A1.
15. "Allen's Heist Highest Ever in Post-Season," *Los Angeles Herald Examiner*, January 1, 1973 (scrapbook clipping), GAC.
16. "Redskins Rated Early Favorite," *Baltimore Sun* via the Associated Press, January 1, 1973, C2.
17. Jimmy the Greek [Jimmy Snyder], "Greek Likes Redskins," *Washington Post*, January 3, 1973, D4.
18. George Solomon, "Rosenbloom Charges Big Ones Freeze Shula," *Washington Post*, January 13, 1973, D2.
19. Ken Denlinger and Leonard Shapiro, "Hello, L.A.: Allen Returns with a Winner," *Washington Post*, January 8, 1973, D1.
20. Ken Denlinger, "Redskins Go Swimmingly," *Washington Post*, January 11, 1973, E1.
21. "Allen Charts Sun for Super Bowl," *Orange County Register* via United Press International, January 12, 1973 (scrapbook clipping), GAC.
22. Ken Denlinger, "Redskins Shut Out California's Lures," *Washington Post*, January 7, 1973, C5.
23. Jennifer Allen, interview by author, December 7, 2020.
24. Dave Brady, "Shula Parries Press," *Washington Post*, January 10, 1973, D1.
25. "Shula and Allen a Study in Contrasts; Don Loose, Confident, George Somber," *Baltimore Sun* via the Associated Press, January 14, 1973, B2.
26. Tex Maule, "17-0-0," *Sports Illustrated*, January 22, 1973, 20.
27. Len Shapiro, "Allen Blasts Reporters for Causing 'Worst Practice,'" *Washington Post*, January 13, 1973, D1.
28. Exchange between Allen and Perkins recalled by Len Shapiro in interview by author, October 23, 2020.
29. "Shula and Allen a Study in Contrasts," B2.
30. L. Shapiro interview.
31. Maule, "17-0-0," 20.
32. L. Shapiro, "Allen Blasts Reporters for Causing 'Worst Practice,'" D1.
33. Boswell, *Redskins*, 99.

34. Shirley Povich, "Allen, Shula Spread Rival Sunshine in Rainy California," *Washington Post*, January 10, 1973, D1.
35. B. Allen interview, March 28, 2020.
36. *Winning Is Living, Losing Is Dying.*
37. *Winning Is Living, Losing Is Dying.*
38. B. Allen interview, March 28, 2020.
39. Hermeling interview.
40. Larry Brown, interview by author, November 6, 2010.
41. George Solomon, "Allen Treasures 'Great Season,'" *Washington Post*, January 16, 1973, D1.
42. Solomon, "Allen Treasures 'Great Season,'" D1.

14. Cruising with George Allen

1. "Pressure on Kilmer Called Key Factor," *Baltimore Sun* via the Associated Press, January 15, 1973, C1.
2. J. Allen interview, December 6, 2019. Subsequent quotes and information are from this interview until noted otherwise.
3. B. Allen interview, February 12, 2020.
4. "Sullivan Quits Redskins after 14 Years with Allen," *Washington Post*, January 28, 1973, C1.
5. Dave Brady, "Allen's Right Hand Will Direct Cards," *Washington Post*, February 24, 1973, C1.
6. Dave Brady, "Sullivan Still Tries to 'Help' Allen," *Washington Post*, October 19, 1973, D3.
7. B. Allen interview, January 3, 2021.
8. George Felix Allen, interview by author, January 3, 2021.
9. Gildea and Turan, *Future Is Now*, 193.
10. Dave Anderson, "George Allen," *New York Times*, November 6, 1972, 57.
11. McVean interview, September 7, 2020.
12. Chris Hanburger, interview by author, December 23, 2020.
13. McDole with Morris, *Dancing Bear*, 103.
14. Hanburger interview.
15. Ken Denlinger, "Redskins Yield Five for Oilers' Houston," *Washington Post*, May 16, 1973, C1.
16. Steve Guback, "And Here's to You, Mr. Robinson," *Evening Star*, June 13, 1973, C1.
17. Steve Guback, "Redskins' Biggest Foe Will Be Team Attitude," *Washington Star-News*, August 26, 1973, S-2.
18. Steve Guback, *Washington Star-News*, 1973 Football Special (scrapbook clipping), SGC.
19. G. Allen, "Hundred Percent Is Not Enough," 76.

20. Gerald Strine, "Allen Took a Loser, Created 7-Year-Long Winner," *Washington Post*, January 22, 1978, D1.
21. Steve Guback, "Redskins Prevail by Yard," *Washington Star*, October 9, 1973 (scrapbook clipping), GAC.
22. Ken Houston, interview by author, October 25, 2015.
23. William Gildea, "Burman Figures Every Third Redskin Uses Pep Pills," *Washington Post*, November 14, 1973, D1.
24. Neil Amdur, "N.F.L. to Check Redskins on Drug Report," *New York Times*, November 15, 1973, 59.
25. Leonard Shapiro, "Allen Denies Pill 'Problem,'" *Washington Post*, November 15, 1973, D1.
26. Shapiro, "Allen Denies Pill 'Problem,'" D1.
27. Joan Ryan, "Nixon Phoned Allen after Cards' Game," *Washington Star-News*, October 23, 1973.
28. Julian E. Zelizer, "The New Enemies List," *The Atlantic*, August 19, 2018, https://www.theatlantic.com/ideas/archive/2018/08/the-new-enemies-list/567874/.
29. "Richard Nixon's Relationship with the Press, His Secret Tapes: Part 1," YouTube, accessed April 17, 2023, https://www.youtube.com/watch?v=2qovLaE3dEM.
30. "Excerpts of Nixon's Question-and-Answer Session," *Washington Post*, November 18, 1973, A12.
31. "Michigan to Recognize Gerald R. Ford as Michigan Football Legend," Michigan Ford School, June 15, 2012, https://fordschool.umich.edu/news/2012/michigan-recognize-gerald-r-ford-michigan-football-legend.
32. George Felix Allen interview, December 18, 2019.
33. Steve Guback, "65-Second Blitz Stuns Redskins," *Washington Star-News*, December 23, 1973 (scrapbook clipping), GAC.
34. Leonard Shapiro, "Allen Kicks Off New Year," *Washington Post*, December 25, 1973, D1.
35. Leonard Shapiro, "Redskins' Year Creditable—and Chargeable," *Washington Post*, December 26, 1973, G1.
36. L. Shapiro, "Allen Kicks Off New Year," D1.

15. "Two Major Egos Clashing"

1. William Barry Furlong, "George Allen's Way: Hard Work, Attention to Detail Give Him an Edge," *Washington Post*, December 21, 1974, E1.
2. Brendan Sullivan, interview by author, February 16, 2021.
3. Thomas, *Man to See*, 25–28.
4. Gildea and Turan, *Future Is Now*, 22.
5. Underwood, "Ice-Cream Man Cometh," 72.
6. *Three Cheers for the Redskins*.

7. Underwood, "Ice-Cream Man Cometh," 72; Thomas, *Man to See*, 290.
8. Sullivan interview.
9. Larry Lucchino, interview by author, January 20, 2021.
10. Lucchino interview.
11. B. Allen interview, February 12, 2020.
12. Ted Marchibroda, interview by author, June 25, 2013.
13. Mike Hull, interview by author, December 7, 2020.
14. Leonard Shapiro and Nancy Scannell, "The Final Plays," *Washington Post*, April 16, 1978, SM17.
15. Leonard Shapiro, "Levy to Coach Chiefs; Allen's Options Fewer," *Washington Post*, December 21, 1977, C1.
16. Leonard Shapiro, "Redskins in the Red Despite High Income," *Washington Post*, September 23, 1976, C1.
17. Thomas, *Man to See*, 351.
18. George Solomon, "Redskins Face Inflated Cost-of-Winning Problems," *Washington Post*, March 4, 1973, C1.
19. J. Allen, *Fifth Quarter*, 174.
20. William Gildea, "Redskins Land Grant of Colts," *Washington Post*, July 9, 1971, D1.
21. B. Allen interview, February 12, 2020.
22. L. Shapiro, "Redskins in the Red Despite High Income," C1.
23. Steve Guback, "Redskins Already Lead the League," *Washington Star-News*, May 30, 1974, D1.
24. George Allen to Edward Bennett Williams, March 28, 1973, GAC.
25. Edward Bennett Williams, memo to George Allen, February 3, 1975, GAC. Subsequent quotations are from this memorandum until noted otherwise.
26. Dave Brady, "Jurgensen Move Correct—Williams," *Washington Post*, May 8, 1975, E1.
27. Williams memo to G. Allen, February 3, 1975.
28. Dave Brady, "NFL Fines Redskins $10,000 for Player 'Tampering,'" *Washington Post*, January 12, 1974, C1.
29. William Wallace, "Allen to Be Fined for Concealment of Player Injury," *New York Times*, January 13, 1973, 21.
30. Thomas, *Man to See*, 352; L. Shapiro and Scannell, "Final Plays," SM17.
31. L. Shapiro and Scannell, "Final Plays," SM17.
32. Lucchino interview.
33. Thomas, *Man to See*, 273.
34. Lucchino interview.
35. Peter Bennett Williams, interview by author, January 2, 2021.
36. Thomas, *Man to See*, 271–72; David Rosenbaum, "Threats by Nixon Reported on Tape Heard by Inquiry," *New York Times*, May 16, 1974, 1.
37. Thomas, *Man to See*, 273.

38. Sullivan interview.
39. Thomas, *Man to See*, 275.
40. P. B. Williams interview.
41. P. B. Williams interview.
42. George Allen, unpublished interview by *Washington Star* sportswriter Steve Guback, January 1978, SGC.
43. Thomas, *Man to See*, 351.
44. Bill Kilmer, interview by author, January 6, 2011.
45. B. Allen interview, February 12, 2020.
46. J. Allen interview, December 6, 2019.
47. J. Allen interview, December 6, 2019.
48. George Felix Allen, interview by author, February 21, 2021.
49. Thomas, *Man to See*, 284–85.
50. Sullivan interview, February 16, 2021.
51. Thomas, *Man to See*, 427.

16. The Fourth Estate

1. *Winning Is Living, Losing Is Dying.*
2. "The Press Box," episode 18 of *Lost Treasures of NFL Films*, NFL Films, November 8, 2002, https://thetvdb.com/series/lost-treasures-of-nfl-films/allseasons/official.
3. *Winning Is Living, Losing Is Dying.*
4. Turan interview.
5. George Felix Allen interview, September 10, 2002.
6. Shirley Povich, "Reporters Occupy Top Spot on Allen's Enemies List," *Washington Post*, November 18, 1973, D1.
7. Bruce Allen, interview by author, March 10, 2010.
8. G. Allen unpublished interview by Guback, 1975.
9. *Winning Is Living, Losing Is Dying.*
10. John Schulian, interview by author, August 4, 2020.
11. L. Shapiro interview. Subsequent quotes are from this interview until noted otherwise.
12. Kilmer interview, November 6, 2020.
13. Mike Hull, interview by author, October 4, 2020.
14. L. Shapiro interview.
15. Schulian interview.
16. Haskins, *Evening Star*, 128.
17. David Israel, interview by author, April 3, 2021.
18. David Israel, "Sonny Makes Allen Cope with Reality," *Washington Star*, May 2, 1975, E1.
19. David Israel, "The Master of Psyche Finally Blew One," *Washington Star*, July 15, 1977, B1.

20. David Israel, "Just Who Does George Allen Think He's Kidding[?]," *Washington Star*, December 21, 1977, E1.
21. George McGovern to George Allen, December 22, 1977, GAC.
22. George McGovern, "George McGovern Responds to David Israel's Column," *Washington Star*, December 23, 1977, A15.
23. Jennifer Allen, interview by author, April 13, 2018.
24. George Felix Allen interview, February 21, 2021.
25. Turan interview.
26. Israel interview. Subsequent quotes are from this interview.

17. Motivation—George Allen Style

1. Dave Reardon, "Former UH Football Assistant John Wilbur Dies," *Honolulu Star Advertiser*, December 10, 2013, https://www.staradvertiser.com/2013/12/10/sports/former-uh-football-assistant-john-wilbur-dies/.
2. *Winning Is Living, Losing Is Dying.*
3. Maher, "George Allen Can Talk, Just Ask the Players," B3.
4. Malinchak interview.
5. Hanburger interview.
6. B. Allen interview, February 12, 2020.
7. Hermeling interview.
8. *Winning Is Living, Losing Is Dying.*
9. Israel interview.
10. Ken Houston, interview by author, November 4, 2012.
11. Malinchak interview.
12. *Lost Treasures of the NFL: Inside Allen's First Season as Washington's Coach* (NFL Films, 2001).
13. Bobby Mitchell, interview by author, October 15, 2000.
14. Wyche interview. Subsequent quotes are from this interview until noted otherwise.
15. Owens interview.
16. Richard Darcey, "Redskins Have Their Cake and They're Eating It, Too," *Washington Post*, September 22, 1972, D6.
17. William Gildea and Kenneth Turan, "After a While, It's Easy Not to Like Allen," *Los Angeles Times* via *Washington Post*, January 20, 1978, D1. Subsequent quotations are from this article.

18. "He's All They Have"

1. G. Allen recorded conversation with Guback.
2. George Felix Allen interview, February 21, 2021.
3. David DuPree, "Redskins Sign Theismann," *Washington Post*, March 2, 1974, C1.

4. Leonard Shapiro, "Two 'Straight Kickers,' Two Sidewinders, after Knight's Job," *Washington Post*, July 18, 1974, G1.
5. Butkus interview.
6. "Butkus Says Bears to Settle," *Washington Post* via the Associated Press, September 14, 1976, D1.
7. Steve Guback, "Sonny Beats Clock in Upset of Dolphins," *Washington Star*, October 14, 1974, D1.
8. William Barry Furlong, "'Tis Teeth-Gnashing Time for Allen's Foes," *Washington Post*, December 20, 1974, D1.
9. "D. D. Lewis Headlines Welcome Back Dinner," Midwestern State University Athletics, August 8, 2011, https://msumustangs.com/news/2011/8/23/GEN_0823114446.aspx.
10. "DCC through the Years," DCC History, March 27, 2028, https://www.dallascowboys.com/news/dcc-history.
11. *1978 Dallas Cowboys* (NFL Films, 1978), https://www.youtube.com/watch?v=pbz7fjN018I.
12. B. Allen interview, March 28, 2020.
13. G. Allen unpublished interview by Guback, 1975.
14. "Roger Staubach, Tom Landry and How the Shotgun Formation Became a Staple of NFL Offenses," *New York Daily News* via the Associated Press, January 14, 2017, https://www.nydailynews.com/sports/football/shotgun-formation-staple-nfl-offenses-article-1.2946590.
15. Drew Pearson, interview by author, April 7, 2021.
16. Leonard Shapiro, "Relaxed Allen Says It's Up to the Team," *Washington Post*, November 28, 1974, C1.
17. L. Shapiro, "Relaxed Allen Says It's Up to the Team," C1.
18. Steve Guback, "Time for Jurgensen?" *Washington Star*, November 30, 1974, E1.
19. Leonard Shapiro, "Cowboy Bomb Shocks Redskins, 24–23," *Washington Post*, November 29, 1974, D1.
20. Pearson interview.
21. Steve Guback, "'Sweet 16' Sours Redskins," *Washington Star*, November 29, 1974, C1.
22. Guback, "Time for Jurgensen?," E1.
23. B. Allen interview, March 28, 2020.
24. Jennifer Allen, interview by author, September 3, 2021.
25. Pearson interview.
26. Ken Stone, interview by author, March 30, 2021.
27. Mike Bragg, interview by author, October 1, 2013.
28. Joe Theismann, interview by author, March 9, 2021.
29. Steve Guback, "The Redskins Togetherness—How Far Will It Lead?" *Washington Star*, December 21, 1974, A1.

30. Steve Guback, “Redskins Turn Over an Old Leaf,” *Washington Star*, December 23, 1974, D1.
31. Brady, “Jurgensen Move Correct—Williams,” E1.
32. E. B. Williams to G. Allen, February 3, 1975.
33. G. Allen unpublished interview by Guback, 1975.
34. Steve Guback, “Redskins Acquire Randy Johnson,” *Washington Star*, April 19, 1975, C1.
35. Steve Guback, “Jurgensen Leaves Believing ‘I Still Feel I Can Do It,’” *Washington Star*, May 2, 1975, E1.
36. Guback, “Jurgensen Leaves Believing ‘I Still Feel I Can Do It,’” E1.
37. Leonard Shapiro, “Teary-Eyed Jurgensen ‘Accepts’ Retirement,” *Washington Post*, May 2, 1975, D1.
38. Kathleen Maxa, “The Fans Rally around Jurgensen,” *Washington Star*, May 2, 1975, E1.
39. Leonard Shapiro, “Sonny Jurgensen, One Year Later: Allen ‘Did Me a Favor,’” *Washington Post*, May 16, 1976, 37.
40. “Statement by Sonny Jurgensen on Retirement,” press release issued by Washington Redskins, August 8, 2019.
41. Ted Marchibroda player-position evaluation of the 1974 season, January 7, 1975, GAC.
42. B. Allen interview, March 28, 2020.
43. Brady, “Jurgensen Move Correct—Williams,” E1.
44. Steve Guback, “Did Redskins Call Off Deal for Kilmer?” *Washington Star*, May 7, 1975, E1.
45. Dave Brady, “Allen Is Wrestling with Giant Idea to Help Redskins,” *Washington Post*, July 9, 1975, 83.
46. Brady, “Allen Is Wrestling with Giant Idea,” 83.
47. Steve Guback, “Redskins May Be Ready to Land a Real Biggie,” *Washington Star*, July 9, 1975, C1.
48. Brady, “Allen Is Wrestling with Giant Idea,” 83.
49. B. Allen interview, March 28, 2020.
50. Joe Theismann, interview by author, February 23, 2021.
51. Leonard Shapiro, “Allen Signs Cards’ Butz to Contract,” *Washington Post*, August 6, 1975, D1.
52. L. Shapiro, “Allen Signs Cards’ Butz to Contract,” D1.
53. Bruce Allen, interview by author, April 5, 2021.
54. “Why Dave Butz Left the Cardinals,” The Big Red Zone: History of the St. Louis Football Cardinals, June 23, 2020, https://thebigredzone.com/2020/06/23/why-dave-butz-left-the-cardinals/.
55. Steve Guback, “New Evaluation for Redskins: Sitting Pretty,” *Washington Star*, September 5, 1975, E1.

56. Kenneth Denlinger, "High-Roller Allen Throws Club Future into Butz Deal," *Washington Post*, September 6, 1975, C1.
57. Dave Brady, "For Better or Worse, Thomas Now Hawaiian," *Washington Post*, September 10, 1975, D7.
58. Underwood, "Why Dave Butz Left the Cardinals."
59. G. Allen recorded conversation with Guback.
60. John Schulian, "Redskins Get Rams' Tackle, Trade Vactor, Settle on Butz," *Washington Post*, September 5, 1975, D1.
61. Steve Guback, "Punchless Display against Eagles Turns NFC East Race into Struggle," *Washington Star*, October 6, 1975, E1.
62. John Schulian, "Redskins Acquire Fill-In for Stone," *Washington Post*, October 10, 1975, A13.
63. Eddie Brown, interview by author, October 25, 2015.
64. Joan Ryan, "Allen and Sudden Death: It's Capital Punishment," *Washington Post*, November 25, 1975, D4.
65. Robert Fachet, "Allen Wants Officials to See Replay," *Washington Post*, November 17, 1975, B1.
66. B. Allen interview, April 5, 2021.
67. "History of Instant Replay," NFL Football Operations, February 15, 2020, https://operations.nfl.com/officiating/instant-replay/history-of-instant-replay/.
68. Bruce Allen, interview by author, April 24, 2021; "U.S.F.L. to Use Replay," *New York Times* via the Associated Press, February 22, 1985, A21, https://www.nytimes.com/1985/02/22/sports/usfl-use-replay-associated-press-united-states-football-league-announced-that-it.html.
69. David Israel, "A Religious Experience Called the Redskins," *Washington Star*, December 1, 1975, D1.
70. G. Allen unpublished interview by Guback, 1975.
71. Ken Denlinger, "This Morning: Allen's Game Plan Made of Pure Gold," *Washington Post*, November 9, 1975, B1.
72. Sam Fogg, unidentified article for United Press International, December 15, 1975 (scrapbook clipping), GAC.
73. Steve Guback, "Allen Says He'll Stay," *Washington Star*, December 2, 1975, D1; Fogg article for United Press International, December 15, 1975.
74. Guback, "Allen Says He'll Stay," D1.
75. Leonard Shapiro, "Williams Flays Rumors: Allen Will Remain," *Washington Post*, January 3, 1976, C1.
76. L. Shapiro, "Williams Flays Rumors," C1.
77. Leonard Shapiro, "Redskins Sign Big Back Hill," *Washington Post*, April 4, 1976, D1.
78. Steve Guback, "Allen Strikes Again—Signs Calvin Hill," *Washington Star*, April 4, 1976, E1.

79. Robert F. Jones, "Will the Payoff Mean a Playoff?" *Sports Illustrated*, August 15, 1976, 20.
80. Ron Reid, "He's Free, but Not Cheap," *Sports Illustrated*, June 7, 1976, https://vault.si.com/vault/1976/06/07/hes-free-but-not-cheap.
81. John Schulian, "Redskins Add Riggins to 1,000-Yard Backfield," *Washington Post*, June 11, 1976, D1.
82. Jones, "Will the Payoff Mean a Playoff?," 20.
83. Larry Brown, interview by author, December 15, 2014.
84. B. Allen interview, February 12, 2020.
85. B. Allen interview, February 12, 2020.
86. Leonard Shapiro and Paul Attner, "Salter Traded, Redskins Gain Scott, Matuszak," *Washington Post*, August 25, 1976, C1.
87. Schulian interview.
88. Steve Guback, "1976 Redskins Preview," *College and Pro Football Newsweekly*, SGC; L. Shapiro, "Redskins in the Red Despite High Income," C1.
89. Guback, "1976 Redskins Preview."
90. Paul Attner, "Best Redskin Team Ever Prophesied by Williams," *Washington Post*, September 2, 1976, E1.
91. Leonard Shapiro, "Defeat Dims Playoff Hope," *Washington Post*, November 15, 1976, D1.
92. David Israel, "After an Autopsy, the Redskins Can Be Buried," *Washington Star*, November 15, 1976, C1.
93. Ken Denlinger, "The String Has Almost Run Out for Yo-Yo Redskins," *Washington Post*, November 15, 1976, D1.
94. Malinchak interview.

19. The Beginning of the End

1. Morris Siegel, "On Any Given Sunday," *Washington Star*, January 22, 1978, D1.
2. George Allen to Jack Kent Cooke, August 31, 1976, and December 1, 1976, GAC.
3. Leonard Shapiro, "Williams Wants Allen Back, Says He Deserves a Raise," *Washington Post*, December 21, 1976, D1.
4. George Allen to Edward Bennett Williams, March 1, 1977, GAC.
5. Leonard Shapiro, "Williams: Allen's Pact 'One of Best,'" *Washington Post*, July 15, 1977, D1.
6. L. Shapiro, "Williams: Allen's Pact 'One of Best,'" D1.
7. Steve Guback, "Allen's Lame-Duck Status Is Causing Him Anxiety," *Washington Star*, B1 (undated scrapbook clipping), GAC.
8. L. Shapiro and Scannell, "Final Plays," SM17.
9. "N.Y. Daily News Picks Allen Coach of Year," *Washington Star*, January 10, 1978 (scrapbook clipping), GAC.

10. Steve Guback, "Are the Redskins Ready? 'I Think We Are'—Allen," *Washington Star*, September 12, 1976, D1.
11. "Pardee Returns to Redskins as the Head Coach," *Los Angeles Times* via *Washington Post*, January 25, 1978, D1.
12. Washington Redskins 1975 press guide, Pro Football Hall of Fame.
13. Ken Denlinger, "The Allen Answer: Redskin Problem; How to Produce Super Bowl Win," *Washington Post*, July 10, 1977, 89.
14. Denlinger, "Allen Answer," 89.
15. Ted Marchibroda player-position evaluation of the 1974 season, January 7, 1975, GAC.
16. Bobby Beathard, interview by author, November 12, 2013.
17. "Joe Theismann Issues an Apology," *Washington Star*, October 28, 1977 (scrapbook clipping), GAC.
18. Joe Theismann, interview by author, May 24, 2021. Subsequent quotes are from this interview until noted otherwise.
19. Leonard Shapiro, "Financial Control Issue Holds Up Allen's Contract," *Washington Post*, November 1, 1977, D1.
20. L. Shapiro and Scannell, "Final Plays," SM17.
21. Lucchino interview.
22. George Felix Allen interview, December 18, 2019.
23. B. Allen interview, February 10, 2020.
24. John Kent Cooke interview.
25. Ted Green, "A Tale of 2 Coaches in Best and Worst of Times," *Los Angeles Times*, July 16, 1978, D1.
26. Jon Hookstratten, interview by author, May 12, 2021.
27. Lucchino interview.
28. G. Allen recorded conversation with Guback.
29. Siegel, "On Any Given Sunday," D1.
30. Morris Siegel, "Redskins Agree to Extend Allen's Contract Five Years," *Washington Star*, May 30, 1977, D1.
31. "Rams OK Knox 'Job Hunt,' Talk with Coryell," *Los Angeles Times*, January 10, 1978, A1.
32. Jim Murray, "Rams Can't Find Pasadena . . . from 6 Inches Away," *Los Angeles Times*, December 27, 1976, D1.
33. Krikorian interview.
34. "Rosenbloom Is Willing to Let Lions Have Knox," *Los Angeles Times*, January 30, 1977, C1.
35. Bruce Allen, interview by author, June 2, 2021.
36. L. Shapiro and Scannell, "Final Plays," SM17.
37. Morris Siegel, "Did Allen Get Himself Fired?" *Washington Star*, January 19, 1978, D1.

38. Steve Guback, "Allen Wants to Stay in Washington, but 'L.A. Is a Very Desirable Place,'" *Washington Star*, January 12, 1978, C1.
39. J. Hookstratten interview.
40. Shirley Povich, "9-5 Record against Softies Raises Questions," *Washington Post*, December 28, 1977, D1.
41. Levy interview, November 15, 2020.
42. Leonard Shapiro, "Levy to Coach Chiefs; Allen's Options Fewer," *Washington Post*, December 21, 1977, C1.
43. Barry Sussman, "Jurgensen All-Time Favorite Redskin: Fans Rate George Allen," *Washington Post*, May 30, 1977, E4.
44. "Rams OK Knox 'Job Hunt,' Talk with Coryell," A1.
45. Skip Bayless, "Bills May Sign Knox; Rams Coryell Talk," *Los Angeles Times*, January 11, 1978, E1.
46. Morris Siegel, "Allen Wants 5% of the Redskins at Its 1969 Value," *Washington Star*, January 13, 1978, F1.
47. L. Shapiro and Scannell, "Final Plays," SM17.
48. Morris Siegel, "How Williams Decided He'd Had Enough," *Washington Star*, January 19, 1978, D1.
49. George Solomon, "'Monday, I Said This Is It,'" *Washington Post*, January 20, 1978, B1; Joe Marshall, "Let's Start the Music," *Sports Illustrated*, January 30, 1978, 18.
50. L. Shapiro and Scannell, "Final Plays," SM17.
51. George Solomon, "Allen Fired by Redskins; Delay on Contract Cited," *Washington Post*, January 19, 1978, A1.
52. Steve Guback, "Bitter Allen Tells His Side of the Story," *Washington Star*, January 19, 1978, A1; George Allen, recorded interview by Steve Guback, January 18, 1978, author's copy.
53. Gildea and Turan, "After a While, It's Easy Not to Like Allen," D1.
54. David Israel, "How Paranoia Finally Caught Allen from Behind," *Washington Star*, January 20, 1978, C1.
55. Bob Messenger, "George Allen Story One of Arrogance," *Greenwood (MS) Commonwealth*, January 20, 1978, 7.
56. Mark Asher and George Solomon, "Pardee Meets with Williams, Emerges No. 1," *Washington Post*, January 21, 1978, C1.
57. Leonard Shapiro, "Beathard Redskins GM; Begins 'Talent Search,'" *Washington Post*, February 25, 1978, C1.
58. Thomas Boswell, "Pardee Quits the Bears, Due Here for Talks," *Washington Post*, January 20, 1978, B1.
59. Bob Oates, "Allen Appears to Be Rosenbloom's Favorite," *Los Angeles Times*, January 20, 1978, D1.
60. Bruce Allen, interview by author, May 16, 2021.

61. Doug Krikorian, “The Great Coach Search,” *Los Angeles Herald Examiner*, January 24, 1973, C3.
62. Steve Rosenbloom, interview by author, April 27, 2019.
63. William Wallace, “Allen ‘Hot’; Pardee Quits Bears!” *Greenwood Commonwealth* via New York Times News Service, January 20, 1978, 7.
64. David Israel, “Protests by Players Dim Allen’s Chances with Rams,” *Washington Star*, January 26, 1978, D1.
65. Israel, “Protests by Players Dim Allen’s Chances with Rams,” D1; “Owner Hedges on Rams’ Attitude toward Allen,” *Los Angeles Times*, January 27, 1978, F10.
66. Fred Dryer, interview by author, April 19, 2019.
67. Dryer interview.
68. S. Rosenbloom interview, April 27, 2019. Subsequent quotes are from this interview until noted otherwise.
69. Teele interview.
70. S. Rosenbloom interview, April 27, 2019. Subsequent quotes are from this interview until noted otherwise.
71. Leonard Shapiro, “Redskins, Allen Talk Contract,” *Washington Post*, January 5, 1978, C1.

20. “Someone Has Cut Out My Heart”

1. Rich Roberts, “Allen Happy to Be Back,” *Long Beach Independent*, February 2, 1978, C1.
2. Roberts, “Allen Happy to Be Back,” C1.
3. Bob Oates, “Allen: We Will Have an Exciting Offense,” *Los Angeles Times*, February 2, 1978, E1.
4. Roberts, “Allen Happy to Be Back,” C1.
5. Oates, “Allen: We Will Have an Exciting Offense,” E1.
6. Leonard Shapiro, “‘Allen: It’s a Dream,’” *Washington Post*, February 2, 1978, D1.
7. Oates, “Allen: We Will Have an Exciting Offense,” E1.
8. L. Shapiro, “‘Allen: It’s a Dream,’” D1.
9. Oates, “Allen: We Will Have an Exciting Offense,” E1.
10. L. Shapiro, “‘Allen: It’s a Dream,’” D1.
11. Leonard Koppett, “Allen Named Coach of the Rams, Who Once Ousted Him,” *New York Times*, February 2, 1978, D15.
12. Roberts, “Allen Happy to Be Back,” C1.
13. Edward Bennett Williams to Carroll Rosenbloom, January 13, 1975, courtesy of Jon Hookstratten.
14. Doug Krikorian, “‘Someone Has Cut Out My Heart,’” *Los Angeles Herald Examiner*, August 14, 1978, D-3.

15. Robert H. Boyle, "The Pleasure of Dying on Sunday," *Sports Illustrated*, December 13, 1965, https://vault.si.com/vault/1965/12/13/the-pleasure-of-dying-on-sunday.
16. Moldea, *Interference*, 77–78.
17. Boyle, "Pleasure of Dying on Sunday."
18. Charles Maher, "The View from the Beach," *Los Angeles Times*, January 26, 1978, D1.
19. Moldea, *Interference*, 199.
20. "Colts Seek Vengeance," *Baltimore Sun*, January 18, 1969, B6.
21. John Underwood, "Sitting on Top of the World," *Sports Illustrated*, September 17, 1973, https://vault.si.com/vault/1973/09/17/sitting-on-top-of-the-world.
22. Mike Klingaman, "Shula's Fateful Loss," *Baltimore Sun*, February 1, 2008, Z6.
23. Jennifer Allen, interview by author, June 1, 2021.
24. George Felix Allen, interview by author, June 1, 2021.
25. Bill Harris, interview by author, April 23, 2015.
26. Morris Siegel, "Williams and Pardee Warn against Attempts to Tamper," *Washington Star*, February 25, 1978, E1.
27. Siegel, "Williams and Pardee Warn against Attempts to Tamper," E1; Nancy Scannell, "Kilmer: 'No Secret' He'd Like to Join Allen," *Washington Post*, February 3, 1978, B5.
28. Leonard Shapiro, "Allen Angrily Denies 'Tampering' with Redskins," *Washington Post*, February 26, 1978, M1.
29. Jim Murray, "Divorce from Redskins Costs George Allen $3,000," *Los Angeles Times*, July 18, 1978, F1.
30. Leonard Shapiro and Dave Brady, "Allen Fined for Statements, Warned of 'Tampering,'" *Washington Post*, July 19, 1978, C1.
31. Murray, "Divorce from Redskins Costs George Allen $3,000," F1.
32. Allen comments to the *Los Angeles Herald Examiner* were quoted in Kathleen Maxa, "Redskins Clip Angry Allen for $14,000 in Old 'Expenses,'" *Washington Star*, June 17, 1978, A1; and Dave Brady, "Redskins Bill Allen for $14,047.94," *Washington Post*, June 17, 1978, D1.
33. "Allen Leaves Rams Fans Out in the Cold," *Los Angeles Times*, July 11, 1978, G2.
34. Ted Green, "Rams Make Deal with Redskins," *Los Angeles Times*, July 25, 1978, G3.
35. Bruce Allen, interview by author, August 1, 2021.
36. Krikorian interview.
37. Dick Young, "Allen Wasn't Fired, He Was Lynched," *San Bernardino Sun-Telegram* via the Gannett News Service, August 18, 1973, D3.
38. Krikorian interview.

39. Ted Green, "Camp Allen, Not Ft. Knox," *Los Angeles Times*, August 1, 1978, F1.
40. Dryer interview.
41. Eddie Brown, interview by author, August 7, 2021.
42. Dryer interview.
43. Mack interview, April 22, 2019.
44. Krikorian interview.
45. Dryer interview.
46. Mack interview, April 22, 2019.
47. Green, "Camp Allen, Not Ft. Knox," F1.
48. Steve Rosenbloom, interview by author, July 31, 2021.
49. Green, "Camp Allen, Not Ft. Knox," F1.
50. Ted Green, "Rams Pass and Pass and Pass—and Flunk," *Los Angeles Times*, August 6, 1978, E1.
51. Krikorian, "'Someone Has Cut Out My Heart,'" D-3.
52. Dryer interview.
53. Krikorian interview.
54. Doug Krikorian, "The Last Day of George Allen; the First Day of Ray Malavasi," *Los Angeles Herald Examiner*, August 15, 1978, D3.
55. Ted Green, "Rosenbloom Gives Allen Quick Hook," *Los Angeles Times*, August 14, 1978, 1.
56. Ted Green, "Rams Offense Takes a Beating," *Los Angeles Times*, August 13, 1978, E1.
57. Green, "Rosenbloom Gives Allen Quick Hook," 1; Krikorian, "Last Day of George Allen; the First Day of Ray Malavasi," D3.
58. Krikorian, "'Someone Has Cut Out My Heart,'" D-3.
59. Gary Rausch, "Surprise! Rams Fire George Allen," *Long Beach Independent*, August 14, 1978, C1.
60. Krikorian interview.
61. Rausch, "Surprise! Rams Fire George Allen," C1; Green, "Rosenbloom Gives Allen Quick Hook," 1; Krikorian, "'Someone Has Cut Out My Heart,'" D-3.
62. Krikorian, "'Someone Has Cut Out My Heart,'" D-3.
63. Rausch, "Surprise! Rams Fire George Allen," C1.
64. Green, "Rosenbloom Gives Allen Quick Hook," 1.
65. Mack interview, April 22, 2019.
66. Green, "Rosenbloom Gives Allen Quick Hook," 1.
67. Green, "Rosenbloom Gives Allen Quick Hook," 1.
68. Harris interview, April 23, 2015.
69. B. Allen interview, August 1, 2021.
70. Harris interview, April 23, 2015.
71. B. Allen interview, February 12, 2020.
72. S. Rosenbloom interview, April 27, 2019.

73. J. Hookstratten interview.
74. B. Allen interview, August 1, 2021.
75. Jennifer Allen, interview by author, August 1, 2021.

21. Uncharted Waters

1. Krikorian, "Last Day of George Allen; the First Day of Ray Malavasi," D-3.
2. "'Do You Think I Got a Chance . . . 2 Preseason Games?'" *Palm Springs Desert Sun* via the Associated Press, August 14, 1978, B1.
3. "Allen Wasn't Fired, He Was Lynched," *San Bernardino Sun-Telegram* via the Gannett News Service, August 18, 1978, D3.
4. Krikorian interview.
5. Vern Buol to Carroll Rosenbloom, August 19, 1978, GAC.
6. S. Rosenbloom interview, July 31, 2021.
7. Bruce Allen, interview by author, April 8, 2022.
8. G. Allen with Maher, *Merry Christmas—You're Fired!*, 25.
9. Paul Zimmerman, "For Allen, This Is Alien Territory," *Sports Illustrated*, March 15, 1982, 37.
10. Jennifer Allen, interview by author, September 8, 2021.
11. George Allen 1978 Los Angeles Rams contract, GAC.
12. George Allen to Carroll Rosenbloom, August 19, 1978, GAC.
13. John Hall, "Together Again," *Los Angeles Times*, August 28, 1978, F3.
14. Hall, "Together Again," F3.
15. B. Allen interview, February 12, 2020.
16. Rich Roberts, "Is It Analysis or Sour Grapes When George Allen Does It?" *Los Angeles Times*, December 20, 1979, F1.
17. B. Allen interview, February 12, 2020.
18. George Allen, "On the Record: George Allen," *Football News*, August 28, 1979, 8.
19. Bruce Allen, interview by author, April 19, 2022.
20. Joe Band, interview by author, November 5, 2015.
21. B. Allen interview, February 12, 2020.
22. G. Allen, "On the Record: George Allen," 8.
23. Dryer interview.
24. E. Brown interview, August 7, 2021.
25. "Rosenbloom Theory Doubted," *New York Times* via the Associated Press, January 16, 1983, 204.
26. S. Rosenbloom interview, July 31, 2021.
27. Billy Reed, "Allen Says He Would Take UK Job, Cites Brown and School's Potential," *Louisville Courier-Journal*, July 13, 1981, C1.
28. Dave Brady, "Vacant Jobs at Illinois Attracted Allen Offer," *Washington Post*, September 30, 1979, D13.

29. Melvin Durslag, "Martin Gives Allen a Vicarious Thrill," *Los Angeles Herald Examiner*, November 24, 1980, D-3.
30. "Allen Interested in Coaching Giants," *Los Angeles Times* via United Press International, December 19, 1978, D2.
31. Paul Attner, "Allen Out; Gibbs Has Inside Track," *Washington Post*, January 7, 1981, D1.
32. Bobby Beathard, interview by author, June 14, 2013.
33. Beathard interview, June 14, 2013.
34. B. Allen interview, February 12, 2020.
35. Don Pierson and Linda Kay, "Halas Vetoes Idea of Rehiring Allen," *Chicago Tribune*, October 23, 1981, 1; David Condon, "Bears Coaching Drama Comes to End—It's Mike Ditka," *Chicago Tribune*, January 20, 1982, https://www.chicagotribune.com/sports/bears/ct-bears-archives-mike-ditka-head-coach-20160120-story.html; B. Allen interview, February 12, 2020.
36. Pierson and Kay, "Halas Vetoes Idea of Rehiring Allen," 1.
37. Condon, "Bears Coaching Drama Comes to End—It's Mike Ditka"; B. Allen interview, February 12, 2020.
38. B. Allen interview, February 12, 2020.
39. Ditka interview, April 5, 2019.
40. Jim Murray, "The Best Coach in Exile," *Los Angeles Times*, February 17, 1981, D1.
41. Israel, "Protests by Players Dim Allen's Chances with Rams," D1; Rich Roberts, "Winning Isn't Everything . . . or Allen Would Be Coaching," *Los Angeles Times*, February 6, 1981, E1.
42. John Schulian, "Football on Allen's Mind . . . and Blackball on His Back?" *Chicago Sun-Times*, 1981 (undated copy provided to the author by Schulian).
43. Schulian interview.
44. Bob Oates, "The Fruit War Is Now," *Los Angeles Times*, June 12, 1979, D1.
45. L. Shapiro interview.
46. Mike Christopulos, "Why Isn't Allen Still Coaching?" *Milwaukee Journal Sentinel*, 1981, 1 (undated scrapbook clipping), GAC.
47. Larry Fox, "George Allen Moves Upstairs; After Giving NFL Owners Fits as a Coach, He's Ready to Take Full Control in Montreal," *Boston Globe* via the *New York Daily News*, April 8, 1982 (scrapbook clipping), GAC.
48. List of George Allen's accomplishments and awards, 1990, GAC.
49. William H. Jones, "George Allen Seeking Jobs for Others," *Washington Post*, April 6, 1979, E1.
50. George Felix Allen interview, March 18, 2020.
51. Douglas Looney, "WHY George?" *Sports Illustrated*, September 24, 1990, 74–78.
52. Greg Allen interview, June 15, 2013.

53. "Allen Is Sworn In as Fitness Chairman," *Washington Post*, September 23, 1981, D2.
54. List of George Allen's accomplishments and awards, 1990.
55. Harris interview, April 23, 2015.
56. George Allen introductory note in a brochure of the United States Fitness Academy, GAC.
57. Harris interview, April 23, 2015.
58. George Allen, *What Is a Workout?*, brochure for President's Council on Physical Fitness and Sports, GAC.
59. G. Allen recorded conversation with Guback.
60. The gift is archived at the Ronald Reagan Presidential Library, National Archives and Records Administration, Simi Valley CA.
61. George Felix Allen, interview by author, September 19, 2021.
62. Ronald Reagan, "The President's Personal Exercise Program: How to Stay Fit," *Parade Magazine*, December 4, 1983, 4–6.
63. G. Allen recorded conversation with Guback.
64. "Reagan Hosts Council at White House," *President's Council on Physical Fitness and Sports Newsletter*, March 1984, 1, GAC.
65. *Winning Is Living, Losing Is Dying.*
66. Fox, "George Allen Moves Upstairs."
67. Paul Zimmerman, "For Allen, This Is Alien Territory," *Sports Illustrated*, March 15, 1982, 31.
68. Paul Attner, "Allen Says He's Investing Now, Coaching Alouettes Later," *Washington Post*, February 22, 1982, C1.
69. George Felix Allen, interview by author, May 20, 2018.
70. Kathy Blumenstock, "Allen Departs Alouettes, Cites Impasse on Sale," *Washington Post*, April 23, 1982, D1.
71. B. Allen interview, February 12, 2020.

22. A New League Comes Calling

1. Michael Shapiro, "Extolling the Joys of Football in May," *Advertising Age*, January 24, 1983, M-4.
2. David Dixon note to George Allen, September 1980, GAC.
3. Steve Ehrhart, interview by author, November 7, 2021. Subsequent quotes are from this interview until noted otherwise.
4. Michael Strauss, "Football League Planned," *New York Times*, May 12, 1982, B6.
5. "Allen Gets 'Feeler' from New League," *New York Times*, June 21, 1982, C11.
6. "Washington USFL Club on Hiring Allen: No Way," *Washington Post*, June 4, 1982, C2.
7. Harris interview, April 23, 2015.
8. M. Shapiro, "Extolling the Joys of Football in May," M-4.
9. Harris interview, April 23, 2015.

10. M. Shapiro, "Extolling the Joys of Football in May," M-4.
11. Dave Brady, "Allen Glows with Health," *Washington Post*, March 31, 1977, 102.
12. Harris interview, April 23, 2015.
13. Reeths, *United States Football League, 1982–1986*, 13.
14. Bruce Allen, interview by author, December 15, 2021.
15. Stan White, interview by author, November 22, 2021.
16. B. Allen interview, December 15, 2021.
17. Michael Wilbon, "Allen to Coach USFL's Chicago," *Washington Post*, June 22, 1982, D1.
18. "Allen in U.S.F.L.," *New York Times*, June 22, 1982, A25.
19. Harris interview, April 23, 2015.
20. Ehrhart interview, November 7, 2021.
21. Chicago Blitz 1983 press guide, Pro Football Hall of Fame.
22. NBC Sports, "The Story of the Chicago Blitz and the Craziest Trade in Sports History," February 1, 2017, https://www.nbcsports.com/chicago/chicago-bears/story-chicago-blitz-and-craziest-trade-sports-history.
23. Ehrhart interview, November 7, 2021.
24. B. Allen interview, December 15, 2021.
25. G. Allen, *Strategies for Winning*, 18.
26. B. Allen interview, February 12, 2020.
27. Chicago Blitz 1983 press guide.
28. Bart Barnes, "Allen's USFL Team Signs Tight End Drafted by Bears," *Washington Post*, August 7, 1982, D1.
29. "USFL Adds Phoenix, Drops San Diego and Signs Bruin Tight End Wrightman," *Los Angeles Times*, August 7, 1982, C6.
30. Chicago Blitz press release, August 19, 1982, GAC.
31. Bart Barnes, "USFL: Tampering Is League-Wide Problem," *Washington Post*, August 14, 1982, D4.
32. Paul Attner, "USFL Déjà Vu: Is Allen Up to Old Tricks?" *Washington Post*, August 13, 1982, C1.
33. Ehrhart interview, November 7, 2021.
34. Barnes, "Allen's USFL Team Signs Tight End Drafted by Bears," D1.
35. Chicago Blitz 1983 press guide.
36. Barnes, "USFL: Tampering Is League-Wide Problem," D4.
37. Chicago Blitz 1983 press guide.
38. White interview.
39. White interview.
40. White interview.
41. B. Allen, interview by author, September 20, 2021.
42. Michael Wilbon, "Allen Sees 43 in Blitz Tryout Here," *Washington Post*, November 28, 1982, D4.
43. Chicago Blitz press release, December 21, 1982, GAC.

44. Steve Ehrhart, interview by author, December 11, 2021.
45. G. Allen, *Strategies for Winning*, 18.
46. Rick Telander, interview by author, November 15, 2021.
47. "A Linebacker Now in Prison for Armed Robbery Wants . . . ," United Press International, August 20, 1982, https://www.upi.com/Archives/1982/08/20/A-linebacker-now-in-prison-for-armed-robbery-wants/9619398664000/.
48. B. Allen interview, December 15, 2021.
49. Rick Telander, interview by author and personal notes, November 15, 2021.
50. B. Allen interview, December 15, 2021.
51. "Will Blitz Be a Hit with Big Name Personnel to Fit?" *Chicago Defender* via United Press International, February 10, 1983, 30.
52. B. Allen interview, February 12, 2020.
53. Don Kojich, interview by author, November 7, 2021.
54. NBC Sports, "Story of the Chicago Blitz and the Craziest Trade in Sports History."
55. M. Shapiro, "Extolling the Joys of Football in May," M-4.
56. Harris interview, April 23, 2015.
57. Ehrhart interview, November 7, 2021.
58. White interview.
59. Kojich interview.
60. "Will Blitz Be a Hit with Big Name Personnel to Fit?," 30.
61. White interview.
62. Leon Shortenhaus to George and Bruce Allen, March 2, 1983, GAC.
63. Kojich interview.
64. Dave Kindred, "Allen's Exile Is Ended with Triumphant Return," *Washington Post*, March 7, 1983, D1.
65. David Remnick, "Federals Blitzed in Debut, 28–7, as 38,010 Look On," *Washington Post*, March 7, 1983, D1.
66. Michael Janofsky, "Allen Wins Again in Nation's Capital," *New York Times*, March 7, 1983, C4.
67. Bill Brubaker, "Nixon Makes It Very Clear," *New York Daily News*, May 20, 1983 (scrapbook clipping), GAC.
68. William Wallace, "Blitz Top Generals in Overtime, 19–13," *New York Times*, May 23, 1983, C10.
69. William Wallace, "Generals Trade Scott to Blitz," *New York Times*, May 27, 1983, A15.
70. "Breakers Rally to Beat Blitz in USFL, 21–15," *Baltimore Sun* via the Associated Press, June 7, 1983, C3.
71. Kojich interview.
72. Kojich interview.
73. Don Kojich, "Blitzes and Bombs: Life in the Precarious USFL," *Culver Alumnus*, Autumn 1985, 11–16.

74. White interview.
75. White interview.
76. White interview.
77. David Remnick, "Allen's Blitz Leads, 38–17, Then Gets Run Over in Overtime," *Washington Post*, July 10, 1983, F12.
78. Reeths, *United States Football League, 1982–1986*, 107.
79. Brian J. Ward, "We Aren't Gonna Lose," *Arizona Living*, March 1984, 50–52.
80. Doc Young, "The Future of the USFL in Perspective," *Chicago Defender*, July 21, 1983, 32; "Blitz Could Be Moved Out West," *Chicago Defender* via United Press International, August 4, 1983, 29.
81. Ward, "We Aren't Gonna Lose," 50–52.
82. Reeths, *United States Football League, 1982–1986*, 141.
83. B. Allen interview, December 15, 2021.
84. B. Allen interview, February 12, 2020.
85. Gabriel interview, April 13, 2019.
86. Alan Risher, interview by author, November 5, 2021.
87. Reeths, *United States Football League, 1982–1986*, 213.
88. G. Allen, "What It Takes to Win."
89. Gabriel interview, April 13, 2019.
90. G. Allen recorded conversation with Guback.
91. Risher interview.
92. Bob Cohn, "Allen Captains Destiny but Ship Leaks a Lot," *Washington Post*, June 9, 1984, G1.
93. B. Allen interview, December 15, 2021.
94. White interview.
95. B. Allen interview, December 15, 2021.
96. Arizona Wranglers 1994 postseason press guide, Pro Football Hall of Fame.
97. Reeths, *United States Football League, 1982–1986*, 194.
98. White interview.
99. B. Allen interview, December 15, 2021.
100. "Wranglers Overcome Gamblers," *New York Times*, July 2, 1984, C6.
101. "One More Thrill for George Allen," *New York Times*, July 3, 1984, B10.
102. Reeths, *United States Football League, 1982–1986*, 194.
103. Bob Cohn, "Allen's Wranglers to Play Stars in Final," *Washington Post*, July 9, 1984, D5.
104. White interview.
105. Cohn, "Allen's Wranglers to Play Stars in Final," D5.
106. Eddie Brown, interview by author, December 8, 2021.
107. "1984 Western Conference Championship: Los Angeles Express vs Arizona Wranglers," USFL Forever, via YouTube, June 23, 1984, https://www.youtube.com/watch?v=pH39wupFRMY&t=7097s.
108. Brig Owens, telegram to George Allen, July 13, 1984, GAC.

109. "Allen to Stay," *New York Times*, August 26, 1984, S7.
110. Christine Brennan, "Allen Resigns, Doubts 'If I'll Coach Again,'" *Washington Post*, September 28, 1984, F1.
111. "Coach Allen resigns Wrangler coaching post to concentrate on responsibilities as chairman of board; coaching great leaves sideline as one of football's most successful field generals," Arizona Wranglers press release, September 27, 1984, GAC.
112. "Allen Resigns as Head Coach of Wranglers; Lanham Named," *Baltimore Sun*, September 28, 1984, 9E.
113. Ehrhart interview, November 7, 2021.
114. B. Allen interview, December 15, 2021.
115. Ehrhart interview, November 7, 2021.
116. William Wallace, "Trump Would Like to Take on N.F.L.," *New York Times*, September 30, 1983, A25.
117. Reeths, *United States Football League, 1982–1986*, 273.
118. B. Allen interview, December 15, 2021.
119. G. Allen, *Strategies for Winning*, 21.
120. B. Allen interview, December 15, 2021.

23. "Are You Kidding?"

1. George Allen, "Ex-Coach Allen Finds Our Kids over the Hill before Teen Years," *USA Today*, March 25, 1986, 3C.
2. Jeff Meyers, "Kids Earn a Resounding F in Fitness," *Los Angeles Times*, May 9, 1986, C1.
3. Tina May, "George Allen Runs the Longest Yard for U.S. Fitness Center," *Orange County Register*, February 14, 1985, A18.
4. George Allen, draft proposal for the National Fitness Classic Program, 1980s, GAC.
5. Robert Hyndman and Lisa Mahoney, "South Coast Gets Fitness Center," *Daily Pilot* (Orange County CA), February 14, 1985, A1.
6. Doug Brown, "Active Millionaire Couple Give Service High Priority," *Los Angeles Times*, August 11, 1985, OC_D1.
7. May, "George Allen Runs the Longest Yard for U.S. Fitness Center," A18.
8. Ronald Reagan to George Allen, June 14, 1985, GAC.
9. John Needham, "Doubt Grows Whether Fitness Center Will Be Built," *Los Angeles Times*, January 2, 1986, OC_A1.
10. National Fitness Foundation Award Honorees list, ca. 1986, GAC.
11. "Fanfare: Allen's Fitness Academy May Be Dying Dream," *Washington Post*, December 19, 1988, B2.
12. B. Allen interview, December 15, 2021.
13. George Allen to Donald Trump, May 6, 1986, GAC.

14. Don Gonyea and Domenico Montanaro, "Donald Trump's Been Saying the Same Thing for 30 Years," National Public Radio, January 20, 2017, https://www.npr.org/2017/01/20/510680463/donald-trumps-been-saying-the-same-thing-for-30-years.
15. George Allen, "Too Often, Our Fitness Programs Are a Joke," August 14, 1986 (includes Donald Trump note written on the article), GAC.
16. Bruce Allen to Donald Trump and Trump response, courtesy of the Allen family.
17. Mark Landsbaum, "An Elusive Goal: George Allen's Game Plan for Fitness Academy in Laguna Hills Has Consumed $2.7 Million but Project Is Still on the Sidelines," *Los Angeles Times*, June 19, 1988, AOC1.
18. "Fanfare: Allen's Fitness Academy May Be Dying Dream," B2 (referencing reporting from the *Orange County Register*).
19. B. Allen interview, December 15, 2021.
20. "George Allen, Council Chairman, Resigns," *President's Council on Physical Fitness and Sports Newsletter*, November–December 1987, GAC.
21. George Felix Allen interview, December 18, 2019.
22. "George Allen, Council Chairman, Resigns," *President's Council on Physical Fitness and Sports Newsletter*.
23. Kiki Kennedy Day, "Allen Stresses Fitness," United Press International, March 29, 1989, https://www.upi.com/Archives/1989/03/25/Fitness-Allen-Stresses-FitnessNEWLNAllen-Lends-EffortTo-Fitness-Parley/2816606805200/.
24. George Felix Allen interview, December 18, 2019.
25. Paul Fine, interview by author, December 22, 2021.
26. George Allen 1986 desk planning book, GAC.
27. Tommy McVean, interview by author, December 5, 2013.
28. B. Allen interview, February 12, 2020.
29. B. Allen interview, February 12, 2020.
30. *President's Council on Physical Fitness and Sports Newsletter*, September 1981, GAC; G. Allen recorded conversation with Guback.
31. "Allen's Morningside Message: 'The Future Is Now,'" NCAA *News*, October 2, 1989, 13.
32. "Allen's Morningside Message," 13.
33. Ken Denlinger, "Once More, Thumbs Up in Sioux City," *Washington Post*, August 11, 1989, F1.
34. G. Allen recorded conversation with Guback.
35. *This Is the NFL: George Allen* (NFL Films, 1989).
36. G. Allen recorded conversation with Guback.
37. "Allen's Morningside Message," 13.
38. G. Allen recorded conversation with Guback.
39. "Allen's Morningside Message," 13.

40. G. Allen recorded conversation with Guback.
41. G. Allen recorded conversation with Guback.
42. Jill Walker and Sally Jenkins, "He's Back: George Allen to Coach Long Beach St.," *Washington Post*, December 20, 1989, C1.
43. Dick Wagner, "Reisbig Quits as Coach of Long Beach Football," *Los Angeles Times*, November 10, 1989, C7.
44. B. Allen interview, February 12, 2020.
45. B. Allen interview, February 12, 2020.
46. Looney, "WHY, George?," 74–78.
47. Bruce Allen, interview by author, January 30, 2022.
48. Douglas Like and Joe Falls, "Famed Coach George Allen Dies at 72," *Detroit News*, January 1, 1991 (scrapbook clipping), GAC.
49. Dabney Coleman, interview by author, February 5, 2022.
50. Paul McLeod and David Haldane, "Allen Expected to Attract Big Financial Help," *Los Angeles Times*, December 21, 1989, LB_J1.
51. Greg Gibson, "49ers Are Media Darlings for a Day," *Long Beach Press-Telegram*, December 20, 1989, C1.
52. Shayne Schroeder, interview by author, January 8, 2022.
53. Gibson, "49ers Are Media Darlings for a Day," C1.
54. "Allen Returns to Coaching," United Press International, December 20, 1989, https://www.upi.com/Archives/1989/12/20/Allen-returns-to-coaching/5476630133200/.
55. Bernie Wilson, "Allen, 71, Returns to Coaching," Associated Press, December 20, 1989 (scrapbook clipping), GAC.
56. Paul McLeod and David Haldane, "Allen Puts Long Beach in Spotlight While Still 0–0," *Los Angeles Times*, December 24, 1989, 18.
57. "Allen Ready to Tackle Challenge," Associated Press, December 20, 1989, C1 (scrapbook clipping), GAC; G. Allen, *What Washington Can Learn from the World of Sports*, 57.
58. Jennifer Allen, interview by author, January 3, 2022.

24. An "Almost Impossible" Task

1. Ken Denlinger, "Allen Over the Hill and Up to the Task: Ex-Redskins Coach Works to Rejuvenate Long Beach Program," *Washington Post*, August 12, 1990, D1.
2. Doug Krikorian, "Heat Is on Allen—in More Ways than One," *Long Beach Press-Telegram*, July 3, 1990, D1.
3. Denlinger, "Allen Over the Hill and Up to the Task," D1.
4. Looney, "WHY, George?," 74–78.
5. Looney, "WHY, George?," 74–78.
6. Bruce Allen, interview by author, January 7, 2022.

7. Steve Lowery, "Allen Seeks One More Miracle," *The National* (sports daily) (undated scrapbook clipping), GAC.
8. Michael Hurd, "Allen Gaining Converts but Needs Miracle," *USA Today*, April 27, 1990 (scrapbook clipping), GAC.
9. Dick Wagner, "Allen Outlines His Game Plan for Improving 49ers' Fortunes," *Los Angeles Times*, March 1, 1990, SE_AJ7.
10. Steve Janisch, interview by author, January 29, 2022.
11. Ray Didinger, interview by author, November 18, 2017.
12. Bruce Allen, interview by author, January 6, 2022.
13. Stephen Nover, "Hyde Is Ready for His Return to Coaching," *Las Vegas Review-Journal*, February 18, 1990, 17E.
14. Doug Krikorian, "Allen Finds Water Murky in Recruiting Pool," *Long Beach Press-Telegram*, February 15, 1990, D1.
15. Krikorian, "Allen Finds Water Murky in Recruiting Pool," D1.
16. Tom Friend, "George Allen Gives Recruiting the Old College Try for 49ers," *The National*, February 16, 1990 (scrapbook clipping), GAC.
17. Tommy McVean, interview by author, December 11, 2013.
18. Chris Tsangaris, interview by author, January 22, 2022. Subsequent quotations are from this interview until noted otherwise.
19. Mark Seay, interview by author, January 10, 2022. Subsequent quotations are from this interview until noted otherwise.
20. "Allen Realistic about Long Beach's Hopes," *USA Today*, August 31, 1990 (scrapbook clipping), GAC.
21. Seay interview.
22. Roger Phillips, "Allen Dinner Is a Huge $ucce$$," *Long Beach Press-Telegram*, May 24, 1990, C1.
23. Dick Wagner, "George Allen's NFL Mystique Has Cal State Long Beach Seeing Stars," *Los Angeles Times*, May 27, 1990, SBB12.
24. Wagner, "George Allen's NFL Mystique Has Cal State Long Beach Seeing Stars," SBB12.
25. Phillips, "Allen Dinner Is a Huge $ucce$$," C1.
26. Jimmy Burch, "KID Stuff: Coaching Legend George Allen, 72, Is Tackling the Toughest Challenge of His Career with Youthful Energy," *Fort Worth Star-Telegram*, 1 (undated scrapbook clipping), GAC.
27. Dan Radakovich, interview by author, January 26, 2022.
28. Pepper Jenkins, interview by author, January 19, 2022.
29. George Allen to Long Beach State players, June 14, 1990, GAC.
30. Ron Orozco, "The Legend Lives on at the Beach," *Fresno Bee* (undated scrapbook clipping), GAC.
31. Looney, "WHY, George?," 74–78.
32. Ken Pivernetz, "Long Beach State Will Look Like a Winner," *Long Beach Press-Telegram*, August 30, 1990 (scrapbook clipping), GAC.

33. *The National* (undated scrapbook clipping), GAC.
34. Shayne Schroeder, interview by author, January 8, 2022.
35. Janisch interview.
36. Dave Sheinin, "Old Redskins, Cowboys Never Die, They Just Fade into Another Flag Pattern," *Washington Post*, June 24, 1990, B15.
37. Scrapbook clipping with no identifying information, GAC.
38. B. Allen interview, January 29, 2022.
39. Janisch interview.
40. Phil Skaggs, "LBSU Confident after Wins," *Las Cruces Sun-News*, October 3, 1990 (scrapbook clipping), GAC.
41. "The Future under Head Coach George Allen," 1990 Long Beach State preseason football outlook, GAC.
42. Tsangaris interview.
43. Radakovich interview.
44. Schroeder interview.
45. Jenkins interview.
46. Schroeder interview.
47. Looney, "WHY, George?," 74–78.
48. B. Allen interview, December 15, 2021.
49. Hal Wells, "Gen. Allen Hits the Beach," *Long Beach Press-Telegram* (undated scrapbook clipping), GAC.
50. Long Beach State 1990 football press guide, Sports Information Department, Long Beach State University (CSULB).
51. Dick Wagner, "The Allen Factor: This Year's Cal State Long Beach Team May Be No Better than Last Year's, but Spotlight Is on the Coach," *Los Angeles Times*, August 30, 1990, SEJ6.
52. Bob Burns, "George Allen's 'Impossible' Job," *Los Angeles Times* via the McClatchy News Service, August 28, 1990, 9.
53. Hoyt Coffee, "Clemson 59, Long Beach State 0," United Press International, September 2, 1990, https://www.upi.com/Archives/1990/09/01/Clemson-59-Long-Beach-State-0/7532652161600/.
54. Tom Friend, "They Call Him Coach Again: George Allen Takes Charge at Long Beach," *The National* (undated scrapbook clipping), GAC.
55. Tom Friend, "Somehow, George Allen's Debut Gives a 59–0 Loss Respectability," *The National*, September 2, 1990 (scrapbook clipping), GAC.
56. B. Allen interview, December 15, 2021.
57. Seay interview.
58. Seay interview. Subsequent quotes are from this interview until noted otherwise.
59. Jim Tuttle, "49ers Win 1st of Allen Era" and "Notes: Allen Gets Game Ball but Gives It to Seay," both from *Orange County Register*, September 23, 1990 (scrapbook clippings), GAC.

60. Dick Wagner, "Long Beach Streak Is 3; New Mexico State's, 22," *Los Angeles Times*, October 7, 1990, C8.
61. Tsangaris interview.
62. Ken Pivernetz, "Canadian Import Really Knows the American Game," *Long Beach Press-Telegram*, October 11, 1990, D4.
63. Tsangaris interview.
64. Ken Pivernetz, "49ers Step Up in Class When They Meet San Jose State Saturday," *Long Beach Press-Telegram*, October 10, 1990 (scrapbook clipping), GAC.
65. Seay interview.
66. Ken Pivernetz, "Allen's Gamble Pays Off for 49ers," *Long Beach Press-Telegram*, November 11, 1990, E1.
67. Doug Krikorian, "Krikorian: Make Allen the Boss," *Long Beach Press-Telegram* (undated scrapbook clipping), GAC.
68. Stephen Nover, "George Allen Has 49ers Fans Fired Up at Long Beach State," *Las Vegas Review-Journal*, November 18, 1990, 8D.
69. Michael Hurd, "Allen Gaining Converts but Needs Miracle," *USA Today*, April 27, 1990 (scrapbook clipping), GAC.
70. Jim Murray, "For George Allen, Life at the Beach Begins at 72," *Los Angeles Times*, December 6, 1990, VYC1.
71. Dick Wagner, "49ers Revel in Finish of Winning Season," *Los Angeles Times*, November 22, 1990, SE_BJ12.
72. George Allen, "My Most Gratifying Year," *Sports Illustrated*, December 3, 1990, 140.
73. B. Allen interview, December 15, 2021.
74. George Felix Allen interview, November 16, 2021.
75. Janisch interview.
76. B. Allen interview, December 15, 2021.
77. Shav Glick, "Warmth of Hospitality Prompts Hawkeyes to Stand Pat," *Los Angeles Times*, December 28, 1990, C10.
78. Dabney Coleman, interview by author, February 6, 2022.
79. Harris interview, April 23, 2015.
80. "George Allen, Coach, Dead at 72; Led Redskins to Super Bowl VII," *New York Times* via the Associated Press, January 1, 1991, 55; John Woolard, "Heart, Not Ice Water, Is What Led to Allen's Death," *Baltimore Sun*, January 3, 1991, https://www.baltimoresun.com/news/bs-xpm-1991-01-03-1991003178-story.html.
81. These details were retrieved from Wikipedia, https://en.wikipedia.org/wiki/George_Allen_(American_football_coach), which reported the information by paraphrasing the sports editor of Long Beach State's newspaper, the *Daily Forty-Niner*. There is no link to the *Daily Forty-Niner* article.
82. Jenkins interview.
83. Harris interview, April 23, 2015.

84. Jennifer Allen, interview by author, February 21, 2022.
85. Butkus interview.
86. Tsangaris interview.
87. Terry Canavello, "Allen Remembered as a Winner: Family, Friends, Associates Recall Coach's Life, Triumphs," *Daily Forty-Niner*, January 18–28, 1991, 4.
88. L. Shapiro interview.
89. Stephen Braun, "George Allen, Coach Who Built Winners, Dies at 72," *Los Angeles Times*, January 1, 1991, VYA1.
90. J. Allen interview, February 21, 2022.
91. *Winning Is Living, Losing Is Dying.*
92. Leta Lynde, "Allen Remembered as a Winner: Family, Friends, Associates Recall Coach's Life, Triumphs," *Daily Forty-Niner*, January 18–28, 1991, 3.
93. Samantha Stevenson, "Allen's Closest Fans Bid Farewell to Coach," *New York Times*, January 5, 1991, 43.
94. *Winning Is Living, Losing Is Dying.*
95. "Rust Fired; Patriots Start Search for a Fiery Coach (Allen)," *Baltimore Sun*, January 5, 1991, 5B.

Epilogue

1. Looney, "WHY, George?," 74–78.
2. Murray, "For George Allen, Life at the Beach Begins at 72," C1.
3. L. Shapiro interview. Subsequent quotes are from this interview until noted otherwise.
4. George Felix Allen interview, December 19, 2019.
5. Pro Football Hall of Fame speeches by Deacon Jones and George Felix Allen, August 3, 2002, https://www.profootballhof.com/players/george-allen/. Permission granted by Elizabeth Jones and George Felix Allen to republish these speeches, which were given on the grounds of the Hall of Fame.

Bibliography

Allen, George. *Strategies for Winning: A Top Coach's Game Plan for Victory in Football and in Life*. New York: McGraw-Hill, 1990.

———. "A Study of Outstanding Football Coaches' Attitudes and Practices in Scouting." Master's thesis, University of Michigan, 1947.

Allen, George, and Joseph G. Pacelli. *George Allen's Guide to Special Teams*. Champaign IL: Leisure Press, 1990.

Allen, George, with Charles Maher. *Merry Christmas—You're Fired!* New York: Simon and Schuster, 1982.

Allen, George Felix. *What Washington Can Learn from the World of Sports*. Washington DC: Regnery, 2010.

Allen, Jennifer. *Fifth Quarter: The Scrimmage of a Football Coach's Daughter*. New York: Random House, 2000.

Bisheff, Steve. *Los Angeles Rams: Great Teams' Great Years*. New York: Macmillan, 1973.

Boswell, Thomas. *Redskins: A History of Washington's Team*. Washington DC: Washington Post Books, 1997.

Butkus, Dick, and Pat Smith. *Butkus: Flesh and Blood*. New York: Doubleday, 1997.

Canham, Don, with Larry Paladino. *From the Inside: A Half Century of Michigan Athletics*. Ann Arbor MI: Olympia Sports Press, 1996.

Carroll, Bob, et al. *Total Football II: The Official Encyclopedia of the National Football League*. New York: HarperCollins, 1999.

Cooper, Charles W., and Jessamyn West. *Whittier: Independent College in California*. Los Angeles: Ward Ritchie Press, 1967.

Curran, Bob. *The $400,000 Quarterback*. New York: Macmillan, 1965.

Davis, Jeff. *Papa Bear: The Life and Legacy of George Halas*. New York: McGraw-Hill, 2005.

Gildea, William, and Kenneth Turan. *The Future Is Now: George Allen, Pro Football's Most Controversial Coach*. Boston: Houghton Mifflin, 1972.

Gilden, Jack. *Collision of Wills: Johnny Unitas, Don Shula, and the Rise of the Modern NFL*. Lincoln: University of Nebraska Press, 2018.

Halas, George, with Gwen Morgan and Arthur Veysey. *Halas by Halas: The Autobiography of George Halas*. New York: McGraw-Hill, 1979.

Haskins, Faye. *The Evening Star: The Rise and Fall of a Great Washington Newspaper*. Lanham MD: Rowman and Littlefield, 2019.

Katzowitz, Josh. *Sid Gillman: Father of the Passing Game*. Covington KY: Clerisy Press, 2012.

Klawitter, John, and Deacon Jones. *Headslap: The Life and Times of Deacon Jones*. Amherst NY: Prometheus Books, 1996.

Kopay, David, and Perry Deane Young. *The David Kopay Story: An Extraordinary Self-Revelation*. New York: Arbor House, 1977.

Kramer, Jerry, and Dick Schaap. *Instant Replay: The Green Bay Diary of Jerry Kramer*. New York: Anchor Books/Random House, 2006.

Libby, Bill. *Life in the Pit: The Deacon Jones Story*. Garden City NY: Doubleday, 1970.

Maraniss, David. *When Pride Still Mattered: A Life of Vince Lombardi*. New York: Simon and Schuster, 1999.

McCaskey, Patrick, with Mike Sandrolini. *Bear with Me: A Family History of George Halas and the Chicago Bears*. Chicago: Triumph Books, 2009.

McDole, Ron, with Rob Morris. *The Dancing Bear: My Eighteen Years in the Trenches of the AFL and NFL*. Lincoln: University of Nebraska Press, 2018.

Moldea, Dan. *Interference: How Organized Crime Influences Professional Football*. New York: William Morrow, 1989.

Nixon, Richard Milhous. *RN: The Memoirs of Richard Nixon*. New York: Grosset and Dunlap, 1978.

O'Toole, Andrew. *Fight for Old DC: George Preston Marshall, the Integration of the Washington Redskins, and the Rise of a New NFL*. Lincoln: University of Nebraska Press, 2016.

Piascik, Andy. *Gridiron Gauntlet: The Story of the Men Who Integrated Pro Football*. New York: Taylor Trade, 2009.

Rand, Jonathan. *300 Pounds of Attitude: The Wildest Stories and Craziest Characters the NFL Has Ever Seen*. Guilford CT: Lyons Press, 2006.

Reeths, Paul. *The United States Football League, 1982–1986*. Jefferson NC: McFarland, 2017.

Richman, Mike. *The Redskins Encyclopedia*. Philadelphia: Temple University Press, 2007.

Ross, Charles. *Outside the Lines: African Americans and the Integration of the National Football League*. New York: New York University Press, 1999.

Thomas, Evan. *The Man to See: Edward Bennett Williams, Ultimate Insider; Legendary Trial Lawyer*. New York: Simon and Schuster, 1991.

Youmans, Gary, and Maury Youmans. *'63: The Story of the 1963 World Champion Chicago Bears*. Campbell CA: Campbell Road Press, 2004.

Index